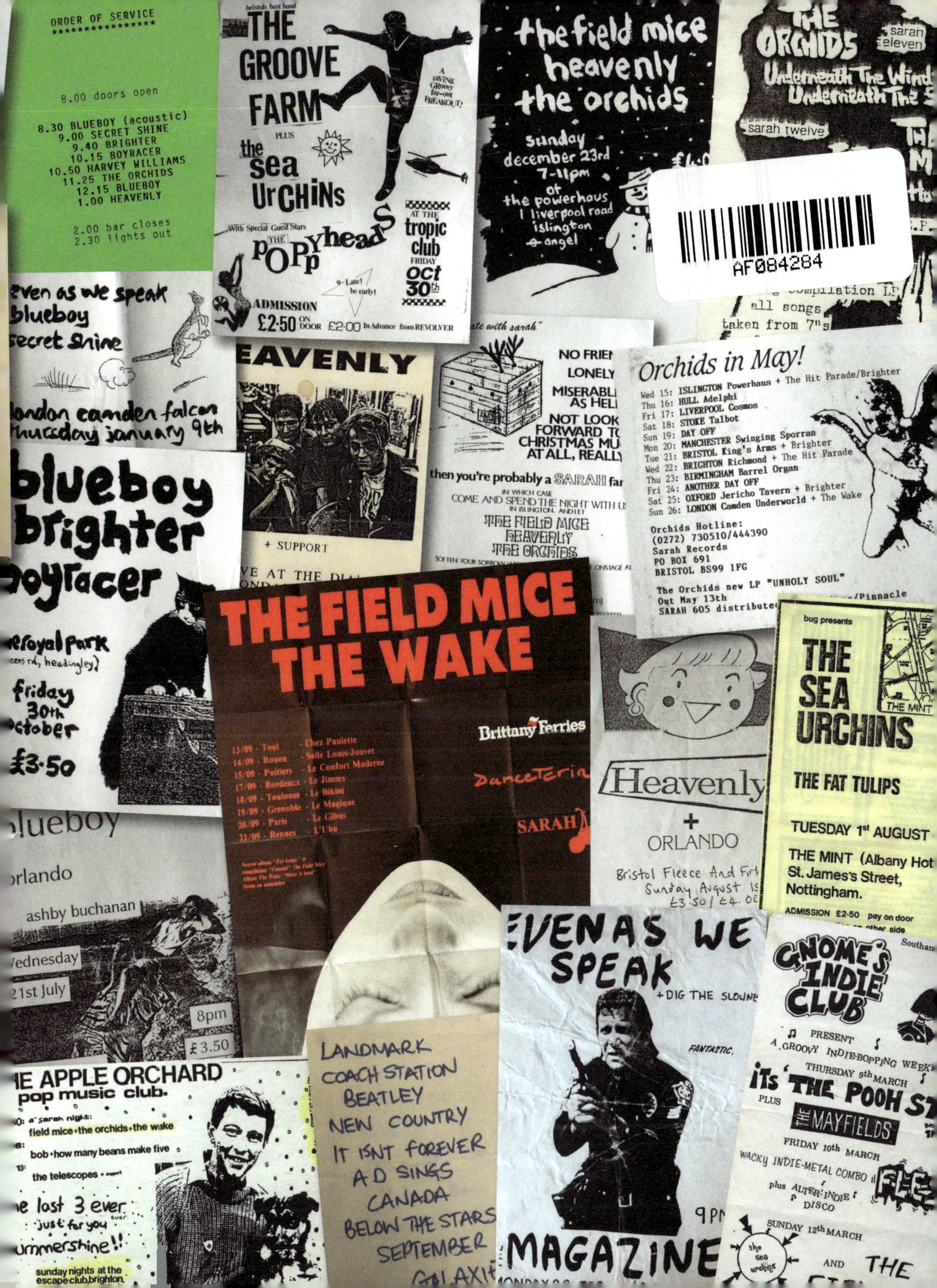
ORDER OF SERVICE
8.00 doors open
8.30 BLUEBOY (acoustic)
9.00 SECRET SHINE
9.40 BRIGHTER
10.15 BOYRACER
10.50 HARVEY WILLIAMS
11.25 THE ORCHIDS
12.15 BLUEBOY
1.00 HEAVENLY
2.00 bar closes
2.30 lights out
bristols best band
THE GROOVE FARM
PLUS
the sea UrCHiNs
A raving Groovy far-out FREAKOUT!
With Special Guest Stars
THE POPPyheadS
AT THE tropic club
FRIDAY oct 30th
9–Late! be early!
ADMISSION £2·50 ON DOOR £2·00 In Advance from REVOLVER
the field mice
heavenly
the orchids
sunday december 23rd
7-11pm
at the powerhaus
1 liverpool road
islington
angel
THE ORCHIDS
sarah eleven
Underneath The Window Underneath The S
sarah twelve
compilation LP
all songs
taken from 7"s
even as we speak
blueboy
secret shine
london camden falcon
thursday january 9th
EAVENLY
+ SUPPORT
VE AT THE
NO FRIEN
LONELY
MISERABL
AS HEL
NOT LOOK
FORWARD TO
CHRISTMAS MU
AT ALL, REALLY
then you're probably a SARAH far
IN WHICH CASE
COME AND SPEND THE NIGHT WITH US
IN ISLINGTON, ANDLET
THE FIELD MICE
HEAVENLY
THE ORCHIDS
Orchids in May!
Wed 15: ISLINGTON Powerhaus + The Hit Parade/Brighter
Thu 16: HULL Adelphi
Fri 17: LIVERPOOL Cosmos
Sat 18: STOKE Talbot
Sun 19: DAY OFF
Mon 20: MANCHESTER Swinging Sporran
Tue 21: BRISTOL King's Arms + Brighter
Wed 22: BRIGHTON Richmond + The Hit Parade
Thu 23: BIRMINGHAM Barrel Organ
Fri 24: ANOTHER DAY OFF
Sat 25: OXFORD Jericho Tavern + Brighter
Sun 26: LONDON Camden Underworld + The Wake
Orchids Hotline:
(0272) 730510/444390
Sarah Records
PO BOX 691
BRISTOL BS99 1FG
The Orchids new LP "UNHOLY SOUL"
Out May 13th
SARAH 605 distributed
blueboy
brighter
boyracer
royal park
friday 30th october
£3·50
THE FIELD MICE
THE WAKE
13/09 - Toul - Chez Paulette
14/09 - Rouen - Salle Louis-Jouvet
15/09 - Poitiers - Le Confort Moderne
17/09 - Bordeaux - Le Jimmy
18/09 - Toulouse - Le Bikini
19/09 - Grenoble - Le Magique
20/09 - Paris - Le Gibus
21/09 - Rennes - L'Ubu
Brittany Ferries
Danceteria
SARAH
Heavenly
+
ORLANDO
Bristol Fleece And Firk
Sunday August
bug presents
THE SEA URCHINS
THE MINT
THE FAT TULIPS
TUESDAY 1st AUGUST
THE MINT (Albany Hot
St. James's Street,
Nottingham.
ADMISSION £2·50 pay on door
blueboy
orlando
ashby buchanan
wednesday
21st July
8pm
£3.50
EVEN AS WE SPEAK
+ DIG THE SLOWNE
MAGAZINE
LANDMARK
COACH STATION
BEATLEY
NEW COUNTRY
IT ISN'T FOREVER
A D SINGS
CANADA
BELOW THE STARS
SEPTEMBER
GNOME'S INDIE CLUB
PRESENT
A GROOVY INDIE-BOPPING WEEK
THURSDAY 9th MARCH
ITS THE POOH S
PLUS
THE MAYFIELDS
FRIDAY 10th MARCH
WACKY INDIE-METAL COMBO
plus ALTER-INDIE DISCO
SUNDAY 12th MARCH
AND THE
HE APPLE ORCHARD
pop music club.
a sarah night:
field mice + the orchids + the wake
bob + how many beans make five
the telescopes
the last 3 ever
just for you
summershine!!
sunday nights at the escape club, brighton.

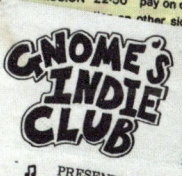

These Things Happen
The Sarah Records Story

By Jane Duffus

> ❝ The most important things in the world are cooking, personal hygiene and cigarettes. Records come joint 27th, equal with *Cagney & Lacey*."
>
> **Letter from Heavenly drummer Mathew Fletcher to me, 1994**

These Things Happen: The Sarah Records Story

First published October 2023 by Tangent Books. This edition November 2023.

Tangent Books
Unit 5.16 Paintworks, Bristol BS4 3EH
0117 972 0645
www.tangentbooks.co.uk
richard@tangentbooks.co.uk

ISBN 9781914345272

Author: Jane Duffus
Publisher: Richard Jones
Design: Joe Burt
Text copyright: Jane Duffus/Tangent Books. All rights reserved
Cherries cover photo copyright: Akiko Yamauchi
Other photo copyright belongs to the individually named people in the captions

Jane Duffus has asserted her right under the Copyright, Designs and Patents Act of 1988 to be identified as the author of this work. This book may not be reproduced or transmitted in any form or by any means without the prior written consent of the publisher, except by a reviewer who wishes to quote brief passages in connection with a review written in a newspaper or magazine or broadcast on television, radio or on the internet.

A CIP record of this book is available at the British Library.

Printed on paper from a sustainable source
Print management Akcent Media

For my mum,
Caroline Mornement

CONTENTS

Chapter 1: Introduction	9
Chapter 2: What was Sarah Records?	17
Chapter 3: Bristol: Maritime City	49
Chapter 4: Unlike Every Other Band on Sarah...	67
Chapter 5: Fanzine Culture	97
Chapter 6: The Power of the Press	119
Chapter 7: On my Radio	155
Chapter 8: Fashion	181
Chapter 9: Partly Political Broadcasts	197
Chapter 10: Letters from a Lifeboat	221
Chapter 11: Recording Studios	235
Chapter 12: Art & Design	263
Chapter 13: Record Shops	285
Chapter 14: Going Out: Bristol	305
Chapter 15: Going Out: Britain	339
Chapter 16: Going Out: All Over the World	379
Chapter 17: Even As We Sleep	409
Chapter 18: The End of the Affair	433
Sarah Records Discography	453
Index	455

Author's Notes to the Reader

1 – *These Things Happen* is an oral history of Sarah Records and the world around it. As such, the stories in these pages are largely led by people's voices. Clearly, I didn't interview 116 people at once because… can you imagine?! Some bands were interviewed together, some separately, it depended on their availability and preference. But when people in different bands have talked about similar things, I have grouped them together to create a more seamless narrative. It should all become clear once you start reading.

2 – Inevitably, people don't always remember events the same way. When interviewees have given me wildly contrasting accounts of the same memory, I have largely opted not to include it at all so as not to cause any bad feeling on either side. Some may say that's cowardly but I prefer to think of it as peacekeeping. See also why I am not making any reference in this book to the many stories of, err, 'romantic' relationships I have heard. NB: Some of the people I interviewed are terrible gossips.

3 – I am including Talulah Gosh as a Sarah band for several reasons: a) they were one of the key 'cutie' bands that influenced this scene, b) most of the band's members later signed to Sarah as Heavenly, and c) Sarah did release a compilation of Talulah Gosh radio sessions and therefore, technically, they *are* a Sarah band.

4 – While the majority of my interviewees are people who were directly linked to Sarah, I have also included a few people who were around the scene to add a bit of texture. For instance: music journalists, academics who were fans, people in sympathetic bands (such as Duglas from the BMX Bandits, and Jyoti from White Town), fanzine writers and so on.

5 – During the process of writing this book, several Sarah fans told me they'd be interested to read a 'where are they now?' section. I'm not doing that for several reasons: the main one being that numerous people from the bands asked me not to share what their day jobs are so as not to shatter the pop star illusion.

Chapter One

Introduction

My older brother Adam Mornement introduced me to Talulah Gosh in 1992 when I was 14. He loaned me his LP of *They've Scoffed The Lot* saying he thought I might like it. And I did. I loved it. "You were obviously interested in music and I remember being very taken with Talulah Gosh when I first heard them, especially the shouty bit on 'Testcard Girl', so it seemed like a logical thing to do," Adam says now. "I was introduced to Sarah by a school friend, Guy Sirman [future manager of The Sea Urchins/Delta]. I think it was 1988. Guy went to Bristol and came back with the first Sarah compilation, *Shadow Factory*. He was a portal to an alternative music culture."

Sarah Records was home to bands with funny names (14 Iced Bears, Christine's Cat, Even As We Speak) and anti-heroic song titles ('I'm In Love With A Girl Who Doesn't Know I Exist', 'The Sadness of Sex', 'My Life is Wrong') that generally lingered longer than the songs lasted. But Adam says it was a welcome antidote to the Sisters of Mercy, Fields of the Nephilim and the largely goth tones of the times. "It took a while for me to become aware of Sarah as a kind of club, or network, with a social and political voice. The key was John Peel. Music was a huge part of my identity at the age of 16-20 and Sarah was a formative part of the story. It was a low-key and unthreatening introduction to the idea of a label with a particular sound and identity. Sarah's defiantly DIY approach was an inspiration. I'm sure that my fanzine wouldn't haven't happened without Sarah. And the Brighter flexi I put out certainly wouldn't, given they were a Sarah band."

> ❝ I discovered Sarah Records yesterday, via Adam's Even As We Speak 7"s … I proceeded to unearth his ENTIRE 7" selection of theirs and am working my way through it. By this process I eased my nagging doubt and can rest assured that Heavenly are Talulah Gosh and they kept Amelia Fletcher."
> **My diary, 11 April 1992**

Talulah Gosh proved to be a gateway drug. I was mesmerised by songs such as 'Beatnik Boy' and 'Break Your Face' but wanted more. I discovered that, although the band had split in 1988, many of the members had reunited in a band called Heavenly and had signed to this label called Sarah. So I scoured through Adam's meticulously alphabeticised 7"s to find what I needed: 'I Fell In Love Last Night' and 'Our Love Is Heavenly'. My teenage indie antenna was twitching fast.

With no online shopping cart to place orders in, I would buy records by writing a letter and giving my mum the money to write a cheque. And when the 7" brown card envelopes arrived at my home in Somerset, they were invariably accompanied by carefully written letters, drawings and postcards that Sarah co-founder Matt Haynes sent me. As such, we built up a friendship that extended to phone calls and sometimes meeting up in Bristol for a chat in Revolver Records or a walk on Brandon Hill. I had an open invitation to come and stay with him and Sarah's other co-founder, Clare Wadd, if I wanted to see a band in Bristol, although I was too shy to ever take them up on it.

The letters were always handwritten on the back of scraps of paper, which didn't mean much to me at the time but, looking at them now, they're little pieces of history. One letter is on the reverse of an estate agent's details for houses around the corner from where I lived while writing the bulk of this book. Another was on the back of an early drawing for a Sugargliders tape insert. While one from September 1994 is on the reverse of Matt's subs demand from the Windmill Hill Labour Party; he was overdue to the tune of £15.

In 1995, Matt sent me the final Sarah newsletter with a note to say that the label was closing. It was quite a shock. For the past three years, the label and Matt had become a key part of my life. In that time, I'd gone from being a gawky 14-year-old to someone who published a fanzine, worked in a record shop, occasionally put on gigs and was now driving a car and thinking about university. Sarah saw me through all this, while subtly introducing me to feminism, socialism and the knowledge that if you believed in yourself, then you could do anything.

In 2015, Sarah was celebrated in a documentary called *My Secret World: The Story of Sarah Records* by director Lucy Dawkins. "When Lucy got in touch, we were initially very sceptical and somewhat suspicious," admits Clare now. "She came up to London and we all went to the pub for the afternoon and got a bit drunk, and Matt and I came away very reassured and really quite excited. Initially, I don't think it was going to be a full-length film but she got a bit carried away with it. I had a fabulous time for a few months travelling around going to film screenings and doing Q&As. As well as various UK ones, I went to screenings in New York, LA, Madrid and Barcelona, all of which were enormous fun." Matt adds: "It's been fantastic revisiting the Sarah years because so many people we used to know or write to have popped up, usually with less hair and more offspring but otherwise still the same, and they're just as excited about the film as we are."

Since the release of *My Secret World*, and a Sarah retrospective exhibition at Bristol's Arnolfini gallery in May 2014, I have written quite a few articles about Sarah for books, magazines and websites: largely potted histories of the label, or about my relationship with it. I've been overwhelmed by the response these received and the people I connected with as a result. My initial blog had thousands of people clicking on it from all around the world. This was something a humble fanzine writer in the early 1990s could never have anticipated: that you could write something, publish it immediately and instantly receive messages from fellow fans in Japan, Australia, Germany, wherever… One person even tweeted to say he had a copy of my fanzine *Arketino* right next to him at that very moment. It was bizarre.

Why I'm writing this book

Music critic Simon Reynolds told me that, when he started writing about the 'cutie scene' in 1986, it was because it was an interesting aesthetic at a time when the only viable alternatives were electropop or goth: "I'd already done a couple of cover stories for *Melody Maker* but [cutie] was something that was really interesting to write about, there was certainly something going on." So perhaps it is not entirely surprising that post-punk, C86 and the indie-pop scene have been the subjects of a number of books. In Michael White's *Popkiss*, Sarah Records already has one book dedicated to it. Why write another one?

With *These Things Happen*, I've treated Sarah like the subculture it was. It had its own ecosystem of communication, fashion, gigs, politics and creativity, for which the music was occasionally just a by-product. A number of people interviewed for this book told me that gigs were often events they went to just to socialise and that sometimes they paid little attention to the bands because they were too busy chatting. While other people told me that the gigs and records formed the centre of their world. An impressively high number of people told me they are still good friends with many of the folks they met during this time. In other instances, I was able to reunite former band members who had accidentally lost touch. What I heard loud and clear in more than 130 interviews is that it was the individuals who made this scene and so I've centred their voices in this book.

I also wanted to bring Bristol to the foreground and look at the world that surrounded the people who were on Sarah. Because the late 1980s and early 1990s were significant periods in society, for good and bad reasons. In many ways, Sarah can be seen as the last analogue record label, operating in a sphere where a fax machine was the most fancy piece of technology imaginable. More than anything, I wanted to celebrate the daftness of Sarah and explore the brilliantly silly things Clare and Matt did to thumb their noses at the mainstream music industry. I was a teenage Sarah fan and I wanted to celebrate the intoxicating fervour with which only a teenager can become all-consumingly obsessed with a music scene.

There were countless unexpected joys involved with researching and writing this book. One highlight was being introduced to Christine Grant of Christine's Cat, who not only gave me her first-ever interview but also dug out some never-heard-before Christine's Cat songs and posted them on YouTube after our conversation. A small corner of the internet went wild

> ❝ Christine of Christine's Cat fame is still a friend of mine if you want any info from her as well."
> **Email that blew my mind from Peter Claughan, The Golden Dawn, July 2021**

> ❝ "I always knew there was a cat but never realised there was also a Christine."
> **Email from Matt to me, July 2021**

that weekend at the news of two new tracks a mere 32 years after the first – and only – one. At this rate, we can look forward to the band's debut album being released in 2053. Which is exciting.

Also exciting was being able to say 'Well, yes' to all the people who, expecting me to say 'Ah, no', asked if I'd managed to get an interview with the elusive Bobby Wratten of The Field Mice; a man who would much rather focus on the music he's making now than revisit the past. Bobby was very obliging, although he did confirm: "I absolutely do view The Field Mice as baby pictures, I couldn't think of anything worse than singing songs I wrote 30 years ago."

It's been an absolute blast and a privilege to speak with so many indie-pop legends in the name of research and to strike up unexpected friendships with some of them. For instance, teenage Jane would never have imagined that 40-something Jane would become parkrun buddies with Clare Wadd and Scott Purnell (Secret Shine); or that Amelia Fletcher and Rob Pursey (Heavenly) would give me a big 'thanks' on their post-Sarah compilation *Under The Bridge* after inviting me to interview all the bands for a promotional fanzine; or that I'd end up going to gigs in Newport with Sian Allen Huntley (The Rosaries); or that my collection of 'Art Postcards From Indie-Pop Stars' would grow so large. And a myriad of other unexpected joys. But yet, these things happened...

It's almost time to begin the story. But before we celebrate the launch of Sarah Records in November 1987, let's quickly whizz back to the post-punk explosion of DIY bands and labels that informed the world we're celebrating in this book. Because almost everyone cites Postcard Records and the Scottish scene as major influences, along with a certain tape that the *NME* put out in 1986.

The Sound of Young Scotland

Before there was anything else, there was Scottish indie-pop. Specifically, the much feted Postcard Records in Glasgow, run by Alan Horne who famously used his sock drawer as a filing cabinet. Although Postcard coined the tagline 'The Sound of Young Scotland', Alan's irreverent label wasn't the only post-punk sound to emerge from there. Equally significant was Bob Last and Hilary Morrison's Fast Product in Edinburgh.

The first wave of punk didn't last long. The Sex Pistols had imploded by January 1978, and in their wake they left a slew of bands such as Siouxsie & the Banshees, Buzzcocks and The Clash, the latter of whom would namecheck Fast, Factory and Rough Trade in their 1981 single 'Hitsville UK'. The song contrasted the integrity of the UK's emerging indie scene to the "slimy deals with smarmy eels" of the majors. The minute punk became commercialised, with middle-class kids seeking out disinfected safety pins to put through their noses, the energy and vitality of the true punk spirit of the disenfranchised working-class kids was dead.

Post-punk emerged while the embers of the original movement were still spitting out sparks. In London, John Lydon had ditched Johnny Rotten to re-emerge as the frontman of PiL. Gang of Four rose out of Leeds. And Joy Division came from Salford, although it was a band Hilary Morrison had rejected for Fast because she found their name deeply objectionable: 'joy division' being the term for the women who were routinely raped by high-ranking Nazis. Frontman Ian Curtis' death by suicide in May 1980 could be seen as creating a change in the way music fans saw things. Perhaps his death meant that the dark, industrial edge of punk and early post-punk bands was suggestive of something more sinister. In that sense, perhaps a throwback to the lighter pop and rock of the 1960s was exactly what young people needed, and what labels such as Fast and Postcard provided.

Fast came first and was created by Bob Last and Hilary at their Keir Street flat in Edinburgh. They were inspired by the DIY ethos of Buzzcocks' 'Spiral Scratch', which is commonly hailed as the first self-released record. Bob and Hilary wasted no time in issuing their first release in January 1978. Along with a DIY attitude and socialist outlook, they also understood the importance of branding. Their artwork was distinctive and made use of bright pink or neon green, as well as enormous text and cartoons. This sat beautifully with Fast's intention to prioritise lo-fi aesthetics while ensuring their records were easy to spot in a crowd. Some influential bands who made their debut on Fast include The Human League, The Dead Kennedys and Gang of Four.

Tony Wilson would credit Fast as an influence on his own Factory Records label, which he set up in Manchester in 1978 and to which he signed Joy Division after Fast had rejected them. Bob recalls in the documentary *Big Gold Dream* how Tony would regularly ring up to ask how to do things, saying: "Fast 13 was Factory, that's my view. I just never told them I had a catalogue number until now." Even though Fast preceded Postcard and was home to several soon-to-be-huge bands, it's a label that not many people remember. You can Google 'Fast Product' until you're tartan in the face but you won't turn up many original interviews or video clips that relate to the label, its founders or bands. It wasn't until Grant McPhee's *Big Gold Dream* documentary in 2015, and subsequent *Hungry Beat* book in 2022, that some retrospective articles began to appear. Many of these credit Bob with doing the bulk of the work, casually forgetting Hilary's equal involvement. Is this an example of women yet again being written out of rock? And is this a reason why Sarah, also run on equal terms by a heterosexual couple, would end up having to go to great efforts to ensure that both its co-founders received equal acknowledgement?

> " What we now know as indie music was invented in Scotland. If you think about Postcard, Fast Product, you know, that's the seeds of labels like Creation, that's really been the template for indie music to this day."
>
> **Simon Reynolds in the documentary** *Big Gold Dream*, 2015

Over in Glasgow, Alan Horne was sitting in his flat at 185 West Princes Street and deciding to form a label with his pal Edwyn Collins, an endeavour they would call Postcard Records. Alan was less concerned about subverting the status quo than Fast was; instead he wanted to put out chart-worthy pop records that were produced on a shoestring. He signed Edwyn's band Orange Juice and put out records by fellow Scots Aztec Camera and Josef K, as well as a lone single by Australians The Go-Betweens.

Realising that there was only one way to grow, Orange Juice left Postcard and signed to Polydor. Their 1983 single 'Rip It Up', featuring a Chic-style funk bassline, would be their biggest hit, reaching No 8 in the UK, and was a song that Edwyn would never be able to escape… at least, not until he released 'A Girl Like You' as a solo artist in 1995.

Rob Pursey of Heavenly expands on the reasons why we all love Edwyn so much: "I think Edwyn has a lot to take credit for because he was very un-macho. He made really beautifully crafted pop songs, played them quite badly but had really good lyrics that weren't afraid of being literary. He used words that you might read in a book. There was a shamelessness to that. With pop, people don't pretend to be more stupid than they are. Whereas in rock, they do." Reinforcing this, music critic Simon Reynolds says: "Orange Juice were always really into disco and funk as well as the Velvet Underground. The cuties took all of the Velvet Underground stuff from Orange Juice and the imagery and the wordiness, the romantic and quite literate love songs. Like in 'Consolation Prize' where Edwyn says 'I'll never be man enough for you'. And then what Morrissey did with The Smiths, that kind of went into the cutie moment, too."

> " Wouldn't you like to feel, just the once, that you could die for a pop record? … *Make It Loud* is that record."
>
> **Sharon O'Connell reviews The Wake in *Melody Maker*, 1990**

Another icon from this scene was Clare Grogan, the singer with Altered Images, who also emerged from the dregs of punk in the late-1970s. Amelia Fletcher of Heavenly was so enamoured that she named her first band Talulah Gosh after Clare told an interviewer that the name would make a great alias. Amelia adds. "I think what indie-pop did, and Postcard had already started this, was to take the aesthetics of pop but make it DIY and cool." By the way, when I interviewed Stewart Anderson of Boyracer for this book, he was sitting in front of a massive framed poster of Clare Grogan. Swoon.

Altered Images came close to being signed to Postcard and just imagine if that had come to pass. "If I had had my way, we would have been," says the band's original guitarist Gerard McInulty, who is known by his nickname of Caesar. "Alan Horne invited us over to have a chat at the flat. It was decided it would be me and [manager] Jerry McElhone who would go. So I went along and had a great day there, chatting to them about The Go-Betweens and Orange Juice and Josef K and getting on really well with them. I really wanted to do something with Postcard. But looking back, there wouldn't have been much point as everyone was second fiddle to Orange Juice."

Caesar graduated from Altered Images to The Wake, which in turn graduated from Factory to Sarah. He muses: "When music is a personal thing, you need a sympathetic label. And that's what labels like Sarah were really good at doing. It was to do with real life. A lot of pop music is based on illusion and fantasy, which isn't that healthy in the long run. It's a good thing when people do it well, as the pop stars of the 1960s did and it created a fantasy life, but reality soon hits home for most people. It's not even a reality for most pop stars in the end. That's a good thing about the independent labels, it was a very real thing. Even looking at Buzzcocks, their manager had the far-sighted idea to think, 'We're not going to sit here waiting for A&R men to tell us they're going to give us a ticket to the pop star life, we're going to do it ourselves'. That was the feeling behind it."

Sarah Records: Punk Rock

Clare and Matt have always called Sarah a punk rock label. But, of course, there are limited parallels between the sound and look of bands such as Buzzcocks and X-Ray Spex, and Brighter and The Field Mice. Clare explains: "Punk meant DIY spirit as well. In some ways, the whole thing we were battling against was the CD sound in the early days, against people like Dire Straits. You don't need to be able to play music, you need imagination. You don't need a big budget, you just need spirit. And anyone can do it but that doesn't mean everyone should do it."

Matt continues: "The point of punk is about doing your own thing rather than doing everybody else's thing. To us, punk is the opposite of spending a week in a 48-track studio trying to smooth out all the lumps. The sleeve of the first Buzzcocks EP notes the number of takes required on each track: 'Boredom – 1st take guitar dub; Breakdown – 3rd take no dubs…' and so on. Four songs, recorded in one day, one bit of 7" plastic, punk rock. There's another thing: Pete McNeish took the name Shelley after his favourite Romantic poet. There's the true spirit of punk rock for you. Punk rock is… romance, poetry, wit, fearlessness in the face of ridicule, rawness in sound and emotion, short and sweet and short and sour, breaking taboos not creating new ones, imagination. 'Full of wrong notes and wrong chords but crammed with right Everything Elses,' as it says in the *Shadow Factory* sleeve notes, though that was possibly a mistake, as it let people confuse urgency with ineptitude. Basically, I think the greatest punk rock group were Orange Juice."

> ❝ Like you, I wasn't 'there' in '76 or whenever but I do remember what it was all supposed to stand for. I still believe in the punk rock'n'roll dream."
>
> **Letter from Matt to fanzine writer Pete Williams, May 1986**

Pre-Sarah, the flexi label that Matt was a part of, Sha-La-La, prided itself on its punk credentials, which might have come as a surprise to any mohawked Penetration fans who stumbled upon the label's Poppyheads flexi. One of Matt's co-conspirators in the project, fanzine writer Pete Williams, elaborates: "Sha-La-La was very much anti the established indie music industry, it was very punk rock. It was more than just putting some flexis out because we liked the music, it was quite ideologically driven, even though if you sat us down and asked us to explain what that ideology was it would be contradictory. The term 'punk rock' was almost used provocatively, exactly because the music was quite soft and not punk at all but the attitude was punk. It's interesting thinking about the way punk was used. It already seemed like this distant thing, even though it was only about seven years before. So for me and some others, using the term 'punk' was like saying 'this is our punk.'"

Music journalist Pete Paphides adds: "Different people have wildly differing definitions of punk. And I guess your definition of punk is partly contingent on when you grew up and when you needed to have a version of punk in your life. But I think the way some older people talk about punk is how I relate to the aesthetic that was ushered in by C86 and carried on by Sarah."

Meanwhile, Simon Reynolds has quite literally written the book on the post-punk scene, with his excellent 2006 tome *Rip It Up & Start Again*, the title again taking us back to Orange Juice. Talking about how the cutie scene slots into the wider post-punk world, Simon tells me: "It sort of picked up on the scratchy, noisy, scrappy, lo-fi, DIY thing. There's a whole range of precursors but it tended to be less the kind of people who were trying to do weird, twisted funk music, and more the people who were doing this scrappy, jangly sound. TV Personalities were huge precursors to this. While for groups like Bogshed and The Membranes, The Fall was the great precursor. There was a line being made through music history that went from The Velvet Underground to The Fall and to Orange Juice. And then Swell Maps and onto The Pastels, The June Brides... So it's a sort of narrowing in a way. There are so many different strands to punk and I think the fact that it is all under one word hides its great diversity of aims and impetuses. But [cutie] is like punk without all the nastiness."

And on that discordant note, let's crack on with the Sarah story...

*****

These Things Happened:
Josh Meadows, The Sugargliders
"My impression was that Clare and Matt were pop purists, they were principled and they were not afraid of doing stuff that they believed in even if it wasn't going to be popular. I had the impression that Sarah Records was a place where people who weren't hip and cool, but who loved pop music and wanted to be liberated by pop music, could gravitate to. It was very much a time of idealism and it was a time when it was alright to be idealistic. That's often used as an insult but for Sarah Records it wasn't: it was something you could aspire to."

Chapter 2

What was Sarah Records?

Sarah was a record label that signed the acts no major label would touch but who you wanted to hear. It put out a board game, produced cut'n'paste fanzines and stuck two fingers up to the mainstream music industry. It was your secret world and it was located in the heart of Bristol. Sarah lasted for seven years, nine months and 11 days.

"For me, rock is about revolution, uprising and kicking against the establishment. It's not about making icons out of iconoclasts," says Jyoti Mishra of White Town, who remains a big fan of the label. "So Sarah comes along and it's basically this cat that you think, 'Are you going to let me pat you or are you going to scratch my eyes out?' Because you never know with a Sarah record what it's going to be. How many labels could do that at the time? Was there anything on Creation that had the potential to be as soft and open as something on Sarah? I can't think of anything." Academic and writer Sukhdev Sandhu adds: "'Sarah' is like a code word. If you meet somebody and it emerges that they know of Sarah Records, you automatically lean in and think 'You are part of a tribe, let us speak, forever friends!' That was part of the joy."

If asked to define the Bristol music scene, the names that spring to your mind might include Massive Attack, Tricky and Portishead. Only the more astute music fans might add Sarah Records. Back to Sukhdev: "There is a way in which they are another Bristol sound. If not the original Bristol sound, then a really important element of it. And if you go back to something like Everything But The Girl, you could say that Tracey Thorn's work with Massive Attack brings together Cherry Red's version of independent music and independent Bristol with more multi-racial, polycultural stuff."

Based first in a Clifton basement flat and later in a house overlooking Bedminster train station, Sarah was, between 1987 and 1995, the most independent of indie labels. Co-founders Clare and Matt were driven by feminism, ethics and a passion to truly embrace the DIY ethos of the post-punk scene. And fans were drawn to the label right from day one. I've even seen copies of two handwritten letters from a Polly Jean Harvey in Dorset wanting to buy a copy of *Shadow Factory* ("or as you informed me

> ❝ I'd known for years I wanted to do something in music, but that I could never actually be in a band."
> **Clare**

Clare and Matt came up with the idea for what would become Sarah Records in the summer of 1987.
Courtesy of Sarah Records.

of its proper name, *L'Usine des Ombres*") back in February 1990. I hope she still has it in her collection.

Clare and Matt were not concerned with forming a capitalist monolith to rival Virgin or EMI. Instead, they were eschewing the posturing and vanity of the pop charts and focusing on promoting the kind of bands that the major labels would be too scared to touch. When Sarah launched in November 1987, Clare was 19 and still at university, while Matt was 25 and a physics graduate who had been working as a car park attendant after graduating. The couple lived in a tiny, rented basement flat at 46 Upper Belgrave Road opposite Clifton Down and were scrimping and saving to make ends meet.

The pair were fanzine writers who met after Clare tried to sell Matt her fanzine at a Julian Cope and Primal Scream gig in the Bristol Bierkeller in the autumn of 1986. But Matt said 'no' because he already had a copy. They became a couple in summer 1987 after Clare popped round to ask Matt about the practicalities of getting a box of flexis back on the coach from London to Leeds. Before long, Clare had moved out of halls and she and Matt launched Sarah as a 'fuck you' to the money-grabbing major labels that just wanted to rip fans off rather than celebrate great pop music. Thinking back to how the spark of Sarah was ignited, Clare says: "After the excitement of putting out the flexi [with

> " I know what I want to do. I want to set up a record label but am hampered by: a) Lack of money in vast quantities; b) Living in Bristol; c) Being too shy to get up and do anything by myself."

Letter from Matt to Pete Williams, early 1986

Kvatch], and the response it got, putting out a proper record was the obvious next step, and The Sea Urchins were the obvious first band. I'd got to know Jamie [Roberts, The Sea Urchins] quite well through letters, so I wrote to him with the news we were starting the label and asking them to be our first proper release."

In the summer of 1987, Matt wrote to his former Sha-La-La ally Pete Williams and mentioned the new label that Clare and he were starting: "You mentioned wanting to be a 'proper' record-company, one day… Basically, I've been discussing this with Clare and she wants to get involved with 'proper' records – she's now based permanently in Bristol (at this address, to be more precise, though don't ask me how long that will last!!) and approaches have been made to The Sea Urchins about recording a three or four track 7" EP, to which the answer so far has been a tentative 'yes'. So things could be happening…" Things were definitely happening.

Julian Cope's show at the Bristol Bierkeller on 29 October 1986 was a landmark moment in the history of Sarah Records given it was where Clare and Matt first met.
Courtesy of Adrian Millard.

"I remember spending the summer of 1987 walking around Clifton village and it was endless sunshine, which sounds unlikely, planning out what we were going to do," says Clare. "And it wasn't like we had a plan that we were going to do 100 7" singles and then throw a big party but we always knew we wanted to do more than one, we weren't just putting a record out, we were starting a record label. I think right at the start we always knew that fanzines would be a part of it and they'd be our contribution and the equal to records, maybe the written version of a 7" single."

Bristol's Subway Organization was certainly an influence on Clare and Matt's thinking that it would be entirely possible to run a record label from the South West rather than London, and they admit that asking Subway's Martin Whitehead for advice might have been the smart thing to do. "I'm sure he'd have given of his time freely and been really brilliant, but we never even spoke to

The EEC Punk Rock Mountain team (see Chapter 14) turned the Julian Cope gig into an away day.
Courtesy of Adrian Millard.

him about it," says Matt. "It's sort of madness. But I think part of the problem was I'd spent several issues of my fanzine criticising him." During an interview with Mark Goodier on BBC Radio 1 in 1992, Clare confirmed that part of the impetus for setting up Sarah was "we looked at other record labels and thought, 'No, they're all doing it wrong, we can do it better'. So that was a motivation as well, we wanted to do it from the fan's point of view."

Although Clare was still at university for the first 18 months or so of Sarah, she was still working equally with Matt on building up the label. To help with the finances, Matt signed up for the Enterprise Allowance Scheme, one of the few good things that Margaret Thatcher's government implemented. "It meant we were 'official' and had a bit more income than from Matt signing on and my grant and holiday jobs," says

Although not officially a logo, early Sarah records were recognisable by the artwork displayed in this picture.
Courtesy of Sarah Records.

Clare. "It helped us make the switch from hobby to whatever version of business we finally arrived at, both mindset-wise and with a bit of extra cash. It also made us more legit and dealt with the question about when to stop signing on. With something like Sarah, because everything was reinvested, it was very hard to see if you were making money until the end of the year, so to know you were no longer unemployed was quite hard." Matt adds: "It made it feel like this was definitely a proper, legit business, rather than a hobby that had got out of hand. Having the £40 coming in each week, regardless of how many records you'd sold or not sold, meant you never lost sight of that. It was also a comfort financially, obviously. But the money just went in the pot with everything else, to be spent on staples such as food and Letraset. And staples."

Talking about the initial ethos of Sarah, Matt says: "The label was in opposition to the capitalism of multi-format releases on the major labels. We were an anti-capitalist business, changing the world through the power of the 7" single. CDs in 1987 were £15, and major labels wanted everyone to re-buy their record collections. While 7"s were £1.50 so they were accessible and affordable." It was so affordable that in the mid-1980s you could put out a fanzine with a two-track flexi disc on the cover priced at 50p and still expect to break even. Everything that could be done by Clare and Matt themselves *was* done themselves, even if it took five times as long, because it was the only way to keep costs down. But they rankled the music press, who hurled an astonishing amount of venom at the label for a huge number of reasons (for more on this, hold tight until Chapter Six). Clare muses: "You like to hope that some of the journalists might now be a bit embarrassed about some of the things they wrote about us."

Now, let's quickly address the issue of the label's name because it really got on some people's wicks. "Matt said 'What shall we call it?' and I said, 'Sarah'. And the only rationale I've ever had for that is I was reading Jane Austen's *Emma* at the time, and I thought if a book could be called *Emma*, a record label could be called Sarah," says Clare. "As for why Sarah rather than any other name, I don't think we were thinking about gender politics. I don't think we were thinking about fighting the masculinity of the music industry at all. I think we'd have had a much easier ride if we'd called it something else but I'm really pleased that we called it what we did and we had those fights and really pissed off those people. I think we were

> "Sarah is a terrific label that suffers from a lot of people making their minds up about it without thinking, probably without listening to the records."
>
> **Bobby Wratten, The Field Mice, in *Kitten Frenzy* fanzine, late 1980s**

always going to get a load of shit because I was female but we really amplified it by calling it Sarah."

Perhaps there might be an argument that it was naïve to think that giving an indie record label a female name was not going to attract attention, sand I don't think I'm alone in this view. Long-time Sarah contributor Harvey Williams observes: "If you give your record label a person's name, you're asking for trouble. That should have been the title of their first compilation album, *Asking for Trouble*." That said, Sarah wasn't the first label to adopt a woman's name. There was American soul label Sue in the 1950s, as well as Anna in the 1960s, which was run by Berry Gordy's sister, err, Anna. There was also Paula in the 1960s, as well as Dawn, which ran into the 1970s, a decade that also spawned Caroline.

At 46 Upper Belgrave Road, Clare and Matt pose beside a door decorated with the artwork from the pre-Sarah Sha-La-La flexis.
Courtesy of Sarah Records.

Frustratingly for Clare, she had to get used to people assuming that she was called Sarah when answering the phone; or, worse, that because she was a woman she must be the receptionist, and they would therefore ask to speak to the person who made the decisions. "And I'd say, 'Yes, you are speaking to them.' And they'd sort of go, 'No, the person who really runs the label,'" she sighs, eyes rolling all over the place. "That used to drive me absolutely mad." However, Sarah didn't have a home phone line initially. Instead, they'd go to the phonebox down the road to make calls. Clare remembers lamenting the fact that Ric Menck of the US-based Springfields had a drawl so slow that they had to feverishly fuel the phone with 10p coins in order to catch the end of his sentences.

Marcus Törncrantz co-ran the *Grimsby Fishmarket* fanzine in Sweden and he sent Sarah a postal interview which Matt responded to. Although this correspondence is undated, it is clear from the context that it was written in the early days of the label and I am including a chunk of it here so that Matt can tell you what was going on in his own words from the time: "The label is run jointly by me and Clare ... We wanted to run a POP label, ie make it all FUN and CHEAP – hence no 12" singles, just 7"s, free posters with all the records, EPs wherever possible – little details like a picture of BRISTOL on the centre of each record and so on!! We wanted to set ourselves apart from the rest of the 'record industry' – too many "'independent' labels seem to want to pretend they're MAJOR labels – spend all their money on NICE OFFICES, HEADED NOTEPAPER, FANCY EXPENSIVE PACKAGING – all the wrong priorities!! ... It's not possible to make a living just on the

> ❝ Sorry for the rather unsatisfactory phone call last night – it's not easy talking when you've got some guy pacing up and down outside the box."
>
> **Letter from Matt to Pete Williams, spring 1987**

7"s, no, but with the compilation LP and maybe other LPs, mini LPs it is just possible! But not for both of us, so we shall probably work part-time when Clare finishes at university. Of course, if our sales continue to increase, we shall make a living! That would be good, because it really takes so many hours each day, we couldn't work full-time as well!! ... Other bands we'd like on the label [include] Talulah Gosh if they reform. ... It's far more exciting putting out the first single by an unknown band, than the fourth single by a band everybody knows... and when we stop being EXCITED by the records, that's the time to stop!!! But I genuinely believe that, at this stage in their 'careers', a band like The Field Mice are better off with a small label like us – more bands have been ruined by TOO MUCH money than TOO LITTLE."

Sarah was pretty much the only label at that time to have a woman as its co-owner, while no label anywhere was owned solely by a woman. However, a few years later, Sarah was joined by a handful of others that included women at the helm, including Ché (Vinita Joshi), Hemiola (Justine Wolfenden) and Slampt (Rachel Holborow). "We were opposed to the sexism of the music industry," says Clare. "It got more important to us when we realised what we were up against. It feels like feminism is at the fore at the moment, which is great, but nothing has really changed. I feel like I've been whining about the same things for 30 years."

Clare's experience is echoed by Vinita, who co-founded Ché with Nick Allport in 1991, eventually securing financial backing from Seymour Stein's Sire Records. It wasn't always an easy experience: "Working with the backers was quite horrible looking back, they were quite bullyish, demanding 'Oh, Vinita, make the tea', like I was thick or something." She adds: "I was always really good at maths, which is why I think the businesses have survived, because doing the accounts is such a big thing. If you haven't got a head for figures you're never going to really succeed in the music industry, you can't be throwing tons of money at a project that doesn't sell, at some point you've got to pull back. It wasn't easy." Proving her various skills, Vinita has been successfully running Rocket Girl Records since 1997. Reinforcing her point, it's probably no coincidence that Clare's post-Sarah life has seen her become an accountant.

Even now, there are still hardly any record labels run by women. A 2018 report in *Rolling Stone* identified that of the 26 most significant record labels in both the UK and US (all of which are owned by either Universal, Sony or Warner), only four have women executives running or co-running them. *Rolling Stone* goes on to miserably spell out the gender pay gap for these positions. In short, men earned almost 30% more than women for running a major record label in 2018. Of course, on both sides of the Atlantic there are independent record labels up by or run by women but, with the exception of Jeannette Lee at Rough Trade, these are much smaller enterprises.

As time went on, Clare and Matt would be inundated with demo tapes from hopeful bands. But in the early days they had to

FUN FACT: 'Pristine Christine' was named after guitarist Robert Cooksey's mum, err, Margaret, who was "such a fusspot," says the band's keyboardist Bridget Duffy, "she was a real pristine Christine." So now you know.

seek bands out. The Sea Urchins launched the label with 'Pristine Christine', a majestic whoosh of pop that brilliantly introduced Sarah to the world.

Nobody was asked to sign a contract, things didn't operate in that way. This meant the bands were free to leave at any point, and that the label was free not to put out any further records by a particular act. "I suppose no one really had any security," says Clare, "but it also meant no one was forced into doing anything they didn't want to do. We never wanted to put records out because we thought they would sell, we always wanted to put records out that we thought were absolutely brilliant and *hoped* they'd sell." Which is why, in May 1988, Matt was writing to The Orchids asking: "I take it you do want to do another single??? And, assuming you haven't been offered vast sums by EMI, would you be happy doing it with us? We're a bit unsure." And a few years later, Clare wrote to The Orchids to let them know that labels including Go! Discs and Food were interested in the band: "Assuming you have now quit the label as it were (or even if you haven't), they might be worth following up." Being The Orchids, the band stayed put.

> "All I ever wanted to be is a Sarah band so I'm certainly not going to start moaning about it being an obstacle. My musical horizons only go as far as Sarah's do and that's fine with me, thank you very much. What more could a boy want than to be on Sarah?"
>
> **Keris Howard, Brighter, in *Pretty Potty* fanzine, 1989**

The Houses of Sarah

Clare and Matt initially lived in a tiny rented flat at 46 Upper Belgrave Road. It was a very small space but in a prime location, facing the beautiful Clifton Down. "The flat was about £80 a month when I moved in," says Clare. Being a basement, No 46 felt especially dingy given it only had one window. "It was a glorified studio flat. The kitchen had no windows and no heating, so the only way of getting any warmth was to turn the oven on," adds Matt. This may explain why mushrooms sprouted in the damp bathroom: "That was our privileged middle-class life back then," says Matt with his tongue in his cheek, in reference to the fact the music press seemed to think they were trustafarians playing at indie-pop.

There was also the small issue of their rental tenancy meaning that they were not *technically* supposed to be running a business from the residence. Although they later found out that their landlord's agent had known all along that they were doing so from the property and he couldn't have cared less. One clue might have come on the day that Clare and Matt accidentally set fire to the kitchen when they went out to collect records from the warehouse for sleeving, having forgotten that the oven was still on with the grill pan inside. Clare and Matt returned from the warehouse in two taxis, unloaded boxes of records onto the pavement, and watched in horror as smoke billowed out of their home while the Fire Brigade was dealing with everything. And the agent looked on…

Sometimes strange things happened while working from home. "We heard *Shadow Factory* coming through the wall once before we released it and it

Top: Upper Belgrave Road: surely the most famous address in indie-pop history?
Middle left: In 1992, Clare and Matt bought a house at 31 Gwilliam Street.
Middle right: At 45 Upper Belgrave Road, this humble table served as a desk.
Bottom: This 1992 view of Gwilliam Street is virtually unchanged today.
Courtesy of Sarah Records.

completely freaked us out. No one had a copy so how could we be hearing it through the wall?" says Clare. Their next door neighbour turned out to be Mike Gartside, who was the indie music writer at Bristol's listings magazine *Venue*. Mike had taken his promotional copy of *Shadow Factory* home to review. "I looked at the address at the bottom of the record and was like, 'That's next door to me!' It was a real shock," remembers Mike. "I was at No 45, and the partition between the two walls was practically non-existent, so I could put on a record in my flat and I'm sure they heard it almost perfectly in theirs. I deliberately put it on loud so they couldn't possibly *not* hear it."

While living in the small basement flat, Clare and Matt also rented office space. The first was really just a cubicle in a big room in Kingswood where Clare would go because it was easier to work without the two of them being on top of each other. The next office was a 10ft x 10ft space near Horfield Prison, but Sarah had the bad luck of being burgled at both this office and the flat in the same week. They didn't keep the office for long.

When next-door neighbour Mike decided to move on from No 45 Upper Belgrave Road, Clare and Matt jumped at the chance to upgrade to the slightly bigger premises. Moving day fuss was kept to a minimum since everything was transported internally, via a door in Mike's bathroom that linked the two flats together. Fun fact: Mike sold Clare and Matt his sofa for the bargain price of £5 and many visiting indie bands used it as a makeshift bed: including four Orchids who somehow managed to all sleep on it at the same time.

In April 1992, buoyed by a few healthy cheques from albums, Clare and Matt decided to do the grown-up thing and buy a house. They moved to the only house they viewed: 31 Gwilliam Street in Windmill Hill, south Bristol, overlooking Bedminster's commuter train station.

The house on Gwilliam Street was somewhat deceptive. It looked like an ordinary two-storey, mid-terrace house from the front but, when you went inside, because it was on a steep slope, it turned into three storeys with a garden at the back and you could look across the whole of the city from the Clifton Suspension Bridge to Temple Meads Station. Clare says: "We wanted to buy somewhere to give us more stability. We'd got quite a big cheque from the distribution company, and we were conscious that you could get moved on at any point when you were renting, and that made the whole address thing quite difficult when we were clearly running a business from a flat we shouldn't have been running it from. So we got the money for a deposit and we obviously weren't going to buy anywhere in [expensive] Clifton, so we were looking for somewhere affordable. I don't think I'd been to Windmill Hill before."

Describing the house, Clare says: "You went in the front door and you'd got a living room which was Matt's office and our not-much-used living room. And then you went straight ahead and

> ❝A belated reply, I know, but you caught us in the middle of moving house and everything has been rather chaotic..."
>
> **Letter to me from Matt, April 1992**

you got what was meant to be the dining room which, when we moved in, had a dark brown carpet, dark brown walls and this massive dark brown fireplace, and that's where we kept all the stock and where I worked. The basement was the kitchen and an enormous bathroom. And a bedroom and living room on the top floor, with a view over the city. For the first two years we didn't have any carpet or anything to sit on in that top room."

Julian Henry of The Hit Parade wrote his song 'The House of Sarah' about the label's move from Upper Belgrave Road. "I used to go down to see Matt and Clare to talk about stuff until we started going to Japan. They had piles of records everywhere. Very messy. One time, I hadn't phoned and just turned up at Upper Belgrave Road and they weren't there. They'd only moved house but I was mulling nostalgically as I do," says Julian. "It seemed the label was growing, becoming something new and unknown. I always memorialise the past so I thought I'd write a song about the place where the idea had been born. The talking at the start of the song is a lift from *Brideshead Revisited*, the story of another famous house left empty to decline."

A day in the life of Sarah

"An awful lot of running a record label is incredibly dull," says Clare. "Mostly, it was the two of us on our own at home, folding bits of paper in half, or writing letters to people, or Matt doing really intricate artwork, or me on the phone, organising tours or trying to get press." While Matt adds: "There was a lot of going to the post office involved." Clare looks slightly traumatised as she adds coldly: "And constantly buying parcel tape."

Never mind how dull Clare and Matt might maintain their day-to-day record label life was, I want to try to recreate a typical day in the life of Sarah Records.

8am – Clare and Matt get up to greet the postman: "There was always post coming to the house. We would always be reading the post over breakfast. The post was a huge deal, everything revolved around the post." In later years, Sarah invested in a PO box and Matt would cycle to the depot on Wine Street to collect the mail and trudge back up the steep hills to Clifton, weighed down by demo tapes.

9am – The pair settle down to their tasks for that day. If artwork needed to be done, they would decide the concept together based on any suggestions or photos that the bands might have sent. The creation of the physical paste-up was almost exclusively Matt's role, though. "Matt's got a natural affinity for it and a lot of patience. Plus he is a perfectionist and I'm not," says Clare, who was busy looking after the majority of the accounts for the label.

11am – "There was always a lot of going out," says Clare. "We would go to the shop that sold the cheap parcel tape or we would be going to buy all the artwork stuff. Everything was done the slow way round to be cheaper, so everything was extremely time consuming. We probably worked 100-hour weeks." Going out might mean heading off to Hatcher's to do some photocopying, or over to CliftonPrint to pick up sleeves.

1pm – "I did most of the talking to people and most of the press and stuff," says Clare. Nine months into Sarah's life, a phone was installed, as described in a letter Clare wrote to The Orchids' Chris Quinn in March 1988: "There's a blue telephone on our wall. They haven't switched us on yet of course, but it's there and it plugs into a socket and I do hope they switch us on today so we can play with it all evening and bankrupt Sarah. ... Oh will you just look at that telephone – one of those one-piece ones with the buttons on the receiver bit, but still quite lovely and it sits in a little (wee) bracket and has a blue wire. Oh, I wonder what the ring sounds like. I bet it's horrid." Once the label had invested in a car, as the only driver Clare was responsible for going backwards and forwards to the distributor and wherever else they needed to go. However, it's worth remembering that for the first few years of Sarah, there was no car and Clare and Matt ferried boxes of records around in taxis. "A lot of time from 1991 onwards was spent on the motorway," says Clare. "The bands played a lot more gigs in the latter half of the label, and we had a car and more money and merch to sell, so we went to a lot more gigs. Which meant an awful lot of late-night drives home, or to wherever we were staying, trying to stay awake."

£1.55 on photocopying? Sarah Records really knew how to splash the cash.
Courtesy of Sarah Records.

3pm – If there was a mailshot to be done, Clare and Matt would brace themselves for a lengthy handwriting session. With no computer or printer, thousands of envelopes needed to be addressed by hand, and the stamps individually licked, because this was in the days before stamps had morphed into stickers. "We did buy one of the spongy things they have in the post office in the end," says Matt, "and we've since discovered other labels roped people in to help." These days, if you want to send a mailshot out, you simply write an email, BCC it to however many thousand people sit on your database, and within 10 minutes you're onto a new task. But not in the Sarah era. "I think we had a couple of thousand people on our mailing list on a card index," says Matt. "We also bought the cheapest possible, gummed envelopes so you'd have to lick 1,000 envelopes and your tongue would end up bleeding."

5pm – There was the daily packaging up of orders to be done, and then traipsing down to the post office every afternoon. By the time Sarah had moved to Gwilliam Street, the closest main post office was on East Street in Bedminster. "We used to take it in turns to go every day," says Clare. "But there was one guy, if he saw us come in, he'd go and open up another counter for us at the end. So we didn't really have to queue at that point." While they were out and about, whoever had been to the post office would also buy discounted groceries for that day's supper, which they took it in turns to cook.

8pm – This time was spent writing letters to the bands or to people Clare and Matt had become postal friends with, rather than the shorter notes that went in with orders from people they didn't know. John Peel would be playing on the radio throughout the later part of the evening and, if they felt like putting their feet up, they might watch a bit of television. "We had a portable black and white TV from about 1989, it was a Christmas present from my parents," says Clare.

To wrap up, Matt says: "People seemed to think that we just released records, went to gigs and that was all there was to it. It was always slightly frustrating for us that people didn't really understand that most of it was just really mundane grind work." They even had a few work experience people but, on the whole, Clare and Matt didn't trust other people to do jobs like folding record sleeves as neatly as they themselves would, so they just got on and did everything on their own. Like heroes.

Pressing Matters

Sarah 1 had an initial pressing of around 1,000 copies, followed by a second pressing of around 600 (pressing numbers are never precise) and that was that. So no wonder copies of 'Pristine Christine' fetch such a pretty penny on Discogs. There was no deliberate decision to keep the numbers low to create collectable items, it was simply that each record needed to fund the next one, so there wasn't much time to be spent looking back at past releases when there were new records to think about. Later single releases would run to an initial pressing of 4,000 which, by the time CD singles were reluctantly introduced with Sarah 71 in 1993, were split evenly across 2,000 7"s and 2,000 CDs, which explains why some of the later Sarah 7"s are almost as hard to come by as the early ones.

Talking to a fanzine writer at the time, Clare said: "None of the records have been limited edition, with the exception of the fanzine/flexi packages, where it's impractical or even impossible to re-press. With each of these packages we've done 1,500. With the hard vinyl the intention has always been to sell as many as possible, and so most of them have been re-pressed at some time." In the same interview, Clare is asked for the sales of each record to date and she gives the following figures: Sarah 1 – 1,600; Sarah 2 – 1,000; Sarahs 3-4 – 1,500 each; Sarah 5 – 1,100 and Sarah 6 – 1,000, while "the compilation LP

> ❝ I never thought I'd live to see the day we'd be scheduling our releases to tie-in with the dollar-yen exchange rate. But then, I never thought we'd be employing scab labour or sending YTS kids up our chimneys so there you go, don't people change, eh?"
>
> **Sarah Newsletter No 8, July 1994**

will probably end up selling 5,000". That was *Shadow Factory*, which, Matt later told *Waaaah!* fanzine had sold around 8,000 copies by that point.

"We were in a position where people would write off for the next five or 10 records before we even knew what they were," Clare tells me now. "So you always knew that, whatever stage of the label it was, you could sell 3,000 of any 7" single and you never wanted to put out one that wasn't good enough because then obviously people would stop buying them ahead of release. So the economics worked because we were really quite certain in our sales."

> "We weren't averse to being successful or making money, it was just there was a way of doing it and a way of not doing it."
> **Clare**

Clare continues: "A lot of people have ended up thinking we weren't really trying to sell records but we were always trying to sell records, and we wanted as many people to hear every record as possible. But within our criteria. So we weren't going to try and get you to buy our records three times over because what's the point of that? But if we could get three times as many people to buy it through legitimate, decent means, then that's absolutely what we wanted."

This leads us to the thorny issue of formats. Sarah launched as a 7"-only label but after time it became clear that, in order to grow, Sarah was going to need to consider other formats. This didn't stop some of the hardened fans from calling Clare and Matt to account, though. The band Brighter notably did this via the medium of song with 'So You Said'. Songwriter Keris Howard says: "I thought doing 12"s was a sell out, simple as that. The trouble is, you start off with an ethical standpoint and that's what defines you against other record labels. And then you have the problem that, later on, you maybe need to do some of those things you said you wouldn't to continue to operate as a label. But you can't sidestep the fact that you have started doing things you said you'd never do. I thought it was disappointing that they released a 12", no matter how great 'Missing The Moon' is. When you saw it, it just looked like anything else from any other label." 'So You Said' is thinly veiled as a song about a girl who used to have a soul but I think we can all agree that nobody was fooled as to who the girl

The quibble strip was fairly self-explanatory. I hope Andy enjoyed his copy of *Sunstroke*.
Courtesy of Sarah Records.

in question was. "It was a poorly disguised attack on selling out on your principles and us getting frustrated with that," says Brighter's Alison Cousens. Nonetheless, Clare and Matt still put the record out.

Sarah fan Jyoti Mishra adds: "What's been lost from music is this thing that Sarah Records had, which is to get the fuck out of the way. It was the angriness, the politics, the vision of 'this isn't good enough', shitty repackaging, reissues, stickers on fucking records, major-level marketing bullshit, and that's all back again. Nothing has changed because capitalism just swallows whatever is problematic and shits it out the other side, like Creation did. That never happened to Sarah. They just did their thing."

One – of many – curious Sarah quirks was the brief introduction of quibble strips, which provided an opportunity for irate Sarah fans to grumble. "People were, quite rightly, always determined to hold us to account whenever they thought we'd strayed, and we felt it was important to take these criticisms on board," says Matt. "I had, after all, just written six fanzines complaining about the way other labels did things, and Sarah was, in part, me now putting my money where my mouth had been. Eventually, we decided to streamline the whole complaints procedure by including little tear-off strips on the 7" inserts so that people could, very literally, tear us off a strip." He explains: "Basically, they could quibble with a lot of what we did by ticking a little box alongside the statement 'I would like to quibble with a lot of what Sarah Records does'. And the strips soon became known as quibble strips. I should point out here that they existed only on the insert with Sarah 34. And that, sadly, there was no room for anything except the tick box. Or technically two, as there was also a box to tick if they didn't want to quibble."

FORMATS

1 – FLEXIS

In 1994, the *NME* called flexis "the most Luddite of formats", which is surely a recommendation for the format rather than a criticism?

From 1963, The Beatles had been issuing festive flexis to everyone in their fan club and, from then on, the format spiralled into common use. They were cheap to produce, cheap to circulate and had a delightful novelty appeal, even if the sound quality wasn't the best. But what could you expect from a thin bit of plastic that was 10% of the weight of a traditional vinyl 7" single? In the early 1980s, there was even a magazine called *Flexipop*, which gave readers a cover-mounted flexi with every issue. While for its first release, the Sha-La-La flexi label chose Mighty Mighty's 'Throwaway', summing up this ethos of disposable pop just perfectly.

"It goes back to the way that people were in touch with each other by mail," says Greg Webster of Razorcuts, meaning that

> ❝ Flexis are made of recycled plastic dustbins rolled out flat – hence the phrase 'throwaway pop'."
> **Letter to me from Matt, spring 1993**

The complete collection of Sha-La-La flexis, as well as the flexi that came with the final issue of Clare's *Kvatch* fanzine: all of these records are now highly collectable items.
Courtesy of Sarah Records.

because everyone was writing to each other it was much cheaper to post someone a flexi than to post them a 7". Razorcuts was one of the bands to put out a flexi on Sha-La-La, a release they shared with Talulah Gosh. Speaking to Roger Holland of *Sounds* in May 1987, "Sha-La-La supremo" Matt was enthusing about the power and magic of the six-and-a-half-inch piece of flexible plastic to transform the music industry, leaving Roger to sum up: "Matt and Sha-La-La Records firmly believe that the simple economics and the special intrinsic charm of the flexi-disc make it the best possible way to re-inject the spontaneity and brilliance and beauty back into pop music." It certainly worked because the eight Sha-La-La flexis have now become highly sought after collectors' items selling for huge sums, which is extraordinary given they cost 13p each to produce.

Matt told *Sounds*: "Basically, this release [The Poppyheads' four-track EP] sums up our entire attitude towards the music business. The band formed, wrote the songs, recorded them, gave the tape to us and we pressed the record all in the space of 28 days. So, yes it's raw, rough, the drummer gets in a tangle and the backing vocals seem to have been recorded at gunpoint. But it's still wonderful. It makes me happy!"

> **❝** Sturm und Drang? Ah, the one your brother did, you mean? We know more about you than you think... [Evil cackle].
>
> **Letter from Matt to me, January 1993**

Matt didn't have the monopoly on pre-Sarah flexis, though, because Clare put out a flexi via her fanzine *Kvatch* that featured The Groove Farm and The Sea Urchins. The latter were a band that Clare had been introduced to via her school friend Matthew Eaton, who would later be in Pram, and who attended university in Birmingham which was where The Sea Urchins hailed from. "I went to a gig in Birmingham the night before I started university in Bristol, and visited a fair bit, and Matthew started talking about The Sea Urchins and their singer Jamie [Roberts], who was a first year at Birmingham," says Clare. "Matthew and his friends put a Sea Urchins gig on at the end of November 1986 which I went up for, and I really loved them. I met Jamie at the gig and we started writing to each other. His letters were smart and funny and all in different coloured felt tip."

A friend suggested to Clare that she include a flexi with the next issue of *Kvatch* and The Sea Urchins were the obvious band for her to approach, alongside The Groove Farm, who were, as Clare says, "this brilliant, exciting Bristol band I'd seen play live a few times". She continues: "I suggested the idea to Jamie and he sent me the famous tape with 'Cling Film' and 'Summershine' on, and I was just blown away by 'Cling Film'. I mean, I liked 'Summershine' but it seemed much more obvious, not as sophisticated or atmospheric."

When Clare refers to "the famous tape", she means the tape that she didn't realise had also been sent to Sha-La-La for consideration although, by a lucky turn of events, both *Kvatch* and Sha-La-La opted for different songs for their flexis. Clare explains: "I had no idea they were offered a flexi by Sha-La-La, and Sha-La-La didn't know about me. Matt and I both found that out when I went round and asked him about getting my flexis home on the coach from Lyntone [a pressing plant in London], asking how big and heavy the box would be. Luckily we'd picked different songs. I got *Kvatch 6* printed up and the flexis made in the Easter holidays, and it came out in April 1987."

A month or two after their appearance on *Kvatch*, The Sea Urchins shared the fifth Sha-La-La flexi with The Orchids. The Urchins' keyboardist Bridget Duffy remembers the label's co-founder Pete Williams writing to invite them to contribute a track and artwork. "Pete sent us really detailed things about how printing worked and how we should make sure we were aware it was in reverse, and I think we wrote back to say 'Just because we're from Birmingham, we're not entirely stupid,'" Bridget laughs, adding: "We just thought it was cool to have something out. We were all about 17 and it felt cool to have something you could actually put on a record player." Bridget and Pete are now married, by the way: a true indie-pop love story.

"I quite liked the idea that it was a disposable thing," says Tim Vass of Razorcuts about the Sha-La-La flexi that his band released with Talulah Gosh. "So we didn't spend loads of money recording it. We went with the Talulah Gosh crew to a tiny studio in Oxfordshire, and spent most of the time chucking balls at each other in the garden rather than actually doing the recording. You play it a couple of times and move on to the next thing." His bandmate Greg Webster adds: "It was completely outside of the normal structures of the music business, that you could just have this bendy little thing that would go out with the fanzine. It was really in line with the mood of the times." Back to Tim: "It's ironic that it had this fantastic sleeve that Liz [Price, Talulah Gosh member and future Turner Prize-winner] and Mathew [Fletcher, drums] did, and it looks really iconic now. There's a silly little flexi inside but it looks like a brilliant indie-pop artefact."

In 1990, my brother Adam Mornement put out a Brighter flexi as the lone release on his Sturm und Drang bedroom label with 'Next Summer' as the lead song. Adam had previously interviewed the band's frontman Keris Howard for his fanzine *Pretty Potty* and, after seeing Brighter play at the Fleece & Firkin in Bristol (at the infamous Four Bands and a Fight gig, and for more on this turn to Chapter 14), Adam and Keris got chatting. "Keris explained that there were issues with Matt and Clare," says Adam. "Some differences of opinion about direction or something. I can't recall how the idea of me putting out a flexi came up, but I do remember thinking that Sarah might be a bit annoyed although Keris calmed my nerves on that. I decided on a flexi because I had no money and that's what people did at the time as flexis were part of the DIY culture. It did really well, sold out quickly, with the Rough Trade shop in Ladbroke Grove buying up at least half of them. Keris was, very sweetly, concerned that I'd lose money on the venture but that didn't happen."

Keris adds: "I was keen to release some of the stuff that didn't fit into the mould of where we were going with Brighter on Sarah, and I had a few songs which hung together quite nicely in terms of what was released on that flexi. I always thought 'Next Summer' was a really great pop song, so it was good to be able to get some coverage on that. In those early days, it was lovely that people came over and said

"There's nothing magical about a bit of plastic that's 7" across..." says Matt. Oh yes, there is.
Jon Craig.

nice things about what you were doing, I never would have had the confidence to do that. To have someone willing to put work in to release our stuff was amazing."

2 – 7" SINGLES

"The point about vinyl for us was that it was the cheap format to buy and therefore it was accessible," says Clare. When Sarah started, a vinyl album would cost £5 to buy while a CD album cost £15, so it made sense to produce music on the more affordable format. "We were strident initially about being a 7"-only label, we said everything would always be available on 7"," says Matt. "There's nothing magical about a bit of plastic that's 7" across, we just wanted something that represented the aesthetics and ethics and style and attitude of what we thought a pop record should be. And at the time, a 7" single was the closest to representing that."

That statement also reflects the fact that, at the time Sarah launched, Clare and Matt could have had no idea how successful the record label would become, nor how long it would last. So while some people gave them stick for later releasing music on other formats, it would be unrealistic to expect two kids in 1987 to know that, eight years later, they would still be going. And, of course, Sarah would not have lasted for eight years if they had stuck to only releasing 7"s.

The label's initial statement that it would be 7"-only was a big draw for lots of people, not necessarily because of any love for the format but because of the principle. Josh Meadows of The Sugargliders explains: "It was such a refreshing thing for there to be a label that believed in stuff and wasn't just about shifting units or having a particular style. They weren't doing it to get into the *NME*, they were doing it because this was what they believed in."

Boyracer's Stewart Anderson agrees: "I loved the idea of 7" singles and that being a pop artefact, it's two or three songs [or six, in the case of Boyracer's 'From Purity to Purgatory EP']. I liked the idea of creating something disposable. I run my own record label today [Emotional Response] and a lot of the things that Sarah instilled in me are still things that I believe to this day: pop music should be instant, you shouldn't have to think about it too much, it should affect you immediately, it should be disposable."

> Records are for playing, not for keeping in pristine condition and waiting for them to increase in value. You can do that with wine or shares. It's not what records are for."
> **Clare**

The Wedding Present famously released a 7" every month throughout 1992, yet frontman David Gedge surprises me when he says: "One thing we didn't share [with Sarah], though, was that

Sarah 1 was 'Pristine Christine' by The Sea Urchins. But I'm fairly sure you already knew that. Pictured above, right, is the original artwork for that record's label.
Courtesy of Sarah Records.

obsessive worship of the 7" single! Don't get me wrong, I *love* 7" singles. But I also like 12" singles and 10" singles." David was interviewed by Mark Carnell for the *Are You Scared To Get Happy?* fanzine and, afterwards, Mark told David that the interview left him feeling "not a little puzzled and disturbed." David explains: "That was because of my fairly flippant answer to his question about 7" singles. I said: 'I have no truck with people who prefer 7"s for aesthetic reasons. I prefer 12"s because they're bigger in your hands and recall childhood when *everything* was big in your hands. I don't like two tracks on one side of a 7" because the record gets quieter with closer grooves.'" Having just re-read this fanzine interview, David tells me: "On a later page, there was an editorial with the headline 'Why David Gedge Is Wrong'! That made me smile."

> ❝ You could be quite trainspottery and have lists of the singles and what you had yet to buy, and it was like indie Pokémon."
> **Jyoti Mishra, White Town**

One argument that could be levelled against the idea of disposable pop is that you are unwittingly creating a culture of collectability. Clare and Matt have always stated that they do not believe in limited editions and never intentionally created exclusive records, although the exorbitant prices that many Sarah records now achieve on the second-hand market are in unfortunate contrast to this. In 1993, when someone gave me a copy of 'Pristine Christine', Matt was flabbergasted that I'd received it as a gift: "Somebody gave you a 'Pristine Christine'????? I hope you realise people pay anything up to £60 for copies these days…?!?" In 2023, there is a slightly damaged copy on Discogs selling for £240 plus postage.

Talking about the appeal of the 7" versus *spits on floor* the 12", Bobby Wratten of The Field Mice says: "When we first joined Sarah, I was pretty much on side as far as 7" singles were concerned. Especially the antipathy towards three-minute pop songs being put on 12" singles, which was a common occurrence. However, I was still a big 12" fan and had grown up with them as the perfect format for a lot of the music I liked, be that Factory releases by Section 25 or 52nd Street or records by Peech Boys or Grandmaster Flash. In fact, I'd argue the perfect independent format was the four-track 12". Put simply, I think Sarah could afford to have a blind spot to other formats because they weren't really concerned with the types of music that flourished outside of 7" singles. The 7" idea did seem a slightly backwards looking, nostalgic thing at the time, which is an odd stance for them to take considering nostalgia has always been a bugbear of theirs."

This leads us very neatly to…

3 – 12" SINGLES

The most controversial thing in the entire history of Sarah Records is that they released two 12" singles. The evil, corporate, money grabbing sell-outs. Gah! "It was really difficult to say to bands 'You can't do this', when they could see their friends in other bands putting out 12" singles and being told that they won't get into shops if they're not doing a 12","" says Matt.

The first 12" single on Sarah was 'Penetration' by The Orchids in 1991, which the Scottish band pushed for because it seemed as if everyone on every other label was putting them out. Clare and Matt are at pains to point out that there are five songs on 'Penetration', making it extremely good value for money. "When we finally did a 12" single, we didn't want it to have a spine because that's what we didn't like about 12" singles, it gave them a self-importance, we just wanted them to look like large 7"s. We didn't realise it would cost more because everybody else has spines on their 12"s because then you don't have to reset the machines to do it," says Matt, notching up an early entry in the catalogue of expensive mistakes that Sarah made in the pursuit of integrity. Clare adds: "I remember going down to the Revolver warehouse on the bus to fetch a box back, and hadn't twigged that a box of albums is 100 (four boxes of 25) but a box of 12" singles is 160 (four boxes of 40, if you don't put a spine in), and I couldn't really carry it. By the time I got to the bus stop, my arms were bruised down the insides."

> ❝ It shouldn't really come down to formats. It's the content that counts. A brilliant song on a 12" will always be better than a terrible song on a 7"."
>
> **Bobby Wratten, The Field Mice**

'Missing The Moon' by The Field Mice followed later in 1991, a track so long it wouldn't have fitted on a 7" anyway. Despite the length of the song (seven minutes), Clare and Matt felt so guilty that the 12" only contained three songs that they sold it for the price of a 7", which must have made it hard to break even. "I suspect all of us would be richer if we'd made it a 12" price," considers Clare. "But my guess is we started with quite a high pressing because it's The Field Mice and I'm guessing we did an initial 4,000, and it's much cheaper to do 4,000 in one go and leave the machines on than it is to press 2,000 and another 2,000. So it probably broke even. But we wouldn't have made any money on it."

Bobby elaborates: "I always credit Michael [Hiscock, bassist] with persuading

Sarah to put 'Missing the Moon' out on a 12" over the course of a phone call he had with them. They seriously suggested trying to release it on a 7" at one point but it was seven minutes long and would have been squashed within an inch of its life. 'Missing the Moon' was quite clearly a 12" song."

So while these are the only two 12" singles in Sarah's eight-year history, Clare and Matt still got a lot of grief from those who felt the label had sold its soul in the process. However, 7" singles had stopped being cool by the early 1990s and many shops just weren't stocking them anymore. What's an indie label to do?

4 – 10"S

Ahh, the 10". Another divisive format. Sarah released just three 10" singles and seven 10" mini-albums, yet someone on Twitter still wanted me to quiz Clare and Matt about why they put out "so many". Ten 10"s over eight years doesn't strike me as *that* many. Perhaps there were *so few* because they are a very expensive format to press since, rather than using two inches less vinyl, as one might imagine, they are a 12" vinyl that's been cut down to size. "We made a lot of expensive mistakes despite trying to be frugal," rues Clare. While Matt explains: "We thought a 10" would be a nicer thing than the 12", and naïvely we thought it would be cheaper because it's smaller, but they have to reset all the machines for both the sleeves and the vinyl, and there's a £450 setting-up charge for that, and again every time you repress."

Cute 10"s were not without other problems, too. Record shops didn't like them because they were too big for the 7" racks and too small for the 12" ones, meaning they ended up getting tatty and never sold as well as other formats because nobody could find them. And it was extra hard to find them when certain bands refused to put any text on the front. (*coughs* Snowball.)

5 – ALBUMS

Shadow Factory was Sarah's first album, a compilation issued in 1988. The first band album was *Lyceum* by The Orchids in 1989, which was an adorable 10". "The albums really came about because the bands had got to the stage that they wanted to do albums," says Clare. "And you'd either stand in their way and frustrate them, which just seemed unhelpful, or start doing albums. The first compilation was driven by the fact the early records weren't available and it was a way of making everything available again at a very low price." She adds: "Compilation albums were a really good way of getting the music out to more people and getting them in the shops that didn't really rack up 7"s very much. And obviously we priced them incredibly cheap but they were a good way of sorting the finances of running the label. Once bands got to the stage they wanted to do albums, and we were able to do that for them, it was really the only thing that generated money."

Some people were upset that the long players also came with barcodes, complaining that this transformed the music into A

> **"** Given we're a 7"-only label, it's a shame our new releases are mostly all LPs."
> **Sarah Newsletter No 6, January 1994**

Product. Matt says: "That's why our first-ever record with a barcode has an on-sleeve dedication to frequent correspondent Chris from Poynton. We knew the sell-out would upset him."

Clare and Matt refused to put any songs on albums that had previously been released as singles, so that fans didn't feel ripped off about buying the same music twice. Although, in some instances, this philosophy caused a bit of tension with the bands, such as when The Orchids wanted to release 'Peaches' from *Unholy Soul* as a single, and there's no arguing that the song would have made an absolutely blinding single. The band's producer Ian Carmichael explains: "I could see where Sarah were coming from about value for money for the fans but, when it came to 'Peaches', we all agreed it should be a single and Sarah said 'No, we don't do that, we're not releasing a single from the album.' I thought, 'What a tragedy. This is a career for these guys, it could be really blossoming with this hit single.' But it didn't happen."

An exception to this rule came with Even As We Speak's *Feral Pop Frenzy* LP which *did* include two singles, because Sarah hoped the album would make its way to the band's native Australia where the singles hadn't been released. To appease their guilt, Clare and Matt issued the generously-filled 17-track album as a mid-price LP. However, the fact Even As We Speak couldn't put an album track out as a single in the UK was frustrating, as singer Mary Wyer says: "We couldn't take singles from *Feral Pop Frenzy*. We wanted to put out 'Falling Down the Stairs' which was getting BBC play and have it actually as a single, and we couldn't do that." Keyboardist and guitarist Julian Knowles adds: "I remember some quite funny discussions where they were also reluctant to release anything on CD because they didn't think that the fans would be able to afford them because they didn't own CD players, which seems so charming in retrospect."

6 - CASSETTES

I'm not sure anybody associates Sarah with cassettes but there *were* some releases on tape, mostly tied to the European market. "They were always an ugly format," says Clare. "The first ones were made for French release and we imported a few to the UK, then later we made our own for some or all of the albums, when we were selling decent quantities overall and there was demand for all formats. The French abbreviate them to 'K7' ['kah' 'sept'] and that's the only interesting thing I have to say about cassettes." Tapes. Nobody's favourite format.

> " We've given up doing cassettes... I always thought they were nasty little things."
> **Sarah Newsletter No 1, October 1992**

7 - CDS

The first CD single was Sarah 66 in 1992, The Orchids' 'Thaumaturgy', "to test the waters," before CD singles became de rigueur from Sarah 71. Record shops were removing their vinyl racks, 7"s were seen as very uncool and the news was full of reports that it was the end of days for vinyl. Well, the news wasn't exactly *full* of those stories but it had a few vinyl-is-dying stories hidden among the ones about, I don't know, rioting all over England, Damien Hirst's pickled shark and the Queen's annus horribilis. For this reason, the final 30 singles were split evenly between 7" and CD format. "I don't think many people have much love for CD singles anymore," says Clare, "but that's how lots of people were buying music back then."

I've seen a letter that radio DJ John Peel sent to Clare and Matt in 1989. It addresses the fact that sooner or later Sarah were going to have to consider CDs. He wrote: "I know what you mean about CDs but they exist and you'll have to come to terms with them somehow – and the sound is good. Even unglamorously recorded sound comes out better. What I'm saying is that eventually Sarah will benefit from CD in some form or other." He was right.

The first CD album was the *Air Balloon Road* compilation in 1990, which featured Akiko Yamauchi's famous cherries photo on the cover, a version of which became adapted as the label's logo. "Because that was our first CD, we didn't quite know how to make a CD insert and we thought we could just have one sheet of paper inside it rather than a fold-up booklet and that must be cheaper, but again it wasn't," laments Matt, chalking up yet another entry in the list of failed money-saving decisions. "They had to actually print the two bits and cut them in half and just put the single sheet in. So again, our attempt to save money completely backfired."

But it wasn't just putting the sleeve together that was a learning point, as Matt continues: "It was our first CD and a lot of engineers didn't know how to compile a CD, so we took it to a studio somewhere in east Bristol, run by a guy who used to work for the BBC. We took all the tapes in and copied them and he spliced them together on an old reel-to-reel machine, and we sent it off. But he'd joined the bits together using sticky tape, as you did with reel-to-reels, and that doesn't work for CDs because you need a continuous data stream. But he'd never done one before either. So they had to send it back and say 'Can you do a copy of the whole tape in one continuous piece'. And you had to put markers in between each track. Everybody was learning as they went along at that point, even supposedly experienced engineers.

"Our compromise, in terms of ideals and politics, was to insist that each CD single contained exactly the same tracks as the 7"," continues Matt. "And obviously we weren't going to start releasing two-track CDs, so that sometimes meant the CD version would combine two 7"s into one. Sadly, making CDs back then meant plastic jewel boxes, rather than cardboard slipcases or digipaks, so they're not nice things, and obviously anyone buying the CD didn't get the inserts."

A knock-on effect of dividing the 7" and CD allocation for singles was that it was no longer financially viable to continue producing sealed sleeves for the 7"s, which was why Clare and Matt returned to the fiddly business of folding covers and

> ❝ I, for one, regret every single album we've ever released, not because they're not all as good as *You Can't Hide Your Love Forever* but because we never <u>wanted</u> to release albums, that wasn't the POINT of Sarah. Unfortunately, it's impossible given the way the music industry exists at present, for us to survive doing just 7"s. But that doesn't mean we should lose sight of what we're trying to do – our political agenda as it were – so: flexi discs, fanzines, board games, post-war theme parks – come on down!"
>
> **Sarah Newsletter No 2, January 1993**

FUN FACT: There was no CD player at Sarah HQ, meaning that Clare and Matt used to post a copy of every CD they released to Harvey Williams in London to play and check that it sounded alright, because he was the only person they knew who owned a CD player.

assembling the 7" packages by hand which they'd abandoned at Sarah 30.

There's also a story about the production of Secret Shine's *Loveblind* CD, which was used as the subject of a late-night documentary by local television station HTV. This, bizarrely, involved a 7am trip across the River Severn to reach a CD pressing plant in Cwmbran, and footage of Matt and Secret Shine's Scott Purnell and Jamie Gingell being obliged to wear head-to-toe sterile white clothing so as not to infect the CDs with anything that wasn't pop music. "Because, of course, THAT'S how you make a CD – you take your master tape IN PERSON to the pressing plant, where you show your artwork to a receptionist, and then they take you to meet the engineer IN PERSON but only after you've put on a plastic smock and hat, and then you watch while they make your CD for you," says Matt.

RUN-OFF GROOVES

For decades, musicians have been etching secret messages into the run-off grooves of their records. George 'Porky' Peckham is a well-regarded engineer who worked on records from the 1960s onwards and his many records have been famously etched with the words 'A Porky Prime Cut'. But often, the band or artist will want some input on the wording. A few classic examples include the four sides of The Clash's *London Calling* LP begging fans to 'tear' 'down' 'the' 'walls', while Joy Division's 'Love Will Tear Us Apart' 7" implored 'Don't disillusion me' on one side and 'I've only got record shops left' on the other. Not to be left out, some Sarah artists enjoyed adding a little something into their run-off grooves. After all, it didn't cost any more to add a short message, so why not? "We always asked bands if they wanted anything, but a lot weren't really that bothered, which seems a shame and slightly inexplicable. Why would you not?" asks Matt.

The most famous example is on the *Glass Arcade* compilation, which has "Sarah Records unequivocally supports a fully integrated light rail rapid-transport system for the Greater Bristol area" across both sides; as all good Sarah fans know, this was supposed to say 'rapid-transit' but, well, you can't always get what you want. Matt muses: "Noel the engineer spent most of his days cutting records for PWL, as the cutting room was in part of their building, and I don't think Kylie Minogue ever requested any interesting run-off groove messages. He also did lots of stuff for Earache Records. It was us, Napalm Death and Stock, Aitken & Waterman, so we always felt he must have had a very odd take on contemporary music."

I've read every single Sarah record run-off groove to save you the trouble, and here's a quick round-up:

- **Tributes**: A run-off groove can be a touching way to celebrate someone, as

"Mathew did a wee wee from a treehouse." Heavenly celebrated drummer Mathew Fletcher (pictured above, second from the right) in the run-off groove to 'So Little Deserve'.
Alison Wonderland.

Brighter demonstrated on *Laurel* when Alison Cousen's shero Tracey Thorn got a shout out. Or as The Orchids showed on *Unholy Soul* when singer Pauline Hynds Bari's daughter Fahria was mentioned. While The Springfields' 'Sunflower' stated 'For Elaine', which was a nod to Matt's ex-girlfriend who had loaned the label some money in its early days.

- **Cultural references:** The Field Mice paid tribute to Sylvia Plath on 'Emma's House' but sadly the engineer included a typo meaning that "I do it so it feels like hell" is missing that crucial final 'l' on the last word, "leaving people to decide for themselves whether it was a typo for 'hell' or 'helping' or 'helicopters are attacking me from all directions which leaves me weirdly euphoric'," sighs Matt. The 14 Iced Bears had 'Safeways Here We Come' etched onto 'Come Get Me', which is a delightful take on The Smiths' album as well as a nod to their own supermarket roots. Tramway's 'Maritime City' had 'Goodnight Irene' etched into its grooves, in acknowledgement of Bristol Rovers' fan anthem. While Action Painting! put messages for Bouncer the dog from the soap opera *Neighbours* on the run-off grooves to both 'These Things Happen' and 'Classical Music'. On 'Fireworks', Aberdeen included a reference to the American cartoon series *Pinky & the Brain*. But my favourite is Blueboy's cinematic pun 'My Own Private Walthamstow', which appears on their single 'River' about the actor River Phoenix.

- **Political digs:** The Orchids had the immortal words 'Fuck the Poll Tax' etched onto 'Underneath The Window, Underneath The Sink', to sit alongside their anti-poll tax song 'Defy The Law'. While The Golden Dawn took a stab at the government by quoting The Jam on 'My Secret World' with: "It's the kidney machines that pay for rockets and guns and I don't want what this society's got." Not to be outdone by their bands, the Sarah compilation LP *Shadow Factory* said: "Looking forward to the revolution."

- **Self-referential, err, references:** Some bands wrote messages that were about themselves, and why not? "It's been a long time coming" wrote The Sea Urchins on 'A Morning Odyssey', which was true as it had been two years since their previous record. Even As We Speak quoted themselves on *Feral Pop Frenzy* with "Nothing but clear skies coming your way". The Talulah Gosh compilation *They've Scoffed The Lot* has the hopeful message "They're back, back!! Back!!!" on side one, before dashing fans' hopes on side two with "Except they're not!" Pish. While Blueboy were so delighted to be on their favourite record label that their debut single 'Clearer' comes with the etched message "Our dream come true", which is sweet. Lastly, and almost exactly last, were Shelley, who modestly wrote "Unique, young, unrivalled, smashing" and "We're bloody marvellous" on 'Reproduction Is Pollution'.

- **Ignoring the haters:** As we know, Sarah had more than its fair share of doubters and some of them were acknowledged in the run-off grooves. "Well, we're still here" said the label bosses on the *Temple Cloud* compilation. While Heavenly's 'Atta Girl' single proclaimed "Sing if you're glad to be girlie". And Boyracer's 'Pure Hatred' simply said: "Very Sarah Records ... Like, we're bothered."

The economics of it all

During an undated interview with *Waaaah!* fanzine, Matt said: "We work every hour of every day, and we worked out a little while back that we were actually 'living' off £15 a week. So we obviously don't do it for the money. I can't imagine doing that in 10 years' time, not on that sort of level." However, this is not to say that Sarah was unsuccessful.

> ❝ Time isn't money, time is just time and there's never enough. Money is just money and we haven't got enough. We've lost money so far and are about to plunge £3,000 in debt."
>
> **Letter from Matt to Pete Williams, autumn 1988**

For the first year of Sarah, Clare was getting her student grant, before spending the summer of 1988 working for the civil service in order to fund the next batch of releases. Meanwhile, Matt was receiving £40 a week from the Enterprise Allowance Scheme. Filling in a tax return showed Sarah had made £5.25 profit during their first year of business, "but by the time I graduated [1989], it was just about supporting us both," says Clare. "Then we got to the point where we started doing more albums. It was a successful label, it did make money." Matt expands: "We were turning over a quarter of a million pounds at the peak. It used to annoy us when people would call us small, and we'd say 'But we're turning over a quarter of a million, we're not that small!' But we lived pretty frugally, and turnover isn't the same as profit." He adds: "Another thing that annoys us is when people say we went bust at the end. But if we'd gone bust, we wouldn't have taken out £5,000 of adverts in the music press to announce the fact, or stopped neatly at number 100." With which there is no arguing.

Clare and Matt often resorted to hitchiking as a means of getting around the place, and here's their very own multi-purpose sign.
Clare Wadd

Hitchhiking was a key mode of transport for these cash-strapped record label bosses, not just in the early days of the label but for many years to come. "With Clare being a student and me not having made millions from my time with NCP [National Car Parks], we used to hitch a lot in the early days to save money," says Matt. "We hitched up to Birmingham for The Sea Urchins' recording, and down to Exeter in a crisp lorry for either the second-ever Field Mice gig or a really early Orchids one, I can't remember which. And then we hitched up to Manchester when The Field Mice played Rawtenstall. And we tried hitching out of Portsmouth after recording 'These Things Happen' with Action Painting!, but gave up after about an hour in the rain beside the M275 and took the train.

"We hijacked a car once," recalls Matt. "We'd hitched back from somewhere and got stranded in Filton and it was raining and we'd resigned ourselves to walking all the way back to Clifton [five miles], and then somebody pulled up to ask directions and I pretty much said 'Can you give us a lift?' and started opening his door." The

> "They were serious about doing things properly. Integrity for them was everything."
>
> **Pete Momtchiloff, Heavenly**

helpless driver ended up taking the two soaking record company executives all the way home and Matt muses: "Even later that evening, I couldn't believe I'd done that. Essentially rattling his door handle and saying 'Can we come with you?'" Anyone who has ever met Matt will agree that this is hard to believe, given what a softly spoken and mild-mannered chap he is. "We must have been the worst hitchhikers," says Clare, "because people who pick up hitchhikers probably want to chat, and then they get us who are shy and don't know how to chat."

Even catching a lift with the bands wasn't without risks. Clare once squeezed into the back of The Field Mice's van after a gig in Leeds. Never mind that it is illegal to travel in the back of a van for safety reasons, but the bottom of this particular van was so rusty that she could see the Tarmac of the motorway whizzing past beneath her. "You look back and think, 'Were we utterly insane?' Was it youthful enthusiasm or was it a different world?," muses Clare.

With Clare and Matt being vegetarian, at least food wasn't expensive. I noticed a trend for recipe tips in their writing over the years, and here are a few choice meals that any culinary inclined readers are welcome to whip up for themselves if they wish to recreate authentic indie-pop suppers:

- Pizza: scone base with cheese and sage, onion, ketchup, sweetcorn, cheese. Presumably with a glass of... (*Lemonade*, Sarah 14)
- Carrot and breadcrumb pie (insert 31)
- Potatoes with beans (Josh Meadows' diary records a supper at Sarah HQ)
- Tea and margarine (smudges identified on a letter from Clare to Chris Quinn, The Orchids, March 1988)
- White chocolate choc ices, presumably shop bought (insert 84)
- "You always seem to ring up at tea-time, and I know that if I try to argue then my chips will crisp, my courgettes sag and my yolks cease to move." (Unappetising letter from Matt to me, September 1994)

Academic and fan Sukhdev Sandhu muses that the frugality with which Clare and Matt lived was "close to hardcore punk. This is like Fugazi. Obviously the music is very different but this is anarchism." He considers that the politics involved here were to do with not being reliant on anybody for survival: "On one hand, it sounds very romantic doing a record label, and of course it's mostly not romantic, especially the way they worked. And they were just incredibly hard working and devotional at a period when a lot of people of their age, including maybe some of their bands, were going out. I guess this is one of the paradoxes of entrepreneurialism. This thing which some people think about as anti-Thatcher is partly a function of cheapness. They were really, really hard working. And even if they turned a profit, good for them, they were never ripping anybody off." Music journalist Pete Paphides agrees: "It must have been really hard work. All those extra bits you used to get with the record, with short stories and these wonderful discursive streams of consciousness typewritten... They were quite hard on themselves really, weren't they? I love that almost incidental militancy about how Sarah went about their business."

> "Of all the labels that we've ever had anything to do with, Sarah has been by far the most thorough with their accounting."
>
> **Josh Meadows, The Sugargliders**

I was touched to see that, at the end of 1988, Matt added a PS on a letter to Chris Quinn of The Orchids to say: "Don't worry about sending SAEs in future." And the thought of a band being considerate enough to cover postage costs for their own record label is almost enough to break your heart. I don't suppose Kylie Minogue was sending SAEs to Pete Waterman in 1988.

The economies that Clare and Matt were making were not overlooked by some of the bands they supported. "They had less money than anyone else I knew," remarks Pete Momtchiloff of Heavenly. "They often went to gigs with their bands to look after them, because a lot of the bands were quite feckless and didn't really know how to deal with people and would be a bit feeble about getting paid and so on." In this sense, Clare and Matt would go to gigs partly to run the merch stall but partly to be a record label presence. "The people who ran record labels, who I met quite a lot of, tended to be either chancers who knew that they were not doing things honestly but didn't care too much, or innocents who said, 'Oh well, I didn't really think about the finances much, I just did it for the love of it'. And that's great but bands would often come a cropper with both of those types of people. But Matt and Clare weren't like either of those. They were in it for the love of it but they weren't innocents." Pete's bandmate Rob Pursey agrees: "They are the most trustworthy people I've ever dealt with in anything."

This sentiment is echoed by The Sugargliders, with Josh Meadows saying: "They gave us records of how many singles had sold, it was all handwritten and faxed to us, and they always recouped to the band what was owed to us." Joel Meadows adds: " It was split so, after expenses, the profits were shared between the band and the label. Big bands might strike deals like that but not little bands with little labels. We still get royalties from them, it's amazing they continue to honour that. It felt like there was no sense that they were trying to be successful. They were trying to be honest."

Just one of the quirks of Sarah was that when they signed The Springfields in 1988, Clare and Matt agreed to send the band's Ric Menck a copy of every Sarah release instead of a cheque. An agreement they honoured right until the label closed in August 1995. "I had no idea that they would end up putting out so many records," admits Ric now. "I'm pleased to say, they were good to word. I still have one copy of every single they released. I didn't love everything on the label but most of it was fantastic. Some of it sounds better to me now than it did back then, which is a testament to the fact that the music is really good. It has held up over time." Clare adds: "He still doesn't let us send him money even though we no longer have any records to send him instead. If he'd sold them all at the right point, he'd have been substantially up on the deal."

Musical Merchandise

Sarah was very clear about not wanting to rip the fans off, and was also aware that many of the fans were students and wouldn't have had much money. But there were still a few bits of merchandise that crept out. There were t-shirts for the bands who played live a lot and, of course, for the Sarah cherries, although they never played live. "T-shirts were a nightmare as everything had to be in four sizes, and sorting through four sizes of black t-shirts in black bin liners under a table in the dark while people are accidentally spilling their beer on them is not fun," moans Matt.

And that was the main trouble with merchandise, it needed to be sold. "Standing around in desolate pub car parks with the night's merchandise takings stuffed in plastic carrier bags alongside unsold t-shirts, waiting for the person who'd promised you a lift to show up…" rues Matt. "We managed to get a parking ticket in Barking while loading t-shirts. But that's rock'n'roll."

It was Mark Dobson who came up with the idea of The Field Mice printing up their own t-shirts to sell on tour. "We couldn't hitchhike or go on the National Express because we had equipment. We needed to put the equipment in a van and we needed petrol to put in the van," says Mark. "So I got these t-shirts done and, to everyone's amazement, we sold quite a lot, and the money we made from t-shirts was putting petrol in the van or buying food for us to eat. So suddenly they were like, 'We knew there was a reason we put this guy in the band!'"

In addition to t-shirts, other merchandise included a mountain of pastel-coloured butterfly badges promoting *Le Jardin de Heavenly*, which was also accompanied by a bright yellow plastic bag if you bought the LP from an independent record shop in the Chain With No Name. "I know we had dilemmas when we did the plastic carrier bag," says Matt. "We were worried that people who bought it in Virgin or Our Price would be sulking because they didn't get the plastic carrier bag, so we only did it on condition that we would also send people the bag through the post if they wrote to us and said they didn't get one." Clare muses: "It's interesting how well they've lasted, isn't it? Oh shit. Plastic doesn't decompose... We've got all these 30-year-old plastic bags that will still be around in another 30 years."

Curiously, in the *One Page Fanzine* that was part of the June 1992 'Le Grand Tour de Heavenly' flyer, it says: "Anyone who pays £20 for a yellow plastic carrier bag in five years' time is plainly stupid." And yet, 30+ years later, those bags are rarer than a copy of 'Pristine Christine' so, when they do pop up on resale sites, go for a lot more than £20.

> ❝ We always dreamed of one day producing some Sarah mugs and maybe even a teapot."
> **Matt**

The fact that Matt's parents lived in London was very helpful, as they provided a place to stay when Clare and Matt were in the capital to go to recording studios, to the cutting of records or just to gigs. Mr and Mrs Haynes were largely supportive of the Sarah enterprise. "They didn't really understand it," says Matt. "They were slightly too old to get pop music or understand what it was about. But I think they were just happy that I was doing something that I enjoyed and that was actually bringing in some money, because they'd obviously worried about me when I was leaving university as I clearly wasn't going to be a career physicist and then I went to work in a car park."

Matt recalls his mum getting rather concerned when she answered the phone one day "and it was the 14 Iced Bears, ringing from the studio to ask if they could have another £100 as the recording was over-running. I think, even then, she was anxious about my finances. But she also understood how important it was to get a good snare sound so she gave them the go-ahead." And on another occasion: "She had a long chat with Amelia [Fletcher] about whether I was eating OK, and Amelia assured her that I was."

He continues: "We gave [my parents] a copy of every single record that we released. We never included the inserts or the fanzines, because I don't think I could ever have explained to them what a fanzine or an insert was. But they knew what a

Top: The kitchen/living room/office at Upper Belgrave Road. Matt notes: "Fax machine far left on top of fridge. I've always thought this photo was very evocative of the early life of a small record label – we bought the washing machine out of our first profits. Collection of Clifton Suspension Bridge postcards just visible on left-hand wall. Niche for coffin to left of front door." **Bottom left:** *Le Jardin de Heavenly* came with a limited edition plastic bag if you bought it from certain shops. You'll hate to know that I once had about 30 of the things thanks to my job in an indie record shop... and I binned most of them years later. Sorry. **Bottom right:** No self-respecting indie lapel was seen without a button badge.

Top: Courtesy of Sarah Records. Bottom left and right: Jon Craig.

record was although they had no record player." As a very sweet afterthought, Matt then tells me: "We gave them everything and I never knew what happened to the records. When my dad died in 2020, we were going through all his possessions and we found the complete Sarah Records collection that he'd got up in his little office, along with a scrap of paper on which he'd noted which catalogue numbers were missing, ie the fanzines."

In 'A Day for Destroying Things', the half-page advert that in August 1995 announced the end of their record label, Clare and Matt made it clear that there would never be any encores. So there will be no deluxe box sets, no re-releases, nothing to make you spend money on what you already have. As Matt explains: "A lot of the bands want their material available and it would be wrong of us to stop that happening, but we wanted the 100 records to be the end. So there will be no more Sarah records ever. But a lot of the stuff we released is available for download and that's fine with us. It's not important to have the 7" single decades later, it's about the music not the product."

*****

These Things Happened:
Dickon Edwards, Shelley

"Matt and Clare were both softly spoken and aloof, to the point where I first mistook them for fans rather than the label. But they were friendly and serious about what they believed in. I think I tried to get them to be interested in my musical exploits for some time, and they weren't keen on those. The early Orlando, which became Shelley, had played a few gigs with Blueboy and other Sarah-related bands by then, so we were on the same page mentally. I admired them so very much, they had integrity without being humourless. Sarah Records was a kind of Bloomsbury Group scene, really."

Chapter 3

Bristol: Maritime City

Bristol in 1987 was a city embedded in Margaret Thatcher's Conservative Britain and, in June of that year, the Iron Lady had just been voted in for her third term. National unemployment was around three million, which might have been the *lowest* figure for years but was still horribly high and indicative of the gulf between the wealthy and the poor in the UK. This was a year in which bomb and terrorism threats to mainland UK were ongoing from the IRA, there were riots in Leeds, a massacre in Hungerford, and an average of one death a day across the UK from AIDS-related illnesses. It's little wonder that in the summer of 1987 the Justified Ancients of Mu Mu independently released an astute pop-hip-hop album called *1987 (What The Fuck is Going On?)* populated by political rap alongside samples and beatboxing. 1987 was a year in which Madonna, Whitney Houston and Rick Astley were riding high in the pop charts while Australian comedy *Crocodile Dundee* and the James Bond film *The Living Daylights* were topping the box office.

> "At the end of the evening, I left the venue with a smile on my face as broad as the Clifton Suspension Bridge."
>
> **Letter from Keith Girdler, Blueboy, to Scott Purnell, Secret Shine, January 1992**

This was the wider world in which Sarah Records was dreamt up in the summer of 1987. "I think Sarah was unusual in not emerging from a local scene. There *was* a scene but it wasn't geographical. The members were scattered around the country, some in small groups, others just by themselves," explains Matt. "What they shared wasn't geography, it was an attitude, an aesthetic. And they didn't meet at a local club, they 'met' by writing to each other, exchanging fanzines, putting on bands, and hopping on National Express coaches to sleep on each other's floors when those bands played. Sarah's role in all this was, I suppose, to be one of the things that held that web together. To some extent, we could have been based anywhere, whereas Factory had to be based in Manchester, Postcard had to be based in Glasgow, and so on. Maybe that's why, weirdly, it's often regarded as a Bristol label by everyone outside Bristol, but people actively involved in the Bristol music scene never seem to have heard of us."

Supporting this idea of people in disparate small towns uniting through a shared love of the scene, Pete Williams of *Baby Honey* fanzine and the Sha-La-La label says:

Top: What do you think of first when you think of Bristol? Chances are that hot air balloons are pretty high on your list. **Bottom:** Between 1974 and 2007, the Ashton Court Festival was a landmark event in the calendar of fun-loving Bristolians. Here we have The Brilliant Corners doing their thing in July 1989.

Top: Rich Kenington. Bottom: Wendy Stone.

"I began to go up to London to go to gigs and started meeting like-minded people. I grew up in Kent, near Sittingbourne, which is a nowhere town. So although I had friends who liked punk music, I didn't know anyone who was really into the bands that I was into, so through letters I made quite a lot of friends. There was a little scene of us who would come up from small towns around London and meet up for gigs. Like Jo [Johnson] and Jon [Slade] who went on to be in Huggy Bear, and David Christian who was in Comet Gain and all these people. I'd get the train up to London on my own, and miss the last train back and have to hang around Victoria Station until 3am to get the paper train. That was really exciting at the time."

Let's take a moment to consider Bristol in the context of the UK in 1987. Despite being significantly smaller than London, it still managed to sustain one university, a polytechnic, a multitude of live music venues and a diverse population of 524,000 that was heavily influenced by the influx of young people who descended on the city to complete their higher education. Which was exactly how Clare (from Harrogate) and Matt (from London) came to Bristol.

Born and bred in Bristol's Avonmouth, a working-class suburb near the docks, Davey Woodward of The Brilliant Corners says: "If you think economically and politically where we were, it was the Falklands war and the miners' strike, then you have these bands making pop music for fun. The imagery was bright and throwaway, and there was an element of harking back to a time when things were simpler. We needed some enthusiasm and joy."

> 66 Listening to this after a trip on the New York subway is nothing less than heavenly."
>
> *Puncture* magazine (Oregon, US) reviews Tramway's 'Maritime City', 1992

The summer of 1987 was one of endless festivals and carnivals for Bristol. From the World Wine Fair in the old transit sheds on the dockside to reggae band Black Roots headlining at St Pauls Carnival, there was something for everyone. The much-missed Ashton Court Festival was in its heyday, and the 20,000 people who attended in 1987 enjoyed a packed line-up of local bands including Jonah and the Wail, Vin Gordon and the Authentics, The Seers and The Brilliant Corners. With a 'pay what you can' ticket system, it was also potentially free to attend.

Even the water was a place for entertainment. A boat called Thekla was moored on The Grove and had recently been converted from a floating theatre to a music venue and nightclub. There was also the former Scottish mailboat The Old Lochiel, which functioned as a floating pub and nightclub on Welsh Back.

In June 1987, the harbour was packed with boats for the annual powerboat races, while the Harbour Regatta would attract more than 100,000 people, with further crowds flocking to the funfair and traction engine rally on Canons Road. Up on Durdham Down, the annual Flower Show pulled in around 40,000 people, while the Ashton Court Kite Festival had the added attraction of children's TV personality Timmy Mallet. Also at Ashton Court, the world-famous Bristol Balloon Fiesta was enjoying what would be one of its golden years thanks to the perfect weather that summer. On one morning alone, 129 balloons took off in just 65 minutes.

But it wasn't all speedboats and hot air balloons. The gap between the haves and the have-nots was widening by the minute as the government was privatising state-owned industries and encouraging entrepreneurial types to sign up to get-rich-quick schemes that ranged from buying into privatisation share issues or property speculation. And all the time, house prices kept on soaring.

There was also the issue of race to be addressed in Bristol, a city that has a thorny history in that area spanning centuries. When the statue of slave trader Edward Colston was toppled in 2020, it prompted some necessary citywide conversations about the way Bristol has faced its part in the slave trade, but there were other race issues to be tackled in the 1980s. Bristol has a large immigrant community but community relations have not always been easy, and then there was the race riot in St Pauls in 1980 following a police raid of the Black and White Café on Grosvenor Road, an important social hub for the West Indian community.

"Geographically, Bristol almost seems set up that if you are white and live in Clifton or Redland or Stoke Bishop, there is nothing that needs to take you through St Pauls, for example. For me, I had never heard of St Pauls until the riot happened in the early 1980s," says Rob Young of The Poppyheads, who grew up in Bristol. "It's an amazing multicultural city but somehow the way the traffic flows, and the way it's fallen in terms of the geography, means there's not as much integration as there should have been." Rob Pursey of Heavenly also grew up in the Bristol area: "The Bristol that I knew as a kid was much quieter and more insular than the Bristol we know now. People didn't move there from London. It's a weird city because it keeps its working-classes over a hill where nobody can see them, and the Georgian splendour of Clifton and the rest of it is very much what gets presented to you."

> ❝ Oh, isn't Bristol the most wonderful place in the whole wide world? Look at that white sky with bright blue streaks, those greenish red rooftops still a little shiny from the overnight downpour and all those chimneys with their pinking-sheer tops."
>
> **Letter from Clare to fanzine writer Mark Taylor, 1987**

Martin Whitehead of the Subway Organization and The Flatmates spent his formative years in the affluent suburb of Westbury-on-Trym and says Bristol in the early-to-mid-1980s "was nowhere near as fashionable as it became. There were three bands in Bristol in my view: The Flatmates, The Brilliant Corners and The Blue Aeroplanes. But you go to similar-sized towns and they have far more bands. Bristol was seen as a bit of a provincial hippy town that was too far away from London to be of any interest. In my view, it only became fashionable when Massive Attack and Portishead became known. Even in the late 1980s, we'd do interviews with the national music papers and they'd ask why we didn't move to London. But London is only two hours away. And Bristol is a nicer place to be than being stuck in a cheap bedsit in Kentish Town."

Andrew Jarrett of the Bristol-based band The Groove Farm adds: "I remember Bristol as being nothing like what people's memories of it are now. There seems to be this nostalgic glow that has been painted as if everyone was running around Bristol with floppy fringes and anoraks but I don't remember it like that at all. I remember it as quite a dark, slightly miserable place." He continues: "Our first record cost £50 to make. But we were living on nothing, we were signing on. Now, it feels like the indie scene was very middle-class, a lot of white boys with pointy boots and Rickenbacker guitars. Rickenbacker guitars! There's no way The Groove Farm would have ever had a Rickenbacker. We found our equipment in the cheapest possible places, we were pulling it out of skips."

Sarah comes to town

Having moved from London to Bristol for university in 1980, Matt soon felt at home in his adopted city. In the later issues of his fanzine *Are You Scared To Get Happy?*, he increasingly wrote about Bristol as a character. As Rob Young of The Poppyheads notes: "It was almost like an indie-pop psychogeography type of writing, and opened my eyes to some places that I had either not been aware of, or walked past and taken for granted in Bristol. It was interesting seeing my city through his eyes."

Although Clare and Matt moved to London after they ended Sarah, they remain enormously fond of Bristol. "If I wasn't living in London, Bristol would still be my top city to live in," promises Matt. "London is where I'm from and I was starting to miss it. But I miss Bristol as well. In an ideal world, I'd have a house in both. Bristol is lovely because it's a self-contained big city. You can stand on Brandon Hill and there's greenery all around. So even though you're in a big metropolis, it doesn't take ages to get out of it."

Clare chose to study at the University of Bristol as a compromise to mollify her parents, who wanted her to apply to Oxford or Cambridge. "Bristol and Durham were the third and fourth universities at that time and who would want to go and live in Durham?" she says. "I just wanted to go to gigs and I thought there wouldn't be any if I went to Oxford but actually I'd have got there at the exact point of Talulah Gosh and Razorcuts, and it would have been fabulous."

> And just as I get sad, a roaring in the distance. Sounds like a lawnmower down below. And then I remember this is Bristol, not the leafy Harrogate of my youth, and down below is not lawns, but Tarmac and houses, and so I look out of the window to see what the roaring can be, and then I remember THIS IS BRISTOL and a yellow balloon fills the space above the rooftops and then passes out of view."
>
> **Clare, *Sunstroke*, 1989**

Although hailing from Oxford, Heavenly's Amelia Fletcher (who is so Bristolian by ancestry that her grandmother went to Fairfield Grammar School with the city's most famous son: Archie 'Cary Grant' Leach) insists there was a really strong Oxford/Bristol connection for a while during the mid-late 1980s, in no small part due to Subway. "We felt a bit Bristolian right from the start, or linked in to the Bristol scene," she says. "And while I was in Talulah Gosh, I sang with The Brilliant Corners for a bit and went on tour with them." Her bandmate Rob Pursey adds wryly: "That's not saying a lot. There weren't many indie LPs that escaped your input."

THE SUBWAY ORGANIZATION

It would be remiss to omit this other Bristolian independent record label from this book, considering it was operating at a similar time to Sarah and there was a certain degree of overlap in terms of interests, although the labels had different goals and attitudes in some regards. But at least one of the same bands.

When he was 17 years old, Martin Whitehead had started a fanzine called *Underground Romance* which morphed into *The Underground*, a fanzine with a circulation of 2,000 that stretched to six issues and scooped an early interview with The Smiths. Martin soon started a cassette label, putting out tracks that bands had sent him to review for the fanzine. But his real dream was to run a record label. "I used to think what my label would be like," he says. "I was really into Stiff and all their slogans and packaging and slightly weird marketing, and I thought that was the kind of label I'd like to have, for people to become fans of the label and for it to have a strong identity of its own." Having made a bit of money from putting gigs on at Thekla, Martin saved up £600 to press a Shop Assistants 7" in August 1985, the first release on the Subway Organization.

Talking about his vision for Subway, Martin says: "I intentionally never wanted to be a Bristol label, it just happened to be a record label that was based in Bristol. The first two releases were by Scottish bands to make that point." The Shop Assistants' first single sold 11,000 copies off the back of an initial pressing of 500. The plan had been to sell those first 500, recoup the money and press 500 copies of another band's single. But then Revolver picked up the 7" for production and distribution, John Peel played it a few times and suddenly the orders were flooding in.

"I was 21 when I started the label, living with my parents in Westbury-on-Trym," says Martin. "I remember sitting in my bedroom folding bits of paper in half and breathing in vinyl fumes. My parents didn't have a clue what I was doing, they probably thought I was selling drugs. I told my dad I was running a record label and he said 'Don't be so stupid'. But a few years later he asked me if I had any jobs going!" Just as Matt would do in the early days of Sarah, Martin signed up to the Enterprise Allowance Scheme to help Subway get started. "It kept me legal and off the streets," laughs Martin, who had given up his day job by this point.

Just as Clare and Matt say it is impossible to pick a favourite record on Sarah, Martin also cannot choose a favourite on Subway. "They're all like children, the records. But Razorcuts' first single 'Big Pink Cake', I like that simplicity. Apparently it became a bit of a hit in San Francisco gay clubs. And I loved that a whole different scene was getting into the stuff that we were doing, and that a completely different culture was embracing it on the other side of the world."

It is fair to say that Subway had a different philosophy to Sarah, in that Subway was more interested in "trying to give the majors a bloody nose," as Martin says. Although Sarah had the philosophy of wanting to show the majors how it should be done – a view shared by Subway – they were less interested in making their fortunes from the label than in making their points. Subway, meanwhile, wanted to show the majors that they could release brilliant records, have hits with them and still care about how it worked. "People at the majors could have been working in Sainsbury's for all they seemed to care," says Martin. "I'd ring them up and they didn't seem to know what bands were on their labels. It was my mission to go and slap these labels in the face by being some 21-year-old kid running a label from his bedroom and getting into the charts." It wasn't long before Subway started putting singles out on 12" as well as 7", which caused a few feathers to be ruffled in the indie camp, because true indies felt opposed to what was seen as the exploitative nature of the 12" format. Martin explains it was all part of his plan to try and get Subway bands more exposure: "If I could have run a record label entirely on 7"s, I would have loved to. But Revolver were the paymaster, they were paying for all the production costs and fronting the releases. Revolver were acting as the record label, and I was acting as the A&R man in that sense. So when they said they needed to do something to make sure I paid that money back to them, I did it because a lot of time I was in debt to them from month to month."

Thinking about Sarah Records, Martin adds: "I'd known Matt and Clare for several years and always got along with them. I do remember when I was living in a flat off Cranbrook Road with a friend, Dave Squire who was the keyboard player in The Five Year Plan, and talking about Sarah Records with him and he'd go 'Hello trees, hello sky, hello flowers'. We liked Matt and Clare but we'd make jokes about the nature of some of their records. I've never admitted that to anyone before! A lot of people think we had some angry rivalry but I've always liked Matt and Clare personally."

THE WIDER APPEAL OF THE CITY

Dickon Edwards, who would one day be in Shelley, moved to Bristol from Ipswich in the autumn of 1990 and stayed there until early 1994. He settled in a bedsit at 132 Cheltenham Road, in the artistic Montpelier area, and says it was the romantic picture of Bristol painted by Clare and Matt that led him to the city: "I was drawn to the romance of Bristol projected by Sarah, with its place names on the compilations, and its Temple Meads Station jigsaw cards in that run of singles. I wasn't quite ready for London and knew that the larger city would wait." Having first stumbled across Talulah Gosh via their album *Rock Legends Vol 69*, Dickon fell in love with the music and wanted to know more. "A school friend who was into hip indie music told me that the band were now called Heavenly and were part of that Sarah Records scene," says Dickon, who promptly went out and bought the first Heavenly single, the *Temple Cloud* compilation and The Field Mice's *Snowball*. "I was fascinated by the feeling that the label had an aesthetic

> ❝ Sarah made locality and regionality cool. Because of them, there are people from America and Japan making pilgrimages to train stations in Bristol. They've made Temple Meads into their Penny Lane."
>
> **Jyoti Mishra, White Town**

Top: Air Balloon Road in east Bristol's St George, AKA the title of an early Sarah Records compilation.
Bottom: Do you recognise this image? It's the modern-day view from Bristol Bridge that features on the cover of *Shadow Factory*.
Neil Phillips.

of its own, which was clearly separate from the rest of the indie music world, the one documented by the music press. It had a touch of the Factory Records feeling, and I was a big New Order fan at the time. But this was quieter and more secretive. And indeed, more sensitive. Very soon I bought a map of Bristol and put it up in my Ipswich bedsit, and counted down the days 'till I could live there."

Telling this story of Sarah's geographical influence on Dickon to Clare, she says: "I think Dickon came round really soon after he moved to Bristol. But I don't remember ever knowing anything about him until he arrived at 45 Upper Belgrave Road and said he'd just moved to Bristol." Matt adds: "I think we've heard other people say similar things, that they came to Bristol because they really liked the sound of it and a lot of it was the Sarah connection."

Dickon was quickly reassured that he had made the right choice: "Bristol had so many places to see bands of all levels play. But really it was about hanging out in the same record shops and at the same gigs, then exchanging fanzines, and perhaps exchanging addresses. Or writing letters. And oh, were there letters! And homemade cassette compilations, or mix tapes as they say now, made to go with the letters. It was what I needed at that particular time. Something bigger than Ipswich, with more to it but not quite the sprawling metropolis of London. I never felt unsafe, which was important. Manchester was being hyped as the city of that era but I was put off by the crime, and indeed the rain. Bristol can be very pretty, particularly Clifton Down in the snow."

His Shelley bandmate Tim Chipping echoes these romantic sentiments: "I don't think Clare and Matt made themselves part of the Bristol music scene, their version of Bristol was their own. They created a fantasy Bristol in the artwork and flyers and fanzines. I don't think they paid that much attention to what else was going on. Bristol was part of their world but I don't think they were part of Bristol in that way." He adds: "One of the appealing things about them for me was how snobbish they were. No one was ever quite good enough for Clare and Matt. They had such an intolerance for when people got it wrong. Both Dickon and I really liked that as we were similar in our demand for perfection."

❝ Successful though they undoubtedly are, don't all Sarah bands conform to the stereotype of being sensitive Ribena drinkers?"
Bristol listing magazine *Venue*, 1991

Someone who had lived in Bristol before Dickon had even pinned up his map of the city was Even As We Speak's Mary Wyer, who spent a year living at 45 Maple Road in Horfield with her then-partner and still-bandmate Matt Love in 1988. Mary and Matt decided to up sticks from Sydney and spend time in the UK to see if they could make it big. Having initially settled in a "dire" squat in London, they jumped at the chance to move in with some friends who had a spare room in Bristol. Although this was the year after Sarah had formed, the label wasn't yet on Mary's radar. Rather than go to gigs, she and Matt were so poor that they took any job they could get just so they could afford time in recording studios and childcare for Mary's young son. When they had clawed together enough money, the couple would take a coach up to London and Divine Retribution Studios, which was where 'Goes So Slow' and 'Nothing Ever Happens' were recorded: these would become very early Even As We Speak singles on Australia's Phantom Records in 1989.

Given how enormous Australia is, Mary and Matt were amused by the English interpretation of distances. "Sydney and Brisbane were 17 hours on a bus at that time, and Melbourne was 12 hours on a bus, and we just did that regularly," says Mary. "But when I lived in Bristol and you talked to the neighbours, and they'd be 'Oh, I've never been to London.' But seriously, it's two hours away! I was so shocked. You'd get onto the bus, the announcement would say, 'Ladies and gentlemen, welcome aboard the National Express Rapide service from Bristol to London' and they'd bring out the trolley and be serving refreshments on a two-hour bus trip! The most we ever got on our 17-hour bus trips in Australia was they'd stop once and kick you out at a petrol station to go to the toilet, get something to eat, get back on the bus." National Express phased out the Rapide in 2000, although not before the service was immortalised in The Divine Comedy's 1998 top 10 hit 'National Express', complete with "a jolly hostess selling crisps and tea".

Mary and Matt were so focused on making ends meet and trying to get as much studio time as possible that they had few opportunities to engage with Bristol. "I saw very little music then," remembers Mary. "We were too poor. I remember Horfield Common that was out the back of the house, and one day a hot air balloon landed in our backyard and hit our fence." But despite that tough year, Mary remembers the city fondly: "I do have a soft spot for Bristol, I really do, and I would love to come back again. I think especially for Matt and I, Bristol will always hold a pretty special place because it's where we lived when we made music that helped us to end up where we are now."

The unofficial Bristol Tourist Board

Sarah Records did a sterling job for the Bristol Tourist Board, unintentionally putting the city on the map at a time when, if a tourist was going to go anywhere in this neck of the woods, they were going to go to nearby Bath and take in the Jane Austen Museum and the Roman Baths. "We always thought we should get paid by the tourist board because so much of what we did was a love letter to Bristol," says Clare. "We used to judge guide books to England by how many pages they had on Bristol in relation to how many pages they had on Bath. We felt the need to bang on about things like, 'Bath might have the Royal Crescent but we've got Royal York Crescent and it's just as good'. Hence not putting the Clifton Suspension Bridge on anything until Sarah 100, because that was the only thing that people knew about Bristol, although I had a collection of about 60 postcards of the bridge."

Sarah 50 was a board game called Saropoly that featured a large, fold-out hand-drawn map of Bristol and involved the

> 66 Who couldn't love a label that released a board game?!"
> **David Gedge, The Wedding Present**

BRISTOL: MARITIME CITY

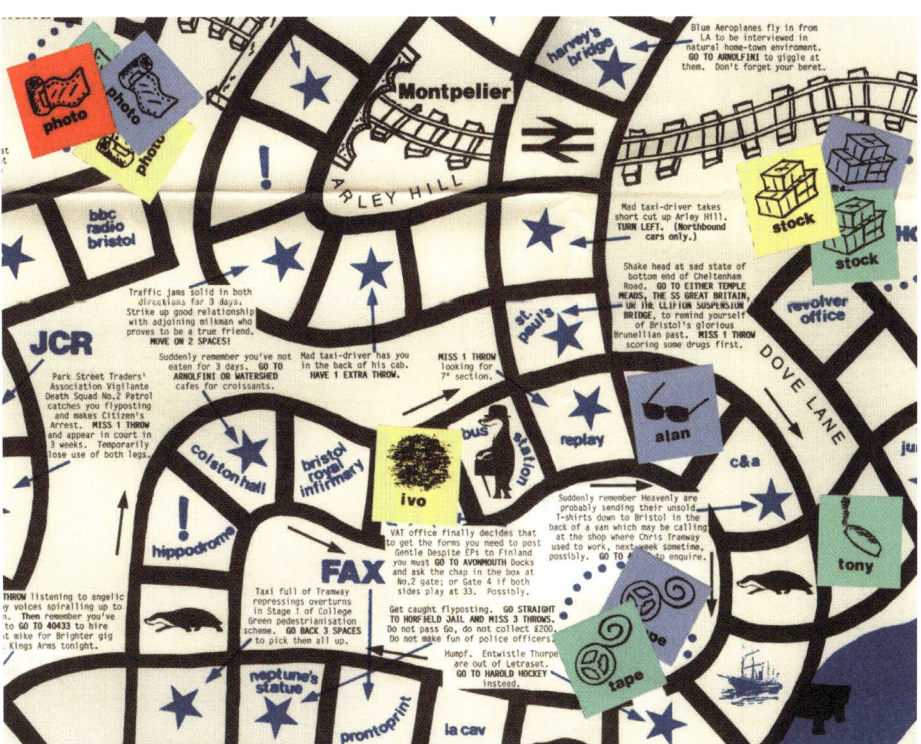

A tense moment in a game of Saropoly as Alan McGee and Tony Wilson race to collect their master tapes from the PO Box while Ivo from 4AD loiters at the bus station, contemplating sabotage.
Sarah Records.

players running an independent record label in the city, along with all the pitfalls that entailed. "We obviously had to play it a huge number of times to make sure it worked," says Clare. "We thought it would take people an hour or so to play, and then everyone complained that they could never get to the end of it because, of course, we'd got really good at playing and we knew the layout of Bristol really well, but if you live in Birmingham and you've never been to Bristol… I think people found it a little frustrating because no one ever won."

In the Sarah 100 flyer, Clare and Matt wrote: "We genuinely couldn't think of anything we could do which would be more exciting than Sarah 50, our board game Saropoly. We even toyed with doing another one – we were going to do Sarah Cluedo, with the scenario that Sarah had had to come to an end because we'd been murdered by one of our bands at an unspecified indie nite-spot, and now the other bands were travelling around the country in hired Sierras being indie supersleuths and asking questions to find out who'd done it and what the murder weapon was, eg Brighter at the Derby Dial with the bucket of water and dodgy amp lead, or Gentle Despite at the Duchess of York with the falling PA stack…"

Each 7" single from Sarah 71 to Sarah 80 includes a photo on its centre label of the Bristol bus with a route number matching the catalogue number. My favourite is Sarah 75; the photo on this East River Pipe single shows the No 75 bus from Bristol city centre to Hartcliffe on its journey down East Street, a stone's throw from the Gwilliam Street house. Matt notes that the pressing plant even took the trouble to send a note saying how much they liked that particular centre label.

Sarah also named all of its compilation albums after lesser-known areas of the city and surrounding districts. Here is a list of their titles, which I will spoil by sharing the reality of the seemingly romantic places after which they are named. As is folklore by now, the catalogue numbers for these records correspond to the number of the bus that would take you there. Please note, timetables may have changed in the past three decades so do check the First Bus website before travelling.

Saropoly came complete with coloured strips that players cut up in order to create the playing pieces. Very DIY, innit?
Courtesy of Sarah Records.

- *Shadow Factory* (Sarah 587). Shadow factories were the consequence of a 1935 government scheme to discreetly manufacture extra aircraft in the build-up to World War Two. This particular shadow factory was a Rolls-Royce site in Patchway, although the picture on the front of the LP is of former brewery buildings in Bristol city centre and completely unrelated. Much more amusing is that *Melody Maker* presumed the album title was an anorak-esque piss-take of Stock Aitken & Waterman's *Hit Factory*, which was achingly popular in 1988.

- *Temple Cloud* (Sarah 376). Temple Cloud sounds blissful. But it is really a rather unremarkable village in Chew Valley that you access by driving down the A37 (or taking the 376 bus if you are travelling in 1990).

- *Air Balloon Road* (Sarah 545). The annual Bristol Balloon Fiesta is always a sight to behold. Air Balloon Road is a big street in the St George area, so big that it's really an A road, the A431 to be precise. It is not a sight to behold.

- *Glass Arcade* (Sarah 501). A lovely spot in the beautiful St Nicholas Market in the old part of town, Glass Arcade is the glass ceilinged, err, arcade that still houses independent market stalls and food traders, just as it did in the 1740s.

- *Fountain Island* (Sarah 583). A magical sounding name with implications of a serene desert island adorned by a beautiful stone fountain. It's not. It's a small, triangular traffic island at the top of Blackboy Hill that used to have a drinking fountain on it. But doesn't anymore.

- *Engine Common* (Sarah 628). Perhaps a communal green space that was built with the intention of providing fresh air for the Victorian working classes? Nah. Engine Common is a small commuter village near Yate, just on the north of Bristol's boundaries.

- *Gaol Ferry Bridge* (Sarah 530). This bridge takes pedestrians from the south side of Bristol to where the gaol used to stand and was much more convenient than having to wait for the ferry that used to shuttle people and prisoners over. It's a 1930s wrought iron suspension footbridge that is rather rickety but *probably* won't fall down when you're on it.

- *Battery Point* (Sarah 359). Battery Point is in the coastal town of Portishead. There's nothing romantic or alluring about the name Battery Point so let's cut to the chase. Battery Point is a small metallic lighthouse on the cliffs that offers a view of Wales.

- *There & Back Again Lane* (Sarah 100). There & Back Again Lane is an alleyway in Clifton that houses some industrial bins belonging to nearby restaurants. There and Back Again Lane is so short that there is barely enough room to fit the street sign on the wall. It is a good name for a road that doesn't go anywhere. And, evidently, a record. Indies keep stealing the street sign. Bristol City Council must hate Sarah fans.

The Actual Bristol Sound

Of all the bands signed to Sarah, only two actually came from Bristol: Tramway and Secret Shine.

Tramway were from Henleaze and put out two 7"s in 1991, 'Maritime City' and 'Sweet Chariot'. When Sarah ended in 1995, a farewell feature in *Melody Maker* listed the top five "boss" songs on Sarah, of which 'Sweet Chariot' was one (although this is the name of the EP rather than a track on it). Clare said in the article: "Our entire audience loathed it and felt really alienated." It is true to say that Tramway were not most people's favourite Sarah band.

"I genuinely think that 'Maritime City' is absolutely marvellous, I love it," says

Top left: Glass Arcade opened as a covered market in the 1740s and is still operating as such today.
Top right: Gaol Ferry Bridge: a 1930s wrought iron footbridge that is quite beautiful in the right light.
Middle: Badgerline buses ceased business in June 1995. Presumably they had heard that Sarah was about to close and that trade from indie fans keen to hop on route 583 to Portishead would be diminishing thereafter. **Bottom left:** Battery Point in Portishead. Built in 1931, this metal lighthouse was an important defence post in the war. **Bottom right:** One of the most famous street signs in Bristol.

Top left, top right & bottom right: Neil Phillips. Middle: Courtesy of Sarah Records. Bottom left: Jane Duffus

Clare now, although it is impossible to get either her or Matt to say a bad word about any of the songs they released. "It must be said, Tramway were not our most popular band but we really liked them. Matthew [Evans] was previously in Panda Pops."

Panda Pops morphed into Tramway in a fit of ego, according to band member Nancy Horlick, who says they were worried that, when they hit the big time, the soft drink manufacturer of the same name would slap a lawsuit on them. Frontman Matthew Evans explains that: "Tramway was the name of the café in the bus station in Bristol and we had a song named after that." The first Tramway single was originally going to be on Cosmic English Music, which was Greg Webster and Liz Price's label, but the pair later decided "it wasn't really what they wanted." So the recordings were sold to Sarah, a label that Matthew had been a big fan of, especially in its early years.

"I love both Tramway singles and I love the fact that the sleeves are inspired by the Bristol Rovers shirt, and the b-side of the second single is a tribute to Bristol Rovers. And then it ends up with 'Goodnight Irene' which is the Bristol Rovers song," asserts Matt, who supports Leyton Orient. "We had no rivalry with either Bristol club and I always had a soft spot for Rovers rather than City because I like the fact that Rovers always seem more down at heel and down on their luck than City." He adds: "I'm still not sure how many people got the Bristol Rovers reference in the sleeve design, largely because the band insisted on using silver rather than white, presumably out of some self-sabotaging desire not to make any money and destroy the label. Metallic inks are hideously expensive, and I'm really not sure why we agreed... And then I think some people didn't realise the second single was a new record, rather than the same record with the sleeve colours changed to look like a slice of Battenberg. In retrospect, I'm not sure we really had our marketing and finance hats on when it came to Tramway. But that's the joy of being an indie label, you can wear whatever hats you want."

FUN FACT: Panda Pops had a song called 'Bristol Fashion' and another called 'Tramway'. They also had a guitarist called Scott Purnell who would later be in Secret Shine.

Tramway are a band so embedded in Bristol's history that they have a road named after them
Jane Duffus

Tramway disbanded not long after Sarah closed, after putting out a further single and an album on a different label. Matthew says: "I think we decided when it started that when the oldest band member reached 25, that would be it. When you're young, you think 25 is too old to be credibly still doing it."

Some bands were such massive fans of Sarah that they deliberately created what they hoped was the sort of demo that would appeal to Clare and Matt, even if that wasn't the sort of music the band wanted to make long term. And in 1991, Secret Shine fell into this category.

Vocalist Jamie Gingell says: "Scott [Purnell, guitar] and I wanted to get on Sarah Records, and we intentionally wrote a demo quite specifically for the label. I was happy with any of the indie labels but Scott liked a lot of the material on Sarah. So we put a demo together. It was intentionally Sarah-ish in sound and they liked it. I just

> Certain cities are very cyclical, they go in and out of fashion. I mean, Bristol was at the forefront of C86 with Subway and The Flatmates and Brilliant Corners, which was cutting-edge for the time. Even now the legacy of that lives on with Sarah Records, and we're putting Secret Shine on at Sound City ... Secret Shine was the one I really wanted."
>
> Radio 1 DJ Steve Lamacq in *Venue*, 14 April 1995

remember getting the letter back from them to my parents' address in Bristol [...] I always remember they signed off by saying 'You're almost definitely not going to get rich.'"

Scott also remembers receiving the letter: "It felt fantastic. It was the first and only time I've seen Jamie look excited. He doesn't show his emotions very much one way or the other. We ran around his parents' garden, jumping and laughing. Part of it was the excitement of being on a label we loved but also the fact that the plan worked." He continues: "I loved the Sarah sound, I'd absolutely die for it but we wanted to do something heavier, more shoegaze, ultimately. We did a demo to get on Sarah. I don't know if we had a plan that eventually we would change the way the music sounded to be more shoegaze. It just seemed to happen that way."

Secret Shine are still going strong and, in 2021, celebrated their thirtieth anniversary. The Beatles could only dream of such longevity.

*****

THESE THINGS HAPPENED:
Gemma Malley, Blueboy

"Sarah was something else. The music mattered but it was about the audience, and the bands had been invited to play to the audience. In the beginning, I found it quite impenetrable. It's a bit like going into a new job and I had to figure everything out. I thought it was about fans and suddenly realised no, it was about this entire subculture, and there was layer upon layer, and it almost had its own language and its own communication channels. To a certain extent, I went along for the ride, it was so much fun. I was in a band with some really cool people, playing fantastic music to lovely people and we got to record stuff."

Top: One of Bristol's most favourite bands, Tramway perform at Le Cav on 22 December 1990.
Bottom: Another of Bristol's favourite bands, Secret Shine commune with nature in a Bristolian park.
Top: Wendy Stone. Bottom: Courtesy of Secret Shine.

THESE THINGS HAPPEN

Chapter 4

Unlike Every Other Band on Sarah...

The picture of Sarah that was painted by the UK music press was one of fey, wimpy, pathetic childishness. The word bandied around more than any other was 'twee'. Therefore, the implication of signing to Sarah could have been something that put many bands off. But it wasn't. In fact, many bands saw it as a badge of honour. But you know what? There was no typical Sarah sound. Not all the bands sounded the same, and pretty much none had a "twee female singer" (despite what David Quantick and his pals at the *NME* thought).

"I hate it when people make Sarah this monolithic thing from the outside and go, 'Oh, it was all that twee rubbish,'" says fan Jyoti Mishra of White Town. "Have they ever listened to a Sarah compilation? They will hear mad stuff going off on one, to very delicate stuff. How is 'Sensitive' a twee song?! In a weird way, 'Sensitive' was The Field Mice doing their Big Black, because at the end of that, it just goes on and on and on, and then the snares go all the way through, and you don't want it to ever end when you're dancing to it." While friend-of-the-label Ken Sweeney, who released music as Brian, adds: "Lots of people were very sniffy about Sarah. But I was listening to Harvey [Williams]'s 'You Should All Be Murdered' recently and it's so subversive. Fucking hell! That would be banned on every American radio station. It's such an offloading, it's brilliant."

> **❝** I honestly don't know what you'll think, but (and I don't mean to sound all big-headed here), when I heard the finished thing, I was a bit... excited, because it's exactly the sort of thing I'd like to go and buy."
>
> **Letter from Michael Warner, Eternal, to Sarah, enclosing a demo tape, 1990**

Being branded as 'just another Sarah band' was understandably infuriating for the groups, who had their music dismissed by naysayers before anyone had even heard it. Bobby Wratten of The Field Mice told *Waaaah!* fanzine: "We don't feel part of any scene. I guess it gets more annoying as time goes by to still be seen as an archetypal indie band or just another Sarah band. We hate all that and think our music is diverse enough for people to realise it isn't true."

THESE THINGS HAPPEN

An early band shot of The Sea Urchins. "I attended a music production course in 1985 and we recorded an early version of 'Summershine' in the studio there as The Quimbys," says Robert Cooksey.
Courtesy of Robert Cooksey.

IN THE EARLY DAYS

The Sea Urchins had featured on a flexi that Clare released with her fanzine *Kvatch*, and the group later had a track on a Sha-La-La flexi. The Birmingham band was already well known to Clare, who had struck up a friendship with frontman James Roberts a year before and this was what led Sarah to snap the Urchins up as the label's very first release. However, The Sea Urchins had already been offered a contract with Jive Records, which they turned down on principle because the label was also releasing records by glamour model Samantha Fox. However, The Urchins also had hopes of being picked up by Creation, as keyboardist Bridget Duffy explains: "In our heart of hearts, we were thinking of Creation, that would have been exciting, but Lawrence [Hayward, Felt] told Darren [Martin] that Bobby Gillespie had said 'no' because he thought we were too similar to Primal Scream." Bobby had attended a pre-Sarah Urchins gig at the Black Horse in Camden and that was very exciting for the band, as was the fact that one of the other 15 people in the audience was Icelandic almost-superstar Björk. Although, at another London

> "Going to the Sensateria tonight ... Bumped into The Quimbeys, they told me that they have split that band and are now going to be The Sea Urchins. Had a bit of a chat with them and then went off for a dance. Had my go-go boots on that I got from C20th Style. My hair is looking a bit like Valerie Singleton's. Too much Boots hairspray."
>
> **Bridget Duffy (The Sea Urchins)'s diary, 30 January 1986**

gig, supporting Talulah Gosh, Bridget got so tired of someone in the audience yelling that The Urchins were Primal Scream copycats that she grabbed the microphone and shouted "Fuck off and watch Primal Scream then!"

Her bandmate Robert Cooksey remembers the band debating choosing between signing to a label that Hugh McGuinness from Mighty Mighty was proposing setting up... or Clare and Matt's new label. "Considering our situation, we felt [Sarah] to be the better option as we were sure they had a ready-made fanbase that had bought their fanzines and flexis, as well as the fact we thought they were genuine fans. We liked Matt and Clare and were excited to be the first release on their new label. I remember thinking it was going to be the new Postcard or Creation but became disappointed quickly with most of the bands they signed after us, to be honest. The Springfields were probably my favourite other band on Sarah."

Of course, back in 1987, The Sea Urchins could have no idea what a highly desired record 'Pristine Christine', aka Sarah 1, would become and at the time it was just exciting to have a hard vinyl record out. Bridget says: "It seems strangely amusing that 'Pristine Christine' has become such a legendary single but it does sound good and it's nice when you suddenly hear it on Radio 6. There were only 1,600 made, so I'm not surprised it fetches so much money, it's a bit like an early Mary Quant piece." Frontman James Roberts adds: "Getting a proper hard record out was all it was for us, and Clare and Matt seemed nice and into it. For us, we were young kids of 17, 18, 19, getting our first proper record out. We loved it. Whether we were any good or not was something else but we meant it and we loved it, and it was everything to us for a few years. It was that thing when you're young, when you're absolutely passionate about something and you're so blinkered with it."

Sarah 2 was by The Orchids who had also had a track on a Sha-La-La flexi. "I remember staying up all night as I turned 20, putting that first Orchids record in sleeves," says Clare, giving an early example of the hard work and sacrifice she and Matt would put into the label. Drummer Chris Quinn says: "I've still got the letter from Matt that he sent saying they'd put our record out, I still remember opening it, the excitement of it, 'Wait a minute, somebody's offering to put out a real single?!'"

Sarah 3 was 'Anorak City' by Harvey Williams under the guise of Another Sunny Day. Again, Harvey was known to Matt from the fanzine network. "Matt and I had struck up this pen friendship and it just seemed like the next stage to send him some songs," says Harvey. "The music he was writing about was inspiring what I was doing but equally I was drawing from other sources as well. So it would be this dialogue between fan and musician. That was the reason for his fanzine existing."

Sarah 4 was an untitled fanzine, the first in a series of occasional numbered fanzines that formed part of the Sarah 100 series. The fanzines were very much regarded as equals of the records because Clare and Matt felt that "the literary equivalent of a pop single was the fanzine". In an ideal world, there would have been more than the handful of fanzines there turned out to be but the busier the label

14 Iced Bears' frontman Rob Sekula is getting rather tired of being asked where his band's unusual name came from. "Not that old chestnut," he sighs before inventing a fanciful story.
Courtesy of 14 Iced Bears.

became the harder it was to find the time.

It was with Sarah 5 that things began to change, because 14 Iced Bears were an established band that had had records out on other indie labels. Clare thinks the band sent Sarah a tape because "we wouldn't have dared approach them". Matt adds: "We very much waited for bands to come to us." Although, as we will see later in this chapter, there were a handful of exceptions to that rule. Chief Iced Bear Rob Sekula thinks that the initial approach *did* come from Clare and Matt but, whichever version is true, it doesn't really matter because the end result was 'Come Get Me' in 1988. Rob had heard of Sarah via the fanzine network and had bought 'Pristine Christine' when it came out. "When they got in touch to say they wanted to release us, we were really chuffed. It was perfect timing as I don't think we had a label at the time," says Rob. As to why 14 Iced Bears only released one single on Sarah, it is simply that the band was keen to put out an album which Sarah didn't want to do at that point. "It was a shame but we understood where they were coming from. There were no bad feelings," says Rob.

Sue Freeman was manager of 14 Iced Bears at the time and, when the group went into the studio to record 'Come Get Me', she ended up playing keyboards. She remembers: "I didn't know what the hell I was doing. But I really liked having fun with effects pedals wired up to the keyboards, and I recorded these noises to go on that single and became part of the live act for any track that required

> " Enclosed: one Poppyheads EP. Is this the most important record ever made??? Four songs on one 6½" flexi!!! PUNK ROCK! It just looks so cute."
>
> **Letter from Matt to Pete Williams, spring 1987**

effects." And it was Sue who did all the toing and froing with Sarah. "They were an absolute delight to deal with, so sweet and friendly," she says. "If you contrast what it was like to deal with them to what it was like for me as manager dealing with a lot of other people in the industry, it was really strongly predominantly male, and you just constantly came across some very big personalities, very arrogant personalities, and that was all a little bit of a battle."

As to where the name 14 Iced Bears came from? "Not that old chestnut!" sighs Rob. "I used to like coming up with weird stories about that to make it more interesting but it seems silly now to carry on. Sainsbury's used to do 15 Iced Bears biscuits and something in my head clicked when I saw the packet, so I changed it to 14 as it was the number my favourite footballer, Johan Cruyff, used to wear for Holland in 1974. And then I got abducted by aliens outside Sainsbury's car park."

Before Sarah 6, The Poppyheads also

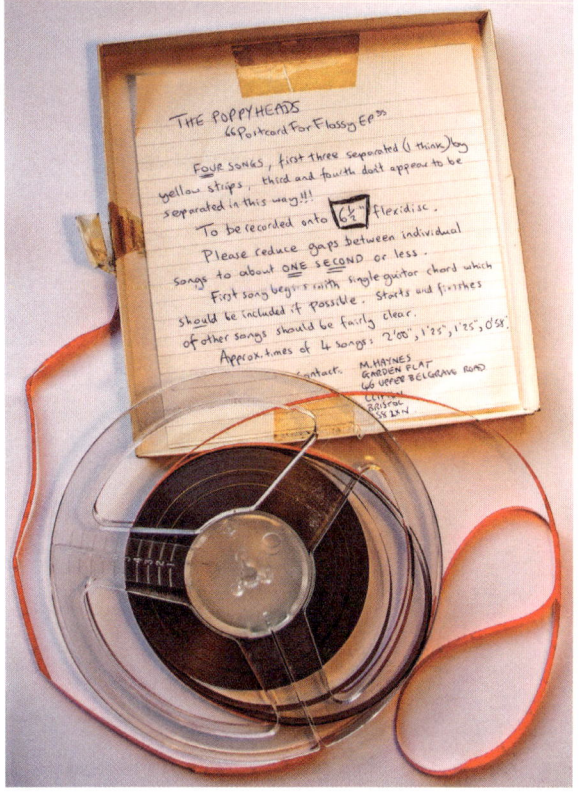

The reel-to-reel master tape for The Poppyheads' flexi.
Courtesy of Sarah Records.

had a track on a Sha-La-La flexi. The band's guitarist Rob Young had met Matt at a Biff Bang Pow! gig at Bristol's George & Railway pub in March 1987. Rob had been clutching a bag containing The Poppyheads' demos and was looking for likely characters to hand them out to.

"I just loved the idea that, because they had four tracks that were all so short, we could put all four of them on one side of a 6.5" flexi disc. And I thought that was such a fantastic symbol of what you could do with pop music essentially," says Matt about the Poppyheads' Sha-La-La flexi. "You could literally put four songs on a flexi disc and sell it for 50p with a fanzine. And isn't that just a wonderful statement?" A wonderful statement it might have been but that didn't stop the 'Postcard for Flossy EP' being seen as everything that was wrong about twee pop. To the extent that someone in Glasgow went to the trouble of defecating into a plastic bag and posting it to Matt along with their unwanted copy of the Poppyheads' flexi. "And that's just one of the problems if you put your home address on things," sighs Clare. They had clearly mentioned the incident in a note to John Peel because, in a letter the DJ sent to Sarah in 1989, he commented: "Sorry about the bag of shit – I used to get quite a few Jiffy bags of the same from the NF/BM [National Front/ British Movement] set, cross that I was playing Black music. Not, as you say, a good start to the day."

After setting up Sarah, Clare and Matt were seeking more bands for their new record label and asked The Poppyheads if they would like to put something out, which was how 'Cremation Town' came to be Sarah 6. The band had recorded more demos by this point and Sarah stumped up the cash for them to go back into the studio. "Money was not the factor at all. It just wouldn't have been discussed," says Rob. "It was done for the love of doing it and the need for having these things out there. Sarah was a real ideological operation. It's a cult really, a cult of the anti-capitalist world of releasing music."

Duff demo tapes

Before long, Sarah was receiving more demo tapes than the label knew what to do with. "We couldn't listen to them all, there were just so many," says Matt. The pair estimate they received an average of 20 tapes a week, which is more than 8,000 tapes across the label's eight years. "There were certainly more than we could cope with," says Matt. "There would be a couple in every post," adds Clare. "We'd also get some completely inappropriate ones. We'd get heavy metal and all sorts. You'd think, 'Why are you sending this to us?'"

Inevitably, a handful of rejected bands would go on to achieve greatness elsewhere. The most famous example is the Manic Street Preachers. "They wrote fabulous letters and had amazing spirit and attitude, but at that point the music just wasn't quite…" says Clare, leaving us hanging as to what the Manics were not quite. "We saw them really early at the Fleece around the time that their first flexi came out and we didn't have regrets." Matt adds: "I can still picture the tape. I always loved the idea of the Manics and enjoyed reading interviews with them but the music just always felt so clichéd. And, to this day, I have no idea what motorcycle emptiness is. But the interviews were great and hopefully demonstrate why they thought Sarah was in tune with what they were doing, politically if not musically."

Music journalist Simon Price, who wrote the Manics' biography *Everything*, says: "Nicky [Wire] was into 'indie schmindie' music. In a weird way, I think they'd have been comfortable being an antagonistic voice in that world. I think part of them would have been really happy putting out a few 7"s in plastic bags on Sarah that were well received by people in the know, and then their failure would prove them right: 'We were too good for this world.'" The Manics certainly started in that world: their first gig in London was with some other indie-pop bands. And that's where Bob Stanley of Heavenly Records saw them and it all grew from there. "Even though they made a point of almost being performatively corporate, there's a part of them that definitely came from a Sarah-esque world," says Simon.

> ❝ We've just filled four large dustbin-liners with demo tapes and chucked them away. You'll probably throw up your hands in horror at this waste of young talent but we were sick of the bloody things … The thing is, if you've never had to sit down and listen to four bin-liners full of demos, you really can't imagine what a soul-destroying business it is."
>
> **Sarah Newsletter No 10, January 1995**

Also on the 'no' pile were Galaxie 500, who had sent a copy of their Aurora Records 7" 'Tugboat', because the b-side wasn't all that, and The Auteurs. "I remember listening to The Auteurs being interviewed on the Evening Session and them saying that they hated the music industry so much they weren't sending out any demos," says Matt. "Which, given I was looking at an Auteurs demo tape at the time, felt a bit disingenuous." An early version of Pale Saints also received the thumbs down, "but it was a very early incarnation, before they went shoegaze, so just fairly standard jangly stuff," says Matt.

> **Brighter? Sort of ching ching, twiddle twiddle, ching ching... You know the sort of stuff. Same as the rest.**
>
> **Letter from Matt to fan Julian Bester**

Clare and Matt quickly developed a sixth sense as to which tapes would be worth their time. And it wasn't the ones that came with glossy photos and a well-designed sleeve. Instead, the tapes that came with handwritten letters were usually more up the Sarah Straße. "I remember Brighter's one coming and thinking, 'This will be interesting' based on the drawing Keris put on the front of it," says Matt. "It was a 'wot no' thing over the wall."

Keris Howard of Brighter says: "I was always fascinated by music, obsessed by it, and it may have been just seeing when 'Pristine Christine' came out, seeing that in the music press and presumably being played on John Peel and Janice Long, and being drawn in that way. And the *Shadow Factory* compilation, seeing how everything held together and getting a sense of the label as a whole. Me and Alison [Cousens] had started to get really into indie music at that time. I'd come from an Echo & The Bunnymen, Cocteau Twins, The Smiths, New Order background and then, in the mid- to late-1980s, was getting into The Wedding Present, McCarthy and Felt and all the Creation bands. Sarah Records was taking it a little bit further in terms of the jangly, tey pop stuff. It was an untapped market that really spoke to me."

However, Keris didn't even think he was sending in Brighter's demo tape for consideration as a Sarah release. "When I sent them a demo tape, I sent it asking for an opinion, and I now wonder what I was doing!" he says. "I had a real respect and admiration for where they were going with music, I decided that when I wrote stuff that maybe they could tell me where I might be going wrong." Guitarist Alison adds: "We were about to go and see *Who Framed Roger Rabbit* and Keris went, 'I've just come off the phone from Clare from Sarah Records. I think I've got a record deal.'"

Buff Demo Tapes

Of course, sending in a demo tape was a perfectly good way for bands to attract Clare and Matt's attention. "A friend of a friend came up to us in an indie club and told us they knew someone who was starting a record label and we should send them our demo," says Ulric Kennedy, vocalist and bassist with The Golden Dawn. "I ended up with the piece of paper that had the now-famous garden flat address on it, sent a cassette to Clare and Matt and that was that. They got back to us really

Top: Brighter (Keris and Alex are pictured here) were a band whose demo tape really shone out when Clare and Matt first heard it. **Bottom:** Gentle Despite were thrilled to be on Sarah Records. "We were looking at each other going 'Wow!'", remembers Paul Gorton.

Top: Grimsby Fishmarket, Marcus Torncrantz. Bottom: Courtesy of Gentle Despite.

soon afterwards and asked us to do a record. In retrospect it all seems too easy." His bandmate Peter Claughan adds: "We had no real notion of what being a Sarah band meant and I'm pretty sure we would not have wanted to be pigeonholed in that way anyway. We were never intentionally a pop band really and were probably happier making a bit of noise like the Velvets or Sonic Youth." Vocalist and guitarist Kenny Forte chimes in: "Eugene [Dawydiak] and I came across the first letter that Sarah had written to us, and it was saying something like, 'You sent us a tape. You didn't say what you wanted us to do with it. And we're thinking we'd quite like to bring a single out but we're not 100% sure yet.' I think they'd only released two or three singles at that point, so it must have been that we were sending off tapes with no explanation of what they were, other than a return address." Eugene concludes: "When Clare and Matt replied super positively and said they were interested in releasing an actual EP, that was just fantastic and certainly exceeded my expectations. Very close to this time, BBC Radio Scotland had also contacted us about playing tracks on their *Rock on Scotland* alternative music show, so the prospect of airplay *and* getting a record out was tremendously exciting."

Gentle Despite also found their way onto Sarah via the tried and trusted demo tape method. The band recorded a demo on a four-track but thought the sound was a bit "dry", so singer Simon Westwood called up his friend Ian-Masters-from-Pale-Saints who had "one of those reverb things". Guitarist Paul Gorton explains: "Ian was a few years older, so we looked up to him as Pale Saints were on 4AD and breaking through." Ian invited Gentle Despite to re-record their demo on his four-track while he played bass, which he ended up doing on the duo's first single for Sarah although, because he was signed to 4AD, he could never be properly credited. "He brought an EBow effect, the thing Robert Fripp used to use to get endless long notes. He played that on 'The Darkest Blue'," reveals Paul.

Simon sent a copy of the original demo to a fanzine writer who gave the songs a glowing review and suggested the boys send the tape to Sarah. "We didn't think we'd be good enough but Matt loved it and said he'd send us some money to go to a studio and we couldn't believe it," says Paul. "We were genuinely chuffed to bits. We were looking at each other going 'Wow!'"

It was a sadness for Paul and Simon that none of their friends in Leeds seemed remotely interested in their fledgling music career: "We were like, 'Wow, we're on Sarah' and nobody was bothered. Nobody we knew cared." Paul explains: "It sounds unreal now if we say we had a Sarah deal, but nobody was interested at the time. Sarah wasn't considered a great label. But then 30 years go by and people can see what an important thing it was. A continuation of the punk ethic. I'm really glad it's survived the test of time. Generally the label was young people expressing their emotions. That carries on to the next generation."

> ❝ As promised, here are a couple of songs for you to listen to ... Vocals – we couldn't actually find Simon [Court] this weekend so they're just instrumentals (but I'm sure you can work out the vocal pattern). They're pretty fast and furious, but I'm sure they'll record really well."
>
> **Letter from Stuart Vincent, The Sweetest Ache, to Sarah, 1990**

This is a copy of the insert that The Rosaries made to accompany their demo tape.
Jonny James.

Over in Coventry, The Rosaries had been formed by Welsh guitarist and songwriter Mark James (now known as Jonny), with Laura Kinsey on vocals and percussionist Sian Allen Huntley. They were soon joined by drummer Robert Dillam, who recorded under the pseudonym of 'RP McMurphy' because he was moonlighting from his Creation band Adorable. It would be fair to say that Jonny and Robert were the two more accomplished musicians in the band, and that Laura and Sian were mostly there for the fun of it. "When we had the communication from Sarah Records saying 'Will you record something?', [Jonny] was overjoyed and I was distraught!" laughs Laura. "I was not a singer and I was like, 'I can't do this! I can't even sing let alone record something.'" Jonny remembers: "Clare and Matt sent back a two-line letter on the back of something else that said, 'If we promise to answer your letters a bit faster in future, will you be Sarah 62?' I think we got it on a Saturday morning and were pretty excited by it. I've never been a person to demonstrate really strong emotions but we thought it was really cool. It was an affirmation that there was something that we'd enjoyed doing that was valued by someone else." Sian adds modestly: "In some ways, we did a disservice to [Jonny] because he was so committed and so keen and so talented but also really patient with us. My role was mostly just to walk around in a duffle coat and bang the tambourine! Like Laura says, when it all became a bit serious, it was horrifying."

Some Sarah bands didn't even think they were "a proper band," as Christian Savill from Eternal tells me. He and a few teenage mates had booked a recording studio "to give us a deadline to work towards" and the results of that session became their demo which was sent to Sarah. Of course, having Sarah say 'yes' to recording the single was great news but, as Christian says: "We literally had no idea what we were doing, we couldn't play our instruments. Our ambition would have been to just get a record out and that would have been enough. They were so enthusiastic, which was really nice because in Reading where we were playing everyone was very unenthusiastic and putting bands down, it was not a nice atmosphere. Sarah said they would pay for us to record it properly and I think we felt guilty that they were going to spend money on us. We were aware they didn't have any money."

Eternal didn't last for long, with bassist Stuart Wilkinson saying the initial demo was recorded at Weston-super-Mare's White House in December 1989, before being re-recorded for Sarah in February 1990. By the time the Eternal 7" was released in the summer of that year, the band had already split up because Christian's other band Slowdive had signed to Creation. And that was that.

Going down the demo tape route also worked for Action Painting!, who released records intermittently throughout Sarah's lifespan, starting with Sarah 28 and then leaving a big gap until Sarahs 73 and 87. The studio experience was a new one for the band, as guitarist Lee Christopher explains: "It was so alien to us. Sarah originally were thinking about releasing the original demo as a single but there's just something missing from it. We re-recorded it and it turned out really different, not as echoey, it's much rawer and punchy."

Talking in issue three of the *Red Roses For Me* fanzine, the band's frontman Andy Hitchcock expanded on how they came to be signed to Sarah: "We were getting a bit worried after 12 days but then we had a phone call from Clare. I went to see Primal Scream the night before and I woke up the next morning with a massive hangover and had this phone call. They say 'um' and 'rather' a lot. 'Um we'd rather like to do it... we think it's rather good actually.'" When

Lee Christopher and Andy Hitchcock of Action Painting! always knew how to look good.
Darren Hawkins.

asked if Sarah was the ideal label for them, Andy responded: "Yes and we're the ideal band for them, hopefully." He went on to explain that they had deliberately made what they considered "a Sarah single", telling the fanzine: "We thought we'd come up with the classic Sarah single as Matt likes stuff like Fantastic Something, all this stuff from years ago and if they didn't like this then Sarah were definitely down the drain." Evidently Sarah was not yet down the drain because 'These Things Happen' came out and proved to be extremely popular with the fans. Andy explained how the sound had been reached: "It is bombastic and melodramatic. We wanted to put on as many layers as possible... It's really good, like a jigsaw. It's like an Etch-A-Sketch of sound brilliance."

Writing about Action Painting! years later, Lee elaborated on the signing process. "So we sent a cassette tape complete with a handmade cover to Sarah Records. They would understand. They were new and they were young and so were we." But the band's demo was initially rejected by Sarah, so the boys went away, polished up their efforts and tried again: "Down a back alley in Southsea, Portsmouth, was The Crystal Rooms, owned by Steve Hoff. The majority of our early recordings were done there, not in the actual alley, but you can smell the piss on the tremolo build-up of 'Mustard Gas'. The live area was up two flights of stairs above the control room and you'd watch the others play their parts via a small, fuzzy low-grade black and white monitor above the mixing desk. We recorded the two songs we had and yeah, we were happy with them. We all jingled my grandmother's collection of brass bells

The Field Mice would become one of the most enduringly popular bands on Sarah.
Lisa Wratten.

throughout 'Boy Meets World' and I struggled to play 'These Things Happen' on the high-action 12-string, but hey, happy we were. We sent a demo to Sarah Records, they would understand. And this is what they said. 'YES!'"

Bobby Wratten of The Field Mice first heard about Sarah after John Peel and Janice Long had played 'Pristine Christine' on their shows "and I liked it enough to buy it. Then I was out one weekend doing my usual record shopping and I saw The Orchids' single. I hadn't heard it but recognised the label so I bought it." He continues: "These two releases approximately coincided with Michael [Hiscock] and I recording the first Field Mice demo in November 1987. So I put three songs on a cassette and sent it to the address on the singles. I had no idea about the world I was approaching and the fanzines that provided the backdrop to this scene. Matt wrote back. I still have the letter tucked in my Sarah 4 fanzine. He quite rightly pointed out that our songs meandered a bit but said there was something there and if we recorded anything else they'd like to hear it."

And that was the moment when the indie universe tilted ever so slightly on its axis. "Someone had asked to hear us," says Bobby. "Michael and I then recorded a second demo just for the purpose of sending it to Sarah. This was the actual recording of 'Emma's House' that ended up on [our debut 7"]. Complete with Dr Rhythm drum machine and a cold-ridden vocal. The tape also included 'The Last Letter' and 'Fabulous Friend'. Matt wrote again and asked us to do a single. We'd never played live. Only Clare and Matt had heard of us. We had no profile but we were going to be on a label that was getting airplay and reviews."

Bobby and Michael met Clare and Matt for the first time on 10 September 1988, when the four of them went to engineer Ian Catt's studio and mixed four songs in a day. "The new version of 'Emma's House' didn't cut it as far as Clare and Matt were concerned but the other three songs went on a 7" with the demo version," says Bobby. "At the session we asked if we could do another single and they said 'yes' and so we moved on to 'Sensitive'."

> "We'd sent a few tapes out but had got nowhere. It then occurred to me that here was a new label run by people who might not be so jaded that they'd actually listen to demos."
>
> **Bobby Wratten, The Field Mice**

For many of the bands who would release songs on Sarah, it was an all or nothing approach. "They were the one and only label that we sent a demo tape to," guitarist Stuart Vincent told a fanzine during the height of The Sweetest Ache's popularity. "They liked it and we agreed to record a couple of singles. Things went on from there and we did another single and we're going to do an LP."

Stuart had been friends with vocalist Simon Court for years and, despite still being teenagers, the two had already been in various bands. After forming The Sweetest Ache when they were 18 or 19, the two "started to do very rough recordings on an old Fostex four-track demo machine, which was quite cutting edge at the time, the fact you could record four tracks at the same time was fantastic," Stuart tells me now. "So we had a drum machine and a really quite primitive sounding demo tape of various songs with Simon singing. When I started to listen to some of the Sarah stuff, I thought our stuff was quite similar to their sound, the structure of the songs, the lyrics of the songs, and the lo-fi recording of the songs. I thought I'd be cheeky, I thought I'd try and blag my way by giving Sarah a demo tape."

Now, there is some discrepancy in the story about how that demo tape reached Sarah. Some people claim it was posted in the traditional manner, while others claim they made a road trip from Swansea to Bristol and handed it over at the infamous Four Bands and a Fight night at the Fleece & Firkin. Regardless, one way or another, that tape ended up in the hands of Clare and Matt who liked what they heard. "Sarah said they loved the songs," says Stuart. "It was a demo of 'If I Could Shine' and a couple of acoustic tracks, and Sarah asked if we'd like to record a single for them. I was absolutely over the moon."

Keith Girdler and Paul Stewart had been playing in bands together around Reading for a few years. When their band Feverfew split up, the two friends regrouped as The

Top: Blueboy frontman Keith Girdler was an extremely photogenic chap. **Bottom:** As time went on and their popularity grew, Blueboy evolved to become a five-piece.

Top: Courtesy of Blueboy. Bottom: Alison Wonderland.

Art Bunnies and, recognising this was an appalling name, changed it to Blueboy. "Keith and I went back to basics and talked about the kind of sound we wanted to develop, and it was beyond the scope of a little local indie band," says Paul. "So we wrote some songs specifically for the next project and did three songs that we recorded in a mate's shed, one of which was 'Clearer'. It was a bit more melancholic, a bit more serious. I was getting more into guitar effects and atmosphere and texture, rather than having a verse and chorus and a verse and chorus and a jolly bit and an end."

> "Sarah's not like a record label really."
> **Paul Stewart, Blueboy**

In an undated letter to Swedish fanzine writer Marcus Törncrantz, Keith, who died in 2007, wrote: "Since leaving Feverfew, Paul and I have been writing the odd song as the Art Bunnies, we have recorded a demo and we plan to go back into the studio soon... Paul and I share a great love of bands like The Wake, Dif Juz, The Sea Urchins, The Field Mice, Bad Dream Fancy Dress, The Cocteau Twins, Felt and a few others. When I'm not daydreaming about The Art Bunnies, I work as a nurse in the operating theatre at a hospital in Brighton which means I'm usually very, very busy."

Without Paul knowing, Keith had sent their demo tape to a few labels, one of which was Sarah. "He rang me up one Sunday and said 'I've got some good news, Sarah Records have decided to do a single,'" says Paul. "So that's how that began. We felt the size of the label and the music and the artists and bands on the label were within our grasp, so we felt as though we weren't shooting above ourselves."

In another letter to Marcus, Keith said: "Since I last wrote to you, The Art Bunnies have changed their name to Blueboy and we have a single coming out on Sarah sometime towards the end of September, we are Sarah 55. The A side is entitled 'Clearer' and is backed with a song about a girl called 'Alison'. I'm very, very happy and incredibly excited about the single. I'm so pleased that it's on Sarah because I think it's the best label since él Records, don't you agree?"

It seemed like a very relaxed relationship, working alongside Clare and Matt. "They're smashing people. They're so behind the music. We had almost complete freedom to record what we liked," says Paul. "They came and saw us live a few times and would chat to us afterwards and say 'We really like the new stuff, let us know when you want to record another single or album'. They were really easy to work with. We weren't trying to please them and they weren't trying to please us but it just fitted and it just worked. It was a dream come true for us really. We never signed a single piece of paper, nothing."

THE EXCEPTIONS TO THE RULE

There's always an exception to the rule and, in this case, the key exception was Heavenly. While almost everyone else had to cross their fingers and hope for the best in terms of attracting Sarah's attention, Heavenly were instead approached by the label. In the early days, Matt had told *Grimsby Fishmarket* fanzine that his dream

> "Some people did singles for Sarah just to do a single for Sarah. We always saw ourselves as a band on Sarah and I don't think we ever dreamed of going anywhere else. We were quite affronted when they stopped."
>
> **Amelia Fletcher, Heavenly**

signing to the label would be Talulah Gosh if they ever reformed. *cue wavy-lined dream sequence*

When Talulah Gosh disbanded in 1988, there was a break of a year or so before most of the members regrouped as Heavenly. But what happened in that fallow year? Frontwoman Amelia Fletcher finished her degree and made a one-off disco record "because I thought I was going to be the new Yazz". But her self-funded recording of 'Can You Keep a Secret?' failed to excite those who heard it, who promptly *did* keep it a secret, and the single never saw the light of day until Fierce put it out in 1991 after Amelia had gained more attention thanks to Sarah. But we've skipped ahead. Let's go back to Amelia trying to launch her solo career as a disco pop sensation. Amelia watched as guitarist Pete Momtchiloff and bassist Rob Pursey from Talulah Gosh started a new band called The Umbrella Birds... with a woman who wasn't her. Amelia admits: "I started getting quite jealous!" To cut a long story short, she decided maybe she could be in a band again after all, wrote some songs to tempt Pete and Rob back and, as if by magic, The Umbrella Birds flew away and the world was given Heavenly. Phew!

Clare and Matt went to the first Heavenly gig, which was at London's Camden Falcon on 28 October 1989, with a view to trying to sign the new band. Friend-of-the-label Mark Dobson, who would later drum with The Field Mice, advised Clare: "You should sign these. The drummer can smoke and play at the same time, and they have the best socks in showbusiness." At this point, Heavenly were entertaining the idea of releasing their new music themselves and had already had a conversation with Revolver Distribution in Bristol. So, when she saw Clare and Matt in Camden, Amelia went over to ask their advice about self-releasing a record, only for Matt to say: "Hmm, are you sure you wouldn't like to be on Sarah?" Amelia says it hadn't even occurred to them that Sarah would be interested because Heavenly's sound was "a bit punkier even then than the average Sarah band". But it didn't take them long to say 'yes'. Pete Momtchiloff picks up the story. "The reason why we decided to put out our record with them was because they were anti-music business and we thought they were good people. We liked the idea of them doing it on their own terms."

Heavenly's first single, 'I Fell In Love Last Night' in 1990, was the first time Sarah had actually released a single with a female lead vocalist, despite all the music press complaints about twee girl bands. Heavenly stayed with Sarah right until the final moment. "We were pleased they stopped because it was a good artistic statement," says Amelia. "But we were a bit affronted because we didn't know who to do our next album with and we had to go and find someone. So if they'd have carried on, we'd have done the fourth album with them, no problem whatsoever." That fourth album, *Operation Heavenly*, came out in 1996 on Wiiija, which was owned by Beggars Banquet, so it was still an independent label but it had more gravitas. Rob says: "Out of all the thousands of tragedies associated with Mathew's death [drummer Mathew

Mathew Fletcher was Heavenly's very entertaining drummer.
Credit: Grimsby Fishmarket, Marcus Torncrantz.

Julian Henry of The Hit Parade had released six singles on his own label before joining Sarah.
Credit: Grimsby Fishmarket, Marcus Torncrantz.

Fletcher died in June 1996], when we did that last LP just before he died, we had the potential to go on to even bigger things. But it's almost like we've never had to answer the question of what we would have done next because it couldn't be asked."

Heavenly weren't quite the only exception to the rule. The Hit Parade had released six singles on their own label before signing to Sarah, explains frontman Julian Henry: "Matt wrote to me and said he liked my approach and our songs, and he had already written about us in *Are You Scared To Get Happy?*. We'd been rejected multiple times by then so it was nice to feel wanted." He continues: "I have plenty of bad memories of people in A&R departments in London promising us things that never materialised. Our third and fourth singles had been played on the Radio 1 night-time shows, Japanese fans were writing to us, too, so it was obvious something was happening. We'd recorded a second LP and had been invited to Tokyo to play live; we flew to Japan in 1990 to tour with The Milkshakes, it was fantastic but still didn't make us appealing to any London label so I gave up on all that. It was then that Matt and Clare asked if we'd give them a song for Sarah Records. They were straightforward, sincere and the idea of being on Sarah Records was appealing as I quite liked the records they'd been releasing."

In addition to fronting The Hit Parade, Julian has a flourishing career in public relations with some very high-profile clients. He says: "I've always had two sides to my career. One allows the other to exist. I gravitated towards PR work and put the money into recording and trying to establish myself. As I got on, the thing I discovered was that I was buying my own freedom with my band. Be it the guitar, the recording time, or whatever... I was buying myself a platform to express myself, and that's what it became and what it continues to be today." Julian adds: "There's been a few odd times when my two worlds of PR and pop have collided. People are surprised when they discover my other side. I've spent ages studying how a story is told within the structure of a three-minute pop song. The ingredients. But not just words and music. The motivation. How it all looked so natural and easy. These fast narrative constructions follow the same principles as advertising and marketing, and films and books for that matter. It's about hooking people, seduction."

Another band with an existing fanbase that found an offer being extended from Sarah was Northern Picture Library, which rose from the ashes of the cremated Field Mice. Although, as frontman Bobby Wratten admits, maybe going to Sarah with their new band wasn't the smartest move. He says: "Relations with Sarah had almost broken down completely. There was no one reason, just poor communication and a fair amount of sulking and different ideas of what the band should be and arguments about the size of the band name on [The Field Mice album] *For Keeps*! [Clare and Matt would] be at shows and neither of us would speak to each other which was a sad state of affairs." He continues: "So, when Anne Mari [Davies] and I were looking for a label, I knew in my heart of hearts not to approach Clare and Matt but I approached them anyway, only for them to rip our demo to shreds. We'd been on the label but now we were outsiders and fair game for destroying. I like to think at this distance there was a fair amount of politics involved. We weren't even talking and yet I chose to send them a six-song Northern Picture Library tape." Concluding the story, Bobby says: "The handful of gigs that Northern Picture Library played were often with Sarah bands and we ended up doing half a dozen dates in France with Blueboy. Clare and I got to spend time together and realised we still liked one another and still got on really well. Around the same time, unbeknown to me, Mark [Dobson, drummer] had been speaking to Sarah saying that I'd written some songs that were more accessible than the LP [*Alaska*, released on Vinyl Japan]. I assume Clare got to hear 'Paris' and 'Norfolk Windmills' live and agreed with Mark. The result of all this was we were back on Sarah. Despite everything that had happened, I had to admit it felt like I was back where I belonged. There was always something that felt right about making records for Clare and Matt."

Off the back of earlier singles

Some of the bands had a few releases to their name on other small labels before they approached Sarah, and were able to use those early releases as calling cards.

Norwich band Ivy had an early version of their track 'Wish You Would' on a four-track compilation EP on Noisebox. A copy of that 7" made its way onto the desk of Steve Lamacq at Radio 1 who ended up playing it a few times on the Evening Session, where Clare and Matt heard the song and offered the band two singles. The first, Sarah 91, was a re-recording of 'Wish You Would'. "Matt and Clare wanted to re-issue the original recording. But bands being as they are, 'Wish You Would' had been written three years earlier and we were sick of it," says guitarist Julian Cator. "The Sarah version was better produced but I just think the other had a better, indie-ish charm. We had new songs that we liked more. We had a song 'Avenge' that we all wanted to put out as well." 'Avenge' would be Ivy's second Sarah single.

The only time Ivy met Clare and Matt was at the Astoria in London, where Ivy had been supporting The Wedding Present. "I walked past them in the venue and then they followed me and said 'Hello, we're your new record label!' And I was like, 'Oh my god, Matt and Clare!'," laughs vocalist Spencer Harrison. "I felt really stupid, and then we sat and watched The Wedding Present together."

Australian band The Sugargliders had had one single out on a UK label called Marineville and three singles on a Melbourne label called Summershine, but "we were such a fish out of water in Melbourne in that time," says Josh Meadows. "It was the grunge era and we were these two brothers playing gentle guitar-driven stuff." The Sugargliders were Josh and his younger brother Joel, who had been brought up listening to the folky records that their parents enjoyed by acts such as James Taylor, Carole King and The Carpenters. "Melody was very important to us from a very young age," says Josh. "I think important to The Sugargliders right from the start

Top: Ivy caught Clare and Matt's attention after the band was played on Radio 1's Evening Session.
Bottom: The Sugargliders had a few records out on small labels but were delighted to be on Sarah.
Top: Courtesy of Spencer Harrison. Bottom: Courtesy of The Sugargliders.

was this naïve political concern as well. And, once we got to know a bit more about Matt and Clare, we learned that political pop music was something that was really important to them, too." Joel adds: "There was something about rejecting the overly masculine big heavy guitars. Just not wanting to do that. I hate the term 'twee' but we liked that something can be both gentle and incredibly powerful. Something can be done softly and absolutely rip you to shreds, and it was that kind of thing with the Sarah songs. It doesn't have to be huge to have a huge impact."

So the Meadows brothers sent their Summershine singles to Sarah in the hope Clare and Matt would see something in them. While waiting for a response, they went into a studio and recorded 'Letter from a Lifeboat' which they also sent to Sarah, asking if the UK label was interested in putting it out. "We got a phone call from Clare on my 22nd birthday saying that they loved it and wanted to do it. We were absolutely rapt," says Josh. "We went overnight from being Sarah fans to being a Sarah band."

Coming from overseas

Most of the Sarah bands were UK based, but a handful came from other corners of the globe:

Aberdeen	Los Angeles, California, US
East River Pipe	Queens, New York City, US
Even As We Speak	Sydney, Australia
The Harvest Ministers	Dublin, Ireland
The Springfields	Urbana, Illinois, US
The Sugargliders	Melbourne, Australia

But in the pre-internet age, how did news spread around the world about this tiny independent label in Bristol? In the case of The Springfields, whose single 'Sunflower' was Sarah 10 in 1988, it is especially interesting when you consider the absolute infancy of the label. "I was really into all the bands on Postcard Records, and I suppose that is what ultimately led me to the indie stuff that began to emerge in 1985 and 1986," says drummer Ric Menck. "I started writing letters to Alan McGee [at Creation] and we became pen pals. I eventually began writing to Martin Whitehead at Subway and Matt and Clare at Sarah. Choo Choo Train ended up putting out records on Subway, The Springfields records came out on Sarah, and Velvet Crush, which came later, were on Creation. There weren't very many American bands on those labels. We were unique in that way."

The Springfields' first 7" was released at the same time as Ric's and vocalist and bassist Paul Chastain's other band, Choo Choo Train, put out their first single on Subway. "I don't know that there was an indie scene in Illinois when Paul and I

Top: Ric Menck of The Springfields (pictured on the right) settled for a unique method of payment for his work: music rather than money. **Bottom:** East River Pipe's FM Cornog was inspired to contact Sarah following a conversation with a record shop owner friend.

Top: Courtesy of The Springfields. Bottom: Courtesy of East River Pipe.

were making The Springfields and Choo Choo Train recordings. There were a lot of 'alternative' or 'college rock' bands back then but we didn't really feel any kinship with them. We were kind of lost in our own little world and not really a part of any scene," says Ric. "I initially heard of Sarah when I bought The Sea Urchins' single. That was a huge record for me. I finally met them in person when Choo Choo Train went over to England to tour with The Flatmates. By then I was paying very close attention to all the indie stuff in the UK."

Fellow American FM Cornog joined the Sarah family in 1993 under the guise of East River Pipe. FM was living in Queens, New York, in the late 1980s when he met Barbara Powers. She started Hell Gate Records solely to release his music, initially on cassette. "She had a kind of burning desire to get my music out there into the world. It was like she was on a mission or something. I had very mixed feelings about the entire thing but I kept writing songs and I semi-cooperated with her plan," says FM. In 1991, East River Pipe released the first of three 7"s on Hell Gate and "during this time it was becoming evident to Barbara and me that East River Pipe and Hell Gate were really two sides of the same coin."

> "My association with Sarah was wonderful. They treated me with lots of respect."
> **Ric Menck, The Springfields**

Via a record shop in Hoboken, New Jersey, called Pier Platters, FM and Barbara met Tom Prendergast, who ran the shop as well as an indie record label called Bar/None Records. "Tom could be very intimidating. He'd stare you straight in the eyes, as if he was reading your inner thoughts," says FM. "Tom said that he had listened to the singles and liked them a lot. And then he asked us if either one of us had heard of a label in England called Sarah Records. We'd never heard of Sarah Records. Tom suggested that we send the Hell Gate singles over to Sarah. So, rather innocently, we sent the records over, not expecting anything to happen."

But FM was wrong: "A few weeks later, we received a handwritten note from Matt and Clare on official Sarah Records stationery. The note was direct and simple, it said, 'Do you want to make a record?' We were stunned. It seemed unbelievable. A real record company in England wanted to release East River Pipe? Are you fucking kidding me? It seemed impossible. We said, 'Yes!'"

On the other side of the US is California, where Aberdeen had been formed in Palm Desert by Beth Arzy and John Girgus. Sarah came to Beth's attention in the early 1990s thanks to her friend Brandt Larson who was fully immersed in the indie world. "Brandt was the social hub of music, he was the glue that brought us all together," says Beth. "He would introduce you to this band, or say you should play with that band, and you guys should know each other, and he introduced me to Sarah Records."

It was Brandt who encouraged Beth to send an Aberdeen demo to Sarah for consideration. "Matt responded with a letter saying they really liked this track and they'd like to put out a single. I was like, 'Holy shit, for real?' And that's how it started," says Beth. "As you know, Matt can be great with correspondence and where I worked we had a fax machine and we used to fax each other all day long, about music and everything and putting out the record. I was made up to be signed to Sarah, we were on top of the world. The other people that we knew that were into Sarah, they were all a bit jealous I think. Our friends were like, 'They're not really good enough to be on Sarah.' And maybe we weren't. But we were over the moon."

John adds: "It felt unbelievable to be signed to Sarah. It's not like 'My god, we've made it!' Something that wasn't possible is actually happening now. One of the things that I really identified with in the first place was that it was accessible. Realising that everybody on the label had your same limitations and aesthetics. Signing to Sarah is not a thing you would ever think about happening. It's really hard to describe how mind blowing it was."

A FRIEND OF A FRIEND

Word of mouth is a good way to get ahead. I know someone who knows someone who knows Clare and Matt quite well, that sort of thing. And this leads us to the story of how Irish band The Harvest Ministers found themselves signed to Sarah. "It would be fair to say being based in Dublin had its advantages, in that we were left alone! And disadvantages, in that we didn't get to go on tour as such with any of our fellow label pals," says frontman Will Merriman. But before we hear how the Ministers were signed, let's first meet their friend Ken Sweeney.

Dublin-born Ken, under the name Brian, had recently released his single 'You Don't Want a Boyfriend' on Detzi to a very tepid response. So tepid that he dumped a load of the unsold copies in his local Record & Tape Exchange in London. On the back of the sleeve were four lines of text about a young American woman called Alma Reynolds who had beaten her fiancé to death with an encyclopaedia in 1989. A friend of Clare's was flicking through the crates in the same Record & Tape Exchange, when he stumbled across this unusual story written on the back of a 7" and bought a copy of the record. He liked the music so much that he told Clare about it, and she liked it so much that she rang the number on the back of the record and got through to Ken.

"I hadn't been in London long and the phone rang, and this soft spoken lady said 'Is that Brian? This is Clare Wadd from Sarah Records.' I thought she was messing. I put the phone down on her and told my friend off for ringing me up and pretending to be Clare," says Ken. "And then I realised Clare actually had rung me up. I'd heard of Sarah Records because a friend of mine wrote for *Select* magazine, and he came up to the house one time with this Brighter 10" album and I thought it was amazing." Ken rang Clare back, and she said that she and Matt loved the music and were interested in putting it out. But she was too late: Setanta had snuck in and just signed Brian. Nonetheless, Clare told Ken that she was going to see a band play at the Camden Falcon the following week and he should come along, too.

Thanks to mutual friend Ken Sweeney, Dublin-based The Harvest Ministers found their way to Sarah.
Courtesy of The Harvest Ministers.

"I was really shy, I had no self-confidence," says Ken, in a sentence that could have been uttered by any one of 500 people involved in this story. "I went to the bar around the corner first and got drunk. Then I went to the gig and met Matt and Clare. They'd heard the 'Boyfriend' single and really liked it, and then Oliver Reed came through the door... this mad, drunk, Irish guy." It wasn't the best of first impressions. "Sarah gigs are the most English thing I've ever been to," says Ken. "There'd be someone in the corner selling a fanzine, everyone had their head down in little chats, it was a very introverted scene. I think Clare and Matt were a bit horrified by me, but Harvey Williams was also there and he reassured them I was fine. Harvey realised what I was like sober."

Ken got back in touch with Clare and Matt and said that while they'd missed the boat with Brian, they should definitely look up his friends The Harvest Ministers. "There were eight or nine of them, they were every Irish music journalist's favourite band," enthuses Ken. "But this was a point in Dublin when U2 were really big and everyone had these loud guitars. Will sent me over their first single, 'You Do My World The World of Good', and I loved it and sent it to Matt and Clare. I wanted to tip them off. That was the incredible thing, because the Ministers got a call to say 'We love it, we're going to put it out' and they were stunned someone was going to put out their record. Suddenly Sarah were putting out this weird Irish band."

Ken adds: "Any other record label, if they miss out on signing a band, all they do is slag the band off. But everything at Sarah Records is the opposite of what labels

"They thought we were signed to annoy people," laughs Boyracer's Stewart Anderson (pictured left).
Courtesy of Boyracer.

do. There was a Sarah Christmas party, and Matt and Clare asked me for copies of 'Boyfriend' and handed them out to everyone at that party, and that was before [my album] *Understand* came out, and that meant there was an audience when it came out because they already had this single."

THE WILD CARD

Boyracer frontman Stewart Anderson remains convinced that Sarah only signed his band to underscore the label's reputation as cantankerous mavericks. He had been putting on gigs in his home city of Leeds, including many touring Sarah bands, and Boyracer would often open the show for them. "When we were asked to do a record, I think a lot of people thought it was just because we'd put a bunch of Sarah bands on," says Stewart. "People thought there was another reason other than the music we were making, because we were very sloppy. They thought we were signed to annoy people!"

Prior to Sarah, Boyracer had had a single on Fluff and a flexi. "At the time, I didn't even have a telephone. I was living in Harehills in Leeds, and I got a letter from Sarah that said 'You've got a song called 'I've Got It & It's Not Worth Having', do you want to put that on a single?' And I remember going down the pub that night and my friends saying 'You don't want to

❝ I was definitely very surprised when they asked us to do a record."
Stewart Anderson, Boyracer

do a single for Sarah, what are you thinking about?' It was considered a joke label at that time. They weren't taken seriously, especially in the music press. But I liked a lot of the Sarah bands and I wanted to do some records."

Was Boyracer the only wild card on the Sarah roster? Some would say The Golden Dawn and Gentle Despite also were. And, if so, doesn't that render the category of wild card obsolete? Discuss. Eugene Dawydiak of The Golden Dawn says: "Many years later, I ended up working with someone who had been in the band Remember Fun who had released on Sha-La-La and were staying with Clare and Matt when they played our demo for the first time. From what he said, and also from what Matt and Clare had said at the time, they did genuinely love the tracks and wanted to release a record on the strengths of the music alone. However, narratives do have a tendency to develop and change over time and I do get the impression that we gradually became the 'outsider' for Sarah and the core fans."

THE END IS NIGH

The last 'new' Sarah band was Shelley, whose 7" 'Reproduction is Pollution' was Sarah 98. Shelley was the band Orlando in disguise; they felt that they needed to adopt a change of name so that the Sarah stigma didn't affect their chances of being taken seriously as pop artistes. Guitarist Dickon Edwards explains: "I wanted Orlando to be a proper pop band, or at least try and be one. I worried that having a record out on Sarah would just confuse a lot of music journalists, and it was a time when music journalists had a lot of power." However, the band's love for the label meant they jumped at the chance to be one of the final releases. Singer Tim Chipping explains: "Dickon had this band called Orlando and what he really wanted to do was find the prettiest boy in Bristol and ask him to be the singer in his band, and he would treat him like he believed Bob [Stanley] and Pete [Wiggs] treated Sarah Cracknell. He really liked Saint Etienne but, because he shared Clare's politics, he thought there was something icky about the fetishising of the pretty 1960s singer they do. But he wasn't a woman so he couldn't reverse it in that way. I know for a while he was wandering around Bristol following pretty boys but he never found the courage to ask them."

Hold on. Dickon was following pretty boys around Bristol in the hope of finding his band's frontman? "I wonder…" muses Dickon. "It sounds like me. I was obsessed with the idea of boys being in bands for their looks, in a kind of reverse of the girl-fronted-band cliché. Some of the Sarah songwriters were beautiful enough anyway: Bobby Wratten certainly was and still is! It was a pastoral, arcadian aesthetic, made all the more appealing by the image of the bands and fans being somehow asexual or virginal. What it was, of course, was an intense aloofness, the kind that only comes from a subculture."

Tim had previously fallen into being in various bands, which was how he and

The final band to be signed to Sarah was Shelley, who released 'Reproduction is Pollution'.
Courtesy of Shelley.

Dickon crossed paths. "Dickon was aware I was singing and I was aware he was in Orlando, and having failed to get this beautiful singer he wanted he settled for me," says Tim. Because both were big Sarah fans and were friends with many of the bands, the early Orlando/Shelley gigs were supporting their friends in Heavenly or Blueboy, and both Dickon and Tim took turns duetting with Amelia on 'C is the Heavenly Option' "because that's what you had to do at that point, take the Calvin [Johnson] role," says Tim. Clare and Matt said Sarah wanted to do a single with Tim and Dickon after they supported Heavenly at the Fleece & Firkin in Bristol. "We were really confused," says Tim. "We just didn't think we were good enough and didn't think we were going to be this band for long. But this was our last chance to be on Sarah." He adds: "The single finally went into profit a few years ago and Matt sent us a cheque for £10 each."

'Did you ever find out who Christine's Cat was?'

During all the interviews I carried out for this book, people asked me two questions more than any other. One was, 'What on earth is Matt up to these days?' (given Clare's career in finance is fairly well known) and the other was, well, the subheading for this section kind of spoiled the suspense. The mysterious Christine's Cat, aka Sarah 13, released a one-track flexi called 'Your Love Is' in 1989 and then disappeared into thin air. The band was never heard of again. Who were they?

Several people wondered if Christine's Cat was actually Clare and Matt themselves. "Sadly, much as I'd like to say Christine's Cat was an enigmatic front for a supergroup containing members of My Bloody Valentine, Teenage Fanclub, Primal Scream and the Brighouse & Rastrick Brass Band, it was actually just a side project of Robert from The Golden Dawn," says Matt. "So nothing to do with me and Clare at all. Unless, of course, I am also a side project of Robert from The Golden Dawn."

So with that rumour put to bed, I can confirm that Christine's Cat was Robert Smith and Kenny Forte from The Golden Dawn, along with their friend Christine Grant on vocals. Christine, as you might have guessed, had a cat and that cat was called Babushka. Does Christine still have a cat? "Yes, I do, it would be strange not to," she tells me in what is her world-exclusive first-ever interview.

Although Robert seems to have gone off grid these days, I tracked down Kenny and Christine for a chat about their brief foray into feline sound adventures on flexi. "It was such a short and sweet pop song that I can almost understand why people would like it," says Kenny. "Robert and his girlfriend at the time would come round to ours, and we'd sit and drink wine and play music and record stuff, so it probably came out of that collaboration." Christine adds: "Christine's Cat was a kind of accident. I was Kenny's girlfriend at the time and I knew some of The Golden Dawn before that. I started going out with Kenny and was singing along when he was strumming and he was quite taken aback that I could hold a tune. He must have said to Robert that I could sing, because Robert asked if I wanted to record some of his songs with him so I thought 'Why not? Sounds fun'. I hadn't recorded anything before in that way so it was really good." Although Robert wanted to call the project The Idyllic Days, Christine and Kenny stood their ground that this was a group project and not just Robert's baby, so a new name was dreamt up... "I wasn't sure about the band having my name on it, it seemed like I'd been revealed in some way," Christine admits.

> "God, who else is on this label?"
> Sarah Newsletter No 2, January 1993

Christine and The Golden Dawn boys would often hang out at Glasgow's Griffin Bar, which attracted all sorts of bands to play and in this way the group saw an early version of The Field Mice when they were still a duo. "I was amazed that Sarah wanted to put one of the Christine's Cat songs out," says Christine. "It hits me more now than it did at the time, because I look back and think 'I've actually got a flexi single, how did that happen?!'"

But it wasn't the easiest process recording the songs, as Christine explains: "I think women have been silenced a bit when men are around. I did feel that, especially with Robert, he was quite controlling. The Golden Dawn was his thing, that's fair enough, but Christine's Cat was the three of us. I don't think I could have continued working with Robert because he was too controlling. I think it's because I was a woman and because he liked to be in charge. In some of the songs, I'd have liked to have been involved in the production because, when I recorded the songs, I was quite happy with them but then when they were mixed, he had tweaked my vocals up a few pitches and I didn't like it. If it was me, I'd have said 'Can we change that?'

Kenny Forte and Christine Grant made up two thirds of Christine's Cat: the most mysterious band who ever joined the ranks of Sarah Records.
Christine Grant.

but I wasn't able to say that to him. When I listened to it, I thought 'That isn't me.' It was like he wanted a wee girlie, squeaky voice, something like Kylie Minogue – Robert really had some terrible taste in music! I do think it's a shame. Women have to be in control of everything themselves to get the music done the way they want it to be done, because somebody like Robert just wanted women to do what he wanted to do. It's very difficult for women, it still is."

Along with a few other songs, 'Your Love Is', which would appear on the one-track flexi in 1989, was recorded on a four-track at Robert's house. Talking to Christine for this book prompted her to dig out some of the other songs that were recorded that day and, more than three decades after they were recorded, she finally uploaded some of them to YouTube, most notably the beautiful pop song 'Like A Summer's Day'.

As for the enigma surrounding Christine's Cat…

"It's always nice to be a mystery," says Christine. "It's nice to know that it was more of a mystery and more cool than The Golden Dawn! It was better being Christine's Cat but I never knew that was going to happen, that it was going to become a mystery. But I think it's pretty cool, yeah." She adds: "The whole period was so amazing. I think I was really lucky just to be there at that time. Glasgow was an exciting town to be in at that time. Just about everybody I knew was in a band in Glasgow."

As for what Matt is up to these days? I couldn't possibly say but I've got a copy of his *Unchartered Streets* book on my desk right now. Dammit, I've got a copy of his SECRET new book on my desk right now. *discards membership form to join the Secret (Shine) Service* 🍒

*****

THESE THINGS HAPPENED:
Rob Sekula, 14 Iced Bears

"They were putting out some of the best music at the time, so we were proud to be on Sarah. It also meant a lot more people got to hear us, which has carried on to this day. If it wasn't for Sarah, we'd be even more obscure! When we reformed in 2010 and were playing places like Northampton, Massachusetts, people would come to see us who only knew of our Sarah stuff. So I'll be forever grateful to Clare and Matt. They genuinely don't want to rip their artists off as they really care about the music, rather than the profit. Over the years, they've been excellent in all the dealings we've had with them."

Chapter 5

Fanzine Culture

In the olden days, when the internet and email were just twinkles in the sky, the best way for music fans to share their love of the things that rocked their world was via self-published fanzines. The modern equivalent of a fanzine would be a blog but the ephemeral nature of them – and the changed means of production – creates an entirely different dynamic, so it's not a perfect comparison.

The origin of music fanzines is commonly dated to the punk heyday of the 1970s, although fan magazines go back to the 1930s. The thinking is that fanzine writers typically have an opinion that is in opposition to that expressed in the mainstream media, hence the need to self-publish. Fanzines also enable fans of a particular thing to find and communicate with each other, thereby opening up a dialogue that would never otherwise have been possible.

To buy a music fanzine, you would tape coins to bits of card and post these all around the country. You might hear about fanzines through adverts in things like *NME* or *Melody Maker*, or more commonly from the tiny slips of paper that fell like colourful inky snow from inside your most recent mail-order fanzine delivery. It was the habit of fanzine writers and flexi producers to create these tiny ads, squeeze as many as possible onto a sheet of A4, and photocopy this onto coloured paper. Then cut these sheets up and send batches of the ads to other fanzine writers to distribute. This, along with reviews in more established titles, was how we heard of other people's fanzines. It was a very successful and introverted network of quiet people making silent contact with one another. Most of us would never meet face to face and were quite happy about that.

> ❝There are only three reasons for writing a fanzine. a) To make money. b) To boost your ego. c) To communicate your love/hate for things to as many people as possible. And if you're doing it for any reason other than 'c', then you're doing it for the WRONG reason and should stop now."
>
> **Letter from Matt to me, August 1994**

The other tried and tested method for selling fanzines was at gigs, so long as you lived in a town that put on gigs and you had the courage to go up to strangers and demand they hand over 30p in exchange for your photocopied musings. Mark Taylor was the editor of the popular *Smiths Indeed* fanzine, which he ran from his parents' home in Bristol and sold all over the country. However, he remembers one of the pitfalls of having a successful fanzine: "I didn't think about the weight of coins after

Fanzines were an absolutely essential part of this music scene. The bottom picture shows three of the most influential titles for many of the people interviewed for this book.
Jon Craig.

selling 100 or 200 fanzines. I'd have to try and get through the gig without my jeans falling down!" Although this level of success wasn't something most fanzine writers needed to worry about.

Chris Tighe and Robert McTaggart mostly sold their fanzine *Far Out And Fishy* at gigs and, according to Chris, would "just walk up to hundreds of total strangers, butting into their conversations, sticking a piece of printed paper under their noses, saying 'Hey, would you like to buy a fanzine? It's only 25p!' and getting told to 'fuck off' once in a while." He adds: "I wasn't exactly an outgoing person and I've got a slight stammer, so it baffles me that I was able to do it."

Rob Sekula of 14 Iced Bears tells me: "It was great to see fanzines being sold at gigs, they added to the excitement. Similar to how football programmes added to the sense of occasion when I went to Tottenham as a kid. They were a more immediate, less industry way to find out about good new bands and discover things like great records and bands from the past, from people who had similar tastes. Along with John Peel they were pretty useful in the days before the internet."

Davey Woodward from The Brilliant Corners adds: "I always thought fanzines were a great thing to happen because I felt we were very close to going back to a time where big multinational labels just ruled the roost in terms of what happened. And I think, in those Thatcherite 1980s, there was a definite reaction against that. People thought, 'No, I am going to do my own thing, I'm going to make it the way I want to make it.' It was important in the wider scheme of things to create a scene for a group of people."

Simon Barber, bassist with The Chesterfields, agrees: "Fanzines were so important. The difference between fanzines and the music press is you only write about something in a fanzine if you love it. If there's a good review in the music press, you don't know if it's been paid for." He adds: "I bought every fanzine going. If someone was going round a gig selling a fanzine, I'd buy it, those guys were the best." Simon still has all his fanzines and kindly loaned me two enormous boxes of them while I was researching this book.

Ric Menck of The Springfields was based in Illinois and says: "The fanzine network meant everything to me back then. I was more interested in fanzines than the British weeklies. The fanzine writers weren't trying to be cool. They just wrote about what they loved. Before computers came around, fanzines were the way to hear about cool new stuff. The fanzine network was always crucially important to underground music."

Influential fanzines that came in the years immediately preceding Sarah included the following three, all of which certainly made an impact on readers and bands. Their editors also all went on to make their mark on the world of pop culture in one way or another. Tellingly, these are all by men.

- *Attack on Bzag* was run by James Brown from Leeds, who would go on to write for *NME* and *Sounds*, edit troublesome lads' mag *Loaded* and men's monthly *GQ*. He later become editor-in-chief for the Sport Newspaper Group which, despite the name, has nothing to do with football but everything to do with topless women and absurd sex stories.

- Meanwhile, John Robb from Lancashire was running *Rox* when he wasn't in punk band The Membranes. John told online magazine JSNTGM: "The best fanzines were out of control, quite literally out of control! They wrote in their own style about their own music and were not filtered by the music business ... I love cut and paste artwork which very much matched the cut and paste nature of the punk and post punk music." John went on to write for *Sounds*, *Melody Maker* and various national newspapers. These days he runs the music website Louder Than War.

- Jerry Thackray launched a fanzine that was called *The Legend!* and – bizarrely – he also put out the first single on Creation. After his fanzine finished, Jerry wrote for *NME* (as The Legend!), before moving to *Melody Maker* and adopting the pen name of Everett True. "I guess I was quite idealistic," says Jerry now. "But maybe that's what separated some of the fanzine writers apart. Some of us really did believe that passionately in what we wrote about." Talking about the way that he adopted a different approach to many of his contemporaries, Jerry says: "I saw all these post-punk fanzines and they all had interviews in. And I was like, 'These interviews are fucking crap, they're just really bad versions of the music press'. I couldn't speak to people and it just so happened that music was easily the thing I was most passionate about so I wrote about music, and that's all I've ever done my entire life." He still writes about music and teaches music journalism in London.

Fanzine favourites

"We were amazed that people would take all that time and effort to write about us in their fanzines, and I've still got a lot of letters people sent," says Chris Quinn, drummer with The Orchids. Guitarist John Scally adds, with bewilderment, how amazed he is by the efforts fans would make: "The people who showed up to a gig before we even put the gear in, that always surprised me. I didn't realise until years later that that was the mindset of a lot of Sarah fans. That amount of effort really surprised me because I don't put a lot of effort into many things. If I can't get the bus within 10 minutes of waiting, I go home again." John almost shakes his head in disbelief.

But thank goodness those fans did put the effort in. Alison Cousens of Brighter says: "I would buy fanzines at gigs to keep abreast of what people were writing about on the ground. And discovering gems of songs on some of the cassettes that would

St Christopher's Glenn Melia (pictured above, left): "Fanzines are an essential part of the big pop plan."
Grimsby Fishmarket, Nicklas Brunzell.

come with them. We missed out on the original fanzines that Matt and Clare had done so, the first time we went to Bristol, Matt showed me some of the stuff they'd done and I remember loving the cover of *Are You Scared To Get Happy?* four. So the front cover of [our album] *Laurel* became a homage to that front cover."

Razorcuts found the fanzine network hugely important for boosting the profile of the band and getting themselves out there, given their scant coverage in the national music press. "There was a time when I seemed to get new fanzines arriving through the door on a daily basis that had stuff about Razorcuts in them," says bassist Tim Vass. "We were fanzine favourites and I think it was partly because I replied to all the letters. Whenever anyone wrote to us, I assiduously wrote back and we were always happy to answer questionnaires and meet people to do interviews." Guitarist Greg Webster adds: "The fanzine culture really reflected the pop underground and that's what we were into. It wasn't controlled by corporate interests so it really appealed to us."

Tim expands on how hard it must be for 21st century teenagers to understand the importance of an independent music press. "You couldn't even explain this to a 19-year-old now because everything is dictated by social media," he says. "But in an era when social media didn't exist, this was a really special thing. It's almost inexplicable how people came into contact with each other and how this scene grew. When I think back to it now, I think it's really quite odd how that whole scene propagated itself. People felt that they knew us and could trust us, so we would get these letters from people and they would tell us all about the shit they were going through in their lives. It was quite nice when we did gigs, because people would pitch up a few hours before the gig started to help us unload our gear or have a drink with us. And that was largely because of this whole thing of people exchanging fanzines and sending letters to each other."

Glenn Melia of St Christopher told a fanzine writer in 1989: "Fanzines are an essential part of the big pop plan. Bands like ourselves owe so much to people who have written about us and hence spread the word. I greatly admire the people who write 'zines as I see them as crusaders for all that we hold dear in pop. On the other hand, you have the national music press, whose writers on the whole seem to be ego-tripping, holier-than-thou punters, soulless people, seemingly determined to belittle anything that resembles pop as 'twee' and 'inconsequential', usually because there is a distinct lack of rock apparent, or the band is not the product of the American underground scene ... In general fanzines are created by genuine enthusiasts who really care. I guess most of them lose out financially, which makes it an even more admirable crusade."

The Field Mice were certainly a fanzine favourite and for a while appeared in almost every new fanzine before suddenly vanishing from view. Frontman Bobby Wratten tells me: "I'm not sure I ever deliberately stopped giving interviews to fanzines. Rather, fanzines seemed to wane in popularity the longer I was involved in music and also the requests to do interviews came to a halt. Michael [Hiscock] and I definitely did not come from the world of fanzines. We never distinguished between interviews, fanzines or otherwise. The fact that someone was interested enough to want to talk to us was enough. It didn't matter if it was *Melody Maker*, BBC radio or a fanzine that would have a print run of 20 copies. But obviously the DIY aspect of fanzines did make you realise that the person in question was really committing to something in a way that someone sent to review you for the *NME* may not be."

Bedroom culture

Fanzine production involved fans sitting on their bedroom floors armed with a typewriter and a Pritt Stick to create mini tributes to their favourite obscure bands. Friendships were formed with the most unlikely people, tapes of the strangest music were swapped, and all kinds of opportunities opened up. It was a brilliantly exciting time. You didn't need to live in London for something to happen. "I'm always impressed to read fanzines that are not London or other big city-centered. I really don't envy people stuck out in the back of beyond with virtually no transport to get to the nearest 'big' places," wrote London-based Dee in the third issue of her fanzine *All About D & Friends*.

Growing up in Gloucester, future-academic Sukhdev Sandhu was a fanzine-

People's bedrooms became the key site of cultural production. Here's the bedroom of Rob 'Poppyheads' Young back when he was, err, young.
Rob Young.

reading Sarah fan who understood the disadvantages of living in the provinces if you had an interest in things that didn't typically reach the provinces. He says Bristol seemed "a million miles away" (it's actually only 35) and, as a teenager, he had never been to the cinema never mind a pop concert. "We didn't have any money in my parents' house, so we didn't have a record player or anything like that. So you had a radio and a tape recorder. You'd press 'play' and there's all the surface noise of your mother saying 'Do your homework' or 'Come down and get your meal', or traffic going on outside, so they're field recordings as much as they're high-fidelity recordings of records," he explains.

And the places where we created our provincial fanzines were our bedrooms. The importance of the teenage bedroom is a topic famously explored by Professor Angela McRobbie and other academics, some of whom have written about how this has changed in the digital world that contemporary teenagers inhabit, and most of whom have found that music is an integral element in the creation and evolution of youth culture within the domestic setting. For many Western teenagers, the bedroom is your space. It is the one part of the world over which you have control. You can put what you want on the walls, you can arrange the furniture as you choose, you can keep your secrets under the loose floorboard, and you can play what you want on the turntable.

I grew up in a rural village where nothing happened. As such,

> ❝ I really mourn the demise of fanzines, the real, old-fashioned, on-a-photocopier-at-work type stuff. I just think they were wonderful things."
>
> **Spencer Harrison, Ivy**

My bedroom in early 1995: a place to sit on the floor and Pritt Stick fanzines together while listening to records until the very wee hours of the morning.
Jane Duffus.

like anyone who could afford to, I learned to drive the second I turned 17. Having a driving licence and a tenth-hand car gave me unfettered freedom to explore, go to new record shops and bigger gigs further afield. But, until I turned 17, my bedroom was my world. I spent an inordinate amount of time in my bedroom, as was common for introverted teenagers in isolated villages and market towns up and down the country. In the late 1980s and early 1990s, there was no internet, no Wi-Fi, no mobile phones, no text messaging. When we were in our bedrooms, we were alone. If we wanted to speak to someone, we either needed to come out and talk to a family member or pick up the telephone. Even then, we couldn't take the receiver into our bedrooms for privacy because it was wired to the wall in another room.

Teenage bedrooms increasingly became a space of cultural production, whether this was somewhere to write in your diary, make art, create your fanzine, learn to play guitar, tape your self-penned songs on a crude cassette recorder, write stories or… whatever. Over time, this led to a transformation in sex norms. Previously, guitar playing or music making would have been seen as boys' activities but, within the self-regulated bedroom, girls could do what they liked with no outside influence exerting its control and limitations.

When I spoke to Pennsylvania-based music fan Lara Cohen for this book, I had a strong feeling that she and I had lived parallel lives on opposite sides of the Atlantic. We're the same age, we both felt like oddballs at school because we were into obscure indie bands, we wrote fanzines and we hung out with bands as much as we could.

For us, the bedroom was the centre of our universe. Lara was behind *Runt* fanzine and in this way she got to know Heavenly when they were over in the US touring with Lois and Bratmobile. "The thing with Heavenly that really struck me was that it was very clear that they were intellectuals," Lara says. "They were hilarious and fun to hang out with but the jokes they made and the way they spoke, it was all happening at this level that really stunned me. It felt like a very separate life that I led outside of school. I really had a sense that my life was split and there was this world of school that I did during the day, and then there was the music and the fanzine that consumed all the rest of my life."

In his autobiographical 1992 book *Fever Pitch*, Nick Hornby asserts that women are incapable of being record-collecting obsessives in the way that men are and, worse, that women rely on men to shape their tastes. Nick expands on this in his 1995 novel *High Fidelity*, saying that he has never met a woman with a large record collection, or one that is

Heavenly were clear fanzine favourites on both sides of the Atlantic.
Courtesy of Heavenly.

alphabetised, and claims that the women he knows have either lost their records, or that they rely on a man to take responsibility for the music in their house. Incensed, I wrote to Nick in 1995 to let him know how patronising this was and received a handwritten placatory postcard in response. He wrote: "First, I wasn't saying that they were, you know, a good thing, these record collections. I stand by my generalisation but if you want to claim equal rights to be an anally-retentive emotional retard, be my guest!!" Not that he will ever read this but, if he did, I think Mr Hornby would have to concede that there indeed *are* many women who are just as obsessive about music as the men he writes about. He clearly just hasn't met the right women.

There were whole bedrooms full of us record-collecting women all around the world. One of whom was Blueboy's Gemma Malley. "The scene was very boy," she says. "There is a particular male view of the world, and it's in Nick Hornby's *High Fidelity*, it's the ordering of things and the keeping of things. I think Sarah really played to that. That was the thing that really struck me at the very beginning. I loved the music, and performing and travelling and hanging out with these guys. I loved recording and the ability to try things, it was so much fun. But when we went to the gigs, that's when I realised this is actually about the fans. They were all boys but, I can tell you, none of them were there for me. I don't think at any point in my entire time at Sarah Records, and I say this happily, I was ever

> 66 This is just a quick note to say thanks for the fanzine, it's good. No... it's very good. I'm really looking forward to getting the flexi."
>
> **Letter from Andrew Jarrett, The Groove Farm, to Clare, 1987**

objectified. I didn't feel female! There was no one checking you out. They were there for the music, the band, the fanzines, the Sarah thing, for everything else. It was a religion, I think that's the best way to put it. You were in the choir but the deity was Matt and Clare. I contributed my little bit but I never felt it was about me and not really about us as a band. It was an ecosystem and everybody played their part."

Kvatch

Clare started her fanzine *Kvatch* while still at school in Harrogate in 1984. As someone who loved both music and writing, Clare decided to combine the two after hearing Kid Jensen on Radio 1 talking about fanzines. "I loved writing and I'd got really into music, and then suddenly I heard about these things called fanzines so, at that point, having never seen one, aged 16 I decided I was going to do one." To do some homework, she sent off for fanzines such as *Rox* and *Attack on Bzag*. "I wrote off for ones where people didn't seem very far away," she says. "I think it felt more accessible. Down south was this scary foreign country of posh people. I was probably also looking for some community. I'd started to go to gigs a little bit but had to get my parents to drive me, growing up in a smallish town. And I suppose I thought maybe I'd get to know some people as well."

James Brown of *Attack on Bzag* met Clare and they spent an afternoon discussing how fanzines were put together. She then asked the headmistress of her school if she could use the school photocopier to run off the first copies of *Kvatch* and "she was like 'Ooh, yes, we can do this for you, this is great'. And then I said I wanted to do 1,000 copies, and she was like 'Oh my god, no, you can't put that through our photocopier!' I think they probably thought I wanted to do seven and give them to my parents," says Clare. As *Kvatch* grew in stature, Clare quickly progressed to sending her artwork to printers to produce.

The first issue of *Kvatch* (the phonetic spelling for the German word 'quatsch' meaning 'nonsense') got mentioned by Kid Jensen and John Peel on their radio

Clare put out six issues of her fanzine *Kvatch*.
Sarah Records.

shows, and Clare also sold issues at gigs and independent record shops. She began producing the fanzine every six months or so, eventually putting out six issues. "It was basically, do one fanzine, get your money back by selling them, reinvest the money in the next one, print more copies, make them bigger," Clare says. "I was so ridiculously young and knew I wanted something that was about music and politics. I did anti-smoking articles, one on Greenpeace, one on the Bhopal disaster, and I grew up near the Menwith Hill American Airforce base so did one about the Menwith Hill Peace Camp. I always knew I wanted it to be more than music but, because fanzines always had The Membranes in them, I interviewed The Membranes through the post before I'd ever even really heard The Membranes. I was trying to do what it was you were supposed to do. I was discovering music and interested in everything at this point."

A flexi shared between The Sea Urchins and The Groove Farm that came with *Kvatch 6*.
Clare Wadd.

The Wedding Present were one of the bands that Clare interviewed and frontman David Gedge recalls: "We were more than happy to do fanzine interviews and stuff because we loved the culture. Clare came to Leeds to interview us in the summer of 1986 for her *Kvatch* fanzine and I've kept in touch with her, off and on, ever since. She recently said that she's known me longer than anyone else apart from her family members!"

Ivor Cutler was another musician who Clare interviewed for *Kvatch*, which came about after she met him at the Ilkley Literature Festival. Clare remembers coming home one evening to a message saying that Ivor had telephoned and feared that he had hated the finished article, but she couldn't have been more wrong. "He'd just had a nice chat with my mum about how impressive what I was doing was, and then he sent me a picture he'd drawn," says Clare. "I interviewed Ewan McColl, and Peggy Seeger picked me up at the station. I interviewed The Housemartins when they were No 3 in the charts. I reviewed a Radio 1 roadshow when I was on holiday in Tenby. There was this real mix of being a kid and grown up at the same time."

Looking back on her time as a fanzine editor, Clare admits that for a while she felt a bit embarrassed about 'Kvatch', in the way that many people do when they revisit something they did in their younger years. But she also feels very proud of what she achieved, given she was still at school: "It wasn't just writing the fanzines, but figuring out where to get them printed, learning about offset litho, photo scans, switching to a different printer to get better quality, getting my own typewriter, collating thousands of bits of paper on my bedroom floor, cutting my fingers selling them at gigs when they were side-stapled... most 16-year-olds weren't doing all that."

The sixth issue of *Kvatch* came out in the spring of 1987, which was really how Clare and Matt met, when she decided to include a Sea Urchins flexi with what would be her final fanzine and, now at

❝ I was pretty determined and self-confident. And I was doing all this alongside four A Levels and a Saturday job.❞

Clare

Matt admits that *Are You Scared to Get Happy?* was in no small part influenced by *Hungry Beat*.
Jon Craig.

university in Bristol, put a note through Matt's door asking how heavy it would be to transport all those flexis back on the coach.

Are You Scared to Get Happy?

When Matt and his university friend Mark Carnell started their fanzine *Are You Scared To Get Happy?* (named after a Hurrah! lyric) in Bristol in 1984, they were openly ripping off Kevin Pearce's *Hungry Beat* fanzine because they didn't know any better. Matt says he had always known about fanzines, dating back to punk and *Sniffin' Glue*, but he had never actually seen one until he read an article in the *NME* about *Hungry Beat*, which prompted him to send off for a copy.

Mark was the only person Matt knew who liked the same bands as him. "We'd started buying some of the early Creation bands, and suddenly we saw this picture of a fanzine cover in the *NME* and it had a list of band names on the front which was pretty much exactly a list of the bands we loved, and as far as we were aware nobody else was writing about them," says Matt. "And, having seen it, we thought we could do something like this and in the end did something *exactly* like this, which was a bit of a mistake." He adds: "It wasn't until we saw that piece on *Hungry Beat* in *NME* that we realised we weren't alone. What I'm saying is that being a music fan in those days was really hard work and that kids these days

> ❝ Well, there are 19,000 sheets of paper in my kitchen, 3,500 flexi discs in the bedroom, 3,500 flexi sleeves in the passage, unfolded… HELP!!!❞
>
> **Letter from Matt to Pete Williams, autumn 1986**

don't know they're born."

In the name of research, and spurred on by *Hungry Beat*, Matt and Mark sent off for other fanzines, including *Slow Dazzle* by Chris Davidson, with whom Matt exchanged many letters. Chris encouraged Matt to start producing his own fanzine. He introduced Matt and Mark to a would-be fanzine writer called Alison who was also in Bristol, and the three met up at the café at Temple Meads train station to talk through ideas and "it was another little nudge to make us actually produce something," says Matt.

Lee Christopher of Action Painting! notes: "The fanzine culture was something special, especially when you're scrabbling around looking for an identity and sense of place in the world. You'd Sellotape a 50p piece to a scrap of card, put a self-addressed envelope into another envelope, and send. Eventually they'd flop through the letterbox. Never knowing what to expect, whether the flexi would be any good or the writing but it didn't matter so much, that wasn't the point. It was about communication, about sharing ideas. Matt wrote to me once apologising about the lateness of his *Are You Scared To Get Happy?* fanzine. To prove that he wasn't making stacks of money (those 50ps can really mount up) and wasn't lounging about in a guitar shaped swimming pool in the sunny climes of exotic Bristol, he wrote the reply on the back of his Housing Benefit claim form."

As Jerry Thackray did with *The Legend!*, Matt didn't often publish interviews with bands, and many of his articles were only very loosely about the bands in question. Matt tells me: "I know *Are You Scared To Get Happy?* used to annoy people because I'd stick a load of band names on the front and they'd expect an interview with those bands or at least a review, and what they'd get was a piece about catching the 376 bus to Wells or walking round Clifton in the rain. But my argument was always that if you liked the Razorcuts, you really should also appreciate a bus ride through Somerset and that it was a lot more interesting than asking Greg [Webster] what his influences were. The first issue was 300 copies but the print run was 2,500 by the end."

> The first couple of issues of my old fanzine had interviews in but it always just seemed such a waste of space, because nobody ever said anything interesting so we ditched them thereafter."
> **Letter from Matt to me, January 1994**

John Peel definitely helped to get the message out to many more people. In fact, Clare heard about *Are You Scared To Get Happy?* on the radio and sent off for the fourth issue as a result. "I was quite baffled when I got it because it was like no fanzine I'd ever seen before," she says. Matt expands: "The fact our fanzine didn't look like other fanzines was very deliberate. Personally, I was reacting against all the fanzines that had an interview with The Membranes, were printed in black and white, and were basically looking as close to *Attack on Bzag* and *Rox* as possible. All the political articles would be the same, all the music articles would be the same and I just wanted to do something that wasn't like that."

Harvey Williams of Another Sunny Day was another one who heard about *Are You Scared To Get Happy?* via John Peel. On a visit to London, Harvey spotted a copy of the fanzine on the wall of Rough Trade and "there was this list of interesting looking bands and Microdisney were on the list, and they were probably my favourite band along with The Smiths. I picked up a copy and it was the first fanzine I bought. There was all this amazing incendiary prose inside. This seemingly passionate, monomaniacal writer had a very fixed idea of what pop was. My view on pop tied into that as well. I used to be passionate about it and I knew what it should be. It's always quite nice to say 'This is how it should sound'. So I started writing to Matt and buying all the records he recommended, and it seemed like it was all about setting up a dialogue between people and the bands."

The final issue of *Are You Scared To Get Happy?* included a mini fanzine by Bristolian schoolgirls Magz Hall and Amanda Burston, whom Matt had met at gigs. The bonus fanzine was called *373 Miles Is A Very Long Way*, in reference to the distance between Bristol and Glasgow. "Amanda was friends with all the fanzine writers around the country and we went up to Scotland to stay with the BMX Bandits," says Magz. "We went and interviewed loads of bands up there and stayed at Norman Blake's house in East Kilbride. There were interviews with BMX Bandits, The Clouds and Stump. It also had our real addresses in, which is insane. We're young girls with our actual home addresses in the fanzine!"

Unfortunately, Matt's co-editor Mark was diagnosed with Hodgkin's Disease during his final year at university. He returned home to Sheffield after graduating and continued contributing to *Are You Scared To Get Happy?* for a few more issues until he became too unwell to do so. "After the first issue he was slightly distracted by other things, as you might imagine," says Matt. "So for the second and third issues, it was notionally both of us doing it but it was him playing less and less of a role. And from the fourth one onwards it was just me but he gave his blessing to me to carry on."

Mark died in 1989 but is remembered on St Christopher's debut Sarah single 'You Deserve More Than a Maybe', which has 'For Mark' etched into the run-off groove. Matt explains: "St Christopher's previous incarnation, Vena Cava, was based in Sheffield, and Mark kept track of them and told me about the stuff they were now recording as St Christopher. We were keeping the run-off groove a secret because I really wanted to surprise him by sending him a finished copy, but I had a phone call from his mother between the test pressing and the finished copy to say he'd died, so I never got the chance to send him one, which is really sad. Sheffield bands were mostly without fault in Mark's eyes. Even Def Leppard, who were partly without arms."

> ❝ This is what POP should be about, not ugly rip-off Soup Dragons 12" debut singles and all the rest. I hate all that, it sickens me, I want something pure and simple and PERFECT, untainted by grubby music industry scheming … A flexi-label would remind people what punk rock (YEAH, it still means something to me!) once meant."
> **Letter from Matt to Pete Williams, June 1986**

SHA-LA-LA

The idea for Sha-La-La grew from letters between Pete Williams of *Baby Honey* fanzine and Matt back in May 1986. Pete remembers: "Matt wrote these enormous, very gushing letters. He was thinking of putting out a flexi and so was I, and through these letters we hit upon this idea of it being a flexi label and Matt got very excited about this, because it was quite punk rock, having a record label that just released flexi discs. And it was a good idea." Pete has generously shared about 50 pages of these letters from Matt with me and they form a unique and fascinating insight into how a post-punk DIY project is both born and killed within the space of a year, which in itself is very punk rock. "In the course of the next few months, we started putting out these flexi discs," says Pete. "And it was quite easy because there were a lot of bands who were coming up on the second generation of indie bands, and they'd be sending demos to fanzine writers like us, and we'd hear this pretty amazing music like 'Summershine' by The Sea Urchins and 'Jenny Nowhere' by The Clouds. We had to act quite quickly because, within a few weeks, real record labels were approaching them and in a couple of cases we lost bands. So we produced these flexis and they wouldn't just be a disc stuck onto a fanzine, they'd have sleeves and a record label identity and would be sold with three or four other fanzines. So between us, we'd be able to sell 2-3,000. And it was quite successful initially."

Although only privy to one side of the conversation in these letters, it is clear that Matt exudes extreme passion and drive for this project, and is brimming with ideas to ensure that every tiny detail is attended to, from the catalogue numbers to dreams of etching messages into the run-off grooves. There was also intense debate about whether song run times should be listed as 120 seconds or 0'120", in line with Matt's conviction that the perfect pop song would never exceed two minutes and "I just like the idea of songs stopping dead as soon as they get to that TWO MINUTE barrier". And while debating the name they would give the label, Matt wrote to Pete in the summer of 1986 to say: "I reckon Sha-La-La is a BRILLIANT name for a flexi disc record label, it's just so anti-everything the independent record INDUSTRY has come to stand for."

Expanding on this, Matt wrote to Pete in early 1987 to further express his vision for the flexi label: "The thing is, while obviously Sha-La-La is there primarily to put out CLASSIC POP MUSIC, there is the secondary objective of showing-up the defects in the current music INDUSTRY and making people realise there is an alternative. For that we need lots of publicity and lots of records to back it all up! And everything has to be CONCENTRATED into this summer."

From the third issue of *Are You Scared To Get Happy?*, Matt and Mark included flexis via the Sha-La-La label with the fanzine. The first two flexis were shared by The Clouds and Mighty Mighty,

Original artwork for the sixth Sha-La-La flexi release.
Courtesy of Sarah Records.

Sha-La-La's Baby Lemonade flexi became a *Melody Maker* Single of the Week.
Courtesy of Sarah Records.

and Talulah Gosh and Razorcuts. Two flexis and one fanzine made a very appealing package for customers and it wasn't long before production runs were rising.

The responsibilities for Sha-La-La were ultimately shared by Matt and Pete, plus Jim Kavanagh of *Simply Thrilled* and David Payne of *Trout Fishing in Leytonstone*, and batches of flexis would also be supplied to other sympathetic fanzines for distribution. Matt says: "Flexi distribution was a bit random. By the time I was doing issue four, I was printing 2,500 copies of the fanzine, so I took the whole batch of the flexis for that. For the earlier ones, I took 1,000 and somebody else took 1,000… So it was this nice idea that we could actually run 'a proper label', in inverted commas, but using flexi discs so it would be cheap and we could give them away with the fanzines, so we wouldn't have to go through any distribution network and we could do it all ourselves. It did seem to work."

Some of the flexis even attracted coverage in the music press with the Baby Lemonade track being named single of the week in *Melody Maker* and getting played on the radio. "When I sent John Peel the first flexi, I included the usual Sha-La-La manifesto about making pop music cheap and accessible, and how it only cost 12.5p to make a flexi disc," says Matt. "Which he chose to interpret as meaning people should send us 12.5p [so] lots of people sent us 12.5p and no postage." Oof. Matt adds: "Any mention on Peel would bring in a huge response because, in the absence of any internet, we all became quite adept at picking up on the slightest mention of anything that we thought might interest us, and following up on it. Because we had to, basically. Back then, if you missed something, it was gone."

My introduction to fanzines

My brother Adam Mornement produced a solitary issue of his fanzine *Pretty Potty* in 1989 and this was my introduction to the DIY pop ethos: that anyone could make anything happen, even from a sleepy thatched farmhouse in a quiet village in Somerset. *Pretty Potty* was rather ramshackle and badly photocopied with different coloured ink on each page, and was crudely folded rather than stapled, then inserted in a sandwich bag to keep the pages together. But it was the first time I'd ever seen or heard of a fanzine and, to a music-loving kid who enjoyed writing, it sparked something in my imagination.

Adam may not have intended it but his earthy fanzine has more in common with traditional punk fanzines than my future fanzine *Arketino* would. *Pretty Potty* conformed to the more anarchic design of its punk predecessors, with its use of Letraset, handwriting, typewriting and stencilling. We didn't have a home computer or even an electric typewriter, so Adam was reliant on a prehistoric manual typewriter if he wanted anything typed. A couple of the keys didn't work properly, so those missing letters needed to be filled in by pen later. It tied in to the sort of fanzines that were designed to be a deliberate snub to the professional and capitalist publications available in WH Smith and other newsagents.

"*Pretty Potty* was ill-conceived and took amateurism to an extreme," says Adam. "I was an introverted teenager using alternative music to shape my identity. I had no musical ability so 'writing' a fanzine was a way to participate in a subculture that I was drawn to. Any alignment with post-punk fanzines, or anything else driven by a sense of purpose, vision or agenda, is entirely coincidental." So there you go. Not everything has a deep and meaningful reasoning. But this was definitely not the way that I wanted to go about producing my first fanzine in 1994. For *Arketino*, I wanted higher production values, a colour card cover and staples. I also made good use of my mother's newly-purchased electronic typewriter to create strips of text to photocopy to the correct size at my dad's office and glue down on the pages.

'If I can do it in Nara, anyone can do it'

Akiko Yamauchi, who now runs the Sugarfrost label in New Zealand, is originally from Nara in Japan, which didn't have a significant music scene of its own. But she found that starting her fanzine *5,000 Miles From George Square* in 1987 made her realise that she was capable of making something happen if she wanted to. Akiko says: "Since I started writing the fanzine and subsequently started something bigger, I always had in mind that anyone can do it without living in Tokyo. The main point was to start something without the aid of being in a big city, not doing something everyone's doing. That was important to me.

> ❝ Writing a fanzine and expecting people to give you money for it is arrogant. So is being in a band. But if you didn't think you were better than everybody else, hopefully you wouldn't be doing it. DON'T BE MEEK. Meek is BORING."
>
> **Letter from Matt to me, January 1994**

Keith and Paul from Blueboy pose in Brighton for a photographer from *Grimsby Fishmarket* fanzine.
Grimsby Fishmarket, Marcus Torncrantz.

If I can do it in Nara, anyone can do it, that was my message."

Although she was in Japan, Akiko was a regular customer of Rhythm Records in the UK, which had a thriving mail-order wing, and via Rhythm she was well-supplied with fanzines and records. "I bought many of my indie records from there. That's why my knowledge of indie-pop went a lot further than any of my friends, who were buying from import shops," she says. "My experience is far from typical in Japan. Those British fanzines were never available in Japan, we didn't even have the music press like the *NME*." Inspired by *Are You Scared To Get Happy?*, Akiko decided to start her own fanzine. "It's bilingual and mostly my words and how I felt. Issues one to three were made in Japan, the fourth was done in Liverpool [while at university] and that was the last, before moving on to Sugarfrost. On the back of [Clare's fanzine] *Sunstroke*, I had the honour of a dedication for my fanzine. That was and still is precious to me."

Over in Sweden, Marcus Törncrantz and his friend Nicklas Brunzell were running the bilingual *Grimsby Fishmarket* fanzine and tape label, and were big fans of the Sarah and él labels. "At the time, people put in loads of flyers with the records and fanzines and cassettes, it basically said 'Send us £2 and we'll send you a cassette back', sometimes we made swap deals," says Marcus. "It was a really healthy environment. People wanted to help each other. I didn't feel like there was much competition. You could tell some people were doing fanzines because they wanted to be picked up as a writer for the *NME* but most of them that were good, they were much more humble in the way they wrote."

Marcus struck up a pen pal friendship with Blueboy's frontman Keith Girdler via the fanzine network, and this meant that a trip to Brighton to see Keith and Blueboy was on the top of Marcus' list of things to do during a visit to the UK. Blueboy's guitarist Paul Stewart remembers going with Keith to meet Marcus for the first time. In a fit of laughter, Paul tells me how Keith mischievously suggested to Marcus that they hold the interview on Brighton beach, forgetting to mention that he was taking them to the nudist beach. "As Marcus was writing the answers down, people kept walking past with no clothes on. And he was asking 'When did you form...?' while watching these naked people walk by and his mouth falling open," laughs Paul.

Of course, one of the main reasons for setting up a fanzine was as an excuse to get closer to your heroes and, long before she became a staple interviewee in other people's fanzines, Heavenly's Amelia Fletcher came up with the idea of running her own to meet her idols. She laughs: "I started a fanzine when I was 15 that I don't know if I ever had any intention of actually publishing but I just wanted to meet pop stars and interview them. So I interviewed Pigbag and Echo & the Bunnymen, I don't think it even had a name. We never actually wrote it." Which strikes me as a genius idea and I wish I'd thought of it myself.

Prior to forming Action Painting!, Andy Hitchcock and Lee Christopher wrote a fanzine called *Waking Up To Nothing* while they were still at school in Gosport, which "ironically slagged off some of the Sarah stuff," laughs Andy. The two friends were really into Sha-La-La and early Sarah "but we'd criticised some of the earlier releases and it was just a no-no then to criticise anything on Sarah. And actually we got quite a good response with people saying 'Thank Christ, you're saying something different.'" Andy and Lee used the school photocopier to run off copies of their fanzine, promising the school some money that they never delivered, and instead used the profits to fund their travel to gigs. "After that we thought, you can't slag something off without putting something back. If you're slagging somebody's creativity off, you've got to show them what you mean." And so Action Painting! was formed.

Sukhdev Sandhu was another Sarah fan who became a fanzine writer, although for him a large part of the appeal was his fascination with the photocopier. A fascination I shared because, as a young child who sometimes used to have to wait at her dad's office after school, I was drawn to the photocopying room and enjoyed helping the woman who worked in there, even dreaming that one day I would grow up to photocopy stuff for a living. Sukhdev's photocopier fascination almost led him to own the means of production. "My dream as a kid was to have a photocopying machine," he sighs. "There was one in a local newspaper that was being advertised on sale for £10 and I couldn't believe it. When I rang the number they said 'Oh sorry, it's a misprint, it's actually £1,000'. I was devastated."

Sarah's fanzines and inserts

"I loved Matt and Clare's fanzines and I still do now when I read them," says Field Mouse Anne Mari Davies. "I think the writing that I really like is the bits that Clare has written. It's poetry and political and it was a real eye opener to me when I was 16 and 17, when I first started reading them. I had never come across anything like that before but it really rang true. It just really felt like, 'Yes, this is how I feel, and nobody else has expressed it before and they're expressing it for me and that is brilliant.'"

Clare and Matt had intended that they would produce more fanzines than they did as part of the Sarah 100 catalogue, but the more successful the label became the less time they had to spend on creating their own work. The initial plan had been to put out one fanzine for every 10 or so 7"s, but they became victims of their own success and there was just no time for Clare and Matt to write these alongside running the record label, organising the tours and everything else they were doing. However, in the later years of the label, there were a few contributions, such as the *One Page Fanzine* in 1992 that was printed on a Heavenly tour leaflet, and even a fanzine in French to coincide with some French dates.

> ❝ I'd forgotten all about the 'Jeff Barrett Knew My Father' thing... I can't remember why I wrote that – and I don't think it's especially well written, because it was in the days before we had a word processor, so the only way to get it to fit the space was to keep typing it out over and over again, changing a few bits each time, until it was the right length. By which time, of course, it had ceased making sense. Real writers don't have this problem... but then I guess I'm not a real writer."
> **Letter to me from Matt, April 1994**

"I do remember someone criticising the French in it but I don't think many record labels were producing fanzines in French, so maybe they could have thanked us for bothering instead," remarks Clare, who can speak French very well.

And speaking of translating things into French, one of the early 7" inserts saw Clare and Matt translate their entire discography into intentionally bad French. Meaning, for example, that St Christopher's *Bacharach* album became *Bergerac*, and The Golden Dawn single 'George Hamilton's Dead' was rechristened 'Monsieur Hamilton Il Et Mort'. This insert is a source of absolute joy and I urge each and every one of you to seek out a copy post-haste. Which reminds me, does anyone have a spare copy of 'La Maison d'Emma' by Les Souris des Champs for sale?

In the early days, the inserts with the 7"s were just the offcuts from the posters and are pretty minimal. But by the time Clare and Matt had moved into sealed sleeves with Sarah 31, they were printing a unique 7" paper square for each record containing writing and images, like a very mini fanzine. Matt says: "Maybe the best example of what we were trying to do, missing hyphen aside, was the *One Page Fanzine* we did to promote Heavenly's *Le Jardin* tour. Shame it took us till 1992 to do it! Looking back, it would have been brilliant to have put that out as a single-sheet fanzine and given it a catalogue number."

*****

THESE THINGS HAPPENED:
Harvey Williams, Another Sunny Day

"Part of me wishes the records could have been better but I'm extremely glad that part of my life happened. Even now, I still see Clare quite a lot and most of my friends originated from that part of my life. I wish I'd put more thought into what I was trying to say on those records but I was just going along with what was happening. I've got lots of good memories and a few bad ones but the good outweighs the bad. I was just glad that there was something going on and I was a part of it, and that it's something that people are still thinking about 30-odd years later. Without a doubt it shaped me into the person I am now. I would be a very different person if I hadn't walked into Rough Trade that day and seen Matt's fanzine on the wall. I might even still be living and working in Penzance. It was all because of that fanzine that I moved to London."

THESE THINGS HAPPEN

Chapter 6

The Power of the Press

During the Sarah era, if the mention of something obscure caught your attention, you had to take a punt and ask your local record shop to order it for you. In this way, the influence of music reviewers was vastly heightened compared to now. As Matt says: "The music press had such power then, which is hard to get your head around these days. They were utterly in control. Back when we were doing Sarah, we needed the music press and they didn't need us, so they could abuse that position of power. The music press that exists now is so anodyne and feeble it just prints whatever bands want them to say."

There was something rebellious about being a Sarah fan because, on the whole, the music press despised the label so vehemently. "Getting stuff together for the [*My Secret World*] film meant re-reading old reviews and sometimes I'm amazed we actually kept going," Matt says. "People often say the internet has made the world a nastier place but no one now would have to cope with the sort of vicious bullying we received from the press." There was also a feeling of what goes around comes around, as Andy Hitchcock explains when talking about the reviews Action Painting!'s debut 'These Things Happen' generated in the three weeklies: "*NME* and *Melody Maker* gave it good reviews but *Sounds* didn't. And then the next week *Sounds* folded, so we went 'Ha ha'. But two out of three ain't bad."

Bobby Wratten has a more philosophical outlook on The Field Mice's lack of decent coverage: "We got lucky a few times with singles of the week but we knew we were never going to be press darlings. In fact, *NME* never did a full feature on The Field Mice. But, 30 years later, it really doesn't matter as the music press are gone or have had their power diluted to such an extent they're almost meaningless. If someone is interested in The Field Mice, they listen online and make their own mind up. Being on Sarah did draw attention to the bands even if the results were often negative. Some of the reasoning behind the hatred was no doubt questionable... sexist, macho nonsense. But some of the journalists just simply didn't like the music and, compared to a lot of forward-thinking

> ❝ At the moment, we just can't seem to get enough reviews, possibly because the Music Press seems pretty contemptuous of small independent labels – so we want to prove we mean business."
>
> **Letter from Matt to Chris Quinn, The Orchids, 26 May 1988**

Some may consider this to be a fire hazard, but I considered my piles of *NME*s and *Melody Maker*s to be a gateway to a very significant musical education.
Jane Duffus.

cutting-edge music, they had a point."

Sarah fan and friend-of-the-label Ken Sweeney was living in London where the music papers, like other magazines produced from the capital, were available one day earlier than in the rest of the country. So he would phone Clare in Bristol and read out some of the reviews to her. "It was horrible because the reviews were horrific. Just the grief they got. It became a cliché to slag them off," says Ken. "The stuff they had to put up with was outrageous. How could those journalists live with it, writing that sort of stuff?"

In a Christmas card sent to me in 1994, Ivy's frustrated singer Spencer Harrison wrote: "We are convinced that the *NME/ MM* don't even listen to the Sarah Records singles that they review – they just see the words 'Sarah Records' and reel out the age-old anorak wearing anecdotes! Julian [Cator] is really annoyed about this. I think we should get Matt and Clare in on the joke and release a heavy metal single – I bet they'd still write 'jingly jangly anoraks'."

Tellingly, a 2005 review in *Uncut* of three Field Mice reissues by LTM Recordings imagines how different the media reception of the band would have been had they initially been on Factory. "Untied from the apron strings of the [Sarah] aesthetic and reissued alongside the FAC fodder of the LTM catalogue, a different band emerges," writes Stephen Troussé, before issuing a string of four-star accolades to the band's Sarah work. "The music press now is way more intellectual," says Blueboy's Paul Stewart. "Even if something is bad, they will write about it intelligently and be constructive, not one sentence that says 'This sounds like my food mixer when I put my dog in it.'"

As a teenager, I always preferred *Melody Maker* because it seemed more inclusive, more trustworthy and more about music. While the *NME* felt akin to a laddish comic filled with in-jokes, something that just wasn't aimed at female readers. From the references to male bodily fluids and male genitalia, to the generally aggressive stance, even many of the adverts seemed to assume the readers were male. When I mentioned this to former *NME* writer David Quantick he looked a bit hurt… and then conceded his wife had also preferred *Melody Maker* for similar reasons. Yet when I had the same conversation with former *Melody Maker* scribe Simon Price, he insisted that it was *Melody Maker* that was the nastier of the two. Huh.

Both titles were published by IPC Media by the time Sarah started, from adjacent floors in the sky-scraping Kings Reach Tower on London's South Bank, and produced by IPC's Ignite! brand, which boasted the strapline: "IPC Ignite! – Better Men's Media." Yes, the UK's two leading music papers made no pretence of the fact they were written for – and mostly by – men. Speaking in 2001, IPC Ignite!'s marketing director Vijay Solanki told the trade magazine *Campaign*: "The strapline 'better men's media' tells you what we do and how we intend to do it." Unfortunately, 'better men's media' did indeed tell people exactly what the *NME* and *Melody Maker* were trying to be.

An Abuse of Power

"I always really liked the Sarah ethic and it pissed me off when people would be dismissive of them. It was such macho bullshit," says Christian Savill of Eternal and Slowdive. "I reckon a lot of people who wrote that stuff would now be a bit embarrassed about it. I get that some of the music was a little bit fey but why is that a bad thing? Sarah was still quite punky and it was inclusive. I just didn't understand why they were so vitriolic about it. They should have respected that Sarah was uncompromising, they didn't give a shit, they were still going to keep doing what they wanted to do, which was really admirable." Similarly, Clare says: "The people who worked [at the music press] are now in their, what, early 60s, and are probably terribly woke and probably still journalists in some way. People bully people at school and I'm sure they grow up and think, 'Oh my god, that was awful' and regret it. But these people were already adults, and are they just pretending they didn't write those things? What's their internal narrative?"

When John Peel spoke to Matt and Clare at Radio 1's Sound City event in Bristol in April 1995, he asked: "Does it spur you on, the fact that Sarah Records does get the mickey taken out of it quite a bit?" To which Clare said that it was "wearing a bit thin". Matt expanded: "It depresses us because it obviously means we don't sell as many records as we could sell because people don't take us seriously as a record label because we get this criticism the whole time."

Perhaps all of this was frustrating for Sarah and its bands because they were people who had grown up loyally reading and trusting the same music papers that were now attempting to rip their hard work to pieces, for no better reason than that it was easy to do so. "To a lot of them it was sport," says Matt. "It was just fun to lay into Sarah Records and have fun at our expense rather than reviewing us properly." He continues: "I would have hated the US-style music press or most of the foreign music press, which was fawning. I loved the fact that our press was angry and argumentative and witty. When I grew up, all my education in literature and politics came through the *NME* and it was fantastic." He wasn't alone in this. Although activists during the Rock Against Racism campaign in the late 1970s and early 1980s, were producing their own fanzines and organising their own events, it was only once the *NME* and *Melody Maker* got on board that suddenly the campaign exploded and this once-small organisation was able to bloom into a massively important powerhouse. And that's what the music press could do when it used its power for good.

Paul Stewart says: "I got to thinking that it was almost like when you have the odd kid at school and people take the mick out of the odd kid, and then everyone joins in. It was probably the worst time to be releasing twee pop records, when [the mainstream] was going through a big macho thing with bigger bands and rocky sounds. We just hated that. It was almost like the antidote to that really."

Paul's bandmate Gemma Malley elaborates: "We just weren't cool. We weren't rock'n'roll enough for the music press. The Sarah fan is an easy target. If you're swaggering down the school corridor, the Sarah fan is the one who's easy to push into a wall as you walk past and laugh. Sarah had its own ecosystem. If you went to a Sarah gig, you knew you were at a Sarah gig. So if outsiders, like reviewers, come in, they're suddenly in a different world and that might be a bit discombobulating, so it's easier to reject it."

Heavenly's Cathy Rogers found that rejection breath-taking: "I was always a bit shocked at how angry and hateful people could be in the press. We were just making nice songs and playing them. It should have been more obvious to me about how much of a subtext there was to all that. I'm sure there are some super-powered people who aren't bothered by reading horrible things about themselves, but mostly people hate to be slagged off and hate to have motives attributed to them that are just so far from what they feel like. The power that a few individuals had at that time to decide the fate of bands and music and what was cool and what was not cool was, in some ways, worse than social media today."

Her bandmate Amelia Fletcher had this to say of the particularly unpleasant attitude towards women that began to show its head in the music press: "When Sarah Records and Heavenly started, there was generally a lot of lad rock. I don't think it was particularly sexist at that point, it was just there were a lot of male bands making a lot of noise. It fed through to Britpop later. We and Sarah were both reacting to these male rock bands who were super popular in the press because they did what the press was expecting a band to do, which was be all male, make a loud noise and have pretty rubbish songs, but men could go along and have a drink at the bar." Sarah's bands definitely did not fit that mould.

This culture became more widespread until, by the middle of the 1990s, the 'ladette' had become the only acceptable type of woman. The noxious 'lads mag' *Loaded* launched in 1994 with former *Attack on Bzag* fanzine editor, and later *NME* editor, James Brown at the helm. "The worst thing about *Loaded* in my view was that it was effectively launched by the *NME*, with a lot of *NME* writers contributing to it," says Clare. "If you'd ever thought the music press might be for you, now you were damn sure it never had been and you felt a bit of a mug. Though there was no women's music press you could have read instead."

Loaded was followed by *Nuts* and *Zoo*, with the three titles joining the ranks of other toxic men's magazines such as *FHM* (*For Him Magazine*) and *Men's Health*, all of which celebrated images of surgically enhanced women in their underwear. "The role of the ladette was invented to mean you could drink as much lager as the fucking idiot sat next to you and you didn't mind people making jokes about your tits," sighs Heavenly's Rob Pursey. While bandmate Pete Momtchiloff elaborates: "It can be hard to appreciate how different the music biz was then. It has changed in three related ways. First, in the last 20 years the music biz has come to cherish, even fetishise, the idea of the creative woman. This is not always a healthy thing, it often takes the form of excessive attention to their appearance and other personal rather than musical factors. But music biz people and music journalists understand now that they are supposed to respect creative women, and they are quite good at pretending to. Another way the music biz has changed is that it is no longer dominated by a ROCK ethos. An aggressive sound and attitude is now just a style option, rather than a criterion for how serious or authentic a band is. Finally, the bogus notion of street credibility associated with ROCK has been discredited. So it is no longer necessary for middle-class journalists to hunt down signs of middle-classness in order to discredit bands."

Former fanzine editor Jerry Thackray worked for both *NME* (as The Legend!) and *Melody Maker* (as Everett True) during Sarah's lifetime, and therefore has an insider's perspective on all this. "The *NME* and all the music press very strongly perceived itself as socialist working-class. So there was this thing happening at Sarah which was challenging them on several fronts. The fact it was male but in a very different way was so alienating for the *NME*, the idea that sex didn't have to be at the heart of rock'n'roll, that it was OK to be quiet and awkward and stuff. The *NME* is very proud of its street cred and working-class and socialist credentials and it's going to use that as a means to attack Sarah. But that wasn't really the reason they disliked Sarah." Jerry believes the real reason they hated the label was because its DIY ethos undermined the corporate structure that held the music press in place.

In March 2015, the *NME* had quite a *volte face* in its ongoing hatred of this inoffensive independent label that seemed so comfortable in its own skin. The *NME* published a list of the greatest independent record labels of all time and, unexpectedly, Sarah Records was at No 2 (sandwiched between 4AD at No 1 and XL at No 3). Poor old Rough Trade, Creation and Factory were left wallowing at the lower end. Speaking about the complete change of heart towards Sarah with this accolade, Clare says: "I don't understand why we weren't number one, obviously! It was nice but it would have been better if they'd been a bit more decent at the time."

However, there are two sides to every story and perhaps there was an element of it being a useful marketing tool to be perceived as the underdog. Mark Dobson of The Field Mice certainly thinks that, while the music press did treat Sarah and its

FUN FACT: The only Sarah star to grace the front of a music paper was Tim 'Shelley' Chipping, who made the cover of the 25 November 1995 issue of *Melody Maker* with a handful of other musicians marked with the 'ROMO' tag. "Being on the front cover of *Melody Maker* doesn't make someone big or clever, just a bit garish," cautioned one of the final Sarah newsletters. So that's Mr Chipping told.

bands appallingly, there was also a sense of the label doing nothing to discourage such bullying. "Matt in particular was incredibly antagonistic towards the music press, he'd slate them at every opportunity," says Mark. "With hindsight, I get that if you want to get people into a musical movement and get loyalty, setting yourself up as anti-establishment and an outsider and the little guy fighting against the big guy, that's really clever and people buy into that."

Music writer Kitty Empire joined *NME* shortly after the Sarah era ended, but looking back on that time as a reader, she says: "A lot of [the negative reviews] were performative but there really wasn't any filter [at that time] on the damage that writers could do by the things that they wrote. People got away with saying terrible, terrible things. There was a real culture of impunity. Those words made and broke careers. The macho performative culture of music journalism. So however nice or decent or interesting these male journalists might have been one-on-one, as a pack trying to outdo each other in print every week, that tended to amplify a toxic writing style that felt the Sarah Records bands were fair game. Obviously not all music journalists did this, some were advocates for Sarah Records. There were some journalists articulating why these bands were good as well. It's a nuanced picture. Without the music press, I would never have discovered Sarah Records. For everyone that was outraged and making fun of Sarah Records, there were enough voices saying these people were really cool and the aesthetic was interesting and the records sounded great."

Setting the scene

In September 1986, Simon Reynolds wrote the first of three features for *Melody Maker* about the 'cutie' scene. He calls the aesthetic a quaint throwback to an Arcadian lifestyle as narrated by Edith Nesbit in her pre-war children's books such as *The Railway Children*, and posits the 'cutie' scene as the antithesis of the Americana that was flooding the UK at the time.

'Younger Than Yesterday', 'Ladybirds and Start-Rite Kids' and 'Regressive Rock' were the three features, and the titles give away a lot of the content. Simon had been freelancing at *Melody Maker* for only a relatively short time at this stage. He tells me he liked some of the music in that scene, bands like The Go-Betweens, The Smiths and Jesus & Mary Chain. But the more jangly end of the spectrum was where he struggled: "I was sort of ambivalent about it. I felt like it wasn't as ambitious as I thought music could be. But I liked the cultural qualities. It was something to write about that you could really get your teeth into." He elaborates: "It seemed to me like a kind of protest or deferral of growing up, and having to lead a conventional life, settling for less. In some sense, an attempt to create a kind of folk culture in which everyone participated, rather than just being a consumer. Everyone's either in a band or doing a fanzine or running a little label or something."

Simon's third feature was more critical than the first two had been. "Having written these fairly supportive pieces about the scene, I did write another piece, it's kind of quite mean I suppose. It was called 'Regressive Rock' and basically I was saying I had my doubts about a lot of the music but essentially celebrated the cultural politics of it and style. I said it was an ever-narrowing lineage and very fixated on the past and on a rather tight canon. I called for bands to be more expansive and listen to, I don't know, the second Roxy Music album or Jimi Hendrix or whatever. Not exactly calling for a new progressive rock but calling for a more expansive idea of what music can be."

Between university and joining the music press, Simon had spent time on the dole and writing a fanzine called *Monitor* with Chris Scott from Talulah Gosh. But the texts he had read at university by the likes of Dick Hebdige and Stuart Hall were still fresh in his mind when he started writing for *Melody Maker*. "And lo and behold, fantastic, a subculture pops up right in front of my eyes," says Simon now. "At that time, this idea of homology, the mirroring effect of different levels in a culture, would have actually been a sort of analytical tool. There's a congruence between how people dress, the way the records are packaged, the choice of names that artists and bands take, the things they write about, their approaches to playing instruments, whatever, it's all congruent and interlocks and it means something that you can read. And it's like a living text. And so that really excited me and I was very grateful that there was something that I could sink my teeth into as a writer."

Former *Melody Maker* writer Pete Paphides adds: "It used to really annoy me when people would imply that people like Harvey Williams and Blueboy and Bobby Wratten were presented as these people who were living in denial of adulthood, that they want to be children forever. I mean, if you're going to try and contextualise Sarah, it was almost like a kind of art movement. This aggregation of people who, with shared values, who rejected machismo, rejected a certain version of how you had to be as an adult, all of those things. For something that was actually more inclusive and gentle and, god, more than ever gentility is something that we need today. So that's why I would often try and write about these artists like they were brave. I quite like using that kind of language about people that look and present like that, because they are brave."

Meanwhile, despite all his frustrations engendered by his perception that Sarah and its bands were playing at being children, journalist David Quantick told me: "Looking back, [working at the *NME*] was just like being a child. It's bizarre now when I go abroad and I have to book my own tickets and pay for them and somebody doesn't pick me up at the airport. Most of us, we left school or university and went straight to the music paper and it was like never leaving home. The only people we ever met were other journalists, or we met PRs whose job was to make us feel good, so we'd have expensive lunches, and our general reaction was ingratitude. We were part of the music industry, we just didn't like to admit it."

Press releases

Quite reasonably, Clare wonders whether Sarah's press releases are what led the music press to despise the label so much. "Is there something about the fact we always took quite a combative attitude with the music press?" she muses. "Our press releases, particularly in the early days, were frankly bizarre." Yes, let's have a look at some of those press releases.

The very first Sarah press release was effectively a four-page mini fanzine in red and black ink, with a cover that boasted the early logo of a large flower with the label's name spelled out on children's building blocks. In the visual style of *Are You Scared To Get Happy?*, the press release began by introducing a disaffected young man called Mr James C Urchin who grew up to front a band called The Sea Urchins and then the text explodes into an impassioned tirade about how the band sound like a "jangly splatter of happy-hearted guitars". A page later, the reader is given a furious rant about just why this new record label was formed and why the "short-sighted capitalist cheats" of the music industry needed this kick up the bum: "Please throw us the crumbs from your table, Mr EMI, when I grow up I want to be soooo like you." And added that this was a label that "sneers and spits contempt on the hypocritical Tory-bound values you (dear reader) hold dear". The press release ended with the suggestion that the reader "fucking die", before being signed off by Clare and Matt with a kiss.

> ❝ Five boys, one girl, refugee babies from the Cod War, cast adrift by thankful parents in an open margarine tub and forced to eat each other's haircuts till only one remained."
>
> **Sarah press release for The Sea Urchins, 1987**

The second press release followed a similar format, ending with a teaser for upcoming releases including 'Cremation Town' by The Poppyheads: "This much-loathed band, returning to prove that life is not all beer and squirrels." The press release for Another Sunny Day's 'Anorak City' berated the reader as "stupid and jaded and sweetly bereft of all, what's that word, IMAGINATION ... You're a jerk, basically." Oh, and it ended with the words: "It's designer made for your snappy critique, go on, squiggley wiggley, I dare you ... We think you're a real fuck-up." Despite this, 'Anorak City' was made single of the week twice. Perhaps the journalists didn't have time to read four pages of vented spleen. So maybe the *NME* missed the genius final line on the back page that stated: "This record is affectionately dedicated to James Brown. Both of them."

By the time 14 Iced Bears were in need of promotion, the four-page tirade had, implausibly, become even angrier. And even more venomous towards the music press. It closed with the challenge: "We hope, dear reviewer, that there is some tiny part of you left intact that isn't a journalist and which can still love and cherish noise." Clare and Matt had stopped signing the press releases by this point, and there

THE POWER OF THE PRESS

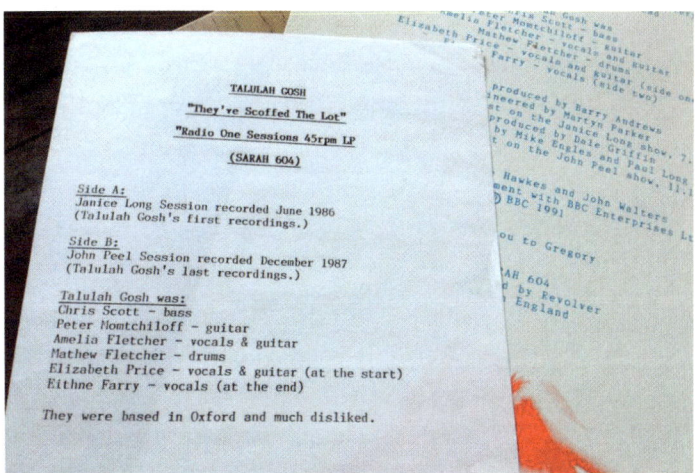

The press release for Talulah Gosh's Sarah compilation. Short and sweet.
Courtesy of Sarah Records.

was definitely no kiss for the music press. And certainly not in the next press release, which addressed the reader as "Rat Face", although went on to describe Glaswegian band The Golden Dawn as "noisy cunts from Seydhisfjordhur" in a dig at how the music press was falling over itself to celebrate Icelandic newcomers The Sugarcubes. This entire press release, which announces four new Sarah singles, brilliantly presents fabricated gibberish about every band, gives deliberately incorrect song titles and generally takes joy in being daft. Of The Springfields, it says: "Their early (US release only) single 'My Uzi Ain't Heavy, It's My Brother's' sounds really silly in the light of Public Enemy, rather like Public Enemy."

In 1989, Clare sent a copy of The Orchids' 7" 'What Will We Do Next' to a reviewer with a note that said: "Advise hanging on for a bit before taking it down the Record & Tape Exchange. Sarahs 1-6 now selling for up to £30." Which is hilarious. Because, of course, lots of music journalists were topping up their meagre incomes by selling the freebies they'd been sent for review. And the person who sent me a copy of the note only had it because he'd bought the 7" second-hand.

The press release for the 1991 Talulah Gosh compilation *They've Scoffed The Lot* takes a more minimalist approach, simply listing the tracks and the band members before closing with the eight-word biography: "They were based in Oxford and much disliked." While by the time Another Sunny Day's sixth Sarah single, 'New Year's Honours', was released in 1992, the press release had become a conventional one-page, typed information sheet about the record. Except, of course, this was Sarah. So the typed text was scribbled out by a marker and had the following words scrawled on the top in pen: "Two fucking good pop songs by Another Sunny Day." Job done.

It's not hard to see why John Peel once contacted Clare and Matt to suggest they tone down their dislike of the music press. In 1988, in response to the sleeve notes on the back of *Shadow Factory*, he wrote them a letter that said: "Admire, if I may say so, the fact that you never lose sight of your original vision. May I though voice one small criticism – the notes at time verge on petulance. Surely grumpiness and Sarah should be worlds apart? It's just that people might feel a little alienated."

The World Service

The music press's loathing of Sarah seemed to be a UK-only thing. Ireland is hardly a million miles away but the perception of the label there was quite different. For instance, articles about The Harvest Ministers in their native newspapers would refer to Sarah as a "hip label". The band's frontman Will Merriman agrees: "Sarah was not exposed to similar treatment in Ireland. The press here [Ireland], in the main, took any record on its own merits, regardless of what label released it. I guess at the time, the British press wielded an almost crusade-like power in pushing a band they championed, which guaranteed a certain amount of sales but this never bothered or affected us." Similarly, French music magazine *Les Inrockuptibles* reviewed The Field Mice's second single 'Sensitive' by taking the unprecedented decision to not only declare it as the magazine's first ever single of the month, but also to have the magazine's entire editorial staff sign the review in endorsement.

"The hostility of the UK music press sure did come across," says Josh Meadows of Australian band The Sugargliders. "It was quite disturbing because it seemed so unfair. I felt this at the time and I feel it even more looking back, but it was just unfortunate that Sarah emerged at a time when grunge music was the most popular strand of alternative music in the world."

I asked American musician FM Cornog of East River Pipe for his opinion of the more cruel reviews of his music in the British music press. "What do I think of when I read stuff like that? Well, not much. You *do* learn to roll with it after a while. East River Pipe has been described by so many music critics, in so many different ways. Also, British journalists use language in a more subtly aggressive way than Americans. The British will find 20 or 30 different ways to indirectly call you an asshole. Americans are less artful and more direct with language. Americans will just walk up to you and call you an asshole. In the end, you try not to pay too much attention to this sideshow journalism and just do your work."

He continues: "I do remember that critics would often mention Sarah in their reviews of my records, which I thought was strange. I mean, who gives a fuck what label a band's music is on? But evidently the British music press cared a *lot*. The reviews for East River Pipe were generally very good but often there was some kind of direct or indirect dig at Sarah. I remember several critics who lamented about how sad it was that East River Pipe was on Sarah, instead of on a hipper indie label where the music would be seen

❝ Bits of 'Untouched' could almost have been what The Stone Roses did next, had they borrowed an angelic voice belonging to someone called Kathryn Smith ... Secret Shine are a definite candidate for best debut of 1993."
Charlotte Observer **(North Carolina, US), reviews Secret Shine, 29 September 1993**

as much cooler. They would imply that most of the music coming from the label was barely worthy of consideration. There was always this somewhat stiff anti-Sarah headwind blowing in but I didn't give a shit."

THERE'S NO SUCH THING AS BAD PUBLICITY?

Some of the bands didn't mind that their records were slated, they were just pleased to be written about. "I would way rather have those awful reviews than a modern blog review that's trying so hard to be nice that it can't say a bad word," says Aberdeen's John Girgus. "The only thing I can hope to see in a review is that somebody listened and put their own thoughts into it. You can tell when someone's afraid to do that and I don't think anyone is better for it."

Keris Howard of Brighter thinks along similar lines: "The fact is, we were getting reviewed and that's an incredible thing. I don't think I was ever that bothered about the quality of the reviews. As somebody who religiously read the *NME* from about 1980 onwards, just to be there, to be reviewed, to be in the indie charts was absolutely unbelievable, it was so fantastic." He adds: "Some of my most cherished reviews are the really bad ones. We were described as being as dull as Nanette Newman's dishwater at one point and I thought that was hilarious. I didn't expect these guys writing for the music press to like it. To be honest, if a lot of these journalists had liked it I probably would have been a bit suspicious. The cruellest thing they could have done would be to ignore stuff."

> ❝ It was quite funny to be in the *NME* in the first place. They could have written what they liked, which obviously they did. We weren't bothered by it."
>
> **Matthew Evans, Tramway**

REVIEWING THE SINGLES

When you think about how many hundreds of singles must have poured into the music press's offices each week, it is both staggering and impressive that Sarah's records were consistently chosen to be one of the 15 or so selected for review every time a new one came out. And that, on its own, says quite a lot about both the depth to which Sarah had burrowed under the skin of the journalists and the begrudging respect the writers probably secretly harboured for this little label that they suspected could take it on the chin. Or it says that the records were easy for lazy journalists to write about.

When I spoke to former writers from both *NME* and *Melody Maker*, they confirmed what everyone always suspected about the process of reviewing the singles. There would be around 50 singles to choose 10-15 from. Some reviewers would skim through the pile and pull out a handful to consider, based on whether they had heard of the label or band, or if there was something about the package that made it stand out. Others would try to listen to at least 30 seconds of all the singles, and maybe group a few similar records together in one review to get more records onto the page. "But you'd also try to take a broader view of what was going on musically and subculturally," says Simon Price. "So there might be three records, two on Sarah and one on another label, and you might review them all together in one paragraph as a little update to what's going on in that world. And if you've been seething with something spiteful about something you wanted to say about that world, here was your chance to let it out."

> Indie bands are only indie bands for one of two reasons. They're either too crap or too radical to get a record deal. End of story."
Steven Wells in *NME*, 9 January 1988

David Quantick tells me: "If I'd been going through the singles pile and seen a Sarah record, I'd have no idea about it but at least I'd probably have something funny to say about it. I've probably written half the review before I've played it, and then you play it and you've got the choice of saying 'Unlike other Sarah records…' or 'This is a typical Sarah record' and it goes from there." David confirms that "everything you've heard is true" and he never listened to more than 30 seconds of a 7" when he was reviewing it "unless I liked it because I believe that, with a single, you should probably get the gist of it, so no I probably only listened to a bit of it."

But judging the records before they had been played was only part of the problem with reviews, because there was also the tedious matter of record reviews being an excuse for the writers to indulge in a spot of something that was more like flash fiction than a music review. "Yeah, that's always an issue when writing. I always try to do a bit of both, personally," says David.

There are certain contemporary big-name journalists who have it written into their contracts that their copy must not be touched by the sub-editors, and I wondered if that was ever the case at the *NME*, thinking that perhaps this was a reason why in-house bully Steven Wells got away with as much as he did. So I asked David if some writers were above the subs. "Absolutely not, that's not how it worked at all," he says firmly. "There was a slap down culture at *NME*, in the sense that in the early 1980s we'd had Paul Morley and Ian Penman, and during punk you had Danny Baker and Julie Burchill, we'd had the concept of star writers but that had been reduced. If you look at old *NME*s, the writer's name used to be on the cover. It would be 'ABC by Paul Morley' or 'Iggy Pop by Julie Burchill'. And they got rid of that in the 1980s, much to the annoyance of the writers, because the paper didn't want that star writer thing." He adds: "Everyone got subbed. It's very good for the soul. I learned how to write through being subbed."

1 – The Good

You might be surprised to know that Sarah chalked up 15 singles of the week across *NME*, *Melody Maker* and *Sounds*, although these were mostly in the first quarter of the label's life. "The music press was fine on day one," admits Matt, "It was on days two and three that things changed." Talking about the debut Another Sunny Day single, Harvey Williams says: "I remember when 'Anorak City' came out and flicking through *Melody Maker* that week and seeing a review. It was completely the last thing I would have expected to be there, and it was quite a pertinent review. It was single of the week," he says. "And the next week it was single of the week in the *NME*. And then I was looking through *Sounds* the week after going, 'Where's my review?!'"

> ❝ These four terrific unassuming little tunes … Whoever plays the piano on 'The Last Letter' is getting free drinks all night if I ever meet them."
>
> **David Cavanagh reviews The Field Mice in *Sounds*, 1988.** (Field research: engineer Ian Catt is the person who deserves those free drinks)

Before he was a pop star with Saint Etienne, Bob Stanley was a music journalist and he awarded 'Pristine Christine' the single of the week spot in the *NME*, something which contributed to the label's debut record selling out within weeks. That and the fact 'Pristine Christine' was played several times by John Peel and Janice Long. "In a way, we couldn't have had much more support," says Clare. "We got off to a good start and people knew we existed." Robert Cooksey of The Sea Urchins recalls: "Getting single of the week in the *NME* changed everything of course and suddenly we had a lot of fans around the country. It meant we could do shows outside of Birmingham and usually play to a lot of people. The downside was that egos became inflated and an arrogance quickly started to develop within the band. We were quite young after all and now we were very minor pop stars."

So it wasn't all bile and spite from the music press. In the pre-Sarah days, while he was writing *Are You Scared To Get Happy?* and co-running Sha-La-La, Matt got a note from the *NME*'s Jerry Thackray (aka The Legend!) seeking an invitation to Bristol to interview him. Thinking there was safety in numbers, Matt enlisted Rob Young from The Poppyheads, as well as fanzine writers Magz Hall and Amanda Burston, to join him for moral support. Rob says: "It was really great they were noticing what we were doing, but also 'Oh God, it's the *NME*, they're not going to get it right!' There was a desire to be taken seriously but an instant protective shell as well, they're never going to get it." In the spring of 1987, Matt wrote to his Sha-La-La co-conspirator Pete Williams to bring him up to speed: "The Legend! interview went OK, though I think I would rather have had someone I could actually argue with than someone who agreed with us… but the bastard still hasn't written it up 'cos he's busy moving house."

Fast forward to the 21st century and Matt recalls: "I remember seeing [Jerry] for the first time when he was selling his fanzine from a plastic carrier bag at the Living Room in London, and not really believing it was him because he was so unlike his stage and fanzine persona. I just didn't expect him to have a plastic carrier bag. I also

In early 1987, *NME* writer The Legend! (aka Jerry Thackray) came to Bristol to interview Matt about the Sha-La-La flexi label. Here they are, striding across Durdham Down near Upper Belgrave Road.
Rob Young.

remember Bob Stanley saying a similar thing about me when we first met. I was trying to sell fanzines at Central London Poly but with little success, so I'd resorted to strong alcohol. And he came across me drunkenly haranguing people on the stairs, demanding that they give me 50p. Selling fanzines really was no fun at times."

Sometimes, when a new Sarah release accidentally made its way in front of a journalist who wouldn't normally have an awareness of the label, good things happened. Such as the time, in September 1991, that the *NME*'s dance music writer Ian McCann reviewed that week's singles and declared The Field Mice's 'Missing the Moon' to be the "total absolute single of the week" and waxed lyrical about it for melding pop and acid house. One imagines that Ian got a lot of stick from his colleagues for this. But it also goes to show the value of music journalists taking the records at face value, even when the writer freely admits that this is a band "about whom I know nil". Field Mouse Anne Mari Davies says: "It was just ace. It was always a very interesting relationship with the music press. There were one or two journalists that were supportive but, by and large, it was a running joke for them. They could always diss Sarah Records because everybody knew that Sarah was twee and childish and skipping down the road with flowers in your hair. And so it was a caricature of Sarah that they used. It was lazy journalism."

> ❝ Look, I'm sick of having to make excuses for this band, so if you know you despise them and everything they stand for, just fuck off and go and read yet another tedious Clash retrospective."
> **Ian Watson reviews Talulah Gosh in *Melody Maker*, 23 March 1991**

Australian band Even As We Speak were already very familiar with the influence of the British music press. Guitarist Julian Knowles admits they had it pretty easy compared to some of their labelmates: "The support we had from *NME* and *Melody Maker* was unusual for Sarah, they loved everything that we did." He explains:

"A lot of us as young people, as teenagers, were following the music scene and the post-punk scene, and so we would get old sea-mail copies of *NME* and *Melody Maker*, I used to religiously read that stuff. We couldn't listen to Peel's shows because there was no internet radio back then but you could read the British music press so we knew how influential they were. So once they started to support us, that felt like we'd hit the big time."

The appreciation of the British music press was the same in the US, where a young Ric Menck had started reading the imported papers in the 1970s. "I was very clued into what was happening in Britain from an early age. I was well aware of the fickle British press from reading the weeklies. I knew they hated anything that sounded 'twee'," says the future stalwart of The Springfields. "I was quite honoured when Bob Stanley awarded 'Sunflower' single of the week in the *NME*. I don't think I ever saw a review for the second single. To be honest, I sort of took the British press with a grain of salt. I knew even then that good music lasts much longer than some stupid review in a magazine. It did make me kind of mad that the press really seemed to hate everything on Sarah but Matt and Clare got the last laugh. The Sarah catalogue is beloved because of the great music."

Another band that got off lightly were The Sweetest Ache. "It might be selective memory but I don't remember being trashed in any way," says singer Simon Court. "One review really stood out and the footnote was that The Sweetest Ache came out shining like diamonds in a dustbin. And that stayed with me, I thought that was really good." That line was from a review of the single 'Tell Me How It Feels' in *Melody Maker*. Simon adds that reading a review of his record in the music press was validation of what the band was doing: "I remember standing in [newsagent] WH Smith reading that and it blew me away. Finding your record reviewed in the music press seemed more real than the record itself."

> ❝ Secret Shine seem to back up the legions of fanzine fumblers with a double A side single which deserves to have them queuing All Around The Fountain to purchase ... Here's to more surprises as pleasant as this."
>
> **John Mitchell reviews Secret Shine's 'Honey Sweet' in *Venue*, 8 May 1992**

James Roberts of The Sea Urchins had his own experience in the newsagents: "Seeing 'Pristine Christine' be single of the week, that was definitely one of those moments that will live with me forever. I'd got some crappy job in Birmingham at the time and had gone into WH Smith at lunchtime and was hunched down in the magazine aisle because we'd been told it might be reviewed. We didn't know it was going to be single of the week, and I was reading it thinking 'Oh my god, that's amazing!' I was too broke to buy the bloody thing! I read it about 10 times in the shop and then had to put it down and leave. That was a lovely thing."

Boyracer capitalised on their fast and loud gigs to pull in some glowing live reviews. "I think we often came across as being pretty bratty and we would play very fast live," says frontman Stewart Anderson. "We did some shows that were actually pretty good, where we were reasonably confident. People often thought 'Oh, it's a Sarah band' and then we'd come on and make this big racket and they weren't expecting that. I never bought the music weeklies very often. I don't need validation

> Blueboy may turn out to be this stupidly ignored little label's forlornest, finest semi-acoustic romantics yet. God, I love Sarah. God, I feel embarrassed writing that."
>
> **Paul Lester reviews Blueboy's 'Clearer' in *Melody Maker*, 1991**

and I don't care if someone doesn't like it, that's fine. There's plenty of things I don't like."

Alongside Jerry Thackray and Bob Stanley, there were a handful of other music journalists who gave Sarah bands a fair hearing, one of whom was *Melody Maker*'s Pete Paphides. "It would have felt like a betrayal to turn on that stuff. It felt like that music had helped me too much in my life," says Pete. "I felt like I understood why that music was made, what it was a response to, what its manifesto was. I thought there was a kind of bravery in that. When I left *Melody Maker* and joined *Time Out*, I remember writing a review of a Northern Picture Library record and, whenever I reviewed those records, I really tried to make their creators sound almost like soldiers because I thought it was quite funny, that disjuncture between what they were, how are they presenting, and actually how brave it was to be that way. I was inviting people to consider this idea that bravery isn't being like one of those guys on *SAS: Who Dares Wins*. Bravery is having the courage of your convictions and really not giving a fuck if someone, who isn't paying close attention anyway, thinks that you're in a state of arrested development."

2 – The Bad

The sexism and misogyny of the music press cannot be overstated. I mean, a quick flick through a pile of old *NME*s while writing this chapter led me – in less than two minutes – to stumble upon a three-page feature from 9 May 1992 entitled 'The Witch Report', which nails its colours to the mast. Purporting to be a celebration of women in rock, the standfirst further gave the game away: "Hips, Lips, Tits, Power! Meet the new breed of enchantress, the spell-binding women who are taking the male bastille and giving it some earthly female perspective. Betty Page greets the new PMT dawn with a deep, personal review of Women in Rock and lets the new women of substance have their say. Let's frock!" I mean… there's a lot to unpack here but it's all so unsubtle that I'll leave you to do it yourself.

The main picture on this feature is a close-up of Curve singer Toni Halliday's face as she sparks a cigarette using a lighter that is shaped like a woman in a bikini. And the article closes with a top 10 list of the worst "gender traitors in rock", ie women whom the *NME* felt had let the side down by being too sexy (eg Wendy James and Kylie Minogue), or by allowing themselves to be exploited (eg teenager Annabella Lwin, who was indeed exploited in 1981 – by 35-year-old svengali figure Malcolm McLaren, who persuaded the 13-year-old child to pose naked on a single sleeve, among many other predatory things). There's nothing like a spot of victim blaming.

What this tells us is that, in 1992, the *NME* was riddled with misogyny and tired old attitudes to women. Even though it had commissioned a woman (who had adapted as her pen name that of an exploited pin-up) to write the article. And the misogyny and sexism that the entire music press showed to Sarah and its bands was phenomenal. Unable to accept a record label that was run on equal terms by a woman and a man, and one that had a woman's name, the music press tore shreds off it week after week, safe in the knowledge that because Matt and Clare were in Bristol there was little risk of the journalist bumping into them at The Camden Falcon and having to make amends. Which is also known as bullying, given how much power the press had in their role as gatekeepers.

On a number of occasions, feeling increasingly frustrated by the attitudes of the music press, Clare contacted the letters pages. Writing to *Melody Maker* in August 1991, she said: "Your treatment of women reinforces the status quo of a woman's role being largely decorative – an object, a stage-prop to be placed at the front of photos (for boys to wank over), a puppet to smile and dance while the boys at the back (the 'brains') pull the strings ... Everett [True] – you're not an individual at a gig experiencing normal lusts; you're a journalist, in a position to change things. Instead you reinforce them. While there aren't an equal number of women with such power, you need to think before putting pen to paper." Thinking back on that letter, Clare now says: "I called up *Melody Maker* the next week to try and make sure something was going to be reviewed or included as news, and whoever answered the phone sniggered and said 'Ah, you want to speak to Everett, don't you?' I said I didn't, but he passed me over regardless, with the express intention of making me as uncomfortable as possible and punishing me for daring to complain."

"We could survive all the sexism, homophobia and patronisation because we'd already established ourselves," says Clare. "If they'd done that from Sarah 1, it would have been very different. My understanding anecdotally is that journalists were rather afraid to stick their heads above the parapet and say they liked us because they got bullied for it. So the people who did like us, and it seemed like there were quite a few people who liked us, weren't really willing to put pen to paper as they were afraid of being typecast as Sarah fans. Which I think is why so many of the reviews say 'Unlike every other Sarah record this is quite good' because it's them covering their arses."

Matt says: "We wished we'd collected all the reviews that said 'This doesn't sound like a typical Sarah release' because every

"We could survive all the sexism, homophobia and patronisation because we'd already established ourselves," says Clare.
Courtesy of Sarah Records.

> 66 Amelia Fletcher's arrival onstage causes, of course, as much of a stir as the words 'Hello, we're Heavenly' ... The owner of indie-pop's finest angel-in-a-teacup voice seems to be cutiedom's ultimate pin-up. Not that she's sexy or anything (new vocalist Kathy [sic] is tons cuter)."
>
> **Ian Watson reviews Heavenly in *Melody Maker*, 1991**

> " I know just what you're expecting. You won't get it. ... A stunner."
>
> **Melody Maker reviews The Golden Dawn's 'George Hamilton's Dead', 1989**

single review said it. Every single band was unlike most other Sarah bands, so there's a typical Sarah band that doesn't actually exist that everyone doesn't sound like. When The Wake were on Factory they got dismissed as Joy Division clones, and the minute they signed to Sarah they got dismissed as Orange Juice clones. But it's the same band making the same music." However, The Wake's frontman Caesar says: "Early on we did really well in the press. But as time went by on Factory, we were not reviewed that much. By the time we were on Sarah, I remember getting a few reviews, and we came out of it OK compared to what we were getting at the latter stages of Factory. So for us it seemed quite complimentary."

Readers sometimes hit back as well, as happened after Jon Wilde reviewed new singles by Heavenly and Tramway with these thoughtful lines in *Melody Maker* in 1991: "Another brace of astoundingly crap releases from Sarah Records. Interesting how all their records sound like a gang of remedial teachers attempting to whip up a bit of enthusiasm around the campfire at the end of term." In response, reader Verity Watson from Cornwall sagely wrote in to say: "Leave Sarah Records out of it for a moment and consider the individual merits of Heavenly and Tramway. You cannot criticise two bands with the same line, just because they're on the same label. Do The Pale Saints sound like The Pixies? Do Ride sound like The Telescopes? Well then. Shut your fucking mouth." Well said, Verity.

Simon Price joined *Melody Maker* in 1988 and stayed there until 1997. "It was quite intimidating at first, quite a bit like a bear pit. There was a real take-no-prisoners attitude," he says. "You had to join in with all the banter and personality destruction that went on in the office, and if you couldn't handle it you didn't make the cut, and I found that quite difficult at first. It was very male to begin with. Certainly when I started, there was only one female on the staff, who was Carol Clerk the news editor." Carol died in 2010 but, in *The Guardian*, her former colleague Caroline Sullivan described a kind-hearted woman who drank, smoked and swore like a trooper, writing: "In a way, she was blokier than the blokes. It was partly her nature, but I suspect she also exaggerated her toughness to fit in. Men vastly outnumbered women in the music press then and she had few role models to follow, so she became one herself." Which rather confirms our suspicions of what it was like to be a woman at the music press.

Simon continues: "I think they found me endearingly peculiar, I was a very shy goth kid from South Wales. Particularly at *Melody Maker*, some of the writers had this Hunter S Thompson tough guy attitude. It was all about taking no prisoners and being brutal. I found myself trying to fit into that and, in some ways, by doing that, I was trying on clothing that was not mine. The way you made your name was by being as vicious as you possibly could."

Pete Paphides joined *Melody Maker* towards the end of 1992 and says "it was terrifying to start with". He agrees: "The first few months I was there, not many people spoke to me. They were very hierarchical. And I was absolutely desperate to not screw this opportunity up. So I just silently went about my business and made myself available for any work that was going. *Melody Maker* was quite dysfunctional. Some of the office banter was really unpleasant. You could definitely see the beginnings of that lad culture in some of the conversations that were happening in *Melody Maker*. I think the women, especially the young women, that got ahead at *Melody Maker* had to be quite pugnacious and laddish, almost more man-like in a way."

It wasn't only the staff who found the music press offices to be alienating and unfriendly. When trying to conjure up press coverage for 14 Iced Bears, manager Sue Freeman recalls the *NME* as being an especially toxic environment. "Ringing up the *NME* was an absolute nightmare," she says. "There was a guy on reception who was just so difficult to get past. I was always pretty determined when I rang up, I wasn't a pushover, but it was particularly difficult dealing with the *NME*." While Clare says: "I only went into King's Reach Tower [where *NME* and *Melody Maker* were based] once to drop off records and try and get them reviewed. I went to both papers and both were equally unwelcoming and intimidating. I never did it again." So that was that.

You want another tale of a woman reluctantly stepping into the offices of the music press? No problem. Vinita Joshi from Ché says: "I remember being taken around *Melody Maker* and *NME* offices by our PR company when we did The Pooh Sticks' record. I barely said a word, it was a horrible, horrible experience. I barely looked up, shuffled in and shook their hands. I was annoyingly shy. Meeting the music press I found very difficult. I remember offering [Jerry Thackray] a drink at the PowerHaus and he said 'whiskey'. We were quite broke but we'd have to do that. So I got him a whiskey and he was pissed off because it had ice in it. I felt like journalists held so much power, and back then you would wine and dine them, and take them to a gig abroad so you'd get a live feature."

> " I wanted to mix nuts and bolts into the Ribena doubtlessly consumed by each band present tonight. Give them some metal and they'll be no further trouble."
>
> **Penny Anderson reviews The Field Mice in *NME*, 1989**

Photographer Alison Wonderland agrees with these stories of the music press offices not being places that welcomed women. As well as being Heavenly's go-to photographer, Alison was a freelancer for *Melody Maker*, taking photos of bands for the new acts section, *Advance*. "The music press didn't treat me great," she says bluntly. "It was a man's world and, in that *Melody Maker* office, it smelled of man's world. I was so scared of going upstairs to the *Melody Maker* office that I used to hand my stuff in to reception then run away, and phone them from the phone box around the corner to say I'd left the pictures in reception! That's how terrified I was. Men wouldn't be like that, of course they wouldn't."

Alison continues: "There were certain people that you had to shag if you wanted to get ahead and I wouldn't do that. That's why I didn't get the front covers. It's kind of shocking when you think back, because it really was like that. If I'd have been one of the boys..." She adds: "I'm quite a strong feminist but for some reason I just put up with it. The job was valuable to me and I think I was a bit scared of losing it."

Heavenly by Alison Wonderland, who was that rare beast: a female photographer at the music press.
Alison Wonderland.

However, there were a few occasions when Alison's work stepped beyond the *Advance* pages. Thanks to Riot Grrrl, certain bands were increasingly requesting a female photographer for their shoot but there weren't many on the books. And, in some instances, Alison recalls how pairing a female photographer with a female journalist led to the sort of insight that it seems hard to imagine a male pairing achieving. She recounts the time that she travelled to the US to cover a piece about Bis, for which Alison was teamed with the journalist Eithne Farry (previously a vocalist in Talulah Gosh). Over at the *NME*, Bis were routinely ridiculed by Steven Wells who threw verbal stones at frontwoman Manda Rin's figure. So the band must have particularly appreciated the more humane touch offered by Alison and Eithne on that trip. "Eithne and I worked together, we talked about the feature and how it should be, and I actually think that's far better than sending you with a bloke journalist who's just being a complete letch and not even talking about what they're going to write," says Alison. "Whereas it was a lovely collaboration, and we were hanging out with the band and it worked so well. They could have used that collaboration with other bands and features but they just didn't. I think that's when I was the most excited about working for *Melody Maker*, and when bands, mostly female bands, were asking for me to do their photos."

Amelia Fletcher recounts the time when Heavenly's album *Le Jardin de Heavenly* was guest reviewed by Shampoo in the *NME*, who gave it one star out of ten: "I pretended it was annoying but actually it was quite funny," she says. "There's an associated story, when my brother [Mathew Fletcher] happened to be at a gig in London where Shampoo were. So he marched up to them and said 'Why did you give Heavenly one out of 10 in *NME*?' and they said 'That's one more than you deserved'. Which is such a cool answer. I have no problem with Shampoo giving us one out of ten, or even nought out of ten. But the general inability to get features, I did get frustrated with that. I could see other bands that I thought we were as good as, or better than, getting lots of attention and it did annoy me because I felt it was unfair."

Andy Hitchcock of Action Painting! tells me: "Lee [Christopher, Action Painting!'s bassist, who was also Shampoo's guitarist] would come back from his adventures with Shampoo and we'd get an idea of how the London music scene saw Sarah, and they saw them with absolute disdain. Later on you realise there was an annoyance because they were doing things their way. When we got the Steve Lamacq Show single of the week [on Radio 1], apparently the rest of the music business was asking how we got that. Their noses were out of joint. We were on the naughty step. We didn't have a plugger and we were doing our own publicity, but Steve Lamacq had actually bothered listening to the record and made his own mind up. It made you realise how fake the so-called indie scene was. It was very conformist and people were frightened of saying the wrong things to the wrong people. Whereas, to their credit, Matt and Clare just did their own thing for better or for worse."

3 – The Ugly

At its absolute worst, the relentlessly negative press levelled at Sarah groups could tip a band into quitting doing what they loved rather than endure yet another round of public humiliation. "This sort of record is the most compelling argument imaginable for the reintroduction of national service," wrote the *NME* about Gentle Despite's debut single 'The Darkest Blue EP'. "We were on a bit of a downer about it, our egos were crushed," says guitarist Paul Gorton. "We were quite upset about that, and Simon [Westwood] was probably more upset about it than me because he was the singer. I admired him for having the guts to sing, I couldn't do that. It really knocked our confidence, we were only 19 and 20 at the time. It was an ego thing for the journalists." Simon sadly died in 2015, which is why we don't hear his voice in this book.

> **"** The critical reaction to Sarah was ludicrous. Why be so hateful to people making records? It seemed way over the top."
> **Caesar, The Wake**

That crushing *NME* review was followed by an even worse *Melody Maker* one for a gig at the Duchess of York in Leeds. Dave Simpson called Gentle Despite an "absolute disaster" and, with a sigh, Paul concedes it was "unfortunately the worst gig we ever did". The band didn't have a great deal of live experience but had been persuaded that if they did some good live shows then they would shake off the bad reviews their single had received. The plan backfired.

With a clutch of bad write-ups, Paul and Simon were struggling to find the momentum to keep their band together, especially when the *NME* reviewed their second single by saying: "It sounds like middle-aged bank clerks tryna pretend to be kids so as to impress their teddy bears. Clueless dickheads, every one of them," which was extraordinarily mean. "Matt and Clare were the only people who encouraged us at all," says Paul. "We loved them because they were only a bit older than us, they were indie kids who put out music they liked. We didn't feel any pressure from them. They were like a light for us at the time." But that support wasn't enough to keep Gentle Despite going and, after two singles and nothing but negativity from the press, the band reluctantly called it a day. "The bad reviews contributed to Simon wanting to not do it anymore. It was really awful. You're so sensitive at that age and take it to heart. He was really upset," says Paul. "It was disheartening. I don't think they realised the damage they were doing. We were so sensitive. We had religiously read *NME* and *Melody Maker* since we were kids and, when you're in them and they slag you off, it doesn't do your confidence much good."

There certainly seemed to be a cult of the ego in the music press, with certain writers spending more time talking about themselves than whatever band it was they were purporting to write about. Even As We Speak's Julian Knowles says: "When I looked at what was going on, I thought 'God, half of their reviews were about themselves rather than the bands and they often took shots as a way of trying to be notorious or something. The music journalists wanted to be the subject of attention

Gentle Despite were driven to abandon their dreams following relentless bullying in the music press.
Courtesy of Gentle Despite.

rather than the people they were writing about. I had to get a little bit older before I saw the classist and gender thing. And then I went, 'Wow, they were in control, they were pulling all the levers on the careers of musicians at that time'. It was quite a revelation."

Secret Shine was the band which was arguably dealt the lowest blow when, in 1993, the *NME*'s Steven Wells reviewed 'Loveblind' in six words by saying: "This isn't music, this is cancer." But that wasn't a review, that was attention seeking. "It never seemed to cross their minds that they were essentially killing a band's entire career with a supposedly witty remark," says Matt. "Secret Shine were about 20 at the time and they had their single reviewed as being like cancer. What does that do to a band when they're just starting out?"

> "We felt anxious every time we released something because we knew it would go one of two ways."
> **Paul Stewart, Blueboy**

Steven Wells was a writer who made a name for himself by being performatively outraged by everything. That was his schtick. He died from cancer in 2009 and, in the obituary by James Brown in *The Guardian*, Steven was described as "the most impossible person to work with because he knew no form of compromise, had little true interest in music, was narrow-minded". And this was the problem: the music press at this time was employing a lot of men who were more interested in themselves than in music. And if they wrote in a confrontational and controversial manner, they knew that might make a name for them at the expense of their subject matter. For that reason, Sarah and its bands were easy targets.

Secret Shine turned a hateful review into something positive, which says a lot about them as people.
Courtesy of Secret Shine.

In the absence of being able to ask Steven about his writing, I asked his friend and colleague David Quantick how he would feel if he was in a band and his record was described as being like cancer. "I wouldn't like that at all," he says honestly, before asking me whether or not this was something he had written himself. I say that Steven wrote it and David says: "What you've got is an extreme writer writing about something that they consider to be extreme. Sarah created an emotional reaction. I'm not saying anybody would have killed to get those reviews but there were millions of labels who you'd get a record from and go 'I don't know what this is going to sound like because this label means nothing to me'. Whereas with a Sarah record, as you've suggested, whether it sounded like that or not, you only had to look at it to have an opinion of the record, rightly or wrongly."

Secret Shine generously say they tried not to be offended by it and instead recognised that it gave them a leg up that they might not otherwise have received. "Based on that *NME* review, John Peel said something like 'If a band elicits that much wrath, it's worthy of attention', so it actually made him listen to us and he made 'Loveblind' single of the week and it then got in the indie charts," says singer Kathryn Smith. Bandmate Jamie Gingell adds: "It's like the Oscar Wilde quote, 'There is only one thing in the world worse than being talked about, and that is not being talked about.' That's what made John Peel notice us."

Guitarist Scott Purnell says he might have felt more angry if Jamie had not urged him to see how ludicrous it was. "He persuaded me not to get upset about it," he says.

"I could have been offended but because of events that quickly took hold after that, I wasn't. The music press, it's just opinions, isn't it? It ended up being a good thing." Jamie continues: "I also realised, as most people did, that it was an intentionally machismo attitude that they had towards Sarah, and it was very chauvinistic, very male-driven, at the *NME*. It was bullying but they thought they were being funny. I didn't respect the *NME*." Kathryn adds: "You're a bit powerless once a record's out there. There's a hope that you're going to get some coverage and reviews every time you bring something out, but when you're met with that, well, what can you do? It's slightly mortifying when I look back. But like I say, because things grew from it, it actually did us a favour in a perverse way." To my mind, the members of Secret Shine are showing themselves to be particularly generous people.

Clare says: "I always thought, because Steven Wells was left wing and we were trying to run a record label in line with a left-wing ideology, that he should have been supportive of us. My fanzine had fitted into that *Attack on Bzag* and *Rox* northern, quite vocally left-wing world he had come out of, so there should have been a link there. For me, it comes back to gender politics and the fact that the history of the labour movement is a very male history. And here were we, with a girly name and a woman 50% behind the label. Sarah just didn't compute in people like that's worlds." Matt adds: "Steven Wells was a ranting poet. He criticised one of Slampt's records for being political but not being his idea of what a political record should sound like, which was shouty, belligerent and macho but instead he got this soft, acoustic political record, and he said it couldn't be a political record because it didn't fit his idea of what a political record could be."

> ❝ I probably said bad things and I would happily apologise for them but it was a virtual reality. Music journalists were like people playing a computer game. We're shooting people and hurting them and, to us, it wasn't real."
>
> **David Quantick, journalist**

The Wake's Caesar picks up the thread about the writers taking centre stage in their reviews of other people's work: "The writers thought they were the stars and they took great pleasure in slagging people off, and the more brutally they did it the more famous they got. Paul Morley became more famous than a lot of the bands he was writing about, and Danny Baker was getting famous as well but his schtick was slagging off the things you were meant to like. Writers were creating stardom for themselves. And they all became media figures and writers of Sunday newspaper columns and novelists. Music was just there to serve them and, by the 1990s, Steven Wells was a perfect example of that. It became really unpleasant. The function of writers should be to analyse things."

Clare muses about Steven: "Now he's dead it does become more difficult to say anything bad about him. But he was absolutely awful to us. Inspired largely by sexism and pretty much every other prejudice going, too. It's astonishing, given how much he purported to hate us, that he ploughed on in the same repetitive abusive furrow, reviewing the records into our last ten singles, isn't it?"

On other occasions Steven simply couldn't be bothered to read the sleeves

> "Why in hell does Steven Wells think *he* has the right to lecture *us* about feminism? The man writes in the most belligerent macho style, hysterically peppering his prose with gratuitously male language and relentlessly selling maleness as something we should aspire to."
>
> **Clare writing to the *NME*, February 1994**

properly. While 'reviewing' Northern Picture Library's 'Paris' 7", he insisted on calling the band 'Norfolk Windmills' (that being the song on the b-side). Quite what this showed, other than that he couldn't be bothered to turn a 7" square of cardboard over, is unclear, especially since there was a note at the end of the 'review' saying the actual name of the band. His schlocky rant about the single being "YET ANOTHER streak of flailing ineffectual tish/tishing wispy-wispy billycooing maggot piss aimed at adolescent male failed-suicides who couldn't get a shag in a nearly bankrupt brothel with a credit card stapled to their pimply foreskins" was a rehash of his weekly effort at stringing a bunch of unrelated, offensive terms together and putting a few in capitals for maximum effect. But it didn't tell you anything except that the writer was in need of a hug.

Every time I see this review, I keep coming back to the phase 'failed-suicides' and staring at it in horror. Of all the truly appalling things that I have read aimed at Sarah bands in the music press (and I have read an astonishing amount of sexist, homophobic and violent content about this label), this is the line that really offends me. "It's jaw-dropping stuff, isn't it?" says Matt. "I know humour is subjective and all that, so it's silly to say I never found him funny, but he was just so unimaginative, with such a restricted vocabulary. He'd recycle the same images over and over, most involving male bodily fluids. But clearly someone at the *NME* thought he was Big and Clever. It really is a complete dereliction of duty, both on his part as a journalist and on the part of the various editorial staff at the *NME*, right up to the editor himself. Going ahead and publishing a review which you know has the band name wrong...?" To which, David Quantick says: "It's funnier to mock Steven Wells than correct him. The subs have corrected the information and now they're just mocking him, which is a regular thing at the *NME*."

But then there was the time Steven reviewed Action Painting!'s single 'Mustard Gas', on which the band name is written in English and the song title in Japanese directly underneath. Therefore, Steven titled the single 'Some Japanese Figures That I Can't Do On This Keyboard'. Again, all he had to do was turn the 7" over to see the name of the single in English. His review concludes: "I'm willing to bet that if Action Painting weren't on Sarah Records they'd be very, very good indeed." So, it *is* a good record then? "So the music's alright but by being on Sarah Records it magically becomes rubbish? Oh, fuck off," says the band's frontman Andy Hitchcock, not unreasonably. "You can't even build up a cogent argument. You don't like the label and you're not going to admit when you're wrong. He decided, like some sort of recalcitrant six-year-old, 'That's it, I don't like you, I'm going to put my fingers in my ears.' It was really depressing, because all the worst things you heard about the London media seemed to play out at that time."

I ask David Quantick what he thinks about the sentiment that if a particular record wasn't on Sarah then it would be quite good, which pops up a handful of times. "That's an example of the label being bigger than the band," he says. "It's often an issue, particularly in the 1980s and 1990s, that the label would be bigger than the band. It was an issue for Factory that, if you weren't a Joy Division-type band on Factory, you would never make it because people didn't want it. There was a 1970s funk act on Factory who were apparently brilliant, but absolutely nobody was interested because they didn't sound like a Factory band. And that happens a lot if you get signed to the wrong label. And with Sarah, there was an identity, real or imagined, and if you weren't that kind of band then people weren't interested. If you're not a Sarah-sounding band, maybe you should have signed with someone else?"

Amelia Fletcher decided to address the Steven Wells issue head on by inviting him to interview Talulah Gosh, which he did over one full page in the 9 January 1988 issue of *NME*. "I knew what I was doing and I knew he would hate us," she says. "But I wrote him a letter because I was desperate to get an interview in *NME*." In that letter, Amelia wrote: "We are aware that it is *NME* policy only to print thoroughly rude and offensive pieces about us. We also appreciate that you are the king of writing such pieces. We are therefore wondering if you would care to interview us?" Steven took Talulah Gosh up on the offer but naturally it was pretty nasty; for instance, Mathew Fletcher is referred to as "the hippopotamus drummer". "It was quite a big piece, in which he said that we were Hitler's Aryan children, which was a bit weird for my Jewish dad to read," says Amelia. "It was a pretty unpleasant piece but it was a big piece and that's what I wanted to get so it was, I guess, effective." Ahem, what Steven actually wrote was: "On stage the Gosh are one lump of lard, two indie geeks and two angelic Super Aryan blondes." Which is hardly better.

> **❝** I thought of most music journalists as failed novelists. So, who cares what a failed wannabe novelist thinks about music?"
>
> **FM Cornog, East River Pipe**

Although Steven never wrote about Talulah Gosh or Heavenly again, that didn't stop Amelia from confronting him about a particularly misogynist piece he had written regarding one of her labelmates: "I wrote him a letter and said, 'You think you're right on but you are totally sexist and this is completely inappropriate behaviour'. And it obviously touched a nerve, because he wrote back 10 sides of a handwritten letter trying to justify himself."

On hearing this story, Beth Arzy of Aberdeen says: "Back in the day, nobody knew that Amelia was super smart and would go on to have all these degrees in economics and a CBE. They just saw this adorable girl in a short dress and skinned knees singing. And they thought, 'OK, I'm going to have a go.' And then she would come back at them and people would shut up. You don't mess with Amelia Fletcher! I always loved it when she would put people in their place and use words bigger than they even imagined were out there in the world. When I met her and Cathy [Rogers], I just thought 'Man, those girls have balls!' They were not what I expected. I thought they were going to be all cutesy and they were just like raunchy Riot Grrrls. I learned

Spencer Harrison, Ivy's singer, was yet another performer on Sarah Records who had to endure a truly nasty write-up in the music press.
Gavin V Woollard.

my place in the food chain after meeting Heavenly and it was not very high up."

Ivy was another Sarah band that suffered at the hands of a reviewer wanting to create some notoriety while not bothering to consider the implications for the band in question. Which is extra unforgivable when you realise that the person who reviewed Ivy's single 'Avenge' in *Melody Maker* was Therapy? frontman Andy Cairns. As a musician himself, Andy should have known better than anyone the effect a stupid review can have, not only on a band's perception in the public eye and therefore on record sales – but also on the confidence of the band itself. Andy wrote: "[Spencer] needs to suffer a bit – servant, heat the poker. Spanish Fly, some motoring tools and a hot fire are what is needed now."

Looking back on the review, frontwoman Spencer Harrison says: "It was quite violent and it was so inappropriate. At the time, I was really shocked and hurt by his comment. He didn't even put it in a clever context, it was just violent and vicious and nasty. It felt horrible to read that. That feeling stayed with me for a week or so. It was very personal and it was violence against women, and it's quite outrageous." Guitarist Julian Cator adds: "Bloody hell, you wouldn't say that nowadays. It was just horrible. But he thought he was being really funny."

David Quantick reviewed Ivy's second single 'Avenge' in the *NME* by saying:

"Ten years this awful label Sarah have been going and still they can't work a simple recording studio. Or sign a good band. Or stop using twee female singers. Or anything." Overlooking the fact that Sarah had only been going for seven years at this point, Clare and Matt were so amused by this bizarre review that they had it pinned to their wall and used it in a future press advert. "I'd love to put him on the spot now and say, 'What exactly did you mean by twee girl singer?' You don't know what Spencer looks like, the lyrics aren't twee..." says Matt. Indeed, Ivy were essentially a goth version of the Cocteau Twins, and there's nothing twee about either of those things. So I *did* ask David when he meant by 'twee girl singer' given how un-twee Ivy was, and pointed out that Sarah only had five bands fronted by women (David's response: "Wow!"). After re-reading his review, David conceded that he would go away and play that track again. Well, he would find it on YouTube: "Of course I don't still have the record!" he laughed.

"Sarah had an identity. That's a big thing for a label," says David. "The whole twee thing... at the time, I just loathed it. I liked grown-up music, I liked pop music. I don't like the sexism and viciousness of heavy metal and a lot of the rock scene, and I would call myself a feminist. But I saw twee as almost the opposite of macho in a sense that it rejected sexuality and growing up in favour of pretending to be a child, removing maturity and the horribleness of sex, and the difficulty of relationships in favour of pretending to be a child."

Former *Melody Maker* journalist Simon Reynolds was not a particularly cruel reviewer although he can understand why some of his colleagues were. He suggests: "There was a thing of doing a crushing review of a polarised thing, like you raving about things saying it's fantastic, going too far that way, and then going too far the other way. A lack of proportion. But it made for entertaining writing, I think. I suppose the thing with Talulah Gosh is they took it as far as anyone. If you didn't like the culture, then they were the most extreme example of it, and then there was a sort of meta element, you know, like 'The Day I Lost My Pastels' Badge'. I thought that was funny but some people would say that was insufferably cute."

PS: There's a withering review of Brighter's 'Around The World in Eighty Days' from *Melody Maker* that calls them a bunch of "lads". Which is a pity given Brighter was one of the few Sarah bands that actually *did* have a woman in, albeit not behind the microphone.

The Amelia Factor

"If you had to name a twee label at that time, everyone would say Sarah," says David Quantick. "I don't know who ran it, I can vaguely remember the names of some of the bands, but I've always remembered the name of a woman who was famous on it who had a very Sarah Records name, who had a very clear aesthetic: Amelia Fletcher. The name 'Amelia' to me sums up Sarah Records."

If we really want to boil down the problem the music press had with Sarah into just one word, it wouldn't be 'cutie' or 'twee' or 'anorak'. It would be 'Amelia'. Because, boy oh boy, the music press really had it in for Amelia and what they felt she represented. Of course, it's also worth remembering that Talulah Gosh were not on Sarah (although the label did put out a compilation of radio sessions in 1991), and Heavenly did not join Sarah until 1990, by which time the label had been going for three years. It's also worth pointing out that Heavenly had a higher profile than most other Sarah bands due to the attention Talulah Gosh and, therefore, Amelia had received a few years before. So maybe it's all being pinned on Amelia because she's the only one some of these people had heard of?

> If Amelia Fletcher had been the lead singer of Girlschool, I don't think her background would have been of any interest to anyone because she'd have just been a frightening heavy metal person whose background was irrelevant. But because it's indie…"
>
> **David Quantick, journalist**

In his review of the album *Le Jardin de Heavenly* for *Melody Maker*, Simon Price wrote: "Singer 'Amelia' (oh yeah, I *bet* that's her name)…" Almost 30 years later, he tells me: "Nobody was called Amelia where I grew up. Most people were called Karen. A lot of my writing, then and now, is informed by class. I come from nothing, so when I see people who've grown up with every advantage and privilege of the southern English bourgeois, and they're feigning underdog status for subculture reasons, it rankles with me, and that more than anything is what bothered me about that whole scene." But Amelia and co did not deny their backgrounds or their education. In fact, it's possibly their *refusal* to hide their backgrounds that is the real problem, if the journalists would only be so honest as to admit it. Because it was much more fashionable to come from nothing than to unashamedly own your privilege.

Simon also wrote in his review that Amelia "has spent her entire adult life pretending she doesn't menstruate. The rest of her band, too, look like the sort of fanzine autistics who still wear dungarees at 30." Which is pretty offensive on a number of levels. As Clare says: "It was extraordinary. Amelia was probably lecturing at Oxford University at the time, for fuck's sake." While Amelia tells me: "It fitted with the idea that songs should be about sex and our songs weren't." However, to underscore the fact it was all just performance, Simon says: "When I was handed that Heavenly album, I'm sure the reason they gave it to me was that I should give them a kicking, because whoever gave it to me would have known that I'd hate it. Some of what I wrote would have been calculated to impress certain people there. But a lot of that review I absolutely stand by." Although he does at least say that he would no longer use 'autistic' as a slur.

Let's go back to David Quantick, who had already mentioned his issues with Amelia several times in our conversation before saying this: "The real focus for rage, and I want to go back to this, is the name Amelia. [The name] seems to suggest a kind of upper-middle-class, public school, moneyed background. Class is such an issue but when you put all these things together… With indie you've got all these weird, vague notions on both sides of what is integrity and what is morality? And there's that

Amelia Fletcher performing with her band Heavenly at the Fleece & Firkin in Bristol (above, left). Amelia recalls of her image: "I didn't want to have to play sexy or angry or tough."
Left: Guy Sirman. Right: Karen Pudner.

whole 'You say you're independent but your parents are rich' thing."

Pete Paphides, a voice of reason who wrote for *Melody Maker*, says: "I felt like that aesthetic was wilfully misunderstood by people who just thought that these people that made these records were in denial of adulthood, that they lived in a Neverland of their own making and that they never wanted to grow up. And actually, hindsight has shown that to be patently untrue." Going on to talk about the extraordinarily number of high achievers from that scene, Pete muses: "How do you explain Amelia? Amelia is a genius in her field. You only need to see what a lot of those people have gone on to do, to know that it's where you really can't make those sorts of generalisations." And it's not just Professor Amelia Fletcher OBE and her Heavenly bandmates who have gone on to be high achievers, plenty of other Sarah folks have done very well for themselves. Off the top of my head: James Moody (The Orchids) is the Regional Manager for Consular Affairs in Northern Europe for the Foreign & Commonwealth Office; Mary Wyer (Even As We Speak) is a Nurse Educator for Biopreparedness; Gemma Malley (Blueboy) is an acclaimed best-selling novelist; and the list goes on.

Amelia also took umbrage at a slur aimed at a labelmate when a male band was dismissed as "effeminate". She says: "I think many journalists were as antagonistic to the non-macho and introspective nature of the music made by the male bands on Sarah, as they were to anything I ever did." She adds: "I can't remember what Sarah band it was but that led me to send a used Tampax to the journalist that had written the review. "I just got so cross that he somehow thought that effeminateness was a vile thing, so I thought I would send him a used Tampax to say, 'If you think

FUN FACT: At the time of writing, the name Amelia was recorded as the second most popular name given to baby girls in the UK. So she must be doing something right. Just think of all those new parents out there who want their daughters to grow up to be adored indie-pop stars and respected economics experts.

effeminateness is disgusting, here's something actually disgusting'. I don't know what was in my mind!"

It seemed only fair to invite Amelia to respond to the above comments by David Quantick and Simon Price and this is her reply: "My dad was born in East End poverty to Jewish parents who had escaped from Polish pogroms. They were keen to anglicise and fit in, so they changed their name from Fleischer to Fletcher and called their four sons Aubrey, Wallace, Reginald and Winston.

I think my dad was basically doing the same thing in calling me 'Amelia'. He thought if I had a posh name then I would fit in. It's a wonderful irony that the name in fact got me ostracised! My dad was successful in his chosen career [advertising], perhaps fearful that he would follow his own father to prison and penury, or his own mother to death by failed lobotomy to treat schizophrenia. So it is true that I was brought up fairly comfortably.

"That said, I will admit to being deliberately provocative in terms of holding onto a certain childlike quality within my image. I was keen to avoid slipping into the usual female stereotypes that fitted the expectations of male journalists and male fans about what women in pop should be like. I didn't want to have to play sexy or angry or tough. My favourite bands included women who were just themselves, from Clare Grogan to Dolly Mixture to The Marine Girls. I wanted to be a pop star like that.

"Later in Heavenly, my feminist outlook hardened with the emergence of Riot Grrrl. We didn't sound like an archetypal Riot Grrrl band but the lyrical content of our songs changed and we felt very much part of that movement. We played a ton of shows with Bratmobile, the band who actually invented the term 'Riot Grrrl' in their fanzine *Girl Germs*, and my brother Mathew was in Huggy Bear for their first few shows.

"I think it is worth remembering that there were quite a few journalists in the music press who positively liked both Heavenly and Sarah Records. We never felt we got our fair share of coverage but we did get some good reviews and features. For those journos that did have a problem with me, I'm sorry that other Sarah bands got tarnished with the 'Amelia' brush. It mainly indicates incredibly lazy journalism but I feel a bit bad about it retrospectively nonetheless."

Music journalists: What were they thinking?

"Sarah was the epitome of a certain thing taken to the extreme," says Simon Price, who wrote for *Melody Maker*. "You had all those C86 bands that came slightly before. But Sarah distilled it all down to such an extreme that if you wanted to have a go at that subculture, that's where you went to let rip and 'give it a kicking', to use the terminology at the time. So maybe that's why Sarah were disproportionately covered and loathed." He adds that the fact that Sarah had also emerged from fanzine culture would have rankled the music press, who would have been disdainful of the fact that something could have happened without their permission, to paraphrase Huggy Bear.

The *NME*'s David Quantick adds: "Sarah were a cartoon target, which is always easier to hit. I remember Swells [Steven Wells] saying to me, 'Oh, people go on about "Oh, that's an easy target", well good, that's what targets are for. Who wants a hard target?' It's much easier to attack a cartoon because they're well defined. If you have a go at Island Records, people don't get it, what's the joke? But if you say 'Sarah Records' people go, 'Oh yeah, running around in their print dresses, skipping through fields, drinking lemonade and having bun fights'." I suggest that labels like Creation and Factory also had a clear identity, but they didn't receive the same relentless bullying. David muses: "I suspect there's some truth in that. Although Factory used to get mocked for being Nazis because of Joy Division. And I hated Creation. But with Sarah, there probably was some misogyny involved because it appeared to be groups of women being twee. And that would be a factor in it."

Did the journalists ever stop to consider what it was like for the bands to read these hateful things about themselves? No. "We're talking to the reader," says David. "We see ourselves as a corrective against the lies of the music industry. And it would be hurtful to bands but then we thought, 'We don't care. They're in the *NME*, they sent us the records to do what we want with.' There were limits and I do maintain that the *NME* was a slightly more thoughtful place than possibly other places but we didn't think about the bands."

> ❝ *Melody Maker* had a culture of performative viciousness."
> **Simon Price, journalist**

Simon Price is brutally honest when he says: "In terms of being cruel and harsh, I'm not sure I regret that as much as you might think. As a critic, your first duty is not to the artist but the reader. You want to write something that's entertaining and makes them think about music in a way they didn't already, and I would say that your duty to the band is some way down the list." He continues: "I don't often feel bad about being harsh. Ultimately, records in those days were quite expensive. Quite a lot of your wages or your student grant would be taken up with gig tickets or records, so you wanted to tell people not to waste their time. I listened to *Le Jardin de Heavenly* yesterday and it didn't make me as angry as it did in 1992 but I still found it irritating and worthless."

Pete Paphides counters that given most music journalists are not in bands and can't even play an instrument, they probably have a spot of jealousy. "Being in a band looks like way more fun than being a music writer," he says. "So if you're in a band, I think from a music journalist perspective, why would any band care that much about what music journalists say about them? Sometimes when I slag things off, maybe, on a subconscious level, that's how I justify it to myself. I didn't really think I was capable of ruining anyone's day. I didn't think I was significant enough to have any sort of effect on the day of the musicians whose records I was reviewing."

Advertising

Given that the music press wasn't going to give fair coverage to the label, every so often Clare and Matt took matters into their own hands and paid for an advert. And while some of those adverts were along the traditional lines of announcing a band's new album or tour, others were more unusual. Most notably, the 1992 'Capitalism' advert and the famous 1995 'A Day for Destroying Things' advert. Although, true to form, Sarah didn't realise they were supposed to barter the cost down. "We'd ring up and say 'How much is it?' and they'd give us the rate-card fee, £2,500 for a half page or something, and we'd go 'OK' and send them a cheque for £2,500, not knowing nobody else does that," says Clare. "We spent an awful lot of money advertising in the music press because they weren't good at writing about us, so we paid for it instead. It was kind of a win-win for them."

The 'Capitalism' advert was published to mark five years of the label and was a quarter-page slamming all that was corporate and hateful about the mainstream music press with the word 'CAPITALISM' printed in, err, capitals, and concluded with the words "To come home each night smelling of bonfires" after inciting the reader to find the politics within themselves. Alison Cousens of Brighter says of the advert: "People define rock'n'roll behaviour as something anti-establishment or anti-authoritarian, and in that sense the very act of being on Sarah, you were hoping and aiming for it to be a bit anti-establishment. I remember being so proud, and Keris [Howard] saying that he was so proud that we were a part of that in however small a way. I wouldn't change that moment when we opened the music press and saw that."

The 'A Day for Destroying Things' advert was a half-page piece published in August 1995 to announce the closure of the label. Across a photograph of the Clifton Suspension Bridge, the fanzine-style advert returned to the theme of being so angry you must burn things. "Clare and Matt were remarkable in taking out hostile adverts in the press and calling it like it was," says Heavenly's Rob Pursey. Matt says: "One of the things I'm proudest of is the 'Day for Destroying Things' advert. I think that still stands up after all these years. And I still agree with everything we wrote in it."

The adverts were part of what Clare calls the "narrative" of Sarah, and supported the label's message that, despite what the music press said, this was a successful independent record label who could afford

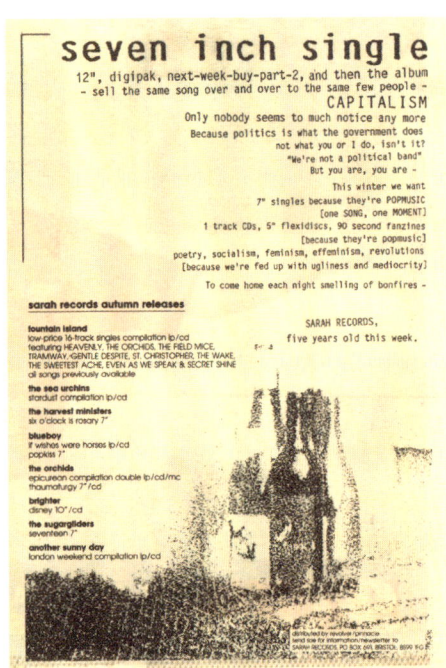

Sarah's famous music press advert marking their five-year anniversary.
Courtesy of Sarah Records.

THE POWER OF THE PRESS

The even more famous advert marking Clare and Matt's intention to close the label.
Courtesy of Sarah Records.

to take out expensive adverts. "It was a sort of 'fuck you', which didn't really work as we were giving them money," says Clare. "But fuck you, you won't write about us so we'll just pay for adverts because we can afford it because we're successful. I'm really pleased we did it at the end of the label because people just assumed we went bust, but of course labels that go bust don't take out big adverts to announce they're stopping. Record labels end by selling out to majors or starting to put out shit records that no one buys, or by going bust. Which is why we invented another way."

And another thing

At the end of our conversation, I ask David Quantick if he is surprised to learn that Sarah Records has become the subject of two books and a documentary film, given what an inconsequential and talentless scene he considers it to be: "It doesn't surprise me in a way because people take inspiration from things that have a strong image. And I think Sarah's impact, rightly or wrongly, is bigger than its actual success. I'm sure nobody on the label ever made any money." I interrupt David here to tell him that, at its height, Sarah Records was turning over £250,000 a year. "Bloody hell!" he exclaims, before laughing: "That's because they're all middle-class posh people. Only joking! I think it's good that it's had an impact. Because just as I've got my own version of what Sarah Records stands for, which is negative, an awful lot of people, like you, have got a positive image of what Sarah stands for and it becomes a touchstone." He adds: "It's weird because I know so little about what Sarah was or what it actually stood for, or if it did stand for anything at all. My views of it are based on a mental image but I cannot tell you where I got it from."

*****

THESE THINGS HAPPENED:
Anne Mari Davies, The Field Mice

"The band made me who I am in a lot of ways. Nobody can ever take that away from us. I remember when 'Missing the Moon' got really high in the indie charts, I thought that would always be the case and it was a really lovely feeling. I listened to 'Where'd You Learn to Kiss That Way?' again recently and there was song after song where I thought, 'No wonder people still listen to this' because Bobby's song writing is bloody brilliant. You take the music away and they look like a great piece of poetry. He's got a really unique way of writing music because he's not musically trained in any way, so he quite often shoves in a chord that you would totally not expect. I've talked to him at length about this, asking 'What made you put that chord there?' He just giggles and says 'I thought it sounded right.'"

CHAPTER 7

ON MY RADIO

It would be impossible to write a book celebrating an independent music scene without tipping our cap towards the legendary, much-loved and much-missed radio DJ John Peel (aka John Ravenscroft). Before YouTube, streaming services and downloading, it was hard to find new music. You might read about new artists in the music press or fanzines but you could only hear new artists if you took a chance and bought their records, or if Peel played them. "If you didn't get a review in one of the three music papers or played on John Peel, nobody knew your record existed," says Matt. Peel played music he honestly believed in, he wasn't swayed by trends, and this meant his listeners trusted him implicitly.

For bands, getting Peel to play your single was a landmark moment. For fanzine writers, having him expound the merits of your photocopied pages was a phenomenal boost. For listeners, meeting Peel at a gig was humbling. When he died suddenly following a heart attack in 2004, it was a collective time of sadness for music lovers everywhere. Do you remember where you were when you heard John Peel had died? Of course you do. I was working in a London newsroom when it flashed up on one of the massive TV monitors that streamed the global news 24/7. People stopped what they were doing to talk about how much they had loved Peel growing up.

It might be difficult for younger generations to appreciate how one man could have such a lasting influence on so many people and for so many decades. "He really was a crucial figure that's never been replaced," says Caesar of The Wake. "John Peel knew how to spot people who were doing it for the right reason. When we did the first Altered Images session, Jerry-the-manager took delight in telling me that John Peel says he doesn't even like a lot of the records he played. I think he meant he doesn't sit in judgement of them, as if to say 'I approve of this', but that he was looking at the spirit behind the records and why people were making them, and that's what he approved of. He knew that what was important in music was the spirit more than anything else."

> ❝ John Peel played 'Clearer' last night – it's out next Monday and I'm quite optimistic about it. For a long time I've been really scared about people's reactions and reviews but even the smallest positive thing like it being played on the Peel show fills me with hope (not that I listen to his show – someone rang me up)."
>
> **Letter from Keith Girdler, Blueboy, to Marcus Törncrantz, 30 September 1991**

Top and bottom: Even As We Speak having a great time recording their John Peel session at Maida Vale in 1993. The band would go on to record three sessions for the famous radio show.
Even As We Speak.

As a BBC employee, Peel was evidently taking the corporation's remit to inform, educate and entertain seriously. Via his late-night show on Radio 1 from 1975 to 2004, Peel brought together a nation of misfits who were huddled around radios in the dark hours listening to the eclectic mix of the often-bizarre records he would introduce them to. By the late 1980s, he was pulling in around 250,000 listeners each week. And by 1987, he was the only one left at Radio 1 who had been part of the initial pool of DJs when the station had started in 1967. By this stage, he was becoming so treasured by the nation that, in addition to his radio show, he also had a weekly column in *The Observer* newspaper, was writing articles for the BBC's weekly magazine *Radio Times*, and hosting a show on the World Service.

Australian band Even As We Speak were the Sarah group to benefit the most from Peel's patronage, with three sessions to their name. Speaking to Sydney's FBi radio in November 2012, guitarist Julian Knowles said: "He kind of occupied this role as the maverick show on what was, for the rest of the week, really kind of quite mainstream. It was very, very commercial. His view was that if he retired they wouldn't replace him with someone doing that kind of show. And he said he was the only BBC radio announcer on Radio 1 who was never told what to play ... He was quite a character and he was able to occupy this maverick position because he had discovered so many huge bands." Singer Mary Wyer adds: "He took people at face value, he took music at face value. He was very, very good to us.

Mary Wyer of Even As We Speak taking a break between recording tracks at Maida Vale in 1993.
Even As We Speak.

The time that we went to have lunch with him at Peel Acres, he showed us the room that had all these tapes in it and he had to listen to them all. He told us this story about how he had his car stolen once and there were two boxes of cassettes in the back of the car and even though he wanted to listen to everything he was kind of glad that they got stolen because that was two boxes less that he had to listen to. Because it took so much time, not because he didn't want to listen."

Peel had cut his radio teeth while working in the US for a few years, but it was on the North Sea where he really made a name for himself. Peel was one of the original pirate radio DJs, having established his show on the offshore Radio London station in March 1967. By September 1967, Radio London had been closed down and Peel took a job with the brand-new BBC Radio 1 station – and right from the off he could be relied upon to play a broad selection of music.

Heavenly's Rob Pursey explains: "John Peel was really important. But it wasn't about him as a character, it was about the fact that he kept this gateway open. It was a lifeline. For me, it was where I would have first heard bands like Josef K and The Fall. He famously loved The Fall and so did I." Bandmate Amelia Fletcher adds: "What people forget now, because he is so venerated, is that at least once every three years the BBC threatened to sack him because he didn't do what the BBC wanted. And every time, there was such an uproar among all the people that loved him that they kept giving up their attempt to sack him."

Almost all of the musicians interviewed for this book talked about Peel with such reverence, grateful for the education he gave them and the blessing he later bestowed on them by playing their records on his show. "I'd listened to Peel since I'd been about 16, usually on my own in my bedroom, so it meant a lot personally to be asked to do a session," says Rob Sekula of 14 Iced Bears. "John Peel had to be one of the most important people in UK, and ultimately world, culture in the 20th century through his discovery and endorsement of new music." While Bobby Wratten of The Field Mice says: "I was an incredibly loyal John Peel listener. I hardly ever missed a show after discovering him around Christmas 1979. One night I turned the radio on and a track from *London Calling* was being played. This piqued my interest as it was one of the records I'd got for Christmas. This was my first introduction to John Peel. I can honestly say that life was never the same again. The music I was exposed to, the records I bought, the ideas I was introduced to, his humour."

> ❝ It's good how these people seem to actually want to be independent of the independents."
> **John Peel, 17 March 1987 about Sha-La-La**

You would be hard pressed to find an independent music fan of a certain age who didn't spend their teenage years taping songs from Peel's two-hour show. Amelia Fletcher laments that as a teenager she would have to get up early for school, which meant that she was listening to Peel in the dark from her bed with one hand sticking out of the covers, ready to press 'record' at a moment's notice when an interesting song came on: "I often would wake up the next morning with my hand still on the 'record' button." Harvey Williams of Another Sunny Day was another one: "I've still got cassettes of Peel sessions upstairs. All those nights from 1985 through 1987, just listening to it every night and having your finger poised over the 'pause' button, waiting for the next song to come on and tape it and keep it. Knowing that song wouldn't exist anywhere else in that format. It was never going to be released on a single and it was only going to be broadcast once or twice, and you could listen back to it whenever you wanted." And Paul Stewart of Blueboy makes three: "I used to have a little transistor radio that I hid under my bed and I had an earpiece just in one ear. So I threaded the wire round the back of my bed and under my pillow and I could listen. So if my mum or dad would come in to check on me, I'd go 'Yeah, I'm asleep.' But I'd be listening to the Peel show."

Absolutely everyone was listening to the show by the time Sarah was in full flow, from bands to fans to the label itself. "You always needed to listen to John Peel because, if you missed it, there wasn't a way of finding out if he played your record or not," explains Clare. "David Gedge [The Wedding Present] used to stay with me quite a bit and it was funny the first time we listened together because we both stopped talking when Peel started talking. It's a habit we'd both formed over years of listening, knowing he might, and hoping he will, mention us. You didn't talk when John Peel was talking because, if you missed what he said, there was no way of finding out what you'd missed." However, Matt admits: "We'd sometimes put a tape on for the end of the show so we could go to bed." Which was very sensible. After all, these two needed to be up bright and early to greet the post person when they brought the next day's sack of letters and tapes.

Peel's show was about more than the records and sessions, though. It was also an education in a myriad of things. One of which, it turns out, was geography. Rob Pursey explains: "In my head, I've got this romantic version of what other parts of the country were like, so Manchester with this amazing landscape with Joy Division and The Fall walking about, and even East Anglia was exciting because there were people like The Farmer's Boys or The Higsons you might bump into. So you got this very strong sense of different parts of the country yielding different bands. You could hear the accents of the bands and he would tell you where they were from, and the labels were often from the towns where the bands were from. I remember when we first started touring and going to places like Norwich or Manchester or whatever, and thinking, 'Now I'm here, this is the place that I've heard songs about and from'. It was almost like my map of the British Isles was formed by the bands that I'd heard on Peel."

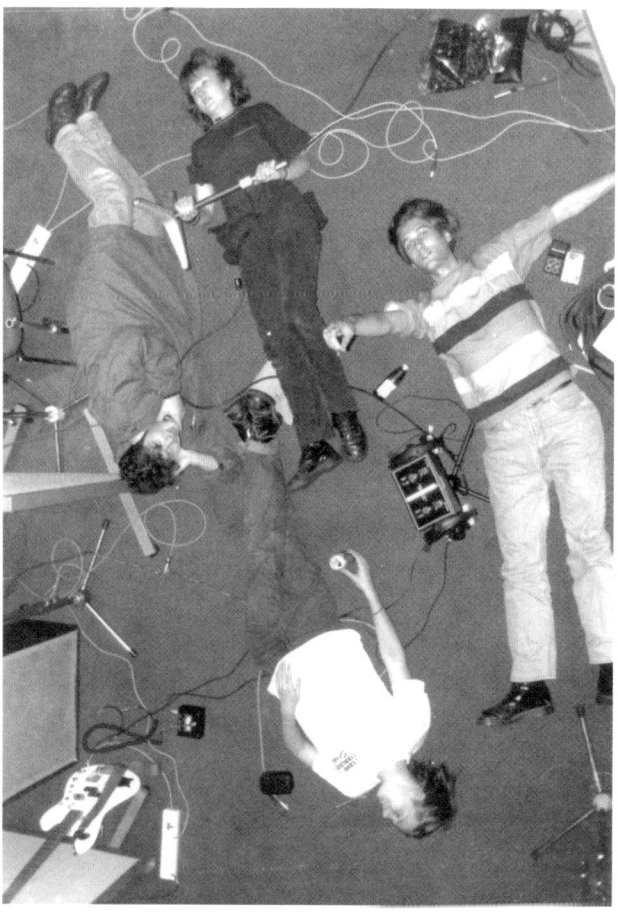

"Well done, lads, punk rock." John Peel gave the band Boyracer his seal of approval, which frontman Stewart Anderson still treasures.
Debbie Kaye.

More than that, Peel had a genuine love for the bands he supported and a complete lack of pretension. For instance, after a spell of hearing Half Man Half Biscuit on Peel's show, the band de jour was booked to play at Bristol's Tropic Club on 21 January 1986. It was the hottest ticket in town and the massively over-capacity crowd snaked down several roads in the insalubrious Stokes Croft area, with 300 unlucky people turned away at the door because there was no more room at the inn. Matt was one of the lucky ones in the top half of the queue who did manage to make it in, and while he was waiting he suddenly noticed that, about 20 places ahead of him, was none other than Peel: "He could obviously have said, 'I'm John Peel, I've been playing this band on my radio show' but he just queued up with everyone else and paid to go in. And I thought that was fantastic. How many other Radio 1 DJs would stand out in the queue?" Clare adds: "So many of us took a lot of our morality from people like him. He was just so self-deprecating and so decent."

Stewart Anderson of Boyracer had a similar experience with Peel when putting on some shows in Leeds during the BBC's Sound City week there in 1996. Just as they did for Sound City in Bristol in 1995, the BBC neglected to book any local bands to play, so it was down to people in the local music scene to organise some fringe events to promote home-grown talent. Stewart says: "Blur and bands like that were playing a big show but where were all the Leeds bands? None of the Leeds bands were booked." Which was how Stewart found himself organising three consecutive nights at the Pack Horse, "a pretty small, gritty northern venue, an upstairs room in a pub." Pulling up outside the venue, ready to set up and soundcheck, Stewart noticed a familiar face. And there was Peel, waiting on the pavement, eating a bag of chips. Peel came to all three shows at the Pack Horse and Stewart says: "I remember him saying 'I should be doing something with Radio 1 right now but I came to see you guys instead.' We played a Boyracer set, and we played 16 songs in 22 minutes, came off stage and John Peel said, 'Well done, lads, punk rock.' And that was the greatest compliment I've ever had in my life."

For fanzine writers

While he was a teenager, Marc Leverton, who would go on to manage The Sweetest Ache, was living in the wilds of Swansea. He recalls: "I used to listen to John Peel a lot. I remember him playing a Sha-La-La flexi and he said 'You can send £1 to Matt at the Garden Flat, 46 Upper Belgrave Road…' and that really stood out. I remember thinking I was going to get that'. It seemed very unusual that he was putting out someone's address on the radio. So I then bought that flexi and started writing to Matt." NB: if only Peel had told people to send £1 to Matt but instead Peel said the price was 12.5p. Oops.

Matt wasn't the only fanzine writer benefitting from Peel's benevolence. Clare had been introduced to Peel via her friend Rosie Cuckston, who would later be in Pram. Initially, Clare found Peel's musical choices "a bit weird" but, as time went on, she became as gripped with his show as almost everyone else in this book. "I must have listened more in the holidays because I remember loving 'Reel Around The Fountain' from the first Smiths Peel session, which was 1983, and being confused I couldn't buy the song, and going to the local record shop in Harrogate and trying to buy 'Teenage Kicks' and learning the sad reality that records got deleted. When we were about 15, Peel DJed at a school in Wetherby so we went and met him, which was very exciting."

By the time Clare was writing her fanzine *Kvatch*, she had become a dedicated listener of Peel's show. "He plugged a few issues of that, including the first one, which made a massive difference to mail order sales. The grown-up brother of a classmate sent off for it, surprised to find a fanzine from Harrogate and even more surprised to find I was doing Further Maths A Level with his sister."

Bristol-based *Smiths Indeed* fanzine editor Mark Taylor says: "Whenever John Peel would mention the fanzine on his show, about two days later a post van would arrive with a sack of mail. Literally. Not many people get bags of mail when they're 17. The weight of it was phenomenal because people were taping coins to bits of cardboard. I spent hours chiselling those coins off the cardboard."

Peel's fame and influence was worldwide. On a trip to Stockholm, he bought a copy of the Swedish fanzine *Grimsby Fishmarket* from a record shop... as the fanzine's co-editor Marcus Törncrantz was later told by the impressed record shop staff. "He did mention it on his show but it didn't lead to extra sales," rues Marcus.

For Bands

Peel favourite David Gedge tells me: "I think The Wedding Present were always destined to have become a 'Peel band', so I think it's more a case that I'd have been heartbroken if he hadn't liked us! Before we released our first single in 1985, we'd sent demos to record labels but had not received any positive results. We struggled to arrange concerts outside of our hometown of Leeds and, when we did, hardly anybody would turn up to watch. Once Peel had played 'Go Out And Get 'Em, Boy!' a few times, though, our world changed completely. People were suddenly contacting *us* offering shows and inviting us to be interviewed by the *NME* and stuff." David adds: "If I'm honest, though, I think he probably had too much power. It wasn't like today, where new bands have so many ways to promote themselves. In those days, if you had any kind of non-mainstream sound, Peel playing your record on BBC Radio 1 was basically your primary route to a wider audience and that meant international exposure, too. So he was a bit like Emperor Nero in the arena with the bands being the gladiators. If his thumb went up, you'd be taking the first step on the road to fame and possible fortune. If his thumb went down, you'd be fed to the lions."

> ❝ Having two entries in the Festive Fifty can never be taken away. It's one more than U2."
> **Bobby Wratten, The Field Mice**

Right from day one, Sarah Records had Peel's backing. Over eight years, he played all the Sarah singles on his show. Prior to signing with Sarah, Even As We Speak put out two singles, 'Goes So Slow' and 'Nothing Ever Happens', on Australian independent labels, which Peel picked up on. In Brighton, listeners Donna and Gordon heard him play them and contacted the band in Sydney to say: "John Peel's been playing your song, we think it would fit with Sarah Records, do you want us to act as your management to go to Sarah Records?" Singer Mary Wyer tells me: "We didn't know who Sarah Records were but we said 'That sounds exciting' and next minute we get a letter from Sarah Records saying 'We'd like to put out the 'Nothing

Ever Happens' compilation of those songs.'"

Sarah bands didn't cause too much trouble to Peel's annual Festive Fifty. However, The Field Mice made the grade twice: once in 1989 with 'Sensitive' and again in 1991 with 'Missing the Moon'. Talulah Gosh scraped in at No 50 in 1987 with their eponymous single, and Heavenly hit the heights of No 33 with 'Atta Girl' in 1993. "I remember 'Sensitive' coming on the Festive Fifty when I was back home in my childhood bedroom over Christmas one year and that being amazingly exciting," says Clare, proudly. Bobby Wratten adds: "I still remember hearing him read out the name 'The Field Mice' over 'Pickin' the Blues' [his theme tune] for the first time. It meant everything to me. I phoned Michael [Hiscock]. Clare phoned me. 'Sensitive' making the Festive Fifty was the icing on the cake. I'd grown up with the Festive Fifty. It was such an education."

Knowing they had Peel's attention and support, Clare and Matt would send him copies of their new releases with handwritten notes telling him, more often than not, that the record enclosed was one of the best records ever made. And Peel would read the note out before playing the record. Although there is an urban myth that he accidentally renamed Gentle Despite 'Genital Desperate', the band's Paul Gorton says it was really just 'Gentle Respite'. Which is a shame, because Genital Desperate sound like the sort of band that would have been invited in to record at least two Peel sessions. Speaking of which...

Peel sessions

A notable feature of Peel's shows were the sessions that he invited bands to record specially for him. Over the 37 years that Peel broadcast on the BBC, more than 4,000 Peel sessions were recorded by more than 2,000 artists. That's a phenomenal output. Until 1988, there had been restrictions on the amount of commercially available music that the BBC was permitted to play, which was why the corporation had been booking bands for specially recorded sessions since the mid-1960s. Typically, a band would be invited to the BBC's Maida Vale Studios in London, where a team of engineers would assist with recording four songs. Of course, other radio DJs were also booking in bands for sessions for their shows but it is the Peel sessions that were the most coveted by up-and-coming bands.

Back to David Gedge: "Even before The Wedding Present had formed, one of my main dreams had been to record a Peel session at Maida Vale and join that list of artists whom Peel had judged to be worthy. In the end, we did several, and I got to know the studio and the engineers and producers quite well. Because you had to record and mix four tracks in a day, a Peel session was kind of in between a normal recording session and a live recording. You essentially played live and, although you could do a couple of takes, you weren't able to spend hours getting

> " Come on! It was a dream come true. It was this thing that you would never expect to happen and it was happening. Three times!"
> **Harvey Williams, Another Sunny Day**

something exactly right. I think that gave Peel session versions more urgency than a normal studio recording."

Pete Momtchiloff recorded sessions with Talulah Gosh and Heavenly, as well as his post-Sarah bands. "For most of us, you'll never be in a studio like Maida Vale again," he says. "I remember, when we went there on one occasion, there was a big orchestra and choir in the big hall and then you'd go for your lunch, and the orchestra and whoever else was in there would all go to the canteen, too. So you really felt like you were in the heart of British musical culture. It could have been very intimidating but I don't remember it as being like that." While Caesar from The Wake says: "Maida Vale had really long corridors, where you thought, 'What's going on in that room?' There were thousands of rooms in that place. You'd open a door and there'd be some guy playing a violin with a dinner suit on, it was a really strange world." (Can I really be the only person who now has a mental image of the penguin in *Gregory's Girl* shuffling from room to room?)

There were several Sarah bands who would go on to record Peel sessions for the show during the label's lifetime:

BAND	RECORDED	BROADCAST
The Field Mice	1 April 1990	23 April 1990, 14 June 1990
The Orchids	8 April 1990	8 May 1990, 28 June 1990
Heavenly	17 March 1991	14 April 1991, 8 June 1991
Even As We Speak	9 Jan 1992	16 Feb 1992
Even As We Speak	31 Jan 1993	20 Feb 1993
Even As We Speak	18 July 1993	11 Oct 1993
The Orchids	24 Feb 1994	9 April 1994 11 March 1995
Heavenly	9 April 1994	7 May 1994, 5 Nov 1994
Boyracer	Date unknown	31 July 1994
Blueboy	Date unknown	30 Oct 1994

As previously mentioned, Even As We Speak benefitted the most from this good fortune of several lucrative sessions. "John Peel knew we needed money and he knew that the BBC sessions paid well," says the band's Julian Knowles, who told a Sydney radio station in 2012 that one session paid the equivalent of 10 gigs. "He made sure we had a steady supply of Peel sessions. We were pretty star struck. John Peel was someone [who] as a teenager I thought, 'Wow, this guy's at the centre of just about every piece of music that I love'. To Australians, if you were a music fan, you would know who he was." When I spoke with The Orchids, John Scally agreed that the session money was very helpful for a cash-strapped band: "It was one of the best

One of the most famous locations in musical recording history.
Jane Duffus.

paid things we've ever done. You get paid well because it's musician union rules, and because we had to travel so far we got paid accordingly. It was about £2,500 the first time and every time it got played we got royalties." Even As We Speak also recorded a session for Mark Goodier at BBC Radio 1 and, in 2014, released the joint sessions on their *Yellow Food* album.

Even As We Speak's singer Mary Wyer remembers: "You don't meet [Peel] at the Peel sessions, so the first time we met him was at the Phoenix Festival in 1993 when Paul [Clarke], Julian and I went there to give him the 'Blue Eyes Deceiving Me' single." Paul had managed to get backstage passes for the three of them and Mary explains: "We bumped into Courtney Love screaming at people around us, and we got to go into the mosh pit to see Hole play and all that sort of stuff. John Peel was DJing on the main stage between the bands so, between Sonic Youth and Julian Cope, he said, 'I just received the latest CD by a band who should have been playing here and I'm going to play it now'. We're standing there and nobody knows who we are, and we're looking around going, 'That's our song!'. That was pretty special."

Boyracer's bassist Nicola Hodgkinson also ran into Peel at a festival, this time at Reading. After spotting her wearing a Boyracer t-shirt, Peel commented, "Oh, Boyracer, excellent!" to which Nicola replied that she was in the band. So Peel promptly invited Nicola and her friend Justine Wolfenden of Hemiola Records into the pop-up studio to have a chat with him on air, while he played a test pressing of 'He Gets Me So Hard', which Nicola hadn't even heard herself at the time. The band's Stewart Anderson says: "One of the things I liked about John Peel was he would invest in so many tiny little indie bands, and knew all the tiny little details about them. He must have had such an encyclopaedic memory."

As a consequence of their meeting at the Phoenix Festival, Even As We Speak were invited to Peel's home for lunch. Julian recalls: "We were quite disarmed by his unpretentiousness and his charm. What was amazing was we were a little indie band from Australia on Sarah, and he felt warmly enough towards us to invite us to his house for lunch with his family. That was quite extraordinary. I look back on that now and just think, 'Wow'." There is a photo of Even As We Speak with Peel and his dog in the garden at Peel Acres and the band look rather forlorn in it. "We're in such scabby clothing. We look like we haven't washed," says Mary with horror. "Because we were sleeping on people's floors, we would sometimes have to go and have showers at the local pools. But I don't think we'd done it that day because we look pretty scabby!"

During the interview with Sydney's FBi radio in November 2012, Even As We Speak guitarist Matthew Love explained: "[Peel] really liked things that were different and unexpected, so the more out there we went, kind of the more he liked it. ... We'd get into the BBC and we were like kids in a candy shop. The BBC facilities have unlimited microphones, we'd get in there and say 'bring us this microphone and that microphone' and they'd dutifully go away and wheel in a timpani for us and then we said, 'oh, we'll need the piano'. We basically had the run of the place, it was really good, and then to add to that there was a music hire shop in London not far away where you could hire all sorts of weird things. We hired a 1970s' vocoder and all sorts of weird and wacky things, we'd just load up with the weird and wonderful and arrive at the studios and just have a go at it."

Clare and Matt only attended one of their bands' Peel sessions themselves, which, by law of averages, was an Even As We Speak one. "We just dropped in because we'd never been to a Peel session," says Clare. "I remember having lunch with Even As We Speak in the canteen. We were there so briefly. And they only get a day to do four songs, so we didn't really want to interrupt, but it was so exciting to get bands doing Peel sessions, and you get [Peel's producer] John Walters calling you up as well. And I suppose you don't realise that until you get a phone you're never going to get an offer to do a Peel session, because someone needs to speak to you to organise it." Which might explain why it took a while before the label scored any Peel sessions for its bands.

Harvey Williams also got to record three Peel sessions, one each with The Field Mice, Blueboy and Trembling Blue Stars, although the third was post-Sarah. Part of the magic of the Peel sessions for Harvey, both as a listener and a musician, was their ephemeral nature. Although some bands would later release their session tracks, most didn't, which meant that the specially recorded songs had an exclusive quality. For The Field Mice's session, four brand new songs were recorded that were not available anywhere else and never played live. "If the sessions are released, it does take the specialness out of it a little bit because it's quite nice to know that those songs only exist in that format on that broadcast," explains Harvey. "But these things have a habit of being there anyway. If you want to listen to The Field Mice session it's on YouTube but the point was to not have them to release, and the point should still be to not have them released. Bob was so prolific around that time. Songs were just pouring out of him and he had songs to spare. So he could afford to have these four songs which were just for that, and there were plenty more where they came from."

Anita Rayner of Even As We Speak behind the drums while recording at Maida Vale.
Even As We Speak.

Talking about the session, the band's Bobby Wratten explains: "It was incredibly exciting. We were maybe a little reckless with the opportunity it presented. We definitely didn't approach it with a careerist attitude. We were about to release a new record but didn't want to just re-record tracks from that. So [...] we decided we'd write material that would remain exclusive to the show. It was so special to us that we maybe lost sight of the fact that the next four songs you come up with aren't necessarily going to be your best. We wanted to make a statement. Then you add to this that, because the songs were brand new, I hadn't realised that a couple of them were in the wrong key for me. But, changing a melody here and speeding up a backing track there, we got through it. All this time later, the songs still crop up from time to time on BBC 6 Music, so the trauma of the day has been replaced by the fact that it's simply our Peel session. I'm still happy that we tried to do something different. I still like the fact that those songs have never been released elsewhere. We have been asked but it always feels like it would be a betrayal of our youthful idealism."

Anne Mari Davies adds: "Bobby wrote a lot of stuff, he was a very prolific songwriter. At some points he was churning out a song a day, and that's why we quite often played something live that we never played again or we'd never recorded or we might have played something two or three times and then it disappeared. He was always bringing new material to things. He didn't want to re-record anything that we'd already recorded or that was earmarked for being recorded, he wanted it to be special. He was never looking backwards."

But this wasn't an esoteric idea that Bobby dreamt up all on his own: he had unashamedly borrowed it from The Wake. That band's founder Caesar has recorded three Peel sessions in his career, two with Altered Images and one with The Wake, pre-Sarah. Talking about The Wake's Peel session, Caesar says: "We did three songs instead of four, which was unusual but our songs were pretty long and they were all songs that we never did anywhere else. That made a big impression on Bobby Wratten, who went on to do that as well for his Peel session. He did songs that were never recorded anywhere else and were only written and recorded for the session, and Bobby said that was a direct result of us doing that."

14 Iced Bears recorded two Peel sessions shortly before signing to Sarah. Frontman Rob Sekula explains: "Peel and producer John Walters said they liked our first single

Even As We Speak were famously invited to Peel Acres to have lunch with the man himself.
Even As We Speak.

'Inside' so were interested in us. It was great to be there and be working with someone like session-producer Dale Griffin from Mott the Hoople. He said he liked our song 'Cut' in the session, which felt amazing. The sessions only have four hours for the recording and mixing of four songs. But they definitely know what they're doing! When the songs came on the radio, they sounded totally professionally recorded. They obviously have great equipment, too. When the session was aired, Peel raved about each song, saying things like '14 Iced Bears, my kind of band' and 'I like these Iced Bears, all 14 of them!' You can imagine how that felt. Global recognition of our little band was just around the corner. Only it wasn't. But I'm forever grateful to him for the endorsement he gave."

The Bears' second Peel session was organised by the band's new manager, Sue Freeman. "I remember having to liaise with John Walters and that was one of the most nerve-wracking phone calls. I was living in a shared house in Brighton and it was a communal phone, and I remember having to call up Walters… and just to be calling this enigma who was one step away from Peel was quite a big deal and I had to build up to it. And he was like, 'Yeah, well I suppose it is about time we gave you guys another one, OK then.' So it was surprisingly easy in the end, but the build-up to calling was quite something."

Talulah Gosh's lone Peel session was broadcast on 11 January 1988. Bassist Chris Scott says: "If you'd told me when I was 15 that

> **“** I was in dreamland. It seemed like life was about to change in a big way."
>
> **Rob Sekula, 14 Iced Bears**

The Wake saw a Peel session as a good opportunity to experiment. This photo shows the band live at The Underworld in Camden in 1991, because they didn't think to photograph themselves in Maida Vale.
Wendy Stone.

I'd do a John Peel session by the time I was 25, I'd think 'Right, that's life sorted! That's my ambition done and dealt with!'" Frontwoman Amelia Fletcher adds: "Talulah Gosh were not competent when we first went there. We did a Janice Long session when we'd only been going about three months, even before the John Peel session, and we were so incompetent but somehow they managed to make a really good session out of it. It was incredible."

As Heavenly, Amelia and her bandmates would record two more sessions, and bassist Rob Pursey remembers: "The engineers there would do the session at incredible speed and skill. They're amazing guys. Every week, John Peel was sending them another bunch of sometimes really quite incompetent musicians to record a radio session and they would make a good thing out of it." Bandmate Cathy Rogers agrees: "It was a combination of all the best bits of being in Heavenly. It was like the wonder of being in Japan, plus that freedom and space of being in a recording studio, and feeling in just such incredibly competent, seasoned hands of experts, that you felt like whatever you did it was going to come out amazing. And a proper Hammond organ! I think it's the only time I've ever seen a Hammond organ in my life, let alone played one."

Radio sessions were a good place for bands to experiment, says The Wake's Caesar, because "you could hear what you were writing and playing live, and then hear it properly in a studio and it gave you a good idea of what stage you are at for a song." The quickfire, no-nonsense nature of the sessions also forced bands to focus their attention if they were to record four solid songs in just one day. "When you got a John Peel session you felt really excited," says Caesar. "But they were really well organised. It was all done very quickly. You had a producer and engineer from the BBC. You did four songs as quickly as you could, and they were technically so good as engineers that they could make it sound the way you wanted it to very quickly. A lot of people feel they did their best stuff in sessions. The more time you have to sit and navel gaze, the more you get wrapped up in the details of it. But there was no time for that."

Heavenly's Pete Momtchiloff picks up this thread: "Some bands found the sessions quite stressful and difficult. The BBC want to record the whole thing live, they don't want to do overdubs. The engineers will spend quite a lot of time, maybe a third of the whole session, just setting up and getting the sound right. So you get to lunchtime and you haven't really done anything. I think some bands get quite stressed out because they want you to play each song a couple of times and then they'll keep one of those and that's it. They'll overdub the main vocals but they don't really want to do any other overdubs. Even with bands who are not very technically competent, it almost always works really well because the engineers are so good, and because they understand how to work with bands who are not professional musicians. A lot of bands think they never sounded as good as they did in the radio sessions."

> Like the last bungalow in a terrace that developers urgently want to demolish to build a motorway, [Sarah Records] will hold out for as long as it can ... Only on a Peel show is it possible to hear the cherubic jingle-jangle of The Orchids in such close proximity to the calculated ultra-violence of Compton's Most Wanted."
>
> **David Cavanagh in his book** *Good Night & Good Riddance*

The Orchids did two Peel sessions, and when John Walters rang drummer Chris Quinn at his parents' house, Chris remembers thinking: "Is this somebody winding us up?" He explains: "I was a huge John Peel fan, I'd listened to John Peel for years while I was at school, so for his producer to ring up and say 'Can you do a session?' was incredible. Us from a scheme in Glasgow going down to record in the BBC studios with Dale Griffin, it was just bizarre." Bandmate John Scally says it took them a long time to decide which songs to do for the sessions because they wanted to do new songs as well as one or two that people would already know: "All I remember is being so nervous we tuned our guitar every bloody minute and Dale Griffin lost it with us, 'Your guitar's in tune! Leave it alone!'" He adds: "The BBC was intimidating. The studio was just sublime, it was beautiful. And we looked up on the wall and there was a plaque saying this was the last place that Bing Crosby had ever recorded in... and it was covered in wet toilet roll balls that had been thrown at it. But it was totally intimidating."

The band's second session was a little more relaxed because at least they knew what to expect this time around, and Ronnie Borland, who John credits as being "a calming influence," was now in the band. Although John adds: "We got on with it a bit more efficiently than we did the first time but it was still intimidating and nerve-

The Orchids' drummer Chris Quinn hangs out at Maida Vale during a recording session.
The Orchids.

wracking. You always walk away thinking you could have done better, it's like an exam."

Paul Stewart of Blueboy was overawed by the reality of going into the famous BBC studios in Maida Vale: "It's off the scale. It's another thing we never dreamed would happen. It was such a privilege." For the Blueboy set, the band did two acoustic songs and two electric songs. "We were very pleased with them," says Paul. "But as you listen to it, you can tell the vocals are really straining on the last one we did because we started at 10am and you're going through to 7pm and you can tell the difference between the performance." His bandmate Gemma Malley agrees that "it was a dream come true," even if her excitement wasn't shared by everyone. "I remember getting the phone call saying we had a Peel session and I was so excited. I was living at home and I went into the kitchen and said 'We've got a Peel session!' and there were these blank faces from my parents! You felt the sense of it being historic, it mattered. We weren't going to mess it up."

Although that didn't stop the band from being a bit cheeky. Paul remembers: "When we went in, they'd pointed to this drum kit in the corner and said, 'Don't touch that drum kit, it's just been set up for the Paul Weller band, so please don't go near it.' So our drummer Martin [Rose], who's a massive mod and Jam fan, went over and he just did this crazy thing, hitting all the drums on the kit." Martin laughs: "How could I resist? It was the chance of a lifetime." He adds: "I was living in West Kensington at the time and so I didn't have far to go to Maida Vale. I remember rocking up in my light-blue Nissan Micra thinking I was going to be mega famous because I was about to do a John Peel session. It's mind blowing going in there. I went off for a little wander and I went down this corridor, opened a door and saw this massive orchestra playing. I was just in awe."

Another one who was determined to enjoy every second was Stewart Anderson of Boyracer, who entered Maida Vale clutching a 24-pack of Heineken. "I don't know how he did this," says Stewart, "but John Peel called my mother. I was in Bristol recording with Tim Rippington, and my mum had given John Peel the studio number. So he called the studio and I remember Tim handing me the phone, and saying 'Hey, John Peel's on the phone.' And I was like, 'Yeah, sure he is.' And sure enough, it was him, and he invited us down to do a session for the show. I was definitely star struck. I met him a few times after that, and he was a very charming man."

Talking about the actual recording, Stewart says: "Dale Griffin was the producer, and he was telling us to take our time because our guitars were so out of tune. At the

While recording their second Peel session, The Orchids spend time in the engineering room.
The Orchids.

time, the recording wasn't as important as just being there. I definitely got a sense of some of the history of the room, just knowing that Queen, Joy Division, Nirvana recorded in here, these huge, huge bands. It clearly didn't go to my head in any way because I'm still talking about the 24 cans of Heineken we drank that day!" He adds: "When it was broadcast, we had a little party. And that was really validating. When you hear yourself on the radio for the first time, it's bizarre. You have that moment when you're hearing yourself how other people hear you."

Peel's general support

It was clear that John Peel had a soft spot for Sarah Records. From sending out birthday greetings to Clare via his show or reading out their Christmas card messages, Peel made time for the label. In a letter to Clare and Matt in 1989, Peel wrote: "Fight the good fight. I'm on your side really." Heavenly's Amelia Fletcher says: "He was really supportive of Sarah bands and Sarah as a label. Some of the music may not have been up his alley but the ethos was totally up his alley." Bandmate Rob Pursey adds: "I think he admired Clare and Matt. He had spent his life incurring hostility. When he first played reggae, famously, white rock fans were angry that this repetitive Black music was being played. And he played punk. He'd probably seen it all before. He'd seen interesting new music come up, which was quite often confronted by a lot of resistance by the rock music establishment, and he would play it. And also I think he was not fussed about production polish. So if your record was produced to

> We were being bullied and abused in the press but there was validation from John Peel."
>
> **Clare**

the sort of level that you could if you were a low-budget indie band, he would just listen through that to the song."

Clare confirms: "It meant everything to have John Peel's support. The fact that 'Pristine Christine' got played by John Peel and Janice Long, I think if that hadn't happened with that, the whole trajectory could have been different. I think we put out a brilliant first record but I also think we put out a brilliant last record and every record in the middle. So John Peel's consistent support all the way through, particularly in that phase where everything was either getting ignored or slagged off in the press, it just felt like you'd got an ally but you also got that publicity. I think there was something psychologically great about having John Peel's support as well."

Talking realistically, The Wake's Caesar says: "John Peel was just another DJ. He was a good DJ but he was just another DJ. But he was a guy you could get in touch with. When we were on Factory, we used to stand outside the BBC at midnight and wait for him to come out so we could give him our singles. He gave me a lift back to our hotel in London one night as he felt so sorry for us. He was a very nice man. By the time of the Sarah bands, John had become this special figure whose approval you sought. It says a lot about Matt and Clare that he really supported them."

When BBC Radio 1 brought its annual Sound City event to Bristol in April 1995, Peel interviewed Clare and Matt on air. This was in the run-up to Sarah 100, although at that time nobody knew the label would be closing. Peel told them: "Well, I hope you keep going. I take heart from your continued activities. I don't like everything that you put out, obviously it would be madness to claim that I did, but at the same time it always encourages me to know that you're throbbing away down here."

Peel was in Bristol for a number of days for Sound City and his activities included hosting a pop quiz at Watershed media centre with teams featuring Pulp, *The Guardian* and Radio 1. Pulp won, by the way. Poor old Peel had to entertain himself, though, after Clare and Matt unintentionally snubbed his advances for entertainment. "John Peel rang up to ask us what he should do while he was in Bristol, and we were really busy putting some records out or something, so I was like, 'Oh, you could look in the record shops on Gloucester Road'," says Clare. "And when we came off the phone, Matt said, 'I think he was looking for us to suggest we meet up'. But we were quite busy and we were just so shit at that sort of thing."

Peel also came along to the first Sarah Christmas party, which was in 1990 at the PowerHaus in Islington. He stayed long enough to listen to Heavenly, who cleverly played a song from Talulah Gosh's recently released Peel session while adding that they themselves had not yet had a Peel session. They got one soon after. Bassist Rob Pursey admits that meeting Peel at the bar that night was the only time he has ever been truly starstruck. "This person was the conduit for all things that were any good throughout all my young life, and I couldn't believe he was there," says Rob. "I couldn't think of anything to say to him. I was just like, 'Huh, thanks for coming'. And I shared this comment with a few other people who were in bands who'd also had John Peel come to their gigs, and I realised that John Peel spent his entire life being approached by shuffling incoherent idiots because nobody could ever think of anything to say. He probably never had a conversation with anyone because it was just all these people like me going 'Oh, hello' and then running away. Every night of his life."

He's on the phone

What comes up repeatedly is that John Peel spent a lot of time phoning people. "I remember him ringing up when we released *Shadow Factory*. I answered the phone one evening and he just said 'It's John Peel here', which is a slightly disconcerting thing to happen when you pick up your phone," says Matt. "And he was saying thank you for sending the album but saying we shouldn't criticise people as much as we do. I don't know if that was a reference to the notes on *Shadow Factory* because they were dedicated to 'our friends in the independent record industry without whom none of this would have been necessary'. But the fact he'd just rung up to say this to us was quite extraordinary." Clare adds: "He used to ring up occasionally when we were in Gwilliam Street. But we'd often have a bottle of wine on a Saturday night by that point, we were a bit better off and homeowners, and we'd call-screen and you'd think, 'I don't really know whether I want to pick up because I'm a little bit drunk and it's John Peel on the phone! Oh my god, it's John Peel on the phone!' So he would just ring up for a chat sometimes."

Proving what a different world the BBC was in the good old days, Tim Rippington says: "When I was in the Beatnik Filmstars, we used to just phone up the radio station late at night and you'd get through to a porter, because everybody else had gone home. You'd say, 'Can I speak to John Peel?' and he'd say, 'Hang on' and then put you through, and the next thing you knew you were either talking to him or John Walters. There was no BBC machine in the way to say, 'Oh no, you can't do that, he's a famous DJ.'"

25 October 2004

Of all the people interviewed for this book, none knew John Peel better than David Gedge of The Wedding Present, who recorded an astonishing 13 sessions. David recalls the sadness of hearing about Peel's sudden death:

"I still think about it all these years later. On the day his death was announced, I was in the village of Alfriston in Sussex and there was no mobile signal. As soon as we reached a more urban area my phone started beeping like crazy as dozens of voicemails arrived. 'Have you heard the news? Are you OK?' There were messages from news outlets like *The Guardian* asking me if I'd like to make a comment but I didn't call anyone back because I couldn't really speak about it. Later, we were invited to play at the Keeping It Peel tribute evening at Maida Vale. The concept was commendable, to celebrate the life of a man who had meant so much to everybody. But celebration and sorrow don't combine particularly well for me, and Peel's death had had a profoundly upsetting effect that had become even more intense the minute I'd re-entered the studios where I'd recorded so many sessions for his programme. The weirdness was amplified by the stress of having to prepare to play live on national radio! Just to even be in the same room as Damon Albarn, Polly Jean Harvey, Gorky's Zygotic Mynci as well as many old friends including Peel's family, Clare Wadd, Graham Coxon, Melys and assorted BBC acquaintances, all at the same time, was, quite simply, surreal.

"Our performance was anything but tranquil. For 10 intense minutes, I took out all of my misery and frustration on my poor guitar as we hammered our way through three songs, including 'The Queen Of Outer Space', which I dedicated to John's widow, Sheila. It was the strangest concert I've ever played and I was relieved when it was over. An excited friend of a friend came bounding up to me afterwards to tell me how much he'd enjoyed it and began firing off a volley of questions about the then newly resuscitated Wedding Present. But, unfortunately for him, I was in no mood for jovial chitchat, and I quickly wandered off to hang around sullenly, listening to the various tributes. Then Sheila appeared and we embraced for a long time. I remember thinking how small and frail she felt in my arms."

Janice Long / Evening Session

Of course, John Peel wasn't the only influential DJ at BBC Radio 1 who could help a new independent band. David Jensen, who was unable to shake off his 1970s' nickname 'Kid', had been with the station since 1976 and remained there until 1984, hosting the evening show and having regular sessions recorded for it. Janice Long joined Radio 1 in 1982 as the first woman with her own daily show (the initial 15 years of the station had been almost exclusively male) and, between 1984 and 1987, she hosted the Janice Long Show in the early evenings to profile new music and current affairs. In this way, she was able to get up-and-coming bands in to record sessions. Janice also went on to be the first female presenter of *Top of The Pops* in 1983, which had been a boys' own club for its first 19 years, and she remained the only female presenter in that particular boys' brigade for the following five years. Janice was also the lone woman presenter during the BBC's extensive coverage of Live Aid in 1985. The BBC evidently had something of a problem with women, as demonstrated by the fact that the Corporation sacked Janice in 1987 because, gasp, she became pregnant while unmarried.

"I think Janice does get a bit overlooked next to the giant figure that was Peel but there's no denying that her support was also invaluable," says David Gedge. "I think she brought, shall we say, the less *extreme* alternative bands to a different audience than Peel's but, like John was, she's a genuine fan of music as opposed to just wanting to hear herself talk on the radio."

The BMX Bandits recorded two Janice Long sessions, one each in 1986 and 1987. Prior to one session, the Bandits' debut single, 'E102', caused such a consternation when it was played on Janice's singles review show that she ended up spending more than 20 minutes trying to convince her guests Neil Tennant and Nick Heyward that it wasn't "absolutely awful." Chief Bandit Duglas T Stewart feels there was some rivalry between Janice and Peel: "Janice has this theory, and I can imagine it being true, that she got to BMX Bandits first and so his nose was slightly out of joint by that. Janice liked John a lot but she'd say, sometimes, she felt if she got a record first, just by a fluke the postman delivered to her first, John would not be interested."

Musing on why Janice might keep being excluded from the story of independent music, Duglas says: "In those years 1985 to 1987, I think for an awful lot of the bands she was the person who really supported them. I sometimes wonder if part of the reason Janice's support of an awful lot of bands of that era isn't documented so well is partly because she's a woman. But I don't think that's the whole thing. John Peel's this historical man and his contribution is massive but I do think part of it is the way people were trained by culture at that time, cultural norms and gender norms, so their perception would be swayed by that. I do think that Janice doesn't really get the credit that she's due for her contribution to supporting a lot of that music."

I had been trying to line up an interview with Janice for this book but unfortunately this coincided with a decline in her health and Janice sadly died in December 2021. I asked Simon Barber of The Chesterfields about his reaction to her death, given how supportive Janice had been of his band: "I think people totally believed that every record played on her show she loved and had chosen it herself. The same as Peel. In a way that no other radio show was that. You just felt that she squeezed as much in that she loved into every show and believed in us all," says Simon, whose band recorded two sessions for her. "It just felt brilliant to get the sessions. It was like an endorsement. Going to Maida Vale and recording a BBC session with the drummer from Mott the Hoople?! We thought we'd made it! We were getting all that airplay on Radio 1 in the evening from someone who obviously loved us. It was a brilliant experience."

Simon continues: "I was gutted when Janice died. We were about to receive some test pressings of our new album and I wanted to send her one as she was always interested. When Davey [Goldsworthy, singer] died [in 2003], she got in touch and asked me to pass on her condolences to Davey's family, which was such an amazing thing to do. Davey's mum knew who Janice Long was and she was really appreciative." He adds: "Janice was the one, more than the label or anyone else who was involved, who gave us a career. I don't know what would have happened without her. She just helped propel The Chesterfields beyond what we were expecting."

The mid-week evening show would continue to provide a space for bands to record sessions. For instance, Ivy benefitted from the patronage of Jo Whiley and Steve Lamacq on their evening show, which picked up the original version of 'Wish You Would' when it was first released on a Noisebox compilation EP. This led to Ivy being invited to Maida Vale to record a four-song session for the Evening Session that aired in January 1994. "It all happened so quickly that we didn't really get a chance to take it in," says guitarist Julian Cator. "One minute you've done a gig with a drum machine at a local venue and, within nine months, we had a session on the Evening Session. It was a real blur." Blur recorded two Peel sessions, by the way.

Peel picked up on Ivy after they had been on the Evening Session and he was so enamoured that he got hold of singer Spencer Harrison's phone number. "Jo Whiley was playing the record so much and saying how much she loved us and couldn't wait to see us," Spencer says. "John Peel then started playing 'Wish You Would'. He really liked us and he called me twice. The first time, my mum was visiting and picked up the phone. She had no idea who it was and said, 'A man wants to speak to you' and I took the phone. Then he said, 'It's John Peel here.' And I was going to my mum [mimes hand over mouthpiece, excitedly pointing at phone] 'It's John Peel! It's John Peel!' and she had no idea who it was or why I was so excited. I wish I could tell you what we chatted about but I know that he was quite looking forward to seeing the band. Although he never did come."

At BBC Scotland, The Orchids recorded a live session for Peter Easton of Rock On Scotland, a show which promoted underground Scottish music. Although backing singer Pauline Hynds Bari wasn't able to make it to London to record the Peel sessions because of her commitments to her children, she was able to join the BBC Scotland session and took her daughter with her. "I think that was the only radio show that I did, because every time they were doing something I always had a baby with me," says Pauline. Most of the artists involved with Sarah were not yet at the stage of life where they had children of their own to consider and, given the majority of the musicians on Sarah were male, would likely have had wives or girlfriends to take charge of the childcare for them anyway. But Pauline's example highlights one of the difficulties of being a parent and an aspiring pop star when you don't have the budget for nannies. It makes it much harder to go away on tour, for one thing. Pauline was invited to join The Orchids for a gig in Paris but she was reluctant to leave her new baby at home and, even though the band was encouraging her to bring the child with her, she decided it would be too complicated and missed the show. "I was too caught up with my family to gig with them much at the time," says Pauline. "When the finished records came, I'd think 'I'm going to keep this and pass it on to the kids when they're older'. So my whole life at that time was about the babies."

Welsh band The Sweetest Ache have beautiful memories of hearing themselves on the radio.
Courtesy of The Sweetest Ache.

WE'RE ON THE RADIO!

"It was great to hear your band on the radio, everyone will say that," states Pete Momtchiloff of Heavenly. Matt adds: "It impressed my mum as well, because she knew who John Peel was. And later on, she'd listen to him on Radio 4. So, to her, that was impressive. It was the real world, it was a world she understood, BBC radio." Kenny Forte of The Golden Dawn agrees that Peel had the parental nod of approval: "John Peel played us at one point and even my dad recorded that. It was good to be played on John Peel. Even though I wasn't a great fan of his programme, I really liked the guy. He was *the* person for cutting edge music, so to get played by him we knew we'd made it and were going to be big!"

Sian Allen Huntley of The Rosaries says excitedly: "I do remember John Peel playing the single and he played it at the wrong speed. We were all so excited and he did his usual grumpy comment but we were so chuffed about that. For me, being played on John Peel was the best thing ever."

Lee Christopher of Action Painting! adds: "I first heard us on the radio on the car stereo of a white VW Polo … Jo Whiley could clearly be heard sniggering disdainfully every time Steve Lamacq played a track from our three-song EP. We didn't care, we were all over the airwaves, like proper bands. When I left home, I had told my father the next time he would see me would be on *Top Of The*

> ❝ I remember the first time I heard 'Pristine Christine' played on John Peel. I was having a bath and jumped out excitedly to tell Bridget."
>
> **Robert Cooksey, The Sea Urchins**

Pops. Getting there, I thought."

And sometimes the whole thing was just magical. "Hearing your tracks on the radio meant everything," agrees Stuart Vincent of The Sweetest Ache. "John Peel played us quite a few times. We'd been to Bristol to see Galaxie 500 play [at The Bierkeller, 7 February 1990], and we were driving back down the M4 with John Peel on the radio, and I remember him saying 'This is the new single from The Sweetest Ache on Sarah Records'. And that moment was just fantastic." Stuart describes the scene: "We sat there in silence, all four of us just listening to the track, which I'd heard 1,000 times before but it was the fact it was on the radio, it sounded slightly different, it was more exciting on the radio, it had a different warmth to it. And listening to that and thinking, 'Wow, that's just fantastic'. The song was 'Tell Me How it Feels' and it was dark and late, it just fitted the moment really nicely. I couldn't have asked for a better moment to hear it back, with three great friends, coming back from a great gig, dark, probably raining. Such a simple thing meant so much."

> " To this day, hearing one of my records on the radio is still something I can't quite get my head around. It never ceases to be special or a thrill. I guess that may be because it remains a bit of a rarity."
> **Bobby Wratten, The Field Mice**

Even As We Speak also enjoyed their fair share of daytime airplay on Radio 1 when one of their songs made it onto the playlist. "You're driving along at 10am and 'Falling Down The Stairs' would come on Radio 1, and you'd think 'Woah,'" says the band's guitarist Julian Knowles. Although the irony wasn't lost on him that while his band could make the daytime playlist of one of the UK's biggest national radio stations, local stations in their home country wouldn't touch them.

Sarah stars in your eyes

With all this talk of the wireless, you would be forgiven for thinking I had forgotten the magical glowing box in the corner of your living rooms. Well, fret not because here's a run through of Sarah stars on the telly.

From as early as their second single, the existence of Sarah was bothering the small screen. On 12 February 1988, for a whole six seconds, a photo of The Orchids was displayed on Channel 4's *The Chart Show* to acknowledge the band's new single 'I've Got A Habit'. "The words 'THE ORCHIDS' were splashed into a million homes," wrote Matt to drummer Chris Quinn a few days later. "I know it's not much but it is television. Hope you saw it. I was excited!!!"

As a rule, *Top of the Pops* was never troubled by anybody from Sarah, given that the records never made their way into the mainstream Top 40. Except… hang on, look again at the time bubble gum pop punks Shampoo graced the studio stage in July 1994 for their performance of 'Trouble'. Who's that miming on guitar? Why, it's Lee Christopher from Action Painting! and I invite you to watch the clip on YouTube because he really does look great. Lee explains: "Shampoo released 'Trouble' in the beginning of 1994. It became a proper smash hit record the world over. Now, instead of playing the Free Butt [a pub in Brighton], I began miming on *Smash Hits* tours, miming on *Top Of The Pops* (fuck you, Dad, I told you) sitting in hotel lobbies despairing as Boyzone constantly practiced their scales and East 17 prowled around like kings."

Over on Channel 4, Heavenly's Amelia Fletcher famously sang backing vocals when Huggy Bear performed 'Her Jazz' on *The Word*, and for the full story on that I suggest you turn to Chapter 16. But if you're desperate for more stories about Amelia on the telly right this second, don't worry. In 1993, in an early episode of ITV police drama *Inspector Morse*, who is that you can spot cycling down a street in the background of the scene? Yes, that's right! It's indie-pop queen Amelia. Biff! "And you need to watch on in the same episode because Rob [Pursey] is in it, too. Staring through a café window," says Amelia. Bang! And the indie stars of *Morse* don't stop there because: "A further indie fact is that the guy I am talking to, before I get on the bike, is the brother of Steve Queralt from Ride." Pow! As a bonus piece of indie-pop telly trivia, Rob Pursey was the script editor of two episodes of *Morse* towards the end of the hit show's run.

Oh, and don't forget that Heavenly's Cathy Rogers had a glamorous career post-Sarah on both sides of the Atlantic due to being the creator and presenter of *Scrapheap Challenge*, or *Junkyard Wars* as our American friends called it. 🍒

*****

THESE THINGS HAPPENED:
Julian Knowles, Even As We Speak
"There was no business plan but what's really interesting is clearly John Peel respected Clare and Matt and there's a lot of handwritten correspondence between them. So they were actually pretty well connected into some of the major players in the scene. I'm sure there would have been a lot of other indie labels that would have been chomping at the bit to have the sort of warm relationship with John Peel that Matt and Clare had. And that did more for us than any business plan might have done, quite frankly. That's the reality. Sarah was interesting because it created a space for the outsider. It seemed to me that Sarah was a magnet for people who felt outside of something else and it gave them a home. We were outsiders, too, so we were in that home."

Chapter 8
Fashion

In his *Dream Inspires* fanzine, Chris Tighe asked Pete Momtchiloff of Heavenly if he thought the band had encouraged stick with "the anorak thing", to which Pete replied: "We certainly hope we have. If there's one thing we are 100% in favour of in the music biz, it is stick. Incidentally, we are now prepared to reveal that 'anorak' is a code word for LSD."

Sarah 3 was a 5¾" inch flexi disc by Another Sunny Day called 'Anorak City'. The song was a 138-second blast against the post-C86 scene that adorned itself in anoraks, flowery skirts, tea dresses and bowl haircuts, and added handclaps and fuzzy guitars to every song. The flexi vowed to self-destruct after a mere six plays, although my copy is still going strong several decades later. Throwaway pop is less disposable than it used to be.

Another Sunny Day was the band name for Harvey Williams, a man who cemented his status as an integral part of the Sarah Records story back in the Sha-La-La days, when he became pen pals with Matt and used to pop up to Bristol from Penzance to go to the EEC Punk Rock Mountain (which will be properly explored in Chapter 14). With 'Anorak City', Harvey

> ❝ I wear my anorak with pride because I haven't given in, because I've got better things to spend my money on than a new coat before this one wears out."
> **Clare, *Lemonade*, 1989**

unintentionally wrote the anthem for his generation. "I wasn't necessarily poking fun at it," says Harvey in response to my suggestion that the song could perhaps be catalogued alongside The Pooh Sticks' 'On Tape' or 'I Know Someone Who Knows Someone Who Knows Alan McGee Quite Well'. He explains that by the time he wrote 'Anorak City' he had moved to London and was going to as many gigs as he could. He saw an article in *Record Mirror* about what was termed the 'cutie scene', prompting Harvey to think: "So this is a genre now? It's a movement? And I thought, do you want to be part of a movement or do you want to not be part of a movement? And it was that ambivalence that led to that song. Although I probably thought about it more just then than I did when I was actually writing that song. It was nice that I could get the joke in before anyone else did."

The *Record Mirror* article that Harvey mentions is hilarious. A lazy attempt to

Harvey Williams makes his way around Anorak City. (Not really. He's quite clearly pictured in London.)
Grimsby Fishmarket, Nicklas Brunzell.

find a bandwagon and jump on it, the feature includes a handy guide to what bands you should be listening to (The Shop Assistants! Primal Scream! Orange Juice!), what you should be carrying (Sweets! Colouring books! Crayons!) and a quiz to help you decide if you are in the 'cutie contingent'. It was just one step short of providing a telephone helpline for those who achieved a positive score. Although there was also a whiff of truth about it: after all, Stephen Pastel *did* wear a Tufty Club badge, The Soup Dragons *were* named after characters in a 1970s' kids' show, and the women in Talulah Gosh *did* wear bright, childlike clothing.

'Anorak City' was initially submitted to Matt for consideration for Sha-La-La in the summer of 1987. In a letter to the label's Pete Williams, Matt initially deemed 'Anorak City' to be "unreleasable". He wrote to Pete: "I think it's a joke but even if it is a joke, there's fairly obviously no way we can release a song called 'Anorak City'! Maybe if they changed the title..." A short time later, Matt had changed his tune and was contemplating putting 'Anorak City' out as a one-track 5" flexi with the final issue of *Are You Scared To Get Happy?*, writing to Pete that: "We've picked up so much of the anti-anorak/cutie flak, the perversity of releasing ANORAK CITY appeals. And of course it is an anti-anorak song itself... and if people miss the irony, well, the joke's on them. It's also a perfect flexi song, and the idea of putting it alone on the smallest possible flexi – the EXTREMITY, the symbolism, a final two fingers to the record industry, APPEALS."

> ❝ *What do you make of the twee reputation that Sarah has acquired?* "It's completely unfounded in that they're not twee but at the same time they're cantankerous and they love to annoy people. They haven't made any attempt to get rid of it."
>
> **Amelia Fletcher, Heavenly, in my fanzine** *Arketino*, **1994**

What is also interesting is that Matt is also telling Pete about Sarah Records in this letter ("the 'PROPER' record-label set up by me and Clare, with debut release an EP, available on 7" only, of course, by The Sea Urchins"). He was finishing off his fanzine and Sha-La-La while he and Clare were still dreaming up their vision for Sarah, so this was an intensely creative and exciting time for Clare and Matt.

By early 1986, John Peel was also talking about the 'cutie scene' on his Radio 1 show, having had The Soup Dragons in to record their first session for him that March. In his book *Good Night & Good Riddance*, David Cavanagh comments on how much Peel liked bands such as The Soup Dragons and The Pastels, having long been a fan of precursors such as Orange Juice and Fire Engines. Scottish indie-pop was clearly on Peel's list of likes and he would become a great supporter of the scene and its bands via his show.

Duglas T Stewart of the BMX Bandits observes: "Sarah and Sha-La-La almost embraced the thing of twee. And then Kurt Cobain would be going on about twee. It was a thing to be celebrated. But when it initially came about, it was used as an insult. It would be journalists and rock fans saying it. A slightly younger generation of musicians came along and said, 'We want to be twee'. Not that they wanted to act in an exaggerated, fey way but they wanted to associate themselves with something that they liked and connected with. But for Stephen Pastel, he was like 'We're not twee, don't call us that. We're not children playing at this.' It's a bit like punk. Punk was initially an insult but then everyone was like, 'Yeah, I'm going to be a punk.' What? You want to be this thing that's derogatory? For some people it was a contrivance but for some people it was an expression. In some ways it was probably a reaction to that overtly sexualised image of women in pop. So some of the things they liked culturally would be films with people like Rita Tushingham and Hayley Mills, and they looked at the way these people were dressed and thought, 'Oh, I like them so I want to dress a bit more like them.' But you're always going to get some people who don't really have their own style and it's almost like a misunderstanding, so 'I need to get an anorak if I'm going to go to this club' rather than thinking 'I think I'll wear this jacket, this would be quite good'. If you went to a punk rock gig in 1976, not everybody was having safety pins through their nose and big massive mohicans. But eventually, they went, 'If I'm a punk rocker, I'd better have a safety pin, I've got to have bondage trousers.'"

> ❝ It was weedy men in specs wearing macho-ish clothes that make them look un-macho. And girls looking androgynous in ill-fitting anoraks and, not deliberately un-sexy, but anti-sexy clothing. Well, that's how it looked to me."
>
> **Rob Pursey, Heavenly**

There were a lot of anoraks to be found at Sarah gigs. There was even a German fanzine run by Peter Hahndorf called *Anorak: Can I Just Say Sweatshirt*, established in 1988 and taking its name from a Pooh Sticks' lyric. Heavenly's Amelia Fletcher once bought an anorak for her super-cool American friend Calvin Johnson of Beat Happening and laughs that "he tried to wear it for a bit to be polite" but, well, it wasn't really him.

When Clare left her jacket attended, anorak-denier Julian Knowles jumped at the chance to try it on for size.
Even As We Speak.

"Anoraks became the cool item of clothing to wear, to us anyway, for a while around '85, '86, due in no small part to the influence of Scottish bands such as The Pastels and Primal Scream whose early records we loved," says Robert Cooksey, guitarist with The Sea Urchins. "I seem to remember we all had an anorak by 1986, mine being an exquisite autumnal colours number."

But the anorak was a trend that not everyone bought in to. Before Heavenly, Rob Pursey was briefly the bassist in Talulah Gosh. "The fact that women were at the front of the band and it was a woman-driven band felt good, I liked that," he says. "But I just couldn't quite face wearing an anorak at the time. I was an anorak refusenik."

And Rob wasn't the only one. "We weren't English, we didn't wear anoraks, we weren't part of that whole fey thing. We were Australians," insists Julian Knowles of Even As We Speak. "The focal point of that English Sarah culture was the anorak for us. Coming to it from Australia, we'd come out of a scene that wasn't really anything like that. Mary [Wyer] and I argued about this the other day because she said Matt [Love] had an anorak." Mary interrupts insistently: "We both did, Matt and I!" Julian is shocked: "You had an anorak?! I never had an anorak. The anorak was the symbol of the Sarah fan and as Australians we used to talk about them as The Anoraks." After a beat, Mary says: "We were going to call our album *Anorak-nophobia*." But as much as Julian may have been an anorak abstainer, there was at least one time he was persuaded into one. "There is a funny picture of one time when Clare came to see us. She was backstage and she'd left her anorak behind and it was a beautiful anorak," he says. Perhaps Julian doth protest too much about his hatred for the aforementioned waterproof jacket?

The Sixties look

The opposite of "self-consciously dressing up like you're in a fucking Ladybird book," as Rob Pursey puts it, was self-consciously dressing up like you were in a 1960s' West Coast rawk band. Skinny leather trousers, winklepickers, jet black hair, that kind of thing. And a few of the early Sarah bands definitely fell into that category.

Just look at The Sea Urchins, who embraced the leather trousers look to the amusement of the less sartorially savvy Orchids, as drummer Chris Quinn says: "It seemed to be that fashion was more important to them than the music almost and we found that strange as we were totally the opposite of that." The Orchids managed to turn the tables, though,

❝ The more cravats and eyeliner the better."
James Roberts, The Sea Urchins

"This photo with Trish from Broadcast was taken in Brighton in late 1987/early 1988 at a Sea Urchins show. I distinctly remember wearing the arran polo neck to this gig as it was cold. Trish told me many years later that we had inspired her quite a lot which was nice to hear. Captain Sensible also showed up at this show and offered us to be on his Deltic label," says Robert Cooksey of The Sea Urchins.
Courtesy of Robert Cooksey.

when they invited The Sea Urchins north of the border for some gigs in Scotland. "We did make them play football against us once, that was funny. We forced them to play football in Glasgow. We beat them easily," says Chris proudly. While guitarist John Scally notes: "We got them some shorts and things but we couldn't get them football shoes to wear, so they were playing in shorts and their mop tops and winklepickers. Trying to kick a ball. So it was quite funny."

Robert Cooksey remarks on how The Sea Urchins' fashion muse changed over the years: "By 1987, the influence of contemporary bands started to wane and from there on it was pretty much all '60s rock that we listened to and '60s fashions that we wore. Simon [Woodcock], James [Roberts] and I had flirted with '60s fashions since 1983 while still at school, wearing paisley and polka dot shirts, and de rigeur Beatle boots. By 1987, we were all wearing '60s fashions and starting to look very dandy. Cravats, Beatle boots, purple polo necks, corduroy trousers, leather jackets, white Levi's were all worn by us regularly. Two of my favourite items of clothing were an original orange paisley Mr Fish shirt and a purple Jon Wood button-down shirt. Darren [Martin] favoured a fetching suede fringed cape with cowboy hat which gave off a cool West Coast vibe. Bridget [Duffy] had been wearing '60s fashions for quite some

> Let's do the timewarp yet again... The Sea Urchins display idiosyncratic variations on the Sixties period costume that's inescapable in the indie world – they sport crazy cravats and extravagant sideburns. In their music, too, they grave rob imaginatively."
>
> **Dave Jennings reviews The Sea Urchins at The Deptford Fountain, 1990**

"This was taken at St Phillips Cathedral in central Birmingham, 1990. I'm wearing a green Nehru collar suit that I picked up in a charity shop in Walsall and wore quite a bit at the time. It was very cool and I still have it," says Robert Cooksey of The Sea Urchins, who is pictured on the right.
Courtesy of Robert Cooksey.

time, influencing us heavily." He adds: "Both James and I had clothes tailored for us during this period as well. I had a white silk satin shirt made that was styled on a shirt that Jimi Hendrix wore in 1967 that I wore to many shows. I also had a pair of black bootcut trousers made that I wore a lot, often with a black polo neck jumper, black boots and suede jacket that was very Beatles. My absolute favourite outfit, however, was a green '60s suit with Nehru collar, which I miraculously found in a charity shop."

Bridget Duffy remembers seeing Robert and James at a gig at Birmingham's Mermaid before she had joined The Sea Urchins. When they walked past, she said to her friend: "Check them out, they think they're in the Mary Chain!" Her diary notes that she curtly told the boys: "Try harder." James Roberts says: "Bridget and Robert were the main movers and shakers on the fashion front, they influenced how the rest of us went along, they were the cool ones. Musically we did quickly go down the obscure 1960s rabbit warren and that was reflected in what we wore. When we started on Sarah it was the old anorak thing but very quickly we were poncing around in cravats and all the rest of it, we were just into that psychedelic 1960s look and music. We had a period when we were all dressed head to toe in complete white, which was a reference to John's Children. It was important to us but, when you're a kid, clothes are a reflection of who you are and how you perceive yourself. It's a showy thing and we had that peacock-ery about us. Where we came from, there wasn't anybody else who looked like that, which we got hammered for quite a lot, it could get unpleasant."

> "I'm sure we looked totally ridiculous to outsiders."
> **Rob Young, The Poppyheads**

Music journalist Pete Paphides grew up in Birmingham with The Sea Urchins on his doorstep: "They were a very visible presence on the Birmingham indie scene. They were very distinctive, all dressed like each other. They all had brown suede jackets and their fringes brushed halfway down their noses. The only one that looked different was Bridget who even then was unbelievably stylish, had impeccable hair and was just a star."

The Sea Urchins were playing up to the sense of performance about that whole leather-trousers-and-rock-star look at Bristol's Fleece & Firkin in April 1990, which was a gig at which Action Painting! were mocking the band for pretending to be something they weren't (for more on this, turn to Chapter 14). A few weeks later, Clare and Matt saw a pre-fame Manic Street Preachers also play at the Fleece "and they were there in their full combat gear covered with slogans," says Clare. "It was the cabaret thing of The Sea Urchins appearing in their 1960s' reinvention wardrobe and then the Manic Street Preachers appeared in their almost-punk clothes. And it just felt like you were watching this succession of people playing dress-up."

The Poppyheads were another early Sarah band that looked like they had stepped out of the past. Guitarist Rob Young says: "We went absurdly down that route, we got very obsessed with that kind of vintage clothing. David [Barbenel, vocalist and guitarist] used to go around in an anorak, drainpipe trousers and winklepickers, he had this real Jesus & Mary Chain shock of hair on his head, and always looked incredibly sullen. Nigel [Blackwood, drummer] was a little bit the same. When I got to [the University of Cambridge], I used to see these two. I didn't know who they were but they looked really unusual wandering around the precincts." Rob adds: "There was a lot of stuff that people in the 1980s suddenly decided was out of fashion. That's why we were all buying vintage, semi-acoustic guitars and Vox amps and all this stuff, because it was relatively cheap at the time. I was gradually growing my hair and had very pointy boots on and drainpipe trousers. We really loved old photos of bands like Love and The Byrds and The Stones from the mid-1960s. It was an absolute, unashamed homage to our retro heroes."

The Golden Dawn, who also joined Sarah's ranks in the early years, really embraced the retro look. Guitarist Kenny Forte says: "The fashion thing was a big, big part of it for us. That's just the way we dressed all the time in those days. In Glasgow it seemed we were quite distinctive. Glasgow was quite narrow-minded in those days, even wearing a pair of sunglasses you'd get comments from certain types of people in the street. We were influenced by the 1960s, which weren't that long ago, and the bands from that time, The Velvet Underground and things. A lot of people in that indie scene wore stripy t-shirts and tight jeans that you had to take in yourself because they didn't make them that way in those days. I did it myself, I learned how to use a sewing machine. I did Ulric's jeans as well."

Jumble sale chic

The Marine Girls were a key influence on the post-C86 bands, with their jumble-sale style and nonchalant attitude. Heavenly's Amelia Fletcher says: "The look of Talulah Gosh was the 1950sy, shabby, second-hand shop chic that had been The Marine Girls' look, combined with out-and-out Ramones-style punk, and a bit of The Pastels' anorak look. I guess we nicked those three aspects." Amelia credits Bobby Gillespie of Primal Scream and Stephen Pastel for making the anorak the go-to garment for the indie crowd: "What I found interesting about Bobby and Stephen when they wore their anoraks, and it kind of is what we tried to copy, is they wore their anoraks with leather trousers, so it was a combo of the rock and the punk with the childish. It was almost 'We're grown up but we're not going to do what we think grown-ups are supposed to do, we're going to do something different.' Unfortunately people looked at us and thought we were just arsing around like kids. But there was a more political, more positive intent."

> ❝ We dressed somewhere between child and old lady."
> **Amelia Fletcher, Heavenly**

Recalling the features he wrote for *Melody Maker* about this scene, music critic Simon Reynolds tells me: "I remember someone saying that the greatest triumph was to be able to get on a bus and pay the child fare. But children generally want to look older than they are. I think it's a sort of game and the play acting is a way of putting

The clothing choices of Amelia Fletcher and Cathy Rogers of Heavenly caused quite a stir in some quarters of the music press. Which seems utterly baffling to comprehend.
Top: Courtesy of Heavenly. Bottom: Nicola Rainey.

off adulthood... But in the end, Amelia gets a proper job and she rises to this great level of achievement. Real life came beckoning. They got married, had kids, but it's a way of deferring that moment and preserving adolescence."

NME journalist Kitty Empire expands on the look of the Sarah era: "Amelia was so, so cool. There was a fantastic way in which Amelia was very much in charge of her music. She wasn't wearing bovver boots and being Tank Girl. She was being gamine and '60s-ish but still had this charisma and groundedness and presence which I found wonderful. Finding your way of being female is perhaps one of the most difficult riddles to solve. And this effortless way in which Amelia seemed to know exactly what she was doing and how she was going to do it, while retaining a sense of humour and standing for her values, was very aspirational." Kitty adds: "A certain kind of man is very upset by female agency. It's an ongoing, unrelenting battle with the patriarchy. I am absolutely sure that what Amelia was, and how Amelia was, and how articulate she was, and how carefree she was, [led them to think] 'How dare this woman?'! That is alienating to a certain type of male. And it is, at the same time, a clear call to anyone who is onside with that. The signalling was clear. Amelia and Heavenly stood for a set of aesthetics and feminist values that, if you agreed with those things, it was an invitation to step right this way. If you disagreed, it was open season. So I really feel for the terrible things that people said about them, it's appalling."

> " In many ways, the cuties embodied more of the original ideals of punk than any sub-culture before or since – the idea that anybody can get up on stage, the idea that you create music for the joy of creation, the pop ideal (rooted in the '60s) of music being played out of enthusiasm rather than for financial reward, anti-image as image."
>
> **Jerry Thackray in** *Melody Maker*, **1991**

Sue Freeman of 14 Iced Bears was another fan of second-hand-clothes shopping and says: "In those days there were so many vintage shops in Brighton, and I would also rummage through my mum or my grandma's wardrobes. I got lots of 1960s stuff from my mum or dad. And black lace-up Doc Martens, I don't think I wore anything else in those days. Black tights, a shortish dress or skirt and some kind of vintage coat or jacket. This was the time before clothing got too branded, so people came across as more original in those days. There were tight drainpipe jeans, the odd cagoule anorak... At the age we were, we were students or working in low-paid jobs, and no one had money for clothes."

Taking her commitment to second-hand chic one step further, The Sea Urchins' Bridget Duffy, who now runs a business selling vintage clothing, says: "I'd go to jumble sales and buy mostly 1960s things. It was just so good to go to a jumble sale, spend £1 and come away with six outfits. There was this woman who'd come to one jumble sale and she had a really cool 1960s coat and I used to think, 'Please die soon so your clothes will go to the jumble sale', which is awful! In the 1980s, you could pick up 1960s stuff really easily in the charity shop. I got Mary Quant jackets and all sorts."

Kitty Empire adds: "I absolutely loved the clap back to the '60s that was going on. It was fresh and different to the mainstream. It was well thought through in terms of how people wanted to present themselves. I know it threatened a lot of men, that's one thing I liked about it. Poly Styrene of X-Ray Spex wore little old lady, 1950s' housewife clothes sometimes, which was, even within punk, such a radical statement. That cardigan aesthetic is absolutely reinforced by Sarah Records' bands. The defiance of it is exquisite." She continues: "If you understood what they were signalling, it was divine. There's a real chasteness to it, skirts below the knee, hair grips, 'We're kind of quoting childhood but we're also quoting granny'. These are the years in which women are not sexually available, these are pre-pubescent, post-menopausal female fashions and it's absolutely two fingers up to the sexualisation of women. It's really important that the unsexualised female is at the centre of this aesthetic, which is laudable and fantastic."

The thriftiness of the jumble sale look was a key factor. Most of the people involved in this scene simply didn't have a lot of spare money, and what they did have they prioritised for records and gig tickets. Lee Christopher of Action Painting! explains: "We had little money, our clothes dirty. I see that in the pictures of the time. I had torn Sellotape strips round my boots, ground in stains in the seat of my trousers. We cut our own hair. The only thing I owned that was even remotely nearly new was a brown suede jacket similar to the one John Lennon wore on the cover of *Rubber Soul*."

The other option was to buy second-hand clothes and customise them, as Clare demonstrates in a quote that should be accompanied by a pictorial guide of how to recreate this look at home: "I made a pink flouncy skirt. I'd got an old sheet at a jumble sale, dyed it pink and put elastic through the middle and that was probably the extent of my clothes making." You heard it here first, fashion fans. She adds: "I think the mainstream world would have looked at us and thought, 'Oh my god, what do you all look like?'"

Matt notes: "I think a lot of it is that it was a very cheap-and-cheerful DIY aesthetic. Anybody could buy a stripy t-shirt and a flouncy skirt and look like the other people at the gig. But most of the people at the gigs just looked like ordinary people. You tend to remember the ones in the stripy shirts and the anoraks because you think, 'Oh there's a kid in an anorak and a stripy shirt', but you ignore the fact that 90% of the people there are actually just in ordinary clothes." Clare adds: "I think we attracted quite a lot of introverts and loners. And one of the things that makes me happiest in retrospect is we seemed to be some sort of convener for people who were quite isolated, growing up in small towns or whatever, to come together in some way. And people found friends through it, as did we, but they were genuinely quite often nondescript, as are we."

Refusing to submit to sexism

Tied to all of this was a political statement about the way that the music industry viewed women. "As females, we were really keen not to have to look sexy, which was obviously a route to growing up for female artists," says Heavenly's Amelia Fletcher. "I was really influenced dress-wise by people like Dolly Mixture and Marine Girls."

> "We egged the twee pudding."
> Rob Pursey, Heavenly

Her bandmate Cathy Rogers adds: "I've always liked that mixture of little flowery dresses with Doc Martens, it feels like a way of taking some control of your femininity. In some ways, I think tropes like the flower hair clips are very powerful to a patriarchal world because they're not allowed, and of course these things operate on an unconscious level and you think you're just wearing a little hair clip because someone gave it to you and it's really cute but you're actually taking a bit of a position."

There was also a contingent of women who opted for clothes that were largely unfeminine and disguised their shapes. Anne Mari Davies of The Field Mice agrees her look was quite androgynous: "There were big baggy jumpers and dresses, nothing that showed off my shape at all. I had this dress with roses all over it that I wore all the time, and always with Dr Martens boots, which frustrated my dad so much. He used to say, 'That dress would be quite nice if you'd wear a pair of white stilettos with it'. But it had to be DMs, didn't it?!"

Ché's Vinita Joshi was just 18 when she moved to London from Rugby, and she used fashion as a way to blend in. "I felt like I wasn't taken seriously enough. I looked very young and I was super shy," she says. Rather than adopt the typical indie kid uniform, Vinita opted for a shapeless, androgynous style to avoid drawing attention to her femininity. "I never wore dresses, I always wore black jeans, pointy boots and really baggy t-shirts. Soon after, I got really into tiny micro 1960s' dresses because of the C86 thing but with really thick 500-denier black tights! I felt like I wasn't taken seriously and I used to think it was because I was young."

But it wasn't just the women who were sick of the male rawk posturing that was dominating the mainstream. "We were frustrated by the machismo around the music scene," says Greg Webster of Razorcuts. "There was this term 'rockism' at the time and that was something that we were reacting against." While Heavenly's Rob Pursey says: "Matt and Clare were always very big on kicking back against the misogyny of the music business. This was a culture in which women in bands were there to be pretty, to be the singer or the frontman's girlfriend. Even in the supposedly safe space of indie-pop tweeness, women were often represented by 1960s' photos of bouffanted beauties in beehive hairdos and miniskirts, looking sultry behind long eyelashes and heavy eyeliner. Women were still very much there to appease the male gaze. If Sarah Records was ever described as being run by 'Matt Haynes and his girlfriend Clare' there would be trouble and rightly so."

The macho nature of rock music in the era that preceded Britpop was pretty suffocating for anyone who was of a more thoughtful disposition. While arena rock was favouring the wide-legged testosterone of all-boy bands such as U2 and Guns N' Roses, the indie kids were seen to be returning to the safety of their childhoods and, if they ventured out, it was not to Wembley Stadium but to the backroom of their local pub where, with 20 other gentle souls, they could quietly watch a local band shamble their way through a poorly rehearsed set played via a shoddy sound system.

Macho rock'n'roll was, and is, focused on sex. It wasn't about romance or love, it was about what men wanted to do to gurrrls. We've all heard endless retrospective horror stories about the abuse men in the industry rained down on women and girls in the '70s and '80s. And then along came an all-female band like The Raincoats who, in 'Life On The Line', wrote about the fears of being stalked by a man, or in 'Shouting Out Loud' addressed the fact that a woman is essentially "a man with fears". Bands such as Talulah Gosh were a clear reaction to the world that bands such as The Raincoats had inhabited.

Over to Heavenly's Rob Pursey: "The vainglorious strutting male in a shit band was something we all hated. But we hated it as much on the grounds of taste as on the grounds of politics because it was preposterous to have a band with a man behaving like that, it was just shit, and the music was mostly terrible, too." Bandmate Amelia Fletcher adds: "It was as much about redefining what males were allowed to do in music, redefining masculinity, as about promoting the female side of things. At least at first. And in a way, they were promoting the ability of men to act in a more traditionally female way, I suppose."

Pete Paphides has a critic's take on things: "What I was interested in, and what seemed important to me, is that aesthetic felt inclusive. It felt not too gender specific, a lot of the clothes that people wore, those were clothes for boys or for girls. I liked all of that. I liked the fact that it was pro-gentility. It was pro-sensitivity. When I heard 'Sensitive' by The Field Mice, it was almost overwhelming. It was brave and so honest, and it didn't really give a fuck if you liked it or not. It was just, 'This is who I am, this is what I want to say, you can laugh at me, I don't care if you laugh at me'. And that was just fantastic. Production wise, I just thought it was perfect. I love that relentless drum machine, which is almost like a passive observer to all this other emotional stuff that was going on around it."

> ❝ It was nice to hear women singing like women. When you first hear Talulah Gosh, it's not the kind of singing you normally hear. It sounded like girls I knew."
> **Jyoti Mishra, White Town**

Another supporter from day one was journalist Jerry Thackray. Although not a die-hard Sarah fan, Jerry says one thing he liked was that Sarah was "trying to address a dialogue around music in a very different way from the traditional Rolling Stones' template that seemed to still rule everything". Having become disillusioned with the rockist turn that Creation had taken, Jerry found something appealing in the world of Sarah: "I liked the concept of Sarah more than a lot of the music. They were my kind of people: we were shy, we were awkward, we found it hard communicating, and this was a voice for us."

Jyoti Mishra of White Town sums it up pretty well: "In rock you'd have a whore: let me sing to you about this whore that broke my heart. And in indie you'd have this perfect goddess woman: she shits sunbeams and spends her summer running through fields being gorgeous, because that's all she's got to do. And it took me a long while to realise they were as bad as each other."

A TRIBE CALLED VEST

As people, we are naturally drawn to others who share the same beliefs, and we learn and take inspiration from each other. If we have a group around us, no matter how small, that can back up our 'unpopular' choices, then that strengthens us to stick to our guns. For this reason, those who grew up in a city always had an advantage over those who grew up in towns or small rural communities.

"You tended to gravitate to people who looked unusual or interesting, and then gradually, when you formed friendships with them, you took bits off each other," says Davey Woodward of The Brilliant Corners. "We were sharing our clothing and styles with each other. It started rubbing off on us. In the early 1980s, there were magazines like *The Face* and they were quite influential in putting kids on the covers, and you'd think, 'Oh, I wear those!' and they were capturing something. But I think generally the indie look has always been, or certainly in the 1980s, was a much more retrogressive look harking back to the 1960s." He adds: "Sarah happened at the right time, right place, and they carried on that punk ethos, the DIY ethos, of you can do it, and it became a collective."

> 66 And then The Field Mice get on stage and there's just two lads that look like plumbers with a drum machine."
> **Jyoti Mishra, White Town**

Lee Christopher of Action Painting! grew up in the garrison town of Gosport. He remembers: "At 16, I was all Muppet Baby Einstürzende Neubauten: black PVC trousers, single row dog collars and grandmother-knitted mohair jumpers. [Bandmate Andy Hitchcock] was paisley shirt, bowl haircut, Chelsea boots and Beatles, Beatles, Beatles. I recall us being both quite awkward in each other's company, slight loners and somewhat set apart from the other kids. I'd run as fast as I could without ever getting anywhere. I won the 1,500 metres [at school] in a Sigue Sigue Sputnik t-shirt and seemed to get in fights without meaning to." Andy elaborates: "We were at school together and people found us an odd match, because I was this quiet, supposedly geeky kid. People thought I was into classical music but I was actually into John Peel and reading the *NME* and starting to buy fanzines. And then there's Lee, who's a punky psychobilly kid. And we started hanging out together." Lee continues: "I was a Picasso-faced strange angular young man, and as my mother, a Picasso-faced strange middle-aged woman, pointed out to me on numerous occasions, 'clothes maketh the person'. I took that idea to the extreme. That I could create/distract/will something into being better than it actually

FASHION

"Two lads that look like plumbers" is one way of describing Michael Hiscock and Bobby Wratten of The Field Mice. The chaps are pictured here while the band was still just a duo.
Grimsby Fishmarket, Nicklas Brunzell.

was. To hide the ugly. I added to my already long fringe-covered face by dressing my eyes with burnt cork as eyeshadow and glued false eyelashes to flutter in time with the one thing I did pretty – pout. The Ivory Maybelline foundation and high-shine lipgloss completed this Quentin Crisp Geisha. All my black clothes were sewn tight as a skin. This was not so much to be noticed but more as a disguise."

In Leeds, Gentle Despite's Paul Gorton also met his future bandmate at school, where an unlikely band t-shirt brought them together: "The first conversation I had with Simon [Westwood, vocalist] about music was at a school camp, and he had a Motörhead t-shirt on and I had a Motörhead badge, and I went 'Oh wow, I didn't know you liked Motörhead' and we just completely connected about Motörhead. We started going to gigs around that time, and the first gig we went to together was Thin Lizzy on their last tour in early 1983. So we're these two 14-year-old kids down the front of the Queens Hall in Leeds, and that night it was like our lives changed, the excitement of seeing a band play live and the whole atmosphere from the audience. It was almost like some baptism into rock'n'roll!" Paul continues: "We were completely music mad after that and went to loads of gigs. There started to be a theme in 1985, 1986 that we started getting into The Smiths, Primal Scream, My Bloody Valentine, Felt, Mazzy Star, Galaxie 500, Spacemen 3, Sonic Youth. We went to see bands who were just a bit older than us and that was exciting. They're not like Jimmy Page or Ritchie Blackmore. They're just thrashing out a few chords, and we thought 'We could do that. We thought we could be in a band'."

*****

THESE THINGS HAPPENED:
Amelia Fletcher, Heavenly
"There will be people that like the Sarah label who don't like one or other single because that's inherent but I think people will have gone a long way with them. They'll have listened to bands that they might not otherwise ever have listened to or even have liked if they'd just heard it on the radio but, because Matt and Clare have given it the seal of approval, they go 'Oh, OK, I get this, this is really good.' Unlike other labels, Matt and Clare were not obsessed with being cool. They very much saw the bands as coming first, they were there in a way to get the bands out there."

Chapter 9
Partly political broadcasts

The politics of Sarah was missed by many people, which is a great shame. Much of it came from Clare and Matt via their fanzines, writing and attitude. But some of it came via the bands who created some furious reactions to the injustices of the time. "The politics was always there but we wanted it to be done with wit and humour rather than be very po-faced," says Matt. Feminism, socialism and anti-capitalism were just some of the issues that Sarah supported. Most people in the indie scene were of a left-leaning nature, even if it went unspoken. Living under Thatcher's polarising Conservative rule had sparked an anger in a lot of people, many of whom embraced indie music and the DIY aesthetic as a means of expressing their frustrations at the monetised, sanitised and corporate mainstream. And this led to a sense of urgency in the output: the sense that this message HAD to get out there NOW, there was no time to refine it, just get it HEARD.

Academic Sukhdev Sandhu states: "Anybody who likes [indie] music but is not interested in politics, it's just a disappointment. You think, 'What were you listening to? Why would you make such a big thing of identifying yourself as a Sarah Records fan if you were just listening to it as music?'" While music journalist Pete Paphides says: "For me, Sarah was important politically because it looked like it was a place where girls were just as welcome as boys and, not even that, but your gender wasn't even that interesting. It was almost a safe place where people could share their passions and it was defined by gentility, and it was defined in contrast to rockism and everything that stood for. The clothes that were worn, and the way people wore their hair and stuff like that, that felt politically important to me, it felt like that mattered."

> ❝ The single most important thing about Sarah Records was their politics. And anybody who doesn't get that is either a Tory, a fool or both. They didn't give a fuck. How can something be twee if it's incandescent with rage?"
>
> **Jyoti Mishra, White Town**

The political climate in the UK around the time that Sarah launched was heavy. The spirit-sapping Conservative government remained in power throughout Sarah's lifespan. Throw in high national unemployment (fluctuating between 10.6% and 8.6% from 1987 to 1995, according to figures from the Office for National Statistics), an eye-watering gender pay gap of 24% (according to University of London figures), homelessness that was rising dramatically and the threat of the egregious Section 28, and nobody should have been surprised that angry young people were educating themselves about what was important and, sometimes, taking a stand.

Many of the bands on Sarah were learning about the world and forming opinions at the same time as the fans were, so it was an educational process for everyone. "The politics of the label were so different from what I had been surrounded by in the village I grew up in, which didn't like anything to be different," says Anne Mari Davies of The Field Mice. "My friends in sixth form were the oddballs, and then you read this stuff and thought 'That's where I fit, even if I can't express myself in the way they're doing, I just love it. All these confusing feelings, they now make sense because of what is written in these fanzines.'"

Tim Vass of Razorcuts and The Forever People expands on this: "Music was political in the sense that it changed my worldview. I grew up on a council estate in Luton, it wasn't exactly a hotbed of righteous thinking, there was a lot of inherent racism and working-class Toryism about the place. The thing that made me react against that was punk. It was buying records by The Clash and hearing them interviewed and the things that they said, it was meeting other punks and meeting Greg [Webster] and people like Greg in the pub, and just the idea that you had to think for yourself and not be dictated to by the media. Punk changed the way I thought. Greg and I took that with us into the bands that we played in."

> There's so little imagination in politics. I do believe that the first stage is to awake the IMAGINATION, to get a general POSITIVE attitude to life – call it 'hope' – then you can deal in specifics."
>
> **Letter from Matt to Pete Williams, autumn 1988**

Whether helping to form people's ideas of the world or cementing ideologies they already understood, Sarah Records was widening minds all over the place. Via the fanzines, the record inserts and the way Sarah acted in opposition to the mainstream music business.

Political songs have been around since music began. One of the UK's most enduring political singers is Billy Bragg, who has blended folk and punk since the late 1970s. His musical and political beliefs are rooted in a tradition that predates his own life. When I interviewed him at Bristol's Fleece in 2011, Billy said: "The reason I'm here is that I work for a man called Woody Guthrie. He never did a gig like this where he had a dressing room and a rider and someone selling t-shirts. He played schools and picket lines and occupations. So I have to do that, too." He continued: "I think the time is coming when you can make political music again, because it's hard to make it without political context. I've managed to keep going because I've found an audience that connects with it.

"The thing that worries me now is that what supported what I did is no longer there, which is the *NME*, *Sounds* and *Melody Maker*. When I was making political music 30 years ago, the editors of those three papers were children of 1968, they believed that music was the alternative lingua franca. That was how we talked to one another, it was how I talked to my parents' generation as a working-class person. The only medium available to me was to buy a guitar and learn to play and write songs. But that's all gone. Even the *NME* pours piss on anyone who's political now."

But just as Billy's way wasn't the only way, neither was the shouty, furious, screeching rage of groups like Black Flag and Crass. "Black Flag were political. Authority didn't like us and we didn't like it," Henry Rollins, the band's former frontman, told me during an interview in 2012. "Punk rock in those days was pretty PC as there were a lot of females in those local scenes. … It is the misogynist, racist, homophobic minority that should be called out, marginalised, voted out, shouted down, whatever way you have to get them out of the way so the rest of us can get down the road."

Meanwhile, Crass were a hardcore punk band formed in 1977 which promoted anarchism as a way of life and a way of supporting feminism, animal rights, anti-fascism, environmentalism and more. They utilised a DIY ethic in everything, from recording to making posters and fanzines. They lived in a commune in Essex and ran a record label that was also called Crass. But if 'anarchy' makes you think of lawlessness and violence, think again. "The anarchy to me was the people who came the next day and swept it all up without being organised. That's real proper anarchy. That's what anarchy is in a political sense," Billy Bragg told me in 2011, in response to a wave of rioting across the UK.

"I think I once said that I saw Sarah as a cross between the Postcard and Crass record labels and I'm still quite happy with that as a statement," says Matt. "I was interested to find out that Bobby Wratten from The Field Mice was also a big fan of Crass in the way they went about things. Most of the music is fairly unlistenable but the actual way they did it... If you wanted politics, there it was. It was big fold-out sheets of dense text and all the records said 'Pay no more than 79p' to make sure that nobody was being ripped off and they would have 10 songs on one bit of 7" vinyl. So the ethics behind it, and the aesthetics as well, was fantastic."

FUN FACT: pop fans may remember that in the early 2000s Henry teamed up with Heavenly's Cathy Rogers to co-present *Full Metal Challenge*.

The thought that you could put out a 7"-sized package of pop, politics and anti-capitalism... hmm, yes, that probably will sound familiar to readers of this book. "The idea that you could put out this package and you'd get your 7" single and it would open out into this vast poster with agitprop stuff on it is fantastic. And low prices. It's a great attitude. That was an influence on me," confirms Matt, surprising nobody.

But there could be an in-between for political music, it didn't have to be either folk or punk, it could be something else, it could be pop. Back to Jyoti Mishra: "In a certain part of the 1980s, your favourite band was The Smiths but you were wearing a Public Enemy t-shirt and that's how everything was intersectional before that was a word. The politics came first. All I cared about was, 'Is this band in the Revolutionary Communist Party or Militant or the Socialist Workers' Party and if they are, like the

Did you manage to collect the set? There are still people in Sarah Records' online fan groups who are trying to find the mising pieces of the famous postcard puzzle.
Courtesy of Sarah Records.

Redskins, I'll buy their records, and if they're Tories, no, that's it'. So when you first read a few fanzines, they're these huge rants and you're like 'Finally, some fucker wants to set fire to everything!' With Sarah, it meant a lot to be able to buy something and know it wasn't by Tories."

Matt picks up the thread: "Although politics was really important throughout Sarah, we didn't want to go down the Crass route of having great screeds of well-meaning text that were ultimately too dull to read. It had to be fun and not spoil things for people who just wanted to hear a nice pop record. Even if that meant that people sometimes missed the politics entirely. So putting postcards randomly into Sarahs 21 to 30 was mocking the capitalist/collector mentality but it also made a jigsaw of Temple Meads station, which is funny. And, although we could have written an insert about how public rather than private transport is the route to a better society, it was more fun to put pictures of consecutive stations on the Severn Beach line on the centre labels, or number compilations after bus routes." And that's exactly it. Pop music doesn't have to be explicit to be political.

Clare continues: "The political point in a lot of our criticism of other record labels was that everyone pretends to be terribly left wing but, when it comes to running their own business, what you're essentially trying to do is exploit money out of kids by getting them to buy your record multiple times by sneaking on one extra track or different versions. So here's our idea, we're going to run our record label how we'd like it to be run were we the fans. Your small 'p' politics have to inform how you lead your life and how you run your business. We talked about things like public transport as being something to be celebrated. It was all designed to be funny and to be a love letter to Bristol. But it was also about how you don't have to move to bloody London. Of course, we then did [after Sarah closed]."

When she was in Northern Picture Library, Anne Mari Davies told *Waaaah!* fanzine: "You have to have talent to write good political songs. We're all interested in politics and social sciences and Bobby [Wratten]'s written one or two more political songs but they've never survived to the recording stage. Mainly because one political song on an LP may look like a token gesture and also he's rarely completely satisfied with the way he's expressed his views."

The politics of a label like Sarah encouraged fans to get up and do it themselves. True to the punk roots that had inspired Clare and Matt to get going in the first place, it was very much a case of the classic punk 'here are three chords, now form a band' school of music making. "For me, the gigs, the bands, the music was the praxis of the theory of the fanzines," says Jyoti Mishra. "Here's this fanzine which is full of rage but it isn't bullshit because look, here's this gig, and look, here's this record, so we aren't just armchair communists, we're actually doing stuff. And if we're doing stuff, we're not special, why aren't you doing stuff? Why aren't you writing articles and putting gigs on? Why don't you form your own band? Doesn't matter if it's shit, just as long as you form one." Elaborating on what Sarah and its music meant to him, Jyoti adds: "Sometimes you just want to listen to something and have a bit of a cry, and you could do that with Sarah music. All The Field Mice music was like getting punched in the face while someone held up a mirror to your shit love life."

Feminism

Clare states: "The worst thing for me is the illusion that women have an active role because you see them on *Top Of The Pops* and you see their pictures in the papers. They're very much front people, often singing other people's lyrics, so they're not speaking their own minds, even though you might think they are. And obviously things are harder for women from the start – lower incomes and things like getting back safely from gigs, and whether or not you want to walk across the park on your own – so everything is stacked against women. I do feel that's something that could actually be changed if anyone was interested in changing it."

> " Indie-pop girls get flowery dresses – and their boyfriend's words to sing – colluding when they should be REFUSING, content with the crumbs."
>
> *One Page Fanzine*, 9 June 1992

This reinforces her stance from a letter sent to *Melody Maker* in August 1991, which also – depressingly – shows that nothing has changed in the intervening 30 years. Clare wrote: "It's hard enough for a woman to carve herself an independent role in music. Stupid basic things like going to gigs on your own and getting back afterwards have to be considered on top of society's everyday constraints, like lower pay, for instance. Add to that the implicit criterion that to succeed you need to be physically desirable. What about the not-so-beautiful, the women who aren't so confident about their appearance/sexuality, having to risk being at best the only girlie not drooled over? Ugly men are acceptable. Ugly women aren't."

Clare was a major feminist influence for many people in Sarah's bands, as well as for those who read her fanzines and writing. Alison Cousens of Brighter was certainly fired up: "That fanzine Clare wrote, *Lemonade*, was really inspirational to me, partly because it resonated with a lot of the reading and the conversations that I was having at the time. Discovering feminist theory was transformative. I did a course at university on women and film, and that changed things for me. Suddenly marrying socialist politics with feminist politics and it then taps into power and assaults on power, and then you have Matt and Clare running a label on equal terms, ordinary people just like us, it was really important. I'm pretty certain when we were in the Bloomsbury Studios there were Page Three images [of topless women] on the walls. You'd go into any studio and they were male spaces. You almost needed to be with males to have any access."

But this newfound openness about feminism could prove challenging when women were still trying to get their heads around some of the ideas, as Anne Mari Davies, who was still a teenager when she joined The Field Mice, explains: "I was really frightened about doing something wrong, like standing at the front of photos. I couldn't carry my amp because it was very heavy and Bobby used to carry it for me and I always felt like, 'Oh, is Clare looking at me thinking Anne Mari should be carrying her own stuff!' I felt like I was a really bad feminist. As an older, wiser woman now, I think Clare is great but I was very intimidated by her. Not because she had done anything that would make me feel like that but just because my political views were much less well formed. I didn't feel like I was her equal."

Alison talks about how everything is stacked against women in the music business, right from even trying to buy your instruments: "I wrote an article for one of Keith [Girdler]'s fanzines called 'I Don't Sing'. It was a raging tirade against the fact that every time we stood up to do a soundcheck, without question the engineer would just erect a mic stand in front of me because, even if I wasn't doing the lead vocals, of course I'd be doing backing vocals, but no, I don't sing." She continues: "It was easy for boys to just go into a guitar shop and buy a guitar. But there's this whole thing where you sit in a music shop, you pick up the guitar, there's everyone walking around, and there's people who are just showing off. And I can never buy a guitar because I don't know how to play, so what's your way into all of that, because

"Discovering feminist theory was transformative," says Brighter's Alison Cousens.
Neil Shumsky.

everyone's looking at you and judging? And even more so if you're female. It was impenetrable. Keris taught me some basic chords, and from there I went and bought an Everything But The Girl songbook because Tracey Thorn was a visible woman in the music industry who spoke to me."

Keris Howard, Brighter's frontman, agrees: "Alison's experience was pretty horrendous at times, given it was supposedly quite a liberated movement we were in. I think she got quite a lot of grief just for having the cheek to be a woman who was in a relationship with somebody who was in a band. Alex [Sharkey] was in Brighter because he was my best mate but Alex never got any grief for that."

This might have been the gentle world of so-called cuties and anoraks but you still needed balls to be a woman in it. As the lone woman in 14 Iced Bears *and* doubling up as the band's manager, Sue Freeman took no shit from anyone: "I was literally travelling around in the back of a van with a load of blokes but I held my own, I would never have hung around with them if it had been in any way toxic or sexist.

It was largely men I was dealing with and most of the other bands we met had blokes in. But I didn't question it much at the time."

Also standing strong as the only woman in her band, Bridget Duffy of The Sea Urchins drew on her Catholic education to find her inner strength. She recalls a nun at school telling the girls: "Do not let any man tell you that you're not as good as him because 'woman' stands for 'woah-man, I'm just as good as you'. So I was never intimidated ever by men." She says: "I think I was a lot more confident when I met The Sea Urchins, I was probably at the most confident part of my life. It was a very boys' own club but I didn't feel like I shouldn't be part of it. Because I was always a have-a-go-hero when it came to playing an instrument. I was the weakest link in terms of any musicality. They were far more talented musicians than I was, but I was like 'Don't worry, I'll have a go!' If you don't try, you don't know."

> We were this tiny little band trying to have a tiny little punch at this beast of swaggering manhood that was a lot of the music industry."
>
> **Cathy Rogers, Heavenly**

But it wasn't like that for everyone. As a young Indian woman co-running a record label, Vinita Joshi had a few awful experiences. Such as the time she went to see one of her bands, The Telescopes, playing at the Fulham Greyhound. On arriving at the venue, Vinita couldn't find the backstage area so asked someone where it was. When she finally found the band "they were laughing going 'Oh, here you are.' And I said, 'What do you mean?' And they said, 'The support band were going, 'Oh, there's some Asian chick looking for you?' What a description! 'Asian chick?!' It probably wasn't said in any malicious way but 'chick' and 'Asian', they could have just said 'There's a girl looking for you.'" Vinita adds: "We worked with so few women in the industry. I've definitely been to some gigs where there were hardly any women. There would definitely be some gigs where I was aware that I was the only Indian person there, or the only person of colour. It was a very white boy thing. It was mostly so male dominated. There wasn't really anyone to look up to, so maybe women didn't think 'Oh, I can do that'. Men really don't understand where we're coming from, and there is an element of us not believing in ourselves enough, and it's not because we're not talented enough but look how long it took us to get the vote! Even now, we're still so behind with pay, there's so few women in any high-powered jobs in government, but look at multi-millionaires, billionaires… You don't hear about women in those positions."

On 29 July 1992, Clare was interviewed on Radio 1 for the Mark Goodier Evening Session. Although it was presented as a live interview, it was actually a pre-record, which meant the BBC was able to edit out one or two of Clare's answers that didn't suit their narrative. Here is a transcript of part of the broadcast:

Mark: "It's great to talk to a lady who runs a small record label because there aren't that many."

Clare: "There's very, very few of us, I think. Which is a great shame but it's the way of the music industry."

Mark: "Why do you think that is? Because clearly you're a music fan and you started because you're a music fan. There must be other women who are music fans and who for some reason don't do it. Not just because they don't see a career in it, surely?"

Clare: "I think it's a thing with role models, that record labels are run by men and it's almost something you don't see that you can do. And I kind of almost did it by mistake. And what we need is more people doing it, and more people bothered about why people aren't doing it and trying to sort that out."

Clare tells me that one of the things the BBC edited out was her irate response to Mark patronisingly referring to her as a 'lady' in his opening question. Which is disappointing because we can be certain that Clare's reply would have been on point. Regardless, the absence of women in the music industry was, and still is, abundantly clear for all to see. Although Sarah wasn't entirely immune from being a male-heavy label, even if it was run on equal terms by a woman and a man.

As previously mentioned, it wasn't until Heavenly came along in 1990 on Sarah 30 that the label finally got its first female-fronted band. So when *Waaaah!* fanzine interviewed Matt during the height of Sarah they asked him about the lack of women fronting Sarah bands. This was his response: "It's sad but a reflection of indie music in general. Most bands are male dominated. There is an unfortunate undercurrent of sexism in most associated things, not quite as obvious as heavy metal or rap, but possibly all the more sinister for that. I suspect a lot of females feel intimidated and lots of sensitive young males drooling over Amelia Fletcher isn't going to make them feel less so." Matt tells me now: "I would have been being defensive because it was true – there *was* a lack of women on Sarah. But that was true of the scene generally, especially on the performing side, so it always seemed a bit unfair to single us out. I assume people did it because we'd taken a strongly feminist stance, and they thought it was hypocritical. But I'm not quite sure what we could have done."

The Wake was one of the bands with a woman at its core in the form of keyboardist Carolyn Allen. Frontman Caesar tells me: "We started in the early 1980s and, because of punk and then post-punk, it was a very standard thing for women to be involved in groups at that time. Not to the extent that it should have been. There weren't the numbers there, certainly the majority was men. But it wasn't unusual for women to be in bands at that point in the way it had been unusual in the 1970s, for instance. By the 1990s, when people started to talk about it in the way that Clare was, it made you think, 'Oh well, it's true, it's not over, it's not a result. This still needs to be addressed.' Why is there still some sort of barrier to people accepting that pop music should not only be about the male point of view?"

RACE

Attitudes to race in the 1980s were less progressive than they are now, although we still have an incredibly long way to go. The indie scene in the mid-late 1980s was very white. There was nobody of colour on Sarah which, of course, wasn't deliberate but, when you look back on that era through a 21st-century lens, is very noticeable. However, it is also not fair to apply contemporary standards to something that happened 30 years ago. "The label wasn't just incredibly white, it was 100% white," says Clare. "And that is a reflection of the scene at the time," adds Matt. "It was a reflection of the type of music as well," continues Clare. "I don't think you could say we hadn't noticed, but I think equally we'd be looking at it through a different prism if we were running that record label now. We were certainly much more interested in gender than we were in race because that was the discrimination I and the label were experiencing." Matt adds: "A lot of it goes back to the fact that independent, underground music was a lot more isolated in those days. It didn't go across the social boundaries in the way that it does now. If you're at school now, you're aware of every type of independent music there is and that will be reflected in the makeup of the people in the bands. But back then, each scene was quite isolated."

> **❝** One hopes that no one who wasn't white felt excluded from the scene but I'm guessing people did."
> **Clare**

Music critic Simon Reynolds expands on this: "Certain kinds of music are kind of self-selecting and you can't force things to be more diverse than they want to be. For me, it was striking that, having lived through Postcard, there was a period when everyone was going on about listening to James Brown and the latest early rap records and being influenced by them, and I was into The Slits who were totally bound up with reggae. And then it suddenly became a much whiter palette and a whiter canon that went back through history."

Unfortunately, there were occasions where some people felt excluded, and Jyoti Mishra of White Town recalls an experience at a gig with a Sarah band member (who I have been asked not to name): "I was outside and went to talk to him after a gig, and I said I really liked his stuff and he said 'thanks'. He had this group of people around him and one of them said, 'Oh, you're in that band White Town, aren't you?' And the others started laughing and going 'What colour's your town? Oh, I don't know what colour mine is'. This went on for several minutes and I just got up and left. He didn't say anything with them but he also didn't say anything against them. I felt really angry, I was embarrassed, my face felt red. I was also kicking myself, saying I should have known better. That's what it's always been like for me in that scene."

However, Sukhdev Sandhu, who has moved from the UK to the US, has a different perspective and sees Sarah as a form of "migrant music" due to how it has since spread to fans all around the world. "I always get disappointed when people call Sarah 'white music' because, since I've been in America, a large proportion of people that I know who own Sarah records are not white. They are Black, they are

Asian, they are Latino. Some of them are much younger. Some of them are a little bit of our generation. I understand why people might think of it as white music but I feel that does Sarah a disservice and it actually does the listeners a disservice, it feels like cultural reduction."

The Brilliant Corners, named after a song by Black jazz musician Thelonious Monk, were unusual in having a Black band member in guitarist Winston Forbes. Announcing Winston's death on the band's Facebook page in 2019, frontman Davey Woodward wrote: "Winston played guitar like no one else ... At the time Winston did not get the credit he deserved for his innovative style of playing. Winston originally played percussion in the band but taught himself guitar in a few months, developing his original style on the way. What also made him different was that he was a Black guitarist in a predominantly white indie scene ... Today we have lost a friend who had a big heart, a lot of joy and the ability to make all of us laugh."

Davey tells me why he thinks there were so few Black kids involved with the indie scene: "From the early 1980s there was a divergence, I saw it in my own friendships, you were either the kid who was the oddball, into your guitar music, or you became a skater, into your basketball, into your New York hip hop. And so a lot of Black kids I knew went more into hip hop and dance music. And kids like me went off into guitar stuff. There were almost dividing lines.

He continues: "If I was to paint broad brush strokes about that indie scene, I'd say something like, well, essentially it was white middle-class kids. But actually, in our band we had a Black member, which was really unusual for that time. We were all working-class kids. And in The Flatmates, Deb [Haynes] the singer lived across the road from me in Avonmouth, she was a working-class woman fronting a band. A lot of people who make things happen, who organise, who enthuse, are often a little bit more educated, maybe they've got a little bit more money that they can invest or can afford to lose, and it was really important to have that cultural mix. And if there's one thing that I think that the whole Bristol indie scene did is it introduced me to a whole different cultural mix of people I never would have met." And this leads us neatly onto the issue of class.

CLASS

What became evident very quickly from talking with music journalists David Quantick and Simon Price was that they were labouring under a long-held misunderstanding of what Sarah actually was. They seemed under the impression that Sarah was an achingly middle-class label populated with indulged bands from the Home Counties who were funded by wealthy parents and that the music was lapped up by people who were just like them. When I mention this to Chris Quinn of The Orchids, he responds with: "Wow! That's funny. They should have visited the housing scheme where we lived and seen how long they survived. We did take

> " I think the fact that Heavenly absent-mindedly leave their correspondence in Tokyo Airport, rather than just on the Tube like the rest of us, speaks volumes about what distinguishes true natural Celebrity from tacky upstart dross: style, panache, complete indifference to other people's feelings..."
> **Sarah Newsletter No 10, January 1995**

an *NME* journalist and photographer through some wild parts of Glasgow once but that was later on, maybe after they'd realised our music was actually OK."

As someone who actually engaged with and understood the scene, former *Melody Maker* writer Pete Paphides suggests: "I think there's an assumption that if someone's making gentle music and is quite literate in their outlook, then maybe they grew up in a comfortable detached farmhouse in Somerset. It's maybe a presumption I made about Sarah, but I didn't really care if the people that made the music I liked were middle-class or working-class or whatever. It wasn't particularly interesting to me. But maybe it was interesting to some people. I think there was a presumption that Sarah was in some way informed by middle-class affectations, that it wasn't engaging with the real world. But to repudiate the 'real world' is as much an engagement as anything."

Alison Cousens recalls the first time that Brighter played in Oxford, and the band driving around trying to find the Jericho Tavern. "Alex [Sharkey] was leaning out of the window and shouting 'Poshos! Poshos!' to everyone," she laughs, in a story reminiscent of a certain scene from *Withnail & I*. "It's that whole educational hierarchy that links into class that links into people that have chips on their shoulders and I'd count us as part of that. We were some oiks from Lancing. Alex was at Thames Poly, and Keris and I had made it to the dizzy heights of Birmingham University, but there was no way we could aspire to being at Oxbridge."

One band who definitely did have an Oxbridge education was Heavenly. But as warm and friendly as the individuals were, the fact they came from a position of privilege was something some other bands, and most of the music press, held against them. And they were aware of it. "If you're in a band, as far as most journalists are concerned, it's better if you're not educated or articulate. And we were the most over-educated band in the world. There were degrees and PhDs flying around, it was ridiculous!" says bassist Rob Pursey. "But also, an awful lot of bands met at college but then did a good job of pretending not to have. So they would be deliberately inarticulate or just deny what their middle-class status was. So that desire for rock to be a primal, uncultured, raw male energy, people went along with that. And we just couldn't or wouldn't."

But is it all down to education? "Both Matt and I were comprehensive kids, although our comprehensives were probably very different," says Clare. "Mine was a huge former grammar school in a nice middle-class town, whereas his London one may have been slightly less academically focused". Matt adds: "I don't even know if Heavenly have public school backgrounds. The only person I know for sure who went to public school was Alan [Bryden], the cellist from Eternal and I'm not sure we can pin much of the blame for Sarah's image on him. He was also only 15, I think, and needed permission from his housemaster to be out of school, which is how I know."

Brighter all held down full-time jobs in addition to being in a band, which made rehearsals and touring tricky. Pictured left to right are Alex Sharkey, Alison Cousens and Keris Howard.
Colin Bell.

Alan the cellist, eh? Bloody Alan. "Did the press all just really hate Eternal's cellist?" muses Matt.

After university, the various members of Brighter found jobs. Alison Cousens became a teacher, Alex Sharkey took a job in civil engineering and Keris Howard worked for the council. This meant that time was very restricted for the band in terms of rehearsals and touring. "It came from our lower-middle/working-class backgrounds where we didn't want to take risks," Keris explains. "Even though we were really young, there was that work ethic that we couldn't take risks because we might end up ruining our lives if we didn't keep our heads down. I think there were some bands who come from a more traditional working-class background and the only way they were going to get to have a nice house and some money was to pursue being in a band. Or you'd get bands who came from white, affluent backgrounds

> "People can assume that if you've been to university or you're singing fey pop about summer fields, that somehow you're coming from a privileged background, rather than it might be an escape from a bleak reality."
>
> **Keris Howard, Brighter**

and had gone to the right schools and universities who know they can play at being in a band and it's not going to have repercussions later because they will bounce back because they've got the connections, they've been to the right universities and stuff. And that doesn't just stand for Sarah Records, that stands for music in general. At the same time it was really difficult because we had lives outside of music and we were scared of mucking those up. Alex was settling down, he got married and was planning a family. It was difficult to think we could somehow use all of our spare time, going to work and then driving off to Oxford or wherever all evening, it was inconceivable."

The Glasgow bands were experiencing a similar struggle. In The Golden Dawn, after going to school near Ibrox Stadium, Kenny Forte and Eugene Dawydiak earned places at university, which was unusual for kids from their school. Kenny studied zoology while Eugene studied astrophysics and psychology, although they discovered that neither degree would equip a working-class man from Glasgow for a job after graduation because there just weren't those sorts of jobs to go into. "I worked at Glasgow Zoo for a year, it was one of those Restart programmes, just trying to get people off the dole, it was great fun," says Kenny. "But after that finished I was unemployed."

The Golden Dawn formed after Kenny and Eugene had graduated from university. "I still didn't feel like I'd grown up," says Kenny. "The school that we went to wasn't particularly good for giving you confidence so I was incredibly shy, and Eugene as well. Ulric [Kennedy] and Robert [Smith] were the more outgoing ones. They did the talking to people, and we just got dressed up. It was a really exciting time, though. There was a lot of unemployment at the time, we were on the brew [dole] for years. We were in another band with the poet John Malley who had a poem called 'Dole Boy Blues', all about being unemployed under [Margaret] Thatcher."

Also in Glasgow were The Orchids, whose friend Karen Albrow speaks about them with great affection. "The Orchids came from quite a rough, working-class area, so they were very different in their perspective of life. They were lovely, almost like vulnerable children, they were so young. And so unworldly-wise." Karen continues: "These middle-class bands, for them it was almost like a profession. For The Orchids, it wasn't. For The Orchids, it was an outlet, it kept them off the street and out of the way of the bad guys. They all lived in council houses. From my perspective, they were quite vulnerable because they were just wee guys."

Glasgow and the nearby towns of Bellshill and East Kilbride are well known for the bands that emerged from there: The BMX Bandits, Teenage Fanclub, Jesus & Mary Chain, Primal Scream, The Soup Dragons and more. As chief Bandit, Duglas T Stewart knew everyone involved. "Places like Bellshill and East Kilbride were very working-class and, at that time, very industrial. So there were a lot of people really struggling and it was pretty dark. Glasgow was very dark at that time, all of

Despite the music press seeming to think most Sarah bands were trustafarians, The Field Mice were certainly not dripping in parental wealth. Here they are at Denmark Hill Station in south London.
Richard Bellia.

the buildings were black – they've now all been cleaned up and look beautiful. But it was almost threatening in attitude."

Mark Dobson, who would become the drummer with The Field Mice, was originally from a County Durham village called Shotton Colliery, which he describes as "very violent". When Mark first heard his future band, it was Bobby Wratten's lyrics that spoke to him because he thought that, in his heartfelt writing, Bobby was sharing something that Mark could identify with but which he didn't hear in many other bands. "Here's this guy writing great pop songs but he's not at all afraid to talk about his feelings. He doesn't like this whole macho environment that I've moved to London to get away from."

Mark finds it staggering that Bobby and Michael [Hiscock] could be called "fey and jingle jangle and twee" given they had

❝ For me, it was a very working-class band, so to be labelled middle-class pissed me off more than the twee or the fey stuff."

Mark Dobson, The Field Mice

grown up on the rough Pollards Hill estate in Mitcham, south London. Mark reflects on his own childhood: "I grew up in abject poverty. My dad was an alcoholic, he put my mum in hospital a few times. My mum was left on her own trying to bring four kids up. I remember having to go to school and stand in the queue for free school dinners, which the divorced kids had to do. So I grew up in this violent, misogynistic, racist, brutal environment. When people labelled Sarah Records as middle-class, I kind of got that. But I had a girlfriend, I had a baby, I had a mortgage, I'd grown up in a much tougher and rougher place than these journalists who were labelling me middle-class and privileged and saying I didn't understand the world."

Mark met Bobby after interviewing him for a magazine piece and the two struck up a friendship. Suddenly, Bobby wrote to Mark inviting him to be The Field Mice's drummer. "I couldn't drum!" says Mark. "I mulled it over and cobbled together about £150, went to the music shop in Streatham and there was a drum kit for about £140. It was a piece of crap but I could afford it. I thought I was only going to be in the band for two weeks and, as soon as they realised I had zero musical ability, I'd be back out again. I even did a deal with the guy in the music shop so that we had the drums for two weeks and, if I got kicked out of the band within two weeks, he would give me £100 of the £140 back in return for the drum kit. As I left the shop I said I'd see him in two weeks! I was paying £40 to rent this drum kit for two weeks."

POLL TAX

The UK's first anti-poll tax song was on Sarah. 'Defy The Law' by The Orchids was Sarah 11, released in 1988 at the start of the UK's poll tax conflict, and the single included a poster collage of anti-poll tax material across which the slogan 'The Orchids Say Don't Pay The Poll Tax' was splashed. As if this didn't make the band's stance clear enough, the runout groove of the single had the words "FUCK THE POLL TAX" etched in angry capital letters.

The controversial tax was introduced in Scotland in 1989 before hitting the rest of the UK in 1990, which put the Glaswegian band in a good position to strike first. Alas, the London-based music press didn't take much notice. Although *Melody Maker* did pick up that 'Defy The Law' was anti-poll tax in its 1988 review, noting: "It has to be said, the sleeve notes on economic policy put up more resistance than the mellotron mewling of this song." I mean, they picked it up but...

The 'poll tax', or the Community Charge as it was officially known, was the Thatcher government's replacement for rates, which taxed a property according to size and location. However, the poll tax was based on the number of people who lived in a property, meaning a small house in a poor area with lots of residents paid more tax than an aristocrat living alone in a mansion, further widening the gulf of economic inequality the Conservative government had created.

> ❝ Myself and James [Hackett], we were quite involved in the anti-poll tax campaign in Glasgow. We used to go to meetings and put leaflets through letterboxes. We used to go to a lot of marches as well."
>
> **John Scally, The Orchids**

PARTLY POLITICAL BROADCASTS

Top: The Orchids released the UK's first anti-poll tax song. **Bottom:** The poster that came with Sarah 11.
Top: Julian Bester. Bottom: Courtesy of Sarah Records.

James Hackett wrote the lyrics to 'Defy The Law': "A three-chords-and-the-truth type of thing."
Jon Cole.

The British public was understandably furious about this; campaign groups were set up and the resulting demonstrations, marches and riots ultimately contributed to the fall of Thatcher. When John Major became Prime Minister in 1990 he set about scrapping the poll tax.

The Orchids were there from the start with 'Defy The Law'. Not so meek and mild now, eh? Fellow Scots The Exploited released comedy punk anthem 'Don't Pay The Poll Tax' in 1990, while English electronic duo Orbital went on *Top of the Pops* in March 1990 to perform their single 'Chime' while wearing hoodies inscribed with the message 'No poll tax'. So whether you were into indie, punk or dance music, there was a band standing up for your rights.

"'Defy The Law' is a three-chords-and-the-truth type of thing. It's just trying to get a point across. I wish we'd done it better but it was what it was," says James Hackett, who wrote the lyrics. "It feels very naïve now but it was a reaction. I don't think that we were aware of how political Clare and Matt were being. We didn't think of it as politics, we just thought it was decency. I came up with that song very quickly just before we recorded it. If I'd spent more time on the words it might have been less embarrassing but at the time it was quite fun to do. It got us a wee bit of recognition from different people, who were pleased we had something to say other than 'I like that girl.' Drummer Chris Quinn adds: "We did get accused of trying to be political to get attention, which was really unfair."

Alongside releasing 'Defy The Law', members of The Orchids also attended awareness-raising meetings, went on protest marches, handed out leaflets and performed at a rally in Glasgow where they were introduced on stage by activist and former Member of the Scottish Parliament Tommy Sheridan, a prominent opponent of the charge. "He was a great speaker, we believed in him, and then we realised he was a big tit and didn't want to be a part of that," says James, referring to how Sheridan was later imprisoned for perjury.

The poll tax riots reached Bristol in early March 1990 when around 5,000 protestors took to the streets. The police tried to arrest some of them but the crowd pulled back and kicked one officer unconscious, while another six members of the public were pulled out of a police van.

By the way, when I spoke to former *NME* writer David Quantick, who thinks that Sarah bands were poshos sitting around drinking lashings of ginger beer, I asked him if he knew that Sarah released the first anti-poll tax song. He looked completely surprised and said: "That's not something you associate with Sarah."

Section 28

Several of Blueboy's songs dealt with the issue of the Conservative government's homophobic Section 28 of the Local Government Act 1988, which was an attempt to prevent "the promotion of homosexuality". For example, it stopped local authorities from portraying "the acceptability of homosexuality as a pretended family relationship" in anything under their aegis, such as schools and libraries. It stemmed from a homophobic British government that may have partially legalised male homosexuality in 1967 but still discriminated against lesbians and gay men. With the arrival of AIDS/HIV in the 1980s, there was a new way for society to display its bigotry towards gay men. This led to a national rise in homophobia, attacks on lesbians and gay men and the introduction of Section 28. "You think the world is on a trajectory to improvement don't you, and Section 28 was such a massive step backwards," says Clare. While Matt adds: "Section 28 is one of those things where you think if you explain this to young people now, would they actually believe that this happened?"

On the eve of the bill being passed, John Peel played Bing Crosby's 1929 song 'Gay Love' at the top of his Radio 1 show, introducing it with the lament: "Presumably, when Clause 28 of the Local Government Bill comes into effect I won't be able to play you this..." Of course, Bing's meaning of 'gay' came from a different era but Peel's point was well made.

Blueboy's protest against Section 28 is most notable on the song 'Clearer'. Keith Girdler quietly sings: "For all the clubs and all the pubs, there's still no love ... Goodbye freedom, goodbye freedom, we've gone back 30 years..." 'Clearer' was the only Sarah 7" that came with a lyric sheet "because we thought the lyrics were so

> " Not very many people were out in the way that people are now. Society wasn't like that. But for fuck's sake, you still know what's right and wrong, don't you? A lot of people seemingly didn't know."
>
> **Clare**

Blueboy frontman Keith Girdler used his band's lyrics to spell out his distaste for Section 28.
Courtesy of Paul Stewart.

important. And they still are. It's extraordinary stuff," says Matt. While 'Fondette', written by Gemma Malley, reflects that: "This is a country where it can be a criminal offence to wink". On the 1994 album *Unisex*, 'Marble Arch' sees Keith sing as if he is a man remembering his youth as a teenage prostitute: "I am young and quite pretty, don't hurt me." To take such a clear-cut attitude and stance in the early 1990s was a bold move. Keith told *Grimsby Fishmarket* fanzine: "Honest emotions are something I try to transfer to my songs, most indie-pop lyric writers tend to be very aloof, very poetic... I try to be more explicit, honest, say what I feel, what I think." Yet *NME* writer Steven Wells still had the gall to review Blueboy's 'Popkiss' single by saying: "Acoustic strumming, feeble, breathless posho whining about being sad." It beggars belief.

Keith, who died of cancer in 2007, was an extraordinary artist. He sang in a delicate voice and wrote beautiful, quiet melodies, and did everything with a hint of sophistication that eluded many of his contemporaries. Keith never publicly made an announcement regarding his sexuality because why should he? However, his lyrics spoke of his feelings regarding the homophobia that was still rife in British society in the early 1990s and the appalling attitude of the government. While Blueboy's labelmates were accused of being limp-wristed or fey in the music press, Keith and co simply presented the public with songs that gently challenged people's

PARTLY POLITICAL BROADCASTS

Blueboy's Keith Girdler and Paul Stewart pictured in Brighton, where Keith was living at the time.
Grimsby Fishmarket, Marcus Torncrantz.

assumptions about whether or not others were gay.

Blueboy's final Sarah single, 'Dirty Mags', saw the band adopt a louder sound and heard Keith snarl: "I want to come inside your eyes, or perhaps your life." The back of the sleeve included some images from the US porn magazine that shared the band's name, although guitarist Paul Stewart insists the band didn't take their name from the magazine and says they are instead named after the Orange Juice song. Paul tells me that he and Keith were driving to Weston-super-Mare to record 'Clearer' and Paul told Keith that he just couldn't be in a band called The Art Bunnies, which was the name they had at that stage. "Keith had a piece of paper and he read out a few alternative names while we were driving down, and there were some other names that were very Keith but very awful," says Paul. "One was The Smiling Monarchs. It sounds like an él band. And then he said 'Blueboy', and I said I really liked that. He said, 'It's an Orange Juice song'. Orange Juice were a big influence for us so I'd say that's the definitive answer but it seemed as though the magazine could fit as well as time went on."

Blueboy wasn't a gay band and Keith was the only member of the band who was gay but, as time went on, his lyrics became more about "his situation," as Paul calls it: "Keith never openly came out as gay. People said to me, 'Oh, were you a gay band?' But what does that mean? If you're a lyricist, you're probably going to write more from experience than anything else and it's right that you do that. We shared Keith's views on things. I'm not gay but I'm not anti-gay either. So equally, there were songs about other things."

Sukhdev Sandhu observes: "I was always interested in gay shame, which is this thing that developed in the late-'80s, early-'90s. Or queer shame, rather than gay pride. And Blueboy, I'm thinking about them as a queer band in relation to some of the more visible and sometimes fantastic artists around today. Music was about skin and vulnerability and wanting. I think queer culture is the best for thinking about the murky world between signals being sent and messages being heard."

The environment

In 1991, Sarah released a charity single, although one suspects that Friends of the Earth didn't see quite enough cash from 'Invisible' by The Forever People to rid the world of plastic, save the bees and tackle all the other issues they work on.

The Forever People was Greg Webster and Tim Vass formerly from Razorcuts, who reunited for this one-off fundraiser. The pair knew Clare and Matt from the indie scene so Sarah seemed the obvious label to go to with their new songs. "Forever People wasn't really a band. We didn't have any other songs and we didn't do any gigs. It was very much conceived as a one-off," states Tim. Greg expands: "'Invisible' is perhaps my favourite song that Tim and I wrote together, I absolutely love that song. I was really struck by how despairing Tim's lyrics are. I find it doubly depressing given the fact that we're decades later and the situation's got horrendously worse."

Razorcuts split in 1987 but Greg and Tim remained good friends. "We got talking about how screwed up the world was and how bitter and twisted we felt about how everything was in terms of politics and the environment, and we had the idea that it would be nice to get together and do some sort of recording that was explicitly about that," says Tim. "I also saw it as a neat way of putting a full stop on the Razorcuts story. We were keen for people not to think that when Razorcuts ended it was because we had fallen out. We wrote a couple of songs that lyrically it was really obvious what they were about, they were about the state of the world, they were about the environment and the fact the human race needed to do something and do it fast."

With just one single and two tracks to their name, understandably Forever People didn't really see themselves as a Sarah band, or even a band. "But there wasn't really any other label that would have been a better fit. Creation wasn't the Creation that we'd spent time with in our earlier years, and other indie labels had come and gone, but Sarah was still out there doing it successfully, so it felt like a good fit." Greg adds: "I don't know whether we were massively embraced by the Sarah audience. It was a bit of an anomaly really."

The insert for the single also deviated from Sarah traditions. Rather than being a piece of prose by Clare or Matt, it was a leaflet about Friends of the Earth. "The Sarah collectors who bought every record, they must have been a bit puzzled by the Forever People single," considers Tim. While Greg adds: "On that insert there's a few paragraphs from Friends of the Earth about what they're doing, and they're saying exactly the same things that Extinction Rebellion and everyone are saying now. But nobody listened." Tim adds: "That record lyrically could come out today. The message is more relevant now than it was then." 🍒

Sarah's only charity single was down to The Forever People with their song 'Invisible'.
Courtesy of Greg Webster.

*****

THESE THINGS HAPPENED:
Cathy Rogers, Heavenly

"What has been the thread through the whole thing is total authenticity. Matt and Clare were doing what they wanted to do, with music that they believed in, signing bands that bought into what they believed in and that hasn't changed. It wasn't a whimsical fashion thing where they swung this way because hardcore was really in, and then rock was really in... they didn't swing anywhere, they kept who they were and what they were about and, as far as I know, that's still who they are and what they're about. It wasn't subject to the vagaries of fashion and changing whims. And what I failed to fully appreciate at the time, because I never read *NME* or *Melody Maker*, looking at it now, the misogyny that existed in the world at large, even in the 1990s, is incredible."

Chapter 10
Letters from a Lifeboat

In the early 1990s, a Glaswegian journalist called Norrie Drummond was working on the *Western Daily Press* in Bristol as a features writer. He had moved to the city in 1988 after spending the best years of his career writing for the *NME* in London during the exciting decade of the 1960s. Former *Smiths Indeed* fanzine editor Mark Taylor remembers working alongside Norrie and says: "He had this incredible background. He was always pissed, and we always thought he was stringing us a line about how he hung out with The Beatles and Rolling Stones and The Kinks. But after he died [in 2005], we learned it was all true."

Mark recalls Norrie telling him what his life was like at the *NME*: "If you wanted to interview The Beatles or The Stones, you'd literally go round to their house. And that reminds me of that time in the early and mid-1980s for those labels and fanzines, that accessibility." The theory could be that, following the initial boom of pop in the 1960s, bigger layers of management came in with the supergroups of the 1970s which built inaccessibility and walls of divide between journalists/fans and the bands. But then punk came along to dismantle it all, meaning that by the time the early/mid-1980s came around the fanzine writers and independent labels that we are interested in for this book were afforded a new bout of accessibility. As Mark says: "It had been nice and cosy and friendly and accessible, then it got overblown into a big monster in the 1970s, then punk blew it all up again, and by the time the indie bands came through they wanted to carry on the punk ethic and you were friends with the bands again, rather than looking up at the stadium stage. Matt and Clare running a label, who'd have thought you'd run a label from a bedsit? I guess those early punk labels started in the same way. There were a lot of mirrors to what had gone on before. They were returning to that grassroots level of producing music and publications."

> ❝ We've kept all the letters we received. They're all in my loft but some of them are a bit mouse eaten. And whenever I try to move them, one falls out and it's always one from Bob Stanley to Matt."
> **Clare**

Pete Momtchiloff from Heavenly echoes this sentiment: "The Clash, The Damned and The Jam, their world was basically the same world as 1970s' rock. They still had managers and people on the doors and groupies and whatever. But the post-punk

Harvey Williams (pictured here in Paris, 1990), possibly singing about bananas and Enya. Possibly not.
Emmanuel Foricher.

era was very much about the ideology of doing it yourself. The Damned and The Clash were not about grassroots independence, they were big-time rock bands. But the groups that came after, yes. That movement definitely had the ideology that you shouldn't be separating yourself off from the fans. And if there are only 50 people at the gigs, it's really easy to talk to the band and they're not going to have a dressing room or anything." He adds: "If you went to these shows where a Creation band played, you could go and talk to them. You would see Alan McGee or Dick Green there. It wasn't like you had to be cool. [Jerry Thackray], who was the least cool person imaginable, knew everyone on the scene. It was such a small scene that it was very easy to connect with bands then. If we'd wanted to, we could have gone up to any of these bands and just said 'Look, we really like your band, can we play with you?' and they probably would have said 'yes.'"

Sarah superfan Tim Chipping made it his business to become friends with each new signing to his favourite record label, saying: "When Even As We Speak signed to Sarah, I was so excited to hear a new Sarah band. I wanted to look them up, write to them, be their friend. I turned up at the studio the first time Even As We Speak were there. They really hoped to see snow when they were here and it didn't snow but it snowed just after they left, so I went out and wrote their name in the snow and sent them a photo of it."

But Tim's devotion did not start and end with Even As We Speak. "I used to do that with every new Sarah band. I would think, 'How the hell do I become their friend?'" he says. "I got to hear about The Sugargliders from [mutual friend] Dave Harris, and I was really harassing Clare and Matt going, 'Have you signed The Sugargliders yet?' until they eventually did. So by the time The Sugargliders came over [from Australia], it felt like they were already my friends."

For fans of the music, it was exciting to be able to write to the bands, which was perfect for the more shy types in their audience who might not have plucked up the courage to approach them after a gig. Record sleeves and fanzines would often include addresses where you could reach the band, as fan Wendy Stone remembers: "It was nice you could write to bands. I used to write directly to loads of bands, even in America, and you'd get a reply. You didn't have to write to the record label because the bands put their home addresses on the sleeves." Indeed, Amelia Fletcher and Pete Momtchiloff's address in Oxford was so well known that they wrote a song about driving home from gigs late at night and called it 'Escort Crash On Marston Street'.

> ❝ In Leicester, we were looking in the window of a guitar shop the day of a gig, and a couple of people came up and said 'You're in Brighter, aren't you?' and it was like, 'Wow, yes!' But that was as close as we ever got to understanding what it was like to be in a 'real band'.
>
> **Alison Cousens, Brighter**

Sarah fan Neil Shumsky showed me a letter he received from Harvey Williams in 1989, evidently in reply to Neil's request for clarification on some Another Sunny Day lyrics. Harvey wrote: "Most people have remarked on the clarity of the words on the EP, so I suggest you listen more closely. However, here are some of the words you may be having difficulty with: times, before, what will be will be, bananas, masturbation, tennis, Enya, do you know what you've done, girl?, I was so shy, kill, muso, she's not worth it anyway, aragh. Hope these have been some help." Which could be repurposed as a WikiHow guide to writing your own Another Sunny Day song.

On the subject of Harvey, the b-side to 'In Gunnersbury Park' by The Hit Parade is a song called 'Harvey' about Julian Henry's good friend Mr Harvey Williams which includes the line: "Down Sinclair Road there's a house that I know, it's where Harvey comes home to each night," giving a tip-off to anyone who wanted to stalk the Another Sunny Day musician. "Me and Harvey have similar ideas about romance, we're idealists, so I wrote a song about him falling in love as I wondered if he'd feel the same as I would," says Julian. "When we played it live for the first time in New Cross, we were supporting Heavenly. They were sitting in the bar next door and when we played 'Harvey', I remember Pete [Momtchiloff] appeared in the crowd. He was listening to my words and laughing. I asked him afterwards what was funny. He said, 'I can't believe you wrote a song about Harvey' as if it was an odd thing to do. That surprised me. Why not write a song for a good friend?"

THE POETRY OF POSTCODES

But it wasn't just writing to the bands that was exciting, it was also fun to write to the record label bosses. Imagine striking up a pen pal relationship with Motown founder Berry Gordy or Columbia Records bigwig Clive Davis and asking them to help with your GCSE coursework. It would be unthinkable. But you could do just that with the people who ran Sarah. Future manager of The Sweetest Ache Marc Leverton was just 16 when he started a letter exchange from Swansea to Bristol with Matt: "To me, this was one of the interesting things about that scene. It was really accessible for young people. Rather than being just a consumer of music, which we all are as teenagers, what made that different was that you could partake in it through writing and buying fanzines and you felt you were part of this secret little club."

It's the exchange of letters with Clare and Matt that many record-buyers remember most fondly of their connections with Sarah Records. Just like me, many fans still have a big envelope stuffed with all the letters they received from Clare or Matt, whichever of the two seemed to correspond with them the most. For me, it was Matt who wrote the bulk of my letters. At one point, I must have asked Matt about the system because he sent me this lengthy explanation: "The way it works is that we do by-and-large try to divide you all into two distinct piles – mine and Clare's – so that whoever answers your very first letter is the one who'll answer all your subsequent ones. The theory is that that way we won't make embarrassing mistakes, eg if you write one time and it's 10 tear-soaked pages about how your one-legged Spanish boyfriend has just run off with a trapeze artist from Gateshead, we don't write back next time and say hey, have you heard the one about the Geordie tightrope walker and the one-armed waiter from Madrid? Because humour's a funny thing and you might just break down completely and, once out of therapy, never buy one of our records again. It's sound economics, basically. So yes, by making sure it's always me that replies to your letters, we can put together a sort of character study, a customer profile, and tailor our service to your own individual needs – we can think of you as a real person, Charlotte Jane, and not just a signature on a cheque.* (*Actually, we have a staff of 35 whose job it is to answer the mail, but they're all under strict instructions to sign themselves 'Matt' and hence give it that 'personal' feel. In reality, there is no such person.)"

Clare and Matt say it would never have occurred to them *not* to include a letter with each record they sent out, and that it stems from their fanzine backgrounds and the way people built up friendships via the post because that was how you found like-minded people. But certainly not all the letters were the multi-sided reams of A4 that I was fortunate enough to receive.

There was a theory that Clare wrote to the male fans and Matt wrote to the female

> ❝ Not laziness or sulkiness, just sheer (if I may) 'overwork'... all the letters that have to be THOUGHT about get shelved till I've time to think about them... and this entire summer was just non-stop fanzine folding, SAEs and writing tedious accompaniments – I'm still getting lots of letters every day to deal with, it's absurd ... this really has gone BEYOND A JOKE."
>
> **Letter from Matt to Pete Williams, summer 1987**

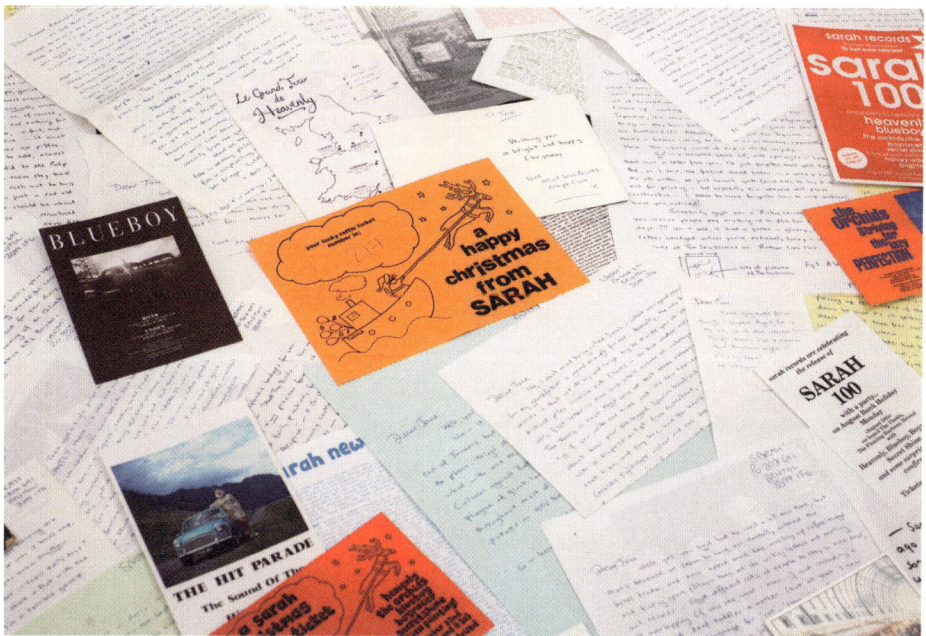

Who doesn't love getting post? These are just some of the many letters that Matt wrote to me during the final years of Sarah, when I really came into my own as a fan of the label.
Jon Craig.

fans but the pair quickly poo-pooed this notion when I put it to them, not least on the grounds that the overwhelming majority of the letters they received were from men, meaning that Clare would have had little time to do anything else had this been the case. "It was probably 80/20, 90/10 even," says Clare of the sex divide in letter writers. There were definitely two categories of letters that were written. The ones that were just perfunctory 'Thanks for the cheque, here's your 7"' letters, and the ones that were much longer and were written to people with whom they'd built up a postal friendship. "The long letters would be the fun letters with people we'd made friends with through the post, so those would probably be done on Saturday night with a bottle of wine," says Clare. "So you'd probably put the people you'd made friends with in the post or who'd sent you substantial letters on one side, and they'd probably get their records more slowly." Matt agrees: "There was a division between letters that were interesting to write and enjoyable to write, and the ones that were fairly perfunctory. We'd grown up in this world of exchanging letters with other fanzine writers and making friends through the post, so it was our social life, writing letters to people."

Clare and Matt were stunned to learn that other record label bosses were *not* spending every spare minute writing to their customers. "It's only in retrospect that we realised it took people by surprise to get a letter because most labels didn't do that," says Matt. The other thing the pair didn't consider was how exciting it

> "On long winter evenings, we often amuse ourselves with tales of times past, and 'I say, old girl, do you remember the time Julian in Newcastle telephoned?' always brings a flush of happy memories."
>
> **Letter from Matt to fan Julian Bester**

was for fans to receive a letter not just from a record label, but from one of the bosses of that record label. "I guess if you're a teenager and you get a letter from a record label, even though they might only be five years older than you, that seems like an extraordinary thing because you're not aware they're only five years older than you," considers Matt.

Clare and Matt are also surprised at all the Sarah fans around the world who have hung on to those letters for more than three decades. When I quoted some of his letters from the Sarah-era back to him during interviews for this book, Matt hid his face behind his hands and muttered: "You weren't supposed to keep them." Clare adds: "I find it quite uncomfortable when people post them on Facebook or Twitter or sell them with the records. Most of this is stuff I wrote when I was barely out of my teens. You kind of hoped people would hang on to the records but I don't think either of us has ever been much of a collector. Although I still have a letter I got from Ivor Cutler so..." However, Clare told me that she still has boxes containing every letter Sarah ever received, which makes me think, given the number of people who still have their letters from Sarah, that someone should piece everything back together as a mammoth cultural and historical study.

Before moving to London and co-founding Ché, Vinita Joshi was living in Rugby, attending school and trying to conceal her multitude of pen pals from her strict mother: "I would look through my bedroom window and wait for the postman pretty much every morning. I'd sometimes see a padded envelope and think it was definitely for me, that's a cassette! And back then there were two posts a day as well. I would sneak down as quietly as possible, take any mail for me and leave the rest on the floor, so my mum wouldn't know I'd retrieved the mail. There was so much post coming for me but Indians are very much like 'You should be studying'. 'Mum, it's Friday night, can I go and see my friends?' 'Why aren't you doing homework and studying?' I was very much under a lot of pressure to study. I didn't let her find out how much post was coming, there was just so much of it. I would read the letters under my duvet in the morning and I would spend all my lunchtimes at school writing letters in the library." Most delightfully, she adds: "I started writing to Stephen Duffy [of The Lilac Time] and, to this day, I write my 'e's like he does, like a 'c' with a line through it."

Wearing his academic hat, lifelong Sarah fan Sukhdev Sandhu has a very considered perspective on the realities of the postal exchanges for fans: "A letter is a relationship, a dialogue. To get notes and for them sometimes to be telling you about things that they're planning to do, that felt like a really nice gesture of sharing, because who am I? I'm just some nerdy boy, I'm not part of the industry, so for you to tell me that kind of thing is unusual. Sometimes they were a little bit bitchy but they were very literate. And that was part of their past and a function of their politics." Sukhdev adds: "At the time, it was unbelievable how much Matt knew about postcodes. He seemed to know where you were before you knew yourself."

LETTERS BE FRIENDS

During the writing of this book, I moved house. And this process unearthed a long-forgotten box that contained, among other things, a lever-arch folder stuffed with about 200 letters from the early 1990s. These were letters from fellow fanzine writers, or people with whom I'd struck up a pen pal friendship via the fanzine network, or occasionally from indie PR companies trying to get a review for their band in my fanzine. I had assumed this folder had been thrown away decades ago, so this was a very pleasant discovery and I spent a few hours sifting through it. Some of these correspondents were people who I'd recently got back in touch with for this book: Pete Dale of Slampt, Pete Morgan of Ivy, Marcus Törncrantz of *Grimsby Fishmarket*, Akiko Yamauchi of Sugarfrost and so on. The letters were a lovely way to return to a precise moment in time, to read people's voices in the moment and to recapture a sense of place. Letter writing was crucial to this world.

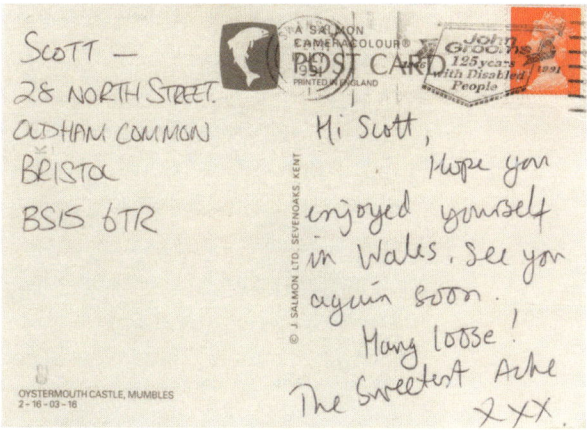

A charming postcard that The Sweetest Ache sent to their friend Scott Purnell of Secret Shine.
Courtesy of Scott Purnell.

Harvey Williams had been corresponding with Matt ever since he first wrote off for a copy of *Are You Scared To Get Happy?* and received a two-page letter with it. "The fact that he'd taken the time to write that letter made me think 'This is clearly someone who wants to do something in a very different way to the way the audience would expect it. He's prepared to put the time in and argue his case,'" says Harvey, who admits that his letter to Matt hadn't been 100% complimentary about the previous issue of the fanzine he had read. "I guess maybe that's why I wrote it, because I knew he was good at arguing. I've always been a devil's advocate kind of person, and even though I'm not very good at arguing I quite like an argument. So maybe I was trying to set up that dialogue. But it was very reassuring to get a two-page letter back from someone who you'd just written to for a fanzine."

The letters from Clare and Matt were never dull. There was always a strong entertainment factor in them, regardless of the subject matter, as Keris Howard of Brighter confirms: "The fact they were there handwriting letters, some of it was to fans and quite newsy updates, others were about booking studios and the business of running a record company. But they did it all in their own way, it was seamless, it almost didn't matter whether you were getting a postcard from them because they were in Paris,

> ❝ Hello again, your record company here.❞
> **Letter from Matt to Chris Quinn, The Orchids, late 1987**

or you were getting a letter which was talking about the next release, they always had the same tone."

Thinking about the business of writing letters, Clare says: "Having both been fanzine writers, sending letters out with the records just seemed obvious to us. We made connections through the post, with bands, venues, promoters and so on, as we always had in our fanzine days. And we made proper long-lasting friendships too – there are people I still see today who I got to know through exchanging letters with them in the late 1980s."

I was fortunate that the letters Matt sent me often extended to several sides of closely written A4, always in beautifully neat handwriting. One time, I must have mentioned that I was writing an essay for school about *Far From The Madding Crowd* because Matt responded with a diagram of the plot complete with exploding sheep. "I'd read that while I worked in the car park," Matt explains now, of his impressive knowledge of Thomas Hardy's 1874 novel. I comment that it seems hard to imagine Alan McGee sending Creation's customers illustrations of the plots of classic works of fiction, to which Matt muses: "I don't suppose he's ever read *Far From the Madding Crowd*." Fair point.

I wasn't the only one who Matt helped with their homework. Jonny James, who would later be in The Rosaries, wrote to Matt asking for help with an assignment for a business studies course he was doing. The task involved coming up with a business plan, so Jonny asked Matt how to set up a record label and received a very long letter in return. "There were pages of how much it cost to get a label printed on a 7", how much plastic bags cost, it was fantastically detailed," says Jonny. "At the end of the competition, we got feedback off these business people and they said 'We can't see how you're going to succeed because you're not going to be able to sign the next U2' and I thought that was funny and interesting, because of course that's the business person's bottom line. And I thought 'Up yours, mate.'"

> ❝ Nancy had a superfan called Alfred, I bet she didn't tell you that. I think he named a park after her in Taiwan."
>
> **Matthew Evans, Tramway**

But it wasn't just Clare and Matt who were writing letters, because lots of the bands were also spending their evenings hunched over a desk, quill in hand, scribbling feverish notes by candlelight, or something like that. Christian Savill of Eternal and Slowdive remembers: "You'd buy these records by The Groove Farm or The Bachelor Pad, and in those days they used to put their address on the records and you'd write to them and they'd write back and it would be really nice, so it was like a little friendly community. Which was nice, because if you're coming from Reading most people are just trying to kick your head in." Which was less nice.

Keris Howard wrote letters to fans in his spare evenings. "It seems incredible now, the idea of sitting down and writing a letter but I wasn't out living a rock'n'roll lifestyle. I was in on an evening if we weren't going to see a band, so I was writing letters to people who had written to Brighter and that was great. But the idea of doing that now would be inconceivable. You had people writing just telling you about doing their A Levels and the pressures of being 19. In what is still a relatively short period of time in terms of music history, things have changed so much in terms of the way people access music and the way they communicate with bands, and how bands can communicate with fans and tell them what's going on with them. It was such a different world then but more special for it."

Sometimes the bands were also writing to each other, such as when Blueboy's frontman Keith Girdler was in Brighton and drummer Martin Rose was in Reading. "Keith was a beautiful soul. He was such a funny bloke, his humour and his wit was so quick," says Martin. "I'm an old mod at heart, I still ride a scooter, and Keith always knew I was into that kind of music. He used to buy the *NME* and *Melody Maker* and he'd go through and find any article or photo of Paul Weller, The Style Council, anything like that, and he'd cut them out and post them to me. Keith was just a gentle soul. It was really sad when he passed but what a top bloke. I always loved being in a band with him."

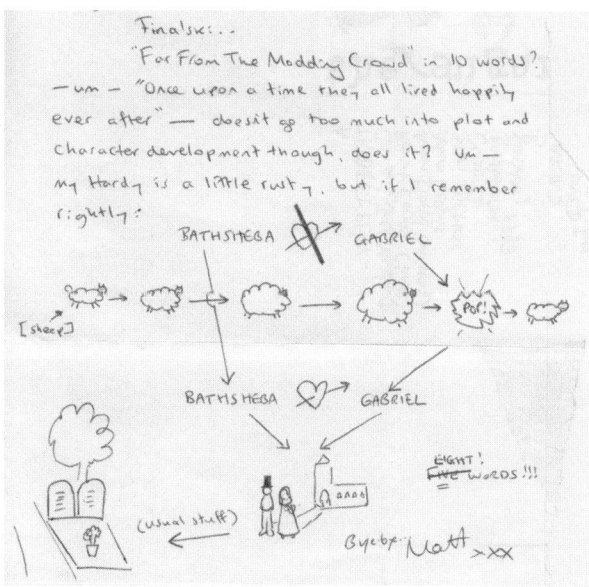

Matt once attempted to explain the plot of *Far From the Madding Crowd* to me... in pictures. It didn't help much.
Jane Duffus.

Nancy Horlick of Tramway remembers being surprised to receive any fan mail and just thinking "What is this?" when it would arrive. But sometimes it would lead to a fun meet-up: "There was a girl in Spain who moved to Liverpool to become an au pair, and we'd written to each other and I arranged to meet her in Liverpool. I got on a coach and went up, and it arrived hours late. I didn't get there until about 10 o'clock at night and had no idea what she looked like. But she was just over the moon that she was meeting Nancy from Tramway on Sarah Records... but it was just me!"

A Christmas gift for you

Clare and Matt were surprised at the volume of Christmas cards they would receive every year. "It would never have occurred to me to send a Christmas card to a record label. And I reckon at the peak we were getting a few hundred," says Matt. "The idea of sending a Christmas card to Creation or Factory, it wouldn't have crossed my mind. But people are sending a Christmas card to friends and relatives and have us on the same list as that, which is really rather nice." I was one of those Christmas card senders and, one year, I got one back, which was fun. In typical Matt style, it wasn't

Top left: Ivy's Spencer Harrison sent me a homemade Christmas card in 1994. **Top right:** This card is resurrected every December. **Bottom:** Tramway had become so prolific by 1991 that they needed a generic Christmas card to send to their mailing list.

Top left: Spencer Harrison. Top right: Jane Duffus. Bottom: Neil Shumsky.

actually a Christmas card, it was the leaflet from the back of the box that tells you what the cards say on the inside. For some reason I was persona non grata with Clare at the time, so the card was signed "Love, all at Sarah Records except Clare x". It was absolute genius. As Tim Chipping commented when he saw it: "What a brilliantly silly man."

There were gifts that came in the post to Sarah HQ as well, including a hammock and a pair of traditional Thai trousers. Friend-of-the-label Julian Bester posted Clare a kaleidoscope for her birthday one year, which went down well judging by the thank-you letter she sent him. But a favourite gift that was sent to the pair was a piece of the Berlin Wall, shortly after it came down in 1989. Clare still has it in her home office and showed it to me during one of our conversations for this book. Matt says: "This was somebody who was literally on the wall the night it came down. The idea that somebody would be on the Berlin Wall in 1989, chipping bits off and suddenly think, 'What shall I do with this? I know, I'll send a piece to Sarah Records.' It's fantastic."

> 66 Speaking of letters... the Christmas card count this year was the worst yet. Do you not love us anymore or something? Or is it simply that you think the commercialisation of The Birth of Our Lord has gone just too far, and this is your way of protesting? If so, could you please find some other way next year, because it's embarrassing when all the other record labels come round on Christmas Eve for mince pies and mulled wine."

Sarah Newsletter No 10, January 1995

THE VISITORS

"I was one of the people who came to Bristol to visit Matt and Clare at home," says former fanzine writer Marcus Törncrantz who called in with Nikolas Brunzell, his partner at *Grimsby Fishmarket*. The Swedish guests went to see the bands Bob and Secret Shine play a gig in Bristol with Clare, before going back to stay at the Gwilliam Street house. "Matt and Clare were really nice," Marcus says. "We asked them if we could help with folding sleeves or something like that. I could see how busy they were but they didn't want any help. I remember we sat in the kitchen, had a cup of tea, then we slept on the kitchen floor."

Japanese fanzine writer Akiko Yamauchi visited a number of times: "On my second visit to the UK in 1987, I visited Matt and Clare at the original Garden Flat. Matt had the Sha-La-La logo stuck on his bedroom door. My second visit to the Garden Flat was a couple of years later and I stayed for a week or so. Which was cheeky!" She adds: "They were surviving on cheap white toast. I was so hungry one day I even went and bought a sandwich from a corner shop and was eating it on a bench in Clifton Down, only to be spotted by Matt! That was a huge embarrassment. One day during that stay, The Orchids dropped in and then went straight out to the pub."

Peter Hahndorf, who ran the TweeNet website from Germany, says: "I first read about Sarah in fanzines, but at the time was buying all my records in shops and the local record shops in my town didn't carry any Sarah 7"s. So my first Sarah record was the *Shadow Factory* compilation, which I bought on 22 March 1989 and loved it. Most often I discovered many new bands through John Peel who at the time had a weekly radio show on my local pop station Radio Bremen Vier, and also one on British Forces Broadcasting Service, as there were still many British troops stationed in Germany at the time." He continues: "On my annual UK trip in the summer of 1988, I had a list of labels and bands I was planning to visit. These addresses were pulled from fanzines. That summer I did an Interrail tour of the UK by myself and came to Bristol. My list had Revolver Records on it which I visited, and also an address for Sha-La-La, even though at the time I didn't own any of the flexis and wasn't really aware of the backstory. So I walked up the long road and ended up in front of 46 Upper Belgrave Road, but there was no shop and no office, just a residential flat. So I did not ring the bell but just walked back down. Too shy, I guess. [Later] I came back and did stay on the famous floor a few times. I remember one time sharing the small front room with all of The Orchids." Were The Orchids ever in their own homes?

Having people come to stay was almost an everyday occurrence for Clare and Matt, who welcomed everyone with genial hospitality regardless of how busy they were running an internationally popular record label with no support staff. Matt

> 66 They'd have an unbelievable knack of showing up the day before the VAT return was due. So it was like, 'If you take that person out for the day, then I'll get the VAT return done.'
>
> **Clare**

apologised for his lateness in replying to me in one of his letters because: "Yesterday rather disintegrated shortly after your phone call – somebody came from Oxford to interview us at lunchtime, and then some Japanese people turned up wanting to look at us – they do that, the Japanese, it's very unnerving. It's a sort of pilgrimage thing – they bow, smile, take photos – I guess we should be flattered! Actually, it's not just the Japanese – there's a German coming to look at us on Monday, apparently. Hmm. The wacky world of pop in all its majesty."

And another time he wrote: "Well, yes, you have had to wait a bit this time, but that's because we seem to have accidentally entered the hotel trade, and now spend more time washing up coffee mugs and finding spare pillows than we do writing letters and mailing out records – FOUR different sets of people to stay in nine days, all overlapping (if you see what I mean...) and including a two-year-old deaf toddler and mother (but at least I now know the sign language for 'cat', 'sleep', 'bath' and, err, 'oh look, mummy's rolling a joint'). But I packed the last one off on a coach to London at 7.25 this morning so, without further ado, here is one Heavenly 'Atta Girl', one EAWS t-shirt, and page one of a Suede interview in Spanish."

As charming as it was having people come to visit, it wasn't always wildly convenient when you were just two people trying to run a business. One problem was that if a visitor had it in their head that they wanted to meet, say, Matt but ended up with Clare taking them on a walking tour of Bristol, that visitor might be a little disgruntled. "There was someone who had turned up and very much wanted Matt and not me and I was having to entertain them because he was doing something only he could do, which may have been the VAT return or may have been some artwork, but needed doing. So I took them off on a tour of Bristol but every half hour they said, 'And when can we go back to the flat and see Matt?' And I was like, 'No, we must go to Sea Mills and see where The Sea Urchins' record label photo was taken'. 'But when can we go back and see Matt?' 'He's doing a fucking VAT return!'"

Taking their home address off the back of records and investing in a PO Box certainly helped to cut down on the number of unscheduled guests. As did moving to Windmill Hill and not giving anyone the address.

Modern Talking

In Sarah's later years, there was a fancy new way for Clare and Matt to contact people, which was via the medium of fax. This was especially useful when bands were based further afield. "We used to communicate with Padraig [McCaul], who rather wonderfully worked in a priests' outfitters. So all our communications with The Harvest Ministers were sending faxes to a priests' outfitters in Dublin," recalls Matt.

"Most of the correspondence that Barbara [Powers] and I had with Matt and Clare was via fax," says FM Cornog of East River Pipe. "This was the early 1990s. They

The very latest in communications technology, AKA the Sarah Records' fax machine.
Courtesy of Sarah Records.

were in Bristol, we were in Queens. Barbara had a telephone/fax machine in the apartment. We'd get really excited when we saw an incoming fax roll out on the machine with Sarah letterhead." They never met during the Sarah era, but Clare did meet Barbara twice, when she happened to be over in New York, although FM wasn't able to make it: "My damaged psyche and drug problems didn't allow me to join her either time. Clare and Matt shared a kind of running joke about whether or not I even existed since they'd never even spoken to me. Later on, Barbara and I both met Clare very briefly in Jersey City at the WFMU radio station. We were all there to see the Sarah Records' documentary *My Secret World*. I bowed before Clare and thanked her for providing East River Pipe with a spiritual home. Then Barbara and I quickly jumped in my old Honda Civic and fled back to our little brick house 15 miles to the west to see our young daughter and our deaf Dalmatian. We're homebodies. So, though we only talked very briefly with Clare and we've never ever met Matt in person, that's OK. You know, it's funny, I really don't think it's necessary to meet people face to face in this life to feel a strong bond, or to love them, or to deeply appreciate them as we do Matt and Clare." 🍒

*****

THESE THINGS HAPPENED:
Joel Meadows, The Sugargliders
"It's an integrity thing. They weren't just wanting the world to be a certain way, they were doing it that way. It was everything from what appears on the covers to how they deal with the finances of the label to the way in which they relate to people and the stuff that they talk about. Sometimes I look back and think it was a bit embarrassing but we weren't pretending to be people we weren't, and I don't think the label was pretending to be something that it wasn't. It was just people living ordinary lives but aiming to do something that was remarkable in a non-showy way. When I listen to those songs from that era, that's what I'm struck by, people being honest."

Chapter 11

Recording Studios

When they started Sarah, neither Clare nor Matt had ever been in a recording studio (despite having put out a number of flexis), so they felt they should find out what it was all about to help them on their path to becoming international music svengalis. Which was why they popped down to a studio near the SS Great Britain in Bristol harbour when Sidmouth-based band The Visitors were recording. "We must have known we were going to The Sea Urchins' recording session and wondered how a recording studio worked," says Matt. The studio was "somewhere on Spike Island when there wasn't really anything there at all." That Spike Island studio was perhaps not a glamorous introduction to the world of recording studios: with a rat running across the carpet at one point and everyone inside wondering if the semi-derelict building was going to collapse at any moment.

The Sea Urchins had two days to record the tracks for the 'Pristine Christine' single, and Clare and Matt hitchhiked up to Birmingham for the second day when the songs were mixed. "I think we went and sat in the background and nodded, we weren't really going to get involved," says Matt. "It was literally the first time we'd been in that situation so we weren't going to interfere because we had no idea."

Guitarist Robert Cooksey recalls the first day in the studio as 27 August 1987: "We recorded 'Pristine Christine', 'Sullen Eyes' and 'Everglades' between 12 noon and 8pm at Rich Bitch Studios in Selly Oak, Birmingham. The first mix of 'Pristine Christine' was scrapped as it was felt my guitar solo was too distorted, so the solo was re-recorded at the mixing session on 2 September using Simon [Woodcock]'s Gretsch Tennessean. I don't remember Matt or Clare coming to any of the recording sessions but I do recall them being at Rich Bitch Studios for the 'Solace' mixing session." A letter from James Roberts to Clare confirms what Robert has said about the August 1987 session, while politely asking: "If you can send a deposit soon that'd just make everything unstoppable – they didn't say how much but I'd have thought about £30-£50 or something."

> 66 Oh good. We've always wanted to release a seven-minute guitar solo with somebody whistling over the top. No seriously – we love it!!!"
>
> **Letter from Matt to Chris Quinn, The Orchids, about 'What Will We Do Next?', 1989**

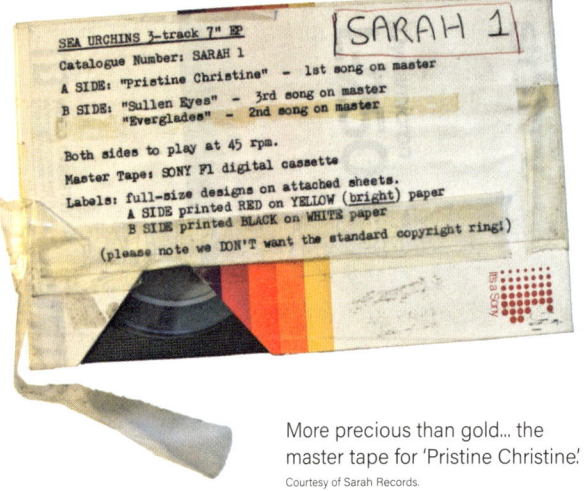

More precious than gold... the master tape for 'Pristine Christine'.
Courtesy of Sarah Records.

Clare and Matt made a point of paying for all of their bands' recording sessions but at the beginning it was a hand-to-mouth existence. Both had now sold the bulk of the last issues of their fanzines, so reinvested that money into studio time for The Sea Urchins. Clare explains: "I think 'Pristine Christine' cost about £300 to record and we scraped that together. If The Sea Urchins, between the six of them, had each put £50 in, they could have paid for their own recording. But I guess what we did was go and get the distribution deal and get it out there, so it's the two things together." Matt adds: "It was always a point of principle that we pay for all the recordings because we felt that's what a record label should do. Because if you're not going to do that, then what are you?"

I asked Clare and Matt if either of them had ever had any aspirations to be in a band themselves and was pleasantly surprised to learn that Matt played keyboard on 'When Morning Comes to Town' by The Field Mice, despite not knowing how to play the keyboard. "It's another example of us trying to save money," explains Matt. "Basically, when The Field Mice decided to do their first demo, they had no experience of recording studios, so they just looked for one that was local and found the address of one literally two streets away from Bobby [Wratten]'s house in Mitcham. This was Ian Catt's home studio, an eight-track set-up in the spare bedroom of his parents' house. And they liked it and got on with Ian, so ended up recording pretty much everything there. And often he'd end up playing keyboards or whatever and charging an appropriate session fee. So when, for their second single, Bobby and Michael [Hiscock] thought 'When Morning Comes To Town' could benefit from some keyboards, Ian volunteered. But he would have charged £40 and, somewhat recklessly, I said that if Bobby sent me the chords, I could try to come up with something. I'd never played keyboards but I'd bought myself a little Casio at some point and I could play classical guitar, so I knew about notes as well as chords. In retrospect, I'm stunned I had the nerve. I think it just came at the perfect moment. We'd gained some confidence as a record label, and the band hadn't yet realised they didn't have to put up with us interfering in what they were doing. I remember Michael looking extremely dubious when I started playing but then he smiled when I got to the higher melody line, so I think he was OK with it. And, in fairness, we'd always said that if it didn't work out, we were happy for Ian to do it instead. The best thing is, we then had £40 to spend on cocaine."

And, reader, you should know that 'When Morning Comes to Town' is not the only Sarah record to which Matt has contributed musically. He also played synth on Action Painting!'s 'These Things Happen'. Vocalist Andy Hitchcock says: "Matt has been a member of Action Painting! He's not bad, is he? I think he must be a frustrated Vince Clarke!"

Matt adds: "My bicycle features on the second Boyracer EP, on the teasingly entitled 'Untitled'. It's just Stewart [Anderson] playing the spokes with a drumstick or something. I'm not sure why." This is one of those things that I'm not entirely sure if Matt has completely made up or whether it might be true. I'm going to go with 'true' but, if it's not, you can all laugh at my naïvety when I'm out of the room. PS: Clare insists she has never played on any records. But I'm not sure if I believe her.

Recording through the night

While there were plenty of small recording studios dotted around the country that catered for local bands wanting to record a basic demo, if you wanted to really toot your horn, you needed to get yourself into one of the bigger studios. And by booking the unpopular graveyard slot, which was often available for 50% of the day rate, and recording when everyone else was tucked up in bed, smaller bands could gain access to better recording equipment, superior instruments and half-decent sound engineers.

Once The Sweetest Ache had agreed that Sarah would put out a 7", the band settled on a budget with the label and then booked Von's in Islington, London. "It was this bizarre place. We got a cheap night session, which meant you started at midnight and went until about 6am," says the band's manager Marc Leverton. "We'd told Matt and Clare that we'd deliver them the master tape with two songs on but then we recorded four songs really quickly. Which was a clever plan. We thought that if we gave them too much music, they'll like that." The plan clearly paid off, because Sarah put out two 7"s by the Welsh band in quick succession.

It wasn't a smooth experience, though. On the road from Swansea to London, the van driven by bassist Dave Walters' dad caught fire, with flames coming out of the engine and everything. The band hastily rescued all of their equipment from the back, as guitarist Stuart Vincent recalls: "I remember being on the side of the M4 with this Mercedes Sprinter van on fire, chucking out drum kits and snare drums and all sorts before they caught fire." In hindsight, Stuart wonders why on earth they went all the way to London to record: "Swansea and west Wales have got an abundance of really good, quite cheap, recording studios. But that was too obvious for us."

However, once they got to Von's, the band found recording to be a pretty fun experience, although working through the night certainly had its challenges and everyone was somewhat snoozy by the end of it. "There is a definite lazy quality to my vocal and the drums were very louche. It worked out alright, though," says

Various members of The Sweetest Ache in the studio, trying not to set fire to anything.
Courtesy of Simon Court.

vocalist Simon Court. Clare adds: "It's just got that sleepy feel to it, it's beautiful."

Exciting as recording may have been, The Sweetest Ache realised they had been lured in by the vanity of recording in a London studio that had previously worked with some of their musical heroes like Slowdive and Lush. "It was the first time we'd ever stepped foot in a recording studio and we didn't have a clue what was going on," says Stuart. "I remember how arrogant the engineers were, it was very much, 'It's your time, you're paying, do what you want'. But when you're in that environment for the first time, you want a bit of guidance."

The band learned from this and, by the time they recorded their album *Jaguar* in 1991, they had moved to The White House in Weston-super-Mare, which was popular with lots of Sarah bands. "Matt and Clare popped down on day three or four. It was really nice having them there. It was quite affirmative when you could play back tracks that hadn't quite been finished or mixed properly to see a reaction. Someone's face speaks 1,000 words when they're hearing something for the first time," says Stuart. "I remember with a sense of pride thinking that they were sounding good and far more polished than we'd managed in the past, because we'd finally found an engineer, Martin [Nichols], who was very supportive."

14 Iced Bears also exploited the graveyard slot to get a better rate when they recorded 'Come Get Me' in Kemptown, Brighton. "That was my first experience of being in a recording studio, apart from at the BBC's Maida Vale," says keyboardist Sue Freeman. "I was fascinated. I was so into my music, it was the be all and end all for me, and just getting involved in that side of it was really interesting." Frontman Rob Sekula adds: "The engineer, Terry Popple, started telling us how he'd just been touring as Van Morrison's drummer. To my shame, it meant little to me at the time. Now I'd feel different after hearing his albums like *Astral Weeks*, which I really love. It was our only time recording with Stephen Ormsby. His looping bass runs towards the end of 'Sure to See' really give the song a lift. I'm sure, like a lot of indie types, I hadn't given much thought to looping bass tracks but what he did is still remarked on by people who talk to me about that song to this day. Maybe he should get some sort of award for services to indie. Also Sue chimed in admirably with some swirly keyboards to give 'Come Get Me' a bit of a psych-y tinge, which was an unconscious hint of the direction we were on towards our first album. I think it cost about £300 to record and mix, which was probably more than they'd budgeted for but they were absolutely fine about it. As I said, a great label to be on." (For clarity, that £300 session eventually became £400.)

The Field Mice were also no strangers to the midnight session. Drummer Mark Dobson tells me about the recording of 'September's Not So Far Away': "The first time I went into the studio with The Field Mice, for some reason Bobby had decided not to use Ian Catt. We went into a studio in north London somewhere. I remember going in and the studio smelled lovely, and it turned out Kylie Minogue had been in there the day before. Because we were operating on a Sarah budget, we could only afford to do it overnight. So we had the studio from 10pm until 8am and everyone fell asleep except me. We had to rescue it by going back to Ian's with our tails between our legs. Ian was fantastic, he did a great job of cobbling together a group of people who, with the exception of Harvey [Williams], didn't really know what they were doing."

Julian Knowles of Even As We Speak recalls: "In 1992, throughout that year we recorded *Feral Pop Frenzy*. It was a bit of a difficult task because Sarah didn't exactly have money. And to record an album in 1992 when you didn't have money was not an easy thing to do because we didn't have computers at home, and you can't do all of the things that you can do now. You had to pay for studio time, and so Matthew [Love] and I were working at the A[ustralian] B[roadcasting] C[ompany], we were working in sound there together and Paul Clarke who was in that iteration of the band was also working there but in a different area. And so we managed to scrounge a little bit of studio time through the ABC and we would sneak in after hours and then, because studio time was the cheapest between midnight and dawn, we would just have to stay up all night, which is not the easiest way of being able to record."

In fact, the massive folder of photos Even As We Speak sent me for this book includes numerous pictures of band members asleep on studio couches at midnight sessions to keep costs down. Sometimes... completely down. "I had a friend who had a recording studio who cut us a little bit of a deal and then we knew people who had the keys to studios, which was a bit naughty," says Julian. "We did sneak in there after hours when no one would know. I remember our friend John, who was doing some engineering on the record. He had the keys to a studio called The Powerhouse which was in Alexandria, and because we hadn't finished a song, we'd run out of studio time, John said, 'Oh, let's go to Powerhouse, I've got the keys'. So we just let ourselves in and got a session or two for free. I hope Powerhouse won't read this book because they'll send us a bill. Back in those days, even the midnight til dawn sessions would probably have been worth about £300 a session." Sarah did, of course, give Even As We Speak some money for recording but it was nowhere near as much as the band needed to record *Feral Pop Frenzy*. Which is quite an involved and ambitious album if you listen to all the different things going on there.

Enjoying recording

Cathy Rogers of Heavenly is someone who "absolutely loved being in a recording studio". She says: "Whatever gadgets and gizmos they had, I loved it. It's a pure sense of space to create and you don't have that in many parts of your life. I had the real sense of the luxury of being on the inside of this place and feeling really happy and lucky to be there."

Presumably her bandmate Amelia Fletcher also loved the studio, given how many records she has both made and contributed to in her career, as Matt commented to me in 1994: "Amelia has done many things under many names... The Catherines of

Arrogance is her, Liz [Price] and Eithne [Farry], and she played recorder for The Carousel. Backing vocals... Pooh Sticks, Wedding Present, Popguns, Brilliant Corners, Hit Parade – and of course it's her exquisite saxophone solo that enlivens the final five minutes of the 12" mix of Jimmy Nail's recent Number One smash." And Nick Heywood's *Tangled* LP.

Martin Rose was drafted in as Blueboy's new drummer after Lloyd Haggar moved on. An experienced musician, Martin was no stranger to the studio. "Normally, when you go with a band to record and there isn't much of a budget, it comes out of your own pocket, so that's why everything was always quick," says Martin. "But I remember coming along to recording sessions for Blueboy thinking 'I haven't got to pay for this!' and it was great. Paul [Stewart] is a great jazz guitarist, he's got a brilliant ear for knowing exactly what should go where and the parts he plays are just amazing. So I always loved recording with him."

Mathew Fletcher of Heavenly: happily talking nonsense about how lyrics get written.
Jon Cole.

Boyracer's Stewart Anderson was a massive fan of The Groove Farm and when he found out that a lot of their records had been recorded at Tim Rippington's Southside Studio in Bristol, that was the only place that he wanted to go to make Boyracer's records. Tim says: "When Stewart discovered that I'd started this studio, he said 'If you're recording in there, then that's where we want to do our recordings because we want to record where Andrew [Jarrett] is recording.'" Stewart adds: "Tim seemed to know what he was doing and was very sympathetic to what we were trying to do. He was just a super fun person to be around. He had a studio in a little lock-up on an industrial estate in Bristol and we'd go down there and it would be great fun."

Southside Studios was just off Whitehouse Lane in Bedminster, a five-minute walk from Clare and Matt's house on Gwilliam Street. However, Boyracer chose to bring their sleeping bags and kip in the studio, after nipping to the mammoth supermarket nearby to stock up on cheap beer. "It definitely became a party vibe, and we would go to Asda and get our 99p breakfasts in the morning and then wait for Tim to show up. We'd probably stayed up all night writing songs," says Stewart.

As engineer and producer, Tim enjoyed his sessions with Boyracer. "They were pleased because they liked to play really loud and Stewart always had about four fuzz pedals that would go completely mad," says Tim. "I think when they'd been in studios before, everyone had just told them to turn it down and tone it down, and when they came and recorded with us it was, 'Do what you want and we'll try and capture it.' So they really liked that and the fact that things got done really quickly. They didn't like the

❝ Only the lyrics tend to get left to the last minute, because we are so lazy and inept. But the songs with 'messages' have usually been a little better prepared and thought out. You can tell a song written in a hurry because it will rhyme 'you' with 'true' and probably be about cat food.❞

Mathew Fletcher, Heavenly, letter to me, summer 1994

Boyracer liked to maximise the studio experience by recording as many songs as humanly possible in the time available. They became extremely proficient at this.
Debbie Kaye.

idea of hanging around for four hours while you mic'd up a drum kit. Studios can sap the life out of you if you're in a big studio and they spend two hours on the snare drum and that kind of thing."

The need for speed meant that, while most bands on a Sarah budget might push to get two or three songs done in 48 hours, Boyracer could easily record up to eight songs in two days. "I used to do my best to make it sound right," says Tim. "I think Stewart sometimes would have just let practically anything go out but we were a proper studio. We were letting them do things fast and loud but it wasn't going to sound like rubbish, and I think he liked that. It was a compromise between the all-out noise and speed but it had some sort of quality control. I used to like to fiddle around a lot with beefing-up guitar sounds, so if they had an idea for a noisy guitar, I'd try and make it sound twice as noisy. But they liked having someone recording who had the same ideas about recording as they did. At a lot of studios, the engineers might be into some completely different sort of music but the sort of music I was making with [my band] Beatnik Filmstars at the time was similar noisy stuff, so we were always developing new ways to capture noise."

James Roberts says that going into the studio was his favourite part of being in The Sea Urchins, much more than playing live gigs. "I found it really, really exciting. To us, that's the kind of thing that

> 66 We don't particularly want you to record in such a mad haste rush that you all have breakdowns afterwards – and only partly because we want you to do lots of gigs afterwards to promote it."
>
> **Letter from Clare to Scott Purnell, Secret Shine, about recording *Untouched*, 1992**

real bands do," he says. "It was all done on the cheap, we were only ever in there for a day for anything we ever did. And most of what we did was knock a live version down of the song, and there might be backing vocals that you'd do on top. We didn't have the time to do anything fancy or layered or what have you. But I always really enjoyed that. You don't have that pressure of the gig or anything like that. You are just getting into it."

FIRST TIMERS

By the time Anne Mari Davies joined The Field Mice at the end of 1990, the band had secured a position as one of the most popular bands on Sarah but there was still a need to keep costs down. The album *For Keeps* was recorded during Anne Mari's two-week Easter break from university in 1991, although she was suffering with tonsillitis and singing was agony. "I really loved recording but I was nervous the first time I went in," she says. "We recorded with Ian [Catt], at his parents', which was a very noisy building and there was always somebody mowing the lawn outside or something. It was on a budget, there's no two ways about it."

Alison Cousens from Brighter echoes this: "There was certainly one time in Ian [Catt]'s studio where we had to let his mum and dad mow the lawn before we could carry on with what we were doing. Everything was a bit makeshift." Brighter went to Ian's in November 1989 to record their second single, 'Noah's Ark'. "That was the first time I'd ever been in a studio and the first time I'd ever met Matt and Clare. So that was a big day for me because I'd been writing to Clare for a while at that point," says Alison. "Not to inflate Matt's ego but it was: 'You are such an iconic figure out in the fanzine world and you don't realise what it is when somebody meets you.' Because I knew how I'd felt when I met them, which was just like 'Wow!' And that stayed with me as we started to play live and we became an entity as Brighter, suddenly realising that people were coming to us with the same sense of 'Wow!' that I'd gone to that first recording in November 1989 with them. We were all just ordinary people just trying to get along." These days, while Ian Catt is still a busy engineer, he works in a studio where the musicians are untroubled by the external sounds of lawnmowers.

Ivy had originally recorded 'Wish You Would' for a compilation EP on Norwich's Noisebox label but headed to Purple Studios to re-record the track for Sarah. "We were on a tight budget," remembers the band's manager and drum programmer Pete Morgan. "It was £99 a day if I recall correctly, and it probably cost less than £200 to do all four tracks. Listening back now, the drum machine is a bit busy, which is my fault, and we all preferred the lo-fi feel of the original eight-track version of 'Wish You Would'. I suspect Sarah did, too."

The gap between being signed and heading into the studio was so short for Secret Shine that they barely had time to think. Although they had done a demo on a four-track in Bournemouth, heading to Sarah's favourite White House was the first time most of the band had been in a proper studio and it led to some unexpected results. "It was cleaner than we wanted, it was incredibly polished and precise and we were not used to that," says singer Jamie Gingell. "I think it took a little bit away from it if I'm honest. We were definitely rough around the edges live. I wouldn't have said I wanted the demo over the recording but it was maybe the shock of someone telling you that you're out of time and you're out of tune and the rest of it."

In the early days, it was just Jamie and his friend Scott Purnell in Secret Shine. "I played every single instrument on the record, which was quite a lot of work, and Jamie just sang," says Scott. "By the time we did 'Honey Sweet' back at the White House, we had a band so I didn't do as much on that one. We looked for somewhere else to record *Untouched* and *Loveblind*, and that's when we found PIJ in Bristol which is Paul Horlick's studio, and a guy called Corin Dingley, who was the engineer who did our last album." "PIJ was great. We were just messing around with getting lovely sounds out of amps and recording feedback, it was all the stuff you want to do in a band, whereas Martin [Nichols] in the White House was 'Do that guitar line. Do it again. Do it again,'" says Scott. "When we recorded all those songs, we only had Jamie singing and then he met Kathryn [Smith]. It sounded like we'd arrived. Jamie is so good at twisting these harmonies around, and good at writing harmonies for Kathryn to sing. It just sounded wonderful."

FUN FACT: Paul Horlick is now married to Nancy Horlick (née Evans) of Tramway, which Scott had been a member of when the band was still called Panda Pops. It's a small world.

Of course, it could be a bit scary having your new record label bosses overseeing your debut recording session, as Scott explains: "The first recording was at the White House, which was really funny because we picked up Matt and Clare on the way. Can you imagine how nervous I was?! I was 18 or 19, picking up these guys in my car who I'd held up as heroes, which wasn't a great car, driving them down to the studio."

In common with a few others in this book, Jamie found recording much more fun than playing live and saw gigs as merely a means to an end. "I was much more interested in the recording process and doing that side of things than playing live. That was always something I had to do to get to the recording of the records," he says. "I liked the possibilities when you went into a studio. A studio was the only place that had all this rack-mount gear and all this tech wizardry that you could never hope to do at home. It's not like now, where you could sit in your bedroom and produce a platinum-selling album. Back then, we literally had a little cassette to record on. So having delays and reverbs and distortion and god knows what, and the quality was a massive quantum leap. So it was that realisation of your art. I guess you don't often get it with other things. If it's painting, you could do an amazing painting at home, it's not going to necessarily be better if you go somewhere else. With recording at that time, there was no way you could do such a high-quality project without going to the studio. I think it's the excitement of bringing your song to life."

Of course, it's one thing to bring your song to life and another to risk drowning it… in the Solent. Secret Shine's album *Untouched* had been mixed in Brighton and,

Secret Shine (pictured here at The Tropic in 1991) enjoyed recording locally to their Bristol homes.
Wendy Stone.

pleased with their work, the band hopped on the last train home to Bournemouth. Only for the train to terminate in Portsmouth and there were no more trains because it was the middle of the night. "I had to phone up my granddad, wake him up and get him to pay a fisherman to row us across Portsmouth Harbour holding this precious reel," laughs Kathryn. "And I was worried because it was worth at least £3,000 in terms of recording time and mixing," says Jamie. "That was a bit hairy."

Here's another recording studio boo-boo. Former Talulah Gosh bassist Chris Scott was working in a shop in Oxford that hired sound equipment and the shop's new Saturday boy was a Bristolian kid called Chris Young, who turned out to be a big fan of Talulah Gosh. "He was in Tramway, one of the less famous Bristol bands," says Chris. "So me and Greg [Webster] went down to produce the first Tramway single, 'Maritime City'. The recording studio had reverb that used to switch itself off, so you'd be going and suddenly all the reverb would disappear. We did this recording and Greg went down to do the mixing and he came back and said, 'The reverb switched itself off and you hadn't noticed. There's no reverb', and one thing we know about these kinds of bands is they love loads of reverb, so we had to go back and do it again." Oops.

On the other side of the North Atlantic Ocean, a band called Black Star Carnival were quids in after winning a local Battle of the Bands competition where the prize was some studio time at the nearby Blue Whale in Palm Desert. Singer Beth Arzy explains: "The studio was basically in this guy's house and it was just a glorified

Over in the US, Aberdeen first entered a studio after winning a Battle of the Bands competition. Courtesy of Aberdeen.

eight-track. But he was super nice and we had a great time recording and did the demo, and I think that's what we sent to Matt. That was around the time we were transitioning to be Aberdeen."

Aberdeen recorded two singles for Sarah, 'Byron' and 'Fireworks', and with the label's backing they were able to go to a proper studio to re-record the songs from the demo for the first single. With just one day booked for the recording, Beth headed into the studio with bandmates John Girgus and Jenni Fields. With Aberdeen having become used to producing their own music, John was alarmed when the studio's engineer sent the band out of the studio while he mixed the tracks: "I was like, 'What? No!' And I was disappointed with how the songs sounded. And Matt was also disappointed. They were really nice, professional mixes but it lacked the creative dynamic and Matt wrote this big fax letter on our mistakes. I read it and I was like, 'Yes, absolutely.'" Consequently, 'Fireworks' was recorded at a studio in Orange County with an engineer who "let us get a little weirder and just have fun in the studio, and that's why 'Fireworks' was more of what Matt wanted. And what Matt wanted was totally what I wanted. I guess if a recording is too tame, it's just not going to be fun to listen to," says John.

By the time Shelley came to record 'Reproduction is Pollution', the band was having fantasies of pop stardom, as singer Tim Chipping explains: "Myself, Dickon [Edwards] and Steve [Jefferis] went into the studio in Camden [London] and, because we were already having these pop dreams, even by that point I'd gone, 'I don't want this single to be entirely jangly and guitar.'" To help with this goal, Shelley approached Sarah stalwart Harvey Williams and asked for his advice, although Harvey drew the line at actually performing on the record. "Me and Dickon had discovered David McAlmont and I wanted us to sound like Thieves but we had no idea how to. I remember hearing Steve asking Dickon why I was now singing in an American accent! I wasn't, I was just trying to sing properly. So even that was a rebellion from what we thought we were supposed to sound like, which is why we thought Matt and Clare would hate us, as we didn't sound like the jangly indie band they'd heard on stage."

'A GROSS MISUSE OF STUDIO TECHNOLOGY'

One of the prerogatives of running your own record label is that you can say if you don't like something and don't want to put it out. After all, a key part of running Sarah was that Clare and Matt were releasing music they themselves liked. The trouble was, this could lead to a few awkward conversations with bands.

Before he joined The Field Mice, Harvey Williams was recording for Sarah as Another Sunny Day but ran into trouble early on with the recording of his second single 'What's Happened?', which just wouldn't sound right no matter what he did: "The only time I ever remember Matt picking something apart was when I recorded my second single in Bristol and the session didn't go very well." Harvey returned home to Penzance to think things over, while Clare and Matt kept the tape in Bristol to study. "They sat there and tried to work out why it didn't work, and they made this list of why it didn't turn out the way we wanted. And that was quite disheartening, the fact they'd actually sat down and thought it out and said 'Why isn't this good? How can we make it good?' It was a grim old couple of days. I went back and re-recorded it and it still didn't work so we used the demo, which I'd done at home on my little Portastudio."

In retrospect, Harvey wonders if it was having Clare and Matt in the studio that put him off his stride. "When I'm working, I'd rather just have me and the engineer, without other people milling around watching," he says. "I was quite shy and trying to do a vocal when you know there are all these people in the other room, listening out for you to make a mistake or not quite hit the note right, that was a distraction."

In the run-up to The Field Mice's *For Keeps* album, the band were told that some of the songs they had submitted for release constituted "a gross misuse of studio technology". Ouch! "We were like, 'Ooh, that's quite harsh,'" laughs Anne Mari Davis with the benefit of almost three decades of hindsight. "There were quite a lot of tensions around what we wanted to do. I don't know how much was down to whether they just didn't like it because at the end of the day they were putting out records they liked." I should interrupt here to say that both Clare and Matt have

> ❝ I think we are quite tough, we do give them a hard time and we do record things and refuse to release them. For us, there's no fun in it if we don't like the music. I mean, it's not a money spinner, it's very hard work, and the enjoyment is the music."
>
> **Clare on the Mark Goodier Evening Session, Radio 1, 29 July 1992**

no recollection of this, with Clare suggesting: "That might have been how Bobby [Wratten] translated what we said when he relayed it to Anne Mari. That might have been what we were trying to say but I don't think we'd have said it like that."

Nonetheless, Bobby agrees with Anne Mari's version of events. He explains: "Things were strained with Sarah and I didn't help by not including a track list! So, 'a gross misuse of studio technology' – it's funny how Anne Mari and I remember the wording exactly – was applied to 'Freezing Point', specifically the ending where all the distorted guitars fade back in backwards. The whole [analysis] of the LP [by Sarah] was full of little digs, such as 'the Killing Joke one' ('Freezing Point' again) and 'we don't like the song but this is a better, slightly harder version' ('Coach Station Reunion') and 'it's a shame the single is a dance track with female vocals' ('Missing the Moon')."

Matt would like to step in here and explain things from Sarah's perspective: "They sent us a cassette tape with no track listing. So calling a track that has no lyrics 'The Killing Joke one'" is purely descriptive, it's not a dig. The comment about 'Missing The Moon' is, I'm pretty sure, a misunderstanding – it's my favourite Field Mice song and obviously it had already been decided that this would be the single. I'm guessing we said it as a jokey comment on the ludicrousness of Sarah Records having to market a dance track, especially when the singer everyone associated with The Field Mice wasn't taking the lead vocal. But the problem with doing everything via letters is that tone can get lost. For a feminist label to object to a female vocal makes absolutely no sense."

Anne Mari picks up the story again: "[Our later Sarah band] Northern Picture Library was more experimental than The Field Mice. It felt like there was a certain freedom from not having to have a Sarah sound or to please the fans. I can't say that Bobby ever wrote to please the fans, he just wrote what he wrote and his influences are far and wide. Depending on what he was listening to, he would write a very eclectic mix of songs. So I don't think he was ever trying to write things that the fans would like or something that would sell well, or that would be a good single. But I do think the Northern Picture Library music was a break; he has got a real experimental bent to his brain and everything he's done since The Field Mice has gone more leftfield."

Talking about the Northern Picture Library songs that were submitted to Sarah, Bobby says: "I got a letter back saying they loved the name but within each song there'd be a lyric that there was no way they could release. 'Lucky' was said to be something that the Mothers' Union could have written. I was mystified. I didn't know what the Mothers' Union was, only that I felt so, so lucky to have met Anne Mari and to have found what we'd found. Also, there were other songs that didn't survive the attacks. They said they wanted revolution and positivity and a certain spirit, not my defeatist numbers." At this point, I will interrupt again to stress that Bobby is saying all of this with a smile on his face and he makes it clear that he bears no bad feelings towards Sarah or to Clare or Matt. He adds: "There's so much positive stuff I could say about Clare and Matt, I owe them so much. They're wonderful people but because we were very close to them, things could get messy. We were not some distant band they'd never met. We were part of each other's lives."

Keris Howard of Brighter was less bothered by suggestions from the label as to how the music could be improved as he was by suggestions that some of his lyrics needed amending. "I remember Matt trying to get me to change the lyrics on a song called 'Out To Sea'. I don't know why he thought he could do that," says Keris. "It's one thing saying he thought we should turn the bass down or whatever, it's another thing telling someone you don't like their line. It's one of those things that, when I think back, I feel quite angry about it. But I don't think I felt that angry at the time, I think I just accepted it, so it's probably not justified to carry a grievance around it. A lot of the stuff was quite heart-on-sleeve stuff, so knock backs and criticism could be quite difficult at times."

When Mary Wyer and Julian Knowles pause to consider if Sarah ever rejected anything from Even As We Speak, the two collapse in laughter. "We were quiet punks," begins Julian, explaining: "If you listen to *Feral Pop Frenzy*, you hear that creative punk attitude in it because it doesn't conform to any sort of conventional idea of what a record should sound like. But when it came to the single for 'Blue Eyes Deceiving Me' and 'Air', which are pretty straight ahead, we did do, as a counterbalance, this thing called 'The Pressurehead', which was a weird spoken word, science-fiction narrative about oppressive forces and people living inside the pressure head that had a processed voiceover from Matt [Love] and then all of this science-fiction background and sound design. I think Matt and Clare thought it was just too out there for them. Fair enough but at the time we were thinking, 'Oh, come on!' We wanted to do things that had a little bit of quiet anarchy going on in them, that we didn't want to just do things that were completely expected the whole time. But that was too much for them."

The Golden Dawn had started strongly on Sarah with two enduring singles but then it all went wrong and the tracks they submitted for their third single were wholeheartedly rejected by the label. "For the longest time, we'd planned our third release as 'Black' and 'The Surf Song' on the a-side, and probably 'Siren Song' on the b-side," says Ulric Kennedy. "I'd already taken photos of Peter and Louise's kitten, named Black after our song, to use as our cover star, and if we'd stuck to that plan it would have almost certainly been our best Sarah release yet but Robert [Smith] had a song called 'Our Children', which contained the line 'Life is so hard in the 1980s' and at some point it was decided that we had to do that instead, as it was 1989 and it was supposedly about to reach its expiry date. So we booked the studio time and decided to do our most ridiculous, rambling tune on the b-side."

The story rapidly descends into the tragic tale of a band's

> ❝ The Golden Dawn had to remix [their new single] because it wasn't unpleasant enough."
>
> **Letter from Matt to fan Neil Shumsky, 1989**

You are invited to enter the strange and mysterious world of The Golden Dawn.
Courtesy of The Golden Dawn.

complete collapse, as Ulric says: "'No Reason Why' was basically designed to be annoying. We were well aware that Sarah would probably hate the song but we probably thought they'd just accept it as us playing the label's pantomime villains, which is how they liked to characterise us. Anyway, we laid down the backing tracks and when the time came for Robert to sing his lead vocal on 'Our Children', he'd changed the lyric to a stream of pseudo-psychedelic codswallop of the most inept variety. The original lyric was bad enough as it stood but the new one was utterly cringeworthy, and was foisted on us in an extremely underhand manner." Put simply: "The band probably died right there and then for me; I didn't even take away a cassette of the tracks to listen to, I was so pissed off."

Poor old drummer Peter Claughan was also pissed off because he got sacked from the band, yet he was the one who seemed to care most about what happened to The Golden Dawn. So how does he remember things? "I did make a desperate phone call to ask Sarah to reconsider releasing the third single, as I believed it to be worthy in a 'Sister Ray' [by Velvet Underground] sculptured noise kind of way but I think we'd drifted too far into the 'noise' side of things. It was all a bit depressing really, the recording had been rushed and one of the songs ('Luminous') had been a recent rewrite of an earlier song and the new lyrics seemed ill fitting and senseless. At some point over the lifespan of the Dawn, I'd started mental health nurse training and was less available for Dawn duties. I had also been going out with my girlfriend, now my wife, for quite a while and I guess it was time to grow up." So there you have it, the sun had set on The Golden Dawn.

Tramway also had their third single rejected by Sarah. "They said they didn't want to put out country music, even though they did elsewhere," shrugs frontman Matthew Evans. "We were quite annoyed they didn't want to do the third single, I thought it was quite good myself. When they didn't want that third record, that kind of affected us a wee bit. We were quite disappointed, which we didn't expect to be and looking back now I can't believe I did feel like that. I can't think why that that would matter but at that age it did have some effect."

Of course, it's worth remembering that while it can't have been pleasant for a band to hear that their label didn't like their new music, it also wasn't much fun for the label to be the bearer of that bad news. "I remember when we didn't release 'Day Into Day' by The Sea Urchins, which then came out on *Stardust*," says Clare. "I was at New Street Station in Birmingham and had to call Robert [Cooksey] and explain why we weren't releasing it and he was sort of playing with me because he was trying to get me to explain exactly what we didn't like about it. That was just the toughest phone conversation of my life."

SARAH IN THE STUDIO

"Me and Clare often sat in on recordings, especially when, like Brighter, it was the band's first time in a studio," says Matt. "We did it partly because we enjoyed it, liked the social side and loved watching the creative process in action but also to make sure that engineers didn't misunderstand what was required or try to impose their own ideas too much. And often we were involved in discussions about what was needed sound wise, more usually at the mixing than at the recording stage. But after a couple of singles we'd normally leave them to it, which I suspect they appreciated, especially Harvey."

Action Painting! weren't entirely sure whether it was really going to be Clare and Matt who turned up though, as guitarist Lee Christopher recalls: "Because it was only our second ever time in a studio, Clare and Matt said they were coming down to oversee the recording. 'We thought it was The Wake playing a joke,' [Clare and Matt] had originally said upon first hearing our demo." Which is hilarious.

> ❝ Harvey recorded us a new single last weekend!!! I finally talked him round and we got the tape yesterday, and it's absolutely and completely wonderful. Sigh! Sarah 60, out February."
>
> **Letter from Clare to fan Mario Suau, November 1991**

Vocalist Andy Hitchcock confirms that 'These Things Happen' was the only recording that Clare and Matt came to. "That was pressured," he says. "I think that affected our performance on the day of recording it. It was quite intimidating. That was the first time we met them. The poor sods, it was absolutely pissing down when they came to Portsmouth, and they were sitting there for hours with us pissing about and things not going right and getting the hump." After messing around with trying lots of different effects, Andy thinks it might have been Matt who suggested adding

"Clare and Matt came to the studio and they were so lovely," says Eternal's Christian Savill (pictured at the back, right).
Courtesy of Eternal.

synths to 'These Things Happen' and then everyone relaxing and agreeing it worked. "I can remember getting the test pressing and playing it over and over again, and just being really happy. If you're 18 and you've got a record, it was a great feeling. You start listening to imperfections and what you could do better but I got a good feeling out of it. I thought, 'Would I buy this record?' Yes, I would and I'd enjoy it. So I was happy with it."

It was in this way that Clare and Matt found themselves having a lovely day out in Reading while Eternal recorded their one and only single for Sarah at the city's Refuge studio. "For some reason, we'd assumed the recording was booked for 10am because most recordings were, so we'd said 'Shall we get there for about 9 o'clock?' and they'd said that was fine," says Matt. What was less fine was that, despite Clare and Matt's 5am alarm call to get the first train out of Bristol, it turned out the recording studio wasn't actually booked until the evening. Meaning the teenage members of Eternal suddenly had to find a way to entertain the grown-up label bigwigs who had come to town for the day and, once you've been to the Wimpy bar, there's not that much else to do in Reading. "At the same time, Christian [Savill]'s other band [Slowdive] was being signed to Creation, who presumably didn't rock up on a train and demand to be shown the sights of Reading," muses Clare.

"They came to the studio and they were so lovely," says Christian. "They were really supportive. I just remember Matt dancing around the studio when we were playing, which was really sweet." But that doesn't mean Christian was pleased with how the recording came out: "I think we were a bit overwhelmed and it was all too much for us, so it ended up sounding absolutely horrible. So we were actually really embarrassed by it in the end. It's only a 7" record, nobody cares. But at the time, we were disappointed with how it turned out. The original demos that Sarah really liked, they came out a few years ago on another label and they sound a bit better."

Clare and Matt ended up staying with 15-year-old drummer Michael Warner and his parents. "I think the cellist [Alan Bryden] wasn't much older," says Matt. "Even Christian was probably still in his teens. Also present in the studio that day were various members of Chapterhouse, just sitting around downstairs. It was the whole nascent Thames Valley shoegazing scene, basically." Evidently, the resulting sound was a success because *Select* magazine's Dan Maier was fully in favour of the "loud, distorted guitars" on 'Breathe'.

Bassist Stuart Wilkinson remembers Christian phoning him up to say Sarah was going to put out an Eternal single "and I was thinking we were going to be like The Beatles". He adds: "It felt like we were playing at being pop stars but we weren't playing gigs and only had three songs. It's testament to Christian being a brilliant songwriter that these songs still pop up now and again." Christian even recorded a version of 'Breathe' with Slowdive.

However, Clare and Matt didn't just visit for the day when Brighter recorded *Laurel*: they stayed with the band for *two weeks*! "It was such a steep learning curve for all of us. Going from not having any sense of how a recording studio worked to at least it being familiar enough," says guitarist Alison Cousens. "The seismic moment was when we recorded *Laurel* for the first time. Matt and Clare came to stay. They just didn't operate like you would expect a normal record label to operate. I think we assumed we all had a similar relationship with Matt and Clare but as time went on, you realised that the different bands had different relationships with them."

Disappointment

Sometimes, things just didn't go the way the band wanted. The Rosaries had a one-day session at the White House to record their lone Sarah EP 'Forever' but unfortunately it wasn't a roaring success. Drummer Robert Dillam, who was moonlighting from his day job in Creation band Adorable, was the only one of the four with any previous studio experience and felt the weight of responsibility when he realised what a tough time his bandmates were having on the day. And it was all compounded by having Clare and Matt in the studio, witnessing things go to pot. "We got to a stage where [Jonny James] had to do a singing part, and he's really into Beat Happening and Calvin Johnson, that means that [Jonny]'s singing voice isn't what you might call a classically trained singing voice and that's why Laura [Kinsey] sang," says Robert. "[Jonny] got into the vocal booth and did his singing part and I thought he really nailed it. But he came out and the engineer flipped. I thought he was really quite angry. [Jonny] doesn't necessarily sing in tune, [Jonny] sings like [Jonny]. But the engineer turned round and said 'I'm not having that singing part on my recording, it's no good.' And I remember looking over at Matt and Clare standing in the corner, looking kind of shocked and looking at the engineer and on a personal level I had a panic and a real loss of self-confidence in that moment because I thought they were

For The Rosaries, their day in the recording studio was a character-building experience.
Courtesy of Jonny James.

going to chuck us out of the studio because it wasn't good enough." He adds: "I did something that I really regret, which is I convinced [Jonny] that maybe we should do it as a spoken-word part rather than a singing part. And in that moment it changed the way that the record was sounding and I feel really bad about it, even to this day. [Jonny] was upset that the music wasn't going in the direction he wanted to, and I should have backed him up and I didn't." Of course, his former bandmates insist Robert has nothing to feel guilty about.

Vocalist Laura Kinsey was also new to recording and admits: "I was so naïve. I remember going into the booth on my own and putting the headphones on, and the engineer said 'Listen to the click track.' And I said, 'What's a click track?' I didn't even know what one was. That made me terribly nervous, thinking 'I don't know what I'm doing.' And then, every time I'd go to sing, I was just so scared and that engineer said to me, 'You sound like a cross between Jimmy Savile and Cyndi Lauper' and I'll never forget that."

Jonny adds: "It was quite harrowing because I was crap at singing, I'd never stood in front of a microphone apart from the eight-track demo. I've got a blurry memory of being pretty embarrassed by my inability to do this thing. I was in one room singing it and they were in another room hearing it, and that was very embarrassing. And what exacerbated the embarrassment was having Clare and Matt in the next room listening to all this."

WATCHING THE PENNIES

"It seems ridiculous to say the entire recording costs of our complete Sarah output probably did not go beyond IR£3-4,000," laughs Will Merriman of The Harvest Ministers. "But the way we record is simple and classic, and a song is either done in two or three takes or else it goes back to the end of the queue. There is no mercy in the studio." The Dublin band were four years into their lifespan when they signed to Sarah and had previously released a few records on their own Crayon label. "A band has two separate entities, a live audience one and a recording one and it was very important to get going on the latter," says Will. "Those days are very special, the basic way of how we recorded 'You Do My World The World Of Good' set the template for every recording since."

Having already had a few years as a Factory band – and having enjoyed the big budgets that came with that – The Wake had something of a culture shock when they came to the more financially restricted Sarah. Yet frontman Caesar says he found this to be a positive thing in terms of his band's creativity. "Factory spent a fortune on things, they would book you into palatial studios like Strawberry Studios and Revolution in Manchester and you could be in there for months, god knows what it cost and if they ever got paid. In a sense, it was a lot more disciplined being on Sarah," says Caesar. He recalls how the recording of 'Crush The Flowers' for Sarah had been booked into a Glasgow studio with their producer friend Duncan Cameron. Only Duncan wasn't happy with the quality of the equipment in the studio and ended up taking the band to his flat in East Kilbride instead. "We were recording in his hallway and getting echo from the bathroom, it was amazing," says Caesar, and this is how 'Crush The Flowers' and 'Carbrain' ended up being recorded. "It goes to show that you can go in a really palatial studio with a good engineer and producer but it's not any better than what you can do in a home studio." Speaking of which...

HOME RECORDINGS

"I've always recorded everything at home, by myself, on a very simple set-up," says FM Cornog of East River Pipe. "I've always used a Tascam mini-studio. It's very low-tech. There aren't many choices to make. I like it that way. It keeps things moving. With a minimum of instruments and recording gear, a song has to stand on its own. There is no sonic trickery available to dress up a shitty song. I just kind of plug my guitar into the damn machine and press record. Simple. Once I've got the skeleton of the song up, I add and subtract, record and erase. I think I work more like a painter." He adds: "So, for the Sarah releases, nothing changed. They left me alone to do my work and Clare and Matt graciously accepted and released whatever we sent them. I do remember at times though, when I was recording, feeling a kind of exhilaration knowing that the songs I was working on were going to be *heard*. I hadn't had that

"I've always recorded everything at home," says FM Cornog of East River Pipe.
Courtesy of East River Pipe.

feeling before. I didn't even care about money or interviews, any shit like that. It was just about getting heard. I thought, 'Wow, people are going to *hear* this, I'm not recording into a void anymore.' It was remarkable."

Jyoti Mishra of White Town had a studio at his home in Derby, and this was where he recorded some tracks with his friends Josh and Joel Meadows when The Sugargliders visited the UK from Australia. Josh and Jyoti had struck up a postal friendship, owing to their shared love of each other's music. "I think the first White Town single came into the record shop I worked in and it had his address on the back and I wrote him a letter," says Josh. Jyoti picks up the story: "We started communicating and I feel like we had a lot in common. We're so different in a lot of ways as well but we were both into politics and pop, and that was enough. I'd known Sugargliders for years back when they were on Summershine and I'd kept telling them they needed to be on Sarah. And Josh was like, 'Oh that's a dream, we love Sarah but I don't think it's ever going to happen.' And then suddenly they're on Sarah."

Jyoti produced two tracks on the band's 'Trumpet Play' single. "Any time people used to kip at my house, I'd say 'Let's record something'. They just did these songs. It was all very spontaneous," says Jyoti. It was so spontaneous that some of the songs had only been written that day in Jyoti's front room. "We tried a few different versions and it didn't quite work, so he brought in a drum machine, he got an 808 going and we played the song along with that," says Joel. "It was a really nice recording, I love it. And then there's a third song that has never seen the light of day, more of a live track and we recorded a version of it, 'If You Can Read You're In Trouble.'" Josh adds: "It's typical Sugargliders in that it's a naïve, political take with a drum machine going and a guitar line. I'm a bit embarrassed by it in a way but it's a reflection of who we were at that time."

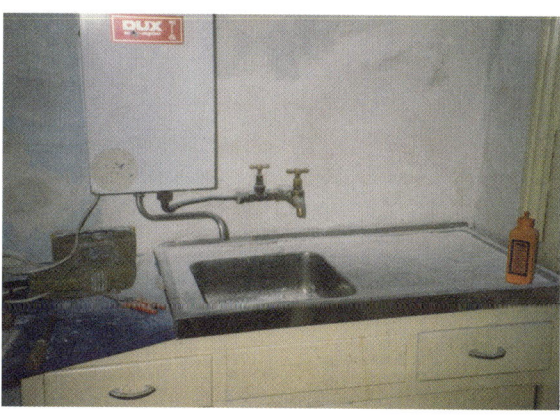

"Is the factory loud now or is that the water heater?" THAT'S THE WATER HEATER! This is quite possibly my favourite photograph in this entire book.
Anita Rayner.

The Sugargliders had form on home recordings, however, with the band's very first ones having been done in their bathroom because the echo made up for the fact they didn't have a reverb unit. Of course, later on the band would progress to working in real studios and had the opportunity of working with the engineer Siiri Metsar at one point. "There wouldn't have been many women working as audio engineers in studios in Australia in the early 1990s," says Joel. Almost as impressive was the time Nick Cave wandered into the back of the studio while The Sugargliders were recording, as he happened to be in the building on the same day. Touched by the hand of goth, as it were.

A last note on home recordings here. As anyone who's heard Even As We Speak's *Feral Pop Frenzy* LP can confirm, there is a spoken line at the start of 'Anybody Anyway' that is Julian Knowles asking: "Is the factory loud now or is that the water heater?" Hearing Julian say this line during our interview was such an unexpected thrill, having played the record so many millions of times over the years. This is because 'Anybody Anyway' was recorded in drummer Anita Rayner's kitchen, with just a stereo mic on the other side of the room. And look! Anita has sent me a photo of the most famous water heater in pop. "If I'd known that at the time, I would have taken a better photo of it," sighs Anita. "This is actually a photo of the plastering next to it, but I guess the wonky vibe fits the song."

TOADS OF TOAD HALL

In Glasgow, The Orchids quickly found their spiritual home at Ian Carmichael's Toad Hall studio. "They were remarkable from the start because of their attitude," says Ian of the time the band first showed up in 1988. "All the bands we'd ever had were young bands who had saved up all their money for months to come and record their demo tape. It cost a couple of hundred pounds for the weekend. Every band that came was so serious and earnest, and they were going to be the next big thing. But The Orchids didn't care. They walked in and they were so blasé about everything and I thought 'Who *are* these people? They're terrible!' I was really shocked by them. And then they started playing and we built up a track gradually, and the more I listened to the music I was thinking, 'This is nice'. And of course, their charm is so infectious. By the end of the weekend, I was thinking, 'I hope they come back, I really enjoyed that.'"

The Orchids did come back, over and over again. Even after Ian closed Toad Hall and moved to Spain, The Orchids kept working with him and still do to this day. "'Underneath The Window, Underneath The Sink' was the first single they recorded with me," says Ian. "That four-track EP was recorded in two days. Most bands are all in the studio, they're all hands on, they're all desperate to have their opinion heard, they want it to be perfect. And The Orchids were going, 'Yeah, that'll do.' Years ago, someone asked me how I would describe The Orchids' ethos and I thought about the path of least resistance, and then I thought it was striving for the lazy perfection, it describes their attitude perfectly."

> ❝ I spent most of my time in the studio with The Orchids with my head in my hands, shaking my head.❞
>
> **Ian Carmichael, sound engineer**

Well, the band certainly had a relaxed approach to recording. "We used to watch *Tom & Jerry* videos while Ian mixed the songs," says drummer Chris Quinn. "And find them extra funny because we were drunk and stoned." While James Hackett says: "It was such a small place, so there was just the mixing room and the playing room. And the playing room was like 6ft long and 4ft wide, so it was very intense and quite claustrophobic, so that's why we'd step out and watch the TV. But it didn't have a TV antenna so we'd just watch the *Tom & Jerry* videos."

Back to Ian: "I remember early on, maybe the second session we had, we recorded the drums and bass, and I got it all tidied up and ready for James to sing the vocals. And I went into the lounge and said, 'James, I'm ready for you now.' And he said, 'In a minute.' And I think I waited 10 minutes and I thought, 'Where the hell is he?' Because they were paying for this time. And he was in there with Chris playing video games! I said, 'James, I'm ready to record your vocals.' And he sighed, 'OK, I guess I need to go and write some lyrics'. And he sat there with a pen and paper writing the lyrics for the single they were about to record. That, for me, was both exasperating and refreshing. It was something so novel to me, to have people so off the cuff that way. I think that was for 'What Will We Do Next?'" In defence of the band, they all had day jobs at the time, so they genuinely were tired when they came to record in the evenings and at weekends. Although the hangovers probably didn't help.

By the time The Orchids came to record *Unholy Soul*, James Moody and Matthew Drummond were getting more into dance music and wanting to incorporate elements of this into their sound, so Ian started to bring in things like drum machines and samplers, which can be heard on the beautiful track 'Peaches' and even more so on the entire *Striving For The Lazy Perfection* LP. But Ian says these developments were becoming a source of conflict within the band, with some members wanting to stick to a guitar sound and others wanting to move towards dance music "and

It would be fair to say that Glasgow-based band The Orchids were not necessarily the most focussed of groups when they were in the studio. Here they are at their home-from home, Toad Hall.
Akiko Yamauchi.

they looked to me to bring all of that together".

Pauline Hynds Bari was a magical addition to The Orchids' sound, admitting that James Hackett says her voice brought "the silver and gold lining" to The Orchids' records. Pauline was already in a band with her husband Rohail Bari, and the pair also recorded in Toad Hall. Ian suggested her when James decided he didn't want to sing the chorus on 'Peaches' and Pauline felt an instant affection for the boys. "Ian said he had a band that needed some backing vocals, so I asked what the band was called and he said 'The Orchids'," remembers Pauline. "And right away I had a really good feeling about it, that sounded really special. It's just such a lovely name." To this day, Pauline remains a regular fixture on records by The Orchids... and hopefully doesn't know that the word 'orchid' comes from the Greek for 'testicles' ('orchis').

Known affectionately by the band as Mother Orchid, having childcare responsibilities at home meant that Pauline didn't have much time to hang out at Toad Hall with the band. However, she says happily, "throughout the years when we've done any recording, for some reason we always end up having fish and chips as a thank you at the end." Ah yes, those end-of-session meals. Ian says in confidence: "You can never tell Sarah Records this but The Orchids would always tell me to add three or four extra hours onto the bill for the recording sessions but then they would use the money to go and buy Indian food and beers!" James

❝ Predictably, the new Blueboy EP is taking longer than expected due to a whole plethora of reasons which, for brevity, we'll just call Keith."

Sarah Newsletter No 11, April 1995

Left: Here we have Jameses Hackett and Moody recording whistling for 'Coloured Stone' from the album *Unholy Soul* at Toad Hall in 1990. **Right:** And here is John Scally, also at Toad Hall.
Courtesy of The Orchids.

Hackett justifies this by saying: "It's the only time we'd put a beer and a curry onto the Sarah budget and I don't think they realised. It's the only time we got anything like a drink and something to eat from them." One would hope that after this passage of time, Clare and Matt would let this go. Although I suspect they probably realised.

Guest musicians

Putting a call out for someone to play flute on a few Blueboy tracks led Gemma Malley to question some of her life choices. The band recorded at a farm near Chipping Norton, which tripled up as a studio run by the farmer's son and a lovely B&B run by the farmer's wife. "You'd be recording and the lambs would be outside your window," says Gemma, confirming everything that the *NME* suspected about the Enid Blyton world of Sarah. "But there was this one funny time where we needed a flautist, so I put a note up at university. This girl contacted me and we had a chat, got into the car and I drove her to Chipping Norton." And then it all went wrong. "She looked at me in total shock and said, 'I thought we were going to London.' And I was like, 'No, no, we record here.' And she basically said the only reason she did it was to get a ride to London! So we had this really grumpy flautist who wasn't actually that good."

Gemma had experience of delivering musical guests to the Blueboy studio, though, bringing her sister Madeleine Townley along to play violin on a few tracks on *Unisex*. Madeline was part of the string quartet that Gemma assembled when they went into the studio to record the tracks, "and that's what I loved, the recording, because it was the ability to spend proper time with each other and just think about the music, which I loved," says Gemma.

Also enjoying a special guest on their record was Gentle Despite, who included Ian Masters from Pale Saints on bass on their records. Guitarist Paul Gorton tells me: "The second single was recorded at Woodhouse Studios in Leeds. Pale Saints were doing the 'Half Life' EP around the same time at the same studio, so me and Simon [Westwood, vocals] went down and hung out with them." Gentle Despite were such good friends with Ian that the band's members were the sole guests at his wedding. "He had a last-minute wedding and invited us to be his witnesses at the registry office. Then we went for a curry after," says Paul, which sounds very jolly.

Sometimes, though, different band members could experience the same thing in different ways, as Action Painting! found when they went to record the 'Mustard Gas' EP at London's Greenhouse Studio, thanks to guitarist Lee Christopher's contacts from his work with pop band Shampoo. "We were all of a sudden mingling with Shed Seven and Suede and Sleeper, everyone was there. And we felt like the charity kids," says vocalist Andy Hitchcock. "I thought the demo for 'Mustard Gas' was much better. We released the demos on a compilation LP so you can judge for yourself. Going up to London and recording, I just felt that if it was a bit dirtier and we weren't under so much stress, it would have been better because it was a lot of pressure and it was a really big studio, and we were used to little studios. We were used to being all together, and all of a sudden Iain's in a booth on his own and Kevin's got to do his bit, and I suppose it was a learning process. I didn't find it fun." Bassist Kevin House adds: "I borrowed Shed Seven's bass because I never owned a bass. I was a bass player in Action Painting! but never had my own bass, I always had to borrow one. Recording was not fun because you could hear yourself playing and realise how bad you actually are." However, Lee's take on the experience is slightly different: "Sometimes I'd sit in the upstairs studio, with only the desk and monitor lights flickering reds and greens in the dark, and think how great this moment was."

As the band with arguably the most commercial sound on the label, Even As We Speak flirted with the majors while they had their year in the UK. "At the time we were in our mid 20s. We would have really liked to have sold a lot more records, because quite frankly some money would have come in handy and it would have been a lot easier to do what we were doing, rather than sleeping on floors," says guitarist Julian Knowles, adding that the band all had jobs during the day, and recorded and gigged at weekends and evenings. "We wanted to make music full time. I had a number of meetings with Paul [Clarke] with the major labels, who were all happy to see us and talk about things. We had quite an interesting

FUN FACT: Madeleine is better known these days as Sophie Kinsella, under which name she has written a string of hugely popular novels in the *Shopaholic* series, several of which have been made into Hollywood films.

Blueboy's Gemma Malley seemed to be the band's go-to person for finding guest musicians.
Courtesy of Paul Stewart.

meeting with Feargal Sharkey, who at that time was the A&R man for Polydor Records. But the punchline from all those meetings was that, in order to do it, we would have had to agree to remain in the UK." And that just wasn't possible for a number of reasons, not least of all that singer Mary Wyer had had to leave her young son behind in Australia and understandably couldn't agree to be apart from him for much longer.

Talking about the disparity in terms between an indie like Sarah and a major like Polydor, Julian notes: "We recorded *Feral Pop Frenzy* for maybe £2,000, all up. But at the first meeting with Feargal Sharkey, he said, 'What we do for a band that's starting out like you guys, is normally we would put up say £30-40,000 for an album and then we would see how that went.' That gives you an idea of the comparison. You can be in a moderately successful indie band on an indie label but what's the gap there between that and the mainstream? And there you go, the gap is £40,000. And that's just the recording budget! It's remarkable that those small labels were able to do what they did with such little money."🍒

*****

THESE THINGS HAPPENED:
Simon Court, The Sweetest Ache
"Getting the finished records felt a bit like imposter syndrome. It didn't feel real. I'd just turned 20. It was all a little bit nuts. I didn't realise how much of a cult following Sarah Records had. I'm still amazed by it now. I didn't realise it was selling all over the world, I had no idea at the time."

CHAPTER 12
ART + DESIGN

During the 1980s, my family had a holiday cottage in North Devon. There was a sprawling beach called Saunton Sands that we liked to visit. On a trip in July 1987, after we had climbed over the mammoth dunes towards the sea, instead of seeing the familiar endless stretches of uninterrupted beach, we saw hundreds of red metal-framed beds, all carefully lined up and with blankets on them. We found out that this was the photo shoot for the cover of Pink Floyd's upcoming album *A Momentary Lapse of Reason* and my brothers and I were very impressed. This was the first time I had ever thought about how record sleeves might be conceived.

> **"** Who are these assholes crediting their hairdresser?"
> **Tim Chipping, Shelley**

The sleeves at Sarah Records did not require anything quite so ambitious as assembling 700 hospital beds on a beach. But they were precise works of art in their own way and emblematic of the era that produced them. "We always gave first choice to the bands," says Matt. "We said, 'Do you know what you want on your sleeves?' And some had no ideas or didn't really care and let us do whatever we wanted but we'd always give first choice to the bands."

Sarah stalwart Harvey Williams says: "I guess the fact they were generally in wraparound sleeves and plastic bags was quite a conscious decision to make them look homemade. Someone had taken this 14" x 7" piece of paper, folded it over and slipped it in a poly bag and put all the other bits, the card or the poster or whatever, in. It was something that had been handmade by a person. There was an element that they were suffering for their art, almost unnecessarily so. You don't have to sit around and do that but it was part of the aesthetic. They were totally committed to it." The wraparound sleeves were actually adopted because they were so much cheaper than sealed ones, and Matt adds: "It wasn't a planned aesthetic, it came largely out of the techniques we were having to use and the fact I have no artistic training whatsoever. It's a product of me doing everything by hand with Letraset and, if it needed text, me or Clare writing it by hand or typing it and then enlarging it on the photocopier. So yeah, obviously things do look a bit similar because of that."

In the days before desktop publishing, artwork had to be sent to printers as physical paste-ups: sheets of card on which text and images had been stuck with Spray Mount or Pritt Stick, with any photos first sent off to be turned into black and white dots ("screened") and any text that wasn't handwritten, typed or Letrasetted sent off to be phototypeset. Matt explains: "We'd receive the typeset words on a sheet of photographic paper from which they had to be cut out with scissors. This cost roughly £40 for a single monochrome screen, and the same for a paragraph of text."

He continues: "Back in those days, if you wanted a picture on a sleeve, you had to send it away to be screened, you couldn't do it at home, and you'd get charged £40 or £50 for every single picture. So we always tried to limit it to one picture on a sleeve if we could, none if possible." Which explains why so few Sarah singles have photos on the covers. "I think it's quite nice to say to bands, 'Don't put a picture of yourself on it, do something interesting'," says Matt, "because it's just so easy to put a band photo on." Clare adds: "But if you're in a band, you've spent your life dreaming of your first record and what the sleeve looks like, and probably a photo of yourself looking cool is what you've always had in mind. But it was a bit like, 'You shouldn't have signed to our label if that's what you want!' Later on, I think we did just send a list of the rules to new bands."

Big record labels print sleeves in full colour, so the machines in the factories are loaded with the four inks used in full-colour printing: black, yellow, cyan and magenta (the "process colours"). If you can't afford full-colour sleeves, and just want to print in one or two colours, you either restrict yourself to those four colours or pay £80 to have one of them replaced with something esoteric and outré like green or red. Or £160 if you want green *and* red. Each time you reprint.

This is why Sarah sleeves aren't littered with photos and make good use of cyan and magenta. As do the labels in the middle. Metallic inks, of course, had extra charges of their own, meaning Tramway were truly blessed with the dominant use of silver on the cover of 'Maritime City'. Tramway had initially planned to release 'Maritime City' on Cosmic English Music, who changed their minds at the last minute and Sarah took the package instead. The band's frontman Matthew Evans explains that, as a Bristol Rovers fan, he had wanted the sleeve to be blue and white but Cosmic had thought it looked too mediaeval, which was why it became blue and silver. "We deliberately chose those colours because blue and white are the Rovers colours. I'm still a Rovers fan, for my sins. You really only support Rovers if you're born into it," says Matthew stoically. "On the second single, we just went for colours that didn't look very nice together, lilac and mustard. You'd be taking yourself too seriously if you put too much thought into the cover, which was what we decided there."

Record Labels

Sarah was also known for the imagery on the record labels themselves, which famously ran in series. However, Clare and Matt made a rather costly rookie error

ART & DESIGN

The record label for Sarah 75: so good that the pressing plant felt it worthy of comment.
Courtesy of Sarah Records.

with their early labels, as Clare explains: "Our first labels all had two non-process colours on them, plus black, so each of those cost us £160 more than it needed to have done in 1987 money". For comparison purposes, the 2021 equivalent is almost £400.

Matt continues: "I think it was worse than that because it was two non-process colours on one side and black on the other, so they had to print both sides of the label separately. We were effectively printing two sets of labels for every 7" single. I think it worked out at one point that we were spending more on the labels than the recordings for those records because we were learning as we went along."

On 12 February 1988, Matt wrote to The Orchids' drummer Chris Quinn to send the band copies of their debut hard vinyl single, 'I've Got A Habit' (aka Sarah 2), eulogising that "the sleeves look bloody wonderful" and gushing over the labels on the actual record: "The picture is a view just round the corner from here – just like the one on the Urchins' record was – a theme!!!"

The record label series of images:
Sarah 1-20   Random shots of (mostly) north Bristol
Sarah 21-30   Shots of consecutive train stations along the Severn Beach line
Sarah 31-40   Along the river from Temple Meads to the Clifton Suspension Bridge
Sarah 41-49   Into Bristol along the cycle path from the Sarah office in Kingswood
Sarah 51-60   The 10 places you have to call in at if you play Saropoly
Sarah 61-70   Windmill Hill and Victoria Park, where Clare and Matt had just moved to
Sarah 71-80   Bus numbers 71 to 80
Sarah 81-90   Castle Park in the city centre
Sarah 91-99   Castle Park to Cumberland Basin, as spotted from the ferry

Hatcher's tobacconists in Clifton had a photocopier. And Clare and Matt regularly popped in to use it.
Courtesy of Sarah Records.

The labels for Sarahs 1-10 are photocopies of photographs, done at Hatcher's newsagents in Clifton, which was close to the Upper Belgrave Road flat. "I took the photos on film camera, got them developed and then photocopied them several times so you get a nice black and white effect," explains Matt. "From Sarah 20, we moved on to train stations and wanted realistic images, which meant we had to get the photos screened at CliftonPrint before sticking them into the paste-up. But CliftonPrint charged us per A4 sheet of photographic paper, so we'd do them in batches: we'd give them however many photos would fit on an A4 page and they'd screen them all together and we'd cut them up afterwards."

Budgetary constraints

In late 1987, even before 'Pristine Christine' was released, Matt was writing to The Orchids to fret about money because the label's budget had been blown by the hedonistic Sea Urchins and their artistic demands: "Money… we will try and send you some to help out with recording, but I'm not sure what at present – we seem to be spending a fortune on the sleeve for this Sea Urchins EP – £20 on [screening] photos today." Which gives an indication of the hand-to-mouth nature of the label at the very beginning. Sarah also included a poster with the first 20 records, as Matt says in another letter to Chris from late 1988: "The Sea Urchins' [record] has the traditional wrap-round glossy sleeve in a polythene bag PLUS a poster. We rather like the idea of a poster in every record, so people can collect the set and stick them on their bedroom walls. Would you agree to this? Basically, a 10"x14" poster, featuring whatever you want but incorporating the band's name somewhere in it."

Never mind what Matt thought, The Sea Urchins themselves had a great time with their artwork, as guitarist Robert Cooksey says: "We were given a completely free hand to design all of the record sleeves that we made with them, which was great fun. The 'Pristine' sleeve was a collective effort and I remember we all gathered at Simon [Woodcock]'s parents' house in Wednesbury to collate the poster, which was undoubtedly influenced by the one which came with The Beatles' *White Album*. The blurred front cover photo had been taken at a session at Brunswick Park in Wednesbury, while the poster featured more shots from this location along with numerous photos taken at the Lickey Hills, a country park south of Birmingham,

CliftonPrint were more used to dealing with wedding invitations and business letterheads than record sleeves but they rose to the challenge.
Courtesy of Sarah Records.

which was the inspiration for 'Everglades'. The horse on the back was an old photograph taken by my grandfather Geoffrey Cooksey and was probably 30 years old at least then."

Another way to avoid expensively screening a photo was to photocopy it with a slightly grainy effect, perhaps blurring it by moving the picture slightly as the photocopy was being made for the authentic DIY look. The people at Hatcher's must have made a tidy profit from their local independent record label, although Charles, who ran the shop, was never curious enough to ask Clare or Matt what it was they were up to with all their photocopied photos of train stations.

Initially, Sarah sent all of the artwork off to an independent printer in Sheffield because it was a small business that was regularly used by people in the music industry, so was familiar with the quirks required by record label folks. But after a while, Clare and Matt switched to a local high street printer and gave their business to CliftonPrint. More familiar with doing headed notepaper for businesses and printing wedding invitations, the staff were initially a little suspicious of the youngsters who came in wanting record sleeves printed up, so asked for the money upfront but, as Matt says, "once the cheque had cleared they were slightly apologetic and the owner drove us back in the van".

For the first Sarah single by The Wake, 'Crush The Flowers', Clare and Matt had the bright idea of screening the same picture twice at different contrasts, then superimposing the two images. CliftonPrint were a little dubious about how this would look when printed but Clare and Matt held their ground and, when the sleeves were printed, they looked so good that CliftonPrint proudly put one of them in their shop window meaning that, for a few months, anyone who walked through Clifton would be greeted by a pinky-red Wake sleeve winking at them.

The principle of printing a picture twice at different contrasts was tried again a few times but it never worked quite so successfully as it did for 'Crush The Flowers'. And without the ability to see expensive proofs before signing off the artwork, there was a certain amount of crossing your fingers and hoping for the best when you sent it off. Clare says: "In the same way as records might arrive from the pressing plant looking a bit warped, sleeves would sometimes come back from the printers not looking quite like you'd imagined they would." Matt elaborates: "At every stage, you sent the artwork off and, because you had to send photos off to be screened, you wouldn't even see what the photo looked like after it had been screened. You'd just have to send them both off and trust the person at the other end to do what you'd told them to do but you wouldn't actually know until you got a finished copy." Clare adds: "To be fair to printers, we were sending off black-and-white photos in a colour world. They were probably very used to screening colour photos but we weren't paying for four films and four plates and four print colours, so they probably weren't very used to working with the sort of things we were sending them to work with." The cost of paying for a proof beforehand was therefore just too expensive to be justified.

Like the text, which was also too expensive to be justified. Typesetting was costly and home computers were something for tomorrow's world, so initially Sarah's record sleeves made good use of typewriters and Letraset to get the words across. On which note...

Letraset with love

Younger readers might be completely baffled by the concept of Letraset. It was sheets of adhesive letters in a range of fonts that you rubbed onto a page using a blunt pencil in order to create a professional-looking design without having to pay a typesetter. Mind. Blowing. Any gig promoter, fanzine writer or, indeed, independent record label boss, would have been well equipped with sheets and sheets of the stuff, or a cheaper own-brand equivalent. So let's take a moment to celebrate the beauty of Letraset: yet another product that has been rendered unemployed by the digital revolution.

The Letraset company was founded in London in 1959 and, by 1961, its dry rub-down instant lettering product had become a must-have item for commercial artists and designers everywhere. The punk movement really embraced the stuff because of how easily it made posters and flyers look that bit better, and so many people appreciated the ease of use of these letters as well as their affordability (in comparison to more professional alternatives) and adaptability for every purpose from school projects to church fêtes.

"Letraset was a full-time job," says Matt. "I could spend an entire day Letrasetting the track list for a compilation LP, which would take 10 minutes on a computer now." With professional typesetting costing an exorbitant £40 a paragraph, there was no alternative for the cash-strapped record label but for Matt to knuckle down: "I would literally spend the entire day staring at my bit of cardboard and rubbing down the letters and then peeling them off again if they didn't go down straight." Nothing was professionally typeset until Even As We Speak's 'One Step Forward' single in 1991, which was Sarah 49, meaning that the entire first half of the Sarah 100 was done with Letraset. Wow.

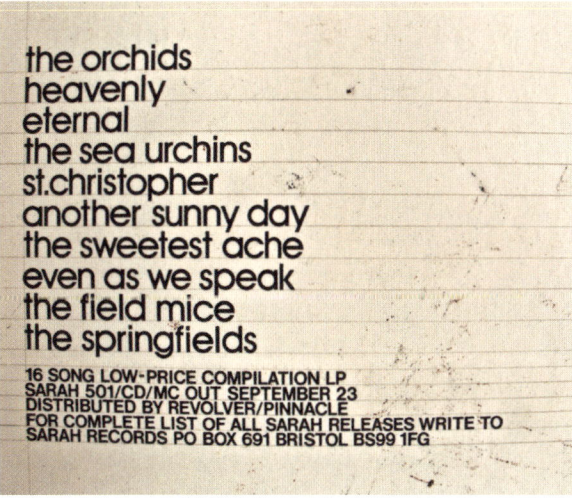

"Letraset was a full-time job," says Matt. A statement demonstrated by his artwork for the *Glass Arcade* compilation. Courtesy of Sarah Records.

Sarah's first compilation album was *Shadow Factory* in 1988, a 16-track record for which Matt, of course, did the lettering. With the best will in the world, the letters are not perfectly straight. When he wasn't in The Hit Parade, Julian Henry was also working for a public relations agency in London, a business where presentation is key. Matt recalls Julian being rather taken by the *Shadow Factory* sleeve: "I remember him being really impressed by the lettering that goes all up and down, all over the place, and he said, 'How did you do that?' Because he's used to professional typesetting and he was wondering how you got that effect, with all the letters on different lines. He thought it must be a really, really expensive design process to get all the letters jumping about all over the place, when no, it was just me thinking I was never going to get it in a straight line so I wasn't even going to attempt it," says Matt with a hint of pride.

The lettering for the 1991 compilation *Glass Arcade* nearly broke Matt, though. "That one was really a menace," he says, which is the closest I have ever heard Matt come to sounding annoyed about something. Having spent the whole day Letrasetting the song titles and band names for this 16-track compilation, Matt spotted an error meaning that the whole job needed to be started again. "You had no natural daylight in that room, for Christ's sakes!" exclaims Clare. "And I was in fingerless gloves," adds Matt, with bonus Dickensian sadness. One can almost imagine a tallow candle stub flickering to the end of its wick beside him, as the last ashes of the small log fire dwindle to grey in the rusty grate.

Akiko's Photo Sleeves

Despite the general inclination to veer away from photo sleeves, a number of photographs by Japanese fanzine writer Akiko Yamauchi would appear on the sleeves of various Sarah records, including these singles: St Christopher's 'All of a Tremble', The Wake's 'Crush the Flowers' and 'Major John', and Even As We Speak's 'One Step Forward'. Akiko's work also appears on the cover of the *Air Balloon Road* compilation CD, which is the famous Sarah Records' cherries-in-a-broken-glass-bowl image.

"Akiko is extraordinary," says Matt. "She was one of the very first people to write to us and there was no indie-pop scene in Japan at the time. As far as we can gather, she pretty much invented it herself." Explaining what a self-starter Akiko was, Matt says: "She used to put on gigs and there were no real gig venues in Japan, so she used to hire local cinemas and things, because it was the only place you could actually get people in. It seems extraordinary that she was doing all this as, presumably, quite a young woman in a very patriarchal society. But as for the photos, she literally was a fan who just sent us some photos and we loved them."

Akiko tells me her side of the story: "I liked taking photos and I sent some of my favourites to Matt. They liked them and used them. It's just as simple as that. Those photos, apart from the one on 'Major John', were taken while I was still living in Japan. With airmail letters as the main communication, there wasn't much detailing and discussions about them between us. In fact, I don't recall any discussions at all. Then one day, one of my friends rang me up from an Osaka record shop, excitedly reporting that the St Christopher single has a credit for 'original photo by Akiko'."

For 'Major John', Akiko, who was now at university in Glasgow, was commissioned to take the cover photo. So she and her now-husband John (with whom she runs the record label Sugarfrost) met up with Caesar from the band to look for locations near where he lived in south Glasgow. "One of the pictures shows Mount Florida Job Club, so we must have started somewhere around there," says Akiko. "Caesar was very pleasant. There was no pretence, not a hint of arrogance, even though he was 'someone' long before Sarah. He was far beyond the age of indie kids, so not everything by Sarah perhaps hit home with him. We walked a long way, with me stopping occasionally to take pictures. It was a thoroughly pleasant experience with a nice man."

The Wake had been signed to Factory between 1982 and 1988. Despite the fact that the band had largely been in charge of their own artwork on Factory, they were happy to leave the artwork up to Sarah and were always pleased with what was produced. 'Crush The Flowers' was "the first time we'd had a suggestion from anyone else that we could use as artwork," says Caesar. "It was quite a sense that there was some kinship here."

Caesar recalls why the Job Club photo was chosen for the 'Major John' single

ART & DESIGN

The Wake's Caesar (pictured on the right) says the sleeve artwork that Clare and Matt came up with for his band showed him there was a "kinship" between band and label.
Julian Bester.

in 1991 saying: "It was a place that a Jobcentre would send you when you'd been unemployed for over a year, it was all the usual nonsense of teaching people how to write CVs and you'd have to go to this club if you wanted to get your dole money. Just another Tory sham, as if they're helping people to get work, when they're just bullying them for being unemployed. Why make people feel so low, why magnify their low self-esteem, why bring them to a space like that?" This particular Job Club was near Caesar's home in Mount Florida: "We know the area quite well because I went to school not far from there and my friend Bobby Gillespie lived there."

Akiko's photo shows an older woman walking past a curtained Job Club window, holding her handbag, head down, and the picture has been given a green wash. "The song was about John Major and his ineffectual premiership, and not really achieving much," says Caesar. "I think, especially up here in Scotland, it was beginning to dawn on people that we were going to have Tory governments for the rest of our lives unless there was a change. That song was picking up on aspects of that. Akiko was really good at just capturing a moment."

Caesar says that the artwork for The Wake's Sarah releases, when he looks back at it now, has a clear thread running through it that shows the beauty in ordinary life. "We weren't going out looking for grimness, it was just real life," says Caesar. "This is where we live, this is what it looks like. This person is walking, you see them every day and this structure behind them, this building has been created by Westminster policy and it won't be here in a few years, it'll be something else. It was a temporary point of contact for people that was never going to last."

The Sarah cherries, as already said, originally came from another of Akiko's photos and made their first appearance on the cover of the *Air Balloon Road* compilation CD. "We just liked it," says Clare simply. "And it fitted quite well on the doughnut on the CD, so we put it on that first CD and then it just seemed to work." Matt adds: "It fitted on 7" labels as well because it hooks around the centre hole. And it photocopies really well. So you can enlarge it up to poster size, put it on all sorts of different bits of artwork, make badges out of it, without having to pay for a photo to be screened."

WHAT TO DO WITH WOMEN

As previously mentioned, bands were largely dissuaded from having photos on the record covers for budgetary reasons, although a few did sneak through, and – with the exception of a blurry Bridget Duffy in The Sea Urchins' group shot, two Northern Picture Library singles with an unidentifiable Anne Mari Davis, and a Boyracer sleeve with a largely unrecognisable image of Nicola Hodgkinson – the band photos that did appear are all of men. Although, obviously, there was a discrepancy on the label between the sexes of band members, which naturally translated into a difficulty in using an equal number of photos of women and men. "There's a Wake single that's got a woman walking past a Job Club on the front but that's allowed because she wasn't there for sexual gratification," says Clare, tongue in cheek. "Although I think if The Field Mice or Blueboy, who each had one woman in, had really wanted a band photo and they'd all been presented as equals, we'd have said 'yes'." Two Heavenly singles, 'PUNK Girl' and 'Atta Girl' do feature images of women, although one is a cartoon and the other is a grainy photo of a feisty looking girl.

As part of the label's feminist stance, Clare and Matt didn't want anything on the label to be seen to objectify women. For the same reason, they discouraged photographers from making any female band members the focus of press shots. However, while well intentioned, this does seem rather like reverse sexism and in conversations with some of the female musicians included in this book, it turns out several of the bands felt likewise.

"I think it's a fair point," says Clare when I raise the issue. "We probably made everything look more male than it was and it was all already pretty male. But so many fanzines would have a 'cool 1960s chick' on the front, and the entire role of women in indie music seemed to be as decoration for sleeves and posters, and then this kind of decoration of backing vocals and singing the band's words as well, because generally songs were written by men, so it was that sort of illusion of a voice but without actually having a voice because you were singing someone else's words, and then people would come up with bizarre defences like 'Oh, but it's not really a sexually alluring image because it's my mum in the '60s, I just thought she looked cool,' but whoever was looking at it wouldn't know it was your mum," explains Clare.

"But of course we ended up with a thing that looked incredibly male."

Beth Arzy of Aberdeen puts her response to this approach pretty succinctly when she says: "As much as I love Matt and Clare, and if either one of them needed a kidney I would step up and give them one of mine, I never really agreed that in photos they would make Anne Mari [or any other woman] stand at the back. I know that it came from a good place because they didn't want to be exploitative of women or sell a band on how somebody looks, but I always thought that that was like positive discrimination. If you're asking a pretty girl to stand at the back then that's discrimination in itself. And if you're saying there are no girls on the covers, that's discriminating against women by not letting them be on the covers. I always thought that was a bit off. I know it came from a good place but I'm not sure what the point was."

While undeniably coming from a good place, it was also undeniable that many of the women involved in bands on Sarah found this rule difficult to accept. Anne Mari Davies was in both The Field Mice and Northern Picture Library and she expands: "I found it frustrating in a way. Now I totally understand that there is an awful lot of the girl pouting at the front while the men look serious in the background because they're the ones who are doing the real music, kind of thing. And I get all of that and I get that when we went for photoshoots, I quite often ended up being put in the front with the lads around me and we resisted that to a point. Then I started getting a bit like, 'hang on, I've got as much right to be at the front as anybody', so it turned on its head a little bit. 'So, you're going to push me to the back because I'm a girl because that's the right thing to do, is it?' I used to get a bit frustrated, 'Oh, it's a photoshoot, I'd better stand at the back', which wasn't great either. But they didn't want it to be about that kind of image. I never got into those kinds of arguments with Matt and Clare but I was certainly frustrated by it. The others thought similarly. It was that whole thing of, 'Are you really, honestly asking me to stand at the back in a photoshoot?' That felt just as wrong as me being at the front."

> ❝ Look through your rag and you'll find evidence of something a little stronger than patronisation. Look at photos of Spiritualized, My Bloody Valentine, World of Twist, Stereolab, Bocca Juniors etc, where the pretty female member of the group has been shoved to the front *TOTP*-style or isolated altogether, despite not giving the accompanying interview or even being the main person in the group. Admitting it's a man's world is one thing, subliminal promotion of men as background Svengalis is serious retro sexism. No other paper equals you in this, so perhaps MM stands for Meat Market? Get responsible, get real, or get out of our lives, scum."
>
> **Letter from Dickon Edwards in *Melody Maker*, 31 August 1991**

Clare explains: "This must have been misconstrued via the photographer, because we never asked for [Anne Mari] to be at the back, we just asked for her not to be treated differently from the rest of the band, to not be placed front and centre. We wanted photos of five people treated the same, not photos of a woman and four men, treated as if they were two different categories of people."

Clare remembers having an argument with a photographer who had been paid to photograph The Field Mice and she had asked him not to put Anne Mari in the middle and at the front. The photographer complained, saying that to not do so would make the photo of the five people, four of whom were men, unbalanced. "I mean, Anne Mari looks fabulous always, but she's one fifth of the band and it's not all about her and the others blurred in the background," says Clare. "The bands and us should all debate it sometime. We probably said 'no' to an awful lot of things. I'm surprised some of [the bands] stuck with us really. I think a lot of it was not wanting photos because they were expensive. I think later on, to save all the hassle, when we signed new bands, we started sending out instructions saying 'This is what we don't do.'"

Beth says: "We had some say in the artwork but they had very strict rules. You couldn't have more than a couple of colours. You couldn't have women on the covers. If it was something you picked that they approved of and fit within their guidelines for Sarah, then it was OK but they had no girls on the front, so if you wanted a picture of Dusty Springfield or some beautiful model from the 1960s then you couldn't really unless it was androgynous. With the first record, a friend of ours took a picture of a bathtub in a forest and it was a nice image we all liked, they approved it, no problem. The second one was a twee little drawing by a friend of mine who came to England to go to university and while he was away we used to write to each other, and I missed him terribly, and he drew this little picture of stars going out the window and sent it to me, and I thought 'That's really lovely, I'd like to use that for a cover'. And Matt and Clare were fine with that, so we never had any issues over artwork or battles or anything. I didn't have any pictures of Hammer Horror models with their boobs out and beautiful long flowing locks. In hindsight, I wish I had."

The artwork for the Talulah Gosh compilation LP *They've Scoffed The Lot* did get vetoed on its first try, though. "That's the only one I ever really remember a row about," says Clare. "They'd gone for a virgin/whore thing. They'd got Amelia [Fletcher] licking a knife and Liz [Price] dressed up as a nun and we were very much 'People are equals, don't focus on the woman.' So the image of Liz is still there but it's covered up and Amelia licking the knife isn't on it at all." Matt adds: "It was a clever joke they were playing on the whole virgin/whore thing but most people would miss the joke and a lot of boys would just like the fact that it was Amelia licking a knife on the cover, and we didn't want to be party to that, which I think was our argument."

FUN FACT: Pop fans are informed that, should they want to see the picture of Amelia licking a knife, they will need to get themselves a copy of her 1991 solo single on Fierce, 'Can You Keep A Secret?'.

The Sugargliders also fell foul of the no-women-on-sleeves rule when they submitted the original artwork for their single 'Trumpet Play', an ink drawing by Joel Meadows based on the Go-Betweens song 'Man O'Sand to Girl O'Sea'. It has a sand man and a sea girl on it but "because her form was a little bit exposed, Matt and Clare had a really clear line on that," says Joel. Josh Meadows adds: "They said they wouldn't want anything that could be interpreted as objectifying women. So we accepted that and respected a principled stance and came up with something else."

But there's also the issue of role models, and the need for fans and young women to see women who they could aspire to be like. Alison Cousens of Brighter says: "My experience of those photoshoots was that you have to look attractive in order to be accepted. In retrospect, you could say that would have been a barrier because, the likes of you and me, we're not getting an image of a representation of a role model coming back to us as somebody who could be there standing on stage and being pictured as in a band. If I think back to who was my role model, then it was Tracey Thorn, and what was important was that I saw her up on the stage, and what you're doing is denying that image of somebody who's there and up on the stage. The thing I loved about Tracey Thorn was she was not your archetypal attractive female, and that's the point. You can be critical in retrospect but if they had put women on the front and made them real women, they would have almost been criticised even more, because it would have been detrimental because those real women would not be your archetypal attractive women."

Alison concludes: "I think it's a valid point and a valid criticism but having been involved in fragments of conversations with Matt and Clare at the time, I understand what they were trying to do in the context of the time. Every decision was carefully thought about [by Sarah] in terms of how it might be received and is the message an appropriate message in terms of representation or politics?"

Before becoming a music journalist, Kitty Empire was a fan of the label and she says: "I believe what they were probably trying to get at was some form of positive discrimination. Images of women are overdone and problematic. It's [nigh-on] impossible to do neutrally. And [if you're Sarah Records] you don't want to sell your product on the back of a picture of a pretty female. So I understand it but it does erase women. The erasure of women in hindsight [seems more] more problematic than selling a product of a photograph of a woman. But that's the magic of Sarah in a way, that these conversations happened at all."

Music journalist Jerry Thackray suggests that "maybe in the concern to do the right thing, maybe some of this is just being completely scared to do it wrong". And there quite possibly was an element of that involved. Sarah was a label that clearly set out its stall on being feminist, anti-capitalist and generally trying hard to Do The Right Thing. But I do think it is perfectly possible to put pictures that include women on record sleeves without those pictures objectifying women.

AN ART SCHOOL EDUCATION

Some of the bands included musicians who had been to art school, had friends who were designers or simply fancied getting creative themselves, and it made sense to tap up their art skills.

For instance, Joel Meadows did most of the artwork for the singles by his band The Sugargliders because he was at art school at the time. 'Letter From a Lifeboat' has a copper-plate etching that Joel had done, while 'Seventeen' has a photograph of a sculpture he made. Joel explains: "That act of creativity was something where we were

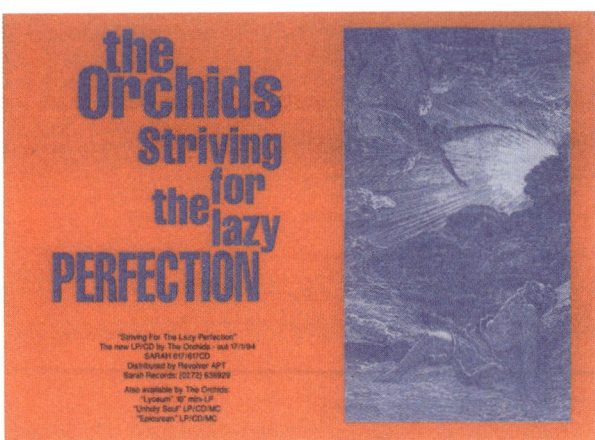

A promotional postcard for the *Striving For the Lazy Perfection* album by The Orchids.
Courtesy of The Orchids.

trying to put the whole thing together. To get a graphic designer to come in and do a cover would be anathema to what we were about." Josh Meadows adds: "Making the artefacts was part of our artistic expression. It wasn't just that the music needed an image to go with it. It was that the photography and etchings and sculptings were part of what we were expressing."

Over in Illinois, The Springfields used a pen illustration of a bird by Ric Menck's father Werner on the cover of the 1991 single 'Wonder'. "He had multiple sclerosis and couldn't move his arms or legs, so he drew the bird with a pen attached to his head. Pretty cool," says Ric proudly. Meanwhile, Clare remembers designing the cover for 'Sunflower' in a particularly dull lecture towards the end of her final year of university. "I love that cover," says Ric. "It perfectly captures the sound of The Springfields."

Meanwhile, up in Glasgow, sound engineer Ian Carmichael was so appalled by The Orchids' initial attempts at sleeve design that he took matters into his own hands. Having been to art school before setting up his Toad Hall studio, Ian took control of the artwork for the band's album *Unholy Soul* and has been in charge of their design pretty much ever since. "Because it was an album, I said they had to have a bit more thought going into this, especially because the cover of [their mini-album] *Lyceum*..." Ian pauses here to consider a tactful answer (and at this point, I would ask Clare and Matt to avert their eyes) and says: "All the text is out of alignment." Ian didn't get paid for his efforts on the band's artwork and when I ask if he even got thanked, he laughs uncontrollably and says: "I don't think The Orchids have ever thanked me for anything, it's not in their nature." Ian does get a secret credit on the sleeves for his artistic skills, though, under the pseudonym of 'Dr Hugo Z Hackenbush' (a Groucho Marx character), while the also-credited 'DAG Wells' is Ian's graphic designer brother-in-law, who pitched in with the fonts and layout. Ian thought it might look a bit egocentric if he took a credit under his own name on the record sleeve, if he was producer, engineer, sleeve designer and so on. Which is a little ironic, when you remember his studio was named Toad Hall, and that the eponymous Toad was the most egocentric amphibian in all of literary history.

But back to *Unholy Soul*, which is adorned with angels, just as *Striving For The Lazy Perfection* would be. "I had this obsession at the time with angels," says Ian. "With The Orchids' music, there was this ethereal quality, this lightness they had in their music, which was such a juxtaposition to their laddish behaviour. I always thought there was something divine guiding them towards this beautiful music they were making, which was so not how The Orchids appeared to be. And so this idea of divine guidance and angels, I thought it was quite apt for The Orchids."

For The Golden Dawn, having control of their sleeves was a high priority. Ulric Kennedy says: "My first job had been in graphic design, and Peter Claughan and I were working on a local newspaper, which gave me access to various graphical equipment and processes, so I delegated myself as designer-in-chief. I did both the sleeves and inserts, but conceded that the centre label should be done by Clare and Matt. It *was* their record label, after all." He continues: "At that time there was an underground movement of 'photocopy artists' and I was pretentious enough to lay claim to a piece of that action. It's a bit of a forgotten byway now, as printing processes have fairly come on since the late 1980s, but the mix of high-contrast images with random artefacts was very appealing to my eye, and of course was all over all the fanzines of the day, too. The idea was simple and effective: monochrome palette, stripes and polka dots. Luckily Strawberry Switchblade had already left town, otherwise they might have had a word with us."

Many record labels had a recognisable image, and the sleeves for 4AD by Vaughan Oliver and for Factory by Peter Saville were particularly notable. While Sarah couldn't afford someone of that calibre, that didn't stop the bands from having aspirations. "I envisaged doing a bit of a 4AD-type sleeve [for 'Breathe'] and we got this sleeve designed, and then Matt and Clare said it could only be two colours and we were like, 'Oh, shit,'" says Christian Savill of Eternal. "So we stuck with it but it ended up looking like a complete mess. It was meant to be a Cocteau Twins-type cover but in just red and yellow it looked really odd." The Eternal sleeve was designed by Steve Jefferis, who would later become a Sarah artist himself via the Shelley single and then sign to post-Sarah label Shinkansen with his band Cody. These days, you can find him in The Warm Digits. Steve says: "I used to cut abstract pictures out of magazines and use them as tape sleeves, and I think that sleeve image came from such a tape I'd done for Christian. I had no idea about the two colour/high contrast process involved on the Sarah sleeves so we were all a bit surprised the way it came back, but it fitted the shoegazing house style so it was probably appropriate enough."

Another Sarah one-hit-wonder band was The Forever People, aka Greg Webster and Tim Vass from Razorcuts. The sleeve for their single 'Invisible' is a very striking graphic illustration that Greg created. Given the single was highlighting the ecological crisis, it made sense that they used an interpretation of the Ecology Flag on part of the sleeve, albeit upside down and in different colours. "That flag goes back to 1969," says Greg, "and was designed by a guy called Ron Cobb who was a counterculture artist in Los Angeles, he went on to be a contributor to *Star Wars* and various other films, he's got quite a history in Hollywood. But at the time, he was a countercultural artist. We liked the idea of that connection. With Razorcuts, after we'd gone through that initial period when it was very much a reaction against the environment, we

Bobby Wratten (pictured left) of The Field Mice was on a mission for minimalism on the band's sleeves. His bandmate Michael Hiscock (pictured right) shared Bobby's less-is-more aesthetic.
Left: Julian Bester. Right: Jon Cole.

were then referencing back to people that we would consider to be like-minded in our music, and going back to the counterculture of the 1960s. We wanted something a little looser and free form, and a lot of that stuff is hand drawn, so it's a little looser and more DIY and more punk rock."

Minimalism

The Field Mice's 10" mini-album *Snowball* from 1989 comes in an entirely blank lilac sleeve, which is an early instance of Bobby Wratten and Michael Hiscock's yearning for anonymity. The band and label would later disagree on the cover artwork to go with the 1991 album *For Keeps*, which ended up being plain blue, with a thick white stripe down the right-hand side and the band name printed at the top, with the album title in tiny letters beneath it. This simple cover was the cause of a great deal of disagreement. "Bobby and Michael wanted the text down at the bottom," says their bandmate Anne Mari Davis. "It sounds like a small thing but it ended up being quite a point of argument. Bobby and Michael didn't care whether anybody saw the name or not, they were just like 'put a sticker on the top'. They wanted minimalism to the point of nothing on their sleeves and I know that Clare and Matt were usually very open to radical ideas in terms of not playing the marketing game." Clare and Matt might have been open to new ideas in terms of marketing but they still needed people to know what the record was when they flicked through the racks at their local record shop. If people didn't know what the record was, how on earth were they going to be tempted to buy it?

Matt comments: "*Snowball* didn't have the band name on at all when we first took the artwork to Revolver, it was literally going to be just the colour. Having the band name on the back was the compromise. Bobby wanted it to be absolutely a plain colour, front and back. And Revolver said they wouldn't distribute it like that, we had to put something on it." Clare adds: "I remember Mike [Chadwick] at Revolver spitting feathers because it was a 10" so no one was going to see it in the racks, it hadn't got anything on the front so nobody was going to pick it out and look at it, and you could sense his frustration because a Field Mice mini-album would probably sell quite well and we did absolutely everything possible, combined with the band, for people not to buy it." Matt reflects: "Most shops displayed it the other way round, so the back was at the front anyway."

Bobby adds some colour to the story: "It's no secret that Michael and I loved Factory and Wire and The Cure and the more mysterious end of presentation. We knew from the start that we never wanted photos or names on the sleeves. That just seemed unnecessary and obvious. However, Sarah was run on an incredibly tight budget, so as much as we'd have loved to have Peter Saville or Vaughan Oliver design our sleeves, in reality we were in a two-colour world. This meant that with *Coastal* [in 1991], for example, we went for a nice post-punk grey with a simple blue font and minimal information. So we went for ideas like *Still* by Joy Division or Julian Cope's Scott Walker compilation on Zoo [*Fire Escape in the Sky*]. Cheap versions of minimalism. I think 'Missing the Moon' worked well. Anne Mari and I would have noticed purple and yellow combined on a Durutti Column sleeve at an exhibition we went to and we obviously squirrelled that away. It was really just working within the limitations that existed on Sarah. These days I think the sleeves fit together as a nice set, although I really wish we could have had the word 'Snowball' embossed in lower case at an angle to really complete *The White Album* feel."

Photo sleeves

Sarah 6 was The Poppyheads' one and only Sarah 7", 'Cremation Town'. The band called up their original singer Melissa, who was one of the handful of people they knew who owned a camera, and invited her to take some photos of the band. "We went wandering around and happened to stroll into a big public garden in Cambridge," explains guitarist Rob Young. "And we saw this cart lying there for no obvious reason, it was in a garden belonging to the university grounds. It just seemed like something to gravitate towards, so we took a bunch of photos around there. It wasn't very premeditated. We were into things like the cover of the first Love album, we liked that band photo, a band hanging around in a slightly strange

> ❝ The photographs of Severn Beach? I like them more now. Maybe it's like anchovies, you start to like them when you get older.❞
> **Rob Pursey, Heavenly**

THESE THINGS HAPPEN

An example of early artwork design for Welsh wonders The Sweetest Ache.
Courtesy of Simon Court.

location. It's funny in retrospect that it has the slightly rustic atmosphere to it, given that I ended up writing about English folk records and things that had a similar tone to them."

With a green wash added to the photo, Rob went away and selected a sheet of Letraset that he thought would do for the band's logo and set about rubbing the letters onto the photo artwork to make up the sleeve. The Poppyheads also provided all of the artwork for the poster that came with the 7". "I liked it, I was very happy with it. It was exciting to be on a record," concludes Rob of his record's sleeve.

"The artwork was left entirely to us," says Harvey Williams. "As Another Sunny Day, I would always give Matt photos and say 'This is how it should look, just Letraset something over the top'. But somehow there would be this uniform aesthetic across a lot of the releases. Generally, most of the time, there would be a sketch and then it would come back. With the *London Weekend* compilation, I remember supplying complete artwork and that would go off to the printer, and by the time of the two solo records, that would have been again finished artwork to Matt. The first singles, I would have been giving him photos and leaving him to come up with a layout."

FUN FACT: The photograph on the cover of 'Gunnersbury Park' is actually taken on Deal Pier, down in Kent.

Julian Henry of The Hit Parade says: "I'm a DIY person, it's my song so I want to do it all. It's the same as the recording to me. I did all the artwork for our singles on JSH Records. I wanted it to be authentic so I laid them out, hand drew the guitars, the Letraset, oversaw the cut, proofed the sleeves and labels, all of that. So when Matt and Clare asked me to do a single for Sarah, I just said 'Yeah, as long as I can do the artwork, too.'"

The first two 7"s for The Sweetest Ache had a very distinctive look, thanks to photographer Lee Jenkins and graphic designer Phil Thomas, who worked to create a coherent aesthetic for the Swansea five-piece. The sleeves for 'If I Could Shine' and 'Tell Me How It Feels' both feature a one-colour image of a single figure superimposed on black gloss. Phil was also responsible for the band's third Sarah single, as well as their LP *Jaguar*, but by this point Lee had moved to London, where he was making a name for himself as a professional fashion photographer. "Lee was just part of our clan," says guitarist Stuart Vincent. "He's a great chap to be around, very funny. I think we all knew he'd do well, although we probably thought at the time we were doing him a favour. Lee would always come to concerts with us in Bristol and Cardiff, he'd bring his camera and a forged press card and he'd get in free." In subsequent years, Lee would go on to shoot images of celebrities as diverse as Eminem, Salman Rushdie and Kylie Minogue for fashionable newsstand magazines such as *The Face*. But remember where you saw his work first, yes?

As part of Shelley's commitment to wanting to be a pop band, singer Tim Chipping drew on the aesthetic of él Records when it came to his band's one and only Sarah single. The flamboyant él look was incredibly theatrical and lavish, being "mostly incredibly poor people pretending to be rich and posh," as Tim summarises. "So me crediting my hairdresser on the back of the record was us attempting to do the él thing. Who are these assholes crediting their hairdresser? It was deliberate but I think it annoyed people." One would imagine that 'Rebecca of Hornsey' still dines out on her fame.

Shelley's rebellion didn't stop there, as Tim adds: "The sleeve was an anti-Sarah thing, too. They didn't really like having the artists on the sleeve, so that's what we did. I was so obsessed with pop music, and I'd discovered Take That by then so I was trying to be like Robbie Williams. I wanted to challenge the Sarah aesthetic a bit." The photograph of Tim was taken by Deborah Harding, assisted by their friend Kenna, hence the design credit to 'D&K'. She remembers: "That photo was taken in Tim's kitchen in Turnpike Lane and we just put up this sheet, because he was very into Kylie Minogue at that point and he wanted it to look more like a Kylie Minogue record and less like a Sarah record." I recently found a letter that Deborah sent me in 1995 and, on the back of a lilac and black A4 photocopy of the picture, she has written: "The first lot of pictures had Tim, flys unbuttoned, hands down pants in sex-sells-records mode... No! We coerced him into a suit and they look much better in a Kylie sort of way."

When Heavenly signed to Sarah, they made it clear from day one that they wanted to do their own sleeve artwork or, more specifically, that drummer Mathew Fletcher wanted to do their sleeve artwork. Mathew had designed all of Talulah Gosh's record sleeves, and he would carry on doing all of Heavenly's sleeves as well. Clare says: "Heavenly always had a clear idea of what they wanted to do and they came up with really great designs. But Heavenly was their second band and most other bands came to us less fully formed. For almost everyone else, it was their first band and they were really embryonic when they got involved with us, so we were probably a bit more dictatorial. Heavenly would send us paste-ups so everything was done, we just needed to add a barcode. Whereas other people might send a bit of an idea, or not really have an

The photocopy of the Shelley sleeve that Deborah Harding sent me with her letter on the other side. This was, excitingly, a month or two before the record was finally released.
Deborah Harding.

66 Enclosed, a Shelley 7", with Tim looking cute as ninepence on the front and Dickon expounding the theory that it is essentially a sad mix of fear and cowardice that catalyses the reproductive process on the reverse. You are going to die. Love, Matt xxx"

Letter to me from Matt, May 1995

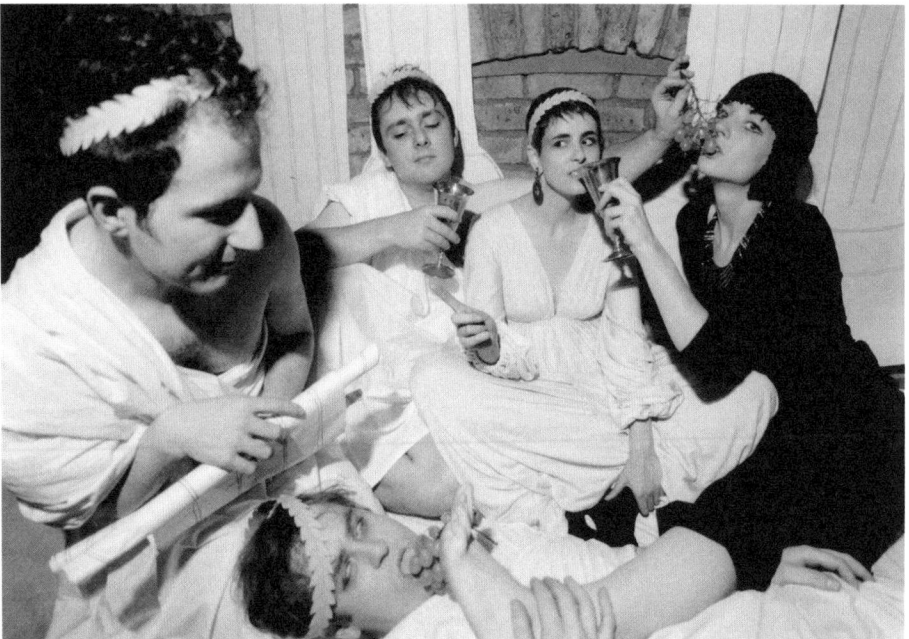

Heavenly became good friends with Alison Wonderland and she was their go-to photographer.
Alison Wonderland.

idea, or want something that we had to veto." Bassist Rob Pursey adds: "We did feel slightly different to other Sarah bands. Partly because we had women in but because we were quite loud live and more like a pop punk band than some of the other Sarah bands, and I think maybe we thought the general Sarah design was a bit drab."

For their later records, especially the albums *The Decline & Fall of Heavenly* and, post-Sarah, *Operation Heavenly*, the band worked closely with their photographer friend Alison Wonderland, who also freelanced for *Melody Maker*. For *The Decline & Fall*, Alison brought the band to her flat in London's Stamford Hill, set up the lights in her tiny kitchen and get to work. "My kitchen was the width of a washing machine, it was the tiniest kitchen you'd ever seen," laughs Alison. "So one at a time, they'd go into my kitchen and play with something, and then we just saw what happened." Which is why the back cover of the album features all the different band members playing with everything from a packet of cat food to the Homepride man. Similarly, the cover photos for *Operation Heavenly* saw the band back in Alison's tiny kitchen, taking it in turns to hold up a checkerboard rug as a backdrop for whoever it was that was currently in the frame. These are the kind of insider details that truly lift the lid on the secret world of Sarah, eh?

The photos on the East River Pipe records were taken by Barbara Powers. "Usually, we would send [Clare and Matt] some photographs that Barbara had taken and maybe a kind of rough artwork idea, and they would do the rest," says FM Cornog. "We were thrilled to let them take over the manufacturing and promotional duties. We were so excited to finally welcome someone else into our tiny circle who shared our aesthetic and that we trusted. We knew that once everything was in their hands, all we had to do was wait." He adds: "Prior to Sarah, all our visuals were simple Xeroxed covers on coloured paper. It was DIY in its purest form. Pretty crude really. *Chickfactor* magazine even made fun of those initial releases. But it was all we knew how to do, and it was all we could afford. We had to fund those initial Hell Gate releases ourselves. We weren't rich kids. We didn't have arty friends with graphic design skills. Anyhow, when the Sarah releases started coming out, all of a sudden we had these beautifully realised actual records. It's hard to express what a huge step up this was for us."

*****

THESE THINGS HAPPENED:
Spencer Harrison, Ivy

"Life was so different then. There was a real sense of confidence, which I don't have now because there's a lot of sadness in life. I don't wish I could exist back in those days but it was just a magical time. I felt like I was swathed in glorious light! Ivy was the best time of my life. I was doing the thing I love and life was a lot simpler then. It was all about music, gigging and the validation of a highly esteemed record label liking our music."

Chapter 13

Record Shops

The centre of the world for any music-lover in the pre-digital age was the record shop. Not an HMV or Virgin-esque corporate but an independent record shop – one that had staff who looked like they worked in a record shop and knew something about music. Some of the key independent record shops in Bristol during Sarah's day were Revolver, Tony's and Replay. But other record shops were available.

In Yeovil, near where I grew up, we had the independent Acorn Records and I started a part-time job there in April 1993 when I was 15. My boss Chris Lowe used to tell me that working in a record shop wasn't just standing around listening to records all day but, in all honesty, a lot of it was. Just as she was going stratospheric, local shero Polly Harvey came into Acorn in May 1993 on the day her second album *Rid Of Me* was released to play an in-store set and do a signing. So I went down after school to help out. You used to see Polly around quite a lot back then, whether in the shops or hanging around at local pub gigs.

In the late 1980s and early 1990s, there were still a lot of choices for record buyers. At the humdrum end of the scale, there was WH Smith and Woolworths. You could even buy some LPs and tapes in Boots the Chemist, along with a new lipstick or some paracetamol. A bit more conventional was the mega chain Our Price, which was later dwarfed by the ubiquitous HMV. There were also plenty of places you could find second-hand records if you were prepared to rummage. It seems hard to imagine now how easy and cheap it was to buy vinyl back then.

> ❝ We don't really go in record shops much because – well, because they're full of people like you, basically. Don't deny it."
> **Sarah Newsletter, January 1994**

Revolver Records

If you weren't insulted by the staff in Bristol's Revolver, then you deserved to feel insulted that you missed out. It was a duel both of you entered into willingly. There were plenty of other great record shops in Bristol but Revolver, at 1 Berkeley Crescent, is the one that stands the test of time in people's memories and hearts. One of the co-founders was Tony Dodd, who sold it to Mike Chadwick in 1976 before setting up his

These days, there is nothing at the site of the former Revolver Records shops to suggest the magic that once happened here. Unfortunately, photos of Bristol's record shops proved very hard to come by.
Neil Phillips.

own record shop down the hill on Park Street. We'll come back to Tony's Records later in this chapter.

Richard King has written an excellent book about his years working behind the counter at Revolver which includes a small section about Sarah and I urge you to read his book *Original Rockers*. Apart from being a great insight into the mechanisms of an unconventional music shop in Bristol, it is also a brilliantly written story about forgotten and unusual records. Richard writes in the book: "Our clientele knew that by entering Revolver their visit ensured the shop was transformed from a liminal space into a threshold, a portal where the shop counter was not merely a location for purchases but a point of departure for the sharing of an obsessional love of music and a wonder at its ability to transfigure the everyday."

In 1984, Mike Chadwick hired a chap called Jeff Barrett to work at Revolver and, alongside the shop, the two also briefly ran a small label called Recreational Records. Jeff told *Going For a Song* author Garth Cartwright about the record shop experience: "I liked what I saw. I liked what I heard. I liked how they smelt. I learned more from record shops than I ever did in school." In the same book, he added: "To me, when I worked in Revolver, it was the most amazing record shop in the world. Record shops can be scary places and this was the scariest of them all: in a windowless building with fag butts on the stairs." Jeff left Revolver in 1985 to move to London, working as a promoter for Creation Records and helping to set up Heavenly Records. Before he left Bristol, Jeff recruited his replacement in the form of Bob Jones, a recent graduate whom Jeff had met several years before when he was managing the Plymouth branch of HMV and Bob was one of his best customers. Knowing that Bob had moved to Bristol after graduation, Jeff headhunted him for the role in Revolver. Bob's new colleagues famously included Grant Marshall – soon to be Daddy G in Massive Attack – who had been the reggae buyer at Revolver since the late 1970s. Bob would largely work under Roger Doughty's ownership of Revolver, but Roger was initially living in Cheltenham so his visits to the shop were sporadic and Bob was pretty much left to his own devices.

> Went to Revolver. I looked around, liked what I saw and took my solitary 12" costing £1 to the counter. "What?!" Mr Revolver Man exclaimed. "How pathetic! Only a pound! Don't you want to buy anything else?!" I meekly mumbled something about not having much money. He went on to say he didn't know why I was buying this particular 12" ['Crystal Nights' by Ornamental]. I replied that I thought it was good. To this he said, "Oh. You like it?" as if that explained everything."
>
> **My diary, 19 February 1993**

Matt moved to Bristol in 1980 and Clare in 1986, and it wasn't long before they each found their way into Revolver. "I'd been in Rough Trade in London but other than that I'd only really been in chain record shops until I moved to Bristol," says Matt. "So Revolver was my first experience of a proper indie record shop. To some extent, it was what I thought an indie record shop was going to be like, quite intimidating and scary. And it's only since then that I've realised most indie record shops aren't actually like that, most have a range of chart stuff as well. If you went in Revolver and asked for the latest chart records, you were going to get laughed at."

Clare adds: "I did Economics and the department was on Berkeley Square in my day, so Revolver was just on the corner of where I studied. I think I would have found it on my first day. And would have taken *Kvatch 5*, which came out just before I moved to Bristol, in immediately. It was mostly Bob behind the counter and he was always welcoming, and I think I felt fairly at home there by the time I first met Roger. I don't remember finding the entrance scary but the shop was very different from Jumbo in Leeds, which is what I was used to, and which was a much more normal indie record shop, if there ever was such a thing."

Being a fan of the independent music scene, Bob was pleased to welcome Matt and Clare whenever they came into the shop with their Sarah Records hats on. (NB: these are figurative hats but imagine what a marketing tool they could have been.) Given Bob worked there from 1985 to 1990, the early days of Sarah very much came under his watch. "That was the heyday of this indie movement, and that's how I got to know Matt and Clare because they were just starting out and they were incredibly shy and nervous," says Bob. "I used to ask Matt what the photos on the 7" labels were of and try to get some banter going but it was quite difficult. I was really into Sarah Records and was pushing it quite hard in the shop. I had to hope that Roger wasn't in on the days they came in, as he was very loud and a big personality. I didn't want him to scare them off!"

Ah yes, that problem of Revolver seeming a bit intimidating to some people. That was a theme that cropped up with many of the people I spoke to, and I experienced it myself to a certain extent when I started shopping there. Revolver famously had no shop front, not even a window, simply a small A-frame board on which Roger would chalk up some of the new releases that week. You would walk up a few steps and into a dark, narrow corridor, the walls of which were papered with posters for local gigs and ads searching for musicians to join bands. That corridor and its posters and flyers is almost as fabled as the shop itself. Davey Woodward of The Brilliant Corners tells me: "That's where we'd advertise for a drummer or a place to play. That was as close as you got to a Facebook page for musicians. I think we went through three or four drummers from that board." And at the end of the corridor was a door on the right which took you into the small box of the shop, a room lit entirely by artificial lighting. It's not hard to imagine what someone might have found intimidating about that entrance.

Martin Whitehead from the Subway Organization grew up nearby and recalls his first visit to Revolver when he was about 13. "I was trying to get some punk or new wave record on coloured vinyl. Mike [Chadwick] was serving and they used to have listening booths to the right of the counter," says Martin. "The place was heavy with rather pungent smoke and I think I asked for this record on coloured vinyl, and Mike said 'We've got it on black vinyl, why do you want coloured?' and these guys in the listening booths with dreadlocks were bobbing away, laughing out loud at how Mike was responding to this kid in his school uniform. I probably didn't go back for several years until I found I couldn't get the records I wanted anywhere else." Nancy Horlick, who would later be in Tramway, also found it pretty intimidating: "I didn't like it because you felt like you were under a spotlight if you didn't know what you were looking at or bought the wrong thing. I went in there to buy something once and Roger wouldn't sell it to me, he told me it was a load of rubbish. And when you're on your own in a shop as a girl, as a teenager, that's not nice... so I stopped going in there."

It's a wonder we all loved it as much as we did. But once you'd plucked up the courage to go in and browse, Revolver became a home away from home for an enormous number of displaced music fans in Bristol. The list of people who told me that a perfect Saturday in that era involved coming into town and working their way through Revolver and the Park Street record and book shops is lengthy. It sounds like an idyllic way to pass a day. A number of people also commented on how Rocker, the drummer from The Flatmates, was a regular fixture in Revolver on a Saturday and how he would come in with a list of songs he wanted after hearing them on the John Peel radio show, hoping the shop would find them for him. Rocker was a big fan of the shop. "It was brilliant," he says passionately. "It was another of these places, a bit like the Tropic Club, where it was almost slightly exciting to go in there. It was an unmarked doorway with no shop front. Then you'd go down this passageway and you'd always have to spend 10 minutes looking at all the new gig posters in the corridor. Because there was no internet, you'd find out about gigs by looking at lampposts and a poster in Revolver. I knew Roger quite well. You'd pick an LP up to buy and he'd say, 'Oh you don't want that one, you want this' and then he'd try to sell you a jazz record because he was a jazz freak."

During my era of shopping there, one of the sales assistants was a guy called Dave Pearce, who was the frontman in Flying Saucer Attack. Talking to Caught By The River (another Jeff Barrett project) in 2017, Dave said: "I can safely say that [Revolver's employees] were all restless, somewhat agitated types ... That restless agitation could also help explain the attraction, at least to me, of the simple chaos of the place." Clare went into the shop one day while Dave was behind the counter and asked if she could put up a poster advertising Heavenly's upcoming tour. To which Dave responded positively, and suggested that Clare cover the entire shop in the bright blue and green tour posters. "The whole of the shop was Heavenly," Clare says. "I was there for about

Picture, if you can, an entire record shop wallpapered in these beautiful butterfly posters.
Courtesy of Sarah Records.

three hours decorating the shop. Which was probably lovely of him but I'd only nipped out for 10 minutes."

Rob Young from The Poppyheads grew up in Bristol and the bulk of his teenage record-buying was done in Revolver, starting in the late 1970s: "I would walk past this building where Revolver was. It had this huge mural painted on the outside and it was someone pointing a pistol like in the James Bond movies and it said 'Revolver'. I remember being really intrigued by that. It was quite scary as well." Rob Pursey of Heavenly grew up in the nearby suburban village of Frampton Cotterell and started shopping at Revolver around 1980: "Revolver was my gateway, I loved that place. I started going into that shop when I was quite young but I was quite scared to go in there because I was a kid in my school uniform, and going into a room full of punks and rastas was a bit scary." However, Rob's friend Tim Rippington, who would later be in The Five Year Plan, Beatnik Filmstars and Arrest! Charlie Tipper, harbours only fond memories: "They would get records in one minute, open the box and go 'Oh, wow!' and if you happened to be at the counter, you'd literally take one out of the box. I remember going down with Rob [Pursey] one lunchtime from school and there were a load of boxes out on the pavement because they had those steps to go up into the shop. And Mike [Chadwick] was there and he asked us to give him a hand carrying the boxes in. It was *Heaven Up Here* by Echo & the Bunnymen. It was like, 'Oh my god! I'm going to be the first person to have one of these records' and we bought it there and then. I just loved that shop, it was amazing. We considered all other shops to be below it. Anything we ever wanted, you'd only get it in Revolver."

For 19 years from 1987, Alan Harwood was a sales rep for Pinnacle, one of the UK's largest distributors of independent labels, and Revolver was one of the shops on his route. As a music fan, Al used to take time to rifle through the racks to see what was new: "I know I was supposed to do my job but I'm also a record collector. Roger was very snooty about records. If he had something in stock and you went to buy it, he would castigate you if he thought it was shit. He'd say, 'What do you want to buy that for? What a pile of shit that is.' Roger would tell you a story about the band or some anecdote about the band and how crap they were, and you'd walk out thinking, 'I've just bought this shit record' but that's what Roger was like." Al adds: "When I sold into him, he would rip the piss out of some of the stuff I was selling. 'What's this crap you're selling me this week?' But if he liked something, he would not stop going on about it. I remember when Carter the Unstoppable Sex Machine released *101 Damnations*, he was obsessed. 'Oh my god, this is so good', he went off on one. He said it was the best thing in the world."

Absolutely everyone I spoke with for this book agreed that Revolver was the most important place for them in Bristol. It provided a hub for those who felt they didn't fit in anywhere else. It was essentially a community centre for the disenfranchised. Former fanzine writer Mark Taylor explains: "Revolver was where it was all really happening. Many times on a Saturday, you couldn't even get in the place as it was so packed with people listening to records and smoking and chatting. It was an incredible place, like a club that was actually a record shop. They would let you put your posters up in the corridor and, as long as you had your own Sellotape, they wouldn't charge you. They'd sell my fanzine [*Smiths Indeed*] and not take any commission. They were the right people. They were so switched on to the whole scene. If it wasn't for Revolver, the Bristol scene may not have even happened." Mark adds: "Often shy people, who didn't know too many people outside of school or work, they weren't the most sociable people. I think a lot of people like me were very insular, bedsit types. But Revolver is where they found solace in fanzines and indie bands, because they're all very similar characters. And when you find a venue like Le Cav or the Tropic, or a shop like Revolver, your whole world opens up because you're with people who are your kind of people. Before social media, this was how you found people. It was confirmation that there were other people like you out there."

Former shop manager Bob Jones agrees: "Record shops had a social purpose to them that's difficult to explain now. Your misfits and shy folks could save up their pocket money and come in on a Saturday, and hang about and listen to stuff that was playing, and the shops had a real purpose to them." The community hub of Revolver was also essential for people in bands. Davey Woodward from The Brilliant Corners tells me: "I hung out at Revolver a huge amount. There was a guy Andy who worked in the shop who later became very involved with helping The Brilliant Corners out. When he moved to London, he worked for [Revolver Distribution] and he'd help us out with gigs. I'd go to gigs with Bob, who was also part of the EEC Punk Rock Mountain. Bristol almost feels like a village, once you know a few people you're running into people all the time, and you'd go into Revolver and hang out, and then see those people at gigs." It was indeed a great meeting place, as I noted in my diary in September 1994: "Went to Bristol. Met Matt in Revolver. Bumped into Al Harwood in there, which was a nice surprise. I found some records, then left with Matt, and we went walking around Brandon Hill so he could show me his house from a distance. Then we went to a café." Dear diary, what a day!

Having opened in either 1970 or 1971 (nobody can decide which), Revolver closed once and for all in early 2000 following several years in which it became increasingly difficult to sustain the business, given the shop's refusal to cave and sell chart releases, DVDs or video games like their competitors had in order to survive in a changing marketplace. But, for 30 years, Revolver was the unlikely spindle of record-buying happiness for the misfits and the socially awkward of Bristol. All of whom treasured what they brought home in those famous red and black plastic bags.

Revolver Distribution

In addition to Revolver Records there was Revolver Distribution, which was a part of the UK's independent cooperative distribution network The Cartel, which formed in the early 1980s as a new means to facilitate the ethical distribution of independent records away from the unaffordable practices of the major distribution networks. There were seven British independent retailers in The Cartel, and Revolver was the South West's link.

While it was relatively easy and affordable for independent labels to record and press a run of records at this time and sell them into local independent shops, it was not so easy for them to get those records into national shops, which was where The Cartel came in. As such, the regional record distributors in The Cartel would offer deals to some of the small independent labels in its area to help them out. Mike Chadwick (who owned Revolver Records at that time) became joint owner of Revolver Distribution in 1981.

The successes of independent bands such as The Smiths (Rough Trade), Depeche Mode and Yazoo (Mute), Joy Division and New Order (Factory) and the Cocteau Twins and Pixies (4AD) meant that, by 1984, The Cartel had access to a large warehouse in London but had also become a distributor to be taken seriously. The Cartel had proved it was efficient and business-like, now distributing to the national chains as well as independent record shops and, as a consequence, it facilitated the rise of even more independent record labels all around the country. Sarah was one such label.

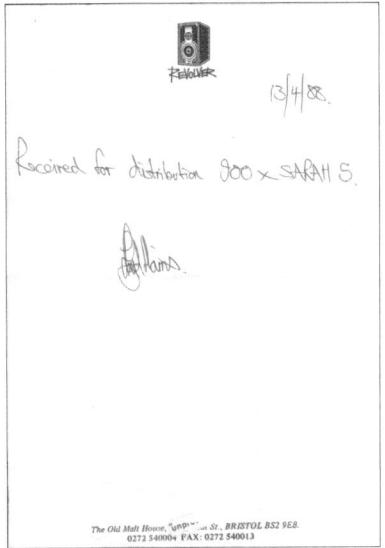

An early note to Sarah from the folks at Revolver Distribution.
Courtesy of Sarah Records.

Clare explains how it came about: "We went to Revolver and asked for a manufacturing and distribution deal, which meant that they would pay to get the records pressed as well as distributing them, and was a really common arrangement. Then they'd take a higher distribution fee because they were taking a risk by paying for your manufacture. Revolver was the obvious first refusal. But we were prepared to be refused because I remember talking about who we'd go to next."

Clare and Matt used the success of their fanzines and the *Kvatch* and Sha-La-La flexis to reassure Revolver Distribution that they knew what they were doing. Clare says: "It was Mike Chadwick we went to see. He was very brusque, and two kids rock up and say 'Will you finance and distribute our record?' And probably because he looked after Subway and Revolver had quite a lot of success with that, he said OK." Matt adds: "I guess they thought if we could sell 2,500 copies of a flexi disc, we knew what we were doing and could probably sell that number of records as well. Mike's other great question was, 'You're not going to put them in those stupid little plastic bags like Subway, are you?'"

In the autumn of 1988, Matt wrote a letter to his former Sha-La-La comrade Pete Williams, in which he helpfully – for us – spells out the financial costs of putting out an early Sarah record: "We only got the go-ahead from Revolver because we presented them with a list of four or five intended releases. They weren't interested in one-off deals. Revolver lend us money for pressing, that's about £500 for 1,000 7"s. Recording is, what, anywhere between £150-£300. Sleeves another £100+. Then publicity, photos etc. Distribution means the Cartel take 35p per copy and we get 80p, so maximum return on a 1,000 pressing is £800. 12"s involve greater initial outlay but you get it back quicker 'cos of the higher profit margin. Fewer sales for the same profit. The Thatcherite definition of ambition. Politics. Simple."

Thanks to Revolver Distribution, one of the local indie bands that was enabled to take the matter of production into their own hands was The Brilliant Corners. Aged 23 in 1983, frontman Davey Woodward and bassist Chris Galvin felt older and wiser than many of the kids in new-ish bands, who were more like 17 or 18. Having a few more years' experience under their belts meant The Brilliant Corners had a better understanding of the punk and post-punk DIY ethos so, after recording their debut single 'She's Got Fever', the band approached Revolver to see if they would distribute the records via The Cartel. As Davey says: "If you were enthusiastic and had energy, you could do whatever you wanted to do. So we came from that set of beliefs."

With Revolver on board to distribute the record, it was just a question of getting the recording pressed onto vinyl, the sleeves printed and then gluing the sleeves together. "It wasn't in a wraparound sleeve and plastic bag," says Davey. "The original pressing was on really stiff card but we destroyed about 100 copies because Bob [Morris, drums] and Winston [Forbes, guitar] glued them together then put the vinyl inside but glue got on all the vinyl. It was that kind of haphazard approach."

The Groove Farm, who started in mid-1986, put out records on their own Raving Pop Blast! label, which frontman Andrew Jarrett is still running today. He recalls that they got the records pressed on an industrial estate in Acton and remembers going up with the band to collect their very first releases, filled with youthful excitement. "We thought it would be amazing, that there would be fairies and elves and it would be a wonderful place," says Andrew. "But it was really horrible! It was a grey day in Acton. There was this old guy doing the cutting who was snivelling and he had a cold and was really miserable and moaning about the sound. He hated the record! And then we had to collect the two boxes of heavy records on the bus, and carry them back through London." He adds realistically: "From the age of eight, I'd been a pop music obsessive and dreamed of being on a record. But of course, I never thought where or how they were made. They're just made in a factory like everything else. It smashed all my illusions."

Revolver initially refused to distribute The Groove Farm's record "on the fact that it was shite and unlistenable and no one would buy it," says Andrew. Undeterred, the band sent copies to Janice Long and John Peel who both played it multiple times. As a result, "we were selling records through mail order and were swamped with people sending us money Sellotaped to bits of cardboard and hidden inside envelopes, and we sold out, re-pressed and that's when Revolver Distribution realised it wasn't unlistenable after all." Hurray!

Continuing to explain how Revolver supported Sarah, Clare says: "I think The Cartel was a good thing. It never occurred to us to be distributed by Pinnacle, because The Cartel always seemed properly indie and Pinnacle always seemed a bit business-like. In retrospect, you think maybe being a bit more business-like might have been a good thing for many of us." Part of the reason for going to Revolver was the Bristol connection but another part was that it had "a fairly neutral reputation", unlike some of the other links in The Cartel chain. "For eight years, Revolver absolutely always paid us on time," says Clare. "We always paid our bills on time, they always paid us on time and it was a functioning business relationship. We had a really good working relationship with them for more than eight years, including them lending us quite a sizeable amount of money at one point. Which we repaid." While that might sound like the bare basics for a business relationship, it would be naïve to think everyone operated in such a straightforward manner.

The whole system changed enormously during the eight years that Sarah was in operation. Back in 1987, there were no pre-orders or advance sales to worry about. Instead, Clare and Matt took The

> ❝ The reason I can't give a more specific answer at the moment is that we've got to go and discuss things with Revolver – we're into ethics and aesthetics, and they're into money – and we have to find a compromise."
>
> **Letter from Matt to Chris Quinn, The Orchids, debating when their next single might be out, 15 May 1988**

Sea Urchins' records down to the distributor as soon as they had put them in sleeves, not realising there was a weekly deadline that they might have just hit or missed, as Clare says: "I don't think we even knew when it was going to be in the shops because we didn't know what the release date was. Whereas later, we knew exactly what our release date was three months in advance and we were counting back from it." So it is unlikely 'Pristine Christine' ever had an official release date, it just started appearing in shops sometime in late-November 1987. "We were very much learning as we went along," says Clare. By the time Sarah was coming to a close, Clare and Matt were having to produce advance cassettes of music for the sales reps to listen to in the car as they went on their rounds, so the reps knew exactly what it was they were trying to sell into the record shops. Which seems a very un-Sarah activity.

Revolver Distribution rapidly outgrew the backroom of the shop on The Triangle and expanded to a warehouse – the first one at the Old Malt House on Little Ann Street, which is where it was when Sarah started, and the second on Dove Lane in Stokes Croft – before settling in a purpose-built warehouse-and-office in Barton Hill. By the time Richard King came to work at Revolver Records, The Cartel era had ended but much of the old stock survived in the shop's damp backroom. He wrote on *Caught By the River* in 2012: "All the detritus left over from The Cartel entranced me. There were enough records to start another shop entirely from the room at the back." Although Alan Harwood was visiting Revolver as a Pinnacle rep several years after The Cartel had folded, he also remembers the ramshackle nature of the shop that was still overwhelmed with old vinyl stock: "Out the back there were piles and piles of records, stacked up, covered in mould. It was an absolute tip. Piles of records that they used to distribute were now piled up in boxes and it was always a total mess behind the counter."

Upgrading to a dedicated warehouse was no guarantee of a more efficient operation, as Clare recalls "hammering on the doors to get in because the music was always so loud". However, "Revolver had a lot of staff by the time Sarah closed," she says. "It was a purpose-built two-storey warehouse and office complex in Barton Hill, a really big building. The previous Dove Lane one was a warehouse you could drive right into, with concrete floors and offices just fenced off to one side with glass doors."

Mike Chadwick seemed to retain a fond bemusement regarding the activities of Sarah, as this example illustrates. "Mike was driving up the M32 and spotted us by the side of the road trying to hitch somewhere," says Matt, "but didn't stop to tell us that the latest pressing was in because he was worried we might think he was stopping to give us a lift." Expanding on Mike's bafflement at Sarah activities, Matt continues: "The other, maybe more poignant story, was when we were standing outside the warehouse having just picked up copies of a new 7" to take back to the Upper Belgrave Road flat for sleeving etc. So there we were outside, with our big pile of boxes, in the pouring rain, waiting for a taxi, or possibly two, when the small door beside the main warehouse door opened, Mike poked his head out, observed us with our umbrellas and increasingly wet boxes and simply said, 'Do you think this is wise?' Which, in retrospect, was quite a good question." Clare adds: "He was great at that sort of thing. I remember one time, he sent us a letter that just said 'Sarah 2 here'. Because we didn't have a phone, we'd go to a phone box, ring up and ask if Sarah 2 was in, and you'd be conscious you were annoying them, so you'd stop ringing and then he'd go 'Their fucking record's here'. He obviously thought we were both idiots and hilarious."

After the collapse of The Cartel, Revolver Distribution merged with rival independent distribution network APT in 1992 and became Vital Distribution. Thanks to Britpop bands such as Oasis and securing business from the likes of Creation, Vital enjoyed a boom in the 1990s. "We had fallen down in their pecking order by then, which was why I think Mike wasn't bothered about us stopping Sarah," says Matt.

In 1994, knowing that the end of Sarah was approaching, Clare took a job with Vital. "I was trying to work out what to do next," she says. Initially thinking of doing a Master's degree in Brighton, Clare approached Mike for a reference but when he saw the size of the form he needed to fill in, his response was along the lines of: "Fucking hell, this will take me ages, can't I just give you a job instead?" And that was how Clare ended up as a sales coordinator for Vital. The job was initially to be based in London before relocating back to Bristol. "It felt like quite an exciting time to be in London," says Clare. "Not for any of the reasons anyone normally says but you'd got Bis and Dweeb and all of those semi-punky DIY bands and it just felt really exciting and like it would be an interesting thing to go and live in London for six months. Being in London obviously came with all the advantages you'd expect in terms of doing press and radio, and I spent time with some of the bands socially. I used to meet Keith [Girdler] from Blueboy on Friday evenings sometimes when he was on his way from Brighton to Reading, and I saw a fair bit of Heavenly."

FUN FACT: Martin Whitehead started working for Revolver Distribution towards the end of Subway's life and in this way he was responsible for the manufacturing of a lot of Sarah's records between 1989 and 1992. "One of my best memories of Sarah is being included on Saropoly," he says. "I felt I had a degree of celebrity there. I've still got it filed away in my 7"s and I'm very proud of it."

TONY'S RECORDS

A short walk from Revolver was Tony's Records, which was largely a second-hand paradise. I remember rooting through a bargain bin of 7"s in the basement once and finding the Human League's 'Being Boiled' on Fast Product for 10p. Despite the very reasonable price, I almost didn't buy it on account of the pen marks on the sleeve. But I'm glad I did buy it because I later realised those pen marks were the signatures of the entire original line-up of The Human League. I still have that 7" by the way.

While 10p is a fair price to pay for a second-hand 7", some of the sums that Sarah's records go for on the second-hand market these days are eye-wateringly steep. These were records that were originally made for as little money as possible so that they could be sold for as little money as possible because Sarah recognised that their customers didn't have much money. "I'll never understand the people who want to pay a fortune for an original 7" of 'Pristine Christine' and stuff like that, because I'm not quite sure what it is they think they're buying," says Matt. "If you were 17 in 1987 and you bought it when it first came out, that's fantastic, it's part of your growing up, it's part of your life, and you can remember the excitement of that being in your memories. But if you're buying a copy now, what are you actually getting?"

I share Clare and Matt's confusion about why people need to physically fill up the gaps in their collections. "You can't buy somebody else's youth just by spending £700 on eBay, so I don't understand that aspect," says Matt. Although Clare concedes: "There are some people who bought it at the time and sold it or lost it or wish they'd bought it. I can remember when we split up our record collection, [Matt] definitely got 'Smells Like Teen Spirit' and I got 'Her Jazz' in return. They were certainly the two we were struggling to split up. So I can see the argument for going back and buying the thing you had but lost. But certainly 'Smells Like Teen Spirit', it's not like you could go a year without hearing it in a shop. In a sense, your world will never be without it."

And all of this reminds me of a letter from Matt to a young Tim Chipping, who wrote to complain that he had seen a 'used' copy of Sarah 3 on sale for £15. Matt responded: "How can you tell it's a used copy of Sarah 3? Is it all covered in nasties they haven't bothered to wipe off, or what? More to the point, what was it used for??" Which is something we should all consider when buying things second-hand. PS, Sarah 3 is the flexi of 'Anorak City' by Another Sunny Day and Tim was lucky to see it for £15, because currently it is going for £180 on Discogs. Yes, £180 for a used flexi that contains only one song which lasts for a mere 138 seconds. That works out as £1.30 per audio second. Which is a lot.

Anyway, now we've considered the concept of second-hand music in general, let's look at Tony's Records in particular. Having been one of the founders of Revolver Records, musician Tony Dodd then set up his own shop in Clifton, which became popular with local punk bands Social Security and The Cortinas. It was in 1984 that Tony moved to the premises on Park Street that many Bristolians will remember.

Tony was known and respected for being a fan of music but you definitely had to be in the right frame of mind before tackling his shop, as it wasn't the most orderly of places. "It was a crate diggers' paradise," says former Pinnacle rep Al Harwood. "If you wanted to look for obscure things and dig around for them, you could spend hours in there. It wasn't really well laid out with an A-Z system. It was more like, 'It might be in that box over there'. Or he'd say, 'I might be able to get you one of those' and jot it down on a bit of paper. He had slips of paper behind the counter with what people wanted and it would be stuck there for months on the off chance he found that record."

As with Revolver, inevitably the shop attracted local musicians to work there and, over the years, staff members included John Langley and Gerard Langley from The Blue Aeroplanes and John Stapleton who, as Dr Jam, was the resident Friday night DJ at the Western Star Domino Club. Rob Young of The Poppyheads says: "John was very cool because he used to play all these weird sound effects with his turntable from the side of the stage. He was a great DJ. He was massively into funk and rare groove."

The shop remained a must-visit destination until Tony called it a day in 1996. However, John now runs Wanted Records in St Nicholas Market.

Replay

Over the years, there were four locations for Replay in Bristol, as well as a fifth shop in nearby Bath. The Bristol shops were at 73 Park Street, East Street in Bedminster, and two branches by the bus station: one on top of the other (the one upstairs specialised in dance music, while the branch downstairs sold new, independent and second-hand records). If you're looking for famous faces, then Simon Price (not to be confused with the music journalist with the same name) and Hugo Morgan from The Heads used to work in the branch downstairs by the bus station. Having worked in HMV in the nearby Broadmead shopping area for a while, Hugo made the move to Replay and stayed there for 15 years until it closed in 2007. It was through working in the record shops that Hugo and Simon met and formed The Heads, while their boss at Replay generously stumped up the cash to finance the band's first few 7"s.

After leaving Revolver in 1990, Bob Jones moved to the branch of Replay by the bus station and became the manager there until the shop closed. "It was not as elitist as Revolver could be," he says. "It was a more normal indie shop. On the whole, I had a great time. The position of the shop wasn't always wonderful because sometimes there was a lot of anti-social behaviour outside, which was a drawback. With independent shops, you've got to be a bit savvy and quite confident. So we didn't get the normal Broadmead shoppers coming over there. But we did have a good fan base. In the heyday we did really well."

Ruth Patterson also worked downstairs at Replay for several years. It seemed the natural career choice for her after she left college, given that for the previous two years she had spent almost an hour a day in the shop killing time while waiting for her bus connections. As a committed indie fan, the ethics of Sarah appealed to Ruth, who remembers Clare and Matt coming in from time to time. "There was also an influx of tourists who would come to Bristol, drawn by the romance of Sarah and eager to snap up anything they could. We used to get Japanese indie kids who would want to buy anything and everything we had on Sarah," says Ruth. "They would buy multiple copies of anything we had. That would happen semi-regularly. They would go to visit all the locations of the records and buy everything they could." Bob adds: "We used to get this one guy who would come over from Japan and he would spend all day in Bristol. He would bring a box on wheels and go round all the record shops, desperate to find obscure Bristol indie rarities that he could flog for a fortune in Japan. That's when I noticed it was a global thing. He would spend hours just going through every record we had, and we had a lot of records in those days. He was very focused."

It was this urgency for buying up the records before they sold out that helped to drive the popularity of Sarah Records. "All the indie records would sell out really fast from Replay," says Ruth. "There was scarcity. I forget as a fan it was hard to get things, because I was so spoiled from working there and I could get whatever I wanted. If we only had two copies of something, I knew I could buy one for myself. So you'd forget the urgency that customers had. The records would sell out but then they would recirculate on the second-hand market."

THERE WERE OTHER RECORD SHOPS, TOO

When Matt moved to university in Bristol in 1980, the very first record shop he went to was WH Smith in the Clifton Down shopping arcade. "It used to have quite a good selection," he insists. "I bought a Psychedelic Furs cassette there. The fact I could buy a Psychedelic Furs cassette in WH Smith is quite extraordinary. But all the chains were a lot better then. The first Sea Urchins single ended up in Virgin, I think that was where we first saw it, in Virgin in Broadmead. The debut single of an unknown label and it's in Virgin!"

There have been three versions of Virgin Records in Bristol over the years. Originally, there was a Virgin down by the bus station, opposite where Replay would open. In the late 1970s, when Virgin first came to Bristol, it was an edgy brand associated with The Sex Pistols. Gig promoter Andy Franks remembers: "They had aircraft seats where you would listen to the music with headphones on, and none of us had been on a plane, so to sit on an aircraft seat in a record shop, you felt like you were on holiday or you were somewhere really different. Virgin seemed like you were in this really hip environment. It was really cutting edge." Later, Virgin upgraded to a shop on Merchant Street in Broadmead. "I remember going in with Kylie Minogue's first single to pre-sell," says sales rep Al Harwood. "I saw the girl in there, and she said they'd take one 7" and one 12". And it turned out to be the best-selling single of that year!"

Despite not anticipating the popularity of Kylie, Bristol's Virgin kept going long enough to sustain the move into a massive Virgin Megastore in 1992 in the shiny new Galleries shopping mall. One of the Megastore's very first employees was Lois Pryce, who came in as Senior Sales Assistant. "I wasn't that into chain record shops, I was more into indie shops like Revolver and Tony's but they never had any jobs," says Lois. "I made it my mission to try and infiltrate my obscure music tastes into Richard Branson's empire. They allowed me quite a bit of input and it was always fun working in a record shop. The 1990s' business model didn't respect the knowledge of the staff or the product, though. It was about bringing in marketing and sales people from other industries and trying to apply it to music, and ultimately it didn't work, as we now know. Although Richard Branson likes to present himself as an alternative hippy, the culture of the company was quite uptight."

Virgin did sell gig tickets though, which meant it was a handy destination for music fans who worked in the centre of town to visit on their lunch break and pick up tickets to whatever was on at the Bierkeller or Tropic that week. And, since they were in there, they might as well buy a few records. I should add that most of the other record shops sold tickets too but, being less central, they were less convenient for office workers. After the Virgin chain of record shops went down the pan nationally, the branch in the Galleries morphed first into Zavvi (a division of Virgin) and then Head (a division of Zavvi). The property is now an arcade.

Sometimes, the chains did manage to make a name for themselves as trusted retailers of good independent music, providing they had the right staff. It was in this way, while both of them were working in Our Price in Swansea, that Marc Leverton met Stuart Vincent, who would go on to form The Sweetest Ache which Marc would manage. In the early 1980s, Our Price was the second-biggest retailer of music in the UK, second only to Woolworths: at its peak, there were 330 Our Prices around the country. In 1994, the retailer merged with Virgin Music but it failed to move with the times and... well, we already know what happened to Virgin.

But in the late 1980s, Our Price was booming and in a prime position to utilise its staffs' personal musical interests to carve out a niche for itself. Marc says: "Spillers in Cardiff was doing a lot of indie stuff but outside of that there was nowhere else you could get it nearby. Downstairs in [Our Price] was commercial and charty music, and upstairs we had a vinyl and indie section, and Stuart and I had total freedom to get in what we wanted." Stuart had been prompted by his mum to apply for the job at Swansea's newest record shop and he sensibly followed up on her idea. "It was a great place to work, it was the hub of Swansea's entertainment scene at the time, and it was a great place to meet people," he says. The teenage staff also enjoyed the kind of freedom when it came to ordering in stock that is unimaginable these days: "Back in the late 1980s, there was no computerised stock system. You were free to order whatever you wanted carte blanche. You'd listen to John Peel, go to work the next day and, all the great records you'd heard, you'd order them in for the shop," says Stuart. "They'd just brought the chart machine into the shop, where you'd scan the barcodes of records you'd sold so they'd get in the charts. So myself and Marc would be scanning multiple copies of whatever single we liked, there was no checking up. It was a great place to be."

Sarah had come to Stuart's attention thanks to The Cartel's sales rep who came in with a Field Mice 7" one day. "He'd always put his pile of records on the counter and, for an hour, he'd try and sweet talk you into taking two or three copies, and you wouldn't tell your boss what you'd bought off The Cartel rep because nine times out of 10 it was rubbish and wasn't going to sell," says Stuart. "I think it was 'Emma's House' or 'Sensitive', and it was the fact that I'd not seen a single in that kind of format in a record store before, which was in a plastic bag and a paper fold-around sleeve, which made you want to pick the record up and study it, you were drawn to it. I said I'd take two copies and played it in the store upstairs and thought it was fantastic."

Now that he had an awareness of Sarah, Stuart started noticing when John Peel played the occasional song or when more singles by the label were sold into the shop. In time, Sarah became one of Stuart's favourite labels and he contacted Matt to see if there were any materials going spare that could be used to make a Sarah display in Swansea's Our Price. "He couldn't quite believe that anyone would want to do that," laughs Stuart. "About a week later, this box arrived with numerous single covers, some postcard inserts of Temple Meads station, just loads of great stuff. Which I thought was fantastic. And I did do a small display in the store but then started to order through distribution companies the backlog of singles as they were coming out. So we started to build up quite a good Sarah Records collection in the store and I told my friends to pop in and have a listen, and the records started to sell, maybe two or three a week. It built up that way pretty much."

Stuart was not the only future Sarah artist to work behind the tills in an Our Price because, in 1984, Amelia Fletcher and Pete Momtchiloff met while working in the Oxford branch. So if it hadn't been for Our Price in Oxford, perhaps there never would have been a Talulah Gosh or Heavenly. Imagine how different the indie-pop landscape would be today but for that fortuitous meeting! "Pete had been working there for a while, and I had a year off between school and university, so I got a job there," explains Amelia. Pete adds: "I knew Amelia as a customer. She came in and bought the sort of records that I liked. Back in those days, I think she was a fan of The Cure, The Bluebells, Orange Juice, Julian Cope…" The pair started Talulah Gosh when Amelia went to Oxford University, from where Peter had already graduated.

FUN FACT: Radiohead bassist Colin Greenwood also worked in that branch, as did Ride's original bassist Steve Queralt. The shop's site should get a blue plaque.

Meanwhile, in London's Muswell Hill, Robert Cooksey of The Sea Urchins was also working in Our Price, "which is where I remember selling a copy of 'Pristine Christine' to a customer who had asked for it. It had just been released and I was surprised that someone came in asking for it, so I was over the moon obviously." Surely there's nothing more exciting than selling a copy of your own record to a fan?! Unless… "Another interesting episode in the shop occurred when I had put The Who's *Tommy* LP on one day and looked up to see John Entwistle of the band in the shop."

Of course, Our Price staff didn't have the monopoly on forming Sarah bands: customers formed bands, too. Bobby Wratten and Michael Hiscock had been friends at school but then lost touch until they ran into each other again in the Croydon branch of Our Price. And after that meeting the two ended up forming The Field

RECORD SHOPS

Can you imagine going into a record shop and seeing Amelia Fletcher working behind the counter? In 1984, that was a very real possibillity. Assuming you went to Our Price in Oxford.
Chris Scott.

Mice. The rest is indie-pop history.

In central London, Sarah fan Deborah Harding would routinely pop into the branch of Rough Trade in Neal's Yard in Covent Garden to do her record shopping, and the manager there quickly noticed this woman coming in to buy every Sarah record. So much so that he would always keep one back for her so that she didn't miss out. That record shop manager was a chap called Stuart Staples who was on the cusp of musical greatness himself as the frontman of Tindersticks.

Further up the UK in Glasgow, future Teenage Fanclub singer Norman Blake had been working in McCormack's Music Shop from the age of 17. When his shift in the shop finished, Norman's best friends Duglas T Stewart [The BMX Bandits] and Sean Dickson [The Soup Dragons] would meet him to hang out and sometimes be regaled with stories of whatever famous people had visited McCormack's lately. And, one day, Norman had the big news that Caesar from The Wake had been in to look at the instruments. "We were all like, 'Wow!' Because at that time, it was the Factory music thing and also he'd been in Altered Images," says Duglas. "So it was like 'Wow! What was he like?' And Norman was like, 'Yeah, he was a nice guy.' When we played with The Wake, I had a little bit of a thing of being very slightly younger than Caesar and thinking, 'He's been there.' He's someone we would have been aspiring to be like.'"

Over in Australia, future Sugarglider Josh Meadows had a weekend job in an independent record shop in Melbourne called Saturdays. "They used to get airmail copies of the *NME* and *Melody Maker*, which were like gold in those days because the newsagents only ever got copies that came the long way. They also had a table just inside the front door with a whole lot of 7" singles on it and they were the new releases that had just arrived by airmail from the US and the UK. It was always exciting to see the new stuff that had just come in, and that was where I first got to hear and buy some of the early Sarah stuff. Another Sunny Day, Field Mice, Sea Urchins… they were exactly what I wanted to hear. [My brother] Joel and I were already into things like The Housemartins, Billy Bragg, Lloyd Cole and Orange Juice but we knew Sarah was a really special label." 🍒

*****

THESE THINGS HAPPENED:
Julian Henry, The Hit Parade
"At the time, I felt Sarah Records was a home for outsiders. A number of us were rejects. People who couldn't find a place in the music industry. Perhaps it was a reflection of the formulaic approach that the major labels favoured with their huge investments. Quite a few people had a belief in pop but couldn't conform to what the music industry wanted and that's what Sarah Records provided. They either liked your music or they didn't. There's a kind of snobbishness to Sarah Records that appeals to me. In my PR job, I've been lucky enough to meet a few stars over the years but my personal tastes have always been less mainstream. I prefer what's happening in the margins. I'm pathetically

nostalgic for the end of the analogue era, the last label of the last century. Labels don't have that meaning anymore. Music has been commoditised. Today the status of a label is assessed by data, everything locked by lawyers, they're not driven by creative instinct or intuition. The dynamic between Matt and Clare was carefully balanced, they were equals. They were honest. This helped them make good decisions. A lot of people start like that but it becomes difficult to sustain it over eight years, and they did it."

THESE THINGS HAPPEN

Chapter 14

Going Out: Bristol

Like lots of cities up and down the UK, Bristol had a clutch of steamy little venues for bands to play in. It also had a listings magazine called *Venue*. "Considering its size, Bristol was incredibly well off for live venues," says Bob Jones, who worked at Revolver and Replay, as well as being a gig promoter. "It's always been a city that absolutely loved music and, for the size of it, it's produced a lot of great bands and artists over the years. You'd get *Venue* and there'd be so much going on. It was a great place for being a music lover. I never felt a pull to go to London because there was enough going on in Bristol." Rocker from The Flatmates would agree because, in his first year in Bristol, he saw around 350 gigs, often managing three in one evening: "There used to be pubs with early nights that were free, and then there'd be a Colston Hall-type gig and then nightclub gigs. I spent all my money on going to gigs. There was a real scene of Bristol bands from 1986."

As a teenager, former fanzine writer Magz Hall spent the years before university going to as many gigs as she possibly could in Bristol: "I lived in a very boring suburban village called Pill. I'd get on the bus to Bristol and that's where my life began. When I look back on it now, it was very fun. Ultimately, I went to London because I wanted to see more bands and there was more of a music scene there but I don't think it was ever as good as the energy that was at the Tropic Club."

Sometimes the social element was just as important, if not more so, than the music. Tim Rippington, of The Five Year Plan and Beatnik Filmstars, says: "In those days, people would go to a gig because they were going out anyway. Most people went out four or five nights a week, so if anybody said there was a gig on, you just went. There were always crowds. I can't remember really poorly attended gigs in those days. Sometimes you'd pay to go in and end up in a corner with somebody and spend the whole time talking to them and forget you'd even paid to go to a gig." Keris Howard of Brighter agrees: "It was so much driven by fans that sometimes bands felt peripheral to it, that gigs were a meeting place for like-minded people to come along and meet up with their friends and sell fanzines."

> 66 The Orchids: Glasgow's finest, they've spent seven hours in the back of a Transit to be here with you tonight, so please don't expect too much."
>
> **From the running order for the Sarah Christmas Party, 1993**

One of the things that made Bristol such a vibrant city for music was its rich cultural diversity. "When I was in The Five Year Plan, we were an all-white band but most of the gigs we played were in venues run by Black men, so the Tropic Club, the Trinity Hall and the Western Star," says the band's Rob Pursey, who would later be in Heavenly. "They were the venues that allowed gigs to happen. They made some money out of us bringing in kids to listen to our post-punk noise but taste-wise we were into each other's music. I was big into dub, partly because of Revolver Records where there was a really good dub section. But the way bands formed is just a reflection of the sub-groups of society. They're nearly always mates. And if you're living in a world like Bristol was at the time, and a lot of Britain still is, where Black and white people don't mix, then you're going to form a band with the people down the road and it's a reflection of where we are." Lifelong music fan Orynthia Thomas, who is Burmese by birth, says: "You would rarely see people of colour at all, apart from me! I can't remember which Bristol gig it was but I remember there was a Black person in the audience and thinking, 'Wow, we never see that!' It was a very white scene."

Here are the most significant Bristolian venues for our purposes, from 1987-1995: sadly, most of them are now long gone. Many of the surviving buildings have since been listed. Ostensibly, they have been listed for their architectural merit but, really, we all know they have been listed due to their importance in indie-pop history. However, the people with power have trouble admitting that kind of thing. They don't want to give away that, beneath their M&S suits, they're sporting natty striped tees.

The Bierkeller

The sudden closure in early 2018 of The Bierkeller due to redevelopment plans by the landlords was a shock for music and arts lovers across Bristol. This dingy, yeasty, scungy cavern was an unlikely hit. I remember sitting on the ancient couch in the manager's office during a meeting and feeling as if I'd sunk between the cushions and slipped right onto the filthy floor. Nonetheless, maybe the extremely old-fashioned, uncomfortable, sweaty charm rubbed off on fans? The condensation would certainly rub off on them if they stood too close to the dripping walls.

The Bierkeller was the venue where Clare and Matt famously met at a Julian Cope/Primal Scream gig and Matt refused to buy a duplicate copy of Clare's *Kvatch* fanzine. The rest is... well, the rest is documented in this book. "It wasn't love at first sight," wrote Clare, bluntly, in the guide to 2014's *Between Hello and Goodbye* exhibition at Arnolfini.

Top: The Fleece & Firkin: so many splendid Sarah shows took place here. **Bottom:** On 24 July 1994, I saw Heavenly for the very first time. At the Fleece in Bristol, of course.
Top: Neil Phillips. Bottom: Jane Duffus.

The Fleece + Firkin

This Grade-II listed warehouse was constructed in 1830 to house the city's wool market and, owing to the stench generated by soaking the wool in urine to soften it, the building was located on St Thomas Street which was – then – a far-out limb of the city. These days, the former Wool Hall is considered to be part of the city centre and, in 1982, was taken over by the now-defunct Firkin brewpub group and repurposed as a live music venue. Now called simply The Fleece, it remains a live music venue and has a large hall with a high ceiling, stone walls and a big stage with good sightlines. In its day, the Fleece was a popular spot for Sarah bands. "The Fleece was a great venue because it's the right sort of size," says Heavenly's Pete Momtchiloff. "The bands couldn't escape from the fans, you were all in there together."

Tramway played a show supporting Heavenly at the Fleece & Firkin and Tramway's Nancy Horlick recounts how they had been just a little bit mischievous. "They had that new song 'Shallow' and we must have heard it, and so we did our own version of it before they played it. I don't think we did the whole thing, maybe we just did a bit of the chorus but that did not go down well." To be fair, I asked Rob Pursey of Heavenly about this and, while he doesn't remember it, he says they definitely wouldn't have minded. So all is well.

On 25 July 1994, I saw Heavenly at the Fleece & Firkin. As my teenage diary attests, it was a big deal: "We got to Bristol at about half eight and parked right outside Fleece & Firkin. I talked to Matt at his stall and bought 7"s by Ivy and Action Painting!, and Heavenly's 'Atta Girl' CD. Put some fanzines on his table. Matt tried to get me to go round selling fanzines. But then Heavenly started so we went up to watch them from the front. When Amelia [Fletcher] first came in, [my friend] James turned round to me and gasped, 'It's Amelia!' I took some photos for the next fanzine. Heavenly were exactly what I expected, and I was even brave enough to dance a bit. Afterwards I sold Amelia a fanzine. She was really friendly and apologised for Mathew [Fletcher] writing a load of crap in his interview. Someone gave me a National Heroes badge like Amelia's."

FOUR BANDS AND A FIGHT

The infamous Four Bands and a Fight night at the Fleece & Firkin has become so embedded in indie mythology that it deserves its own sub-section. So here it is. Much like the fact that absolutely everybody in the world claims to have been there when The Sex Pistols played at Screen on the Green in Islington in 1976, I have been hard pushed to find anyone who was *not* at the Fleece & Firkin the night that The Sea Urchins and Action Painting! had a kerfuffle. It is the stuff of Sarah legend. It has gone down in indie-pop folklore as one of the few times that someone left a Sarah gig with blood on their clothes. It has become a night of such fabled significance that, if it were not for the photographic evidence, the tape recording of the gig and endless first-hand testimonies, I would strongly suspect it had never happened in the first place. But it did.

Writing in *Venue* magazine in April 1990, reviewer Mike Gartside likens The Sea Urchins' drunken headlining performance to the pantomime punk of Tenpole Tudor before laying into the "morass of banter and cat calling" that the evening "degenerates" into. "The drummer wades across the stage and into the audience," Mike wrote. "Then, at a gig for the label with the wimpiest reputation in town – would you believe it? – a fight breaks out!"

The gig in question was a Sarah band night on 29 April 1990 for a bargain £2. The Sea Urchins were joined by Brighter (playing only their third gig) and St Christopher,

Top: Jamie Roberts and Robert Cooksey of The Sea Urchins on 24 April 1990... something was brewing.
Bottom left: The band's drummer Patrick Roberts, shortly before he stepped out from behind his kit.
Bottom right: A poster advertising one of the most infamous nights in Sarah's illustrious history.

Top and bottom left: Wendy Stone. Bottom right: Courtesy of Sarah Records.

as well as Bobby Wratten and Harvey Williams from The Field Mice doing an acoustic set. The audience was also full of Sarah superstars: Amelia Fletcher and Pete Momtchiloff from Heavenly were there, having come down from Oxford with Greg Webster from Razorcuts. As were members of The Sweetest Ache (soon to be a Sarah band), Tim Chipping (who would one day be in Shelley), my brother Adam Mornement with his friend Guy Sirman (future manager of The Sea Urchins), some of The Groove Farm... and Action Painting!, of course. And, presumably, everyone reading this book. And your friends, relations and neighbours.

Brighter had been in Bristol all day, walking around looking at the sights as a way to offset their nerves. "It was that moment when we realised we were part of something much bigger than we'd anticipated because this felt like a proper gig, and the Fleece & Firkin felt like a real venue," says guitarist Alison Cousens. "It's stories like [the fight] which show we weren't these twee, fey people." Frontman Keris Howard adds: "It was the first gig we'd done with other Sarah bands. I remember the gig went absolutely OK and that the evening was fantastically entertaining. I remember there being trouble but you knew what you were going to get with The Sea Urchins, they had a bit of a reputation, but it probably wasn't what I anticipated from my first experience of a Sarah night."

Fanzine writer Mark Taylor saw it all start to kick off after the bands had drunk a few too many lemonades: "One of The Sea Urchins jumped off the stage and then there was a fight in the front by the pillars." Music fan Wendy Stone was also there: "I think The Sea Urchins had drunk a bit too much and had a fight. I've got pictures of Clare trying to pull them apart." Hugo Morgan of local band The Heads adds: "I got there early and thought, 'These blokes following the band are pretty pissed' and it turned out to be The Sea Urchins. It was the last thing you expected to see at a Sarah Records gig."

The Fine Art of Shoplifting fanzine reported: "[The Sea Urchins] weren't very good at all, and acted like idiots, shouting at the crowd etc... untogether and out of tune. I think they were rather drunk, actually. Is this their idea of a joke, or has the fact that they've put out a couple of, gulp, CLASSIC singles gone to their heads? Beats me! On the subject of which, that's exactly what they did to certain members of the audience." While *Jade* fanzine wrote of The Sea Urchins' set: "Aw, it was awful ... They just couldn't be bothered. They came on stage and you could see it in their faces that they'd rather have been at home watching the telly or something! ... It was like one big ego trip for them ... Who do they think they are? People paid good money to see them last night and they were too lethargic to even try to entertain us. And now this morning I'm left feeling disillusioned with it all."

OK, so what happened? Let's pass the mic to Action Painting! frontman Andy Hitchcock who was in the audience with his bandmates Lee Christopher and Kevin House. "It was quite a humid night and our drummer had a big block of gear with him. The Sea Urchins were appalling, they were like a pub band. It was the only time I'd seen them, and they were just playing Jimi Hendrix stuff and it was like, 'Oh for fuck's sake, come off it, you're better than that, stop being dicks.' And Lee was shouting 'You're shit!' And I was heckling as well, saying 'You're shit! You're bollocks!' I think Jamie [Roberts, The Sea Urchins' frontman] said, 'Who said that?' and Lee put his hand up and said 'Me!' And Jamie said, 'Oh, fuck you, you goth'. Lee had had a few drinks and said, 'Come on, then!' So Jamie jumped off stage, waded over, threw a punch, Lee threw a punch and Clare was literally in the middle saying 'Stop it!' like a playground attendant. I think some people dragged them away and I just stood next to Lee laughing. I didn't even have a chance to get stuck in, it was so quick. But you can hear on the recording Clare saying, 'Oh god, the boys are fighting!' and that was it. That's the Sarah riot. For about 10 seconds it looked like it was all going to kick off, because it was right in the middle of the crowd and it takes that amount of time for people to think 'Oh my god, am I going to run away or am I going to try and stop this?'. Clare and Matt never said anything to us after, I think they quite enjoyed it to be honest. They liked that we were naughty boys. We were horrible, it was part of the publicity in a way. Maybe, because they turned down the Manics, we were their Manics."

With the benefit of hindsight, Lee reminisces: "Even though we'd had a run-in with [The Sea Urchins] during one of their gigs at the Fleece & Firkin, they were by far the best thing Sarah ever had. The gateway drug of twee indie. The 16-year-old me cherished 'Clingfilm' and 'Summershine' and 'Pristine Christine'. Absolutely."

The Sea Urchins' guitarist Robert Cooksey tells me: "The four of us drank far too much and it is mostly pretty appalling musically, definitely one of our worst performances. Patrick and Simon [Woodcock] both got into scuffles with audience members and Simon actually got thrown out of the venue at one point during the performance! It's a shameful episode." He continues: "There's not much that I can add to that 'historic' incident apart from the fact that I remember we were drinking Löwenbräu. Yuk! That does explain a lot in terms of the behaviour, as it is pretty strong stuff. I wasn't a big drinker and am really ashamed, in truth, of what went down that night but I guess I can also appreciate the funny side. The bottom line though is the music was pretty awful and the tape that survives is absolute proof of a drunken mess. 'Pristine Christine' sounds like we are playing it at 33rpm!" Robert adds: "I really don't blame the audience in Bristol getting annoyed as they had paid good money to see a reasonably professional concert but got a befuddled horror show. Alcohol is poison basically and over many years I saw the undeniable damage it caused to the band, which is the reason I haven't touched a drop for 20 years."

Vocalist James Roberts adds: "I do remember that night at the Fleece. We didn't know what it was at the time. It was only after the event that we found out it was this other band on the label that I think thought they were doing kind of label-mate bantz. We just thought it was some pissed up guys in the audience that were trying to ruin the gig!"

Having been heckled by Action Painting! throughout their set, The Sea Urchins finally snapped and eventually drummer Patrick Roberts (not frontman James, as Andy thinks) got out from behind his kit while Lee pushed forwards in the crowd. Clare stepped in between the sparring musicians and, with the men not wanting to hit her, that was the end of the fight, although Clare's new striped t-shirt still managed to get a splatter of someone else's blood on it.

The Sea Urchins soldiered on and were still playing when the house lights were turned on and the audience was pouring out, in equal parts baffled and amused by what they had seen. However, in typical Sarah fashion, Matt muses: "My main memory is of the sheer pressure of trying to get four bands on with a 10.30pm finish." At the end of the night, The Sea Urchins refused to accept their £50 fee from Clare, flinging the cash on the floor (from where Clare picked it up) and saying they didn't deserve it because they'd been so shit. "At some point later, they appeared at our flat and said 'Can we have our £50 so we can get some petrol to go home?'," says Clare. "I remember them sheepishly standing in our flat."

The George & Railway

While the British government was busy worrying about European Economic Community sugar and butter mountains in the mid-1980s, Bristol was more concerned by the EEC Punk Rock Mountain. Postgraduate student Gordon Guthrie, the main man behind the team of ten, coined the brilliant club night name and explains: "The idea was that the price of punk rock had dropped so far that Europeans were buying it up to support the market and it was stashed in a giant warehouse. That was it, basically.

"To go and see a band in London, it cost you like £25, so we said 'Why don't we all put £10 in and subsidise the band to come here?' It's not really rocket science," says Gordon. "Having 10 people put £10 in, you're guaranteed to have £100 even if you don't sell one ticket. A lot of it was also to have something to do. My niece once asked my dad why he used to go to the Boys' Brigade five nights a week and my dad said, 'Well, we didn't have a television.' So, why did we put bands on? What else were we going to do?"

Simon 'Chesterfields' Barber kindly gave me his EEC Punk Rock Mountain badge because I didn't have one. What a kind man.
Jane Duffus.

The team of 10 Mountaineers was: Gordon, Matt, Rocker's accountant friend Adrian Millard, Rocking John, John Baxter, Bob Jones from Revolver, French Marion and her boyfriend Michael, Glaswegian Robena "who had good art skills and knew all the Glasgow bands" (says Gordon), and Jeremy Routledge "who was just part of the world we were in." Matt surmises: "I think we were selected Legion of Superheroes style for what we might bring. We displayed the accounts on our final night. And averaged

 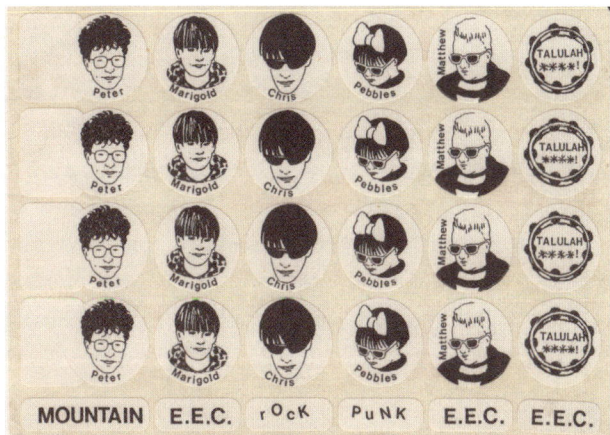

Left: Poster advertising Talulah Gosh's visit to the EEC Punk Rock Mountain on 22 October 1986...
Right: ...and some specially made stickers handed out to guests on the night.
Courtesy of Gordon Guthrie.

out across all the gigs, we'd each lost roughly the admission fee each time, which seemed quite fitting."

The EEC Punk Rock Mountain nights were held at the George & Railway pub, which can just be seen in the cult 1979 road movie *Radio On* as our hero drives into Bristol and over the much-missed Temple Meads rickety flyover, past the pub. The beautiful mid-Victorian building had a big room at the back that was sometimes used for gigs. By the time the EEC Punk Rock Mountain was being scaled in the mid-1980s, some dismal town-planning choices had left the pub stranded on an unsightly traffic island, which gave it the plus point of having no neighbours to annoy but the minus point of being rather hard to access.

"It *was* very difficult to get across the road to it," muses Matt, who was one of the Mountaineers. "Equipment was loaded in and out through the windows at the back of the stage, which probably gave the impression at the end of the evening that the band were doing a reverse runner, climbing out through the window before anyone had the chance to pay them." Matt adds: "I know it had mirrors facing the stage, because The Jasmine Minks were completely freaked out by having to spend the entire gig staring at themselves."

Gordon explains that lots of the big Victorian pubs in London had started putting gigs on as a way to bring in extra income and that it was quite possible that, when starting to think of somewhere to put on gigs in Bristol, he walked out of Temple Meads one day, saw the pub opposite and thought: 'That'll do'. "The George & Railway was really on its knees at the time," he says. "And we needed to find somewhere that wouldn't charge us but that was happy to take money just off the bar. The landlady was quite bemused by it all but

> ❝ I think I'm now involved with promoting gigs in Bristol, as part of a group of eight or nine friends (to minimise loss!). Maybe we can get some live recordings straight from the mixing desk – potential flexi material?!? Possibilities, possibilities, I think we're going to try to open with The Soup Dragons."
>
> **Letter from Matt to Pete Williams, September 1986**

I think they hoped for a more hard-drinking crowd. They wanted 50 people having five pints each, instead they got lots of people ordering orange juice and lemonade. But they grew to quite like us." The George & Railway liked the night so much that they added a special meal to the bar menu called The Mountain, which was literally a mound of mashed potato with a few sausages poked in the top.

One of the main reasons that Gordon was able to access such big names (relatively speaking) as The Jasmine Minks and Miaow! was that Jeff Barrett, who had been working in Revolver, was now the tour promoter for Creation. "He phoned me up and offered me The Loft and all the early Creation stuff," recalls Gordon. "And I was saying, 'I can't do it, I'm trying to get my fucking PhD!'" There clearly had to be a limit somewhere.

People still remember the extra EEC touches. Many people I spoke with had kept strips of Talulah Gosh stickers that had been printed up for their gig at the EEC Punk Rock Mountain, although nobody was able to summon up a 30+ years old sugar mouse or slice of cake that they'd been handed on the door in lieu of a ticket, which is just as well. "As you went in, you were handed a cake at the door with a word on it in pink icing. Most of the words were swear words as I remember," says Tim Vass of Razorcuts, whose band had a single on Subway called 'Big Pink Cake'. His bandmate Greg Webster adds: "I remember 'fuck' certainly being on one of the fairy cakes that I came across." At Christmas, everyone was greeted with fresh fruit at the door. Well, almost everyone. "There were all these oranges and apples and things, and I said 'Ooh look, there's a cabbage'," says Andrew Jarrett of The Groove Farm. "And the guy said they were saving that for Martin Whitehead of Subway."

The night that The BMX Bandits played, everyone was asked to tell a joke as they made their way in and the best joke won a prize. When reminded of this, Matt says thoughtfully: "Yeah, that does sound plausible." While Clare adds: "That sounds like the sort of thing you would hate, Matt!" Chief Bandit Duglas T Stewart elaborates: "That sounds very like us. Someone that I met years and years later told me that he saw The BMX Bandits in Bristol in 1987 and he won a pair of my jeans in a competition. I think it was a pair of some pink or orange jeans and they were signed by the band. And when he told me this years later, I was going [incredulous voice] 'You won *what?!*'"

Razorcuts played the opening night of the EEC Punk Rock Mountain, but the George & Railway staff clearly weren't sure whether or not they were supposed to intervene as hosts, or just leave these kids to do whatever it is they were going to do. Matt explains that at the very beginning of the set, the pub's landlady "grabbed the mic from Greg Razorcut just as he was about to start the first song, and asked him who they were and where they were from. And then he stood beside her looking sheepish as she did her 'Ladies and gentlemen, they've come all the way from Oxford to play for you tonight, let's have a big hand for the Razorcuts…' spiel." Tim Vass says: "I've got a tape of that gig somewhere so she's captured for posterity. She was a bit of a Bet Lynch from *Coronation Street* sort of character, I think she was head-to-toe dressed in leopard skin and had peroxide blonde hair. When she came on, we all looked at each other in bemusement while she introduced us." Tim Rippington from The Five Year Plan was in the audience that night: "I think the landlady did that more than once, that became a bit of a thing. She was good! In those days, people were quite happy to seek out odd places to go and see bands. If you put a gig on somewhere and it wasn't a traditional venue, people were quite excited by that and quite happy to walk around until they found that place. And it was a bit like that with the George & Railway."

Greg and Tim had had a bit of a rush to find the venue, given its mysterious location on a traffic island. "I've been to Bristol recently and I was amazed to discover that it's right next to the station," says Tim. "But we didn't come on the train, we came by car and we drove around looking for it for about half an hour. Swifty [David Swift], our drummer, was already there. I think he was looking forward to the possibility of performing a drum solo instead of the Razorcuts' gig." The gig cost the princely sum of £1.73 to enter and, according to the accounts sheet, the band received £80 for their troubles. "Did we? We got paid £80?! I wonder what we spent that on?" muses Tim. "We'll have to play there again, Tim, that's pretty good," adds Greg, still keeping an eye on the finances.

Coming from sleepy Penzance, music fan Harvey Williams found the idea of seeing a band in a pub's back room in Bristol to be a charming novelty. "I wasn't a regular gig goer in the mid-1980s," he says. "I lived in Cornwall and there were no real venues in my part of the world. But certainly, the idea of seeing a band in a back room of a pub was quite an alien concept for me in 1985 or 1986. It was strange to see a band in a pub and think, 'Oh look, he's just walked past me and now he's getting on stage'. The divide between the audience and the band, all of a sudden that wall came down."

Despite the lasting impact the EEC Punk Rock Mountain had on those who knew of it, there weren't really that many gigs: 14 at the George & Railway, plus two at the University's Grad Club. Nor were there that many people who came. "The spreadsheet literally has ticket prices for every week. So Talulah Gosh got 37 paid tickets, meaning there were 47 people there. And it was a pretty regular crowd, including some people who did travel. People said later, 'Oh, it was really exciting going up to the EEC Punk Rock Mountain from Somerset,'" says Gordon, a little bemused. For those unfamiliar with the geography, Bristol and Somerset are right beside each other on the map. He adds: "The thing that was always important was you really had to believe in what you were doing and think it was important, even if it wasn't particularly important."

Sadly, the now-Grade-II listed former pub has been empty for more than three decades and has become derelict, despite its listed status and prominent location. The matter of its future is a topic that often rears its head in the local newspaper but no solution ever seems to be reached. Bob Jones sighs: "We had some good times down there. I can't remember why we stopped doing those nights now."

Harper's Bazaar

There is one word that people repeatedly use to describe Harper's Bazaar and that word is 'glitzy'. I'm sure 'swanky' is just one breath away. It was on Anchor Road where a casino now occupies the same building, and people are undecided whether Harper's Bazaar was mostly a casino, a nightclub or a comedy venue, but the air of mystery is nothing if not appealing. "There was nothing else around it at that point," says Matthew Evans of Tramway. "That was one of the few buildings still standing there at that point [after extensive bomb damage from the war], all the old warehouses had been cleared."

Primal Scream came to Bristol to do a show at Harper's Bazaar on 29 June 1988.
Courtesy of Gordon Guthrie.

Harper's Bazaar was a larger-scale venue that would sometimes put on gigs with bands such as The Pastels and Swans. Bob Jones from the EEC Punk Rock Mountain team put on Primal Scream and Loop there, again thanks to Jeff Barrett's connections. Music fan Wendy Stone says: "The Pastels, The Vaselines and Loop played, that was an amazing gig. It was a weird place to see an indie gig as it was quite glitzy." While gig-goers Tom and Orynthia Thomas recall: "It was a bigger room than some of the indie venues but it was never very full. It wasn't a sticky back room of a pub. It was quite glitzy. They wanted it to be the place to go, because there was nothing down that end of town, but Anchor Road felt like the end of the world. The Primal Scream one was a really memorable gig."

The Pastels gig with support from The Vaselines (tickets £3.25 in advance or £3.50 on the door) was organised by Rocker from The Flatmates. "It was a pretty horrible venue, it was like a casino," he says. "It was a bit plush and a bit too big. The problem we had with The Pastels gig was that Swans had played there a couple of weeks earlier and it was one of the first gigs the venue had put on. There were security on the door for Swans and it took two hours to get the audience into the place because everyone got frisked, and then Swans were painfully loud and everybody walked straight out again. So that put a bit of a downer on the venue but I'd already booked it to put The Pastels on and we just didn't get enough people in. I lost a lot of money on that night. Harper's Bazaar wasn't open for very long as a gig venue."

GOING OUT: BRISTOL

Here's a poster for the ill-fated gig at the King's Arms, flyposted near the Upper Belgrave Road flat.
Courtesy of Sarah Records.

King's Arms

There was a short period where the Fleece & Firkin was out of action and the bands who would have done shows there needed to be rehomed. Which was why, on 21 May 1990, The Orchids and Brighter ended up playing a gig at Clare and Matt's local pub: the King's Arms pub on Blackboy Hill, alongside Bristol band Hope (tickets £3). The trouble was, the venue had a sound limiter fitted which meant that if you so much as sneezed, the sound would cut out... which made for a frustrating gig. "That gig was a nightmare," sighs The Orchids' drummer Chris Quinn sadly. "James Hackett [The Orchids] spent the entire set looking at the little light on the ceiling to see when it was about to kick out because the moment that light came on, they knew they had five seconds to adjust the sound," remembers Matt.

The Orchids and Brighter had done a series of dates together to promote their albums *Unholy Soul* and *Laurel*. "There was a big joke at the time about Brighter's sound being the most gentle, quiet sound on Sarah but even Brighter were breaking rules on sound and noise," laughs Brighter's Alison Cousens. "I remember it as being absolutely bloody ridiculous! The gig went ahead but I think it kept cutting out right the way through. It was bad enough for us but for The Orchids, who were a proper band, they couldn't even get 10 seconds into a song before it would cut out." Her bandmate Keris Howard adds: "I'm sure we did a cover of 'Just Can't Get Enough' by Depeche Mode where one of The Orchids came over afterwards and slurred 'That was fucking awful'. Which was fair enough."

The Field Mice, still a duo at this stage, performing at Le Cav on 1 July 1989.
Wendy Stone.

Le Cav

Underneath The Crown in the historic St Nicholas Market, deep in the wine cellar, sat a very small venue known as Le Cav. There has been a pub on this site since 1741, but any visiting indie-pop bands in the late 1980s or early 1990s should have been under no illusions of grandeur as it was a very simple affair. Le Cav had stone arches and low ceilings, and was a popular haunt for early Sarah bands, as fan Wendy Stone remembers: "I saw The Field Mice at Le Cav. There was hardly anyone there and they played simply and you wondered why more people couldn't come and enjoy it." Former fanzine writer Mark Taylor adds: "I remember seeing The Field Mice at Le Cav in the early 1990s and there were about 50 people there. You'd go down and it was pretty damp and steamy if it was a busy gig." Clare muses: "It didn't have the world's best sound. But it was a nice little room for really small bands."

In *Lemonade*, Clare wrote about seeing her first gig at Le Cav on 30 June 1988, which was Clevedon-based band Mousefolk plus The Wednesdays and Panda Pops, which included Matthew Evans (who would later be in Tramway) and Scott Purnell (who would later be in Secret Shine). She wrote: "Le Cav, my first trip, the perfect venue, whitewashed basement, long narrow no stage, conversation audible over blaring pop, £1.25 admission." Scott rues: "When we played at Le Cav, I couldn't even have a drink at the bar as I was too young."

Nancy Horlick used to play the Stylophone in the Panda Pops. At Le Cav, her instrument was balanced on top of a beer barrel "and somebody came up at the end and said, 'Oh, you were really good but what were you writing all the way through?'

He thought I was just stood there writing a book!" Her brother Matthew Evans remembers the venue well: "I'd watched The Field Mice play there as a duo, I think they'd just signed with Sarah. They weren't very good that day, just two of them and a drum machine. You used to get a lot of people in because you'd put on three bands and charge 50p to get in. I remember once we played at Le Cav and *Venue* magazine gave us a big write-up but we had a pricing policy that is probably illegal now: you had to pay more if you were over 21. We thought music should be for young people."

The first time Clare and Matt met St Christopher was outside Le Cav on 15 October 1988. "I don't think they're that much older than us but they seemed so grown up because they had proper jobs and cars," says Clare. "Glenn [Melia] gave us a lift home because he was heading our way, and it felt like we were kids and they were grown-ups. Because everyone else on the label was kids as well." Matt adds: "I was just really pleased to be putting out a record by them. There's loads of reverb on the St Christopher records and, at a sound check, rather than doing the 'one two, one two' thing, Glenn would just make a popping noise and count the waves to make sure the reverb was exactly the same as on the record."

Malaap Club

In Bristol's bohemian Stokes Croft area there is a branch of Tesco Express that was so unwelcome when it opened on Cheltenham Road in 2011 that it experienced two nights of furious rioting. Prior to the building's life as a controversial convenience store it was a comedy club and, before that, the Malaap Club.

During the BBC's Sound City week in Bristol in 1995, the Malaap hosted a Sarah fringe event on 17 April where Heavenly, Blueboy and Secret Shine thrilled the audience for a mere £3. Well, all except DJ John Peel who "wanted to come and watch us but he ended up choosing to walk rather than get a taxi and he missed us play," laments Kathryn Smith of Secret Shine. Although the radio host did try to make amends afterwards by phoning vocalist Jamie Gingell to apologise: "One minute I'm watching some crap lunchtime programme on TV, the next John Peel is talking to me on the phone and I'm thinking 'This is a bit surreal.'"

It seems John Peel wasn't the only one who had trouble finding the venue, as Paul Stewart from Blueboy can attest. "I got lost," admits Paul. "I had an interesting encounter on the way. It was before sat nav and Google Maps. I pulled over to this street and saw these two young ladies walking on the opposite side, one was dressed in red leather trousers and the other not wearing that much, and I wound down the car window and said 'Excuse me' and she leaned in my car with a cigarette. And I said, 'I'm looking for the Malaap Club' and she told me where it was, and I said, 'Ah, thanks so much.' And she said, 'I thought you were after a bit of business.' Naïve!" Anyway, Paul got there in the end. As did Peely, who had finished his stroll across Bristol by the time Blueboy came on stage.

THEKLA

Thekla is a German cargo ship built in 1958 that is now moored at The Grove. She was initially repurposed in 1982 as a floating theatre called The Old Profanity Showboat, co-owned by the charmingly eccentric Vivian Stanshall of the Bonzo Dog Doo-Dah Band and his wife Ki Longfellow-Stanshall. In 1986, the boat's original name of Thekla was reinstated and Rocker of The Flatmates was one of the first gig promoters to put music on there. He says: "The Thekla decided that in order to stay afloat financially they'd have to put gigs on, so they very much looked down on the grotty little indie punks who used to hire their venue out." It was the location for two Sarah Christmas parties, plus the infamous farewell party in 1995.

Before putting on indie gigs at the Tropic, Martin Whitehead and Rocker had put on a few shows at Thekla, and the profits from the first few of these went to funding the initial Subway singles. Martin says: "There was a curtain behind the stage at the Thekla with a dressing room with no floor, just a walkway, and if you didn't look where you were going you'd end up in the water. Two of the bands who played there managed to blow the electricity, because the power supply came from the quayside." He adds: "I really wish I had fully appreciated the time I had spent with Viv Stanshall. But his wife told us they weren't having us back as we were all animals, so after six gigs we got thrown off the Thekla."

FUN FACT: This boat remains a beloved gig venue and even had its own Banksy on the side for a decade, which can now be seen in the nearby M Shed museum.

We have already heard the story of the fight that erupted at a Sarah gig between members of The Sea Urchins and Action Painting! but that wasn't the only tomfoolery The Sea Urchins got up to. Just before Sarah launched, the Birmingham band was invited to support The Flatmates at the Thekla. Rocker remembers: "They brought some mates along and one of their mates took all his clothes off and ran around the venue. I remember Debbie Flatmate chasing around this guy holding his underpants, saying 'Put these back on!'. She was like the mother figure suddenly." Bridget Duffy of The Sea Urchins adds with a shrug: "That was a guy who was the equivalent of Bez [Happy Mondays], he used to help with carrying stuff. He was a nice guy but he'd get really drunk and then decide he was going to strip. He did that at a couple of gigs."

The first time Razorcuts played in Bristol was on Thekla. "It had a very loud PA and I think it must have been one of the first gigs that we'd done with [drummer] David Swift, one of the first gigs we'd done as the three-piece Razorcuts, which was like an indie power trio," says bassist Tim Vass. "I remember it being really loud and looking at Greg [Webster] halfway through the first song and thinking 'Wow, this is great.' Swifty was a really full-on drummer." Greg adds: "I particularly remember that gig because my guitar decided to be completely untuneable, so I just hit it a lot."

Prior to being in Heavenly, Rob Pursey was in a number of bands including The Five Year Plan and he lists their support slot for The Housemartins at Thekla as one

Thekla remains one of the most iconic gig venues in Bristol. You've got to visit it at least once.
Neil Phillips.

of the most fun gigs he has ever played. The gig was on 4 October 1985 and Rob says: "They were amazing people, and we had a game of five-a-side football with them in the car park after the soundcheck and it was a great gig." The Housemartins were at that exciting point where 'Flag Day' and 'Sheep' had been low-level hits but the band were yet to hit the top 10 with 'Happy Hour' and make it onto *Top Of The Pops*. Rob adds fondly: "The Thekla was a pretty incredible place. It always had that extra tension when you went backstage because you weren't quite sure if you were going to fall through a hole. The back of the boat felt quite rotten and you might just end up in the dock."

Rob's Heavenly bandmate Cathy Rogers also enjoyed playing on Thekla. "I absolutely love being on boats, even if it's only one inch away from the land it gives me this feeling of freedom," she says. "So the fact of playing a gig on a boat was a total winner for me. And the environment there, you feel like you're in another time and place. It always felt like you were going to have a good time, it was a party boat. Often we would be playing last at those parties and that's quite a lot of time that you've been in an alcohol-filled venue before you play, so it takes quite a lot of self-control to make it all the way to your set. I think of the Thekla and think of being quite drunk."

Don't worry, we will return to Thekla later in this chapter when we revisit the Sarah Christmas parties.

Left: A treasured ticket to see Secret Shine (and friends) at Sound City. **Right:** A flyer for the same gig.
Left: Courtesy of Stephen Nash. Right: Courtesy of Scott Purnell.

The Trinity Centre

In a late Georgian former church in Old Market sits this imposing Grade II listed venue. Deconsecrated in the 1970s, the former Holy Trinity Church was given to the public for use as a community centre and arts space. Responsibility for the building was transferred to the African-Caribbean Community Association, which began a programme of extensive repairs and renovations. The Trinity Centre was opened to the public on 1 July 1978, the same day as that year's St Pauls Carnival. Over the years, bands who would play at the Trinity included U2, Joy Division, New Order (supported by The Wake) and Scritti Politti.

One of Tim Rippington's earliest bands was The Inane, which also featured future Heavenly bassist Rob Pursey. The Inane played a few gigs at the Trinity. "It was all run by West Indians," says Tim. "At the end of the night, one of the West Indian chaps asked us to come back and play again. He got us back to support Jashwha Moses, who was a big reggae artist. So you had these little teenage indie kids playing this really shrill trebly guitar stuff supporting a really professional reggae band in Trinity Hall and that was purely because the guy who ran it had an open mind about music. I can't imagine that happening now."

In 1995, during the BBC's Sound City week in Bristol, the Trinity played host to a number of mighty fine bands. One of whom was the Jesus & Mary Chain, supported by Secret Shine and Belgian band dEUS. The slot came about thanks to the infamous 'cancer' review that the *NME* had bestowed on Secret Shine, which had been so outrageous that it had propelled the Sarah band to the attention of John Peel, Jo Whiley and Steve Lamacq, among others. The band's guitarist Scott Purnell explains: "It was incredible, it's still one of the peaks of our time. It was just wonderful. It gave us a small taste of being on a different level, with the way it was professionally set up. There was a band called dEUS supporting with a rack of guitars and Jesus & Mary Chain with a rack of guitars, and we turned up and the BBC sound engineers were saying, 'You've got a rack over there to put all your guitars on' and we had one guitar each. It just shows how quickly you can step up to a different level but unfortunately it didn't carry on."

His bandmate Jamie Gingell adds: "It was just such a step up, because the BBC were organising it and running it and engineering it, and I don't think I knew what was going on if I'm honest! It was broadcast live on radio and it was terrifying." Vocalist Kathryn Smith continues: "I think we just turned up, panicked for ages, did our stuff and then disappeared again. I do remember really enjoying their gig afterwards when I could relax." Scott adds: "We were well rehearsed for that gig and I thought we sounded quite good. We're not a bunch of amazing natural musicians, so it does become a challenge but that was good. It just felt fantastic. We had lots of friends in the crowd and just to look across a room, and it be absolutely packed and knowing you're supporting one of the bands that you've loved for years, the Jesus & Mary Chain, it was fantastic."

The Tropic Club

Over on Hepburn Road in Stokes Croft, the Tropic Club opened in 1983 and immediately became a vibrant music venue. Being run by the entrepreneurial Burgess family, who had come to Bristol from Jamaica in 1954, it was an oasis of hip in an area of the city known for being a little down at heel. When Bristol's famous Dug Out club was closed by police in 1986, the Tropic benefitted from a lot of the acts that had played there needing a new venue to play in.

Rocker from The Flatmates helped put on gigs there, alongside his bandmate Martin Whitehead, who also ran The Subway Organization, and their friend Mark Simpson. Describing the Tropic, Rocker says: "It was a great venue. As you walked in on the ground floor, it was all very dark, there were no windows and so it was all artificial neon light. The ground floor had a standard disco and that tended to be what we thought was trendy music. Not chart music but disco music and what would become house music, rare groove and stuff like that. Downstairs, we called it The Bunker because it was literally like going down into a bunker. You'd walk down a zigzag set of stairs, and it's basically where the toilets were and you'd carry on a bit and there was a little door that opened up into a cavernous room and the stage had a bright orange backdrop with palm trees. There was a bar area which was quite small and then there was an area where the punters stood for the stage, which was even lower, and a DJ booth to one side and a PA guy to the other but it was very cramped. It was hot as well." Martin adds: "The dressing room at the side of the stage had a sink in and I caught more than one band pissing in there, rather than walk through the crowd to the toilets."

Rocker explains how the nights were a little disorganised, though. "We used to turn up on a Thursday night and the guy who had to come and unlock the place was never there to open up for us," he says. "We'd have all these bands coming down from London and we'd be sat outside on the street for half an hour, an hour sometimes, because they hadn't got someone to open the door. It was all very haphazard. I think the agreement was we got the door money and they got the beer money, and they probably made five times what we did." Martin adds: "I don't think there were any bad bands at the Tropic. I think Primal Scream cancelled and we put The Chesterfields on instead, and we still got 250 people in and they'd only put one single out at that time. It was a 300-capacity venue which functioned well. I can't remember why we stopped doing it. It was a good way for me to find bands for Subway."

As seemed to be common for Bristol venues at this time, the bands rarely came on before 11pm and Matthew Evans from Tramway says that, after moving from the outskirts of Bristol to the city centre, he often used to go to bed for an hour or two and then get up again to go out and see a band at the Tropic. On the day that Clare arrived in Bristol in 1986, rather than try to make friends in her halls of residence or head to the Student Union, she looked to see what bands were playing and headed off to the Tropic on her own to see The Brilliant Corners and to try to sell a few fanzines. However, she hadn't realised that gigs in Bristol started so much later than everywhere else and, by the time the band came off stage in the early hours, the buses had stopped, so she was faced with a long walk home in the pitch black. "So here am I on Stokes Croft, the first day I've arrived in Bristol, at one in the fucking morning and I live the other side of the Downs," she says. "A minicab picked me up and the guy lectured me the whole way back about how I was standing not very far from where the riots had started not very long before and all of this stuff, so I shouldn't be out on my own. I think cities were just unloved and overlooked. They'd still got bomb sites around." That didn't put her off and Clare became a regular at the Tropic: "In my first year in Bristol, I saw Jesse Garon & the Desperadoes, The Fizzbombs, I saw The Wedding Present there but I got kicked in the ankle in the mosh pit and haven't been in a mosh pit since. I certainly saw Talulah Gosh there at least once."

While Davey Woodward of The Brilliant Corners says: "I lived on Stokes Croft, literally around the corner from the Tropic. The Brilliant Corners did loads of gigs with The Flatmates, The Chesterfields... Many great bands of that era played there." Tim Rippington's band The Five Year Plan played at The Tropic at least once a month: "We lived in the Tropic. That was the epitome of the sticky floor. When you lifted your feet up, they were literally stuck to the floor, it was gross. And if it was a packed gig, there was no way anybody was getting out of there. The fire exit was down the side of the stage but it was packed with all the gear and I don't think it had been opened for years."

Amelia Fletcher recalls her early band Talulah Gosh gigging there on 22 October 1987 when she was a student. "I remember it quite distinctly because I had an essay to do for university the next day, so between the soundcheck and the gig I sat in the dressing room and wrote a philosophy essay," she says. "I remember really clearly trying to get Talulah Gosh out of my head to focus on this essay and then I had to get back into Talulah Gosh mode, it was weird." Both Matthew Evans of Tramway and Andrew Jarrett of The Groove Farm were in the audience that night. Andrew says: "On 'Testcard Girl', Eithne [Farry] and Amelia just started screaming into the microphone and the PA was so loud that it was really, really painful. I'm sure that's why I've got tinnitus now! They were brilliant, they were so good, a real punk band."

"Be there, fish face." Your invitation to the launch of 'Pristine Christine'.
Courtesy of Sarah Records.

Despite the mythical status that the Tropic's Sonic Youth gig has since acquired in Bristolian music lore, it was not the biggest show at the venue, despite being sold out. Rocker says: "I think for Sonic Youth we got about 300 in. We were really worried because nobody had heard of Sonic Youth. They asked quite a lot of money for back then, about £200, and we were really worried about charging £2.50 and that it was too much when entry was usually £1 to £1.50." Exceeding the popularity of Sonic Youth was the night that Half Man Half Biscuit played, with The Flatmates as support band. "We'd never known anything like it before," says Rocker proudly. "People queued all the way to the traffic lights at Ninetree Hill to get in and we had to turn away about 300 people."

Sarah unofficially launched on 30 October 1987 at the Tropic with a gig featuring The Sea Urchins, The Poppyheads and The Groove Farm. Technically, it was a Groove Farm gig that Sarah piggybacked and Clare says: "People in Bristol didn't think The Sea Urchins were any good, so we probably needed The Groove Farm to bring some people." However, The Groove Farm were under the impression that it was *their* gig that they'd simply invited The Sea Urchins and The Poppyheads along to, and only realised Sarah had repurposed it as the single launch party once the band saw the flyers! Andrew Jarrett tells me: "For us, that was just a gig. We had played with The Sea Urchins in Birmingham so we kind of knew them, and we asked them to come down to Bristol. We had no idea that Clare and Matt were going to hijack it for their launch for the single, we didn't know that was going to happen until we caught them giving out flyers!" The Groove Farm were already friends with Clare and Matt, though, and Andrew says that if only Sarah had started six months earlier he

Top: Early Sarah band The Poppyheads doing their thing at The Tropic in Bristol. **Bottom:** Also at The Tropic, The Sea Urchins, who are pictured performing on 28 January 1988.

Top: Rob Young. Bottom: Wendy Stone.

thinks The Groove Farm would have signed to them but, as it was, they had already committed to Subway "which was the biggest mistake we ever made". Oops.

Harvey Williams travelled up to Bristol from college in Plymouth to be at the launch party and the event at the Tropic cemented his link to Sarah. "If you spend some time in a room with people who have this shared affinity, it was like being a part of something. I thought, 'I've found my people.'" Matthew Evans was also in the audience, although remembers the gig more for celebrating the launch of The Groove Farm's new single 'Going Bananas With…' and the fact everyone was given a banana on the way in. Although some people chose to employ the more mediaeval approach of using fruit as a weapon… "The Poppyheads decided they would play with their backs to the audience, in some kind of gesture, which meant they were met with a hail of bananas," recalls Matthew. However, Rob Young of The Poppyheads says of the gig: "It felt amazing because it was a venue that I really loved. It was quite fun doing that gig, I must say. With the world we lived in at that moment, a launch gig for Sarah felt important."

In the sleeve notes to *There and Back Again Lane*, Clare and Matt wrote: "The Sea Urchins' van broke down [on the way to Bristol] so they all had to get the coach, and afterwards we turned pied piper and led them back to our flat two miles away at three in the morning, them and lots of their friends, making it 13 in all, all strung out in a line behind us along Redland Road. They spent the night in the kitchen and lined up two-by-two along that long cold passageway we had; I always felt embarrassed about that."

The Tropic closed in 1994 and the building has since been converted into flats.

The Western Star Domino Club

The love people still have for this one-of-a-kind venue is extraordinary. The Western Star Domino Club is even alluded to in Alan McGee's autobiography *Creation Stories*, when Alan, who gigged at the Western Star with his band Biff Bang Pow!, talks about indie nights springing up in the wake of his Splash One night in Glasgow, and how these nights would pop up in all sorts of spots, even in "a space normally used for old men to play dominoes".

The building in St Pauls was where middle-aged, first-generation immigrants from the Caribbean would gather to socialise and play dominoes: a much more rowdy and animated interpretation of the game than the one Brits are familiar with. As such, the Western Star was one of the most important social centres for that social group. It was also a popular live music venue for local and touring bands.

Rob Young of The Poppyheads grew up in Bristol and describes the experience of going to this special venue: "The Western Star really felt like a time capsule of something from the 1960s, an earlier era of Bristol's immigrant population. You'd go past the Spectrum Building [an enormous glass office complex completed in 1984], further down the road, and then there'd be a load of disused parking garages and warehouses, all really run down, it felt like Detroit or something. And then there was this little side road and a door, it was quite hard to find, and you went up two or three flights of stairs, with old, red laminated flooring. And as you went up, you saw into these open doors, and you'd see these fantastic old Jamaican guys playing dominoes. Then you'd go into a bar in an open room. It wasn't a big room. It had a low stage at one end and a bar run by this fantastic Jamaican character. It was full of smoke, and decades of beer and whiskey on the floor. I can summon it up in my nostrils just thinking about it. A really extraordinary place. You felt like it was a bit of an adventure just to get there."

Andy Franks, one of the two bookers for the venue and an early manager for The Brilliant Corners, describes the building: "You went in through the doorway on the ground level, up a double flight of stairs and then into what was effectively the main room. There was a little bar on the left-hand side, there was a very small stage, it was a little working men's club. The stage was a few boxes made into a stage and off the corner of that was a dressing room with no toilet, no access from the outside, so all the bands that played had to come in the same way as the punters to get into the dressing room. The Western Star became a very hip venue." He adds: "If you went to trendier clubs they had high-tech speaker systems but at the Domino Club it was still the homemade speakers that were on the floor from the sound system. They used to be pumping out all this different music. It was such a fantastic place, a brilliant atmosphere."

Reg Evans, the venue's other booker, adds: "They had this banquette seating that they were always very concerned about, you mustn't stand on it. Jim [Williams, one of the venue's founders] was always complaining about people standing on the chairs and anybody smoking weed in there would completely freak them out. They were kinda grumpy but it generated a load of money so it really helped them. You'd go in there in the week and it would either be shut or very quiet. Most of these guys were the bus drivers and the plasterers, and painters and decorators, they were all working men. There were West Indian women there as well, not so many, but their wives would turn up on high days and holidays and birthdays, and they'd invite us to their parties."

FUN FACT: the Spectrum building that Rob just mentioned is featured on the cover of Sarah 530, aka *Gaol Ferry Bridge*. Even though a picture of Gaol Ferry Bridge would have been much more visually appealing.

Rocker from The Flatmates adds: "I saw some great bands there. It was quite a narrow room and they had long leather benches along either side with tables to play the dominoes and chairs around those. So when you'd put the gig on, all the West Indian guys would be moaning about having to move out of the way for the indie kids to come in and if you ever put your foot on the leather upholstery the bloke came running round from the bar telling you off. I was in my mid-20s then and was quite cowed by the characters you'd get in there! They never seemed interested in our music but they loved selling the beer."

Everyone who ever went there feels sadness at the loss of the Western Star Dominc Club. Here it is in June 1989, shortly before demolition, with one of its founders, Jim Williams.
Courtesy of Bristol Post.

The Western Star had been bought by its members in 1982, two years after the riot that had taken place in nearby St Pauls. The club had been run on a voluntary basis since then. It was important for the West Indian community to have a social club in a city that didn't offer them many opportunities. Rob Young continues: "The white people from the suburbs or the villages, where I was from, would drive around or through St Pauls with their windows wound up because they were scared, which was pathetic. So when you went into those places because you were allowed to play a gig there, you felt special because you were stepping over this invisible line that had been set up to keep the white population apart. And although you weren't really mixing culturally, because I didn't learn to play dominoes and none of the Jamaican guys started playing indie music, you were in the same space. We would turn up and bring 100 people who would spend money at the bar and it meant we were helping to pay the rent on the club."

Reg continues: "The Western Star would have opened on that site in the 1950s or 1960s. One of the guys who had founded it became the Lord Mayor, Jim Williams. So we approached him and they thought it would be a thing to make them a bit of money. It was a committee of about eight of them, and they were all old guys in their 60s and 70s, and Mr Allen was 80. They were quite set in their ways but they were very fond of us. I had a lot of good nights down there." Although he adds: "You couldn't get a drink. It didn't matter whether there were 10 people or 200, there'd only ever be three people on the bar and it was just the old guys who ran the club. You could shout at them as much as you like but they would just move at the same speed, which was Jamaican time. 'Can I have a beer?' 'Soon come, man. Soon come.'" Andy agrees: "On domino club nights, they had a good crowd but for some of these shows it was really packed. But you could never get a drink at the bar, they certainly never worked at anything that would be approaching breaking any kind of sweat. Everybody got served in the end though or else the goat curry would come out. They'd always do goat curry, that was their signature dish."

The Western Star could stay open until 2am, which meant that bands rarely came on until 11pm at the earliest but not everybody knew the drill as Matt found out when he moved to Bristol: "It was the first proper Bristol venue I went to. We assumed it was starting at 8 o'clock, so we went down there at half eight and had to knock on the door as it was completely closed. Eventually somebody came and let us in but was surprised to see us. We went upstairs and it was just full of old guys playing dominoes who cleared out when all the indie kids came in." Andrew Jarrett of The Groove Farm echoes this story: "I've no idea why venues started so late in Bristol. The first time I went to the Western Star it was to see The Brilliant Corners and I turned up at half seven thinking that was the time you went to a concert. I got there and paid my entrance fee and there were loads of old blokes sitting around these tables playing dominoes. And I was thinking, 'What's going on?' So I ended up sitting on some steps for about four hours. I even remember the band turning up to do the soundcheck! And at about half past midnight they went on. That's how we managed to see three bands in one night!"

Rob Young saw loads of gigs in Bristol when he was growing up, but one of the stand-out shows for him was Biff Bang Pow! at the Western Star. "It was very memorable because it ended with Alan McGee smashing his Rickenbacker and I was right at the front, right in front of him," says Rob. "They did an encore, I think it was 'I'm Still Waiting for My Time' and they did this feedback ending of it, and then he took his Rickenbacker and smashed it into the amplifier. It was a shame it was only in front of about 40 people. It should have been in a stadium."

Gig-goers Tom and Orynthia Thomas say: "You'd have Mighty Mighty playing at the front and these guys would be playing dominoes at the back up by the bar. John Stapleton used to DJ there for quite a long time. There was a railing with tables and seats along the side, you couldn't really call it a dancefloor but a standing area in front of the very low stage and the bar at the back. It was a very plain room, like a small school hall. It could be quite loud in there because it was this building on its own, everything else around it had been knocked down and it was in the middle of a car park basically next to Broadmead. The Western Star was a funny place but great."

Ah yes, John Stapleton, or Dr Jam as he was known, was as much of a draw as the bands. Reg says: "Dr Jam was our DJ and he's got an amazing record collection, and he played loads of really nice reggae and just sweet tunes, soul and proper dance music. That's another thing that the Western Star was well known for, was that the band would be alright but afterwards you'd have a chance for a really good dance and people would come for a dance."

The men who ran the venue also appreciated some of the music, as Reg confirms: "The old boys could tell if it was a good band. They could spot a good guitar player playing the blues. They could also spot a good indie band. They liked The Brilliant Corners but having Winston [Forbes] in the band probably helped. If you couldn't play and made a horrible racket, they would ignore it. But if you could get an indie band that was good, someone with brilliant pop tunes, the old boys would go 'not too bad, not too bad', and then they'd have a dance."

Talking on a local TV bulletin in 1989 about the impending demise of the Western Star to make way for the Cabot Circus mall, *Venue* magazine's Rock Editor Dave Higgitt said: "The Western Star is not just a venue, it's the best venue for local bands in Bristol. There's plenty of pubs but people don't go to pubs to hear bands necessarily, they do come here to see bands. And it stays open until two o'clock in the morning."

The Western Star was closed following a compulsory purchase order in 1989 and demolished almost instantly. News of the venue's closure even filled half a page of *The Guardian* on 20 June 1989, complete with a large and atmospheric photograph of 74-year-old domino champ James Doyle. Writing about how the community had been desperate to keep the venue open, *The Guardian* said: "The club's 300 members have been trying to stave off the inevitable. Run since 1982 on a voluntary basis, the club cut across age and race barriers. On Fridays and Saturdays, up to 250 people would crowd onto the small dance floor as local bands played. For the rest of the week, it provided one of the few places where older West Indians could meet and play dominoes." Even if the building had to be demolished to build a multi-storey car park, why was the community it displaced not relocated?

Back to Andy Franks: "One of the good things about the Western Star was there was no attitude. It was a great atmosphere and you'd want to be part of something like that." Rocker concludes: "It was a wonderful venue. It got closed down because it had a demolition order on it to flatten that whole area. But they then didn't use that land for about 15-20 years until Cabot Circus got built, so it was a real kick in the teeth."

As an aside, in November 1985 Erasure played their first-ever gig here because Andy had become the tour manager for Vince Clarke's former band Depeche Mode. Andy drove to London to pick up Vince and Andy Bell, drove them down to Bristol for the gig and then drove them back afterwards. But despite Vince's fame with Depeche Mode and Yazoo, the gig was far from a sell-out. "The gig was hilarious," says Reg. "There was hardly anybody there because, in true Bristolian fashion, they thought it was going to be too busy so people didn't bother coming." Andy thinks Erasure took home about £120 between them after their Western Star gig. Which is the price of one solitary ticket to see Erasure live in 2023. How times change.

Happy Christmas!

Here's a round-up of the Sarah Christmas parties over the years:

- 23 December 1990 – The PowerHaus, Islington, London. The Field Mice, Heavenly and The Orchids. Tickets £4.
- 16 December 1991 – Thekla, Bristol. Heavenly, Another Sunny Day & The Hit Parade, Brighter & Blueboy, Tramway and Secret Shine. Tickets £4.
- 22 December 1993 – Thekla, Bristol. Heavenly, The Orchids, Blueboy, Boyracer, Secret Shine and Action Painting!. Tickets £5.

There is a myth that Sarah bands were drippy little wet blankets who hid behind their floppy fringes and would never say boo to a member of Moose. Not true. The queue of 400 well-oiled fans for the Sarah Records Christmas Party on 23 December 1990 managed to snake all around the block outside the PowerHaus. "Not your stereotypical sensitive pop kids that music papers would make you believe," wrote one fanzine. "A mixture of all sorts of people just like at any other gig. I wonder if the reviewers were actually there, maybe they make up half of their reviews?"

Heavenly was one of the bands on the bill, and they played at all three of the Sarah Christmas parties. "We were the closest thing Sarah had to a party band," says bassist Rob Pursey. "I think by that time, Sarah and the Sarah bands, like us and The Field Mice and The Orchids, we'd got quite big and there was a general sense of 'Woah, look at us!' We're not just hiding in a little hole, we're taking over a big London venue and there was a party atmosphere because of that."

A bittersweet memory from the PowerHaus show comes via Duglas T Stewart of The BMX Bandits, who appeared as a special guest of Heavenly's. "We did a version of 'We Are The Champions' as an encore," says Duglas. "And at the very end of it, Mathew [Fletcher] did the thing of throwing the drum sticks into the audience and the first one went in the crowd but the second one, I turned round at the wrong time and the drumstick went [Duglas mimes slapping his eyebrow] and I started feeling slightly strange, and I looked at this kid who'd been wearing a nice white Heavenly t-shirt with the butterfly logo on it, and suddenly I was like 'What's all that red on your t-shirt?' And it was blood from my head. And this poor indie kid in a nice white Heavenly t-shirt was covered in my blood like a scene from *Carrie*."

Heavenly's Cathy Rogers, who had studied medicine at university, patched Duglas up. "I had a scar after that and I ended up writing a song called 'Scar' that was on our *Life Goes On* album. It's going to sound like a strange thing but, after Mathew died, I used to love having this scar. It came out of something that was quite funny, although Mathew was upset about it at the time. The scar's pretty thin now, which

> **❝** I can't really remember much about going up on stage and singing. I can sort of recall not being able to hear anything and the first song being a bit of a disaster."
>
> **Letter from Keith Girdler, Blueboy, to Scott Purnell, Secret Shine, about the Sarah Christmas Party, 1991**

GOING OUT: BRISTOL

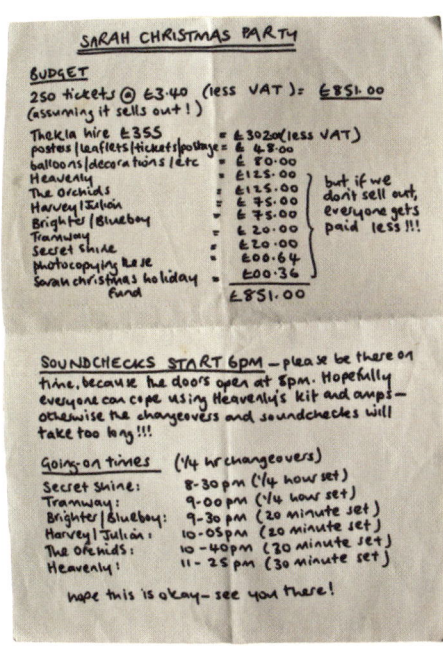

Top left: "Hope this is OK, see you there." The budget for a Sarah Records Christmas Party on board Thekla. It's fair to say that nobody was in this for the cash. **Top right:** My raffle ticket was No 217. It didn't win. **Bottom left:** Roll up, roll up... but be careful that you don't roll in the water. **Bottom right:** My ticket to the 1993 Christmas party.
Courtesy of Sarah Records.

is a good metaphor for how memories begin to get more distant and more faded as life goes on but whenever I do look at the scar, I always think of Mathew in a fond way." Cathy laughs: "At the time of Duglas' head wound, I was probably studying the anatomy of the upper arm! But I love that he made something positive out of the scar."

The Orchids, as was customary, went on stage a little the worse for wear. "I remember being incredibly drunk because there seemed to be a bottle of Johnny Walker Red Label in the dressing room for the first time ever at a Sarah gig and I think we were the only band that paid any attention to it," says guitarist John Scally. "I took it on stage with me and I think me and Matthew [Drummond] might have drunk the best part of it. It was a really good night, everyone really enjoyed themselves."

The Sarah Records 1990 Christmas party was at London's PowerHaus. Here we have Heavenly (pictured top) and The Orchids (pictured bottom) proving that Sarah bands knew how to have fun.
Julian Bester.

The funny thing about memory is that not everyone remembers the same event the same way, which is why Harvey Williams, who was in The Field Mice at the time, remembers this Christmas party as being "quite melancholy, it felt like a bit of a downer." Fellow Mouse Bobby Wratten told *Waaaah!* fanzine: "I used to generally hate playing live and obviously now we're a 'proper' group it is much more enjoyable. When it goes well it is a terrific feeling but when you have fiascos like the Sarah Christmas party you just want to quit playing live there and then. The response has surprised us. You see, when no one writes about you and you hardly ever hear yourself on the radio, you get to wondering if anybody knows who you are. So when 400 people turn up to the PowerHaus or when people literally demand an encore that you haven't prepared for, or anything, you get to thinking, 'Hey, maybe we're almost popular!'"

Thirty years on, Bobby understandably can't remember why he had described the PowerHaus gig as a fiasco, concluding: "It was almost certainly down to a perceived poor performance on our part and very much me seeing the evening through the eyes of someone who stepped on a pedal at the wrong time or something. I remember The Orchids invaded the stage at one point but it *was* meant to be a party. The Field Mice probably weren't cut out to headline Christmas parties." It wasn't all bad though and Bobby certainly takes some fun memories away from the show: "I remember John Peel being there. Unfortunately, or maybe fortunately, he had to leave to do his show before we played. Also, I remember Mark [Dobson, drummer] DJ-ing. I recall very specifically him playing 'The Lonesome Death of Hattie Carroll' by Bob Dylan and remarking, when pressed, that it probably wasn't a big party number [and Mark said] 'It's important stuff. People need to hear this', which seems perfectly reasonable to me now."

Nonetheless, it sounded like a good time was had by pretty much everyone, and footage on YouTube clearly confirms that they did. Plenty of Sarah fans liked to drink. So where better than the annual indie-pop Christmas party to really let their bobs down, shake off their anoraks and party? "Those Sarah Christmas parties were pretty riotous," says Rob Pursey. "I reckon there were well-behaved indies who had been proper and shuffled about at gigs all year, and then at the Sarah Christmas Party it went riotous." His bandmate Amelia Fletcher adds: "There was discussion of sex in the toilets and all this very un-Sarah behaviour." Rob: "I bet more Sarah babies were conceived as a result of those Christmas parties than at any other Sarah-based activity."

Further un-Sarah behaviour came in the form of "a shopping bag full of amphetamines" that Action Painting! brought along to a Christmas party at the Thekla in 1993. "We lined it up in the backstage area and no one else wanted it so it was all for us! Amelia Fletcher was like 'No, no. No, thank you.' Heavenly wouldn't take any but they were always quite chatty and friendly, and you didn't get any arsey vibes off them," says frontman Andy Hitchcock. He adds: "Halfway through the gig,

Action Painting! were achingly stylish, even coordinating their guitars to their tinsel to their clothing.
Wendy Stone.

Kevin [House] managed to break a bass string, he must have been whacking it pretty hard. Stewart Boyracer stepped in and managed to fix it but, in between, I started telling jokes to fill the gap."

Scott Purnell of Secret Shine remembers the 1991 party: "There was a tussling for position in the order of the bands. When Tramway were on before us, I don't think they liked that very much! When they were live, they were a bit more rocky than their recorded songs, and Matthew [Evans] was such a good, engaging frontman. He couldn't sing a note really, to be fair, but it didn't matter, did it? They went on first and he was walking around with a bottle of wine, swigging it, saying, 'No one likes us and we don't fucking care!'"

Matthew Evans responds to this with: "I think we had one stipulation, which was that we didn't go on first. But I think it was probably our best performance. There was a guy at the Christmas party who laid on the floor and held on to my leg and wouldn't let go, so Nancy [Horlick] punched him." Nancy interjects: "We were backstage and I don't know who it was, someone from another band was really drunk and really irritating Matthew, to the point that I could see Matthew just getting angry and I don't know where it came from, I just punched this person in the face. I had to sit down afterwards, it was the first time I'd ever hit anyone and I was shaking! And I remember Clare and Matt were there shaking their heads."

Matthew continues: "There were two youths at the front and they struck me as being like two old people who had gone on a coach tour and had a leaflet of the itinerary, and one of them said 'Oh it's Tramway now, they're not very good', and the other one said 'No, nobody likes them' and I think I happened to walk past them at the wrong moment, and that annoyed me when I went on. So Chris [Scott, ex-Talulah Gosh] gave me a bottle of not-very-expensive red wine because I had to have something to hold because I'd been banned from playing the guitar at that point because I couldn't play and sing at the same time, it was too technical."

On a related point, she technically might have been Tramway's backing vocalist but Nancy admits she just couldn't sing. "At the soundcheck, I started singing and the sound producer was like, 'Stop! There's some awful noise coming out of somewhere', so we all stopped. Fine, it had gone. I started up again and he goes, 'There it is again, this awful noise!' I had to put my hand up, 'I think it's my singing'. So that was the end of that!" Happy Christmas!

Festive cover versions have become the stuff of Sarah legend. Heavenly's frontwoman Amelia Fletcher says: "The most ridiculous one we did was a combination of Lenny Kravitz's 'Are you Gonna Go My Way?' with 'The Smurf Song'. Which involved Lenny Kravitz talking to the Smurfs and it must have been terrible." Rob Pursey interrupts dryly: "We were on last. They were so drunk they didn't care." While guitarist Pete Momtchiloff muses: "I think the audience was more baffled than delighted." The Kravitz/Smurfs medley was during the 1993 Christmas party at Thekla, by the way, which was the same night that drummer Mathew Fletcher massacred 'Goo Goo Muck' by The Cramps while dressed as a vicar. "What was fun about those parties was we all used to gather on stage at the end, all the bands," says Scott Purnell . "I remember being up there with Heavenly and Brighter singing 'Happy Xmas (War Is Over)', the John Lennon song."

Brighter did a Christmas set with Keith Girdler of Blueboy in 1991 that included a number of traditional festive songs. "We knew Keith from Brighton and used to go to the pub with him quite regularly," says Brighter's Keris Howard. "And Keith being Keith was always coming up with fantastic plans for what we were going to do next. 'This will be a great idea, why don't we do this?!' He was definitely an ideas man. I've got memories of everything being out of sync, Keith coming in at the wrong time, everything being quite shambolic and me being hit by a Brussels sprout that somebody threw from the crowd. It was quite hard because it wasn't cooked... Maybe that's where my aversion to brassicas comes from?!" Guitarist Alison Cousens adds: "Those Christmas gigs were lovely, they really were. A joyous, shared love that we had for music and Christmas was coming up, so everyone was in a good mood. I have happy memories of that night."

Blueboy performed at two Christmas parties and guitarist Paul Stewart says:

Top: Secret Shine shunned the tinsel during the 1993 Christmas extravaganza - party poopers! **Bottom:** Heavenly's Amelia Fletcher surrounded by party balloons. Wendy Stone.

"The Christmas parties were great fun. That's the roll call of honour, being asked to play. I think in our favour, even as far back as Feverfew, we were gigging a lot so we were quite a tight outfit live. The Christmas parties were good fun. You'd hear all these different accents because people came from all over the place and abroad. It was quite daunting for us and we were nervous because it was important and we wanted to play well. We played our little hearts out. We did 'Anarchy in the UK' at Sarah 100, I think." His Blueboy bandmate Gemma Malley adds: "The Christmas gigs were fun as they were packed and it was the proper fans. I remember staying up all night after a Christmas party, we were all staying at Matt and Clare's house. And just sitting up all night with all the different bands. That's when you got what Sarah was. It was a whole lot of people who were looking out for each other."

Boyracer played at the final Sarah Christmas party in 1993 and frontman Stewart Anderson says: "I remember getting to Bristol early and being in the bar over the road, and Mathew [Fletcher] from Heavenly was on the pinball machine for, like, two hours and he seemed very focused on that. Maybe that was his way of preparing for the show? The fun thing was meeting people who had written to us. Our friend Ian Johnson played guitar, and he'd never played guitar with us before as Matty [Green] had moved to Spain. So we were playing with a guitarist we'd never rehearsed with but that was kind of what we did then. I taught him the chords in the car on the way to the venue. I watched a lot of the bands that night and I enjoyed all of them. It was a very friendly atmosphere. Everyone was up for having a fun night out."

In case you think I've forgotten it, don't worry, the Sarah 100 party is covered in Chapter 18.

*****

THESE THINGS HAPPENED:
Rob Pursey, Heavenly

"Matt and Clare were both clearly really clever and they both knew the scene, the bands, everything that was happening on that scene really well. The problem with Matt is he's really softly spoken and also he's really tall, and I'm quite short, so to have a conversation with him in any public space is quite difficult because his head's up there and he talks quite quietly. Record labels are a labour of love to some extent. You're not going to get rich running an indie record label and I remember thinking what was amazing about them was that they had quite a well worked out political attitude to releasing music and how it should be done but also a high degree of competence as to how to do it. It was a pretty rare combination. Looking at what they actually put out in the end, it was really quite diverse in terms of the different noises the bands made."

Chapter 15

Going Out: Britain

Rocker from The Flatmates had form on hiring minibuses to chauffeur the Bristol crew to gigs in other cities. Back in 1985, he ferried almost 20 fans down to Plymouth to see the relatively new Jesus & Mary Chain play a 15-minute set, of which "ten minutes was them shouting 'Jesus fuck! Jesus fuck!'," laughs Rocker. "The tunes were almost from the 1950s but with that screaming feedback and it reminded you of punk a few years earlier but with the excitement of hearing something you'd never heard before."

EEC Punk Rock Mountain organiser Gordon Guthrie was one of the Bristol contingent on Rocker's minibus to see the Mary Chain, and he recalls telling the doorman that they had come 120 miles from Bristol and the horrified doorman retorting: "You've come all that way to see this lot?! But they're shite!"

Showing support for their musical friends in Oxford, the team at Bristol's Subway Organization hired another minibus and ferried 14 enthusiastic indie fans up to Oxford to see Razorcuts, supported by a brand-new Talulah Gosh, on 7 March 1986 at Worcester College. The hand-drawn poster for the show, by Talulah Gosh's Liz Price (a future Turner Prize winner), sums up the innocence and anti-rockism of the scene, with little choo choo trains chuffing around the corner of the page. During our conversation, I show Greg 'Razorcuts' Webster a hand-coloured poster that is on my desk and he says: "Is that the one with the trains on it? It's an Elizabeth Price! You're sitting on a fortune!" Alas, it's only a loaned poster but at least I can now say I've touched a priceless Price.

As with so many things in this little world, the night felt just a bit inbred. Liz from Talulah Gosh was dating Greg from Razorcuts and he secured the Goshes the support slot at the Worcester College gig. Having sent Martin Whitehead from Subway a tape, Razorcuts also secured a record deal that night. Greg says: "We'd sent a cassette down to Subway and Martin really liked it. He'd written back and he wanted to come along and see us at the gig. So we got signed to Subway at that gig." Bandmate Tim Vass adds: "It was all part of people vaguely knowing each other. I

> "I wish I had a time machine so I could go back and see Heavenly for the first time again."
> **Beth Arzy, Aberdeen**

The Liz Price-designed poster for the famous Razorcuts and Talulah Gosh show at Worcester College.
Courtesy of Gordon Guthrie.

wouldn't say that all the bands that recorded for Subway were necessarily my favourite bands at the time but it was a good little label and was a way of getting our first singles out."

"I recorded that [Worcester College] gig on my little tape recorder," remembers Rocker, who used to record as many gigs as he possibly could. "And all you can hear is Debbie [Haynes, The Flatmates' singer] stood next to me shouting, 'They sound just like us, what a rip off!' Talulah Gosh had tunes. It's that mix of noisy guitar and tuneful singing."

One of the other people on that minibus to Oxford was Matt. "I'm not sure why I was invited. I think just because I was writing the fanzine and had therefore become part of the Bristol indie scene – and obviously the main rationale for the trip was to see the Razorcuts, who Martin was signing to Subway, so maybe he hoped I'd write about them. I just remember Gordon being completely enraptured by [Talulah Gosh], rather at the expense of the Razorcuts, and me thinking 'He's absolutely right, you know'. All I remember about the trip is sitting quietly at the back and everyone being asleep on the way home. Other than Rocker, who was driving."

Greg adds: "I remember most of Talulah Gosh's gigs being incredible, great fun. It was just a rush. Both Tim and I come out of a punk rock tradition and they were a shambolic punk band in many ways." Tim says: "I absolutely loved them. It was brilliant. We were all mates, we played loads of gigs together, and I loved watching them live. I liked Heavenly as well but, for me, the golden age of that scene was when Razorcuts and Talulah Gosh were playing gigs together. I can remember when we played together in Bedford. Greg and I were up on this table dancing at the back when Talulah Gosh played because we just thought they were great and it was a really nice time."

> I've been up to London for a week, taking in Talulah Gosh in Chalk Farm supporting (ugh!) Slaughter, then again in Brixton supporting the Soup Dragons. They ARE WONDERFUL ... The Brixton gig was only their FIFTH ever (I've been to four!) and they were interviewed afterwards by both *Sounds* and *NME*, and at least three record labels are interested."
>
> **Letter from Matt to Pete Williams, June 1986**

Martin tells me that Talulah Gosh was another band he had his eye on for Subway. "Me and Rocker were going to go to the gig, and then all these other people said they were going to go and wanted a lift, so we took a minibus," he says. "And we stopped somewhere and bought Easter eggs on the way to Oxford, it was ever so twee. It was going to be the gig where I said I'd like to put out records by Talulah Gosh."

Chris Scott was in the audience at that Worcester College gig.

Little did he know that it wouldn't be long before he would be invited to join the Goshes as the bass player after Rob Pursey quit. Chris tells me about how the very last time he saw drummer Mathew Fletcher, at a Heavenly gig in London, the two were talking about when they had met at the Worcester College gig. "Mathew said, 'The first time I met you, I thought you were a complete cunt!'," laughs Chris. "And then, of course we had to live with each other because the rhythm section sticks together. He was a one-off."

Simon Barber, whose band The Chesterfields was also signed to Subway, remembers playing a gig with Talulah Gosh supporting at Bristol University on 10 May 1986. "The NME had just discovered them when they supported us again in London a few weeks later," Simon says. "They'd just been

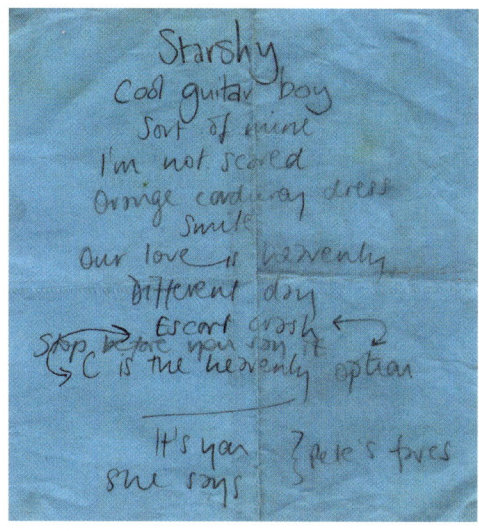

By saving Pete Momtchiloff's favourites for the encore, Heavenly ensured gigs always felt exciting.
Courtesy of Neil Shumsky.

signed to somebody and our gig was not our gig anymore, as they came to see Talulah Gosh who were supporting us at the Enterprise in London [11 July 1986]. It was such a brilliant night, it was so hot and sweaty, and nobody could move because of the amount of people they'd let in to see Talulah Gosh. It was a feeling of being at the start of something special because they were so great. They encapsulated something special at that time." Chris was the bassist in Talulah Gosh by this time and remembers being blown away by the scale of the attention they received after that gig at the Enterprise: "We were in all the music papers and that was it. That was the moment when everyone went, 'Blimey!'" Blimey, indeed. Reviewing the gig in the NME, Jerry Thackray gushed: "The girl in the minidress clasps her hands in front of her whilst singing, the girl in the curtain skirt contributes fervent guitar noise. Pop incarnate – fun, uncontrived, innocent, joyful ... Just for tonight, Talulah Gosh are the best band in the world, no contest!" The poor old headlining Chesterfields didn't get a look in.

Remembering that gig now, Jerry says he was only there by mistake, having been unable to get into the nearby Dr & The Medics gig he was supposed to be reviewing. "So I went round the corner to where Talulah Gosh were playing at Room At The Top in Chalk Farm Enterprise and there were 10 people there," he says. "I thought they were great, I loved them. So I wrote a 200-word review in the NME and a couple of weeks later they were on at the same club but there was a queue three times round the block to go and see them because of this one review I'd done. And I couldn't get in but Amelia [Fletcher] refused to go on stage until I did. It was just really exciting and fun. I really thought they were marvellous."

In future years, Chris Tighe's band Cody (also featuring Steve Jefferis of Shelley) would sign to Matt's post-Sarah label Shinkansen, but in the late 1980s he was a

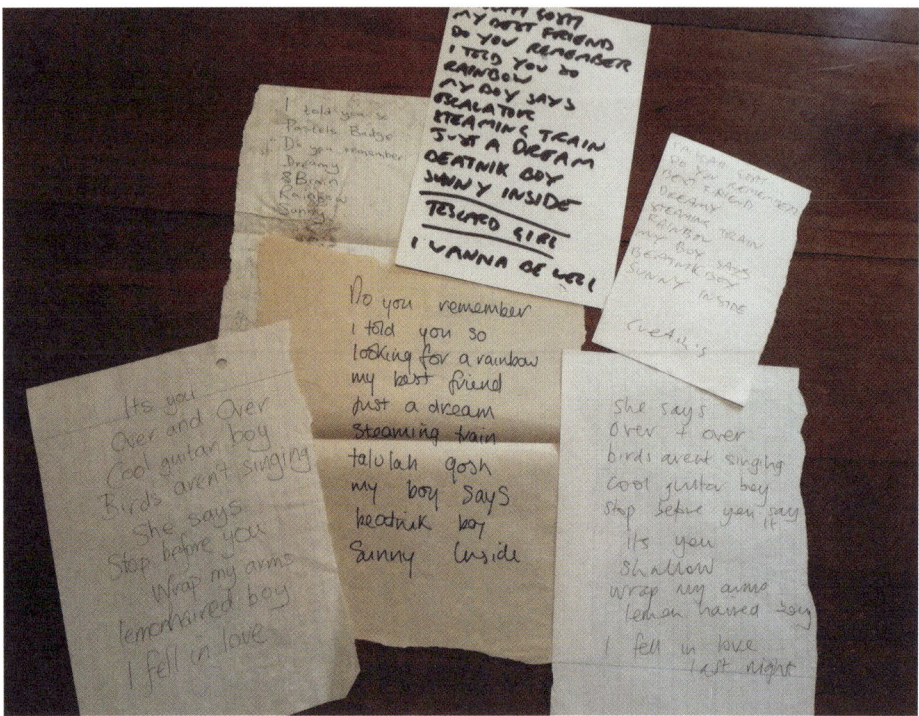

A choir of Heavenly set lists. Can you spot your favourite songs on these scraps of paper?
Courtesy of Tim Vass.

student in Manchester. It was in this capacity that Chris saw Talulah Gosh at the Manchester Boardwalk on 4 April 1987. According to gig promoter Dave Haslam's online diary, the band received £80 for their troubles, were supported by Spacemen 3 and tickets were £1.50. "It was a colourful gig," Chris says. "Partly the clothing and partly just the actual sound. They were obviously playing songs influenced by The Ramones but they also had that 1960s' girl group influence that widened their music out. It meant there was a certain archness to it, as well as being really straightforward. They had the ability to sound like they were taking the piss but also really celebrating the stuff they were doing. That was their secret weapon. They were colourful and they created more excitement than most of the bands I'd seen. Even though there was a lot of excitement coming from the front people, when you looked at Chris [Scott] and Pete [Momtchiloff] at the back, they were just stood there looking really morose and I liked that contrast. Talulah Gosh was a very exciting, colourful mess."

Not everyone was enamoured with the Goshes, though. Future *Melody Maker* journalist Simon Price was DJing at an indie night at his university in London the same night that Talulah Gosh were playing and slammed some records on superfast to make sure the band didn't come back for more. "I'm not sure they would have played an encore anyway but as soon as they went off stage I thought 'What's the most un-Talulah Gosh record I could follow them with?,'" says Simon. "And it was this EMI-manufactured, Giorgio Moroder-produced cyberpunk record by Sigue Sigue Sputnik as a palate cleanser. It didn't go down great to be honest. I was a bit too pleased with myself for having done that."

However, Talulah Gosh did make a big impression on future Ivy frontwoman Spencer Harrison, who felt inspired after seeing them at the Norwich Arts Centre in 1987: "There was this boy who leapt up on stage and I'll never forget the look on his face when Amelia started singing, he just had this look of bliss. And then he jumped down off stage again. He was a real indie boy, floppy fringe, striped Breton t-shirt, very much of the time. That was a clear memory for me. I was looking at them and thinking this was really interesting, and wondering how I could get a band and sound a bit like that."

After Talulah Gosh disbanded, many of the group's former members reunited as Heavenly and built on the influence and ability of their early band to draw audiences. Dickon Edwards of Shelley says: "I saw Heavenly a huge amount of times. I was their regular mad fan down the front. It meant a lot to me at the time. It wasn't just music, it was the need to belong."

Avoiding the clichés

There is a pretty standard formula for most live music shows: one or two support bands play and then the headline act comes on, the front person yells "Hello, Bristol!" and asks the audience how they're doing, and the band then rattles through a set for an hour or so before, maybe, coming back for a few encores. Job done, everyone buys a t-shirt and goes home. And some people, especially some of the bands, find comfort in that routine, as Cathy Rogers from Heavenly says: "I loved the ritual of gigs and seeing the whole process. I remember loading up the gear, and then you get there and fiddle around and do the soundcheck. And then there's this nice downtime between the soundcheck and the gig where you wander around and see some strange corner of a city that you don't know or eat some slightly random food in a slightly random place and then get excited about actually playing. The energy changes over the course of that and I always really liked that."

> **❝** I often find myself thinking at gigs, once 15 or 20 minutes have passed, 'This could stop now and nothing would be lost. Nothing unexpected is going to happen.'"
> **Bobby Wratten, The Field Mice**

But there could be exceptions to the rule. Obviously, that's what the Jesus & Mary Chain were doing with their noise-fuelled 15-minute sets and these also influenced Action Painting!, as frontman Andy Hitchcock explains: "We wouldn't play any more than 15 minutes, which was a C86 thing. Jesus & Mary Chain used to do that but apparently bands in the 1960s would do that as well, they used to do two sets and they wouldn't play more than 20 minutes in each set. And I could see the reason why. It's pop music, for fuck's sake. Quality rather than quantity. Some people got irked by that but tough." Tough, indeed.

Bobby Wratten of The Field Mice prefers to avoid the cliches of gig going.
Jon Cole.

The Golden Dawn played live just five times, and only in Glasgow, so there wasn't a lot of time for them to generate a buzz or even to build their performance skills. But Ulric Kennedy remembers the second gig as being a hoot because the venue was packed to the rafters with every indie kid in town, while the fourth was the worst because "we were given a crate of beer, which made us very sloppy. Our drug of choice was always hashish, which kept us lucid but loose." Drummer Peter Claughan pipes up: "I remember dropping my drum sticks regularly at our first gig in Texas Fever. A lot of Dawn songs are really fast and I was a stand-up drummer of no previous drumming experience, so it was hard work!"

The band made sure that each gig was an occasion, with each being given a title that was used on the posters and flyers. Those titles included 'Musick in Theory and Practice' and 'Playing Soft Tonight'. "Our first gig, with our old drummer Sharon [Scott], was at a Transmission Gallery party, and Robert [Smith] photocopied an illustration from some music paper article as a flyer, even though it wasn't open to the general public," explains Ulric. "I think the piece was about Primal Scream and others of the burgeoning anorak scene. In any case, it had the caption 'The Death of The Love Generation', so that set a precedent of giving our events a title. We were probably inspired by those 1960s happenings, like *Games For May* and *The 14-Hour Technicolour Dream* and thought a name makes it seem like a special event rather than just any old band putting on a gig. Over time, I came up with the idea of incorporating a kind of numerological system, so the third one was a three-word title – *Vanity Is Sanity* – with a triangular design on the poster. We were somewhat mystically inclined, as our name suggests." For those who don't know, the original Golden Dawn was a secret society devoted to studying the occult.

Guitarist Kenny Forte says of the gigs: "They were terrifying and exciting all at once. Before we went on stage, we were smoking furiously to try and calm the nerves. I don't think they were particularly busy gigs but they seemed exciting. Most of the places we played in have since burned down. Texas Fever was a good club. Although that was one of the places that burned down." Hopefully this has nothing to do with the occult. Kenny adds: "We weren't expecting anybody to particularly like us and when we played our live gigs we pushed the boundaries a bit, they were fairly short sets. We were listening to the Jesus & Mary Chain a lot, and I remember [listening to] 'Just Like Honey' the first time and it was a wall of feedback, we thought that was great. Gigs would descend into chaos, we would just keep making noise at the end. The audience was probably glad when we got off the stage."

Stewart Anderson of Boyracer was also happy to rip up the rulebook and do whatever he wanted, so long as he had fun in the process. He says: "All of my favourite musicians are wilfully amateurish. My favourite singers are clearly untutored. You listen to Calvin Johnson: technically he's dreadful but he's absolutely perfect for Beat Happening. And for me, a big part of what makes music interesting is all the imperfections." Stewart continues: "I don't like something that has been laboured over. I'm quite happy to get on stage and sing a song that we haven't rehearsed. We used to do that all time or we'd write songs in soundcheck. Early on, we used to end our shows with a cover that we'd play once at that show and never play again. Just because I liked the idea of something specific to that performance but also because I was challenging myself."

For some performers, the clichés of gig-going and gig-performing were too much. Bobby Wratten from The Field Mice finds the ritual of the gig where the band plays, exits and comes back for an encore and the audience feigns surprise at their return simply tedious. Bobby says his perfect live LP is *Document and Eyewitness* by Wire because "the tension is incredible. This is clearly not what the audience came for... new material, experimental material, even theatre, heaven forbid! Of course, they pretty much split up afterwards. I saw The Cure on the *Pornography* tour and they were playing an album that wasn't out yet. I was mesmerised by the fact that the show ended with two tracks that weren't even on the new record. It was only later that I found out the final song was called 'All Mine' and would never be recorded. But I had that memory of having seen it as a 15-year-old, not really knowing what was going on. The bar was set very high for me, so anything that seems like going through the motions or playing the game makes me recoil. In more recent years, going to more experimental shows has taught me just how safe rock shows are, hence my feeling that it's all a conservative ritual."

Overcoming stage fright

Brighter's guitarist Alison Cousens freely admits she spent most of the band's debut gig hiding behind her long fringe in order to cope with her nerves. "It was the first time I'd ever stood on stage," she says. "I was feeling really, really nervous. I looked up and saw these upturned faces, and was shaking to the point where I thought I was going to lose the ability to make the chords with my hands. So the only way I could get through that gig was by keeping my head down and not looking up or out at the audience." And that cemented Alison's strategy because she admits she was plagued by stage fright throughout Brighter. "From then on, that's what I did. I thought I'd be alright as long as I kept my head down and didn't look out. My fringe became very useful and then it was part of my signature look."

Of course, having a long fringe to hide behind didn't stop members of Blueboy from threatening/joking that they would

> "It was undoubtedly quite a terrifying experience."
> **Keris Howard, Brighter**

Alison Cousens (seen behind Keris Howard) found her long fringe a useful thing to hide behind. Here she is at Bristol's Fleece & Firkin on 29 April 1990.
Wendy Stone.

lop Alison's hair off. "They used to fantasise about getting my fringe, when I was playing with my head down, and getting a big pair of gardening shears and cutting a third of it off to reveal my face," Alison laughs, before adding: "Routinely, I went through agonies of nerves every time I stood on stage and that's why I knew I didn't want to do this as a job. I would wake up on a morning when we were playing a gig wishing I was anyone else, anywhere else, doing anything else and then I'd drive us down to the gig." And Alison wasn't the only one in Brighter who did not enjoy gigs. "When I got involved in Sarah Records, I had never done that with any anticipation of playing live," says singer Keris Howard. "It was always quite a difficult experience and then you add that to being a front person in a band, which is not something I ever, ever would have anticipated doing."

As with so many things, there was an added layer of difficulty for the female performers. Although many people in this scene were not what we might think of as accomplished musicians, it was easier for the men to get away with being inept than it was for the women. Audiences, venues and journalists, whether consciously or subconsciously, assume that women are going to be rubbish, which means women need to work extra hard to disrupt that preconception. "I was always very conscious of my own limitations in terms of being able to ad lib if something went wrong," says Alison. "I never wanted to be exposed as the weak link, even though I know I was the weakest link musically. Part of that taps into being female… Things like tuning up in the middle of a set, I didn't feel confident to do that. And I had a 12-string!"

Alison recounts a gig at the Fleece & Firkin in Bristol, after which Matt pointed out that she had been slightly out of tune the whole time. "We may well have been in tune at the soundcheck but then it got slightly out of tune. If I have a regret, it's that I never became comfortable enough on stage, with all eyes on me, to be able to just go, 'Fuck it, this needs to be right and I'm going to take some time' but I didn't feel confident that I could do that quickly enough."

Nerves are normal but stage fright is debilitating. It's something that can paralyse you. You're standing up there in front of strangers and expected to bare your soul. Maybe you're lucky and can hide behind a drum kit, a guitar or a fringe but, for the singer, there is nowhere to hide. "Simon found the gigs really stressful," says Gentle

Despite's Paul Gorton about frontman Simon Westwood. "He was very self-conscious that things would go wrong or about people looking at him. I don't know how he dared sing. I would stand there with my head down. Looking back, I was horrendously shy. I admired that he could stand up in front of people."

Secret Shine recall a gig at Easton Community Centre in Bristol where their temporary bassist was so terrified that he just played the same song over and over again while the rest of the band tried to work their way through the actual set. "He looked like a rabbit in a headlight," says vocalist Kathryn Smith, adding that afterwards: "Someone from the audience came up to Jamie [Gingell] and went 'That was brilliant!', punched him in the stomach, then spun round and fell down. So I think the audience were maybe too drunk to notice."

Anne Mari Davies of The Field Mice found stage fright beyond debilitating.
Jon Cole.

Sue Freeman of 14 Iced Bears tells me: "I used to find gigs quite nerve-wracking and had to have a pint before we went on. I only went on for the tracks that required my playing. But I was always conscious that I was still the one who was organising it, liaising with the promoters and what have you, and I remember a lot of tiny little backstage dressing rooms. And trying to negotiate what would go on the rider."

However, Anne Mari Davies of The Field Mice was plagued by anxieties to the point that she ended up seeing a doctor during a French tour. "Probably, I'd eaten something that had upset my stomach but I was very unwell and couldn't get on stage," she says of that terrible night. "Added to that, I was chucked out of the club for being sick because they thought I was drunk. The venue tried to get me a doctor, couldn't get one, so they phoned the fire brigade who came along and I sat in their van and they said 'We think you've got food poisoning, you need to go and rest' and so Bobby [Wratten] and I checked into a hotel." While this was happening, the rest of the band had to go back to the venue and do the show without her. "It was just a really hideous night. But the next night, we were playing the last gig of the tour, I think it was in Rouen, and just before we went on stage, I said 'I'm going to be sick again' and I didn't make it on stage that night."

> **❝** The band suffered, they were changing the set list right up until the last minute because was I still going to go on stage?"
> **Anne Mari Davis, The Field Mice**

Blaming it on exhaustion at the end of a long and tense series of gigs, Anne Mari thought that all she needed was a break ahead of The Field Mice's British tour a few weeks later. But no. "I probably only managed to get on stage about 50% of the time. I couldn't stop being sick and it was just horrid," she says. "Half the time, you haven't got a decent backstage area with its own toilet. It got really stupid." Eventually, guitarist Harvey Williams gently suggested to Anne Mari that she didn't have to keep putting herself through this and Anne Mari began to think it was time to quit.

But it was a big decision to make. The Field Mice were attracting regular attention in the music press, John Peel was playing them on the radio and their live shows drew big audiences for a band on the indie scene. Despite this, Anne Mari thought: "I need to stop doing this, I need to resign. So I was intending to do that at the end of the tour. But then there was the night in Glasgow when Bobby just said 'I don't want to do this anymore.' He'd said that a few times before but he really meant it this time." And suddenly that was that, the decision was made for her because The Field Mice were no more. Although Bobby, Anne Mari and drummer Mark Dobson would reunite as Northern Picture Library, Anne Mari never played live again. "By this point, I was really poorly," she says. "It lasted for years. I became agoraphobic and I was frightened to leave the house. I was frightened to get on a bus in case I was sick. I was in a real state." Although this was a truly awful experience to go through, Anne Mari has worked hard to overcome everything and says she now feels almost fully recovered.

And while Bobby Wratten would accept that he is a shy person, he says that it was never a barrier to performing. "I think the shy performer is quite a common phenomenon," he says. "Creative people aren't necessarily extroverts, usually far from it, which is maybe why they start writing in the first place. I never got nervous. The best thing was to not think about it. If you did suddenly become aware of what you were doing then that could derail you. So it was easier to just sail through it in your own bubble. As for singing, I wasn't really operating in a world of good singers, so the bar was pretty low. It was more just communicating rather than trying to impress. It may have looked like I was putting myself in a vulnerable position but emotionally I was pretty comfortable on stage." He adds: "Regarding the personal nature of the songs, that just felt like natural territory. I'd grown up drawn to writers who wrote in a very personal way. The songs weren't particularly good initially, so if anything made me feel vulnerable, it would have been the strength of the material rather than the subject matter."

I'm with the band

The ability to travel to gigs was certainly an obstacle for cash-strapped indie-lovers and Sarah superfan Tim Chipping never got to see any Sarah bands live until he moved to London in 1989. "The first gig was at the Bull & Gate and it was The Field Mice and Another Sunny Day," he says. "The Field Mice became my big obsession. Everything felt a bit different about them. There were lots of bands we all liked but something about The Field Mice was different, we all had to be a bit reverent around them, maybe because Bobby [Wratten] was so quiet and you had to be quiet around him."

Quiet as Bobby may have been, Tim broke the ice by asking if, err, he had any

Tim Chipping (centre) was a regular fixture in the audience at Sarah shows. Here he is enjoying a drink with Clare and Harvey Williams.
Grimsby Fishmarket, Marcus Torncrantz.

Field Mice badges for sale just so he had a reason to talk to him. But the ruse worked: "Then it was easy to start seeing them because we had the Camden Falcon nearby, and at least two bands would play there every month and it was so cheap to get in, it was about £2.50. I just kept turning up and you naturally talk to everyone and realise you now know all these people. At some point Clare and Matt became my friends, rather than the people who ran my favourite record label."

Tim became such a stalwart of the Sarah audience that eventually the bands would expect him to be there. On one occasion, he had gone to Leeds to see Blueboy and guitarist Paul Stewart came outside, saw Tim and exclaimed happily: "Tim Chipping is here! He's come to Leeds!" Tim explains: "They were excited that someone would like them enough to come from London to Leeds. After that they would just pick me up and take me to gigs." In the same vein, Rob Young from The Poppyheads says: "Occasionally, you'd play in, say, Leicester and people had come from Liverpool to see you and that was an amazing experience. You were like, 'Woah, why?!'"

If, for some reason, Tim didn't make it to a show, a band would feel that something was missing. Field Mouse Anne Mari Davis says: "Tim was always at the front. He was sweet, he was always there, it was quite reassuring, it felt wrong if he wasn't down the front shaking his fringe. There were a few like that. There was a German guy called Richard and he popped up everywhere."

❝ There weren't, in the big scale of things, very many fans but they were very dedicated, the ones we had."

Anne Mari Davis, The Field Mice

THESE THINGS HAPPEN

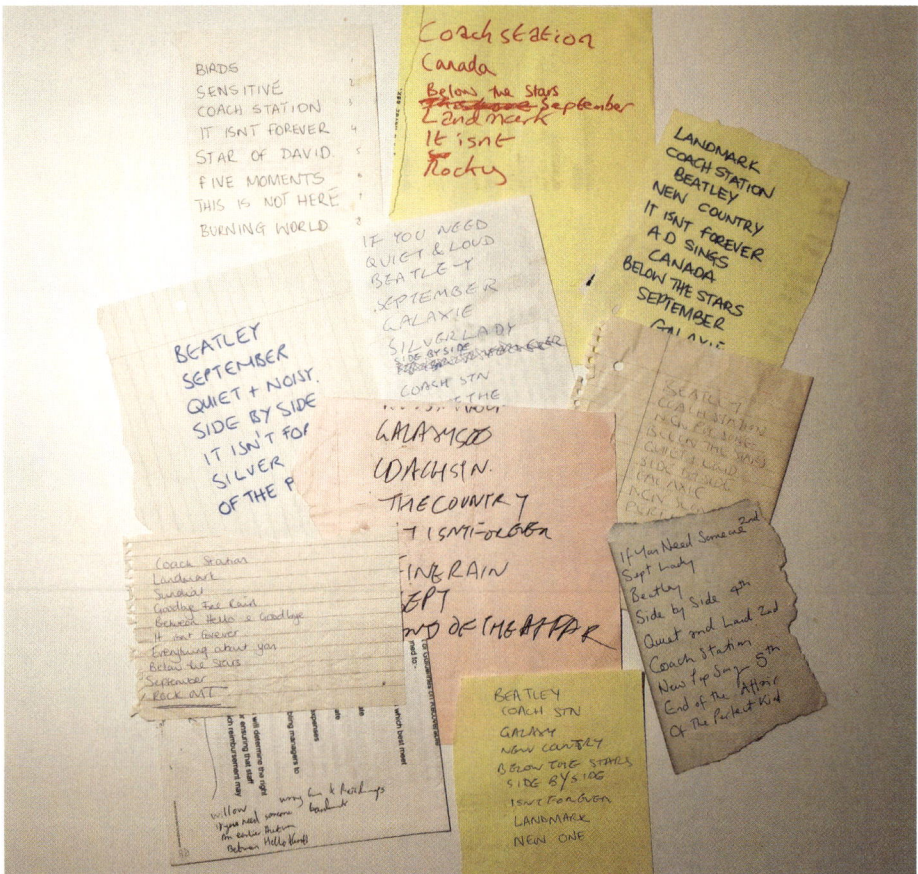

Top: Bobby Wratten and Anne Mari Davies of The Field Mice in their natural habitat. **Bottom:** I'm not sure what the collective noun is for a selection of Field Mice set lists. A nest?

Top: Guy Sirman. Bottom: Courtesy of Tim Chipping.

At the final Field Mice show, at London's Tufnell Park Dome on 21 November 1991, bassist Michael Hiscock dedicated a song to Tim and Harvey Williams later told Tim that he was the band's biggest fan. Which was how all the Sarah bands came to view him and, eventually, bands would just pick Tim up when they were driving around collecting band members to go to their gigs. It was almost like they collected the van and went: 'singer, drummer, guitarist, bassist, Tim Chipping'. "There was a time when Heavenly would pick me up and drive me to their gigs," Tim laughs. "Rob and Cathy were working in London, so would drive to gigs and back in the same night so would just take me and Amelia [Fletcher] would do that as well."

Heavenly's Rob Pursey says that Tim was one of several people who would be given the spare seat in the car or van when the band was heading out of London for a gig. "You'd treat them as if they were in the band almost," he says. "They just become friends. Tim's clever and funny, a smart guy, so he's good company." While Amelia adds that they would also take other people back home to London or Oxford after a gig because those people had stayed for the encore and subsequently missed their last train home and she didn't like to think of them being stranded.

For Rob, this kind of thing is one of the key distinctions about being in the independent scene as opposed to the major circuit: "I remember a conversation with some A&R man and one of the things he said was he'd come to see us at a gig and there was no VIP area. He expected to meet us in the VIP area and one of us was saying, 'Why the fuck would we want a VIP area?' But he thought one of the privileges of being on his label was you'd have a VIP area to hang about in and have people like him to talk to. But that was one of the precise reasons why we did *not* want to be on a major label."

FUN FACT: Clare and Matt confirm that they did indeed walk 18 miles to Bath along the old railway path to see The Groove Farm and that it took all day. They got the train home.

Clare echoes this sentiment: "The bands liked to meet the fans to get to know people. And none of us was famous, really. Part of the enjoyment of it was getting to meet the people who liked the music. Because everyone was so young, you never knew what someone would go on to do. So they might be a student writing to you from a student newspaper and the next thing they're the music editor of *The Guardian*. The bands enjoyed it in the same way we did."

Andrew Jarrett of The Groove Farm remembers Clare being a big fan of his band and that she used to come and watch them play whenever she could. He says: "We played in Bath, which isn't a million miles away from Bristol but it's far enough if you're walking, and she and Matt walked from Bristol to watch us. So you have to actually want to see the band, don't you?," he laughs. "She approached us after a gig and said she was going to do a flexi with her fanzine and did we want to do a song. So we recorded two versions of 'Baby Blue Marine'."

As soon as she'd finished her A Levels, future Ché co-founder Vinita Joshi told her parents that she was going youth hostelling in Scotland with friends... neglecting to mention that the friends in question were The Sea Urchins, who she was joining for a 10-day tour, and that none of them were going anywhere near a hostel. Vinita had started a pen pal friendship with singer James Roberts after buying the 'Cling Film' flexi. Before long, she was regularly going from Rugby to Birmingham to see the band and became friends with them all. "Musically, I loved them," says Vinita. "The lyrics were like poems, they looked great, they were local-ish, I played them all the time. I was so painfully shy that I just wrote to everyone and it was easier to express myself in letters than in person. I used to post Jamie those Ruffle bars, raspberry with dark chocolate, I'd send him sweets all the time and massive letters. I've got all his letters still, he had great handwriting. Jamie said, 'Don't ever not come to a gig because of train times and if you ever need somewhere to stay, then let me know' and I was like 'Wow!' So I'd tell my mum I was staying at my friend's house, she'd probably tell her mum she was staying at mine and we'd get the train. We started going to a lot of gigs at an amazing 1960s' club called Sensateria [in Birmingham]. And then we'd go and stay at The Sea Urchins' house and we'd all sleep in a line in the lounge. The boys would literally be in their briefs and we probably slept in our clothes!"

Thinking about the Scottish tour, she says: "It was very bizarre looking back. It was so much fun but I was so painfully shy. We stayed in Kelvinbridge with Remember Fun and The Orchids, so we were split between their houses. They played Glasgow, Dundee, Inverness... one got cancelled, another on a beach got cancelled. One night we were driving from Dundee to wherever in the middle of the night, absolutely shattered, stopped at a service station, and Mark [Bevin] went back to the car and he'd locked his keys in the car somehow."

Gigging in Reading

During 1991, when singer Keith Girdler was starting to assemble Blueboy, he was also writing letters from Brighton to fanzine writer Marcus Törncrantz in Sweden. In one letter, Blueboy were about to play their second show. This was to be at the Camden Falcon. "Our second-ever gig and a headline show in London, not bad, eh? It all went very, very well. I got a bit drunk and I was so happy!!" wrote Keith.

A later gig at the Camden Falcon was something of an anti-climax, though. The band had just returned from a successful tour of Japan having played to several thousand fans at concerts where the staff wore headsets and looked official, so returning to the Camden Falcon with an audience of just 30 folks milling about was a reality check. As guitarist Paul Stewart recalls: "The sound guy with a fag saying 'You're on at 10, off at half past or I'll pull the plug out' was a reminder of your place in the food chain."

Gemma Malley joined Blueboy around the end of 1990 while she was in her first year at university. Having cut her musical teeth in orchestras and choirs, Gemma fancied something different and one day saw a note on a university noticeboard saying a band

> ❝ I'm looking forward to playing with you in January. God, that sounds pervy. I mean your band."
> **Letter from Keith Girdler, Blueboy, to Scott Purnell, Secret Shine, December 1991**

This shared gig with Blueboy (pictured top) and The Sugargliders (pictured bottom) at The Rising Sun in Reading is widely considered by both bands to be one of their favourite ever shows.
Courtesy of Josh Meadows.

was looking for a singer who liked Everything But The Girl, The Sundays and the Cocteau Twins. "I was like 'tick, tick, tick' so I called the number," says Gemma, adding sheepishly: "I think I took the note down. I'd like to think I left it up but it's quite possible I took it down." She met Keith and Paul in a café in Reading, where they explained that there was a song Mark [Cousens, bassist] had written called 'Clear Skies' which Keith couldn't sing, so they wanted someone to sing that one song, one time. Gemma agreed and casually mentioned that, as well as singing, she could also play cello and keyboards. Suddenly, the boys' eyes lit up. Gemma's first gig with them was at the After Dark Club in Reading "and I sang the whole thing with my eyes closed as I was so scared and overwhelmed by the whole thing." But by that point she was already a member of the band and would meet up with the others regularly to rehearse and run through ideas. "I had no idea what I was getting myself into. It was just something to do one day and then it snowballed."

In a letter to Marcus on 12 November 1991, Keith wrote: "Paul and I are doing our second ever gig in Reading on December 7th at The Rising Sun ... Oh, sometimes life is just full of smiles and sunshine and today was one of those days." The Rising Sun Institute gig was reviewed by David Bratt in the *Reading Evening Post*: "Brightness, skies, happy, smiles, clouds, blue, perfume, falling – these are words which feature heavily in the lyrics of Sarah Records' Next Big Thing. Blueboy ... drew the walls of Reading's Rising Sun Institute even closer together than they already are to create an intimate and comfortable atmosphere. ... Blueboy blend a sophisticated indie-pop, propelled by classical guitar and cello, which in this instance demonstrated a shrewd understanding of the jazz refrain. It was a confident and accomplished performance and the audience, scattered cross-legged beyond the footlights, were overtly captivated by their spell."

Being largely based in Reading, Blueboy played there a lot although it wasn't always a glamorous experience. During one show, the band's original drummer Lloyd Haggar managed to trip and fall off the stage. "I'm fine, I'm fine!" he assured everyone in a very British manner. "He didn't look very fine," Gemma tells me in a dry tone. Lloyd walked himself home at the end of the show but, when Gemma called round to see him two days later, she found Lloyd sporting a plaster cast. "His foot had swollen to three times the size and that was when he realised he'd broken his ankle," says Gemma.

Fast-forward 12 months and the *Reading Evening Post* was still proud of its local kids done good, previewing a show on 21 November 1992 by writing: "Sarah Records double bill with Blueboy, not a band for narrow-minded fools, sexists, homophobes etc, and Sugargliders, one of Aussie's finest indie guitar outfits, at the Rising Sun Institute. Strongly recommended for riot grrrls and boyz everywhere. Tickets £2." That gig would turn out to be a special one for both bands on the bill. Blueboy performed an acoustic set, having just written a lot of the material for *Unisex*, with Paul playing classical guitar, Gemma on cello, Harvey Williams at a lovely old piano that was in the hall and Keith singing. "They lit it all with candles and people sat on the floor, it was a very ambient night, very enjoyable," says Paul. "Who's the really good looking guy out of The Field Mice? Michael Hiscock, he was there. Tim Chipping was there. That was a very memorable night, some people said it was our best gig."

Having flown into the UK four days earlier, The Sugargliders were on their first tour of the UK. "It was a magical night," says the band's Josh Meadows. It was only the band's second show in the UK, having played another gig with Blueboy in London two nights before. "It was a total Sarah home crowd," Josh says. "The place was full, most people were sitting on the floor, and there were candles and lamps in the room so it had a beautiful atmosphere. Both bands just complemented each other so well that night. That was the night I realised how good Blueboy were. Listening to their records from the other side of the world, I hadn't got the sense of how good they were but that night it really shone through. There was something about the audience that night, too, people were just hanging on every note and loving it. It was a great night."

Fellow Reading band Eternal sadly didn't enjoy the same warm reception from their audience when they played the one and only gig of their short life at Cartoons to a… well… to a tepid response. Bassist Stuart Wilkinson tells me: "It was an absolute nightmare, I'm still haunted by it now. Christian [Savill] had sent the demo to Sarah who said they wanted to release it, so we thought we ought to play a gig. I think we tried to make sure we were on first so we could get off quickly. I remember being on stage, looking at people and thinking 'Oh my Christ!' and I was trying to hide behind the amplifier to get out of people's way and didn't realise that Christian didn't feel comfortable being the centre of attention either. He's a really, really brilliant guitarist and uses these really elaborate tunings, and back in the day he probably only had the one guitar. So he'd play one song and then have to completely re-tune, and it seemed to go on for a long time, and in the last song his tunings slipped halfway through, so we had to start again, and oh my god, it was a nightmare!" Christian can only agree: "We did one gig and it was a fiasco. We literally couldn't play." Eternal were the opening act on a three-band bill, which Christian's other band – an on-the-verge-of-fame Slowdive – were headlining, while an early incarnation of Chapterhouse completed the line-up. Summing up Eternal's sole set, Christian says: "It was a nightmare, it sounded horrible, so we shuffled off and thought 'Let's not do that ever again.'" And they didn't.

It was all kicking off in Somerset

Close to Bristol on the map are the counties of Somerset and Dorset. I grew up just inside the Somerset side of the county border, which is why pub gigs in Yeovil and Sherborne have fond memories for me. Simon Barber of The Chesterfields lived nearby and ran a roving indie night in both towns called The Electric Broom Cupboard, which saw a range of indie bands playing in a selection of sweaty pub

Top left: On revisiting this poster design by Simon Barber, Matt noted: "Splendidly enigmatic poster from Simon. I guess if you needed to be told that EBC stood for 'Electric Broom Cupboard', and also where said Cupboard was located, then you weren't the audience he was after." Simon added: "That was in the Woolmington Hall at The Pageant Inn, Sherborne. If it helps, I'm pretty sure Polly [Harvey] went to the gig." **Bottom left:** Simon's poster for the Heavenly gig in Yeovil: one of the highlights of my teenage years. **Bottom right:** "Just found this! My fax to Amelia [Fletcher]." Messages such as this, from Simon, were the sort of thing that really cheered me during the compiling of this book.
Simon Barber.

function rooms and skittle alleys. "I remember being hugely impressed by the James Dean Driving Experience, Bob and The Sea Urchins among others," says my older brother Adam Mornement. "And of course PJ Harvey was at Yeovil College. It was amazing to watch her emergence at close hand. I remember seeing her perform the *Dry* album at East Coker Village Hall."

On 26 November 1994, with the aid of Simon and his other indie night (The Treehouse Club), I helped to organise a gig with Heavenly in Yeovil, in the skittle alley of a pub called the Quicksilver Mail. The Electric Broom Cupboard had also put on a previous Sarah night featuring St Christopher and The Sea Urchins in Sherborne back in 1990, so Simon was no stranger to the Sarah world. My teenage diary tells me that I first mooted the idea for the Yeovil gig in August 1994, when Simon suggested I find out how much Heavenly would need and Matt told me that the sum of £150 would secure their musical services for the evening. In retrospect, £150 seems somewhat low for five professional musicians to drive all the way from Oxford to Yeovil and back in one evening to perform a headline show (approximately 220 miles in total). While interviewing them for this book, I remind Amelia Fletcher and Rob Pursey of the fee for the Yeovil gig and both seem pleasantly surprised. "That's more than we get now! We never thought of doing gigs to make money. It was always about trying to cover our costs," Amelia says.

> An early highlight for me was finally getting St Christopher down and having Brighter turn up in the audience. It was a charming Sarah Records moment that I still cherish to this day. This was just too good, my favourite bands hanging out in my local pub."
>
> **Dave Fennessy, gig promoter**

Regrettably, Simon doesn't remember much about the evening because, as well as organising the show, his then-band Gear were supporting: "I don't like gigs as much if I'm playing and, when it comes to it, I always wish I wasn't playing. If you're promoting and playing, it's the worst thing. I do remember Heavenly being great that night, though. I hadn't seen them as Heavenly before." Amelia, Rob, Cathy Rogers and Pete Momtchiloff don't remember much about it either. Nonetheless, my teenage diary provides some brief insight into what was clearly the biggest night in Yeovil's musical history: "Got there early. I couldn't get over the fact Amelia Fletcher was in my local venue where shit bands usually play. Afterwards I went to see Amelia and she said she remembered me. Pete talked to me about Heavens to Betsy and Pussycat Trash afterwards. Amelia was utterly delightful."

Oxford also had a lot going on

Oxford was a big part of the indie scene at this time, and the city's musical world revolved around the Jericho Tavern. Located at 56 Walton Street, the Jericho is well known for having provided an early stomping ground for soon-to-be-massive Oxford bands such as Radiohead, Ride and Supergrass. Its history as a pub goes back to the 1680s, although the current version of the Tavern was built in 1818 and, as was common for pubs generally, it would regularly welcome entertainers. Over time, those entertainers would include Talulah Gosh, Heavenly, Razorcuts and any number of Sarah bands.

Blueboy wrote 'Too Good To Be True' about driving to see Brighter play at the Jericho. "The message is about discovering something new and personal and beautiful and special, and it can't be spoiled. It's about sharing that experience with someone. It was a great venue," says Blueboy's Paul Stewart. However, for The Sugargliders, memories of the Jericho are tinged with sadness. "Probably one of my great regrets in life was when we played with Heavenly at the Jericho Tavern and Amelia asked if I could take the male part in 'C is The Heavenly Option,'" says Josh Meadows. "But I had only heard the song a couple of times and just said I didn't know it well enough,

Left: A snap of the band room at the Jericho Tavern. **Right:** Even As We Speak's Paul Clarke and Mary Wyer performing on stage with their band at the Jericho Tavern.
Even As We Speak.

so I had to pass up the opportunity. But if it ever comes up again…"

For fanzine writer Chris Tighe, who had recently relocated to Oxford, the Jericho became a regular haunt and it was here that he saw Tramway, whom he didn't have high expectations of liking. "They were playing what was very much generic Sarah music, mid-tempo, slightly electronic but you could feel there was something that had started growing there," says Chris. "Previously, they were playing slow songs because they couldn't play any better but, when I saw them live, they were playing slow songs because they realised that's what they were good at. This was a band that had not impressed me on their recordings and I had gone to see them out of friendly loyalty but it meant that I made a good discovery. A band that I was on the verge of writing off showed that they were worth sticking with and they proved that when the second single came out." Something magical happened at the Jericho that night.

THE WORST… AND THE BEST GIGS

One of the problems of playing live and not having the cachet of, say, Oasis or Blur, was that you were never sure whether anyone would turn up. As Talulah Gosh, for example, found. Thanks to a buzz whipped up in the music press, the band became a big draw early on, but that only seemed to work when they were playing in the larger cities. "The worst gig was Southend, we played there and no one came except my mum, who lived nearby, her husband and a bloke from the local radio who turned out to have been taught by my mother's husband. Apart from that there was just the support band," says bassist Chris Scott. "It was some pub in Southend which had posters for strippers on the wall. And we thought, 'Why are we even here?!' But

Amelia Fletcher, pictured here at The Amersham Arms, had the ability to draw the crowds.
Grimsby Fishmarket, Marcus Torncrantz.

then we played in Edinburgh and did two or three encores, and Amelia wets herself because she's laughing so much. So gigs were very much a mixed bag."

This is a story echoed by lots of bands. "Sometimes you'd play places and there just wouldn't be many people there, and I'd feel guilty for having dragged people out," says Blueboy's Gemma Malley. "Particularly when you had some of the committed people who'd come all the way from London to the middle of nowhere and then they're sat there nursing a pint. I feel more for them when it's cold and dismal and they've heard it all before, and there's no one else there."

But to prove it wasn't always like that, here's a story from The Sweetest Ache, who had been on tour around the UK promoting *Jaguar* and the last night of the tour was at the Hull Adelphi. "They were the most welcoming crowd we'd ever come across on that tour," says guitarist Stuart Vincent. "It was really busy, it was really packed, they were really receptive and when you're playing downbeat, quite slow tracks, to get a crowd dancing is a feat. But I remember them dancing all night long and loving it. I remember getting that energy back from the crowd and doing an encore and all sorts. The energy in Hull was fantastic."

Brighter frontman Keris Howard remembers a really great gig at the Derby Dial with Heavenly in July 1991 that was packed

> 66 Having put up a photo of Heavenly downstairs at The Fountain [venue], the gay pool-playing lesbians had gone absolutely apeshit over Amelia [Fletcher]. I wonder if she was ever aware of the effect she had on Deptford's pool-playing lesbians that night. They helped pack the night out, that's for sure."
>
> **Dave Fennessy, gig promoter**

Keris Howard lists Brighter's gig at The Derby Dial in 1991 as one of his favourite live shows.
Neil Shumsky.

out and went so well that fans were asking them to sign Sturm und Drang flexis afterwards, "which I'm sure we ruined because we were using a biro." He continues: "Things were going really well, it was just after *Laurel* had come out to some good reviews. Everything felt well in the world. It was proof that there are moments where, as somebody who never envisaged playing live, there can be special moments."

The Field Mice's drummer Mark Dobson recounts a truly wonderful night for his band which also happened at the Hull Adelphi. "It was a really good gig, we played well, there were lots of people there. The promoter was delighted there were a lot more people than he was expecting, so we got paid well," says Mark. "We'd come out of the Hull Adelphi at about 11.30pm, jumped into the van, John Peel was on the radio and, by pure coincidence, just as we got to the M62 he played a Field Mice song so we were buzzing. It was the perfect night. We couldn't sleep that night, so we had a conversation about what songs had got us into music and Michael [Hiscock] said that 'Wheels of Steel' by Saxon had changed his life and we all burst out laughing. I thought that was a wind up but it isn't."

Where's our money?

Nobody was getting rich from putting on indie bands, by the way: not the bands, not the venues and not the record label. Everyone was doing it for love and, if they were lucky, petrol money. "We left a London gig once, and we'd sold t-shirts and had some gig fees but, after we paid for fuel and van hire, we had about 10p left, literally," says Kathryn Smith from Secret Shine. Marc Leverton, who managed The Sweetest Ache, agrees: "The whole thing was very hand to mouth, you'd make £50 at a gig and spend £60 on petrol."

> Two people and a drum machine isn't exactly impressive on stage, especially if you have to put up with a bad PA and not being able to hear what's going on. We're seriously thinking about getting a drummer and another guitarist because, apart from our first gig, playing live has been a pretty unhappy thing for us."
>
> **Letter from Bobby Wratten, The Field Mice, to fan Neil Shumsky, 1989**

But sometimes, unscrupulous gig promoters simply didn't want to pay the bands what they were due. Even As We Speak recall playing a gig in Manchester to a packed-out room and the promoter trying to palm the band off with £20. "Matthew [Love] completely flew off the handle and threatened to beat him up," says singer Mary Wyer. "Clare was there and she was hiding in the corner!"

Sometimes promoters would offer the band a guarantee, meaning that however badly tickets might sell, the band would

A lot of gig life involves loading in and out of venues and hanging around in vans. Here we have Even As We Speak doing just that outside London's Dome Club.
Even As We Speak.

still be guaranteed a minimum amount of money. But, at the same time, if the gig was well attended, the band would take home a bigger percentage of the door. "So once the guarantee is recovered, if it's a full house you get quite a lot," says Julian Knowles of Even As We Speak. "But at some of these shows the promoters were not scrupulous, and so you would fill the room and they'd just try to pay you the guarantee. And the guarantee for a show in Manchester would barely pay for the fuel from Brighton to Manchester and back."

The unlikely gigs

When original punks Buzzcocks came to Swansea's Patti Pavilion on 11 October 1990, they wanted a local band to support them. And, despite the disparity in musical styles, The Sweetest Ache were offered the gig. "I said to the bloke, 'Have you actually heard our band before?'," says guitarist Stuart Vincent. "He said, 'Yeah, absolutely, you'll be great, they'll love you.' And I was thinking, 'We're cheap and we're from Swansea, that's why you're asking us.'" One of the deciding factors for The Sweetest Ache was that former Smiths drummer Mike Joyce was now in Buzzcocks and The Sweetest Ache were all massive fans of The Smiths. The Welsh band's drummer Geraint Morris even plucked up the courage to ask Mike if he could

Tunbridge Wells: where indie-pop bands go to rock out.
Even As We Speak.

borrow a piece of kit.

"The gig was terrible!," laughs Stuart. "We probably had a ten-song set and a few of our songs were quite slow at the time, almost acoustic-sounding, and the crowd didn't want to hear slow, acoustic songs, they wanted to hear pogo-y, up-tempo, four-by-four songs and we only had about three of those. I remember being on stage and we had our set list there, and turning to Simon [Court] and going 'This is quite a slow one now, shall we skip this one?' and he'd agree. So then we'd play quite an up-tempo, fast-ish song. And then come to the next one, 'OK, it's quite a slow one, let's skip it again', so in the end we only played about four songs. Out of fear of upsetting quite a stalwart punky crowd."

The headline act was very supportive of the younger band, though, as Stuart says: "We met Buzzcocks, they were smashing. They came out and listened to our soundcheck and said it was really good. They were really accommodating, really nice to meet but if ever there was a clash of different audiences, it's Buzzcocks and it's Sarah Records, it was a bizarre fit." Stuart concludes: "It was the first time my parents had come to watch the band play. I got them on the guest list and they don't really come from a background of music at all. They were horrified by the crowd and horrified by Buzzcocks. They left after the first Buzzcocks song. I remember asking my dad what he thought of the evening, and he said, 'It was very loud, son. It was very loud.'"

> "I remember that night fondly for the bizarreness of the situation."
> **Stuart Vincent, The Sweetest Ache, about their support slot for Buzzcocks**

Buzzcocks also came to see a Sarah band at the Dublin Castle in London, having been tipped off that Action Painting! were pretenders to the throne. "Steve Diggle and Pete Shelley came to see us, and Pete came up to us afterwards and said it wasn't loud enough," says Andy Hitchcock. "I said, 'It's not our fault, there's flippin' limiters!' And he laughed and we spent the rest of the evening with Steve Diggle and Pete Shelley, and I was drinking and getting pissed with them. They were brilliant, really funny, really intelligent, camp as a box of camp things. Because we'd had comparisons to Buzzcocks, Pete wanted to come and see us. We were anointed by Pete Shelley and I enjoyed getting his approval."

And Buzzcocks weren't the only original punk band showing an interest in a Sarah signing. Captain Sensible of The Damned came to see The Sea Urchins in Brighton in 1988 after hearing the band interviewed on the radio. "After the gig he was very enthusiastic about signing us to his Deltic label and arranging light shows for us, though nothing came of this," says guitarist Robert Cooksey.

Fans of BBC Radio 4 and *Private Eye* magazine may associate the staid Kentish town of Royal Tunbridge Wells with the fictional letter writer 'Disgusted of Tunbridge Wells', who used to write angry letters to the public broadcaster about the decline in moral values. Nonetheless, when Even As We Speak rolled into town in 1993 to play at the Tunbridge Wells Forum, the Australians were met by a joyously riotous audience. Maybe it was the Radio 1 airplay the band had been enjoying, maybe there was nothing else in town that night, but it turned out that the good folk of Tunbridge Wells were up for a moshing. "From the very first chord, there were people stage diving, which was unusual at a Sarah gig," says guitarist Julian Knowles. "We all wound up in the audience by the end of the show and our guitars got dented, so we did have a damage assessment the next day. I crowd surfed. And she'll probably never forgive me for this but I remember going, 'Come on, Anita' and getting [drummer Anita Rayner] out from the kit and pushing her out into the audience." Describing the band's *This Is Spinal Tap* moment, singer Mary Wyer adds: "The audience came and got me and threw me out there, I was so scared! Paul [Clarke] threw himself in and the crowd parted and he landed on the floor!"

Health and safety gone mad

One of the most bizarre Sarah gigs was a Blueboy and Brighter show in 1993 at a burnt-out Liverpudlian venue. Planet X had been the main destination for Scouse music fans until the venue suffered a devastating fire that ultimately saw it close down. But between the fire and the decision to close Planet X, Blueboy and Brighter played in a blackened room that still had fire water running down the walls. In a 2013 nostalgia article about the venue, the *Liverpool Echo* surmised: "Planet X stood out like a beacon for anyone who wanted to be a bit different, and in some cases, a lot different." And you don't get much more different than hosting a gig in a soaking wet and sooty safety hazard.

A photo survives of a chilly looking Keith Girdler, Paul Stewart and Gemma Malley, bundled up in coats, scarves and gloves, huddled together on Planet X's stage, wires coming out of equipment that surely can't have been safe to plug into the walls. Guitarist Harvey Williams was huddled up inside his duffle coat and says: "It was just a burned-out shell of a building. There was all this water dripping down from the ceiling and lots of burned-out beams. I think we all thought the venue didn't look safe but the promoter was there waiting for the PA to turn up. I don't remember it being particularly well attended. People probably thought, 'The building's burned down, maybe the gig's not going ahead'. But the show must go on." That's the spirit.

> ❝ I think legally it would be called a condemned building now, but for some reason they still put the gig on."
>
> **Paul Stewart, Blueboy**

Clare and Matt were also at Planet X that night. "At the point that Blueboy and

Top: Blueboy's Keith Girdler, Paul Stewart and Gemma Malley took their lives in their be-gloved hands at a ruined Planet X. **Bottom:** Leaving his anorak at home, Harvey Williams was snuggled up in his duffle coat for warmth.

Courtesy of Sarah Records.

Brighter would have been playing there, they would have been grown up enough to have jobs and you'd kind of assume that if they didn't want to play, they wouldn't play," says Clare. "I don't think it would have occurred to us to recommend they didn't play. And it didn't occur to them not to play. And it obviously didn't occur to the promoter to cancel the bloody gig."

Paul Stewart muses: "We thought they were joking as the water was still coming down the walls from the fire brigade. I was getting my gear ready and I said to the sound guy, 'Is it safe to plug my amplifier in here?' So he plugged it in and turned it on and he went 'Yeah, looks alright.' It was probably one of the most surreal experiences of my life. I just didn't want to touch anything because you'd be covered in black soot and water." Alison Cousens of Brighter adds: "There was water running down the walls. We were plugging things in thinking we were about to be electrocuted. I can't imagine that that would be able to go ahead now with all the health and safety stuff that we have. I felt we were taking our life in our hands every time we plugged or unplugged a guitar into a monitor or anything into the wall."

'ROCK BAND IN CRASH SCARE'

At least when Blueboy and Brighter played in a burned-out venue with water dripping down the walls nobody got hurt. But the same cannot be said of driving endless miles, which The Orchids had to do to reach gigs lower down the UK. "We had probably the hardest travelling to do," says singer James Hackett. "We'd come from Glasgow all the way down to Bristol, and you're getting in and getting a soundcheck, you're having a couple of beers to relax, and you're feeling it 'cos you're tired. It was more a mixture of tiredness and alcohol, and we used to look like a shambles because of it. It wasn't like Harvey [Williams] getting off the train from London with his guitar, all fresh and clean, saying 'Let's go, guys!'"

Matt says: "I think we sometimes forgot how far it was for The Orchids to actually come down and play a gig. We'd arrange a gig for them in London, forgetting that's a 400-mile drive for them for £50. In retrospect, you think 'How did they put up with that?' I think the van crash was the point they thought, 'Why do we keep having to go down to London?'"

In January 1994, the van carrying The Orchids and three of their friends from Glasgow to London for a gig at the Highbury Garage to promote *Striving For The Lazy Perfection* hadn't even left Scotland when it hit ice. James explains: "It was bad luck and bad weather. We hit ice as the sun was coming up and started to skid in front of this big articulated lorry that was heading towards us and we were helpless. Fortunately, the van hit the edge of the pavement, flipped up into the air and rolled down the verge to take us out of the way of the truck. So in a lot of ways we were very, very lucky that we didn't have any real injuries."

I might beg to disagree with James here, given that the van was a write-off and

Given they were based in Glasgow, The Orchids had to do more travelling than most bands to reach gigs. Here they are enduring van life "somewhere in England" in June 1991.
Courtesy of The Orchids.

three of its passengers were hospitalised: James, drummer Chris Quinn and the band's friend Ruth. "Alan [another friend] banged his face and later on he found out his jaw was broken," says James. "I've got a scar on my back. But when you think about it, we were flying through the air and I still remember it and it feels like forever and you don't know where you're going to land. The fact we bounced and ended up on our wheels, and when we counted ourselves as alive, it was so lucky. We were in shock for a while." The story made the pages of the *Scottish Sun* newspaper under the headline: 'Rock Band in Crash Scare'.

Understandably, the crash prompted the band to rethink future long drives. Although not a strategy for making the journeys shorter, they decided to at least make them more comfortable and The Orchids invested in a mobile home to ferry them to gigs that were further afield. But that was not without its own problems: "It was like travelling in a boat, it was swinging all over the place, my anxiety levels were sky high," says James, who ended up taking the train home to Glasgow after the next round of gigs because he couldn't stomach any more time on the road. "I couldn't take it anymore. After that it was really difficult to say 'yes' to gigs, it had to be worthwhile." Fortunately, the post-Sarah rise in budget airlines, while terrible for the environment, has meant it is much easier for The Orchids to get around the country to gigs these days. And, dare I say it, much safer.

For those readers wondering what happened to the band's planned gig in London, here is the answer. News of the crash didn't reach the venue until shortly before The Orchids were due to soundcheck because this was in the days before mobile phones.

Clare has memories of standing in the hallway of Matt's parents' house in London, trying to sort everything out on their landline. Given that Northern Picture Library and Blueboy were the support acts that evening, Harvey Williams and Bobby Wratten volunteered to do a few old Field Mice songs as an opener, including three songs that had never previously been played live: 'Willow', 'An Earlier Autumn' and 'A Wrong Turn and Raindrops'.

Where's our tour manager?

Very few bands on Sarah had a manager, meaning that tours and gigs were either organised by the band or by their ever-helpful record label. But, as Clare explains, having never had 'proper' jobs themselves, she and Matt were not always in tune with the difficulties of trying to fit gigs around study or work commitments. For a band from, say, Glasgow, to get to a Thursday night gig in London, they would need to take all of Thursday and Friday off work in order to undertake the 800-mile round trip, and that just wasn't viable for a lot of reasons. "For us, it was like, 'But we've found you a gig! Why don't you want to do it?'," says Clare. "We understood it in theory but not in practice, that everyone has different work timetables so trying to coordinate everybody's time off is so painful to do."

> ❝ Rang Rob [Cooksley] from a pooy phone box. I told the girl who went in after me that there was a shit in the box but I had not done it."
> **Bridget Duffy (The Sea Urchins)'s diary, 1986**

And never mind not having a manager, some of the bands didn't even have a phone line. James Roberts from The Sea Urchins reflects that "it was ridiculous how it got done". He explains: "It was all done in telephone boxes because we were all living in student accommodation or shared houses, nobody had a phone. I was living in a shared house with friends, the cliché of student accommodation. There was a phone at the top of our road and that's where most of the gigs got organised from. You'd have people knocking on the door saying, 'There's somebody phoning the phone box for you, something about a music gig?' It's surprising so much got done given how chaotic it was, but we did a lot of gigging." Does that phone box have a blue plaque yet? Can somebody look into it?

The one time Sarah attempted to work with an established gig agent was not a positive experience. Gig agents operate by trying to book as many bands into as many gigs as possible because that's how they make their commission. But they don't necessarily stop to think about whether the gig and the band make sense together. The Field Mice ended up playing at a catering college in Liverpool, for instance, and Brighter were booked to play a Young Farmers' ball at Writtle Agricultural College in Essex. Singer Keris Howard remembers: "It was Matt and Clare's idea to try and get us out a bit more. That was when we realised we were cut adrift from the security of a Sarah Records night, which were always nice and cosy, and you were playing to an audience who'd come to see Sarah Records bands, and you often knew the other bands. Suddenly being on bills with bands you'd never heard of, or you'd heard of but thought they were totally inappropriate."

For those who didn't grow up in rural Britain, Young Farmers' Clubs have been around since the 1920s and provide an opportunity for posh, mostly white kids whose parents own farmland to socialise.

When Brighter turned up at Writtle, they drove through a campus that was bursting with drunken students who had been watching a rugby match that afternoon. The organiser approached Keris and said "This could go one of two ways," which, as Matt says, "is not what you want to hear before you go on stage." Alison Cousens says: "The sound engineer looked genuinely scared for us." Keris continues: "It was absolutely terrifying when you're looking out at a decent-sized hall seeing this audience of drunk young farmers who were expecting a good time and just knowing that wasn't something that we had the power to deliver." However, the band got through it by turning up the drum machine and letting the drunken youths dance their hearts out. Keris explains: "It was a bizarre thing. We realised the music didn't matter, what mattered was the beat and as soon as the drum machine came on, everyone started leaping around. We could have just left the drum machine on stage and gone out and had a beer, which would have been far more enjoyable."

Alison says: "I think they must have been so pissed that it didn't matter who it was. We tried to do some of the more upbeat songs towards the end, 'Does Love Last Forever' and 'Wallflower', and they were moshing. And they wanted an encore! I was like, 'Really? Are you sure?' It was bizarre." Brighter took home £100 for their troubles that night which, as Alison says, "was amazing." The band was used to getting £20 or £30 for a gig but, as she adds: "The promoter was just paying us danger money, frankly!"

When Even As We Speak made the decision to come to the UK for a year in 1993, they all quit their jobs in Australia, Mary Wyer left her young son behind and they came over to really make a go of promoting *Feral Pop Frenzy*. "It was a big tour that had been lined up and we had about a million shows booked, mostly at pretty small venues," says Julian Knowles. The tour had been organised by a couple called Gordon and Donna who were acting as their managers but it was an exhaustive diary of dates. "I cried when I saw the list," says Mary. "We got over there and we were sleeping on Gordon and Donna's floor, and they handed us the gig list and I burst into tears! We'd left everything at home and we wanted to play, and I enjoyed it in the end but just seeing it was overwhelming."

Even As We Speak were used to playing twice a week in Sydney, but this schedule had them playing five shows a week with barely any time off in between to work the cash-in-hand jobs that they needed in order to earn enough money to sustain themselves. "I think that was the first time for us that we had ever experienced this idea of just driving and driving and driving and playing and driving just for days and days on end with nothing else in your life, except for loading in and out of venues, driving up and down motorways, and drinking the rider," says Julian. "And having

Has a group of Australians ever looked happier to pose near a van?
Even As We Speak.

kebabs at 3am because you didn't have time to eat."

The experience later inspired guitarist Matthew Love to write 'Our People Travel Many Moons', a song about the band "'travelling around to circumnavigate the sacred rooms', which makes me laugh," says Mary. Of course, Even As We Speak weren't the only band to write a song about the experience of long and late driving after gigs. "Heavenly very much enjoyed playing gigs, so they would probably do a lot of overnight drives back to Oxford and 'Escort Crash on Marston Street' is about them driving back tired," says Clare. The lyrics include the to-the-point lines: "Hey now, Robert, you happy with your smashed up car? And your broken neck bone and your facial wounds? You've murdered Amelia. Pete can no longer play guitar. And Mathew's brain is damaged. But that's not so different. Could you tell at all?" Thankfully, it was not a prophecy.

The Sugargliders didn't have a manager when they came over for their UK tour, so relied on Clare and Matt setting up as many dates as possible. "It's totally not what a record label has to do," says Josh Meadows. "We played loads of gigs up and down the country, and a lot of them were with other Sarah bands like Secret Shine, Blueboy, Heavenly and Boyracer." It was nice for the band to be somewhere different because they'd found they were playing to the same audience again and again in their hometown of Melbourne, and in Australia it was much more difficult to set off on a nationwide tour due to the size of the place. "To actually go and tour around the UK and have completely different people coming to shows [...] was great," says Joel. And it seems like it was also great for those in the audience, if this glowing review from the Union Tavern in London by Ian Watson in *Melody Maker* is anything to go by: "Listening to these songs is like eavesdropping on another's closest secrets. They're here til mid-December. Treat yourself to a slice of real life."

It was the first time the brothers had been to the UK and Joel Meadows says "it was just like *The Goodies* and *The Bill*. We'd seen so much UK TV, so it was kind of a weird homecoming." They spent their spare time travelling on the tube or visiting art galleries and, when they were in Bristol, they were taken on a walking tour of the local sights by Clare. "We went to Revolver record shop and I bought quite a bit of stuff there," says Josh: "They took us out to pubs for a pint of bitter and pub food, and I remember a pub that had a lot of ciders on tap near the Clifton Suspension Bridge. Cider on tap in a pub, that wouldn't happen in Australia. We'd go back to their house and eat a massive dinner made by Matt. Potatoes with beans. They were so good to us, so hospitable and really went above and beyond what a record label should do for its bands." Potatoes with beans, yum.

Talking about going that extra mile, many of the bands also commented on how Clare and Matt would come to as many of their gigs as they could manage, which the bands later discovered was not something many other labels would do.

Support the support band

While on Factory, The Wake often supported New Order on tour. The Wake's frontman Caesar recognises what great opportunities this gave his band, especially for playing venues that might otherwise be out of their reach. "Probably the biggest one was Brixton Academy. Even in Glasgow we played Barrowlands with them several times and could never have played there ourselves. Then, people were really into support bands and you felt you were playing to an audience that wanted to see you. Gigs were real events. Groups used to choose their support acts carefully. Siouxsie & the Banshees and The Cure [who his first band Altered Images supported] didn't get a support band foisted on them, they chose them."

During interviews for this book, The Sea Urchins pop up repeatedly as a support band, although the gigs came with mixed results. Razorcuts played with them quite a few times and the two bands always got on well. "I just think we felt that we were on the same page," says singer Greg Webster. For a gig in Lichfield in 1987, Razorcuts' Tim Vass did the sound for The Sea Urchins and remembers it as "a really good gig," adding that he liked the younger band because "'Pristine Christine' really knocked me sideways." Greg elaborates: "I think they were a punk rock band, so that's why we felt some kind of affinity with them. And they'd gone back to the same countercultural references from the 1960s that we had, so it just felt like we were talking the same language."

> 66 The Sea Urchins live were either really shit or really great and there was no in between, like the Jesus & Mary Chain."
> **Jyoti Mishra, White Town**

Bridget Duffy recalls a time her band The Sea Urchins supported Primal Scream

The Sea Urchins performing at Edinburgh's Potterrow in 1991.
Nicola Rainey.

and had so much fun that she refused to leave the stage after their support slot had ended. "I decided that it was my divine right to stay on the stage and dance and cause a distraction," she laughs. "And then I got teased really badly by Joe Foster [The Television Personalities] and one of the Surf Drums. And Bobby Gillespie did interject and say 'Don't be mean'. I was having such a great time I didn't care."

But sometimes, the choice of support band just wasn't a good idea, especially if it wasn't clear who was the support and who was the headliner. "We fell out with The Sea Urchins," says Simon Court of The Sweetest Ache. "They're cocky shits, much as I love their music, I really do, they're my favourite Sarah band by a country mile." The Sweetest Ache were due to play with The Sea Urchins, or Delta as they had become, at Manchester's Swinging Sporran and it had been unclear which of the two bands was the headliner. "They rolled up and they were their usual cocksure selves. They were rude, arrogant shits. So we refused to play," says Simon. The Sweetest Ache were perhaps not in the sweetest mood having spent the night before squashed up in their van. "I don't think they gave a damn to be honest, they were notorious for not turning up, or turning up and not playing, so they could hardly throw any shade on us. There really wasn't much of an audience at that gig." In the sleeve notes to *There and Back Again Lane*, it is noted that the venue's sound engineer switched Delta off mid-song and someone threw a punch at poor old Hugh McGuinness from Mighty Mighty, who had presumably turned up for what he hoped would be a fun night out.

Although James Roberts of The Sea Urchins doesn't recall the incident in Manchester, he muses: "I think we *were* cocky shits. I don't think we were ever absolutely vile to people, we weren't bullies or anything like that, but we could be wind-up merchants and we could be cocky little fuckers at times, and sometimes you needed to be because you'd have promoters trying it on with you. We could be cheeky little fuckers but half the time we were doing it on purpose and we were giggling behind our hands about it. We were definitely playing a part but we were quite nice boys and girls. But the rock'n'roll thing was what we were about. We weren't trying to be some introspective shoegazey cliché."

Sometimes The Sea Urchins just didn't show up or else they cut it fine. Matthew Evans of Tramway recalls a time when a friend had booked the Urchins to play in a cellar venue in Windsor and, as it was almost time for the band to go on stage but there was still no band, he was on the verge of sending the audience home with a refund "when he saw these pink cords and Chelsea boots coming past the basement window and had never felt so relieved".

Heavenly were, probably, left quietly bemused when support band Even As We Speak rocked on to the stage at the Islington PowerHaus wearing what guitarist Julian Knowles describes as "proto-space suits." Singer Mary Wyer elaborates: "We wrapped ourselves in tin foil and came on stage with a smoke machine. We couldn't find our equipment, we were crawling around on the floor trying to find plugs to plug everything in. And I just think people didn't really get it. Some people have written to us and said they loved it but most people were just like 'What the hell is this?' I don't remember us even talking to any of Heavenly, except for Amelia's brother [Mathew Fletcher]. He came up to us and said 'I love you guys'. He seemed very sweet."

For Gentle Despite, two of their favourite shows were as the support. One of those gigs was with Pale Saints in Bradford in June 1990, in a venue that was much bigger than the band were used to. "Pale Saints had already had their album out and because of that we were in a big venue with a professional PA system and someone who knew how to mix a band," says guitarist Paul Gorton. "We played great and it made us so confident. It was probably the biggest crowd we played in front of, a few hundred people. It was a bit nerve-wracking! Because we had a great sound, we got really into it." Another memorable support slot for Gentle Despite came at the Boardwalk in Manchester where they opened for The Field Mice. "I remember having really good sound there, although it was a smallish venue," says Paul. "There was a dressing room and all the other bands had written on the walls: Inspiral Carpets, Stone Roses, Shaun Ryder."

Boyracer's Stewart Anderson saw Gentle Despite supporting The Field Mice at The Royal Park in his home city of Leeds and was very impressed. "I remember Gentle Despite doing a cover of 'Interstellar Overdrive' by Pink Floyd for 11 minutes. They weren't your typical Sarah band," he says. "I'd seen them play as a very stripped-down acoustic thing and then I saw them play a Pink Floyd song. That seemed remarkable to me. They used to dress in leather jackets and there was something quite mysterious about them. I was actually surprised they did end up on Sarah. It's unfortunate they never did more than they did. Simon [Westwood, vocals] was such an interesting person." Alas, *Melody Maker* did not agree with Dave Simpson writing: "Gentle Despite are a disaster. Tune-ups take longer than songs, songs themselves are exercises in chaos." Ouch.

Boyracer supported Gentle Despite at their final show in Leeds, which was acoustic and saw them do a cover of 'Real Cool Time' by The Stooges as their encore. "That was the last thing we ever did on stage. It took us back to when we first started to get into good music. We did love the first few Stooges albums," says Paul happily.

And, of course, one of the great perks of playing alongside another band is that you can borrow things from each other that you might be missing. Things like a guitar lead, an amp or maybe a drummer. "On one occasion, our drummer didn't turn up, so The Chesterfields' drummer stepped in," recalls Tim Vass of Razorcuts of the night that Dominic Manns joined his band for a one-off special. "The Chesterfields had this bouncy, jolly sound and that was largely the drummer's style. So we played this gig with their drummer and suddenly we turned into one of these jolly bands because of the way he played drums, it was the most bizarre thing."

Fight, Fight, Fight!

It's been said many times but, just as the concept of a Sarah sound was a myth, so was the notion that the bands were mild-mannered meerkats. And that's why I ended up hearing an unexpected amount of stories about fights when I was interviewing bands for this book. Here are a few of the punchier ones...

While playing a gig at the Pentre Legion in the Rhondda Valley with The Sweetest Ache, Secret Shine ended up dodging a near riot that kicked off in the venue. "All the local youths had come out of the disco over the road and gone a bit mental," says the band's guitarist Scott Purnell. "We had to barricade the back of the stage and jump out of a window with all our gear. I think they were just very, very drunk and looking for a fight. They were all the lads, and saw a bunch of indie kids in this hall watching The Sweetest Ache and Secret Shine, and they fancied a fight, and then it turned on the bands. They hadn't even been at the gig. The police were in there like a shot."

The fight at the Fleece & Firkin is covered in the previous chapter and its instigators Action Painting! were getting a reputation for being "quite punchy," as frontman Andy Hitchcock puts it. "But you have to realise both Lee [Christopher] and myself, and to a degree Kevin [House], all used to get regular abuse and attacks for our supposedly feminine appearance because we wore make-up and had big hair. Living in a garrison town [Gosport] made us targets

> ❝ Secret Shine played the Rhondda Valley and had to lock themselves in the toilets to avoid getting beaten up by 'local lads having a bit of fun,' to quote the South Wales Police..."
> **Sarah Newsletter No 8, July 1994**

for being non-conforming males. You end up becoming a bit punchy yourself after being jumped a few times." Lee agrees: "There was only one pub in Gosport that we felt safe to drink in, The Village Home, somewhere pissed-up shore-leave sailors wouldn't feel the urge to question our sexuality with a swift punch to the back of the head … A man was beaten to death with his own garden fence after telling some kids to get off of it, schools got burnt down, and me and Andy would be regularly challenged by packs of kids for the way we dressed. Especially when Andy was wearing my auntie's flower print anorak." Kevin adds: "Action Painting! gigs were sometimes funny but never fun. It was always on the edge of the razor wire of falling completely to pieces, which it did several times. But there was a kind of antagonism between us and them. Them being the audience."

Action Painting!'s punchy reputation was something Andy was not pleased about. "[Jerry Thackray] wrote that people go to see our gigs to see whether we'd split up on stage or fight each other," sighs Andy. "At one gig, there were really dodgy skinheads turning up, and people trying to heckle us and trying to get us involved in stuff, and I was getting fed up with that. There was another gig at the Beachcomber Club in Brighton where there was a heckler and Lee literally put down his guitar halfway through the song, got off the stage, punched the heckler, got on and carried on with the song. Which was great for journalists. And I have to admire the fact that he did it all in time."

Action Painting! were once "hounded out of Norwich" by "locals with blocks of wood". What the heck?! "We played very badly and were very drunk," says Andy about the gig at Norwich Arts Centre. The gig had come via a booking agent, meaning the band had been paid handsomely (£200) as well as getting a rider that included "a hot meal, 24 cans of export larger and two bottles of strong spirits,"

> ❝ 'You're shit, give us our money back! You're shit!'
> **Action Painting!'s audience, Norwich Arts Centre**

according to Kevin, who says they all started playing different songs at the same time when they finally made their way on stage. Andy continues: "Basically, we drank it all before going on stage, so we were absolutely appalling. But we didn't care because we thought 'Fuck you, we've got £200 and we're absolutely pissed.' I'd fallen down halfway through the performance. We got off the stage and there were loads of people shouting at us and chasing after us, and our manager literally shouted 'Get in the van!' And the last thing we saw were these blokes with stones and blocks of woods, trying to chase after the van and chucking stuff at us." Kevin adds: "Iain [Naylor] the drummer always took a golf club around, and he was ready to get out his golf club to get us out of the place. Gigs could either be the greatest thing ever or such a shambles."

While we're on the topic, Andrew Jarrett of The Groove Farm remembers a show that got a bit sticky: "We did a gig in Newcastle and we were halfway through a song when all the power was cut off to the venue. We were at the Whoosh club, which was in a pub called The Broken Doll. And a woman came running in screaming 'Get

The final ever show by The Field Mice (who are pictured here in Rennes) was "an interesting experience". Emmanuel Foricher.

out, get out, the pub's been overtaken with skinheads downstairs!' And upstairs, this room was packed with indie kids, and you could see sheer panic and everyone flocking down the fire escape and us lot with a drum kit trying to get down the fire escape. The things you did back then!"

One of the final Field Mice shows was at The Richmond in Brighton and, while it was not a night of physical fighting, it was certainly a strained night. Anne Mari Davis explains: "What wasn't good for me was tension and conflict, that was probably the thing that triggered it all," says Anne Mari, who struggled with anxiety. "So we played this gig and it was so frustrating. Bobby [Wratten] ended up smashing his guitar up on stage, the neck came off the guitar, and Mark [Dobson] pushed his drum kit off the stage and into the crowd. It was utterly insane but it was borne of frustration and general upset. I just think we were all a little bit over-sensitive and not very robust."

Talking about that drum kit, Mark says: "It was a £140 second-hand drum kit, and it was such a bad drum kit it didn't even have a manufacturers' name on the front. It was like the people who made it were so embarrassed by how bad the workmanship was and how dreadful it sounded, they wouldn't even put their name to it. I was so ashamed of that drum kit. Every time we went out on tour, I asked the support band if they could bring their drum kit, so I'd use theirs. I moved out of London in 1998 and I left it in a street in Tooting Bec. I just put a note on saying 'Free to a good home' and left it there." But none of the other Mice had good kit either, there just wasn't the money for anyone to buy nice instruments. "Michael [Hiscock] had a bass guitar but no bass amp, so when we'd go to rehearsals at Bobby's house, it plugged into Bobby's guitar amp so it sounded absolutely dreadful," says Mark. "Bobby had a Kay guitar which I think he got from the [Kays mail-order catalogue] and he paid £25 for it. We're quite possibly the poorest band in the history of music! Harvey [Williams] on the other hand has a fantastic guitar amp and a Rickenbacker 12-string so, whenever we play a gig, the support band latch onto him because he's the only person who knows how any of the gear works. Bobby eventually got so fed up with his guitar, in a fit of pique at the end of a gig at The Richmond in Brighton, he smashed it. But it took him about eight goes before it eventually started smashing, and then he walked off stage. And him and Anne Mari had to get the train down to Brighton from Croydon the following day to ask if they still had the guitar, and they got the bits and couldn't put it back together."

Fanzine writer Chris Tighe says he had "the great misfortune of seeing the final Field Mice gig at Tufnell Park Dome on 21 November 1991 and that it was "an interesting experience." Like most people in the audience, Chris didn't know that the band had already agreed to split up, and he'd instead heard that this was to be their big London gig with A&R people in attendance and serious record label interest. "So I was bemused," he says, "watching them and wondering why they looked like they wanted to be anywhere other than where they were. There wasn't a great deal of life in the performance. It wasn't a fun experience." I don't think the final Field Mice gig was a fun experience for anyone and video footage just shows a collection of very unhappy people going through the motions on stage, trying not to cry.

Talking about that sad gig, Mark says: "We'd split up a few days earlier but were contractually obliged to play this gig. We could have not done it but we'd have had to pay, so we had to go through with it. It was the last time that the five of us have ever been in the same building together. Until one of us dies, and the other people turn up to the funeral, I can't envisage a situation where the five of us would ever be in the same room again." He continues: "So this last gig, we'd come back from France completely euphoric to find out that 'Missing The Moon' was single of the week in *NME* and Sarah had sold about 10,000 copies. It would have been in the charts if they could have pressed enough. We had major labels sniffing around. But within the space of seven days we managed to completely implode. We've gone from right up high to as far down as you possibly can."

ISOLATION

"Everyone was very guarded at Sarah gigs, it was lots of little cliques," says Stewart Anderson of Boyracer. "Possibly a lot of the bands weren't particularly confident about their position or their involvement. Lee [Christopher, Action Painting!] was an amazing performer, he was also a member of Shampoo so he'd had this taste of the high life. But he was famously rude to everybody. I remember saying to him a couple of years ago, 'I never really got to know you, I thought you didn't like us.' And he said something flippant like, 'I didn't like anyone, I was rude to everyone, don't think you're special, I wasn't just rude to you.' But I've since got to know him and he is very interesting, so much so I am now releasing records by him." Of course, sometimes geography was the reason that a band might not get to know their Sarah labelmates. For example, Gentle Despite were based in Leeds and rarely ventured outside of their home city which made it tricky to meet many other Sarah bands. The band's Paul Gorton and Simon Westwood got to know Stewart because he was also in Leeds but, other than that, their contact with other Sarah bands was slim. However, Paul tells me: "We did a nice gig at the Royal Park in Headingley, which was quite a big indie hub at the time. I played there with The Field Mice and thought they were a nice bunch of guys. It was nice to meet other people on the label and they also understood the anti-Sarah vibe that was going round."

The Harvest Ministers, based in Dublin, were another band that didn't encounter many of their labelmates due to geography. "I met Clare several times and found her to be the most gentle and artistically astute woman," says frontman Will Merriman. "I remember herself and Harvey came to one of our Dublin shows, which was a great night. The only other times we got to meet were at a couple of gigs in London. We played with Blueboy in The Mean Fiddler, which I remember as being a cool evening of song and music. We really didn't get to play much with any of our fellow label bands, which was a pity."

The Sweetest Ache's Stuart Vincent says: "We played with many Sarah bands over the years but I don't think that The Sweetest Ache ever felt part of something. We always felt on the outside a little bit. The bands we played with, there was no camaraderie or togetherness, it was very much 'You're the support band, we're the main band', we sat in different corners, there was no conversation around music. It was strangely distant when you met these bands. I don't know why it was. We didn't not get on, there was no animosity, but it felt a bit distant."

Of course, there's a difference between feeling a bit separate from the other bands and feeling downright targeted by them, as Brighter found when Action Painting! came to see them at The Joiners Arms in Southampton. "They heckled us right the way through. They were just a bit arsey," says guitarist Alison Cousens. "Action Painting! heckling us, it was just part of that culture. Has that changed? I doubt it, because it's all to do with ego and the male ego particularly."

*****
THESE THINGS HAPPENED:
Caesar, The Wake
"Tony Wilson [of our former label Factory] and Matt and Clare had completely different personalities. Matt, you couldn't get him to look you in the eye. We only met him a few times, at gigs. We did all our recording business over the phone. When we met them at any live event, Matt's fringe was the dominant sight, you never saw into his eyes. Once you engaged Clare in conversation, you could talk away to her. But Tony Wilson was the ultimate show off and dominated the room. A lovely man and a huge music fan but a TV personality. There was a lot of hype in his talk. Whereas Matt and Clare were really shy. We were quite like that ourselves. Moving from Factory to Sarah expanded our audience, as we were on two labels that mean a lot to people. It was a move at the time that seemed like a bit of a mistake, as Factory was a well-known label but, in the long run, it was a really good move for us. I'd like to emphasise that."

Chapter 16

Going Out: All Over the World

Most of the bands in this scene didn't have anything as official as a manager, meaning that a lot of the admin was handled in a very ad hoc fashion. For example, some of the bands' tours were organised by the record labels or even by fans. A fanzine writer might send a letter from, say, Lausanne, asking if the band wanted to play a gig there and offering to put them up for the night. And this would then be discussed over a few phone calls before the gig would magically happen. It was in this slightly slapdash way that many of these bands found themselves having all sorts of adventures, not just in the UK but all over the world.

> "We felt like proper pop stars for the first time when we first went to Japan."
> **Amelia Fletcher, Heavenly**

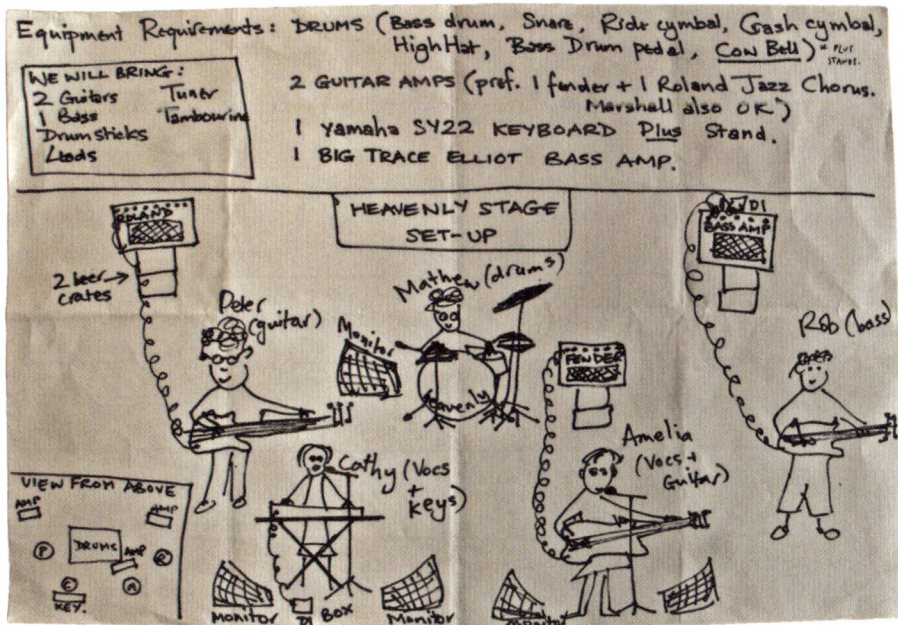

Heavenly's requirements for their stage set-up were so demanding that Mariah Carey was known to take notes for her own tours.
Courtesy of Sarah Records.

France: Brittany

While talking with Harvey Williams, there was a moment when he said: "The Britney tour was one of my best experiences from that whole period." Hold on, what? Sure, Harvey has played with pretty much everyone who's ever made a record but I didn't know that he had toured with Britney Spears. Wow! Oh, *Brittany*... It's Brittany.

Yes, in 1989 there was a mini Sarah tour of three or four gigs in Brittany with Harvey, Heavenly, St Christopher and a handful of Orchids. "It was a pretty unlikely place to go for a tour but we did," says Heavenly's Rob Pursey. "Quite a few people wrote to us from Brittany, especially in the early days. It seemed to be a hotbed of pop fans," confirms Matt.

Rob continues: "One of the places we stayed was this enormous seminary and I guess it was holiday time because there weren't any trainee priests in it but it was vast and it was freezing cold. It was a big, old, dark stone building. We were all in one room, like a dorm, where priests would normally be. But it was quite spooky and then Mathew [Fletcher] woke up in the middle of the night, he'd been quite drunk, and he started sleepwalking. He was ranging around the room, and he opened a cupboard and said 'There's another fucking Harvey band in here!' So for a while, our generic term for bands on Sarah was 'Another fucking Harvey band.'" Mathew's sister Amelia Fletcher adds: "To Harvey's credit, he thought it was funny. There's so many of these fucking Harvey bands! So that seminary was quite something."

After I fact-check this story with Harvey, he smiles and says: "It's so nice to hear that story about Mathew again." He elaborates: "I'd seen Talulah Gosh live before and I was aware of Amelia's legendary status. And then I first met them on the ferry across and it really did seem like, 'Oh right, these are people I want to spend time with'. And to then play some shows with them and to find people who are on the same wavelength as you, who actually had an idea about what music is all about, it was a real eye opener and it was a great week. And to know that Mathew had this dream about Harvey bands, whatever they are. I'd clearly made an impression."

Harvey adds: "We did one show in Rennes and then a couple of more provincial shows. The person in Rennes must have contacted Matt and Clare to say 'Can I bring them over?'. And to make it more financially viable, they organised these other few shows as well. Doing three dates in a small part of France seems completely ridiculous really now. But incredible fun. I'd done occasional gigs with Michael [Hiscock] from The Field Mice, he managed to get Matthew [Drummond] from The Orchids involved, he was almost part of the motivating factor, he said we could do it if he could get a guitarist as Bob [Wratten] didn't want to do it, so he got someone else and it all happened. And it was all based on 'Will it be fun?'"

Heavenly's Pete Momtchiloff confirms: "Going to Brittany was very good fun. It was very out of the way. It was put on by a couple of very young fans and we were playing in places that didn't usually have a lot of gigs. Brittany isn't particularly a backwater, we were playing in fairly well-known towns like Rennes but it was very much the grassroots thing, just put on by fans for fans. It was a really fun outing. It was like a little British seaside holiday in France."

Brittany was also where the infamous 'Fields Festival' took place. This was a three-day music event where, bizarrely, all the bands were playing in alphabetical order. Meaning that The Field Mice were due to play just before The Fields of the Nephilim. Which is a fascinating juxtaposition of bands. "It was the biggest gig we ever did,"

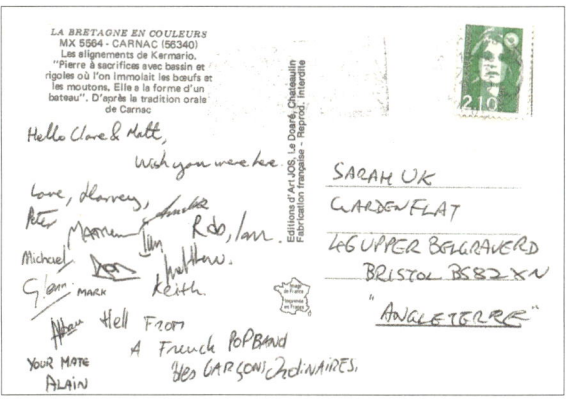

A postcard home from a gaggle of touring Sarah bands. Wish you were here?
Courtesy of Sarah Records.

says the band's Anne Mari Davies. "It was in a hangar, like an aircraft hangar. The promoter came up and said 'We've got a bit of a disaster, The Fields of the Nephilim have split up so you're going to go on in their slot.' And we were like 'We're going to get bottled off the stage'. But that didn't happen. The stage was the size of most of the places we normally played. It was huge. But the sound system... We were always playing crummy venues where you couldn't hear yourself and the monitors didn't work or you kept getting electric shocks from things, and then suddenly you're in this professional place and it was brill, it was amazing. And the crowd was amazing. You just felt like, 'We've made it.'"

Drummer Mark Dobson echoes Anne Mari's enthusiasm: "The drums were enormous, up on this massive riser, so I was looking down on the rest of the band who were like ants. The sound was incredible, the monitors worked, it was like playing Wembley." Mark says The Field Mice ended up going on very near the top of the bill because of some last-minute shuffling but that only added to the band's nerves. "Bobby [Wratten] came in, face white as a sheet, looking like he'd seen a ghost and he said 'It's full!' This aircraft hangar in the middle of nowhere was full of 2,000 people! We couldn't play to that many people!" gasps Mark. The band rejigged their setlist to bump up some of the more atmospheric songs, which seemed more suitable for the massive venue, but that wasn't all... "The guy said normally The Fields of the Nephilim played their entire set in a fog of dry ice and they had the dry ice that nobody was using, so we had their dry ice. We went down incredibly well, people were roaring at the end. People flooded into the dressing room afterwards asking for autographs, there were people from Virgin Records."

FRANCE: PARIS

Of course, it wasn't only the quieter parts of France that welcomed the bands, because people in the country's capital absolutely adored Sarah Records. None more so than Naji Baz, a French advertising executive who was a huge fan of the label and its bands. In January 1990, Naji arranged a mini Sarah festival at a Parisian nightclub called The New Morning. Shelling out for full-page advertisements in prestigious magazines including *Les Inrockuptibles* and *Cahiers du Cinéma*, Naji brought The Field Mice, The Orchids, St Christopher and Another Sunny Day over to the city of romance for a few days. Sacre coeur! "We got a full-page article in *Libération* as well," adds Clare. "Which you'd think we'd have bought a copy of but we didn't buy most of our press because we didn't have enough money."

Naji invited his musical guests to a party at his expensive apartment the night before the show, although it would be fair to say that the Sarah crew found his luxury Parisian lifestyle a little out of kilter with what they were used to. "His friends were there and they were clearly coming from a different world," says Matt. "He invited us to a party and The Orchids thought they'd take some beer. So they bought some cans of beer and turned up. Because that's what they'd do at a party in Glasgow. And when we got there, there was a huge slab of pâté and cooked meats and the posh friends, it was clearly a different sort of party to the parties we were used to."

The Orchids definitely found the experience uncomfortable. "We were just young guys from a scheme in Glasgow and we were in his fancy flat in Paris going 'What are we doing here?'," says Chris Quinn. "He wanted us to come over and some of his friends were there and he'd laid food and drink on for us, we found it bizarre." James Hackett adds: "It was like he was trying to show us off and it didn't sit too comfortably with us. He fed us and gave us a lot of drink and a bit of dope but it was just to have us there so he could impress his friends. We had no social skills for that sort of occasion." Chris adds: "I remember [James] Moody biting all the gherkins and putting the other half back in the jar and he thought that was funny. And we were like, 'What are you doing?!' That was the level of behaviour." James Hackett adds: "Out of all of us, Moody was probably the one who was going, 'I hate this sort of bohemian nonsense, what's he trying to impress folk with five kids from Glasgow for? It's not really that impressive is it?' So he started getting a bit antsy."

Naji certainly sounds like he had fun while the Sarah bands were over, though. "He came to the soundcheck and was playing air guitar to The Orchids' 'Caveman' while they were soundchecking," remembers Matt fondly.

Melody Maker's Bob Stanley (soon to be of Saint Etienne) made it to Paris for The New Morning show and wrote a lovely review for the paper on his return, concluding with how headliners The

> ❝ Christ, I'm knackered; too many sleepless nights. Travelled to Paris overnight on Sunday and then back on Monday; the first night was really cold because the blankets were so small, the second was just full of hyperactive French school children running around. Luckily I was vaguely alert while I was actually there. Probably because Paris was so cold, absolutely bloody freezing it was. Luckily my mother had bought me a coat as an early Christmas present."
>
> **Letter from Clare to fan Neil Shumsky**

GOING OUT: ALL OVER THE WORLD

St Christopher (pictured, top), Another Sunny Day (pictured, middle) and The Orchids (pictured, bottom) at The New Morning show, 21 January 1990.
Emmanuel Foricher.

Orchids got called back for not one but two encores and writing: "While guitarist Matthew [Drummond] seems close to tears at the groups' supposed ineptitude, there are 700 people here intent on dragging him back just one mo' time."

Harvey Williams remembers the New Morning gig saying: "It was quite an adventure. It seemed like the last thing that would happen and the fact that it was for this one-off gig. And it was a really nice venue, had really good sound. And I just remember going over on the train, staying at a nice enough hotel and two days later, you hear all these stories that The Orchids have been chucking tellies out the windows and stuff like that. I was completely oblivious to all that stuff going on at the time." Glenn Melia of St Christopher agrees: "It was fabulous, a real kick, actually being recognised in shops, bars, etc. I don't remember much about the financial aspect of the gig or even how we got there but I reckon the promoter would have broken even at least."

On another occasion, there was a Sarah night at La Locomotive, a club which had certain unusual stipulations. One of which was that the soundcheck needed to be at 6am, so that there was no sound bleed through into the Moulin Rouge above. Another stipulation was that the show would start at 1am, once the Moulin Rouge had closed. A lovely breakfast buffet was laid on for the early doors soundcheck but that wasn't the only take away point: "Somewhere we've got some toilet roll from there because they used to print the next line-up on toilet roll," says Clare proudly.

> ❝ Orchids, Wake and Heavenly in Paris last night – or rather early this morning. Imagine The Underworld but three times the size and twice as dark. Lots of mad people travelled from Switzerland and Germany and stuff… Too much free beer, meaning I'm collapsed this afternoon instead of out seeing the sights!!!"
>
> **Parisian postcard from Clare to fan Julian Bester**

Despite the fact that the bands were more used to playing to a few dozen people in a sticky room above a yeasty pub, they rose to the occasion and played their hearts out to the crowd of 700 who had gathered to see them. And this was more than a sell-out show, this was a show that had sold out weeks in advance. The love for Sarah in the French capital was further demonstrated by the volume of people in attendance who knew the words to every single song from every single band.

The Orchids brought their engineer and producer Ian Carmichael along with them to do the sound at La Locomotive and Ian remembers his first trip to Paris as a total blast: "It was great fun, in that we drove in the van all the way there, went on the ferry. We arrived in France, we did the gig and had a hotel room that night… I do remember being quite overwhelmed by thinking, 'Oh my god, I'm doing the sound in the Moulin Rouge', well, I thought it was the Moulin Rouge. The thing I remember afterwards is we got so trashed, because that's what The Orchids do."

After being up all night, having a few beers, phoning their friends around the world and eventually smashing their hotel room door (wait for chapter 18 for more on this), The Orchids got in their van at 8am and set off for the next stage of their European tour in Germany. Leaving Ian behind in Paris to enjoy one packed day of sightseeing before making his way home to Glasgow. "I ran everywhere," Ian laughs.

"I ran to the Louvre, to the Eiffel Tower, to Sacré Coeur. I'd never been in Paris before, it was my first time and I just ran everywhere to see everything, it was exhausting! The Orchids didn't do a lot of sightseeing but they did go to the pubs."

Less fantastic was The Field Mice's gig in Paris at the end of their French tour with The Wake, when Anne Mari Davis had become so ill that she couldn't even get on stage and Bobby Wratten was desperate to get the gig over with as soon as possible so that he could go and look after her. It was a sold-out show in front of 1,300 fans, and the band was contractually obliged to play for 45 minutes. "There's a cassette recording of that gig that Tim Chipping did, where I played a drum solo for probably about 10 minutes," says Mark Dobson, lamenting the fact that he was desperately trying to

James Moody is the sort of man who is willing to step in and help save a show.
Jon Cole.

string the set out as long as possible so that they hit the 45-minute mark. "The only people on stage by then were myself playing a sort of tribal drum beat and [James] Moody from The Orchids/The Wake who had come on stage and did a striptease. This actually happened. I know we've got to play for another seven minutes or we're not getting paid. And Moody, who I was sharing a room with, who was a bit crazy, understands what's going on. The drum beat isn't going to keep people entertained for seven minutes, so he comes on stage and starts taking his clothes off. Fortunately I can only see this from the back, I've not got the frontal view! I don't know how far he's going to go with this but knowing Moody, he's probably going the full way. That gig ended with Moody taking off his underpants, throwing them into the crowd and walking into the crowd right on the final drum beat. That actually happened."

France was a hotbed of Sarah fans and at one point Clare and Matt were offered a £100,000 advance by Virgin France, however they turned it down in favour of a smaller company called Danceteria who said they would do 500 copies of each 7". But it didn't quite go to plan, as Clare explains: "They did 500 of the first one, then 400 of the next one, 300 of the one after... then went bust. I probably had to do an overnight trip on the bus from Bristol to get the tapes back."

Given that she could speak French well, Clare popped over to France fairly regularly on her own to attend to business matters. But there were no private jets and limos for this record label executive, instead there were a selection of overnight coach trips and choppy ferry rides. Speaking about the visits to France, Clare comments: "There was a point where we were on the cusp of being really successful in France. There seemed to be a while where I could rock up in Paris and just drop the national radio a note beforehand on a fax and go in the studio with the French John Peel [Bernard Lenior]. They always quite liked me because I spoke French."

Amelia Fletcher remembers a time that she was in France with Clare and the two of them were being interviewed on French radio. "We had the option of talking in English but then I realised Clare was actually pretty fluent in French," says Amelia. "So she just went off in French, and I was like 'Oh, maybe I'd better do this as well'. I thought, 'I've got a French O Level, I should be able to talk French'. And I think I got about a sentence and a half in and went [sheepish voice] 'Can I talk English, please?'" Clare adds: "I probably just assumed Amelia could speak French because she can do everything else." Which is a reasonable assumption to make, given how close to world domination Amelia is.

France: Toulouse

Tensions were starting to appear on The Field Mice's 1991 tour with The Wake. Anne Mari Davis and Bobby Wratten had become a couple by this point and it was starting to cause a rift between Bobby and bassist Michael Hiscock. "Bobby was always disappearing and couldn't cope with things and saying he couldn't do it anymore," says Anne Mari. "The more that Bobby and Michael fell out, the more guilty I felt. But it was a very successful French tour. You'd drive to these places in the middle of absolutely nowhere, through fields and fields of sunflowers, thinking 'Well, if we get five locals we'll be lucky' and then it would be a sell-out and everybody knew every word to every song and it was just crazy. Sarah was really popular in France in relative terms. There may have only been 20,000 fans worldwide but they were very dedicated, so they would travel to Toulouse to see us if they were within 50 miles, so it made it feel like we were bigger than we were. And we'd been live on the equivalent of Radio 1 and the equivalent of John Peel [Bernard Lenior]. It was also really crazy that we were driving for nine hours a day and then playing a gig, staying up til two or three by the time we'd packed everything away, a couple of hours sleep, and then driving from Paris to Grenoble or somewhere. We slept in these motels that had a bunk bed with a double on the bottom and a single on the top. That was good enough."

Her bandmate Mark Dobson recalls a gig at the Bikini Club in Toulouse on 18 September 1991 and the feeling of definitely being somewhere very different. "You drive through the gates and there's a swimming pool at the venue with two beautiful women who work there, sat with their legs dangling in the pool, with very few clothes on. We got out the van and were like, 'This is not the Hull Adelphi'. People moved the gear in for us, the sound was fantastic, kids sang along to every song down the front, unbelievable. It must have been a good gig because Bobby agreed to play 'Sensitive'. And I think he only played it two or three times when I was in the band, and that was when it was a really good gig."

Blueboy were another Sarah band that was well received across the Channel. Fresh off the plane from Japan, the band barely had time to do their laundry – and enlist a new drummer in the form of Martin Rose – before repacking their bags and

Top: Blueboy on tour in France. **Bottom:** This time it's Blueboy's turn to pose by a large rented vehicle.
Courtesy of Paul Stewart.

setting off for France to promote the *Unisex* album. Martin says: "Paul [Stewart] rang me up and said, 'What are you doing in about 10 days' time? We're doing a tour of France if you fancy it. I'll drop off a cassette, you've got 14 songs to learn in 10 days, we've got one rehearsal.' I was like, 'You're joking!' And it was always like that. What's quite nice is they probably knew I could pull it off, which is a backhanded compliment but I remember living and breathing those songs, in the car, at home, learning them."

Martin continues: "On the tour, obviously you're stuck in a minibus driving through France, you get to know everybody. I loved that tour. It was the first time I'd played overseas. I was told there was going to be a tour bus and it turned out to be a minibus from Wokingham Van Hire or whatever! We had one for the gear, one for us lot, and we all crammed in it and it was fun." Martin really realised how popular Blueboy were in France: "The first night I think we played in Rouen and I didn't know what to expect. I wasn't used to playing massive venues but it was a big venue, the crowd was great and what I wasn't used to was fans, people coming up afterwards wanting you to sign a CD, and just wanting to hang out, so it was pretty cool. Exciting days. You'd go to a venue, do a soundcheck, drive off with about 10 people in the queue to come in and when you came back, the queue would be right round the venue. And just the excitement of them knowing the songs."

"It was a different vibe in France," agrees bandmate Gemma Malley. "They just really liked the music and the bands. We did the gigs and I remember dancing and it was just fun. And then we had this insane drive back and we hadn't slept for at least one night but we had to get on the ferry, and Paul was driving and was literally falling asleep at the wheel. So we had to keep all the windows open and my job was to keep him awake, and I was literally falling asleep with my eyes open. That's the stuff you look back on and just go 'Oh my god!'"

Oh yes, about that drive to the ferry against the clock… "We'd done our last gig of the tour in France and I was driving the minibus back to get the ferry. And I had work the next day, so we really had to get this ferry and we had overslept so we were miles away," says Paul. "So we piled into this van, smelly, not cleaned our teeth, driving down the motorway, I was falling asleep at the wheel, it was awful and nearly had an accident a few times, and Mark [Cousens] our bass player was desperate for a pee. I said, 'Mate, we can't stop, if we miss this ferry the next one's tomorrow…' It was one of those minibuses where the door slides, so I said 'OK, if I go a bit slower…', so I could still see in my wing mirror Mark leaning out and pissing into the grass of the French motorway. He probably slammed the door closed and said, 'Ahh, that's better.'"

Martin muses: "When we did the French tour, I didn't think it was going to be as big or as busy as it was. And so I remember coming back from France on the bus, and being told that Ride wanted us to go back to Paris and support them, and I remember Paul going 'Oh, no we've just done France, I don't want to go back', and thinking 'But that could be massive!'"

GERMANY

"There was a guy called Lars in a town called Bielefeld in Germany. And he got in contact with us and said he thought he could put on seven or eight German dates, did we want to come across and do it? Of course we did!" says Davey Woodward of The Brilliant Corners. "There was a group of West German kids who were really into the alternative music scene and were collecting every single thing you did. The only place in East Germany you could play was Berlin, other than that it was exclusively West Germany."

Davey goes on to explain the logistics of trying to tour divided Germany in the days when the Berlin Wall was still up: "It was absolutely chaotic. Half the band had never left Bristol, let alone gone abroad! The chaos of having to queue up and sign multiple bits of paper, and the guards come and see what you've got in your vehicle, it just used to be crazy. There used to be this thing called a carnet, and it was a whole set of forms that you had to fill in and, when we played our first German tour, Lars had got someone who was going to be our tour manager and interpreter. Back then they had these things called 'the corridors' that took you through East Germany to Berlin and you could only drive at a certain speed because you were timed to get to Berlin at a certain time. If you got there too early, they were suspicious. If you got there too late, why were you late? You had to get there at a certain time. The guy in charge of us was petrified that one of us would make a wisecrack or do some piss-taking and we'd all be banged up in an East German police cell for 48 hours."

SWITZERLAND

"We played in an old gas dome in Switzerland. It was just a mud floor, an iron dome with some seating and no toilets, that was pretty rank," says James Hackett of The Orchids. "There was no toilet, there was a bucket we had to use. And it was similar for the punters, too." The Orchids were in Lausanne, Switzerland, with The Field Mice and St Christopher and the three bands muddled along very nicely with each other. "The Field Mice were lovely guys, really into music," says The Orchids' Chris Quinn. "Michael [Hiscock] liked a good time but Bobby [Wratten] was pretty introverted at times and liked a quiet time. We had a good time with The Field Mice."

Because The Field Mice were still the duo of Bobby and Michael, they were able to pitch in on hiring a van with The Orchids. And to make things easier still, Bobby's dad came along to drive the van. "It was Bobby's first venture into the rock'n'roll lifestyle and his dad's there watching every minute of it," sympathises James. "It's not very comfortable for him, he was very introverted." Half of The Orchids and The Field Mice went in the van with Bobby's dad and the kit, and the other half piled into a car and everyone basically

> 66 Switzerland was brilliant. Six good concerts and we got to meet The Orchids and St Christopher which was nice. We played various sized venues to various sized crowds, but the beer was free and it was a valuable lesson in playing live."
>
> **Letter from Michael Hiscock, The Field Mice, to fan Julian Bester**

Top left: Here we have Clare with Heavenly, Brighter and The Field Mice at Gatwick Airport on 20 September 1990, en route to Switzerland. **Bottom left:** Squeak! Anne Mari and Bobby give us a wave before boarding the plane. **Top and bottom right:** Backstage at 'La Nuit de Pop Sarah'.
Mark Dobson.

sat on each other's laps for thousands of miles as they drove from show to show. "The St Christopher guys always seemed to turn up late. They had their own van and took a longer route, never seemed to come the right way, and left early and turned up late again. But they were a decent bunch of fellas," adds James.

Lausanne was also the setting for the infamous La Nuit de Pop Sarah show on 20 September 1990, sponsored, rather improbably, by Marlboro, who had provided an enormous tub of free cigarettes in the centre of the venue for everyone to just help themselves. Nobody at Team Sarah had known about the cigarettes though! The Field Mice, Heavenly and Brighter made up the bill. "That was bizarre," says Alison Cousens of Brighter. "It was a moment of insight into what it is like to be on a real label in a real band, playing internationally. I'd only previously flown to Jersey from Shoreham Airport on a tiny plane for a family holiday. So that whole thing about going to an airport, we were wide-eyed with wonder. And then we were turning up with instruments, so it was this glorious adventure, it was fantastic." Bandmate Keris Howard echoes that enthusiasm: "I hadn't been on a plane since I was two, so that was great excitement." Alison adds: "I remember sitting next to the window in the plane and going 'What does this do? and going to pull down the blind and Alex [Sharkey] having an absolute fit, thinking I was going to open the window and we'd be sucked out!"

However, the journey took a turn for the less glamorous, as Keris explains: "This was a moment of being in a band when you suddenly think you've arrived but then you suddenly come down to earth really, really quickly. We were on the train to Lausanne and we saw a guy get on to the train, he was obviously crew because he had a t-shirt on that was advertising the event. A really nice t-shirt that had 'La Nuit de Pop Sarah' on it and it had the bands on it, how fantastic. The idea of being on a t-shirt was amazing. But they had spelled our name wrong. They called us 'Brighters'." He adds: "We got complimentary t-shirts that we continued to wear for many years afterwards as they were really nice shirts." There is a lesson in humility for us all there.

Back to Alison: "And then we rocked up to this bizarre venue in Lausanne. The soundcheck was in this bizarre hangar covered in architectural decor, so there were half limbs of dolls all around you, it was quite surreal." Things became even more surreal when, during a tour of the venue with Matt, Alison split her head open on some of the unusual overhanging bits of rusty decor that had been hammered into the roof. "I sat down and I was bleeding quite profusely," says Alison. "There was a lot of blood. They tried to patch me up with some first aid at the venue but the promoter was saying he thought I needed to go to hospital for stitches. When you go to a Swiss hospital, it's the opposite of an NHS A&E. It was completely empty and pristine with all mod cons. I was whisked into this theatre room with everyone in white coats and all I had was my O Level French that I couldn't remember because I was probably a bit concussed." After putting some stitches in her head wound, the doctor said: "Oh, you're playing that gig tonight?" and asked if he could be put on the guest list. And it was at this point that Alison realised that La Nuit de Pop Sarah was quite a significant event for the town.

Despite everything, Alison was back at the venue in time for the show, and she admits that because she was so busy worrying about everything else it was one of the few times she didn't experience stage fright. That anaesthetic probably helped, too. "I plugged the guitar in and there were all these people in the front going, 'Are you OK? Is your head alright?' And I thought, 'How do you know what just happened?' And just going ahead and playing," says Alison.

Keris adds: "For some bizarre reason, we thought it would be hilarious to go on to Frank Sidebottom's big band music, which was stupid and obviously that went down like a lead balloon. I think some of the audience did know Sarah Records but others were just out for a good night. So starting out with Frank Sidebottom's big band music, and then me and Alex doing a tortuous joke about Swiss Army Knives... so I think we'd already killed the atmosphere before we'd even started the drum machine." Despite all that, Keris concludes: "The Field Mice were always great fun to be around, Heavenly were really nice people, Matt and Clare we knew really well, it was a nice bill and we were going to Switzerland, we were seeing another part of the world, we had our name on t-shirts! Just the idea of going abroad to play gigs felt really exotic."

One fan who made a big effort to be there was Peter Hahndorf, who ran the TweeNet fan site from Germany. He tells me: "The Field Mice, Brighter and Heavenly were playing for one night in Lausanne on Lake Geneva in Switzerland. That was far away and it took me two days to hitchhike there, and I just made it in time for the first band. I think this was the longest I've travelled for any band. But then I also had a crush on a member in one of the bands." Who that was, Peter doesn't say, which is rather enigmatic of him.

Peter was no stranger to making the effort to see the bands when they had taken the trouble to cross the Channel. "I got word that The Field Mice and The Orchids would play two gigs in Germany in May 1989 after a short tour in Switzerland," he says. "But it was near Frankfurt and in Cologne, quite far from where I lived. Nevertheless, a friend and I drove down to both places and both shows were really great, even though The Field Mice was still a two-piece with concessional support from some Orchids members." He adds: "In the following years, I went to see all Sarah bands when they came to Germany, in some cases, such as Heavenly and The Orchids, I went to gigs all over the country."

Japan

Indie-pop found a big audience in Japan as well as Europe. And after touring in Japan, Keith Girdler of Blueboy told *Grimsby Fishmarket* fanzine: "Japan was incredible. People cried and it was just the most amazing place I've been to. I think we're bigger in Japan than in the UK."

"Best wishes for '93." Blueboy's backstage pass for their Japanese shows.
Courtesy of Paul Stewart.

Blueboy went to Japan for a whirlwind eight days as the guests of Quattro, who were licensed to distribute Sarah in that part of the world. "Our records sell quite well in Japan," says Keith's bandmate Paul Stewart. "We're big in Indonesia as well for some reason." Playing six or seven shows while there, it was a busy few days for the band but it was also an absolutely incredible experience. Apart from anything, the band were treated like bona fide pop stars everywhere they went, which was a far cry from the lack of attention their presence normally aroused in the UK. "We'd get people coming up to us in the street in Tokyo. And yet you go into London and nobody has even heard of you," says Paul. "They were very nice people, we got treated very, very well. We had lovely hotels, lunches and things. We went on the bullet train, the Shinkansen, and we did Osaka and Nagoya. We did a few in-stores and were in some of the magazines. It was a fantasy world really. We went

GOING OUT: ALL OVER THE WORLD

Blueboy doing some Japanese sightseeing and posing.
Top: Courtesy of Blueboy. Bottom: Courtesy of Paul Stewart.

> "We knew so well that this was just a little vignette, it would never be repeated, and it was all the more special because of that."
>
> Gemma Malley, Blueboy

into one store and they were playing our CD in the shop!" Talking about a gig in a packed-out sports stadium, Paul adds: "A thousand people came and they were all singing the words, it wasn't even in their own language. I was terrified. But Keith and Gemma [Malley] did exceptionally well, they sang brilliantly together."

Gemma agrees that it was a wonderful experience: "I'll never forget that trip, it was really quite something. Having done Hull Adelphi-type gigs, and then you get to Japan and there are all these signs saying 'Blueboy'. Just going to Japan was big enough. But you go to Japan and do something like that and it was amazing. It was like being famous but only in one part of the world and only for a week, so it didn't go to anyone's head."

That week of rock'n'rolling in Japan might *briefly* have gone to Gemma's head, though... She took the opportunity to channel her inner Suzi Quattro and wear leather trousers on the tour and even had a go at stage diving, having been egged on by a mischievous Keith. "I got a little bit carried away. But you've got to do it once, right, and it was like being Bono!" she laughs. "The gig was full and we finished the song and then there was a bit of silence and then they clapped. So you'd get no moshing, no shouting, nothing, it was so respectful. But I was trying to get a bit of stuff going and Keith dared me to jump off the stage, he never thought I'd do it." Gemma's antics caused panic for the poor security guys who rushed around to 'rescue' her and return her to her rightful place on the stage. "Japan was where we felt proper rock'n'roll. It was like pretending to be in a famous band. I did keep thinking that, at some point, someone was going to say, 'Excuse me, we didn't mean you, we meant these people standing behind you.'"

More confident in their own shoes were Heavenly, who played all over the world including two trips to Japan. "The first tour was brilliant because we went with Duglas [T Stewart] from The BMX Bandits, so we hung out with him loads, which was really fun," says frontwoman Amelia Fletcher. To save money on that trip, which was organised by Vinyl Japan, Duglas travelled solo and a Japanese backing band was found to make-up the Bandits for him. "But he'd never met this band and they learned all their songs off a live tape of the BMX Bandits which included mistakes. So Duglas then had to learn the mistakes the BMX Bandits had made on the day the tape was made," laughs Amelia, adding that, of course, Duglas was roped in every night to sing Calvin Johnson's part on 'C Is The Heavenly Option'. Teetotal Duglas has very fond memories of the trip and says that Heavenly was the perfect band for him to travel with, given that none of them were wild party animals. "I remember being on the plane with them and playing Travel Scrabble because it was a very long flight. And how incredibly good they were at it," says Duglas. "Amelia had a little notepad out at one point and she was doing mathematical puzzles for fun! I liked it. It felt nice and civilised." Amelia adds: "People in Japan were into getting signatures and we felt like pop stars. People did it a bit in Britain and on the continent but in Japan it was a

Heavenly enjoyed two separate trips to Japan, such was their popularity.
Courtesy of Heavenly.

thing. Everyone was so nice and wanted to have their pictures taken with you."

On their first trip, Heavenly had played in just two cities (Tokyo and Osaka). On their second trip, which was organised by Quattro (which added in Nagoya) and felt like pop royalty. Amelia says: "We played in venues that were kind of in shopping centres. They'd make the third floor of a shopping tower block into a venue and you'd go up in the lift to this gig with other indies, which just seemed really weird, and you'd go in and it would be immaculate but then they would put posters on the wall and deliberately tear them because they knew that's what a rock venue looked like." And these were quite big venues, with space for around 1,000 people. "It genuinely felt like being pop stars."

It seems hard to imagine now but, back in the 1990s, Japanese food wasn't a big thing in the UK and Heavenly promptly became "obsessed with ramen, sushi and seafood generally". Amelia explains: "When we went to Japan and saw all this stuff, it was completely new, it was out of this world. This was a Cathy [Rogers] thing but we ended up doing imitations of seafood on stage for the Japanese fans. This isn't something The Field Mice would have done!" Let's all take a moment to pause and imagine vegan Bobby Wratten doing an impression of raw tuna on stage. OK, back to Amelia: "We were doing prawns and octopuses and jellyfish. We had little actions for all of them and

> 66 We had proper hotels in Japan and we'd turn up and it would say 'This hotel welcomes Heavenly.' We were like 'Woah.'
>
> **Amelia Fletcher, Heavenly**

then the audience had to guess what seafood we were." Ever the professionals, the band learned the Japanese words for the relevant seafood so that they knew if the audience had correctly guessed their culinary charades. Cathy explains that the seafood mimes came about because Amelia needed to find something to do to amuse the audience while Pete Momtchiloff was retuning his guitar and, due to the language barrier, chatting in English clearly wouldn't have worked. Charades was the next obvious step. Cathy adds: "As a result, the show felt more like a performance, albeit a slightly weird performance."

Cathy also gives her own appreciation for just how fortunate they all were to be in Japan: "We were the luckiest band in the world. We all did jobs that we quite liked and when we weren't working, we were doing something else that we totally loved. It wasn't like we earned loads of money from it but for someone to pay for us to go to Japan or America, it was incredible." Although the band was playing shows in the evenings, the days were theirs to spend as they pleased and so she says: "We were just wandering around whichever city it was and were in absolute heaven buying weird things and just being proper big-eyed tourists."

Clare and Matt "gate-crashed" Heavenly's second trip to Japan. Clare says: "We'd signed a deal in Japan so it felt quite important to go out there and spend more time with the people we'd signed a licence deal with." Although the whole party nearly didn't make it because their work permits had been sent to the wrong address. "The record label assured us it would be OK because they'd meet us at the airport with paperwork and explain everything to immigration control," says Matt. "But the flight arrived an hour early because of tailwinds so they weren't there. We genuinely thought we were going to be put on the next flight back to London." Clare adds: "We were all hauled off in pairs for questioning. It was really scary, because you're just off an 11-hour flight and then you're in a little room being quizzed about why you're there. I'd never been outside of Europe at that point."

Matt continues: "The bands were treated like rock stars, it was fantastic. You'd arrive at a hotel and you weren't even allowed to pick your own bags up. People would shoo you away if you tried to lift up your guitars." Sometimes, the level of rule-following was a little unnerving, as Clare explains: "The record company guy told us he'd travelled in Europe with his wife before they'd been married and then he got terribly anxious that we would tell anyone he'd basically slept with his wife before they got married. And I remember this Brazilian intern and us trying to clear up after ourselves from snacks, and him saying 'No, no, you can't do that' and us all going, 'No, we've made this mess, we'll clear it up.' And he's like, 'No, it's my job and I will get sacked if anyone sees you doing it.' So we just sat there."

A third Sarah band who enjoyed a trip to Japan were The Field Mice. They went just after teenage Anne Mari Davis had joined the group at the end of 1990. But Mark Dobson opted to stay behind as his girlfriend was due to give birth around the same time. The trip, organised by Vinyl Japan, was just a few days in Tokyo. "We went over on an Aeroflot plane where Michael [Hiscock]'s seat wasn't even bolted to the floor," Anne Mari says. "Although it sounded so glamorous that we were going on this all-expenses-paid trip to Japan. At this point, I was mostly being pointed in a direction and I'd just walk in that direction. I felt like I was the baby of the group. They were all five or six years older than I was and had all been on tour before." She continues: "We spent a couple of days feeling completely bamboozled by the noise and the chaos of Tokyo, there were loudspeakers coming out of every shop, just blaring music and voices and whatever else. Bobby [Wratten] and I managed to find a lovely Japanese garden that was the antithesis of all the noise and chaos. It was also slightly tricky, with him being vegan and me being vegetarian, trying to find stuff to eat. I remember we went to a supermarket and bought a loaf of bread, which we broke open and it had a sausage in the middle. Everything was just kind of funny but difficult."

The gigs themselves were fascinating, not least because The Field Mice's support band was "an indie, heavy metal type thing. And then we went on stage and the audience was so polite and it really felt like we were going down like a lead balloon, and then we left the stage and left the building and there was a beautiful, orderly queue of 200 people asking for our autographs and actually it was just a cultural difference," explains Anne Mari.

United States

While most Sarah bands didn't have the clout or the cash to get to the US, some had a head start by virtue of being American to start with... but conversely couldn't afford to get to the UK to play with the majority of the British-based Sarah bands.

Aberdeen were based in Los Angeles, California, which meant that when a rare Sarah band ventured over to their neck of the woods, singer Beth Arzy might be asked to keep an eye on them, as was the case when St Christopher headed to Los Angeles. "They did a couple of in-stores and stuff, and I was trying to keep track of them," remembers Beth. "I hung out with Glenn [Melia] while they were there and got massively drunk with him a few times." Glenn recalls: "We've been a few times to various parts of the States and had mostly good times, despite the insane amount of travelling required to play perhaps a 35-minute gig, sometimes to just half a dozen people. I thought the scene would actually be bigger than it was, perhaps not allowing for the enormous scale of the US in general."

Of course, Aberdeen largely played around California, given that's where the band was living. And, on a rare occasion, they would share a bill with a Sarah stablemate who happened to be in town. Although these are not some of Beth's favourite memories. "It was horrible!," she declares of the night Aberdeen opened for Heavenly at the Alligator Lounge in Santa Monica, which was on

> **“** In the UK, we were constantly reminded by the music press of how utterly uncool we were. Whereas when we were in America, we felt cool because we were cool by association."
>
> **Cathy Rogers, Heavenly**

Aberdeen performing at Club Boomerang in San Francisco.
Courtesy of John Girgus.

6 October 1994. "When we played with Heavenly, we were really excited to do it but I just thought that we weren't very good and Heavenly were heavenly. I was dying when we met Amelia Fletcher, I had such a crush on her. Well, everybody did. Nerves really ruined it for me and also I didn't think that we were very good, at least not good enough to be playing with Heavenly. I came away from it and I was just like 'Oh, that was awful.'"

Her former bandmate John Girgus adds: "Heavenly were awesome. I have a ton of respect for Heavenly still, they're a real band. All of them were really cool to us. I remember sitting and having a beer with Mathew [Fletcher] in a booth, and he was an awesome dude. We were a bit odd out in the Sarah world because those guys were all professionals. When I found out Julian Henry [The Hit Parade] was this big PR guy, that was mind blowing. He was a legit cool part of the music industry and indie-pop god. That's when I realised these were all pretty impressive people."

Aberdeen's set that night included a cover of Brighter's 'Half-Hearted'. John explains: "I had stepped on the drum machine mid-song by accident but the nature of the drum machine was such that it would reset the programme to zero if you stopped. It probably wasn't a good show anyway but then we do 'Half Hearted', and we come off the stage and Heavenly were all there, enthusiastically watching us and being supportive and smiling and telling us how great the show was, like genuine smiles, even though I had that self-conscious thing of 'We opened for Heavenly and we blew it, we did the dumbest technical problem ever.' And then they look at us, and Cathy and Amelia go, 'Yeah, we could have done without the Brighter cover!' I think it was awesome they came out and said that."

But at least Heavenly were friendly to Aberdeen and made them feel as if they were pleased to be sharing a bill with them. When Aberdeen opened for Boyracer at Jabberjaw in Los Angeles, the situation was completely different. "We didn't fit on a bill with Heavenly and we didn't fit with Boyracer because all those bands were a bit edgy, a bit Riot Grrrl-y, and we were more shoegazey," says Beth. "I think Matt had said, 'Oh, Boyracer are coming, you should get on this bill and play with them'. And we got in touch with Gary [Dent] who owned Jabberjaw and he said 'Yeah, that's fine'. It wasn't our best gig and I don't think people were there to see us. You looked out and there aren't that many people there but they're just looking back at you with their arms crossed, like 'Nah, this isn't my thing'. So I didn't really come away from that thinking 'Yeah, we smashed it'." John adds: "Gary hated us. Nobody liked us in LA. As far as the cool scene in LA, which was the noise punk stuff, there's nothing worse than being the twee band on the rock bill. I don't remember much about the gig, which leads me to think maybe it was one of our bad gigs." Throw in a perceived lack of friendliness from Boyracer to their labelmates, and it was a tough night to be in Aberdeen. NB: I did ask Boyracer's Stewart Anderson for his thoughts but he has no recollection of the gig.

Heavenly became associated with the Olympia music scene, especially in the early days of Riot Grrrl. The band's Cathy Rogers says: "I can't remember being in the States without thinking of the people that we were with. Like Lois and Small Factory and later Bratmobile and Tiger Trap and Calvin [Johnson]. We hung out with them a lot. There was always a big difference."

Because US licensing laws meant that under-21s were denied entry to venues that served alcohol, some bands started putting gigs on in unusual, and unlicensed, venues because the bands wanted to be as inclusive as possible. "There was this subculture that developed around alternative spaces and it meant this was opened up to younger people and others who might come along," says Cathy. "There was a sense of community with people who were trying to make a stand about doing things slightly differently. Around that time, it felt like anything was possible." It was in this way that Heavenly played a show at a branch of Fantagraphics Warehouse in Seattle that included Dave Grohl and Krist Novoselic from Nirvana in the audience. Bassist Rob Pursey says: "I think it was before Nirvana got really big, so when someone told us the two of them were there, we were like, 'That's nice but who are Nirvana?' Looking back, the fact that we were playing in a Fantagraphics Warehouse to a bunch of Seattle slackers, including two of Nirvana, may have been the coolest thing we ever did, were it not for the fact that we also played gigs with Tiger Trap and Bratmobile, which is obviously cooler."

Also cool was a party Heavenly attended in Olympia, at which Cathy spent the evening chatting away to someone while being blissfully unaware of who he was. "I was always more ignorant than everyone else about famous bands," says Cathy.

> "We definitely lived cooler lives in the US than we did in the UK."
> **Rob Pursey, Heavenly**

While in the US in 1992, Heavenly performed in all sorts of venues, such as the Fantagraphics Warehouse, which meant that fans of all ages werre able to attend.
Arthur S Aubrey, used with the kind permission of Calvin Johnson.

"Amelia said, 'Do you realise who you were just talking to?' And I was like 'No, but he seemed quite nice.'" I will interrupt this anecdote to say that, charmingly, Cathy has again forgotten the name of the nice man in question but I have been reliably informed – and seen photographic evidence to back it up – that it was Eddie Vedder, the frontman with Pearl Jam, who were absolutely huge in 1994. "He was the sort of person that if you knew who he was, you wouldn't talk to him because you wouldn't be so presumptuous," muses Cathy.

Another aspect of Heavenly's adventures in the States that stood out, and was doubtless enabled by Riot Grrrl, was seeing some younger fans in the audience, as demonstrated by gigs such as those at the Fantagraphics Warehouse. "There were quite a few people who would show up at a number of gigs and often go with us to gigs, just for company if there was room in the car. It wasn't a very easy life for the fans, they'd be sleeping on the railway station or whatever but when you're young, you can do it," says guitarist Pete Momtchiloff.

For instance, Lara Cohen was just 16 when she joined Heavenly, Lois and Small Factory for a short tour in 1994, justifying her presence by running the merch stall each night. Lara was one of those fans who was denied entry to a lot of venues with a 21+ door policy so, to circumnavigate this, she very enterprisingly got an after-school job at the Khyber Pass venue in her home city of Philadelphia when she was just 15, offering to do odd jobs. In this way, she not only got to see a lot of bands but also interview them for her fanzine *Runt*. "By that point, I was a little bit of an anomaly," says Lara. "I was this weird, dorky, pretty young teenager who had her parents' house that people could stay at. So people came to know that and I was recognisable."

Small Factory were staying at Lara's parents' house the night she turned 16 "and the next day, we were all sitting outside eating breakfast, and somehow they invited me to go on tour with them and sell t-shirts, and somehow I convinced my parents that this would be OK," says Lara, slightly incredulous. "So that summer, I flew out to the West Coast to do that leg of their tour with them and be their merch girl. It was an amazing experience. I think it was later that summer they were playing East Coast dates with Lois and Heavenly and I just tagged along for a bunch of those dates, too. It was really magical. Even now, looking back, I can't really believe that that happened."

Reflecting on the experience, Lara says: "We slept on people's floors and we travelled in a van together. It was amazing. I also wonder, the bands were in their 20s, early 30s, and, to some extent, I think what they were doing was very kind. I couldn't have been that much fun to hang out with. I was a teenager and a pretty sheltered teenager at that. There was a great deal of kindness in that scene that I want to hold on to."

'Fuck you, no way!'

Riot Grrrl was determinedly not about being a girl but a grrrl. A girl was demure, childlike, feminine, pink. A grrrl is angry, creative, inspired, determined, individual, sassy. With Riot Grrrl, the emphasis was on not waiting for somebody else to do something for you but to get up and do it yourself – whether that was forming a band, starting a fanzine or putting on a gig in your local pub's back room. That was what was empowering – the enabling of all young women to get up and do something. They didn't need to be rich or connected or experienced, they just needed enthusiasm. And the more young women who were getting up and doing something, the stronger the revolution would be. Riot Grrrl saw women claiming their space as performers and fans in the male-dominated music industry, with Bikini Kill famously asserting that the front of the auditorium was female only: "Girls to the front."

Alison Cousens of Brighter enthuses: "The Riot Grrrl stuff really inspired me. I had a flyer from a Huggy Bear gig and it was like, 'If you're female, please come to the front because we want to see female faces, if you're a chap, please go to the back'. And it was speaking the truth about mosh pits and standing in a gig. You always knew it as a female who was interested in music but no one had ever articulated that before. It was fantastic." While Heavenly's Cathy Rogers says: "I found Riot Grrrl brilliant and exciting because it made sense of things. I think I was tolerant when I was younger and had let a lot of things slide, and suddenly they were articulating all of these things that suddenly felt so important and obvious and terrible. And it felt like we needed to do something about the problem, to which Sarah wasn't immune, of 90% of people on stage being male. So I loved it. It was the most exciting way of being educated."

> **❝** I came back and told people about Riot Grrrl but they would have heard about it pretty soon anyway. It was just very, very exciting."
>
> **Amelia Fletcher, Heavenly**

A large element of what constituted the Riot Grrrl ethos was being self-sufficient and not being reliant on major record labels or the mainstream media to get the message out. Instead, Riot Grrrls deliberately worked with independent record labels and independent distributors and they created their own media via fanzines. This was a huge call-back to the DIY attitude of 1970s punk and the fanzine culture of that decade. It was also a kick in the teeth to the growing corporate and capitalist culture of the self-serving 1980s.

Heavenly hanging out in the US.
Courtesy of Sarah Records.

In the early 1990s, Heavenly visited Olympia where they became excited by the nascent Riot Grrrl scene. Amelia Fletcher has been credited many times with bringing the scene over to the UK, something she modestly denies. Regardless, she was still a key person in the US/UK crossover. While in Olympia, she united with Calvin Johnson of Beat Happening who had co-founded K Records with Candice Pedersen. Simon Reynolds and Joy Press wrote in their 1995 book *The Sex Revolts* that Riot Grrrl "went beyond do-it-yourself, making a veritable cult of incompetence … Sloppy, out-of-synch, lo-fi: all of these things signal authenticity." While that seems a little cutting, you can also see where they are coming from. K would go on to enjoy huge acclaim after Nirvana frontman Kurt Cobain declared himself a big fan, something he reinforced by having the label's logo tattooed on his forearm.

Heavenly's guitarist Pete Momtchiloff says: "The Riot Grrrl bands were a big influence on us. Any band when they go abroad, it really broadens your horizons and you realise how much else there is that's going on. A lot of the Riot Grrrl movement was specifically for women to the extent of wanting to have a lot of things being more women-only. But it wasn't exclusionary. Some feminists want to keep things just for women but there was definitely a space in Riot Grrrl for like-minded people to join in the fun. Although we weren't an all-women band, and lots of the Riot Grrrl bands weren't, it was quite welcoming if you were a sympathetic man. It was certainly a very enjoyable thing to be around even though it wasn't about people like me."

Songs didn't need to just be about love and relationships, they could be about feminism and politics and all that that entails. As Heavenly's main songwriter, Amelia says: "Certainly, Heavenly got a lot more credibility when we got more inspired by Riot Grrrl and actually our songs were about love gone wrong. They had always been about love gone wrong but then they became more about love gone wrong with a more overtly feminist stance. And at that point people took it a lot more seriously. Which was galling because, in a way, the song writing didn't change that much but, because we were writing about things that somehow weren't just pop, we were afforded extra credibility."

Amelia was very inspired by Calvin and cites their magnificent duet 'C Is The Heavenly Option' as her favourite track on *Le Jardin de Heavenly*. In August 1991, K would release the Heavenly single 'She Says' on its cult International Pop Underground 7" series and I would later order this direct from Sarah, my mind blown by the magic of an exotic American 7" finding its way to my draughty bedroom in a thatched cottage in Somerset. *Le Jardin de Heavenly* became the first Sarah record to be released in the US thanks to K, and Heavenly's gigs in the States to support the release became the first US gigs by a Sarah band.

"It was Candice who thought of signing Heavenly to K alongside Sarah, so we said 'Yeah, that'll be brilliant'. We absolutely loved Beat Happening so we knew about Calvin anyway," says Amelia. "*Le Jardin de Heavenly* was on K and from that album onwards they were taking us over to the US to do short tours. So we would play with bands that were friends of Calvin's or other K bands. And if we did the West Coast, we hung out in Olympia. It was a brilliant scene that fosters creative thinking and has fostered an amazing music scene over the years. It was remarkable going there because it just seemed like there were billions of people in bands and creative people everywhere you went."

Heavenly's second trip to Olympia coincided with the initial explosion of Riot Grrrl. The *Girl Germs* fanzine had just come out, inventing the term 'Riot Grrrl' as it did so, and "there was all this chatter," says Amelia. "Everyone was really excited about this thing that was happening called Riot Grrrl and there were lots of meetings where people were talking about what it meant. We had no idea what we were walking into." It sounds a little like the initial burst of excitement surrounding the second wave of feminism in the 1970s, when there were consciousness-raising meetings happening in women's living rooms everywhere. "It was all anyone was talking about and it was really, really exciting," continues Amelia. "And then we were hearing the music of those bands and they were great, so I remember coming back to the UK and writing to everybody, particularly the people that were in Avocado Baby because I knew that they would love, it but also telling the people that turned out to be Huggy Bear all about it."

Talking about how Heavenly incorporated some of the Riot Grrrl ideas into their own work, Amelia says: "It was a very deliberate decision to take on board the set of issues and some of the musical aspects of the bands that we were hearing and loving and going to all the gigs of. But to nevertheless stick with what we also thought was Heavenly, so to try and combine those two, with the result that actually no one in Riot Grrrl really thought we were a Riot Grrrl band, even though we played with Bratmobile and all these bands. But they never thought of us as Riot Grrrl and in a way that's been bad for posterity because we're not seen as being part of it. But I think the music we made, by combining those aesthetics and that ethos with what we were doing anyway, was the best stuff that we did and just inherently really good."

It wasn't until the summer of 1992 that Riot Grrrl really took hold in the UK, largely thanks to Amelia whether she likes to take the credit or not. In 1994, I interviewed her over the phone for my fanzine *Arketino*. I asked her if she was a Riot Grrrl: "At heart, yes." Then, I asked if Heavenly were a Riot Grrrl band: "No, because certain male members aren't completely behind the idea of Riot Grrrl. If Heavenly could define what was meant by Riot Grrrl then they would be through and through. We feel punk at heart but we know according to everyone's definition of punk we aren't." Lastly, I asked if she was sick of talking about Riot Grrrl: "Well, yes. When it first started it was really exciting but after about two months it felt like you were at the start of something and it was going to get bigger and bigger. Everyone was going round in circles saying all the same things."

Alongside Riot Grrrl, something else was bubbling up in the pop charts. In 1993, Jacqui Blake and Carrie Askew burst out of Plumstead in south-east London with their bubble-gum punk band Shampoo, which soon included Action Painting!'s Lee Christopher on bass. But were they a novelty act or something more interesting? I'd argue for the latter. Looking back to his time with Shampoo, Lee notes: "I played bass considerably worse than I did the guitar, difficult to imagine I know. I had little interest in the instrument; my hands weren't getting bigger and neither was my enthusiasm to learn. I cribbed the failsafe root notes, star jumped on an open E and managed a yawning pout but it paid off… I went to foreign countries, pulled out a decaying tooth on live French television while miming a three-note riff to a soon-to-be hit single. Met Malcolm McLaren and Kylie Minogue, sat in Tokyo snow, got drunk next to a teetotal Adam Ant, sniffed Robert Palmer's hair and thoroughly enjoyed the ride, even when Blur played the cockney piano, and especially when Supergrass got stuffed in the trouser press."

Lee's Sarah labelmates Heavenly bumped into Shampoo in 1994 when both bands were over in Tokyo. Shampoo had just released 'Trouble' and were doing a signing in Tower Records, which Heavenly attended. "We were psyched," Mathew Fletcher told a fanzine writer. "Me and Amelia took notes while Pete learned the Japanese for 'I'm Shampoo's uncle' and stood at the back shouting it. We burst their bubble alright." Reader, I fact checked this with Pete and, brilliantly, he confirms it is true.

Lee was also in Tokyo on that trip and recalls "buying TV shaped rucksacks, Nintendo Gameboys and Superlovers watches, and experiencing the sheer horror of performing hour-long sets in front of people that looked like they enjoyed it. As much as I loved being paid good money to go to countries I would never have gone to, I did always feel like I was lost. I wanted to be with the right gang."

The UK's overlooked Riot Grrrl label

When people look back at the early years of Riot Grrrl, they tend not to think of Sarah – but they really should. "I still maintain that your fanzines, *Sunstroke* and *Lemonade*, should be spoken of in the Riot Grrrl lineage because they're two years before what we think of as the first Riot Grrrl fanzines over in the States," Matt says to Clare during one of our conversations for this book. And he's right. Clare wrote those early Sarah fanzines around 1988, long before Riot Grrrl exploded and those fanzines are brimming with feminist rage. "I found all the boys lusting away over girls in flowery dresses in their fanzines really tedious," says Clare. "It was like they thought the role of girls in the scene was just to look cute, not to participate and to be an active part of things. But somehow, because they weren't macho about it, they thought it wasn't sexist or something. It really angered me."

Matt continues: "Whenever *Girl Germs* or any of the other Riot Grrrl fanzines are mentioned, Clare's never get mentioned at all. It always seems it's the American ones. It's always about Bikini Kill and those bands. But I would still maintain that the best Riot Grrrl records are the two Heavenly singles and Huggy Bear's 'Her Jazz'." He adds: "The cover sheet we did with Sarah 70 [Blueboy] was a great little manifesto, if I say so myself. You tend to forget we even did it, it just came wrapped around the other three fanzines and the flexi disc, but that's very much us being influenced by Riot Grrrl and I think that still stands up. I wish we'd done more things like that because I think that's almost what Sarah should be remembered for. That's almost the essence of what we were trying to do."

> ❝'Lemonade' was certainly embryonic, but then nothing like it had ever been done before I don't think, or not that I'd seen. First Riot Grrrl fanzine? ... I certainly hope things have moved on. The last five years would seem pretty pointless if not."
>
> **Letter from Clare to me, autumn 1994**

Similarly, Sarah fan Jyoti Mishra of White Town observes: "I do think Sarah created the preconditions for our Riot Grrrl scene. A lot of the people I knew who were Sarah kids went straight into Riot Grrrl, they already knew where they were politically and then here comes this thing where this scene is good, but how about girls playing in bands? How about us not just standing at the back holding our boyfriends' coats? That would be nice. How about saying girls come to the front for a gig? I don't think that switch to Riot Grrrl could have happened without Sarah because Sarah was the blueprint in this country. Fair enough, in Washington it was Kill Rock Stars or whoever, but we didn't have Kill Rock Stars, we had Sarah. As if Creation cared about politics! Sarah made it OK to say you were a revolutionary and not get laughed at. If you look at a lot of the later Riot Grrrl fanzines, a lot of those are straight Sarah descendants." While music journalist Pete Paphides admits: "I was slow to realise that there might've been a connection between the Riot Grrrl bands and the Sarah bands. I think maybe I took my eye off the ball. I didn't realise it was probably a genealogical musical connection between the two."

Huggy Bear and The Word

In the early 1990s, *Melody Maker*'s Jerry Thackray was a regular visitor to the US, where he was reporting from Olympia on the thriving Grunge scene for the British music press. Hopping back and forth across the Atlantic, he would bring news over to not only his *Melody Maker* readers but also his friends such as his flatmates Jon Slade and Jo Johnson. Jon and Jo would form Huggy Bear, one of the leading bands of the Riot Grrrl movement on this side of the Atlantic.

To fully show his support for Riot Grrrl, Jerry produced a hastily written fanzine that was sent free of charge to anyone who sent him a stamped addressed envelope. This I promptly did and received a collection of photocopied and unfolded A4 sheets, stapled in the top-left corner. The fanzine was a paean to Huggy Bear and their manifesto. My diary noted on 26 October 1992: "I got two letters today. One from Matt [Johnson] from The Fat Tulips, and a photocopied fanzine thing, which was the second part of an interview with Huggy Bear in *Melody Maker*. Riot Grrrl and all that – all I can grasp is [Jerry Thackray] and Sally Margaret Joy think Riot Grrrl is vitally necessary, and it's about girls in rock standing up for themselves."

Huggy Bear's original bassist was Heavenly's Mathew Fletcher, who quit after two gigs due to the band's refusal to rehearse a song more than once, and Karen Hill took over. "I'd known Chris Rowley in Huggy Bear for years, since I was at school," says Mathew's sister Amelia Fletcher. "And some of the other people in that band, like Jon and Jo, I'd known since Talulah Gosh. And they were also really good mates of Mathew's. But having been in Heavenly the person who never wanted to practise a song more than once, when he was in Huggy Bear and they wouldn't practise a song more than once it was driving him mad."

> ❝ 'Twas indeed the young Ms Fletcher on Huggy Bear backing vox – more to the point, it was also Heavenly's guitar amp. Did you know Mathew used to play bass for Huggy Bear in their early days? Not a lot of people do. Or that two of Huggy Bear share a flat with the deputy editor of *Melody Maker*? I'm a terrible gossip."
> **Letter from Matt to me, February 1993**

Huggy Bear were increasingly influenced by the Olympia imports the band were snapping up in Covent Garden's Rough Trade and adapted their style to match this new American sound. And, in a bid to impress Wiiija Records' boss Gary Walker, Huggy Bear made a demo they knew would be to his taste. Between recording sessions for John Peel and securing support slots with Sonic Youth, Huggy Bear were rapidly growing in reputation. And, by October 1992, the band had released two singles on Wiiija. At the same time, there was an uprising in female-led independent music and writing. For instance, there was a growth of tape labels such as the Slampt Underground Organisation (led by Rachel Holborow and Pete Dale), and fanzines such as *My Little Fanzine* and *Girlpride*. In addition, bands including Pussycat Trash,

Huggy Bear performing at the Jericho Taven, 26 November 1992.
Wendy Stone.

Linus and Mambo Taxi were appearing on the circuit, and Riot Grrrl meetings were taking place in UK cities as far flung as Leeds, Portsmouth and London. Riot Grrrl had definitely arrived in the UK.

On 14 February 1993, Huggy Bear performed 'Her Jazz' live on Channel 4's post-pub TV show *The Word*. The episode became infamous. Although the song itself was performed without any drama, the band and their supporters began a vociferous protest about host Terry Christian's interview with American glamour models the Barbie Twins immediately after their song. The result was that *The Word* was taken off air mid-broadcast while Huggy Bear and the other protestors were ejected from the building. Consequently, Huggy Bear were projected to mainstream attention and the following week's *Melody Maker* ran with a screenshot of frontwoman Niki Elliot on the cover and an in-depth report from Sally Margaret Joy, who had been at the studio.

But look closely, and who's that singing backing vocals for Huggy Bear on *The Word*? Why, it's Heavenly's Amelia Fletcher. During an interview I did with her in 1994, Amelia told me how it all came to pass: "We've known Huggy Bear for a very long time and their first two gigs were supporting Heavenly. They rang up the day before they were on *The Word* saying, 'You couldn't bring us your equipment to play through on *The Word*?' because they used to borrow our equipment." Expanding on what happened when talking to me for this book, Amelia says: "Although Huggy Bear were excellently entertaining insurrectionaries, they were a bit hopeless in that they didn't have any equipment or any ability to drive or much organisational quality. So they got this gig on *The Word*, goodness knows how. They were asked to do it but they didn't have any equipment or any way of getting equipment there, and it was a place you're meant to play live. So they rang me up and asked if I was willing to drive all of Heavenly's equipment down to *The Word* studio so they could then use our equipment to play."

Being the obliging sort, Amelia agreed, and she and brother Mathew loaded up the car, drove everything down to London for a midday soundcheck and set the equipment up. "I think they felt a bit guilty that I was sat there doing nothing, so they said 'Do you want to sing?' and I was 'Yeah, alright'. I knew the song well enough, 'Boy, girl, revolution', so that's what we did. They possibly asked Mathew as well and he went 'No', I don't even remember. It was just completely random on the day. My brother was one of the people heckling on the night and got chucked out. I was mostly laughing so I didn't get chucked out." Amelia adds: "Because *The Word* was run by young people, they hadn't thought about security. They hadn't dreamed that anything like this might happen."

Rob Pursey remembers being at home and watching it unfurl on the TV. "It was brilliant," he says. "It was one of those shows that everyone watched. It was the *Loaded* era. It was where alternative culture turned into populist shit, that's what was going on, it was dismal. But *The Word* always had good bands so you'd tend to watch it. Obviously, I knew that Amelia and Mathew were going to be there and it was kind of exciting. At the time it looked like a bunch of unruly, unmusical kids who shouldn't have been there being put in their place by some professionals but now you think, 'This is a monstrous, sexist, gender stereotyping piece of shit with some people who are trying to tell the truth who get kicked out'. It's aged pretty well I think."

*****

THESE THINGS HAPPENED:
Beth Arzy, Aberdeen
"I thought Matt and Clare were funny little English people, very quaint and very English in their expressions. And also really scholastic. I thought they were like the king and queen of the indie scene, they were smart and charming and had all this power and knew all these bands, and I was like 'Oh my god, they know Amelia Fletcher, they must be really, really cool.'"

Chapter 17

Even As We Sleep

Music journalist Jerry Thackray has joked that, to warrant inclusion on the *NME*'s C86 compilation, a band first needed to have slept on his floor. And in recognition of the time-honoured tradition of pop stars kipping uncomfortably, this chapter is dedicated to all the weird and wonderful places our heroes slept in those halcyon days of true independent music.

It is hard to imagine now, in a world steeped in stranger danger and grisly news headlines buzzed to our fingertips every 10 seconds, that, in the olden days, it was perfectly reasonable to rock up at the front door of someone you'd once bought a mail-order fanzine from and ask to sleep on their floor that night because you were in their town seeing a tiny band. And that they would say 'yes'. Of course, stranger danger and grisly news headlines were as much a thing in the 1980s as they are now but perhaps people were ever so slightly less paranoid, due to the fact news was that bit slower to reach us? I don't know, I can only guess. But I do recall an evening around 1990 when my older brother brought home a fanzine writer called Marcus-from-Sweden who wanted to stay the night. Because why not?

Remember, before the internet, you'd often have no hope of finding a B&B unless you rang the local tourist information office and asked them to hook you up with a place that had a vacant room that night. Budget hotel chains such as Travelodge and Premier Inn were founded in 1985 and 1987 respectively but it would be a few decades before they reached the ubiquitous level that they have these days. So what follows is a trip down Memory Foam Lane to relive some of the strange places that people bedded down in the name of indie-pop.

Sometimes, of course, the solution to where you were going to sleep was simply not to go to sleep at all, which was an option adopted by some of The Field Mice. "I never felt vulnerable because I was always there with my metaphorical older brothers," says the band's Anne Mari Davies, in response to my question about how it felt to often be the lone woman on a tour. "But I remember *not* going to bed more than anything. Bobby [Wratten] found it quite

> 66 Blueboy: Often described as the sort of band you could take home to meet your mother and we'd be much obliged if any of you could put this to the test, as we're a bit pushed for space at our place."
>
> **From the running order for the Sarah Christmas Party 1993**

hard to settle anywhere that wasn't his own house, so he quite often would go for a walk and I didn't like leaving him to go for a walk on his own. So we would just walk all night. We walked all around a lake in Switzerland one night. We just didn't go to bed. I was totally exhausted."

Bobby explains: "Neither of us could sleep, so we just decided to head off into the night. I remember looking across the lake and seeing the lights on the far shore shining. You take such magical moments for granted in the sense that you just think this is what life is meant to be like, night-time in a foreign city. We're in this dreamlike situation while most people are tucked up in bed. I've been back to Lake Geneva a couple of times in recent years and it was strange thinking of my younger self and that night-time walk with Anne Mari. I also remember some nocturnal wanderings in Tokyo which now seems incredible. We were so lucky to be granted such moments. Wandering past shops with speakers playing strange haunting mysterious sounds out into the street. Almost eerie. We really knew we were in a place like no place we'd ever been."

Sleeping on a stranger's floor

Sarah obsessive – and, later, Sarah recording artiste – Tim Chipping sums it up best when he explains that, for most fans growing up in small and suburban towns, there was a fear of having missed out. If you spent your formative years in the middle of nowhere, you had to travel to see the bands you wanted to see and that wasn't always possible when you had school in the morning. So once he moved to London, Tim was determined to make up for lost time. "Everyone else was happy seeing The Field Mice once," he says, "they didn't need to go and see them in Paris as well as London. But I would go to three or four gigs a week, even going overseas. I could afford it by not spending money on anything else."

He adds: "In those days it was easy. There were various places you could treat like London. So you could get the Oxford Tube [a bus that still shuttles between London and Oxford, although it's now rather more expensive] for £1 on a student card, so any Sarah gig in Oxford might as well be in London. Harlow Square [a venue in Essex] was on the commuter belt and, if you were fast enough, you could see the end of the gig, run across the field and get the last train back to London. But it was really scary as there was nowhere to stay in Harlow if you mistimed it." Tim continues: "It was a sort of unwritten agreement that, because we were a part of this culture, we could travel and stay at each other's places. Everyone was poor. We were all eating basic food and travelling the cheapest way, everyone was looking out for each other. It was odd how quickly we all knew each other. A lot of the German guys who ran their own labels used to just turn up and we'd say, 'Oh, of course you can stay, that's perfectly normal'!"

> **"** Oh, of course you can stay, that's perfectly normal!"
>
> **Tim Chipping, recalling the relaxed attitude to having strangers to stay**

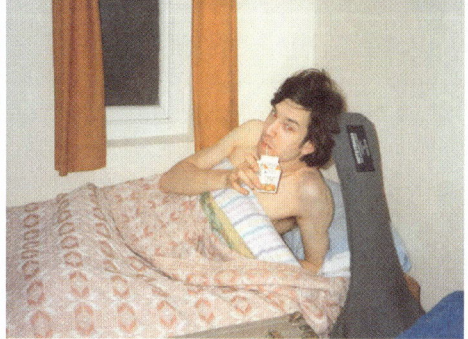

Left: A bedroom/storeroom at 46 Upper Belgrave Road. **Right:** The Rosaries stayed with Clare and Matt at Upper Belgrave Road the night before the band's recording session. Here we have Jonny (pictured top) and Robert (pictured bottom) rubbing the sleep from their eyes.

Left: Courtesy of Sarah Records. Right: Jonny James.

Tim's Shelley bandmate Dickon Edwards agrees that "part of the whole Sarah scene was about being so devoted that you'd happily crash on a floor or sofa just to see one of the gigs." Tim adds: "When I started wanting to go to gigs all the time, I would write to people I'd bought fanzines from and say I was coming to Leeds to see Blueboy and could I stay on their sofa? And because we liked Sarah, we would stay at each other's places. The bands did as well. I had Mary [Wyer, Even As We Speak] living on my floor. To save money, she slept on a rolled mat on the horrible floor in my flat." Mary insists this was just for one night but, whatever, a horrible floor is a horrible floor whether for one night or 100 nights.

Sue Freeman of 14 Iced Bears recalls an audience member putting the band up after a gig in Newcastle and it being a decidedly unique affair. "I was never one for taking drugs but it was like a psychedelic experience," says Sue. "This guy had constructed some kind of surreal entrance to his flat that was like a tunnel and the whole flat was designed like a psychedelic landscape. I asked Rob [Sekula] recently whether I imagined it or if it really happened and he said it really happened. It was bizarre."

Clare and Matt would let people stay with them at their Bristol home with an enormous degree of generosity and equanimity. Tim recalls: "They started letting me stay in their house when I would go to gigs in Bristol. That was nuts! That a record label that was internationally famous would just let people stay in their house! But that's how they got around when they were going to gigs, so it created a culture."

It's hard to imagine many other record label co-owners letting you kip on their floor. Do you think Richard Branson did that while managing Virgin's global empire? It seems unlikely. "Quite a lot of people stayed with us, some of whom we knew, some of whom we didn't," says Matt. "There was a time that The Orchids and The Sweetest Ache stayed with us in No 45, which was quite crowded, and Brighter as well. All at once. But that flat had two decent-sized bedrooms as well as a decent-sized living room. We had a big sofa bed and I think we had four Orchids sleeping on that head to toe. Dickon was there as well."

Harvey Williams used to get the train up to Bristol from Penzance to go to gigs at the EEC Punk Rock Mountain and occasionally had to sleep in the waiting room at Temple Meads afterwards, having missed the last train home. Once he progressed to being signed to Sarah as Another Sunny Day, he upgraded to Clare and Matt's floor when he was in town. The studio flat at 46 Upper Belgrave Road "was an interesting shape," says Harvey. "It had a kitchen at one end with no windows and a long corridor hallway, and Matt and Clare's room was at the back and they had this incredible view of the whole expanse of Bristol because they were at the top of a hill. Somehow they ran a record label from this place."

After one Sarah party in Bristol, Action Painting! slept on the kitchen floor of the Gwilliam Street house, although singer Andy Hitchcock says there wasn't a lot of sleeping going on. "And in the morning, Clare came downstairs at the crack of dawn. She was like Barbara from [1970s' TV sitcom] *The Good Life*, going out into the garden and watering all the plants and the allotment, they were growing their own vegetables. Not very rock'n'roll but I always remember that. The sun had come up and there she was watering the plants and we hadn't even gone to bed yet."

After sleeping at Amelia Fletcher and Pete Momtchiloff's Heavenly house, many people commented on how grown-up the couple's Oxford home was compared to most of the places they stayed. Dickon Edwards says: "I did sleep in Amelia's Oxford house a few times, along with members of Comet Gain. We'd all watch Pastels videos in the morning. It was wonderful really, as this was how you'd find out about music and further gigs. I heard Nico's album *Chelsea Girl* for the first time at Amelia's house. It was the only way to be part of the network. I honestly don't think that world would have been the same if the internet had existed."

The Sweetest Ache band members were also guests on Amelia and Pete's accommodating floor, as manager Marc Leverton recalls: "We were like, 'This is a proper grown-up house'. They had plants and it was lovely. We were 18 and 19 and not at that stage of life." I love how having plants is the barometer of loveliness. The band's Simon Court tells me: "The place that I tend to bang on about as a claim to fame is I slept on Amelia Fletcher's floor in Oxford. It wasn't a particularly comfortable night but I was happy to be there. I've slept in hallways, doorways, cars and vans but that's the one that really sticks in my mind." Meanwhile Rocker from The Flatmates remembers popping round to Amelia and Pete's for a cup of tea whenever he was in Oxford seeing a band. It seems hard to imagine Amelia and Pete managing to do anything else except offer hospitality to passing musicians, yet somehow they also managed to have a popular band of their own and full-time jobs.

These days, Amelia is amazed that people were so impressed with the house, while Heavenly bassist Rob Pursey cautions: "I lived on the same street as Amelia and Pete, and all I'd say is those people were wise not to look in the kitchen too closely." Amelia adds: "It wasn't as clean as they thought but it was maybe cleaner than the average indie house. It was Pete and my house, and we slept upstairs but we had an open plan downstairs, the front and back rooms were knocked together. We deliberately got a sofa bed and it was designed for people to be able to come and stay because we knew that would be fun to do that. I guess people did get treated nicely and we stayed up drinking with them and then left them to it, and made them coffee in the morning."

Pete remembers a time when German band The Bartlebees was playing in Oxford and ended up at their house. Well, sort of. "We said, as a joke, 'Oh, you can sleep in the shed if you want' because there was a shed at the bottom of the garden with electricity in it. And they trooped off there and said, 'Oh this is fine, we'll sleep here!' It did have a carpet, I hasten to add. That was what bands had to do. They were willing to just take their chances." Not everyone got sent to the shed by Pete, though. Chris Quinn, drummer with The Orchids, recalls fondly that when they stayed over: "At the end of the evening, Pete left a bottle of whisky in the middle of the table and said 'Have a good night lads' and went to bed. That's a good memory."

But Amelia and Pete weren't the only ones with a grown-up house, as Even As We Speak's Mary Wyer explains: "One place we slept that was quite interesting was Jyoti [Mishra]'s place. His house was very clean and comfortable." Her bandmate Julian Knowles agrees: "It was very civilised. He had Super 8 film clips of his family, home movies, and he was editing them with sticky tape, and he got a Super 8 projector and put it on the wall of his house, and was playing us all these videos that he was making. Which was fantastic because it was a whole window into another world. Sometimes the fans were making their own music as well. And Jyoti obviously was. It reminds you that a lot of people who are into music also make it, which is fantastic."

As a coda to all this, The Sea Urchins' frontman James Roberts had a blast from the past during a recent break by the sea in Margate. After browsing in a second-hand clothes shop, he went to the counter to buy a shirt and the guy at the till looked at him curiously and asked: "Were you in The Sea Urchins?" After hesitantly confirming that he had been, James was stunned to discover that, many decades ago, he and the other Urchins had slept on this guy's floor after asking from the stage if someone could put them up for the night. A Sarah fan never forgets.

WISHING YOU WERE SLEEPING ON A STRANGER'S FLOOR

While all of that sums up the dedication to the cause, we don't yet have a sense of the truly weird and uncomfortable places people slept. Staying on someone's floor was an absolute luxury compared to, say, bedding down at a train station, as Shelley's Dickon Edwards says: "I think for me, the most extreme place was sleeping on the floor of train stations in London having missed the last train back to Ipswich or Bristol." If Dickon had glanced up from his makeshift bed, he might have noticed Julian Henry of The Hit Parade also camping out on the concourse. "I slept at Euston train station," says Julian. "It was late, after watching a band, I missed the last train home. I had nowhere else to go. I did it a few times. It helped level me out as a person."

Of course, a train station floor was no good for a record label bigwig, which is why Matt ended up sleeping on a bench at Manchester Airport one night, despite not having a plane to catch. Matt had gone to Preston to see Heavenly and run the merchandise stall ("The guy from the local record shop told me off for doing it because it meant people wouldn't buy the records in the shop, which seemed a bit unreasonable"), and then realised he had nowhere to sleep. With another gig to get to the next night, Matt decided to take a train to the airport and bed down on a comfy bench in the departure lounge. Which is actually a pretty sensible plan the more you think about it.

"There's a picture of me at a Blueboy/Heavenly gig in Harlow and you can clearly see on the merchandise stall there's a poster saying, 'Can anybody give me a lift back to Epping Station afterwards?' and luckily somebody did," says Matt. "But if they hadn't, I'm not quite sure what I'd have done. On the same Heavenly tour, I hitched up to Birmingham or somewhere and had this naïve idea I could find an all-night café after the gig. But in the end, Rob [Pursey] and Cathy [Rogers] took pity on me and drove me back to Bristol. To my shame, I fell asleep in the back of the car and only woke up as they were pulling into Gwilliam Street."

Similarly, the bands put up with a lot to make the gigs happen in the first place. "We stayed in some really grim places in Germany," recalls Heavenly's Amelia Fletcher with a shudder. "The worst places are the official places above venues, because they've all been stayed in by really hideous people before you." She recounts staying somewhere in Germany straight after the UK Subs had been there and says that the veteran punks had plastered their band name all over the walls and "destroyed the toilet. It was absolutely hideous," she says. Her bandmate Rob Pursey didn't think much of German hospitality back then either and, given that most of Heavenly were vegetarians, they struggled to get a decent breakfast the next day: "We had breakfast in the same room where the gig had happened the night before, so it smelled of beer and sick. As Germans, they didn't really do vegetarianism at the time, so breakfast was a banana and a hard-boiled egg. A combination of the smell of the egg and banana and the room… it was disgusting."

The Hull Adelphi was an unusual venue from the get-go, being a converted end of terrace, three-bedroom Victorian house. Having been a social club of one kind or another since 1923, it opened as a live music venue in 1984 and is still functioning as such today. The building narrowly escaped a bomb during World War Two but the three adjacent houses were hit and the venue's small car park occupies the levelled bombsite. As unique a music venue as the Hull Adelphi undoubtedly is, it does not make for the cosiest night's sleep, as Harvey Williams, who stayed there after a Blueboy gig, can attest: "The Hull Adelphi is one of those venues that's always been there. It was a fantastic venue but it was quite a bleak place. I don't know where we expected to sleep whenever we turned up at these venues. I think we'd hope that the promoter would have something sorted out or we could find a friend who had floor space. But this night in Hull, for some reason we ended up sleeping upstairs at the venue. I think there were mattresses and sleeping bags on the floor. Venues are stinky places. It was no fun but it was better than sleeping in the car or having to shell out £20 for a B&B, for god's sake!"

But you don't have to just take Harvey's word for it. "I remember Keith [Girdler] going into the bathroom," says Blueboy guitarist Paul Stewart. "He opened the door and beckoned me over. I went in, he lifted up this sponge that was on the side of the bath, and we're talking about the sort of sponge you do the washing-up with, and he lifted it up and it was only clean under the sponge. It was not nice there. I did not sleep well that night. It was revolting." After telling me this horror story, Paul shudders: "I need to have a shower now." All his bandmate Gemma Malley can be persuaded to say on the matter is: "I think I've blocked it from my mind."

> **"** I slept in a motorway arcade game in a service station after hitching back from somewhere once. One of those games you sit in to drive."
>
> **Chris Quinn, The Orchids**

We even have photographic evidence of Even As We Speak upstairs at the Hull Adelphi, including a picture of guitarist Julian Knowles flat on his back on one of the beds, fully clothed, with his boots on his stomach and looking very much as if he was trying not to touch anything. Which, in all fairness, was probably exactly what he was doing. "It was rancid," laughs Julian. "It had cassettes all over the floor and hadn't been cleaned for years. That's a good example of the kind of accommodation you'd get." He turns to singer Mary Wyer and says with a shiver: "Remember the floor…" The kind of floor you wouldn't even want to put your boots on, evidently.

Heavenly toured in America a fair amount, especially once they got close to the K Records crew and the Riot Grrrl scene, and that involved a lot of staying on people's floors. "We were pretty lucky, says the band's Amelia Fletcher. "People were nice but you just do not sleep that well. And particularly in America, you're driving really long ways the next day so you'll stay up partying until 3am, then sleep on a hard floor for three hours and not really get any sleep, then you'll try and have a shower but there'll be someone in the shower or you won't be able to work the shower, and

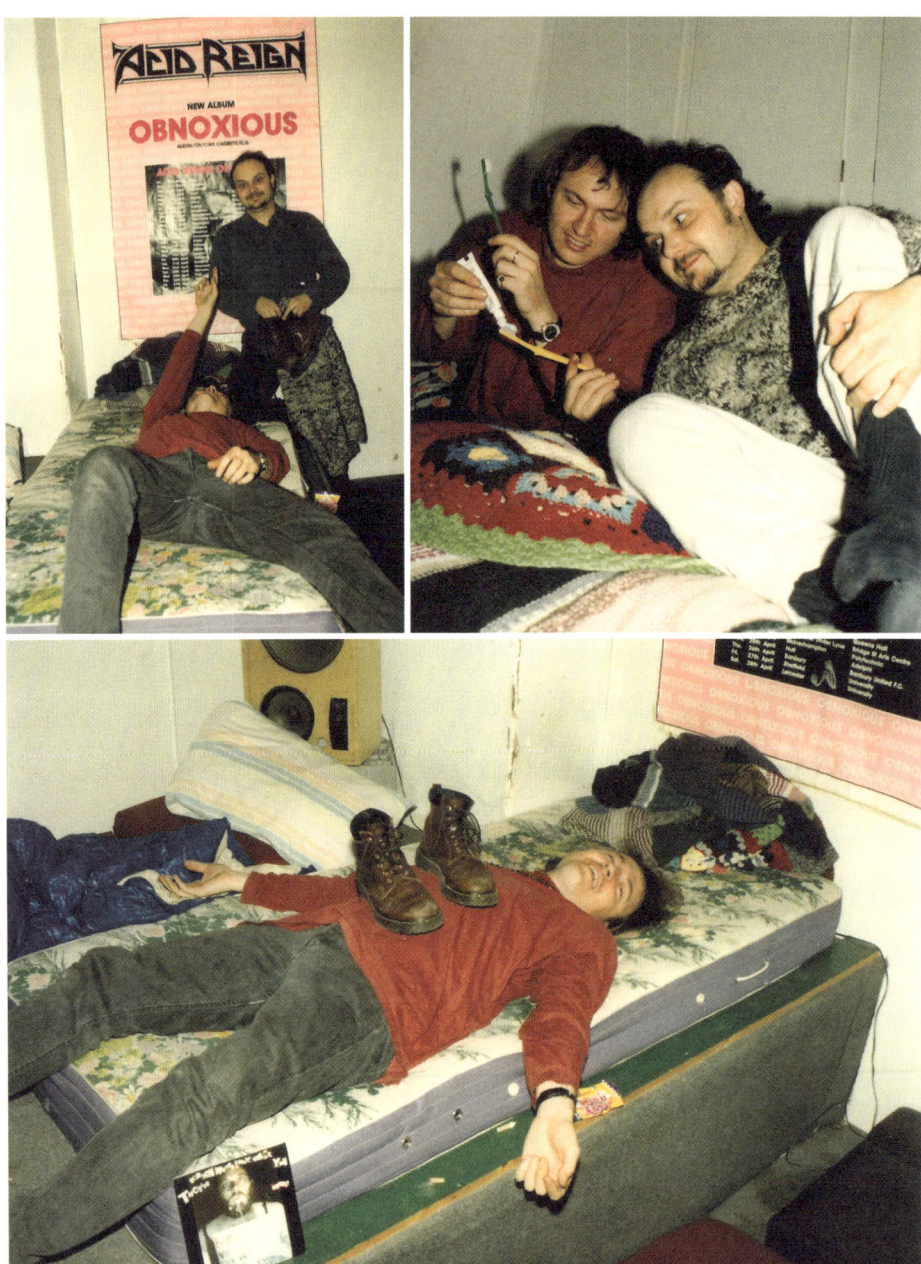

"It was rancid," Julian Knowles of Even As We Speak sums up the accomodation at the Hull Adelphi. Julian and bandmate Rob Irwin tried to maintain standards of personal hygiene, despite everything.
Even As We Speak.

then you'll get back into your car and drive eight hours to the next gig."

Heavenly crammed a lot into their American tours because the band was never over there for very long, having to squeeze the tour in during annual leave from work or during university breaks. This meant the band might do an afternoon gig in a comic shop before an evening gig at a music venue, and repeat this every day for eight to 10 days. "That was pretty knackering," admits Amelia. "Every time we came back from America, we would completely flake out and say we were never doing that again. It was proper work."

Although Clare and Matt were the co-founders of an internationally popular record label, that didn't mean they were lording it about in five-star hotel suites any more than the bands were. One night in August 1989, The Field Mice played in the relatively small mill town of Rawtenstall 15 miles north of Manchester. A fan had organised the gig in a local pub and, because nothing much had ever happened there before, the entire town turned out to see this pop band. Having hitchhiked their way up to Rawtenstall from Bristol to save money, Clare and Matt had hoped somebody would find some floor space for them but nothing was forthcoming so, while the band headed back to someone's house to sleep, "we just slept on the hillside behind the venue". Clare expands: "It was the longest night of my life. We had one sleeping bag. And someone had a very bad cough in one of the houses. It must have been summer or we wouldn't have done it. But it's always much colder than you think if you sleep outside. I think we were just embarrassed that we had nowhere to go, so I don't think the bands ever knew that we slept on the hillside. I guess they assumed we'd made arrangements." The next morning, the cold and tired duo took a bus into Manchester city centre to warm up with a vegetarian fry-up in a cafe and, as Matt recounted that story to me, Clare muttered dryly: "If we'd taken sandwiches, we could have paid to stay the night somewhere." The glamour of the music business.

> "The deal was you played the gig, then you stayed in this fucking horrible room upstairs, and then in the morning you'd come down and have breakfast."
>
> **Rob Pursey, Heavenly**

Side note: fanzine writer Chris Tighe was one of the 20 or so people who made up the audience at the Rawtenstall gig. One of his friends had the big house in Rawtenstall where everyone stayed. "If only we'd known Matt and Clare had nowhere to stay, because we had plenty of room for them," says Chris. Nobody tell Clare and Matt, please. There's a possibility they're still picking the slugs off that sleeping bag.

While recording at the White House in Weston-super-Mare, The Sweetest Ache also slept outside although, unlike their label bosses, at least they had a canvas roof. "Some of the boys could snore really badly, so we put tents up in the back garden," says guitarist Stuart Vincent. "It was quite good fun at the time." The White House was a popular recording studio for Sarah bands and Blueboy drummer Martin Rose was clearly a make-do-and-mend kind of guy, as he recalls improvising a bed in the studio after a session: "I used to bring my sleeping bag, take the pillow out of the bass

Top: The Sweetest Ache were hardy souls who were happy to bunk down on a studio floor if required.
Bottom: Sometimes kipping in a van was a must. To illustrate a band in a van, here we have Clare en route to Glasgow with The Field Mice and a bunch of Loch Ness Monsters.

Top: Courtesy of Simon Court. Bottom: Mark Dobson.

drum and just sleep behind the drums in the studio. There were times when there were seven or eight of us in a really small room, sleeping and drinking. When you look back, it was absolutely brilliant."

After a night out in Birmingham seeing The Sea Urchins, Scott Purnell of Secret Shine and Matthew Evans of Tramway ended up missing the last coach back to Bristol, so they did what anyone would do… they tried to sleep in the photobooth at Birmingham Coach Station. "We got moved on really quickly by the police," sighs Scott, who only wanted to catch a few zeds. "So we walked around Birmingham for a bit and then we went into the coach station, and I think the earliest coach back to Bristol was about 6am, so we ended up sleeping on a bench. And ironically, even though it was so uncomfortable and cold, we ended up oversleeping and by the time we'd woken up, there was a massive queue for our bus, even though we'd been first in the queue at 3am." Reader, relax, they made it on to that bus and got home fine.

> "We ended up covered in slugs by the morning."
> **Matt**

Sleeping in the tour van is a rite of passage but do remember that we're not talking about the kind of luxurious multi-level coaches that chart-topping pop bands tour in, we're talking about a rented Transit with no cushioning. And kipping in a van like that must have been particularly galling when you knew there was a comfortable bed waiting for you, if only you had a sober driver to get you to it. "I remember being in Manchester at the Swinging Sporran," says Stuart Vincent of The Sweetest Ache. "It was part of the *Jaguar* tour and my friend Bob had agreed to drive the van for the two weeks." Someone had offered the boys a bed after the gig, but it was a bit of a drive from the venue and so Stuart was rather surprised when he saw Bob sitting at the bar with a pint in his hand. "I'll just have one beer now and call it a day," promised Bob, shortly before necking several more and rapidly rendering himself incapable of driving. In response to Stuart asking what was going on, Bob wailed: "I can't take it anymore! I've gone nine nights without drinking, I'm going to get smashed tonight and there's nothing you can do about it." With nobody else able to drive, there was nothing for it but to "park up in some ropey area of Manchester, in the back of a van with no seats, just smelly socks and the six of us all piled in the back of the van because the driver couldn't go another night without a beer. I couldn't blame Bob for that, though," says Stuart generously.

Another musician who had his share of van nights was Rocker, the drummer with The Flatmates. "We only did one tour in Europe when I was still in the band, which was in Holland, but you got treated so much better, you got fed *and* paid!" he says. "I remember sleeping on the floor of a nightclub, having to wait until the nightclub ended before we could kip. I've often slept out in the van as well, because you've got so much gear and you're never insured properly, especially if you're not in England. But even in England I've spent nights just sleeping in the van to make sure no one nicked the van."

Anne Mari Davis of The Field Mice chips in with another tale of van life: "People were so helpful putting us up but I slept in the van a lot. I could quite comfortably make myself a little nest and sleep the whole journey." Given that field mice are nocturnal creatures, perhaps she was slowly morphing into her musical namesake?

The five Orchids, who usually travelled with a few extra friends, regularly slept in their Transit van while away from home. "It was pretty horrendous," says drummer Chris Quinn bluntly. "There was a night, somewhere between France and Switzerland, just before the border. We were in the van with all the gear but nobody slept much, to be honest. Condensation was dripping off the metal roof." By the time The Orchids had upgraded to a camper van, things got more comfortable, so comfortable that they occasionally overslept. Such as the time they got a parking ticket while sleeping in the camper right outside the BBC's studios in Maida Vale the night before a Peel session. Oops.

Sleeping on a fan's floor

Even As We Speak's Julian Knowles says grimly: "We did a lot of sleeping on floors." His bandmate Mary Wyer elaborates about a particularly rough night at a fan's place in Sheffield: "It was so disgusting, and it was sticky and there were cigarette butts sticking out of the grill." Julian says: "That was one I remember well! We played at a venue in Sheffield and we didn't have anywhere to stay and, as usual at the end, fans would talk to you and you'd go, 'Do you know anywhere we can stay?' And they'd go, 'Oh sure, you can come and stay at our place.' It was a student house, it was winter, it was super cold, and they couldn't afford to run any heating so it was really, really cold in the house, and the place was just dirty, so we were sleeping on the floor. I remember looking to the side and there's pizza stuck on the carpet."

Is pizza better or worse than what The Orchids encountered on the floor of a student flat in Leeds? "There were mouse traps everywhere," says drummer Chris Quinn. "We were lying on the floor with the mouse traps." Note, he says 'lying' rather than 'sleeping'.

Staying with fans is lovely. It's really generous of people to offer up their homes to a touring indie band who are needing to save pennies and it's also exciting for the fans to have their favourite musicians stay with them. However, as Julian Knowles explains: "The thing that people don't realise is, when you're playing for five nights a week, you're tired. And so you finish a show and all you really want to do is just find a comfortable bed somewhere and crash out and sleep well, because you know you've got to go somewhere the next day. But of course, for the fans it's a night out. And so they'll invite you back to their place and all they'll want to do is party. And so there'll be booze coming at you and all this stuff, and you'll be like, 'I just actually feel like a cup of tea, have you got a cup of tea? I'm cold and tired.'"

Mary Wyer pipes up with a story about staying with fans after doing a show with

The Orchids at Manchester University in 1991. "We got back to the house, Matt (Love, guitar), Anita [Rayner, drummer], Rob [Irwin, bassist] and I, just going 'We just want a cup of tea and to go to sleep,'" she says. "But we got back and alcohol was waiting for us, no one had been allowed to touch it until we got there. The Orchids were staying there as well. We got there and just looked around and were like, 'No, look, we've really got to go to sleep'. But The Orchids were up for it, they drank all of it!"

Simon Barber from The Chesterfields agrees: "We didn't book hotels because our only money was from the gig and t-shirt sales, so you weren't going to spend money on accommodation. Sometimes you'd end up at a student's house and there'd be a party happening and then you'd have to endure the party. When you're on tour, you don't always want to party because you're getting up early the next day. That's why our driver slept a lot in his van." Davey Woodward of The Brilliant Corners offers another reason for why staying with fans wasn't always the perfect solution: "We never liked staying in a block of flats because we learned, after our van had been broken into a few times, that you had to take your stealable stuff from the van into the house you were staying in. I can remember staying in this tower block and carting all our gear up in the lift. It was like we loaded in and out perpetually."

> "Quite often, you'd have four people in sleeping bags in one room, someone upstairs, someone in the bathroom, someone at another mate's down the road. We didn't sleep well but I guess back then we didn't care."
>
> **Davey Woodward, The Brilliant Corners**

Revolver Records' Bob Jones recalls that he and other members of the team who put on the EEC Punk Rock Mountain nights in Bristol took it in turns to host the visiting bands on their floors. "Sometimes they would drive on into the night but mostly they wanted to crash on your floor," he says. "I do remember Stump sleeping on my floor. One of Stump got a bit agitated and wanted to smoke some marijuana and wanted me to drive him to St Pauls to pick some up, and it took ages to say I wasn't going to do it as he'd drunk all my alcohol and it was 2am."

The Wake's Caesar had been in bands since co-founding Altered Images in 1979, so he had more experience in matters of accommodation than some of his younger label mates. "I learned early on, try to get proper accommodation sorted because a lot of promoters are fans who get so carried away with getting a PA and a venue that they forget there are six or seven people who need to sleep somewhere," he says sagely. Caesar would not tolerate a floor, quite rightly insisting on a bed or, at the very least, a couch. However, he notes, "one mistake we made was going with The Orchids to Germany", which they did in June 1991. Some German fans had lined up a tour of small German towns for The Orchids, who invited The Wake along for the trip. "I was the one who was left to do all the dirty work," says Caesar, "like when you went to play at a club and, at the end, the manager says he can't pay us even though the club was packed. I was the one who'd have to stand up to him, while The Orchids were all daft and drunk by the end of the night and would just leave. They were so disorganised."

Another element of disorganisation concerned the sleeping arrangements and,

Caesar had experienced enough dodgy floors to know that he always wanted a bed when he went on tour. Sadly, he didn't factor for going on tour with The Orchids.
Julian Bester.

on one occasion, Caesar was forced to bed down on the floor despite his best intentions. Although this particular floor in Bielefeld might well have been better than the alternative, as Caesar explains: "The gig was in some godforsaken little town in Germany, a really miserable little place. It turned out we were playing at this guy's house for his birthday party but, because his parents worked in the media and were fairly rich, they had built him a venue in the basement of the house. It was this long, rectangular room but it had a stage in it and it looked like a club. It was quite small and it had lighting. I'd never seen anything like this in anybody's house in Glasgow."

With the young fan's parents away for the night, he and his friends enjoyed the show and it was only afterwards that The Wake and The Orchids realised there was nowhere for them to sleep and they were just expected to make do with the basement floor. "Carolyn [Allen, keyboards] threw a tantrum and said she wasn't sleeping on the floor," says Caesar. "So the guy whose birthday it was felt sorry for her and gave her his parents' room. Carolyn went into this room and there was this large newspaper reproduction framed on the wall of when Hitler came to power. It was like that moment when Father Ted goes into a room and it's filled with Nazi memorabilia. We thought, 'Oh my god, we're in a Nazi house!' That was the one time we really roughed it and that was because we let The Orchids organise it."

All The Orchids obeyed the rule about not going upstairs in the house except for singer James Hackett, who demanded that he be allowed to have a shower... and was promptly shown the Hitler picture by Carolyn. "I'd thought she was kidding," says James. He adds philosophically: "But that's what the tours were like. You'd get information from Matt and Clare saying, 'These guys got in touch, they want you to play with The Wake, for example, and have arranged you'll play six dates across two weeks'. So you'd get bits and pieces of information but you don't know what you're actually going to do the next night until you get there."

> " You'd end up in an extreme fan's house and wake up in the morning with their mum and dad coming into the dining room because you're sleeping under the table on the floor."
>
> **Simon Barber, The Chesterfields**

Another strange German experience for The Orchids came in Darmstadt, which drummer Chris Quinn deems "the most bizarre place ever". The building they were in had a mini cinema in the basement that was playing *Cheech & Chong* stoner movies on loop, while the gig venue was on the middle floor and the band were expected to sleep in the attic in bunk beds. But at least they had beds. "We took the rider up to the bedrooms and stayed up all night in there," says Chris. James adds happily that Darmstadt was where the band went to the castle that inspired the name of the title character of Mary Shelley's *Frankenstein* to enjoy "champagne day" in celebration of guitarist Matthew Drummond's birthday. "In the rider, they'd given us fizzy wine. So we saved it for Matthew's birthday and went up the castle and burst it open," says bandmate John Scally. It's only obvious but everyone seems to agree that it was a great day.

> ❝ One mistake we made was going with The Orchids to Germany."
> **Caesar, The Wake**

That said, sometimes you just need a hotel, even if you don't have the budget to get rooms for all of the band. Which was how Brighter found themselves illicitly squeezing four adults into a Liverpudlian Travelodge family room (maximum permitted occupancy: two adults and two children): "We figured there would be four beds somewhere," reasons guitarist Alison Cousens. She and bandmates Keris Howard and Alex Sharkey also had Alex's partner Sara along for the ride, so they definitely needed to accommodate four adults somehow. "We did that comedy thing where I would go and check in on my own, while Keris walked past with some bags, so that they'd only see me," says Alison. "Then I walked back in with Alex and we had to wait until the person behind the reception desk had changed. And then we had to wait until the receptionist had gone away for Sara to run in underneath the counter and hope nobody saw her. And once we got there, the kids' beds were tiny little pull-out cots that were too small for adults, so we were literally four-in-a-bed. We didn't like to break the rules and the anxiety of smuggling people past reception just wasn't worth it in the end." Crime never pays, kids.

Sleeping with the Stars

Of course, it could also work the other way round and bands might sometimes invite fans to sleep on their floors. Swedish fanzine writer Marcus Törncrantz had struck up a friendship with Blueboy's Keith Girdler via letters and would sleep on Keith's floor if he was visiting Brighton. And, if Marcus was in Glasgow, he'd do the same at James Moody of The Orchids' house – a situation made only slightly awkward by the fact that James still lived with his mum, who perhaps didn't appreciate the young Swedish man who would be sleeping on her floor for a week at a time. Marcus recalls: "She didn't like it at all. I didn't have the sense to apologise and say 'OK, after two days it's time to leave!' But she was really nice and understanding, and we took care of the dishes and bought some food."

Unsurprisingly, Clare and Matt would stay with the bands if they were visiting them in their home towns or cities. For instance, the record label bosses slept behind singer Andy Hitchcock's sofa after going to Portsmouth to oversee an Action

The Orchids enjoy "champagne day" at Frankenstein Castle, near Darmstadt, in 1991.
Courtesy of The Orchids.

Painting! recording session. Another time, they invited themselves to stay with Keris Howard and Alison Cousens for two weeks while Brighter were recording *Laurel* in June 1990. "We'd met Keris but we hadn't met Alison and we just invited ourselves to stay for a couple of weeks," says Matt. "What an extraordinary thing to do in retrospect. But it seemed perfectly natural at the time." Alison says: "We lived in a one-bedroom flat and they slept in the front room. I was working at housing benefits at the time, so I must have taken some time off work so we could all go into the studio together. They came and had a mini holiday in Brighton." Meanwhile, Nottingham-based band The Fat Tulips, although not on Sarah, proved to be excellent hosts if Clare and Matt happened to need a bed after a gig in the Midlands.

In 1988, David Barbenel of The Poppyheads had met former Strawberry Switchblade singer Rose McDowall and the two started a brief relationship. Which is how The Poppyheads roped her in as guest vocalist at a few of their live shows. Following one London gig, The Poppyheads stayed at Rose's flat, which was quite the experience. "She had a pet monkey that was extremely smelly," says guitarist Rob Young. "I had this night of staying in a sleeping bag with this monkey in a cage and just feeling the whole air smelled of monkey." He adds: "She had a stalker at that time, so she was being rung up all night by this guy who I think had known her in Glasgow and he was outside in a car threatening to kill himself if she didn't come out, so there was all that going on. And she had this whole bookshelf full of books on psychology, psychotherapy and black magic, as far as I remember. She was very intriguing."

> ❝ We stayed at Harvey's house in London after doing gigs there and it was really cold. To warm the place up, he would light the gas oven and put it on full."
>
> **Paul Stewart, Blueboy**

But sometimes, bands would just go home after a gig – no matter how far away home was – in order to keep costs down. During the year they spent trying to make it in the UK, Even As We Speak members shared a three-bedroom flat in Portslade, on the edge of Brighton ("We mostly had beds but I think Anita [Rayner, drums] slept on the couch," says singer Mary Wyer) and would head back after many of their shows, regardless of where they were in the UK. Bassist Rob Irwin was happy to do the driving so the band would pile into the van after the show and, even if they'd played in Manchester, off they would set on the 250-mile journey through the night.

Likewise, Heavenly were not averse to some late-night long drives. Guitarist Pete Momtchiloff says: "I don't know how many gigs we played a year, maybe 40 or 50. Almost all my holiday time was taken up with music and there were lots of weekends and gigs mid-week where you'd come back and have to work the next day. I remember getting back from a gig in Durham at about 6am and at 6.30am I had to get the bus to wherever I was working. It was particularly tough for the drivers, who were Amelia [Fletcher] and Rob [Pursey]. The trouble with staying on someone's floor or staying at the venue is that it's not very comfortable. Often the people who are putting you up want to stay up and talk or play records. So you're totally knackered the next day."

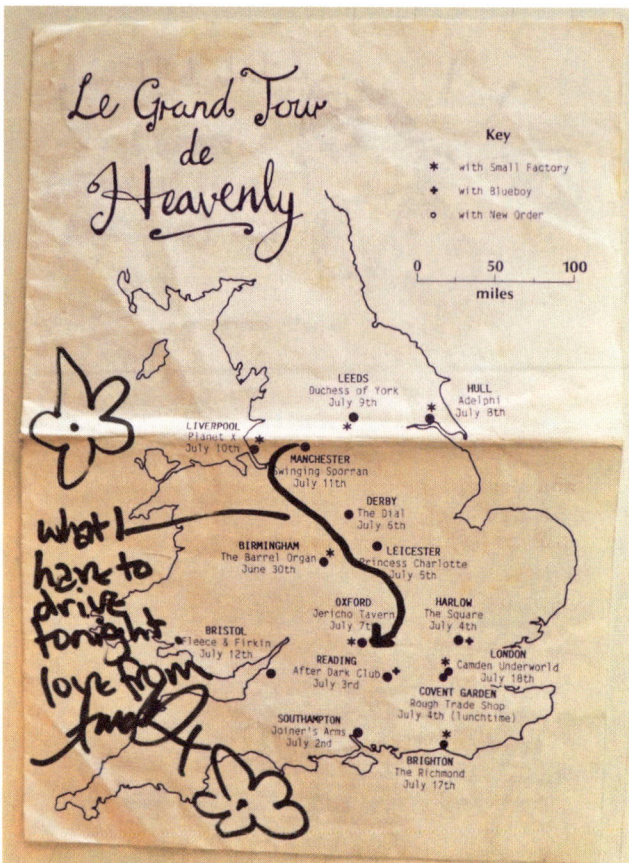

Heavenly often chose to drive home after gigs rather than put up with substandard accommodation, as Amelia Fletcher's note on this fanzine demonstrates.
Courtesy of Tom Deakin.

St Christopher's frontman Glenn Melia reflects on the band's trips overseas: "We'd think nothing of driving overnight to the south of France in a car packed full of gear and then finding a cheap Formula One hotel to rest for a few hours. We stayed in a lovely monastery as part of the deal for playing a gig in Vannes, Brittany. I also remember flying to Las Vegas in order to play gigs in San Francisco and then LA, and literally falling asleep at the wheel several times." Tiredness can kill, take a break.

In the very early days of The Sea Urchins, frontman James Roberts remembers going to see the Jesus & Mary Chain in Nottingham with guitarist Robert Cooksey, but the gig went on so late that the boys missed the last train back to Birmingham. "We wandered down to the railway station and there wasn't a train going back until whatever time in the morning. We must have looked about 12 years old," says James. "Anyway, Jim Reid and one of the other guys and a few of the others, they'd come in looking for food after the gig and they clocked us and Jim Reid, bless his heart, came over. He clocked these two little things that had obviously been to his gig. Long story short, he took pity on the pair of us, he bought us a sausage sandwich and let us kip on the floor in the pub that the band were stopping at. And the Mary Chain at the time were seen as these devil people but he was a real sweetheart taking pity on these two kids, freezing cold at the railway station, so that was a really sweet thing."

To close this section, we have the plight of 14 Iced Bears, stranded at the BBC's studio in Maida Vale after an incredibly long and tiring day recording their second Peel session. "We were loading up the van afterwards and the key snapped in the van door, it literally came apart in two bits," remembers manager Sue Freeman with horror. "To this day, I thank the BBC security person who took pity on us and let all five of us sleep on the floor in reception. I had a little bottle of contact lens liquid that I took everywhere and I had to squirt it out into two BBC polystyrene coffee cups

14 Iced Bears (pictured here at the Tropic Club in Bristol on 17 September 1991) once sought refuge on the floor of the BBC's reception.
Wendy Stone.

for my lenses. We didn't have anything with us because we didn't imagine we were spending the night anywhere." Chief Bear Rob Sekula adds: "The next morning, our mishap was the talk of the studios as various staff and luminaries squeezed past our equipment and lingering, smelly bodies. We never got another session."

Five Go Off To Camp

One of the *Famous Five* stories that Enid Blyton neglected to write was the tale of The Orchids going on an out-of-season camping holiday just outside Stoke-on-Trent in 1988. Inexplicably, the band had three dates in a week that were in the area (June 26 and 27, and July 2) and "we didn't realise they were all a few hundred yards apart," says singer James Hackett.

On their way down to gigs in the south of England, fellow Glaswegians Remember Fun dropped The Orchids off in the field (yes, just a random field... not even a proper campsite) that they would come to call home for a week... and then picked them up again seven days later when on the way back. How this was arranged without mobile phones is a wonder of primitive communication and scheduling.

James explains: "We ended up sleeping in a tent to kill some time. We knew we were going to have some time in the area when we weren't going to be playing. We thought it would be a great idea, because we did some research that said Staffordshire was quite pretty, and we thought that we could find a field somewhere and pitch two

The Orchids were big camping fans. This picture shows them live at Fury Murray's in Glasgow on 7 December 1987.
Courtesy of The Orchids.

tents. So we did. We found a town near Lichfield, Little Haywood, the pub was The Red Lion, there's always a Red Lion." Drummer Chris Quinn elaborates: "I can't really remember why we thought camping was a good idea to be honest, as none of us were experienced campers or anything, as proven by the fact that Matthew [Drummond] borrowed the old canvas-style tent and hadn't even checked it before leaving, hence the laughter when he spread it out, saw and smelled the mould and realised that we'd all need to share the one tent." Yep, the five Orchids were all cosied up in a small three-man tent for a whole week.

Not for the first time, The Orchids would risk their lives in the pursuit of pop: "We had the biggest thunderstorm and we all had to cuddle each other. And then we realised that the tent pole was metal so jumped away from it. The lightning was bouncing yards away from us, we could feel it, so it was quite a frightening time but it didn't last long. So we were able to get ourselves up and go to the pub, eat some frozen pizza and drink some pale English beer."

The band took the bus to Stafford one day "to get a bit of culture," as guitarist John Scally says. While James explains they spent another day walking around the hills because "we needed to stay out of the pub and not be in it from the minute it opened

> ❝ When we went to walk up the hills there was some carry on and [James] Moody threw a big rock from some distance that hit John [Scally] on the back of the elbow. He nearly passed out and we thought we were going to have to cancel the rest of the gigs due to his injury, but he recovered OK and could play."
>
> **Chris Quinn, The Orchids**

up as we were starting to get a reputation among the locals. And English pubs didn't have the same licensing. They chucked us out after lunch and we had to go and find something to do." He adds: "Each time we went on tour we treated it like a holiday."

WHERE THE HELL AM I?

Other odd places people stayed include the out-of-season holiday camp in Devon in which the Flatmates were accommodated. Drummer Rocker tells me: "I think it might have been Devon County Council who put the gigs on, where you played in Exeter one night and then Westward Ho!, so South Devon and North Devon on consecutive nights. And they'd got a Butlins-type holiday camp right in the middle of Devon to put the bands up. In bunk beds." The Flatmates were joined by Razorcuts and The Chesterfields, an experience that Razorcuts' bassist Tim Vass terms "a bizarre Subway Records tour of the West Country." Tim adds: "My biggest memory of that is getting really cross with The Chesterfields because the people who were organising this mini tour left us this parcel of food in the chalets with sausages and fruit and rice and I don't know what in. And The Chesterfields just put the whole lot into a frying pan, including the fruit, and just made this completely inedible mess out of it. And I was really cross about it!"

Anne Mari Davis recalls being in France with The Field Mice for a gig and the band staying in the most unutterably cold farmhouse imaginable. Finally, in exhausted desperation, all five mice lived got into one bed together, hoping that their combined body heat would somehow help them make it through the night alive. Spoiler: it did.

Meanwhile, Brighter were left quite literally asking 'Where the hell are we?' following their gig in Lausanne. The band members were split between two addresses that had been found for them but they lost track of each other and had to keep their fingers crossed that their Swiss hosts would be true to their promise to get everyone reunited in time to travel home. "It was the days before mobile phones and none of us knew where any of the rest of us were, all we knew was we had to get back to the airport for a certain time," says Alison Cousens. "Bear in mind we were so naïve, we'd never really been on a plane before and we hadn't really travelled abroad at all because we hadn't done the middle-class thing of Eurorailing or anything, as we had to work through the summers. Keris [Howard] and I were in this flat somewhere in Lausanne and we'd been told that someone would come and pick us up. We had no idea where Alex [Sharkey] was, we had no way of contacting him. But we did get picked up and met up on the platform of Lausanne train station fortunately."

Another Sunny Duvet

It's important to stress that not everywhere was shit. Clare tells me: "I'd like to put a vote in for the Osaka Royal Grand because the bed in the hotel there was probably the size of our whole flat at 46 Upper Belgrave Road, it was certainly the size of the kitchen." So it wasn't all hillsides and hitchhiking.

The Orchids, scoring an upgrade from a small tent in a thunderstorm, were gifted a mini-break in Carnac one October by a French promoter called Pascal. "That was one of the best times we ever had," says singer James Hackett. "It's in Brittany, it's quite famous for standing stones. It's a World Heritage Site and a beach holiday resort for lots of French folk." The Orchids had played a gig in Paris but had a few days of downtime before the next French dates, so Pascal offered them his parents' holiday home. "He invited his friends down, made us a curry and we got very drunk and ate very well. It was good fun," adds James happily.

> Um… I'm on the scrounge I'm afraid. I wouldn't ask, but you did offer last time The Field Mice played in Stoke… I wondered if you could maybe put me up if I go to the gig? I've got somewhere to stay in Manchester the next day, but Stoke is a bit of a problem."
>
> **Letter from Clare to fan Julian Bester**

Guitarist John Scally picks up the story: "One day, Pascal brought a friend over who was a personal chef, who turned out to be a complete nightmare. We went shopping and he decided he would steal from the supermarket. I couldn't believe it. Because we were Glaswegian and the chef was French but of Indian descent, Pascal decided he would get him to cook us a really good authentic Indian meal, so we had to go to the supermarket to get the ingredients. Obviously we were going to pay. But we were in the supermarket and he just started lifting stuff. He had a bottle of whiskey in his pocket and we were like, 'What's he doing?!' And then he got drunk and never cooked the meal!" Well, as Chris adds: "He did start cooking it but we had to finish it because he passed out on the floor. But it was very, very nice as I remember."

The Orchids also came across Pascal's family's wetsuits and decided to put them on and run into the sea at 4am. "It was pretty damn cold," states James. "You realise, now we're in our 50s, that was dangerous but when you're so young it was just so much fun. I'm glad we did it but glad we got away with it as well. Every time we went away on a tour, we would take as many friends as we could. So we always had two or three friends with us who could come and enjoy it with us. That night, we had a friend called Alan with us and he put on one of the wetsuits and dived into the ocean and we didn't see him resurface, so we did worry about him. We thought he was gone but he came back."

WAKING UP

While speaking to me for this book from his comfortable house in Sydney, Even As We Speak's Julian Knowles reflects: "I think that was one of the hardest things about the whole thing, the level of discomfort. It's why I think a lot of younger bands just burn out after a certain amount of time. I know music managers who manage young artists and they are very mindful that when they send them to shows that the shows will all be good ones and that they'll be treated well and that they'll have somewhere to stay. When you're absolutely exhausted, it's really hard to enjoy what you're doing. And if you're sleeping on a cold floor with no heating, then it's also quite hard to enjoy what you're doing. You tend to be lying there going, 'What the fuck am I doing?'"🍒

*****

THESE THINGS HAPPENED:
FM Cornog, East River Pipe
"It was life-changing. How do you thank someone for pulling you out of utter obscurity and sharing your music with the world? They were the ones that took the leap. And they always *will* be that. East River Pipe on its own is just East River Pipe floating around in the ether but East River Pipe within the frame of Sarah Records has a permanence and weight. Sarah's lasting effect on me was that it cemented my belief that art and commerce are two completely different animals. My stay at Sarah further confirmed my belief that the only thing an artist should expect from his or her work is the occasional joy and release it brings. An artist should expect nothing more than that."

Chapter 18
The End of the Affair

While it would be a push for anyone to describe Sarah Records and its bands as wild-eyed rock'n'roll hellraisers, I was still determined to find some tales of musical mayhem. I knew there had to be some... and I was right. True, these stories are not *quite* up there with the ones of Keith Richards staying awake for nine days straight. And they don't equal the tales of Mötley Crüe band members smashing glass bottles over each other's heads and eating light bulbs. Or the ones about Ozzy Osbourne biting the head off a living bat... or snorting a line of moving ants. As far as I'm aware, not one single member of a Sarah band so much as threw a member of the Television Personalities out of a hotel window. But that's not to say there aren't still a few tales of indie-pop hedonism for us to enjoy at their expense. So here goes...

"My favourite Orchids story was when we all did that tour of Brittany," laughs Heavenly's Amelia Fletcher, recalling the time the two bands played a few shows on the edge of France in 1989 (as mentioned in Chapter 16). "We played in this venue where there wasn't a dressing room so the guy just said, 'Go behind the bar and you can sit there'. And when we were coming out, Matthew [Drummond] was carrying his guitar and his guitar case separately. And none of us even thought about it. When we got back to the seminary [where we were staying], he opened his guitar case and it was stuffed full of beer that he had nicked. And the guy then worked out that he was missing a load of beer and he called up the promoters and was like 'Where's my beer gone?!' and it was like at school when you have to show your stuff to prove you weren't the person that stole the beer. Matthew came out and opened his guitar case and there was all the beer."

> **❝** Seeing The Orchids washing down paracetamol with Guinness before they'd even got out of their sleeping bags was a sight to be avoided at all costs."
>
> **Letter from Clare to fan Julian Bester**

Not to be left out, Heavenly bassist Rob Pursey pitches in with his own tale of drunken debauchery on tour. "The most drunk Heavenly ever got was the first time we played in Spain," he says. "Nobody told us that the bands don't start until 3am or something crazy and, at the club in Madrid, the barman decided that we could design our own cocktails. So we had to draw a glass and ratios of whatever drink would be in it and then we drank them all. We thought we'd be playing like in

England, at 10pm or 11pm but it was certainly after 1am, and by this point Mathew [Fletcher] could hardly stand up."

Stories of drummer Mathew Fletcher enjoying a few light ales are plentiful. While it would get repetitive to print them all, here is an early highlight. It is also worth remembering that Mathew was only 15 when he joined big sister Amelia's band Talulah Gosh, so he was living the rock'n'roll lifestyle from an early age. Talulah Gosh bassist Chris Scott says: "Mathew absolutely forbade his parents from ever seeing us play live. When, bizarrely, we were booked to support The Blow Monkeys at the New Theatre in Oxford, his parents thought they could hide in the audience but he spotted them and at the end of our set, he kicked his drum kit over, sending expensive microphones flying and getting us in trouble with the venue. He then went outside and threw a rock at his mother's car, denting the bonnet." Oh, and here's another anecdote from Chris about his rhythm section colleague: "I think it was the last Talulah Gosh gig, which was one of those places off Euston Road [London], and Mathew had been drinking Pernod and blackcurrant. We'd got literally half a mile down Euston Road and he threw up out the window but it flew back onto his white t-shirt and then he passed out. So we got back to Oxford and he wakes up, and he thinks he's been coughing blood all the way back."

Turning the pint glass upside down, here's a story from fanzine writer Akiko Yamauchi, who moved to Glasgow in 1990 for university. Already a Sarah fan in her homeland of Japan, she was now perfectly placed to hang out with some of the bands and to spend time with The Orchids. I asked her what the band was like. "The Orchids? They drink. They drink. And they drink," she says. "But my funniest experience with The Orchids is definitely watching *Predator* on video with them, on a tiny telly at someone's flat with a cup of tea! How that happened, I have no idea. It was surreal almost, all five members of The Orchids with a Japanese girl watching *Predator* sober!" So not everything was rock'n'roll excess, then.

> ❝ The Harvest Ministers don't do rock'n'roll. We're strictly a cakes and tea band after the show, with maybe a game of chess thrown in."
> **Will Merriman, The Harvest Ministers**

But so much of this was really just youthful exuberance because you have to remember that most of these bands were still teenagers or, at best, in their early 20s. Travelling and playing music with their mates was just fun. "We really liked The Sea Urchins because there was an affinity there between the two bands, because they were both working-class, both out for a bit of fun," says Karen Albrow, a friend of The Orchids who ran the Texas Fever club night in Glasgow. "When The Sea Urchins came up here for a few gigs, they really got on well. Even to us, they seemed younger than us, they seemed more boyish and more badly behaved compared to The Orchids, which was fun. It was like having your wee cousin come up and stay! I remember them staying at [James] Moody's house and it was almost like The Orchids had taken them under their wing to look after them when they were up in Scotland. When they were up here they wanted to go to the sea because they lived in Birmingham, miles from the sea, so that's what they did on their day off. It was nothing to us to nip down to the [River] Clyde but for them it was a big thing. They were dead excited, they were like wee puppies."

The Sea Urchins possibly wouldn't have used the term 'puppies' to describe themselves but they definitely concede that they were having a brilliant time being in a band together. "Having the excitement of being on a record label and having a single out and being giddy teenagers, everyone got a little bit cocky and a bit silly, and if you can't do that when you're 17 and 18, when can you?" asks the band's keyboardist Bridget Duffy, which is an entirely reasonable question. "It all got a bit silly quite often. I think we were a bit bratty but I think it was more the exuberance of youth. I was at the polytechnic at Regent Street and [future author and journalist] Jon Ronson was entertainment secretary [at the Students' Union], and I remember them asking if we could do a gig. I said: 'By the way, we want to support The Television Personalities', he sorted it out and then [TVP frontman] Dan Treacy thought we were all on heroin! None of us were but maybe we sat there too stunned, thinking our dream had come true."

Playing down some of the stories that the Urchins could be prickly, the band's frontman James Roberts says: "I think we always got on with the bands. There was some ribbing and we liked to push the Sarah 1 thing with the other bands just to wind them up and stuff but I don't think we ever felt massively part of that scene. There was never any animosity with people, I don't think. We were doing our thing and they were doing their thing, and occasionally we were on the same bill and that was cool."

Given that Sarah wasn't the most druggy of labels, it was impressive to find two Sarah bands in the *Melody Maker* gossip column one week after members of The Sweetest Ache pinched The Orchids' weed at a Sarah party. "This is the Nineties and, times being what they are, Sarah bands ain't' cute n' winsome and innocent anymore, *right*? Sarah bands are 'ard. Well 'ard. Rock'n'roll 'ard. And they'd just like to say they're sorry to have to disappoint some of their Scottish fans, but they won't be taking their Sweetest Ache tour up to Glasgow because The Orchids have sworn they're gonna beat them up," warned the music weekly. "We were kind of notorious for constantly being inebriated on one substance or another," says Simon Court of The Sweetest Ache. "We drank a lot, we smoked a lot, we imbibed other stuff but we didn't really do anything terribly rock'n'roll. I wouldn't say that we were intimidating but we weren't very accommodating." Chris Quinn of The Orchids scolds his Welsh labelmates with: "Outrageous behaviour!"

What is genuinely outrageous is that The Orchids never get included in the stories of Scottish indie-pop alongside the likes of Teenage Fanclub, Primal Scream, The Soup Dragons et al. While what is genuinely *not* outrageous is the behaviour of BMX Bandits' frontman Duglas T Stewart, who has a lovely story that is the antithesis of rock'n'roll excess, not least because Duglas hasn't touched a drop of alcohol in

> ❝ Mentioning no names... 'bowel relief' into a waste bin in Nice, drunkenly spinning a car around a mall car park near LA, being chased by a bar owner through the frozen streets of a small East German town after losing a 'naked' bet, prostitutes offering their wares to us in a mouse-infested hotel in Marseille... The list goes on."
>
> **Glenn Melia, St Christopher, on their rock'n'roll lifestyle**

Fun lovin' minimals: The Orchids supporting My Bloody Valentine in York.
Karen Albrow.

decades. He tells me about a time the Bandits were on tour with Shonen Knife and ended up staying in the same London hotel as their friends from Eugenius, who were on tour with Urge Overkill. All four bands ended up with the same night off so Urge Overkill put on a massive party in a suite at the hotel to which everyone was invited. Duglas was sharing a room with Eugene Kelly of Eugenius and they were both getting ready to go to the party while the TV was on in the background "and Miss Marple with Joan Hickson's *A Caribbean Mystery* was announced as coming on and I said [earnest tone] 'I've not seen this, this is the first time it's been on, so I think I'm going to stay and watch this because I really wouldn't want to miss it'. And Eugene's like [incredulous tone] 'But we're having this party!' And Eugene swears, as he left the room, the last thing he heard me say was, 'Oh, I do like a good mystery.'"

Of course, not everything with The Orchids was as harmless as taking The Sea Urchins to see the sea. Sometimes, the Glaswegian band members got into trubs when they were away. Here are a few examples of everyone's favourite mischievous musicians...

> ❝ The Orchids, you could always tell they loved being in a band. They loved everything about it but when I look back on it, I found them a little bit scary as well but just that sense that 'For Christ's sake, we're in Paris! It's us five from Glasgow and here we are in Paris and we're going to have fun while we're here!'"
>
> **Clare**

- While over in the French capital for a gig with several other Sarah bands, The Orchids stayed up drinking and accidentally jammed the lock on their hotel room door, trapping themselves inside. There was clearly nothing for it but to smash the door down! "I had to get up at 4am and calm the hotel management down and do French/Glaswegian translation," sighs Clare. In the band's defence, singer James Hackett reasons: "There were quite a lot of us in the room, it was claustrophobic. And it was five floors up with no lift." Guitarist John Scally picks up the story: "We phoned reception, told them that we couldn't get out of the room and they'd have to come up and open the door, and they refused. I decided we had only one course of action and that was to force my way through the door." Drummer Chris Quinn acknowledges: "We did leave Matt and Clare with a bit of a problem." With reference to another Parisian adventure, James says: "We also left them with a bit of a phone bill, I believe." Which is about an infamous phone bill they ran up by ringing their friends back home in Glasgow, as well as James Moody's girlfriend in Sweden.

- The band's dressing room at a Swiss gig was next to a stockroom piled high with beer and chocolate. Faced with a 10-hour drive the next day, Chris admits "we took several loads down to the van. Then, when we were leaving, the promoter said, 'Oh, have some beer and chocolate for your journey'. So after stealing all this stuff, he actually gave us extra stuff as well, so it was quite embarrassing." James adds: "There was also a full cheese wheel and it was thrown in among the beer. There was no need for it, so it sat and sweated in the van for weeks until we eventually threw it away somewhere. I felt guilty about that. You shouldn't waste food."

- "The most rock'n'roll thing was the journey to Nantes on the boat," says John. Following the 1992 general election that saw the Conservatives win again, the frustrated band sank a bottle of whisky on the boat to ease their woes. But it went to their heads... "We were physically fighting each other when we got off the boat, so that wasn't good going through customs," muses Chris.

- Oh, and in Carnac, where the band had enjoyed the mini break between French dates... "We had that wee town to ourselves and we used to drive around drunk in the minibus to get to the beach in our wetsuits. I'll admit we were driving drunk," says John. Chris adds: "It wasn't just that we were drunk, there were only one or two people who had actually passed their driving test." The band are quick to point out that they wouldn't drink and drive these days.

- The band had to remove the keys to their minibus from James Moody when they were in Munich in 1992... because he wanted to use the van to pull a cigarette machine off the wall of a venue. "We were all really drunk, Moody was steaming. He'd got a rope or chain from somewhere and he'd hooked it up to the back of the van, then he hooked it up to the cigarette machine, and was trying to rev the van forward to bring this thing off the wall," says James Hackett. "We had a huge fight about that. It was just before he went to Sweden, so I think he was determined to cause havoc."

- John recalls a time when they were in Switzerland or Germany and, having been cooped up in their van for several days, decided to treat a public swimming pool as a communal bath. "They had rules in the pool about correct lane procedures but we were there for a bit of fun. I don't think it went down too well but it was funny at the time."

- "There was that night we were fighting with the crowd in the gas dome in Switzerland," remembers Chris. "We were throwing bottles and cans into the crowd because they were throwing bottles and cans at us. That was quite scary as well because it was proper menacing violence almost. They were throwing full cans of beer onto the stage and we were retaliating."
- Last but not least, while staying with Clare and Matt after a gig in Bristol, two of The Orchids took a taxi to St Paul's in search of weed but the taxi driver turned the car around because police were blocking the roads. At which point, the driver asked the band, "Oh, are you looking for some of this?" and they got their wares from him instead. "That's Bristol for you," shrugs John.

When I told The Orchids that my research placed them at No 1 in the chart of the most rock'n'roll bands on Sarah, they dismissed the accolade and nominated The Wake instead. "They're below the radar. Caesar gets rock'n'roll when he goes to a football match. That's when he raises his voice," says John. While James adds: "I think because we drank a bit, people thought we were rock'n'roll bad boys but we really weren't." Reader, you can make your own mind up.

WHAT WILL WE DO NEXT?

On 28 August 1995, Clare and Matt threw a big party on the Thekla in Bristol to celebrate the closure of their record label and the release of Sarah 100, a compilation CD called *There & Back Again Lane*. "We were both absolutely convinced we had to stop at 100 because when would you stop if you didn't?" says Clare. "We never just wanted to fizzle out or go shit or sell out to a major or go bust. Where do you go if you don't stop at 100? Because 150 is not really anything, do you go to 1,000? We'd had it planned for a while and were absolutely certain it was the right thing to do. I think a couple of weeks later it probably hit us because we'd got all those new records out, so we were just as busy as we'd always been. But then you're thinking, 'That's the last time our house will fill up with Action Painting! and The Orchids and Boyracer.'"

Clare and Matt were trying to keep the closure of Sarah a secret until they were ready to announce it themselves. Clare says: "I had a tough few evenings on the phone calling them all. Some of the bands had worked it out and some hadn't. I called Heavenly and they were like, 'Well did you think we didn't know?' because we were not announcing what was after Sarah 100. This was also how we discovered the internet. We told someone by post – in Australia I think – and the next week someone in Germany or somewhere asked us about it, but we couldn't work out how news had travelled so fast and it turned out there was this Indie-Pop Mailing List."

Left: "Please take one!" The Sarah 100 booklet. **Middle:** A no-frills flyer to the final Sarah show on board Thekla. **Right:** Balloons do not last well. This 30+ year old item would not stand up to being inflated in the 21st century, sadly.
Courtesy of Sarah Records.

Clare continues: "It wasn't an easy thing to do because it was the only thing we knew, and it was our lives and our social lives and who we were, because we were Clare and Matt from Sarah Records. And it was our income. And it left the bands without any outlet for their music. It was designed to be this big romantic gesture but it was also quite traumatic and quite difficult." Matt adds: "I think everybody respected what we were doing and understood why we were doing it and knew it was our decision, but a few maybe missed out on their next releases because of it." Back to Clare: "We'd never wanted to be 40 with 15- or 18-year-old bands, that felt a bit weird. Most of the bands were roughly our age. But with the later bands, I think Stewart [Anderson, Boyracer] must be three or four years younger, Beth [Arzy, Aberdeen] is a bit younger than me. It felt like there was beginning to be a little bit of an age gap between us and the bands. And if we carried on, the next thing we knew we'd be 35 and ancient."

Matt states: "The most important thing for us was to make it clear we weren't going bust. Which is why we took out the big adverts and had the party. We wanted to make it clear that this was a conscious, definite decision. It's not that we'd given up or sales had tailed off or we were losing money, we wanted to go out with a bang."

> What with you being ensconced at the throbbing heart of the indie-pop universe, or so I am led to believe (albeit almost entirely by your good self), I thought you ought to be the first to hear The News ... Oh, go on, admit it – somewhere beneath that hard, cynical, girlish exterior, you are deeply, deeply impressed. Was a record label ever so pure, so noble, so courageous??? Of course it bloody wasn't. Jeez."

Letter from Matt to me, summer 1995

Almost all of the bands were supportive of Clare and Matt's decision to call time on Sarah, although one or two of the newer signings had not seen the end coming and were left feeling a little stranded with no home for their latest music. But just how did different people feel about Sarah closing?

"It was quite devastating to hear that Sarah was folding," says Caesar of The Wake. "It came out of the blue. What do we do now?! It felt odd. We need labels like Sarah

The artwork for the tickets to the Sarah 100 party.
Courtesy of Sarah Records.

and Factory and the label we're on now, Factory Benelux. So when Sarah disappeared, we kind of disappeared for a while because it was never really an option for us to go back to the major label approach of sending demos to people."

Long-time Sarah contributor Harvey Williams says: "There was certainly a bit of disappointment when they said Sarah was closing. Clare was living in London at this point and I think I'd gone round to her flat to give her a tape of some new songs I was doing, and she almost looked at me apologetically and that's when I found out. I'd made this tape and there was no label now. I certainly didn't feel like it was time to move on."

Some groups who had already disbanded and lost touch with the label found out the same way that the general public did: through seeing the 'A Day For Destroying Things' advert in the *NME* and *Melody Maker*. This half-page announcement was a grand and glorious way for Clare and Matt to tell the world that they were choosing to shut the doors of Sarah Records and they had achieved what they wanted to. "Nothing should be forever," as the announcement said.

That advert was certainly how Simon Court of The Sweetest Ache heard the news: "It was sad but I don't know whether it was entirely unexpected. Things were changing. Everything seemed to have gone in a different direction. It's probably best that they did it the way they did rather than let it pathetically limp off to a corner. It gave it the correct level of kudos."

Blueboy, despite being a functioning band whose single 'Dirty Mags' was Sarah 99 and therefore the last-ever music to be recorded with Sarah money, now concede that the end of Sarah at 100 was inevitable. Guitarist Paul Stewart says: "We figured it couldn't last forever and the digital evolution might have had something to do with it. We were sad about it but we'd heard a whisper from Matt that he was starting Shinkansen and he'd love us to consider being on that label, so at least we had a Plan B. But we felt as though Sarah was part of who we were and in our DNA as a band." His bandmate Gemma Malley thinks it was Harvey Williams who broke the news to her because she was living near him in London at that time. "It was the end of an era but it was more than that. For me, it was the end of a bit of my life. It was this utterly brilliant, chaotic, creative time," says Gemma. "But

> When we were approaching Sarah 50, I remember Mike Chadwick [at Revolver Distribution] saying 'What are you going to do for No 50, anything special?' And I jokingly said we were thinking of stopping. And he was like, 'Christ, don't do that.' As we got towards 100, he said, 'What are you doing for 100?' And I said we were thinking of stopping, and he said, 'Yeah, alright.'"
>
> **Clare**

people had lives and complications, and things were getting a bit tricksy. I had never dreamed any of that stuff might happen, it just happened. And it felt like the right time to not do it anymore."

Secret Shine were also still very much a band and had not spotted the warning signs that Sarah was coming to an end, as guitarist Scott Purnell explains: "I was pretty devastated. I understand why they did it but, for us, we felt we were on the up. You always think your last record is the best one and, at the time, we'd just done *Greater Than God* and we were getting a lot of good feedback and I thought we were in a good song writing place, and we had a lot more material to come that we wanted to put out with them. We felt that was our label to release it on. So I was devastated, it definitely affected us. We went into a bit of a hiatus after that, we didn't really know what to do next."

When Clare and Matt announced they were closing Sarah, The Orchids hadn't released anything for a year and had all but disbanded although, of course, being The Orchids, they didn't quite manage to officially split up. "We were all surprised by it," says James Hackett, reflecting on the news from Bristol. While guitarist John Scally adds: "I think they caught everybody unaware. I think we knew when they put that thing in the press. I'm sure that's how we found out. It wasn't a major impact, as we'd really finished by then." James adds: "We were just treading water and it was becoming quite a bore. We got a bit bored with the 1990s basically. It's like when someone says 'I'll not be phoning you for a while', you think 'Aye, that's OK.'" The Orchids did resurrect themselves to play at the Sarah 100 party, though, and more on that shortly.

> 66 We did worry about Matt and Clare, in case there was something wrong, if that was why they were ending it. That was my first reaction. It was, 'Are they OK?'"
>
> **James Hackett, The Orchids**

For The Sugargliders, the end of Sarah coincided with Josh and Joel Meadows deciding they were ready to try something new. Josh remembers: "I felt sad about it but also totally respected them for doing it their own way. So few bands and labels go out when they're on top. I wasn't devastated, I thought 'Good on 'em'. At the time, I thought 'The Sugargliders has finished, we're on to bigger and better things' but in actual fact, The Sugargliders was the most popular musical period of our lives. And although we've kept on making music, it hasn't ever been as popular as the stuff we did for Sarah."

Given that 'Mustard Gas' had been Sarah 87, Action Painting! were clearly still an active part of the label, so the band's frontman Andy Hitchcock also received a call to let him know that Sarah was coming to an end. "I felt funny about going to the farewell party because I knew I was going to split the band up for a while," says Andy. "I was not entirely shocked when Clare told me but I did feel a bit sad because they were bringing out stuff which, despite the press, was becoming a bit more interesting. I found some of the Sarah stuff not to my liking but they were going out on a high. Ivy was the one I really liked, 'Wish You Would'. It reminded me a bit of the first Hellfire Sermons single. I liked Harvey Williams' piano stuff. We got hate mail from some Sarah fans when we changed our sound, they wanted us to do 'These Things Happen' over and over again. Harvey went from guitar to piano and I think even he got a bit of hassle for that. There was a certain bunch of Sarah fans who wanted one thing over and over again, like pop heroin!"

Aberdeen was the last band to be signed to Sarah as a result of a demo and, with their two singles for the label being Sarahs 93 and 97, they really were there for the final hurrah. "I did know Sarah was folding when we signed because Matt told me early on, so I had to sit on that secret for a while," says singer Beth Arzy. "And I was really sad, I was thinking 'Nobody's ever going to put our records out ever again.'" She continues: "It felt like the death of something really special. It felt like a friend had died. I took it really badly. And coming in at the end, I was honoured to be on the label but when I, as a fan, look back, I kind of think we came in on the tail end of a bunch of releases that I probably wasn't that keen on. I felt the label had lost its way and wasn't as good. I think Matt and Clare knew that as well. And 100 is a good number to stop on. It was sad but I knew it had to be done. But I felt like we never really got a chance to be in that scene and then it was all over. I remember sitting in the car crying when I heard."

Fellow American FM Cornog of East River Pipe took the news in a more stoic manner: "It was inevitable. Clare and Matt did what they had always said they were going to do. They were going to stop at 100 singles and that was what they did, they stuck with their initial plan. Sure, I was a little sad and disappointed at first but Barbara [Powers] and I both respected Matt and Clare immensely. We knew fundamentally that Sarah Records was theirs. It was not ours. We also knew that Matt and Clare were idealists because we were idealists. You see, all idealists must eventually decide upon which way their original dream dies. Clare and Matt had a vision of what they wanted Sarah to be, and they chose to shut the label down while that vision was still intact, rather than continue on and possibly dilute that ideal over time." He adds: "You never know about these things when you're young and you're just starting out, and you're stuffing 7" records with homemade artwork into plastic sleeves. You never know that eventually your young dreams will come face to face with the hard realities of the adult world. Two young people alone in an apartment, be it in Bristol or Queens, can accomplish some very beautiful things. But as Barbara and I have found out, artistic beauty alone won't pay the bills. To pay the bills, you must relentlessly hustle the beauty you create and you must be eager to please. You must willingly play the game. You must send that beauty out into very public places, far beyond those little apartment walls where your dreams began. And when you start to ask the thing you love to make money for you, you often find yourself walking into very different rooms, rooms full of contradictions, and funhouse mirrors, and compromises that are hard to swallow. Where the walls keep pressing in and where that pressure can deform or destroy the very thing you love. I think Clare and Matt saw this heading their way. Barbara and I certainly did. And

FM Cornog: "Clare and Matt did what they had always said they were going to do."
Courtesy of East River Pipe.

we still do."

Bobby Wratten of The Field Mice had been a part of the Sarah story since 'Emma's House' was Sarah 12 in 1988. "I have a vivid memory of Clare giving me the second East River Pipe 10" and it just seemed like a magical object and I really wanted to be involved in music again," says Bobby. "What happened next was Clare asked me how I'd feel if my solo record, rather than being on Sarah, was actually the debut release on a new label. It was then she told me that Sarah was stopping. If I'd actually been in a functioning band on the label at the time it would have obviously affected me differently but I felt outside of things at that point. When Sarah ended, I was already looking ahead to what would be the first Trembling Blue Stars LP. Clare asked me to play at the Sarah 100 party, saying that I'd been a big part of the label and she felt I should be there and play some songs. At this point, I wasn't ready to play live and I certainly didn't want to do old songs but playing a set of new songs probably wouldn't have been in the spirit of the event. I wasn't actually going to go to the show but at the last minute [engineer] Ian Catt suggested he pick me up and we drove to Bristol. I'm happy that we did go because I know it meant a lot to Clare to see me turn up unexpectedly. It was the least I could do for her after everything we'd been through."

Yes, there was going to be a new record label after Sarah because Matt had decided to carry on independently and set up Shinkansen Recordings, which featured several Sarah alumni on its roster. "I'm not sure I was thinking about what I would do after Sarah," says Matt. "What I did do was Shinkansen. By the time [Sarah] came to a stop, I didn't want to leave it all behind completely."

Sarah 100 party: 'I think we got away with it'

On Bank Holiday Monday, 28 August 1995, Sarah threw the queen of all parties onboard Thekla to bid a fond farewell to the label after eight happy years. The running order for the evening was *clears throat*: Blueboy (acoustic set), Secret Shine, Brighter, Boyracer, Harvey Williams, The Orchids, Blueboy and Heavenly. All for the bargain price of £5. Which works out as 63p per band. Wow!

When the tickets went on sale, Clare and Matt were surprised to start receiving orders from places as far away as Hong Kong, Singapore and Canada. "We contacted them and said, 'Are you sure you're coming? Because if you just want the tickets, that's fine but we need to let some other people in as well in that case,'" says Matt. "But they said they were coming and it was lovely. One of them was from Newtownabbey [north of Belfast]. He'd been buying all our records but never seen any of the bands because nobody had ever gone to Northern Ireland [except Heavenly]. And he thought, 'This is my last chance'. So he got the ferry across to Fishguard and the train to Bristol, and turned up at 8 o'clock in the morning and said he could help out." While the idea of people travelling to a landmark gig might seem fairly standard to us now remember that, in 1995, travel was a much more costly and time-consuming business.

> ❝ If you were there then you know what happened, and if you weren't you'd probably rather we kept quiet. I know word's already got round about Harvey and Julian (Hit Parade) performing their set entirely naked, and The Orchids coming on stage as a human pyramid perched atop the handlebars of a Harley Davidson, and the whole evening ended with a 400-strong conga around the streets of Bristol..."
>
> **Sarah obituary, January 1996**

"We tended to price these things to breakeven but then the poor bands only got their travel costs," says Clare about the finances for the Sarah band nights. "Even for the Sarah 100 party, I think we've got the sheet of all the maths somewhere for how much everyone is getting paid and it's literally if you sell every single ticket, which we assume we will, then this is what you pay each of the bands. Sometimes they were awkward buggers but generally they were all thoroughly amenable to all of this."

While Clare and Matt, as the organisers, were doubtless under a bit of stress to ensure the night ran smoothly, some of the bands also had their own anxieties to contend with that evening. None more so than Blueboy, whose members were seriously starting to doubt whether drummer Martin Rose would even show up. "We were all waiting outside ready to go in and soundcheck and he wasn't there," says guitarist Paul Stewart. Given these were the days before mobile phones, there was no easy way to contact Martin. As time ticked on, the band contemplated approaching a drummer from one of the other bands and seeing if they could step in. But, even though The Orchids' Chris Quinn was borrowed for the soundcheck, it would have been unrealistic to expect another drummer to learn the songs in time. With their moment on stage creeping ever closer, Paul and vocalist Keith Girdler contemplated just doing the acoustic set, instead of both acoustic and electric sets, "but I was really disappointed because I thought we were going to lose the opportunity to play," says

By the time Sarah came to a close, Blueboy were easily one of the label's most popular bands.
Alison Wonderland.

Paul. Thankfully, Martin's car appeared at the very last moment. But where on earth had he been? The answer turned out to be very un-Sarah.

Martin had… been arrested and spent the night in a police cell in Reading. "Here's my defence," says Martin with a smile. After attending the Reading Festival to see his hero Paul Weller, and getting extremely drunk, Martin had decided to go home and had tried to get into a minicab. "That's when two policemen came over and said, 'You can't get in that taxi because you didn't book it,'" recalls Martin. Drunk, frustrated and tired, he got a little fresh with his language and ended up being "quite manhandled" by the officers and thrown in the police van. To make matters worse, Martin wasn't free to go until he had attended court the next morning. Well aware that he had the Sarah 100 gig to get to in Bristol that evening, Martin was thinking: "It's only drunk and disorderly, they'll get me in, get me

> You know all the balloons hanging around the Thekla? That was me. I blew them all up. Heavenly played and the earth shuddered, all the other bands played too but I was upstairs hanging out, chilling and being a flirt. Earlier in the day, we went for a coffee, me and the Heavenly kids, at the art gallery café by the waterfront down from the Thekla."

Letter from Dean Talent, fanzine writer, to me, 24 November 1995

fined, get me out." But he was the last person to be seen that day, meaning that the clock was ticking very loudly. "So it was a case of getting in my light-blue Nissan Micra and caning it down the M4 to Bristol," he says. After a quick pint, Martin picked up his drum sticks and was ready to go. "Paul kind of laughed at it and Keith thought it was very rock'n'roll," laughs Martin now.

Paul says of the gig as a whole: "Sarah 100 was bittersweet really. I can compare the feeling to when you leave home for the first time. Matt and Clare, whether they'll admit it or not, they nurtured a lot of bands through their first years. We felt we owed them a lot."

The soundcheck was just as significant as the rest of the evening for Secret Shine. "We had to turn up for a soundcheck at about 5 o'clock, and I walked around the corner with my guitar and there was a massive queue going right out of the Thekla. The doors wouldn't even open until about 7pm," says Scott Purnell. "It was just so wonderful to walk past everyone in the queue with my guitar and go in and soundcheck, thinking we had all those people coming to see us. In the soundcheck, for a laugh, we did a half-speed 'Loveblind' which was good fun, and we did a cover of Barry Manilow's 'Could it Be Magic' with lots of distortion on the bass guitar, a really gritty version."

> **❝** I do remember being quite sad at the end, as was everybody else there."
>
> **Peter Hahndorf, German fan**

As well as travelling from all parts of the UK, fans also arrived from countries such as France, Germany, Greece, Hungary, Japan, Portugal, Singapore, Spain and the US. The nearby youth hostel was sold out to visiting indie-pop fans who soon made friends in the dormitories. In an interesting example of early social networking, the TweeNet Indie-Pop Mailing List and chat room had provided a way for modem-owning fans across the world to communicate, share travel plans and arrange to meet up once they landed in the UK. The Indie-Pop Mailing List had been established in September 1994 by technologically advanced indies including Peter Hahndorf in Germany, Steve Thornton in the US and Robin Humble in Australia, and was housed on the TweeNet website which still exists in a rudimentary form.

Having been a computer science student in Germany, Peter had had an email address since October 1988 and established his first website in June 1994 before setting up TweeNet. Within two months there were 100 members. Peter explains: "There was no Google at the time but, in 1995, the first search engines started and Yahoo! had a hand-maintained catalogue of available sites on the net which listed TweeNet. So there was a lot of word of mouth. There were magazines that reviewed new sites, and books trying to list all sites, which became an impossible task quickly." The idea of buying a book that would provide you with a catalogue of websites sounds wonderfully quaint to our 21st-century brains.

Peter explains that an annual trip to the UK was not uncommon for many German music fans "to see bands and buy records in the motherland", given that not all of the bands and records that they were interested in made it out of the UK. "It wasn't as easy as nowadays with cheap budget airline flights, almost all trips were done by bus, train and ferry, which were always long journeys." By the time Sarah announced it was closing in 1995, Peter hadn't been to the UK for three years, but there was no way he was missing this chance to catch up with his international pop friends: "Since the late 1980s, I had been in touch with an indie-pop kid from Singapore named Alfred, we exchanged tapes and opinions over the years. It turned out he was planning to come as well. I already knew a bunch of people from the past but it was nice to put faces to email addresses. The evening itself was way too short for me. I met up with people I had not seen for years, it was much more a community gathering than a gig, at least for me."

Writing a comprehensive review of the event for TweeNet, Peter created a very picturesque story of how he and his friends spent their days being indie-pop tourists in the UK. In London, they paid homage to Rough Trade Records and Gunnersbury Park, while in Bristol they went on a tour of all the Sarah sights that had featured on the record labels or record covers or that had housed Clare and Matt at various points over the previous eight years.

Meanwhile, Scott Zimmerman came over from the US. Writing on the TweeKitten site, Scott detailed what an exciting time he and his friends had at the Sarah 100 party. Like other first-time tourists to Bristol, Scott went on a walking tour of the city and wrote about how familiar it felt having studied the photos on Sarah's records for so long: "In a way, we were living the life of Matt and Clare for a day," he wrote. And neatly disproving the myth that Sarah fans are quiet little Ribena drinkers, Scott wrote in his review: "The alcohol had finally started to take its toll, showing that fans of Sarah Records really do not act much differently than the moshers at Guns N'Roses shows, once properly inebriated."

From the fan reviews I have found, everyone seems to agree that Brighter's set was the highlight of the evening. "[Brighter] performed a set of pure glory. The applause and screams were huge. What a hit! With that classic jangle, Brighter seems to have one of the simplest sounds of any Sarah band, yet they exploit it so fully. Perfection," enthused Scott on TweeKitten. Having split up three years before, Brighter reformed especially to play at the Sarah 100 party and, on hearing how well their set was received, guitarist Alison Cousens muses: "Maybe absence makes the heart grow fonder? We hadn't played together for three years but it felt like it was important to reform for a one-off as a farewell. It felt OK to get back together and stand on stage one last time but we were fairly certain that would be our last time." She adds: "It was a privilege to have been asked and a privilege to have been part of the Sarah story. We had the summer holiday to rehearse to a point where we felt that we could stand on stage and do ourselves justice. We were probably better rehearsed than we would have been normally! I was sad Sarah Records was finishing, however it was the right time and the right statement for them to finish at Sarah 100, it was classic Sarah. Every ending is tinged with sadness. But I think people were really exuberant and just wanted to drink it in for the last time, that's how I felt. There was a sense of real love for the label."

What comes across from everyone is the celebratory and fun spirit of the night. Although there was a sense of sadness that something was ending, there was also a celebration of all the good times everyone had enjoyed along the way. "It really was celebratory. It was a terrific evening," says Harvey Williams, who was – of course – playing that night. "I met loads of people for the first time. I don't remember feeling sad, it was very upbeat. I was in Blueboy by this stage and a lot of our songs were quite thrusting and dynamic, so that night we did think more about what we were playing. I did a set with Julian [Henry, The Hit Parade] as well and it was a really great night."

Although The Wake were not on the bill, Caesar was in attendance having been drafted in by The Orchids to fill in on bass. "I loved the boat, I thought it was a fantastic place to have it," he says of Thekla. "It felt like a happy event rather than the end of something. It was the end of the label but it was a statement in itself, it felt like a celebration of everything." Caesar admits he spent most of the night sitting outside chatting to Bobby Wratten and Ian Catt. "I can only remember it as a happy event. It felt like something that Matt and Clare had had in their minds for a while. It was a way of rounding things off but not a sad finish."

Secret Shine were on early in the evening "which I always like because then you can relax, have a drink and watch the other bands," says singer Jamie Gingell. Guitarist Scott Purnell adds: "It was absolutely brilliant. It was really packed and really chaotic. There were so many bands playing, I think we had a set of four or five songs but you want to be up there forever. It was raucous and lovely and everyone really loved it. I think we even got a good review for that! Jamie wore that 'My Bloody Secret Shine' t-shirt because a lot of the press at the time were saying we sounded like something off *Loveless* [by My Bloody Valentine]." Vocalist Kathryn Smith adds: "It was just a night full of love and celebration." Jamie continues: "I did feel sad towards the end of the night. It was a party and a buzz but it did feel like the end of something, which it was. I knew that Matt and Clare were never going to resurrect it in any way. Because of their commitment and the way they'd done everything else, they weren't for turning." Summing up the Secret Shine set that night, Kathryn laughs: "I think we got away with it. We always say that when we come off stage, 'Did we get away with that?' And I think, on that night, we got away with it."

Harvey Williams had been linked to Sarah Records throughout every stage of the label's life.
Grimsby Fishmarket, Nicklas Brunzell.

The Aftermath

The Sarah 100 party on 28 August 1995 might have been when the label said goodbye, but that wasn't really the end. A slew of singles had recently been released along with the *There & Back Again Lane* compilation. "There was a lot compressed into that last bit because of realising we'd have to get everything out before Sarah 100," says Matt, while Clare adds that the mail order side of things carried on for another year or so until stock ran out. "The label ended on 28 August but we were still doing as much selling on 29 August as we were on 27 August. Nothing actually stopped," adds Matt.

Both Clare and Matt insist that they do not have any favourites out of all the records and bands they released during the lifetime of Sarah Records. "They come with different emotional attachments and trauma as well that separate the bands from the songs. You're not just listening to music, you're listening to a part of your life," says Clare. While Matt adds: "We are just so close to every single one of them in different ways. To us, it's not just a song, it's everything to do with it: it's the recording, it's speaking to the band before and afterwards, there's just so much to it."

> 66 Hey, it's fun destroying a record label – you should try it sometime. There's lots to choose from."
>
> **Sarah 100 flyer**

In time, the Gwilliam Street house was sold and Clare and Matt moved to London. While packing up their things, it transpired that a record label doesn't actually generate that many things with which to fill a home. "In the Sarah days, we just didn't

> We forced Talulah Gosh to go and live in an old peoples' home in Uttoxeter because we were fed up with her incontinence. She still sends us cards with £5 record tokens tucked inside at Christmas, but she is sadly senile and only ever dwells on her pathetic past, drivelling that she 'used to be pals with that My Bloody Valentine' and stuff. All lies and quite sad really.
>
> **Letter from Mathew Fletcher, Heavenly, to me, summer 1994**

have stuff. We had a black-and-white portable telly but we barely had a table lamp. We didn't have many clothes or books or even records, really," says Clare. "I don't think we ever thought about things being artefacts. Even things like reviews in the music press, we didn't even buy them all. If we were single of the week we'd buy it, but you weren't going to spend 45p on just an ordinary review. A lot of the artwork has been lost because it went to the pressing plant and never came back. But then I'm sometimes slightly surprised at some of the stuff we gave away. We gave away the centre label films to 'Pristine Christine' in a raffle and thankfully Harvey [Williams] won them, so they're still in the family. But you think, 'Fuck, we gave that away? It's "Pristine Christine"! Jesus!' But it seemed nice to give things away." Shaking her head, Clare mutters: "Lunacy."

It was only when Clare and Matt were looking for items for the retrospective Sarah Records exhibition at Bristol's Arnolfini gallery in 2014 that they really started to assess the Sarah memorabilia that they had in their respective attics. Clare says: "I've got the travelcard from the day we recorded 'Emma's House', and most years Bobby [Wratten] emails me and says, 'Happy however-many-years since we met'. And we've certainly got the letter Bobby sent us when he sent us his first demo. In a way you don't end up with that much… we've got test pressings, master tapes."

In April 1996, Matt released 'Abba On The Jukebox' by Trembling Blue Stars on Shinkansen Recordings and began a new chapter in his life. Meanwhile, Clare found work in the music industry in London. But it was certainly a big adjustment after almost eight years running their own business. "I was Clare from Sarah Records and Matt was Matt from Sarah Records, so there's a bit of a personal identity. It's like, who am I now?," asks Clare. "I remember, a year later, at a gig in London, someone came up and said 'Didn't you use to be Clare from Sarah Records?' As if I wasn't Clare anymore. And it was kind of weird. It was literally our whole lives, we did nothing else other than run Sarah. And because the two of us were together as a couple and lived together and worked together, you kind of destroyed the whole thing. I think it was quite a brave thing to do."

Looking back, music journalist Pete Paphides says of the Sarah story: "Its core values are timeless. People will always want to gravitate to a gentle alternative to the pugilistic extremes, what they see happening in the wider world. And in many ways, right now, the world seems like a crueller place than ever. And people will always look for somewhere to escape to, a safe place to escape to, either literally or metaphorically. And there's something about the music that was released on the label throughout that time, and the way that music was presented, which was very important, which I think speaks to younger people. There's just something about that world, what it represents, the aesthetic message that it's putting out, that I think is still relevant. And I think it's timeless."

THE END OF THE AFFAIR

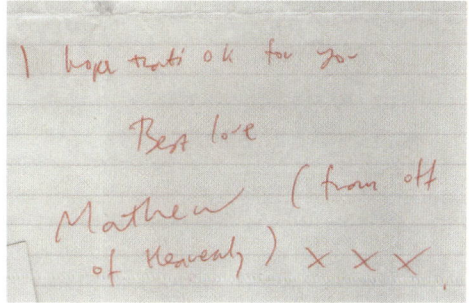

Top: A rare photo of Clare and Matt together. **Bottom left:** The Clifton Suspension Bridge, as if you didn't already know that. **Bottom right:** Mathew Fletcher's sign off on a letter to me in 1994. "I hope that's OK for you. Best love xxx."

Top: Julian Bester. Bottom left: Neil Phillips. Bottom right: Jane Duffus.

*****

THESE THINGS HAPPENED:
Rob Young, The Poppyheads

"It was very much a celebration of the small. It was almost like a badge of honour to keep things on a small scale, perhaps as a defence against the fact it was never very likely to do very well. It made a virtue of the fact that it was almost doomed to fail but it was going to heroically die trying. This is what pop music should be about."

Sarah Records Discography

Sarah 001 **The Sea Urchins** *Pristine Christine* 1987
Sarah 002 **The Orchids** *I've Got A Habit* 1988
Sarah 003 **Another Sunny Day** *Anorak City* flexi disc 1988
Sarah 004 untitled fanzine 1988
Sarah 005 **14 Iced Bears** *Come Get Me* 1988
Sarah 006 **The Poppyheads** *Cremation Town* 1988
Sarah 007 **Another Sunny Day** *I'm In Love With A Girl Who Doesn't Know I Exist* 1988
Sarah 008 **The Sea Urchins** *Solace* 1988
Sarah 009 **The Golden Dawn** *My Secret World* 1988
Sarah 010 **The Springfields** *Sunflower* 1988
Sarah 011 **The Orchids** *Underneath The Window Underneath The Sink* 1988
Sarah 012 **The Field Mice** *Emma's House* 1988
Sarah 013 **Christine's Cat** *Your Love Is...* flexi disc 1989
Sarah 014 *Lemonade/Cold* fanzines 1989
Sarah 015 **St Christopher** *You Deserve More Than A Maybe* 1989
Sarah 016 **Another Sunny Day** *What's Happened?* 1989
Sarah 017 **The Golden Dawn** *George Hamilton's Dead* 1989
Sarah 018 **The Field Mice** *Sensitive* 1989
Sarah 019 **Brighter** *Around The World In Eighty Days* 1989
Sarah 020 **St Christopher** *All Of A Tremble* 1989
Sarah 021 **The Wake** *Crush The Flowers* 1989
Sarah 022 **Another Sunny Day** *You Should All Be Murdered* 1989
Sarah 023 **The Orchids** *What Will We Do Next* 1989
Sarah 024 **The Field Mice** *The Autumn Store part 1* 1990
Sarah 025 **The Field Mice** *The Autumn Store part 2* 1990
Sarah 026 **Gentle Despite** *Darkest Blue* 1990
Sarah 027 **Brighter** *Noah's Ark* 1990
Sarah 028 **Action Painting!** *These Things Happen* 1990
Sarah 029 **The Orchids** *Something For The Longing* 1990
Sarah 030 **Heavenly** *I Fell In Love Last Night* 1990
Sarah 031 **Eternal** *Breathe* 1990
Sarah 032 *Sunstroke* fanzine 1990
Sarah 033 **The Sea Urchins** *A Morning Odyssey* 1990
Sarah 034 **St Christopher** *Antoinette* 1990
Sarah 035 **Another Sunny Day** *Rio* 1990
Sarah 036 **The Sweetest Ache** *If I Could Shine* 1990
Sarah 037 **Even As We Speak** *Nothing Ever Happens* 1990
Sarah 038 **The Field Mice** *So Said Kay* 10" 1990
Sarah 039 **The Sweetest Ache** *Tell Me How It Feels* 1990
Sarah 040 **The Springfields** *Wonder* 1991
Sarah 041 **Heavenly** *Our Love Is Heavenly* 1991
Sarah 042 **The Orchids** *Penetration* 12" 1991
Sarah 043 **Tramway** *Maritime City* 1991
Sarah 044 **The Field Mice** *September's Not So Far Away* 1991
Sarah 045 **Gentle Despite** *Torment To Me* 1991
Sarah 046 **St Christopher** *Say Yes To Everything* 1991
Sarah 047 **The Sweetest Ache** *Sickening* 1991
Sarah 048 **The Wake** *Major John* 1991
Sarah 049 **Even As We Speak** *One Step Forward* 1991
Sarah 050 *Saropoly* board game 1991
Sarah 051 **Heavenly** *So Little Deserve* 1991
Sarah 052 **Tramway** *Sweet Chariot* 1991
Sarah 053 **Secret Shine** *After Years* 1991
Sarah 054 **The Forever People** *Invisible* 1992
Sarah 055 **Blueboy** *Clearer* 1991
Sarah 056 **Brighter** *Half-Hearted* 1991
Sarah 057 **The Field Mice** *Missing The Moon* 12" 1991
Sarah 058 **The Hit Parade** *In Gunnersbury Park* 1991
Sarah 059 **Even As We Speak** *Beautiful Day* 1992
Sarah 060 **Another Sunny Day** *New Year's Honours* 1992
Sarah 061 **Secret Shine** *Ephemeral* 1992
Sarah 062 **The Rosaries** *Forever* 1992
Sarah 063 **The Sugargliders** *Letter From A Lifeboat* 1992
Sarah 064 **The Harvest Ministers** *You Do My World A World Of Good* 1992
Sarah 065 **Blueboy** *Popkiss* 1992
Sarah 066 **The Orchids** *Thaumaturgy* 1992
Sarah 067 **The Sugargliders** *Seventeen* 1992
Sarah 068 **The Harvest Ministers** *Six O'Clock Is Rosary* 1992
Sarah 069 **Brighter** *Disney* 10" 1992
Sarah 070 **Blueboy** *Just As Good As I Should Be, Nice Boys Prefer Vanilla, I Am Telling You Because You Are Far Away* fanzines + *Cloud Babies (live)* flexi disc 1993
Sarah 071 **Secret Shine** *Loveblind* 1993
Sarah 072 **The Sugargliders** *Ahprahran* 1993
Sarah 073 **Action Painting!** *Classical Music* 1993
Sarah 074 **Blueboy** *Meet Johnny Rave* 1993
Sarah 075 **East River Pipe** *Helmet On* 1993
Sarah 076 **Boyracer** *B Is For Boyracer* 1993
Sarah 077 **The Sugargliders** *Trumpet Play* 1993
Sarah 078 **East River Pipe** *She's A Real Good Time* 1993
Sarah 079 **Even As We Speak** *Blue Eyes Deceiving Me* 1993
Sarah 080 **Blueboy** *Some Gorgeous Accident* 1993
Sarah 081 **Heavenly** *P.U.N.K. Girl* 1993
Sarah 082 **Heavenly** *Atta Girl* 1993
Sarah 083 **The Sugargliders** *Will We Ever Learn* 1993
Sarah 084 **Harvest Ministers** *If It Kills Me And It Will* 1993
Sarah 085 **Boyracer** *From Purity To Purgatory* 1993
Sarah 086 **The Sugargliders** *Top 40 Sculpture* 1993
Sarah 087 **Action Painting!** *Mustard Gas* 1993
Sarah 088 **Blueboy** *River* 1994
Sarah 089 **Secret Shine** *Greater Than God* 10" 1994
Sarah 090 **The Hit Parade** *Autobiography* 1994
Sarah 091 **Ivy** *Wish You Would* 1994
Sarah 092 **Ivy** *Avenge* 1994
Sarah 093 **Aberdeen** *Byron* 1994
Sarah 094 **Northern Picture Library** *Paris* 1994
Sarah 095 **Northern Picture Library** *Last September's Farewell Kiss* 1994
Sarah 096 **Boyracer** *Pure Hatred '96* 1994
Sarah 097 **Aberdeen** *Fireworks* 1994
Sarah 098 **Shelley** *Reproduction Is Pollution* 1995
Sarah 099 **Blueboy** *Dirty Mags* 1995
Sarah 100 **Various Artists** *There And Back Again Lane* booklet + CD 1995

TEN-INCH LPs
Sarah 401 **The Orchids** *Lyceum* 1989
Sarah 402 **The Field Mice** *Snowball* 1989
Sarah 403 **St Christopher** *Bacharach* 1990
Sarah 404 **Brighter** *Laurel* 1991
Sarah 405 **East River Pipe** *Goodbye California* 1993
Sarah 406 **Harvey Williams** *Rebellion* 1995
Sarah 407 **East River Pipe** *Even The Sun Was Afraid* 1995

TWELVE-INCH LPs
Sarah 601 **The Field Mice** *Skywriting* 1990
Sarah 602 **The Wake** *Make It Loud* 1990
Sarah 603 **Heavenly** *Heavenly vs. Satan* 1991
Sarah 604 **Talulah Gosh** *They've Scoffed The Lot* 1991
Sarah 605 **The Orchids** *Unholy Soul* 1991
Sarah 606 **The Field Mice** *Coastal (compilation)* 1991
Sarah 607 **The Field Mice** *For Keeps* 1991
Sarah 608 **The Sweetest Ache** *Jaguar* 1992
Sarah 609 **The Sea Urchins** *Stardust (compilation)* 1992
Sarah 610 **Heavenly** *Le Jardin de Heavenly* 1992
Sarah 611 **The Orchids** *Epicurean (compilation)* 1992
Sarah 612 **Blueboy** *If Wishes Were Horses* 1992
Sarah 613 **Another Sunny Day** *London Weekend (compilation)* 1992
Sarah 614 **Even As We Speak** *Feral Pop Frenzy* 1993
Sarah 615 **Secret Shine** *Untouched* 1993
Sarah 616 **The Harvest Ministers** *Little Dark Mansion* 1993
Sarah 617 **The Orchids** *Striving For The Lazy Perfection* 1994
Sarah 618 **The Wake** *Tidal Wave of Hype* 1994
Sarah 619 **The Sugargliders** *We're All Trying To Get There (compilation)* 1994
Sarah 620 **Blueboy** *Unisex* 1994
Sarah 621 **East River Pipe** *Poor Fricky* 1994
Sarah 622 **The Hit Parade** *The Sound Of The Hit Parade* 1994
Sarah 623 **Heavenly** *The Decline And Fall Of Heavenly* 1994

LABEL COMPILATIONS
Sarah 587 *Shadow Factory* 1988
Sarah 376 *Temple Cloud* 1990
Sarah 545 *Air Balloon Road* 1990
Sarah 501 *Glass Arcade* 1991
Sarah 583 *Fountain Island* 1992
Sarah 628 *Engine Common* 1993
Sarah 530 *Gaol Ferry Bridge* 1994
Sarah 359 *Battery Point* 1995
Sarah 100 *There And Back Again Lane* 1995

INDEX

Note to the reader: There are two obvious omissions from this index: 'Haynes, Matt' and 'Wadd, Clare'. The reason for these omissions is that each name generated more than 700 individual references which, quite frankly, is no use to anybody and very tedious to type out. If you would prefer to have an index that includes these names, please reach for a pencil and add 'Haynes, Matt: 9-451' and 'Wadd, Clare: 9-451' in the appropriate places.

14 Iced Bears	9, 46, 70-71, 96, 99, 126, 137, 158, 166-167, 190, 203, 239, 347, 411, 426
4AD (record label)	59, 75, 123, 277, 291
Aberdeen	41, 87, 89, 129, 145, 246, 273, 339, 397-399, 408, 439, 441
Action Painting!	41, 43, 76-77, 108, 115, 119, 139, 144, 177-178, 187, 191, 194, 237, 251, 261, 308, 310, 312, 332, 335, 343, 362, 373-374, 377, 404, 412, 438, 441
Adverts	43, 48, 97, 120, 147, 152-153, 382, 439-440
'Air Balloon Road' (compilation)	39, 60, 272
Albrow, Karen	210, 434
Allen Huntley, Sian	12, 76, 177
Allen, Carolyn	205, 422
Altered Images	14, 155, 166, 302, 370, 421
Anderson, Stewart	14, 34, 92, 133, 160, 164, 170, 241, 345, 372, 399
Anoraks	52, 69, 120, 126, 131, 148, 181-184, 187-188, 190-191, 203, 296, 335, 344, 374
Another Sunny Day	69, 109, 117, 126-127, 131, 158, 162, 181, 223, 247, 280, 296, 302, 332, 348, 382, 412
Are You Scared To 'Get Happy?' (fanzine)	35, 53, 84, 101, 107-111, 113, 126, 131, 182, 227
'Arketino' (fanzine)	11, 112-113, 182, 404
Arzy, Beth	89, 145, 245, 273, 339, 397, 408, 439, 442
'Attack on Bzag' (fanzine)	99, 105-106, 109, 122, 143
Austen, Jane	20, 58
'Baby Honey' (fanzine)	49, 110
Barber, Simon	99, 175, 341, 355-356, 421-422
Barrett, Jeff	116, 286, 289, 314, 316
BBC Radio 1	19, 64, 84-85, 105, 107, 121, 139, 156-160, 164, 172, 174-175, 178, 204, 215, 247, 363, 386
Beatles, The	30, 64, 187, 191, 194, 221, 253, 266, 337
Blueboy	41-42, 49, 64, 81, 85, 94, 105, 115, 120, 125, 134, 141, 149, 155, 158, 163, 165, 170, 215-218, 229, 241, 259, 260-261, 272, 295, 319, 332, 337-338, 345, 349, 352-355, 357, 359, 363-365, 367, 369, 377, 386-388, 392-394, 409, 414-415, 417, 423, 425, 440-441, 444-446
BMX Bandits, The	5, 109, 175, 183, 210, 302, 314, 332, 394, 435
Boyracer	14, 34, 42, 92-93, 133, 160, 163-164, 170, 237, 241-242, 272, 332, 336, 338, 345, 369, 372-373, 377, 399, 438-439, 444
Bragg, Billy	198-199, 302
Brighter	9, 15, 23, 29-30, 33-34, 41, 73, 90, 100-101, 129, 147, 152, 202-203, 208-210, 223, 227-228, 243, 249, 251, 253, 274-275, 305, 308-310, 317, 332, 337, 345-346, 357, 359-360, 363-365, 367-368, 377, 390-392, 398, 401, 412, 423, 425, 429, 444, 447-448
Brilliant Corners, The	51-53, 64, 99, 194, 207, 241, 288, 290-292, 324, 328, 330, 389, 421
Britpop	122, 192, 295
Brown, James	99, 106, 122, 126, 141, 206
Brunzell, Nicklas	113, 231
Buzzcocks	12-13, 15, 361-362
C86	11, 16, 64, 150, 181, 188, 192, 343, 409
Caesar (aka Gerard McInulty)	14-15, 136, 140, 143, 155, 163, 166, 168-169, 172, 205, 255, 270-272, 302, 370, 378, 421-423, 438-440, 448
Carnell, Mark	35, 107
Cartel, The (distribution network)	291-300
Cator, Julian	85, 120, 146, 176
Catt, Ian	79, 131, 236, 239, 243, 443, 448
Chadwick, Mike	279, 285-286, 288-289, 291-292, 294, 440
Che (record label)	23, 137
Chesterfields, The	99, 175, 324, 341, 355, 373, 421-422, 428
Chipping, Tim	57, 93, 124, 222, 230, 246, 260, 263, 281, 296, 310, 348-349, 351, 355, 385, 410
Christine's Cat	9, 11, 94-96
Christmas	28, 92, 120, 158, 162, 171-172, 229-230, 305, 314, 320, 332-338, 382, 409, 450
Christopher, Lee	77, 108, 115, 177-178, 191, 194, 261, 310
Clash, The	12, 40, 132, 198, 221-222
Claughan, Peter	11, 75, 250, 277, 344
Clifton Suspension Bridge	25, 47, 49, 58, 152, 265, 370, 451
CliftonPrint (shop)	27, 266-268
Cocteau Twins	73, 81, 147, 277, 291, 354
Cohen, Lara	104, 400
Conservatives, The	49, 197, 212, 215, 437
Cooksey, Robert	22, 69, 131, 177, 184-186, 235, 250, 266-267, 300, 311, 362-363, 426
Cope, Julian	18-19, 164, 300
Cornog, FM	89, 128, 145, 232, 255, 283, 431, 442
Cosmic English Music	63, 264
Court, Simon	79, 133, 239, 262, 371, 412, 435, 440
Cousens, Alison	30, 41, 73, 100, 152, 202-203, 208-209, 223, 243, 253, 274-275, 310, 317, 337, 345-346, 365, 368, 377, 390-391, 401, 423, 425, 429, 447
Crass	199, 201
Creation (record label)	13, 17, 30, 68-69, 73, 76, 87, 100, 107, 123, 151, 193, 219, 222, 228-229, 252-253, 286, 295, 327
Crosby, Bing	169, 215
Cure, The	279, 345, 370
Cutler, Ivor	107, 226
Damned, The	221-222, 362
Davies, Anne Mari	84, 116, 132, 154, 166, 192, 198, 201, 202-203, 243, 247-249, 272-274, 278-279, 347-349, 375-376, 381, 386, 396-397, 409-410, 420, 429
Dawydiak, Eugene	75, 93, 210
Depeche Mode	291, 317, 331
Dillam, Robert	76, 253
Dobson, Mark	46, 82, 85, 123, 211, 239, 335, 348, 360, 375, 381, 385-386, 396
Doc Martens	190, 192
Dolly Mixture	150, 192
Doughty, Roger	287-290
Drummond, Matthew	258, 333, 384, 423, 428, 433
Duffy, Bridget	22, 33, 68-69, 177, 185, 187, 190, 204, 272, 320, 367, 370, 435
East River Pipe	60, 87, 89, 128-129, 145, 232-233, 255-256, 283, 431, 442-443

455

Echo & The Bunnymen	73, 115, 290	Gorton, Paul	75-76, 140-141, 162, 196, 261, 347, 372, 377
Edwards, Dickon	48, 55, 57, 93-94, 246-247, 273, 281, 343, 411-412, 414	Grant, Christine	11, 95-96
EEC Punk Rock Mountain	181, 291, 312-316, 339, 412, 421	Griffin, Dale	167, 169-170
		'Grimsby Fishmarket' (fanzine)	21, 81, 113, 161, 216, 226, 231, 392
el Records (record label)	81, 281	Grogan, Clare	14, 150
Empire, Kitty	124, 190, 275	Groove Farm, The	32, 52-53, 105, 228, 241, 293, 310, 314, 325-327, 330, 351, 374
Enterprise Allowance Scheme	19, 42, 54	Guthrie, Gordon	312-315, 339-340
		Gwilliam Street	25, 27, 60, 173, 231, 241, 412, 414, 449
Eternal	67, 76, 121, 208-209, 228, 252-253, 277, 355	Hackett, James	212, 214, 258-260, 317, 365, 382, 389, 422, 427, 430, 437, 441
Evans, Matthew	63, 129, 228, 251, 264, 316, 318-319, 324-325, 327, 336, 419	Haggar, Lloyd	241, 354
Even As We Speak	9, 38, 42, 57-58, 87, 132-133, 140-141, 149, 157, 163-165, 178, 179, 184, 222-223, 240, 249, 257, 360-361, 363, 368-369, 411, 415, 420, 425	Hahndorf, Peter	183, 231, 392, 446
		Half Man Half Biscuit	159, 325
		Harding, Deborah	281, 302
		Harrison, Spencer	85, 103, 120, 146-147, 176, 283, 343
Factory (record label)	12-14, 36, 49, 57, 120, 123, 136, 145, 151, 172, 229, 255, 270, 277, 279, 291, 302, 370, 378, 440	Harvest Ministers, The	87, 90-91, 128, 232, 255, 377, 434
		Harvey, Polly (aka PJ Harvey)	17, 174, 285, 356
Farry, Eithne	139, 241, 325	Harwood, Alan	290-291, 294, 296, 298
Fast Product (record label)	12-13, 295	Hatchers (shop)	27, 266-267
Fennessy, Dave	357, 359	Haynes, Deb	207, 320, 340
Field Mice, The	12, 15, 20, 22, 35-37, 41, 43, 46, 67, 78-79, 82, 84, 95, 102, 119-120, 123-124, 129, 131-132, 137, 154, 158, 161-163, 165-166, 178, 192-193, 194, 198-199, 202-203, 211-212, 236, 239-240, 243, 247-249, 273-274, 278-279, 310, 318-319, 332, 334, 343, 345, 347-351, 360, 367, 372, 375-376, 380-381, 382, 385-386, 389-392, 396-397, 409-410, 417, 420, 429-430, 443	Heavenly	9, 14, 42, 44-46, 55, 81-83, 94, 104, 116, 122, 135-136, 137, 139, 145, 148-151, 162-163, 168-169, 171-172, 177, 179, 182, 188, 190, 192-193, 196, 199, 204-205, 208, 219-220, 240-241, 272, 279, 281-283, 289, 208, 319, 321, 332-338, 341, 343, 351, 356-357, 359, 369, 372, 379-380, 384, 390-392, 394-408, 412-417, 425, 433, 438, 444, 446, 450
		Henry, Julian	26, 84, 223, 269, 280, 302, 398, 414, 448
Flatmates, The	52, 64, 89, 207, 288, 305, 316, 320, 323-325, 328, 339-340, 413, 419, 429	Hiscock, Michael	36, 78, 102, 162, 211, 236, 278, 300, 351, 355, 360, 376, 380, 386, 389, 397
Fletcher, Amelia	9, 12, 14, 46, 53, 82, 94, 115, 122, 135, 139, 145, 147-150, 157-158, 168, 171, 179, 182-183, 188-190, 192-193, 196, 205, 223, 240-241, 274, 300, 308, 310, 324-325, 335, 337, 341, 342, 351, 357, 359, 369, 379, 380, 386, 394-396, 398, 400-408, 412-417, 425, 433-434	Hit Parade, The	26, 84, 223, 241, 269, 280, 302, 398, 414, 448
		Hitchcock, Andy	77, 115, 119, 139, 144, 194, 237, 251-252, 261, 310-311, 335, 343, 362, 373-374, 412, 423, 441
		Hitchiking	43, 415
		HMV (record shop)	285, 287, 297
Fletcher, Mathew	1, 33, 82-83, 139, 145, 150, 241, 281, 308, 332-333, 337-338, 341, 369, 372, 380, 398, 404, 406, 408, 434, 450	Hodgkinson, Nicola	164, 272
		Holborrow, Rachel	22, 406
		Horlick, Nancy	63, 228-229, 244, 288, 308, 318, 336
Forbes, Winston	207, 293, 331	House, Kevin	261, 310, 336, 373-374
Forever People, The	198, 218-219, 277	Housemartins, The	107, 302, 320-321
Forte, Kenny	75, 95, 177, 188, 210, 344	Howard, Keris	23, 29, 33-34, 73, 129, 152, 203, 208-210, 227, 228, 249, 305, 310, 317, 337, 345-346, 359-360, 367-368, 390-391, 423, 425, 429
Franks, Andy	298, 328, 331		
Freeman, Sue	70, 137, 167, 190, 203-204, 239, 347, 411, 426		
Fringes	52, 187, 196, 332, 343, 345-346, 349, 378	Huggy Bear	51, 150-151, 179, 401, 403, 405-408
Galaxie 500	73, 178, 196	Hull Adelphi, The	359-360, 386, 394, 415-416
'Gaol Ferry Bridge' (compilation)	61, 328	Hynds Bari, Pauline	41, 176, 259
Gartside, Mike	25, 308	Indie-Pop Mailing List, The	438, 446
Gedge, David	34-35, 58, 106, 158, 161-163, 173-174	Ivy	85, 103, 120, 146-147, 176, 227, 243, 283, 308, 343, 441
Gentle Despite (no 'The')	59, 75-76, 93, 140-141, 162, 196, 261, 372-373, 377		
Gillespie, Bobby	68, 188, 271, 371	Jam, The	42, 221
Gingell, Jamie	40, 63, 142, 244, 319, 323, 347, 448	James, Jonny (aka Mark)	76, 228, 253-254
Girdler, Keith	49, 79-81, 115, 155, 203, 215-218, 229, 259, 295, 332, 337, 352-355, 363-364, 392-394, 415, 423, 444-446	Jarrett, Andrew	52, 105, 241, 293, 314, 325, 330, 351, 374
		Jefferis, Steve	246, 277, 341
Girgus, John	89, 129, 246, 398	Jensen, Kid (aka David)	105-106, 174
'Glass Arcade' (compilation)	40, 60-61, 269		
Go-Betweens, The	14, 124, 274	Jesus & Mary Chain, The	124, 188, 210, 322-323, 339, 343-344, 370, 426
Golden Dawn, The	11, 42, 73-75, 93, 95-96, 116, 127, 177, 188, 210, 249-251, 277, 344	Johnson, Calvin	94, 183, 253, 345, 394, 399, 402-403
		Jones, Bob	286, 290, 297, 305, 312, 315-316, 421
Goodier, Mark	19, 164, 204-205, 247	Joshi, Vinita	22, 137, 192, 204, 226, 351-352

Joy Division	13, 40, 136, 145, 151, 159, 171, 279, 291, 322	Photocopying	27, 97, 113, 115, 285
Kennedy, Ulric	73, 188, 210, 249-250, 277, 344	Pink Floyd	263, 372
King, Richard	286, 294	Pinnacle	290, 293-294, 296
Kinsey, Laura	76, 253-254	Poll tax (see also Conservatives; Thatcher, Margaret)	41-42, 212-215
Knowles, Julian	38, 132, 140, 157, 163-164, 178, 179, 184, 240, 249, 257, 261-262, 361, 363, 368, 372, 413, 415, 420-421, 431	Pooh Sticks, The	137, 181, 183
		Poppyheads, The	15, 32, 52-53, 70-72, 126, 131, 187, 279-280, 289, 297, 325-327, 349, 425, 451
'Kvatch' (fanzine)	19, 32-33, 68, 105-107, 160, 187, 292, 306	Portishead (band)	17, 52
Lamacq, Steve	64, 85, 139, 176-177, 322	Postcard (record label)	12-14, 49, 69, 87, 199, 206
Lemonade (fizzy drink)	44, 151, 310, 314	Postcards	10, 12, 58, 105, 201, 227, 300, 384
'Lemonade' (fanzine)	182, 202, 318, 405	Posters	14, 21, 116, 199, 212, 263, 266, 268, 272, 280, 288-290, 339, 344, 358, 395, 414
Letraset	20, 112, 263-264, 268-269, 280	Powers, Barbara	89, 232-233, 283, 442
Leverton, Marc	160, 224, 237, 299, 360, 412	Price, Elizabeth (aka Liz)	63, 339
Long, Janice	73, 78, 131, 168, 172, 174-175, 293		
Maida Vale (studios)	162-163, 170, 174-176, 239, 420, 426	Price, Simon	72, 120, 130, 136, 148, 150-151, 207
Malley, Gemma	64, 105, 122, 149, 170, 216, 260-261, 338, 352-354, 359, 363, 388, 394, 415, 440-441	Primal Scream	18, 68-69, 182, 184, 188, 210, 306, 316, 324, 344, 380, 435
		Purnell, Scott	12, 40, 49, 63-64, 142-143, 227, 242-243, 318, 322-323, 332, 336-337, 352, 373, 419, 441, 446, 448
Manic Street Preachers	72, 187, 311		
Marine Girls, The	150, 188, 192	Pursey, Rob	12, 14, 45, 52-53, 82, 123, 152, 157, 159, 168, 171-172, 179, 183-184, 192-193, 208, 279, 283, 289, 306, 308, 320, 322, 332, 335, 337, 338, 341, 351, 357, 380, 399, 408, 413-414, 417, 425, 433
Martin, Darren	68, 185		
Massive Attack	17, 52, 287		
McGee, Alan	59, 87, 181, 222, 228, 327, 330		
Meadows, Joel	45, 85, 87, 234, 256-257, 274-275, 302, 369-370, 441		
Meadows, Josh	16, 34, 45, 85, 87, 128, 256-257, 274-275, 302, 355, 357, 369-370, 441	Quantick, David	67, 120, 125, 130, 142-144, 146-151, 153, 207, 215
Melia, Glenn	102, 319, 384, 397, 426, 435	Quinn, Chris	27, 44, 69, 100, 119, 169, 178, 184, 207, 214, 227, 235, 258, 265, 293, 317, 366, 382, 389, 413, 415, 420, 422, 428, 435, 437, 444
Membranes, The	16, 100, 106, 109		
Menck, Ric	21, 45, 87, 89, 99, 133, 276		
Merriman, Will	90, 128, 255, 377, 434		
Mighty Mighty	69, 111, 330	Ramones, The	188, 342
Minogue, Kylie	40, 44, 96, 134, 239, 280-281, 298, 404	Rayner, Anita	257, 363, 421, 425
Mishra, Jyoti	17, 30, 35, 55, 67, 193-194, 197, 199, 201-202, 206, 256-257, 370, 405, 413	Razorcuts	30-33, 53-54, 101, 109, 111, 192, 198, 218-219, 277, 310, 314-315, 320, 339-340, 357, 370, 373, 429
Momtchiloff, Pete	43-45, 82, 123, 163, 169, 177, 181, 221-223, 300, 308, 310, 337, 342, 357, 380, 396, 400, 402, 412, 425	Replay (record shop)	285, 297-298, 305
		Revolver (record shop)	10, 231, 285-291, 295-298, 305-306, 312, 314, 370
Moody, James	149, 258, 382, 385, 423, 428, 434, 437	Revolver Distribution	36, 54-55, 82, 279, 291-295, 440
Moragn, Hugo	297, 310	Reynolds, Simon	11, 13-14, 16, 124, 147, 188-189, 206, 402
Mornement, Adam	9, 33, 112, 310, 356	Riot Grrrl	139, 145, 150, 354, 399-415
My Bloody Valentine (see also My Bloody Secret Shine)	95, 196, 273, 448, 450	Rippington, Tim	170, 173, 241, 289, 305, 315, 322, 324
		Roberts, Jamie (aka James)	19, 32, 68-69, 133, 184-185, 187, 235, 242, 311, 352, 367, 372, 413, 426, 435
'My Secret World' (film)	10, 119, 153	Rocker	288, 305, 316, 320, 323, 325, 328, 331, 339-340, 413, 419, 429
New Order	57, 73, 291, 322, 370	Rogers, Cathy	122, 145, 168, 179, 192, 199, 204, 219-220, 240, 321, 332-333, 343, 351, 357, 395-401, 414
Nirvana	171, 183, 399, 402		
Nirvana	171, 399, 402		
Noisebox (record label)	85, 176, 243	Rosaries, The	12, 76, 177, 228, 253
		Rose, Martin	229, 241, 386-387, 417-418, 444-445
Northern Picture Library	84-85, 134, 144, 201, 248, 273, 348, 367	Rough Trade (record label)	12, 22, 123, 291
'One Page Fanzine' (fanzine)	46, 116, 202	Rough Trade (record shop)	33, 109, 117, 287, 302, 406, 447
Orange Juice	14-16, 136, 182-183, 218, 300, 302	'Rox' (fanzine)	100, 105, 109, 143
Orchids, The	23, 25, 27, 33, 36-38, 41-44, 69, 78, 100, 119, 127, 149, 163, 169, 176, 178, 184, 207, 210, 212-215, 231, 235, 257-260, 265-266, 276-277, 293, 305, 317, 332-335, 352, 365-367, 380, 382-385, 389, 392, 412-413, 415, 420-423, 427-429, 430, 433-438, 441, 444, 448	Sandhu, Sukhdev	17, 44, 102-103, 115, 197, 206, 218, 226
		Sarah Records (record label)	9-451
		Saropoly	58-60, 265, 295
		Savill, Christian	76, 121, 228, 252, 277, 355
		Scally, John	100, 163, 169, 185, 212, 333, 423, 428, 430, 437, 441
Our Price (record shop)	46, 285, 299-300	Scott, Chris	125, 167-168, 245, 340-341, 358-359, 434
Pale Saints	73, 75, 136, 261, 372		
Paphides, Pete	16, 44, 125, 134, 136-137, 149, 151, 187, 193, 197, 208, 405-406, 450		
Pastels, The	16, 147, 183-184, 188, 316, 412		

Sea Urchins, The	19, 23, 32-33, 42-43, 68-69, 81, 89, 107, 110, 126, 131, 133, 177, 183-187, 190, 204, 232, 235-236, 242-243, 251, 265, 266, 272, 294, 298, 300, 302, 308-312, 320, 325-327, 351-352, 356, 362, 367, 370-372, 413, 419, 426, 434-436	'The Word' (TV show)	179, 406-408
		Thomas, Tom and Orynthia	306, 316, 330
		Thorn, Tracey	17, 41, 203, 275
		Tighe, Chris	99, 181, 341, 358, 376, 417
		Toad Hall (studio)	257-260, 276
Secret Shine	12, 40, 49, 61, 64, 128, 133, 141-143, 231, 244, 318-319, 322-323, 332, 335, 347, 352, 360, 369, 373, 441, 448	Tony's (record shop)	285, 295-297, 298,
		Torncrantz, Marcus	21-22, 81, 113-114, 155, 161, 227, 231, 352, 423
Section 28	198, 215-218	Tramway	41, 51, 61-63, 129, 136, 228-229, 244-245, 251, 264, 288, 308, 316, 318, 324-325, 332, 336, 358, 372, 419
Sekula, Rob	70, 96, 99, 158, 166-167, 167, 239, 411, 427		
Sha-La-La	15, 19, 30-34, 49, 68-69, 71, 93, 110-112, 115, 131, 158, 160, 181-183, 231, 292	TweeNet	231, 392, 446-447
		Typewriter	102, 107, 112-113, 268
'Shadow Factory' (compilation)	9, 15, 17-18, 23-25, 29, 37, 42, 60, 73, 128, 173, 231, 269	U2	91, 161, 193, 228, 322
		Upper Belgrave Road	18, 23, 25-26, 57, 160, 231, 266, 294, 412, 430
Shampoo	139, 178-179, 261, 277, 404	Vass, Tim	33, 101 198, 218-219, 277, 314, 320, 339, 370, 373, 429
Sharkey, Alex	203, 208-209, 391, 423, 429		
Shelley	42, 48, 55, 57, 93-94, 124, 246-247, 263, 277, 281, 310, 341, 343, 411, 414	Velvet Underground, The	14, 16, 188, 250
Shelley, Pete	15, 362	Vincent, Stuart	75, 79, 178, 237, 280, 299, 359, 361-362, 377, 417, 419
Shop Assistants, The	54, 182		
Single of the Week	111, 126, 131-133, 139, 142, 376, 450	Vinyl Japan (record label)	85, 394, 396
Sirman, Guy	9, 310		
Slampt	22, 143, 227, 406	Virgin (record shop)	18, 46, 285, 298-299, 381, 412
Slowdive	76, 121, 228, 239, 252-253, 355	'Waaaah!' (fanzine)	29, 42, 67, 201, 205, 335
Smith, Kathryn	128, 142-143, 244-245, 319, 323, 347, 360, 448	Wake, The	14, 81, 136, 140, 143, 155, 163, 166, 168-169, 172, 205, 251, 255, 267-268, 270-272, 302, 322, 370, 378, 384, 386, 421-423, 438-439, 448
'Smiths Indeed' (fanzine)	97, 161, 221, 290		
Smiths, The	14, 41, 54, 73, 109, 196, 199, 291, 361	Walters, John	165, 166-167, 169
Sonic Youth	75, 164, 196, 325, 406	Webster, Greg	30-33, 63, 101, 109, 192, 198, 218, 245, 277, 314, 320, 339, 370
Sound City (BBC event)	64, 121, 160, 172, 319, 322		
Soup Dragons, The	182-183, 210, 302, 313, 340, 435	Wedding Present, The	34, 58, 73, 85, 106, 158, 161-163, 173-174, 241, 324
Springfields, The	21, 41, 45, 69, 87-89, 99, 127, 132, 275		
St Christopher	102, 110, 116, 270, 308, 319, 356, 380, 382, 389-390, 397, 426, 435	Weller, Paul	170, 229, 445
		Wells, Steven	130, 141, 143-145, 151, 216
Stanley, Bob	72, 131-132, 134, 221, 382	Western Star Domino Club	297, 306, 327-331
Stapleton, John	297, 330		
Stewart, Duglas T	5, 175, 183, 210, 302, 314, 332-333, 394-395, 435-436	Westwood, Simon	75 140, 196, 261, 347, 373, 377
		White House (studio)	76, 239, 243-244, 253, 417
Stewart, Paul	79, 81, 115, 122, 141, 158, 170, 218, 319, 337-338, 349, 352, 357, 363, 365, 415, 425, 440	Whitehead, Martin	19, 52, 54, 87, 288, 295, 314, 320, 323, 339
		Wiiija (record label)	82, 406
		Wilkinson, Stuart	76, 253, 355
Stone, Wendy	223, 310, 316, 318	Williams, Harvey	21, 40, 67, 69, 91, 109, 117, 125, 131, 158, 162, 165, 174, 181-182, 223, 227, 240, 247, 251, 263, 280, 310, 315, 327, 335, 347, 351, 354, 363, 365, 367, 376-377, 380, 384, 412, 415, 425, 440-442, 444, 448, 450
Strawberry Switchblade	255, 277, 425		
Stump	109, 421		
Subway Organization, The	19, 52-55, 64, 87, 288, 292, 295, 314, 320, 323-324, 327, 339-341, 429		
		Williams, Pete	15, 18-19, 21, 33, 42, 49-50, 70, 108, 110, 182, 198, 224, 313, 340
Sugargliders, The	9, 16, 34, 44-45, 85-87, 128, 223, 234, 256-257, 274-276, 354-355, 357, 369, 441		
		Wilson, Tony	13, 377
Sweeney, Ken (aka Brian)	67, 90-92	Wolfenden, Justine	22, 164
		Wonderland, Alison	137-139, 283
Sweetest Ache, The	79, 133, 178, 224, 237-239, 262, 280, 299, 310, 359-362, 371, 373, 377, 412, 417, 419, 435, 440	Woodcock, Simon	185, 235, 266, 311
		Woodward, Davey	51, 99, 194, 207, 288, 290-293, 324, 389, 421
Talulah Gosh	5, 9, 14, 22, 32-33, 42, 53, 55, 69, 82, 111, 124, 127, 132, 139, 145, 147-148, 162-163, 167, 172, 182, 184, 193, 245, 274, 300, 313, 315, 324-325, 336, 339-343, 357-359, 380, 406, 434, 450	Woolworths (shop)	285, 299
		Wratten, Bobby	12, 20, 35-37, 67, 78-79, 84, 93, 102, 119, 125, 158, 161-162, 166, 178, 199, 201, 211, 236, 248, 278, 300, 310, 335, 343, 345, 347-348, 360, 367, 375, 380-381, 385-386, 389, 389, 397, 409-410, 443, 448, 450
Taylor, Mark	52, 97-99, 161, 221, 290, 310		
Teenage Fanclub	95, 210, 302, 435		
'Temple Cloud' (compilation)	42, 55, 60		
		Wyer, Mary	38, 57, 149, 157, 161, 164, 184, 249, 262, 360, 363, 368, 372, 411, 413, 415, 420-421, 425
Temple Meads Station	25, 55, 108, 201, 265, 300, 313, 412		
Thackray, Jerry (aka Everett True)	100, 109, 123, 131, 134, 137, 190, 193, 222, 275, 341, 374, 406, 409		
		Yamauchi, Akiko	39, 113-114, 227, 231, 270-272, 434
Thatcher, Margaret (hint: stand down)	19, 44, 49, 99, 197, 210, 212, 214, 292	Young, Rob	52-53, 71, 131, 187-188, 279-280, 289, 297, 327-330, 349, 425, 451
'The Legend!' (fanzine)	100, 109		

458

ACKNOWLEDGEMENTS

The following people kindly gave up their time to be interviewed (in some cases, several times) and therefore their stories help to shape this book: Karen Albrow, Stewart Anderson, Beth Arzy, Simon Barber, Ian Carmichael, Julian Cator, Tim Chipping, Lee Christopher, Peter Claughan, Lara Cohen, FM Cornog, Simon Court, Anne Mari Davis, Eugene Dawydiak, Robert Dillam, Mark Dobson, Bridget Duffy, Dickon Edwards, Kitty Empire, Matthew Evans, Reg Evans, Amelia Fletcher, Kenny Forte, Andy Franks, Sue Freeman, David Gedge, Jamie Gingell, John Girgus, Paul Gorton, Christine Grant, Gordon Guthrie, James Hackett, Peter Hahndorf, Magz Hall, Deborah Harding, Spencer Harrison, Alan Harwood, Darren Hawkins, Matt Haynes, Julian Henry, Andy Hitchcock, Nancy Horlick, Kevin House, Sian Allen Huntley, Pauline Hynes, Jonny 'Mark' James, Andrew 'Arthur' Jarrett, Bob Jones, Richard Jones, Vinita Joshi, Ulric Kennedy, Jon Kent, Laura Kinsey, Julian Knowles, Marc Leverton, Gerard 'Ceasar' McInulty, Gemma Malley, Joel Meadows, Josh Meadows, Glenn Melia, Ric Menck, Will Merriman, Jyoti Mishra, Peter Momtchiloff, Hugo Morgan, Pete Morgan, Adam Mornement, Pete Paphides, Ruth Patterson, Flora Pick, Lois Pryce, Scott Purnell, Rob Pursey, David Quantick, Chris Quinn, Simon Reynolds, Tim Rippington, James Roberts, Rocker, Cathy Rogers, Martin Rose, Sukhdev Sandhu, Christian Savill, John Scally, Chris Scott, Rob Sekula, Keith Sharp, Guy Sirman, Kathryn Smith, Duglas T Stewart, Paul Stewart, Wendy Stone, Ken Sweeney, Mark Taylor, Jerry Thackray, Tom and Orynthia Thomas, Chris Tighe, Marcus Törncrantz, Tim Vass, Stuart Vincent, Clare Wadd, Gregory Webster, Martin Whitehead, Stuart Wilkinson, Harvey Williams, Pete Williams, Alison Wonderland, Davey Woodward, Bobby Wratten, Mary Wyer, Akiko Yamauchi and Rob Young. Phew!

These good souls found letters, flyers, clippings, photos and all sorts to share with me: Karen Albrow, Simon Barber, Julian Bester, Eugene Bryne, Jon Cole, Robert Cooksey, Jon Craig, Tom Deakin, Mark Dobson, James Feagin, Emmanuel Foricher, Gordon Guthrie, Darren Hawkins, Stuart Huggett, Calvin Johnson, Darren Johnson, Rich Kenington, Grant McPhee, Adrian Millard, Stephen Nash, Neil Phillips, Karen Pudner, Scott Purnell, Chris Quinn, Nicola Rainey, Anita Rayner, Chris Scott, Neil Shumsky, Guy Sirman, Wendy Stone, Mario Suau, Marcus Törncrantz, Pete Williams, Alison Wonderland, Akiko Yamauchi and Rob Young.

While these splendid people helped with various parts of the creative, editing, supporting and publishing side of things: Joe Burt, Paul Duffus, Nick Godfrey, Richard Jones and Kim Renfrew. Obviously, enormous thanks to Clare Wadd and Matt Haynes, without whom none of this would have been necessary.

ABOUT THE AUTHOR

Jane Duffus (pictured here in 1994) qualified as a journalist in 2001 and has since worked as a writer and editor for numerous best-selling national magazines and publishers, as well as editing several books for other writers. After relocating from London to Bristol in 2009, Jane founded the award-winning What The Frock! Comedy project in 2012 to challenge an industry that knowingly overlooks female talent. She continues to work as a freelance writer, editor and speaker. *These Things Happen* is her sixth book. Despite being in her mid-40s, Jane's longest-held job remains as a sales assistant in an independent record shop when she was a teenager. And what a great job that was.

Email: janeduffusbooks@gmail.com
Twitter: @Bristol_Jane
Website: www.janeduffus.com